Selling Today

Building Quality Partnerships

Second Canadian Edition

Gerald L. Manning
Des Moines Area Community College

Barry L. Reece
Virginia Polytechnic Institute and State University

H.F. (Herb) MacKenzie
Memorial University of Newfoundland

Prentice
Hall

Toronto

Canadian Cataloguing in Publication Data

Manning, Gerald L.
  Selling today: building quality partnerships

2nd Canadian ed.
Includes index.
ISBN 0-13-084869-7

1. Selling   I. Reece, Barry L.   II. MacKenzie, H.F.   III. Title.

HF5438.25.M35 2001   658.85   C00-930015-5

© 2001, 1998 Pearson Education Canada Inc., Toronto, Ontario

ISBN 0-13-084869-7

Vice President, Editorial Director: Michael Young
Acquisitions Editor: Mike Ryan
Marketing Manager: James Buchanan
Developmental Editor: Laurie Goebel
Production Editor: Marisa D'Andrea
Copy Editor: Kelli Howey
Production Coordinator: Deborah Starks
Page Layout: Jack Steiner
Photo Research: Alene McNeill
Art Director: Julia Hall
Interior Design: Kevin Connolly
Cover Design: Julia Hall
Cover Image: Stone Images

1 2 3 4 5   05 04 03 02 01

Printed and bound in Canada

Brief Contents

Contents

PART II
Developing a Relationship Strategy   48

3. Creating Value with a Relationship Strategy   50

PART IV

Developing a Customer Strategy — 146

7. Understanding Buyer Behaviour — 148

10. Creating the Consultative Sales Presentation

11. Custom Fitting the Sales Demonstration   251

PART VI

Management of Self and Others

15. Management of Self: The Key to Greater Sales Productivity

Preface

A personal selling textbook suitable for the twenty-first century must offer students a blend of time-proven fundamentals and new practices needed to succeed in today's information economy. The second Canadian edition of *Selling Today: Building Quality Partnerships* provides comprehensive coverage of consultative selling, strategic selling, partnering, value-added selling, and sales force automation. These are the major developments that have transformed personal selling from "peddling" to a new level of professionalism that has dramatically changed the way products are sold around the world.

The new age of personal selling requires that we build on past improvements and adjust to the changes that have accompanied the age of information. Learning how to manage and communicate information to customers within a high-trust working relationship is one of the major challenges facing salespeople today. Personal selling in the age of information also involves fulfilling customer expectations through strategic alliances. These alliances, which represent the highest form of partnering, are growing in importance. Strategic alliances have created a new selling environment that requires the use of advanced customer relationship management (CRM) technology. The fundamentals of CRM represent an important new feature of the second Canadian edition of *Selling Today: Building Quality Partnerships*. A number of important components have been retained from the first Canadian edition.

BUILDING QUALITY PARTNERSHIPS

1. The four broad strategic areas of personal selling, introduced in Chapter 1, serve as a catalyst for skill development and professional growth throughout the textbook. Success in selling depends heavily on the student's ability to develop relationship, product, customer and presentation strategies. Salespeople who have achieved long-term success in personal selling have mastered the skills needed in each of these four strategic areas.

2. The partnering era, which evolved during the past decade, is described in detail. A series of partnering principles are presented in selected chapters.

3. Value-added selling strategies are presented throughout the text. A growing number of customers are seeking a cluster of satisfactions that include a quality product, a salesperson who is truly a partner, and outstanding service after the sale. The salesperson is usually in the best position to discover what adds value (in the mind of the customer) and then determine ways to add value.

4. A hallmark of this edition is the use of many real world examples that build the reader's interest and promote understanding of major topics and concepts. Examples have been obtained from a range of progressive organizations (large and small) such as Shred-it Canada, Xerox Corporation, Janssen-Ortho, Windsor Factory Supply, Premdor, Padinox, and many others. Web sites are provided for most of these companies as well as for organizations of interest to sales people.

5. *Selling Today* provides a three-dimensional approach to the study of ethical decision making. One dimension is a chapter on ethics (Chapter 16) titled "Ethics: The Foundation for Relationships in Selling." Chapter 16 provides a contemporary examination of ethical considerations in selling. The second dimension involves the discussion of ethical issues in selected chapters throughout the text. The authors believe that ethics in selling is so important that it cannot be covered in a single chapter. The third dimension is an exciting business game entitled, *Gray Issues—Ethical Decision Making in Personal Selling* and available in the Instructor's Resource Manual. Participation in this game provides students with an introduction to a range of real-life ethical dilemmas. It stimulates in-depth thinking about the ethical consequences of their decisions and actions. Students play the game to learn without having to play for keeps.

IMPROVEMENTS IN THE SECOND CANADIAN EDITION

The age of information is creating a new economy that offers salespeople many challenges and exciting employment opportunities. The second Canadian edition of *Selling Today: Building Quality Partnerships* describes how sales professionals are adjusting to this new economy. Several important improvements appear in this edition and in the support materials. The most significant changes include:

1. Personal selling is presented as a set of transferable employment skills needed by four groups of knowledge workers who often do not consider themselves salespeople: customer service representatives; professionals (accountants, consultants, lawyers, etc.); entrepreneurs; and managerial personnel. Success in each of these employment areas requires mastery of any of the skills used by sales professionals. This new feature helps develop a higher level of motivation among class members who may be uncertain about a career in personal selling.

2. The role of technology in personal selling has been updated and expanded. All ACT! sales force automation exercises have been updated with a new customer database and converted to the Windows operating system. These exercises, featured in nearly every chapter, are now described as

Customer Relationship Management (CRM) exercises. The textbook includes new material on how to use PowerPoint and Excel software to create attractive and effective sales demonstration materials. The impact of the Internet on personal selling is described in detail. Internet exercises are featured at the end of each chapter.

3. The growth of strategic alliances used in business to business selling situations is explained and students learn about the new selling environment created by these alliances. The result of most strategic alliances is a complex sale that requires the approval of several people before the sale can be closed. Information on team selling, an approach commonly used in conjunction with complex sales, has been expanded in this edition.

4. The use of sales planning forms, a popular feature of previous editions, has been expanded. These forms provide the student with important skill development opportunities.

5. Role-play exercises have been added to each of the chapters that deal with the selling process (Chapters 9-14). These exercises give students the opportunity to apply what they have learned during their course.

6. This new edition is a more concise, tightly focused textbook. Information not essential to coverage of the topic or concept has been removed. The finished product is very "reader friendly" because the text is focused on important "must know" information. In most cases a real-world example is provided to enhance student interest and clarify important concepts.

Prentice Hall

7. A new and expanded Web site at www.pearsoned.ca/manning has been developed for use by students and professors. One new feature is an interactive study guide/pretest for students who want to check their comprehension of key concepts in the book.

ORGANIZATION OF THIS BOOK

The material in *Selling Today* is organized around the four pillars of personal selling: relationship strategy, product strategy, customer strategy, and presentation strategy. The two chapters that make up Part I set the stage for an in-depth study of the four strategies. The first chapter describes the evolution of personal selling from 1950 to the present and introduces the four strategies. The second chapter gives students an opportunity to explore specific career opportunities in the six major employment areas: service, retail, wholesale, manufacturing, as an independent agent, and as an inside salesperson. Career-minded students will also find the first appendix, "Finding Employment: A Personalized Marketing Plan for the Age of Information," very helpful.

Research indicates that high-performance salespeople are better able to build and maintain relationships than are moderate performers. Part II,

"Developing a Relationship Strategy," focuses on several important person-to-person relationship-building practices that contribute to success in personal selling. Chapter 4, a new addition to Part II, examines the influence of communication styles on relationships between customers and salespeople.

Part III, "Developing a Product Strategy," examines the importance of complete and accurate product, company, and competitive knowledge in personal selling. A well-informed salesperson is in a strong position to apply the fundamentals of consultative selling.

Part IV, "Developing a Customer Strategy," presents information on why and how customers buy, and explains how to identify prospects. With increased knowledge of the customer, salespeople are in a better position to achieve their sales goals.

The concept of a salesperson as adviser, consultant, and partner to buyers is stressed in Part V, "Developing a Presentation Strategy." The traditional sales presentation that emphasizes closing as the primary objective of personal selling is abandoned in favour of three types of need-satisfaction presentations. Here, the salesperson is viewed as a counsellor and consultant.

Part VI includes three chapters: *Management of Self: The Key to Greater Sales Productivity, Ethics: The Foundation for Relationships in Selling,* and *Management of the Sales Force.*

LEARNING TOOLS THAT ENHANCE INSTRUCTION

The second Canadian edition of *Selling Today* includes several learning tools that will aid both teaching and learning. The design and development of these learning activities was influenced by experiences acquired by the authors in over 1000 seminars, workshops, and conferences.

1. Five video clips from the Pearson Education Canada/CBC Video Library and from Canadian business organizations are provided. Each video segment has an average running time of ten minutes. These videos introduce students to real people and companies in the text, and enhance their understanding of various career opportunities in personal selling. Four of these videos support end-of-chapter cases. Once students view the video, they study case information and answer thought-provoking questions. These videos support end-of-chapter cases for Chapters 3, 6, 12, and 14, and a boxed text in Chapter 15.

2. An optional role play and simulation provides students with a realistic opportunity to apply major concepts presented in selected chapters. They are given information about a selling position in the service industry and required to make several critical decisions and complete a number of tasks. All materials needed for both salesperson and customer roles are provided in this easy-to-use exercise. Easy-to-follow instructions are provided in the text at the end of Chapters 1, 5, 9, 10, 11, 12, 13, and 14. These instructions refer to assignments in Appendix 3. The role play and simulation provides a bridge between classroom instruction and the real world of personal selling.

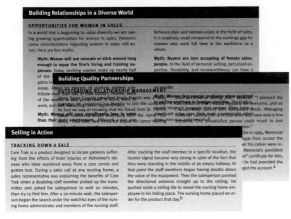

3. Most chapters feature three or four boxed texts, focusing on the themes "Building Quality Partnerships," "Building Relationships in a Diverse World," "Selling in Action," or "Building Relationships through Technology." These explore current real-world examples of what the student is learning throughout the text. This feature gives students a contemporary look at personal selling. Each chapter also includes the following special features that aid the teaching and learning process:

- a list of learning objectives to help the student focus on the important concepts;

- definitions of key terms in the margins next to where they appear in the text;

- a summary that provides a brief review of the most important ideas presented;

- a list of key terms that follows the chapter summary;

- a set of review questions that reinforce the student's understanding of the major concepts presented in the chapter;

- a series of field-based application exercises that will provide students with an opportunity to apply concepts and practices presented (each chapter includes one "Internet Exercise" and each of the six chapters in Part V includes a Role-Play Exercise); and

- a case problem that permits students to analyze and interpret actual selling situations. Each case problem is based on a real-life situation.

4. Every chapter features an insight on the use of sales force automation, now referred to as Customer Relationship Management (CRM) Technology. The trend toward greater use of technology to improve personal selling effectiveness has grown extensively during the past three years and will continue to in the years ahead. In response to this important trend, the second Canadian edition features 17 "Building Relationships through Technology" insights. Each insight explains how salespeople use sales automation to improve quality in the selling process. Optional, easy to complete "Customer Relationship Management (CRM) Application Exercises" have been expanded in this edition to 16 chapters, and CRM Case Studies now appear at the end of eight chapters. These interactive exercises give students the opportunity to use the "Windows" version of the highly acclaimed ACT! Contact Management Software program developed by Pat Sullivan and Mike Muhney, leaders in the field of sales force automation.

See the *Selling Today* Companion Web Site at http://www.pearsoned.ca/manning. The student can use the *Selling Today* Companion Web Site to access the ACT! Contact Management System that features a prospect database and other information to be used by students as they make a range of decisions regarding qualifying prospects, approaching prospects, the sales presentation, demonstration, negotiation, closing, and servicing the sale. Students can print prospect profiles, sales letters, and telephone contact lists; conduct key-word searches to find important references in the database; and do many other things. Simple single-stroke instructions are provided that enable students to experience the many advances in sales automation.

SUPPLEMENTS

Selling Today: Building Quality Partnerships, second Canadian edition, is accompanied by a complete supplements package.

Instructor's Manual

The comprehensive Instructor's Manual includes detailed presentation outlines, answers to review questions, a trainer's guide for the "grey issues" selling ethics game, suggested responses to learning activities, copies of printouts for Sales Automation Exercises, detailed instructions for using the video case problems, and a complete trainers guide for using the role play and simulation.

Test Item File

The author-developed Test Item File contains over 1,000 multiple-choice, true/false, and essay questions. Each question is rated by level of difficulty and includes a text page reference. It is available in both printed and electronic formats.

Pearson Education Canada Test Manager

The Pearson Education Canada Test Manager merges the Test Item File with a powerful software package in the Windows platform. With the Pearson Education Canada Test Manager's user-friendly test-creating abilities, you can create tailor-made, error-free tests quickly and easily. The Test Manager allows you to create an exam, administer it traditionally or online, and evaluate and track student's results—all with the click of the mouse.

Pearson Education Canada Video Library

Pearson Education Canada, the CBC and Canadian corporations have worked together to bring segments from the CBC series *Venture*, as well as video material from several Canadian businesses to support this text. All programs have extremely high production quality and have been chosen to relate directly to chapter content. (Please contact your Pearson Education Canada sales representative for details. These videos are subject to availability and terms negotiated upon adoption of the text.)

Electronic Transparencies in PowerPoint 7.0 and Transparency Masters

Over 200 PowerPoint transparencies, including figures, graphs, and key concepts featured in the text, are available electronically in PowerPoint 7.0.

ACCOLADES FOR THE U.S. EDITION

Selling Today has been the recipient of many accolades over the years. Three of the most important honours will be of interest to current and potential

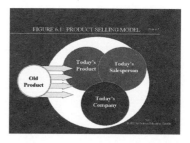

adopters. *Selling Today* was selected by Intelecom for use in its telecourse entitled *The Sales Connection*. An esteemed panel of business and academic professionals spent over two years and $1-milllion to develop this important new college course. *Selling Today* was also selected by Certified Marketing Services International for use with the first international program for sales certification. The International Organization for Standardization (ISO) authorized CMSI to develop and administer this important new program. The major objective of this certification program is to increase the standard of excellence in the field of personal selling. Sales Links/Mentor Associates, a popular Internet Web site for persons involved in major account selling, sales training, and sales optimization selected *Selling Today* as the best overall textbook covering the field of personal selling.

ACKNOWLEDGMENTS

Many people have made contributions to the second Canadian edition of *Selling Today: Building Quality Partnerships*. We are very grateful to Jack W. Linge, who contributed significantly to the development of the sales force automation case study, which is an important addition to this textbook. Special recognition is also extended to Cadalyst Resources and Contact Software International for assistance in developing materials used in conjunction with the second Canadian edition. The text has been improved as a result of numerous helpful comments and recommendations. We extend special appreciation to the following reviewers:

Paul F. Dunne, *College of the North Atlantic*; Steve Lee, *Algonquin College*; Peter Mitchell, *British Columbia Institute of Technology*; Nancy Schappert, *Niagara College*; and Joseph Suarez, *Humber College*.

THE SEARCH FOR WISDOM IN THE AGE OF INFORMATION

The search for the fundamentals of personal selling has become more difficult in the age of information. The glut of information (information explosion) threatens our ability to identify what is true, right, or lasting. The search for knowledge begins with a review of information, and wisdom is gleaned from knowledge (see model in margin). Books continue to be one of the best sources of wisdom. Many new books, and several classics, were used as references for the second Canadian edition of *Selling Today*. A sample of the more than 100 books used to prepare this edition follows.

Blur: The Speed of Change in the Connected Economy by Stan Davis and
    Christopher Meyer
Data Smog: Surviving the Information Glut by David Shenk
The New Strategic Selling by Robert B. Miller and Stephen E. Heiman
Selling the Invisible by Harry Beckwith
Working With Emotional Intelligence by Daniel Goleman
Psycho-Cybernetics by Maxwell Maltz
The Double Win by Denis Waitley
Zero-Resistance Selling by Maxwell Maltz, Dan S. Kennedy, William T. Brooks,
    Matt Oechsli, Jeff Paul and Pamela Yellen
Messages: The Communications Skills Book by Matthew McKay, Martha Davis and
    Patrick Fanning

Spin Selling by Neil Rackham
The Power of 5 by Harold H. Bloomfield and Robert K. Cooper
Secrets of Closing the Sale by Zig Ziglar
Sales Magic by Kerry L. Johnson
Making Contact by Barry Siskind
Seminars to Build Your Business by Barbara Siskind
The New Professional Image by Susan Bixler and Nancy Nix-Rice
Complete Business Etiquette Handbook by Barbara Pachter and Marjorie Brody
The 7 Habits of Highly Effective People by Stephen R. Covey
Integrity Selling by Ron Willingham
Selling With Integrity by Sharon Drew Morgan
Thriving on Chaos by Tom Peters
Secrets of Power Presentations by Peter Urs Bender
Changing the Game: The New Way to Sell by Larry Wilson
The Circle of Innovation by Tom Peters
Business @ The Speed of Thought by Bill Gates
Consultative Selling by Mack Hanan
The Butterfly Customer by Susan M. O'Dell and Joan A. Pajunen
The 10 Natural Laws of Successful Time and Life Management by Hyrum W. Smith
Personal Styles and Effective Performance by David W. Merrill and Roger H. Reid
The Versatile Salesperson by Roger Wenschlag

AN INVESTMENT IN THE FUTURE

Charles Schwab the great industrialist and entrepreneur said, "We are all salespeople every day of our lives, selling our ideas and enthusiasm to those with whom we come in contact." As authors, we suggest that you retain this book for future reference. Periodic review of the ideas in this text will help you daily in areas such as:

- interviewing for new jobs in the future

- understanding and training salespeople who work for you or with you

- selling new ideas to senior management, co-workers, or employees you might be supervising

- selling products or services that you represent as a salesperson

We wish you much success and happiness in applying your knowledge of personal selling.

Gerald L. Manning   *Barry L. Reece*

Gem MacKenzie

About the Authors

DR. BARRY L. REECE, PROFESSOR
Virginia Polytechnic Institute and State University

Dr. Reece has devoted more than three decades to teaching, research, consulting, and the development of training programs in the areas of sales, supervision, human relations, and management. He has conducted over 600 seminars and workshops for public- and private-sector organizations. He has written several textbooks and articles in the areas of sales, supervision, communications, and management. Dr. Reece was named "Trainer of the Year" by the Valleys of Virginia Chapter of the American Society for Training and Development, and was awarded the "Excellence in Teaching Award" by the College of Human Resources and Education at Virginia Polytechnic Institute and State University. Dr. Reece has contributed to numerous journals and is author or co-author of twenty-five books, including *Business, Human Relations — Principles and Practices, Supervision and Leadership in Action*, and *Effective Human Relations in Organizations*. He has served as a consultant to numerous profit and not-for-profit organizations.

MR. GERALD L. MANNING, CHAIR
Marketing/Management Department, Des Moines Area Community College

Mr. Manning has served as a chair of the Marketing/Management Department for more than 30 years. In addition to his administrative duties, he has served as lead instructor in sales and sales management. The classroom has provided him with an opportunity to study the merits of various experiential learning approaches such as role-plays, simulations, games, and interactive demonstrations. Partnership Selling: A Role/Simulation for Selling Today, included in this text, was developed and tested in the classroom by Mr. Manning. He has also applied numerous personal selling principles and practices in the real world as owner of a real estate development and management company.

Mr. Manning has served as a sales and marketing consultant to senior management and owners of over 500 businesses, including several national companies. He appears regularly as a speaker at national conferences. Mr. Manning has received the "Outstanding Instructor of the Year" award given annually by his college.

Dr. H.F. (Herb) MacKenzie, Associate Professor
Memorial University of Newfoundland

Dr. MacKenzie has taught in the undergraduate and graduate programs at several Canadian universities, and has been consulting to both private- and public-sector businesses since 1985. He has over 15 years of industrial sales and sales management experience, and has published many cases, conference proceedings, and articles in the areas of sales management, buyer–seller relationships and distribution channel management. Dr. MacKenzie has conducted professional selling and sales management seminars with the Centre for Management Development at Memorial University of Newfoundland, and with a number of private organizations.

KEEPING CURRENT IN A CHANGING WORLD

Throughout the past decade, professors Manning, Reece, and MacKenzie have relied on three strategies to keep current in the dynamic field of personal selling. They are actively involved in sales training and consulting. Frequent interaction with salespeople and sales managers provides valuable insights regarding contemporary issues and developments in the field of personal selling. A second major strategy involves extensive research and development activities. The major focus of these activities has been factors that contribute to high-performance salespeople. The third major strategy involves completion of training and development programs offered by many respected sales training companies. Among them, professors Manning, Reece, and MacKenzie have completed seminars and workshops offered by Learning International, Wilson Learning Corporation, Forum Corporation, Franklin Covey, and several other companies.

Your Internet companion to the most exciting, state-of-the-art educational tools on the Web!

The Pearson Education Canada Companion Website is easy to navigate and is organized to correspond to the chapters in this textbook. The Companion Website is comprised of four distinct, functional features:

1) Customized Online Resources

2) Online Study Guide

3) Reference Material

4) Communication

Explore the four areas in this Companion Website. Students and distance learners will discover resources for indepth study, research and communication, empowering them in their quest for greater knowledge and maximizing their potential for success in the course.

A NEW WAY TO DELIVER EDUCATIONAL CONTENT

1) Customized Online Resources

Our Companion Websites provide instructors and students with a range of options to access, view, and exchange content.

- **Syllabus Builder** provides *instructors* with the option to create online classes and construct an online syllabus linked to specific modules in the Companion Website.

- **Mailing lists** enable *instructors* and *students* to receive customized promotional literature.

- **Preferences** enable *students* to customize the sending of results to various recipients, and also to customize how the material is sent, e.g., as html, text, or as an attachment.

- **Help** includes an evaluation of the user's system and a tune-up area that makes updating browsers and plug-ins easier. This new feature will enhance the user's experience with Companion Websites.

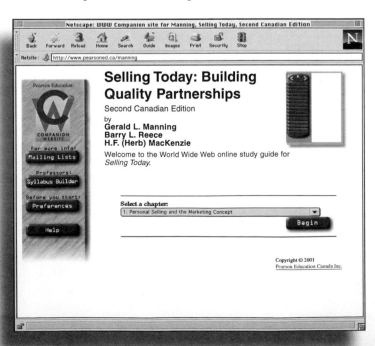

Pearson Education

COMPANION
WEBSITE

2) Online Study Guide

An Interactive Study Guide forms the core of the student learning experience in the Companion Website. Modules for Multiple Choice, True/False, and Internet Exercises are organized by text chapter, providing students with the ability to send answers to our grader and receive instant feedback on their progress through our Results Reporter. Students can check suggested answers after submitting their problems. Role play questions are available for each Part in the book.

3) Reference Material

Reference material broadens text coverage with up-to-date resources for learning. Special **Video Case Studies** provide instructors and students with interesting video segments and stimulating cases for discussion. **Web Destinations** provides direct links to websites relevant to the subject matter in each chapter. **Net News (Internet Newsgroups)** are a fundamental source of information about a discipline, containing a wealth of brief, opinionated postings. **Net Search** simplifies key term search using Internet search engines.

4) Communication

Companion Websites contain the communication tools necessary to deliver courses in a **Distance Learning** environment. **Message Board** allows users to post messages and check back periodically for responses. **Live Chat** allows users to discuss course topics in real time, and enables professors to host online classes.

Communication facilities of Companion Websites provide a key element for distributed learning environments. There are two types of communication facilities currently in use in Companion Websites:

- **Message Board**-this module takes advantage of browser technology, providing the users of each Companion Website with a national newsgroup to post and reply to relevant course topics.

- **Live Chat**-enables instructor-led group activities in real time. Using our chat client, instructors can display Website content while students participate in the discussion.

Companion Websites are currently available for numerous Pearson Education Canada books, including

- Solomon, Zaichkowsky, and Polegato, *Consumer Behaviour*, Canadian Edition.
- Evans, Berman, and Wellington, *Marketing*, Second Canadian Edition.
- Kotler, Armstrong, and Cunningham, *Principles of Marketing*, Fourth Canadian Edition.

Note: CW content will vary slightly from site to site depending on discipline requirements.

The Companion Website can be found at:
www.pearsoned.ca/manning

Pearson Education Canada

26 Prince Andrew Place
Don Mills, Ontario M3C 2T8

To order:
Call: 1-800-567-3800
Fax: 1-800-263-7733

For samples:
Call: 1-800-850-5813
Fax: (416) 447-2819
E-mail: phcinfo.pubcanada@pearsoned.com

Part I

Developing a Personal Selling Philosophy for the New Economy

The two chapters that make up Part I explain the important role of personal selling in organizations, in economic systems, in social reform movements, and most importantly in the personal lives of the millions of men and women enjoying rewarding sales careers in today's services-oriented, information-saturated, global marketplace.

BUILDING QUALITY PARTNERSHIPS

Every employee at Federal Express must be sales oriented and each manager must be an outstanding individual salesperson.

Federal Express

Personal Selling and the Marketing Concept

Personal Selling and
the Marketing Concept

LEARNING OBJECTIVES

When you finish reading this chapter, you should be able to

1. Describe the contributions of personal selling to the information economy

2. Define personal selling and discuss personal selling as an extension of the marketing concept

3. Describe the evolution of consultative selling from the marketing era to the present

4. Define strategic selling and name the four broad strategic areas in the Strategic/Consultative Selling Model

5. Describe the evolution of partnering and discuss how it relates to the quality improvement process

Several years ago, Tony Woodson traded his Purolator courier uniform for the uniform of a Purolator sales representative. Tony's first career was professional football, where he played for both the Calgary Stampeders and the Ottawa Rough Riders. In 1990, following an injury to his Achilles tendon, Tony reassessed his opportunities in football as he was about to move to the B.C. Lions. He ended up in Calgary, where he accepted a full-time job and also began to work part-time in a Purolator warehouse. After one year, he moved to a full-time position as a Purolator courier. Fortunately for Tony, Purolator had developed a courier-sales program in 1993, as part of its commitment to making shipping the easiest part of the day for its customers. In an effort to streamline the sales process and add value for Purolator customers, couriers were trained to sell to customers during pick-up and delivery calls. Tony's performance ranked him number-one across Canada, and he moved to a full-time sales position in 1995. Since then, Tony Woodson has been a three-time President's Club award winner at Purolator.[1]

Sales professionals who represent Purolator are experiencing changes in selling that are shared with salespeople around the world. One area of change is the scope of the competitive selling environment. Today, a one-world market exists for products ranging from courier and consulting services to automobiles and computer equipment. Salespeople need to adopt a global perspective. A salesperson employed by Purolator must compete with salespeople for UPS, Federal Express, Canpar, and Loomis for the opportunity to serve customers throughout the world. Purolator, for example, processes 2 250 000 pieces each week for destinations across Canada and around the world.[2]

A second area of commonality is the need for salespeople to develop the skills needed to sell intangibles. A majority of today's salespeople sell services. Salespeople employed by ADT Security Services, Clarica Life Insurance, Dun & Bradstreet, Ernst & Young, and Marriott Hotels sell services, not physical products. As our service economy continues to expand, so will employment opportunities for salespeople in the service sector.

A third area of commonality is the need for all sales professionals, regardless of employer, to adjust to the changes that accompany the age of information. The age of information is creating a new economy that offers salespeople many challenges and exciting employment opportunities. Learning how to manage and communicate information to customers within a high-trust working relationship is one of the major challenges facing today's salesperson.

Tony Woodson of Purolator is a three-time President's Club award winner.

Personal Selling in the Age of Information

Restructuring from an industrial economy to an information economy began in the 1950s (Figure 1.1). John Naisbitt, author of the popular book *Megatrends*, noted that it was during this period that our economy began shifting from an emphasis on industrial activity to an emphasis on processing information. He recognized we were giving way to a new society where most of us would work

Figure 1.1 The age of information has greatly influenced personal selling. Salespeople today use a variety of information technology tools to gather and process information of value to the customer. They recognize that information is a strategic resource and relationship skills are needed to build a conduit of trust for information acceptance.

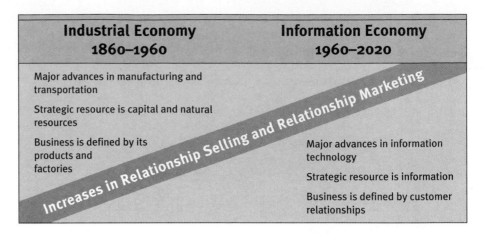

with information rather than produce goods.[3] We live in an age in which the effective exchange of information is the foundation of most economic transactions. Today we are in the latter stages of the age of information, and the implications for personal selling are profound. We will describe the three major developments that have shaped the information economy and discuss the implications for personal selling.

Major advances in information technology. The information age has spawned the information technology revolution. Salespeople and other players in the information age use personal computers, electronic mail, faxes, mobile phones, and other forms of technology to obtain and process information. Explosive growth of electronic commerce and other Internet activities has changed the way we use computers. Stan Davis, futurist and co-author of *Blur: The Speed of Change in the Connected Economy*, says we now use the computer less for data crunching and more for connecting. These connections involve people to people, machine to machine, product to service, organization to organization, and all the combinations thereof.[4] Without these connections, information-age workers cannot do their jobs. People who work extensively with information, such as salespeople, need these connections to carry out their information gathering and information management responsibilities.

Strategic resource is information. Advances in information technology have increased the speed by which we acquire, process, and disseminate information. David Shenk, author of *Data Smog: Surviving the Information Glut*, notes that we have moved from a state of information scarcity to one of information overload.[5] The information age is dynamic, but it can also be disorienting. In an era of limitless data, informed salespeople will be expected to help us decide which information has value and which information should be ignored. Customers who have less time to adjust to new products and circumstances will value this assistance.

Business is defined by customer relationships. On the surface, the major focus of the age of information seems to be the accumulation of more and more information and the never-ending search for new forms of information technology. It's easy to overlook the importance of the human

"One question: If this is the Information Age, how come nobody knows anything?"

element. It is humans, not computers, that have the ability to think, feel, and create ideas. It is no coincidence that relationship selling and relationship marketing, which emphasize long-term, mutually satisfying buyer–seller relationships, began to gain support at the beginning of the age of information. Personal selling provides a human response that counterbalances the impersonal nature of technology.

Today's salespeople are competing in a services-oriented, information-saturated global economy. They must spend considerable time acquiring, processing, and delivering information to customers who are often experiencing information overload. Success will be achieved by those salespeople who employ relationship skills to build a conduit of trust for information acceptance. As the level of trust builds, the customer is more willing to share information that the salesperson must have to satisfy the customer's needs.

Personal Selling—A Definition and a Philosophy

Personal selling involves person-to-person communication with a prospect. It is a process of developing relationships, discovering needs, matching appropriate products with these needs, and communicating benefits through informing, reminding, or persuading. The term **product** should be broadly interpreted to encompass physical goods, services, and ideas. Increasingly, personal selling is viewed as an important form of customer service. In an ideal situation the salesperson diagnoses the customer's needs and custom fits the product to meet these needs.

Preparation for a career in personal selling begins with the development of a personal philosophy or set of beliefs that provides guidance. To some degree this philosophy is like the rudder that steers a ship. Without a rudder the ship's

personal selling Involves person-to-person communication with a prospect. It is a process of developing relationships; discovering customer needs; matching appropriate products with these needs; and communicating benefits through informing, reminding, or persuading.

product One of the four P's of the marketing mix. The term product should be broadly interpreted to encompass physical goods, services, and ideas.

Figure 1.2   Today, salespeople use a strategic plan based on a personal philosophy that emphasizes adopting the marketing concept, valuing personal selling, and becoming a problem solver/partner.

Strategic/Consultative Selling Model	
Strategic step	**Prescription**
DEVELOP A PERSONAL SELLING PHILOSOPHY	○ ADOPT MARKETING CONCEPT ○ VALUE PERSONAL SELLING ○ BECOME A PROBLEM SOLVER/PARTNER

personal selling philosophy
Involves three things: full acceptance of the marketing concept; developing an appreciation for the expanding role of personal selling in our competitive national and international markets; and assuming the role of problem solver or partner in helping customers to make complex buying decisions.

direction is unpredictable. Without a personal philosophy the salesperson's behaviour is also unpredictable.

The development of a **personal selling philosophy** involves three things: adopt the marketing concept, value personal selling, and assume the role of a problem solver or partner in helping customers make buying decisions (Fig. 1.2). These three prescriptions for success in personal selling are presented here as part of the Strategic/Consultative Selling Model. This model will be expanded in future chapters to include additional strategic steps in the selling process.

Personal Selling as an Extension of the Marketing Concept

A careful examination of personal selling practices during the past 40 years of the age of information reveals some positive developments. We have seen the evolution of personal selling from an era that emphasized *pushing* or *peddling* products to an era that emphasizes *partnering*. Throughout this period we have seen the emergence of new thinking patterns concerning every aspect of sales and sales management. Salespeople today are no longer the flamboyant product "pitchmen" of the past. Instead they are increasingly becoming diagnosticians of customers' needs and problems. A growing number of salespeople recognize that the quality of the partnerships they create is as important as the quality of the products they sell.

The Evolution of the Marketing Concept

marketing concept A belief that the business firm should dedicate all its policies, planning, and operation to the satisfaction of the customer; a belief that the final result of all business activity should be to earn a profit by satisfying the customer.

What is the **marketing concept**? When a business firm moves from a product orientation to a customer orientation, we say it has adopted the marketing concept. This concept springs from the belief that the firm should dedicate all of its policies, planning, and operation to the satisfaction of the customer.

The marketing era and the age of information began in the 1950s (Table 1.1). J. B. McKitterick, a General Electric executive, is credited with making one of the earliest formal statements indicating corporate interest in the marketing concept. In a paper written in 1957 he observed that the principal marketing function of a company is to determine what the customer wants and then develop the appropriate product or service. This view contrasted with the prevailing practice of that period, which was to develop products and then build customer interest in those products.

The foundation for the marketing concept is a business philosophy that leaves no doubt in the mind of every employee that customer satisfaction is of primary importance. All energies are directed toward satisfying the customer. As

Table 1.1 Evolution of Personal Selling (1950 to Present)

SALES AND MARKETING EMPHASIS	TIME PERIOD	IMPORTANT EVENTS	SELLING EMPHASIS
Marketing Era Begins *Organizations determine needs and wants of target markets and adapt themselves to delivering desired satisfaction. Product orientation is replaced by a customer orientation.*	*Middle 1950s*	• *John Naisbitt cites 1956–1957 as the beginning of the information age.* • *J. B. McKitterick, General Electric executive, presents a paper in 1957 on applications of the marketing concept.*	• *More organizations recognize that the salesperson is in a position to collect product, market, and service information regarding the buyer's needs.*
Consultative Selling Era *Salespeople are becoming diagnosticians of customers' needs as well as consultants offering well-considered recommendations. Mass markets are breaking into target markets.*	*Late 1960s to early 1970s*	• *In the late 1960s Wilson Learning Corporation develops a sales training course entitled "Counselor Selling."* • *In 1973 Mark Hanan writes* Consultative Selling.	• *Buyer needs are identified through two-way communication.* • *Information-giving and negotiation tactics replace manipulation.*
Strategic Selling Era *The evolution of a more complex selling environment and greater emphasis on market niches creates the need for greater structure and more emphasis on planning.*	*Early 1980s*	• *Strategic Selling is written by Robert Miller and Stephen Heiman in 1985.* • *Learning International, The Forum Corporation, and Wilson Learning Corporation develop sales training courses that emphasize strategic selling.*	• *Strategy is given as much attention as selling tactics.* • *Product positioning is given more attention.*
Partnering Era *Salespeople are encouraged to think of everything they say or do in the context of their long-term, high quality partnership with individual customers. Sales force automation provides specific customer information.*	*1990 to the present*	• *Tom Peters, Larry Wilson, and others popularize the "Lifetime" customer concept.* • *American Media, Inc. produces a training film entitled "Partnering: The Heart of Selling Today."*	• *Customer supplants the product as the driving force in sales.* • *Greater emphasis on total quality relationships that result in repeat business and referrals.*

The foundation for the marketing concept is a belief that a firm should dedicate all of its policies, planning, and operation to the satisfaction of the customer.

noted management guru Peter Drucker once observed, "The customers define the business."

Business firms vary in terms of how strongly they support the marketing concept. Some firms have gone the extra mile to satisfy the needs and wants of their customers:

➤ Canada's National Quality Institute recently recognized IBM Canada with its prestigious Canada Award for Excellence. IBM handled 325 000 hardware and 126 000 software service calls, and recorded 96 percent and 90 percent customer satisfaction levels, respectively. In its report, the institute wrote, "IBM Canada Customer Service of Markham, Ontario, addresses customer inquiries promptly and employees accept responsibility for resolving customer concerns. As a result, they are a leader in the highly competitive hardware and software service and technical support business, consistently increasing market share."[6]

➤ Marriott Hotels uses a blend of "high tech" and "high touch" to build customer goodwill and repeat business. Each of the 5500 sales representatives can sell the services of 10 hotel brands in Marriott's portfolio. The customer with a small meeting budget might be encouraged to consider a Fairfield Inn property. The customer who is seeking luxury accommodations might be introduced to a Ritz-Carlton hotel (a chain that Marriott acquired a few years ago). All reservations go through the same system, so if one Marriott hotel is full, the sales representative can cross-sell rooms in another Marriott hotel in the same city.[7]

MARKETING CONCEPT YIELDS MARKETING MIX

Once the marketing concept becomes an integral part of a firm's philosophy, its management seeks to develop a network of marketing activities that will maximize customer service and ensure profitability. The combination of elements

Wal-Mart views personal selling as an important dimension of its marketing program. This company also realizes the value of relationships in creating repeat business.

making up a program based on the marketing concept is known as the **marketing mix** (Fig. 1.3). These elements are product, distribution, promotion, and price.[8] For a marketing program to achieve the desired results, each function must be executed effectively.

One element of the marketing mix, promotion, can be further subdivided into advertising, public relations, sales promotion, and personal selling. When a company adopts the marketing concept, it must determine how some combination of these elements can result in maximum customer satisfaction.

marketing mix The combination of elements (product, distribution, promotion, and price) that creates continuing customer satisfaction for a business.

THE IMPORTANT ROLE OF PERSONAL SELLING

Every marketer must decide how much time and money to invest in each of the four areas of the marketing mix. The decision must be objective; no one can afford to invest money in a marketing strategy that does not provide continuing customer satisfaction … *across all businesses, more money is spent on personal selling than on any other form of marketing communications.*[9] Firms make large investments in personal selling in response to several major trends: products and services are becoming increasingly sophisticated and complex; competition has greatly increased in most product areas; and demand for quality, value, and service by customers has risen sharply. In response to these trends, personal selling has evolved to a new level of professionalism. Since the beginning of the age of information, personal selling has evolved through three distinct developmental periods: the consultative selling era, the strategic selling era, and the partnering era. We will examine each of these developments.

Product	Distribution
Price	Promotion

Figure 1.3 Each of the elements that make up the marketing mix must be executed effectively for a marketing program to achieve the desired results.

The Evolution of Consultative Selling

Consultative selling, which emerged in the late 1960s and early 1970s, is an extension of the marketing concept (see Table 1.1). This approach emphasizes

consultative selling An approach to personal selling that is an extension of the marketing concept. Emphasis is placed on need identification, need satisfaction, and the building of a relationship that results in repeat business.

need identification, which is achieved through effective communication between the salesperson and the customer. The salesperson establishes two-way communication by asking appropriate questions and listening carefully to the customer's responses. The salesperson assumes the role of consultant and offers well-considered recommendations. Negotiation replaces manipulation as the salesperson sets the stage for a long-term partnership. Salespeople who have adopted consultative selling possess a keen ability to listen, define the customer's problem, and offer one or more solutions.[10]

Although consultative selling is emphasized throughout this text, it is helpful to understand the role of transactional selling in our economy. **Transactional selling** is a sales process that most effectively matches the needs of the value-conscious buyer who is primarily interested in price and convenience. Because the transaction-based buyer tends to focus primarily on low price, some marketers are adopting lower-cost selling channels. Low cost transaction selling strategies include telesales, direct mail, and the Internet. This approach to selling is usually used by marketers who do not see the need to spend very much time on customer needs assessment, problem solving, relationship building, or sales follow-up.[11] It is an unattractive alternative to consultative selling in situations involving high-value customized products with relatively long and complex decision making processes.

Service, retail, wholesale, and manufacturing firms that embrace the marketing concept have already adopted or are currently adopting consultative selling practices. The major features of consultative selling are as follows:

1. The customer is seen as a *person to be served*, not a prospect to be sold. Consultative salespeople believe their function is to help the buyer make an intelligent decision. They use a four-step process that includes need discovery, selection of the product, a need-satisfaction presentation, and servicing the sale (Fig. 1.4). These customer-centred strategies will be fully developed and explained in Chapters 9 to 14.

2. The consultative salesperson, unlike the peddler of an earlier era, does not try to overpower the customer with a high-pressure sales presentation. Instead, the buyer's needs are identified through *two-way* communication. It is very important that the salesperson know the product or service they are selling. Then, the salesperson asks the potential buyer questions in an attempt to learn as much as possible about the person's needs and perceptions.

3. Consultative selling emphasizes *information giving, problem solving, and negotiation rather than manipulation*. This approach leads to a more trusting relationship between buyer and seller. Helping the buyer make an informed and intelligent buying decision adds value to the product.

4. Consultative selling emphasizes *service* after the sale. Theodore Levitt, author-consultant, recognizes that the relationship between a seller and a buyer seldom ends when a sale is made. In an increasing number of trans-

transactional selling A sales process that most effectively matches the needs of the value-conscious buyer, who is primarily interested in price and convenience.

Figure 1.4 The Consultative Sales Presentation Guide. This contemporary presentation guide emphasizes the customer as a person to be served.

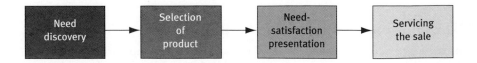

In consultative selling, negotiation replaces manipulation as the salesperson sets the stage for a long-term relationship.

actions the relationship actually intensifies, because the customer has higher expectations after the sale. The personalized service provided after the sale may include making credit arrangements, supervising product delivery and installation, servicing warranties, and following up on complaints.

At first glance, it may appear that consultative selling practices can be easily mastered. The truth is, consultative selling is a complex process that puts great demands on sales personnel.[12] This approach to personal selling requires an understanding of concepts and principles borrowed from the fields of psychology, communications, and sociology. It takes a great deal of personal commitment and self-discipline to become a sales consultant/adviser.

THE ENHANCEMENT OF CONSULTATIVE SELLING

Throughout the past 30 years consultative selling has evolved into a more mature and more focused approach to meeting the customer's needs. With each passing year we have learned more about high-performance salespeople who use this approach; this information has been incorporated into many sales training programs, training videos, and books devoted to personal selling.

The early consultative sales training programs emphasized the development of face-to-face selling skills. These skills continue to be important today, but they must be enhanced with strategic planning and a strong commitment to building partnerships. Today salespeople are encountering better educated and more demanding customers who are asking harder questions and seeking more precise solutions to their buying problems. Time is a precious commodity for most of today's customers. They want to partner with a salesperson who is well organized, well informed, and able to use strategic thinking to meet their complex needs. The remainder of this chapter will be devoted to an introduction of strategic selling and partnering.

The Evolution of Strategic Selling

Strategic selling began receiving considerable attention during the 1980s (see Table 1.1). It was during this period that we witnessed the beginning of several trends that resulted in a more complex selling environment. These trends, which include increased global competition, broader and more diverse product lines, more decision makers involved in major purchases, and greater demand for specific, custom-made solutions, will continue to influence personal selling and sales training.

As companies face increased levels of complexity in the marketplace, they must give more attention to strategic planning. The strategic planning done by salespeople is often influenced by the information included in the company's strategic market plan. A **strategic market plan** is an outline of the methods and resources required to achieve an organization's goals within a specific target market. It takes into consideration all of the major functional areas of the business that must be coordinated, such as production, marketing, finance, and human resources management.[13] Almost every aspect of the plan directly or indirectly influences the sale of products.

The strategic market plan should be a guide for a strategic selling plan. This plan includes strategies that you use to position yourself with the customer before the sales call even begins.[14] The authors of *Strategic Selling* point out that there is a difference between a *tactic* and a *strategy*. **Tactics** are techniques, practices, or methods you use when you are face to face with a customer. Examples are the use of questions to identify needs, presentation skills, and various types of closes. These and other tactics will be discussed in Chapters 9 to 14. **Strategies,** on the other hand, are prerequisite to tactical success. If you develop the correct strategies, you are more likely to make your sales presentation to the right person, at the right time, in a manner most likely to achieve positive results.

A selling strategy is a carefully conceived plan that is needed to accomplish a sales objective. Let's assume you are a sales representative employed by a food service distributor (wholesaler) and you call on full-service restaurants. A strategy might include careful analysis of restaurant menus prior to sales calls. Menu

strategic market plan An outline of the methods and resources required to achieve an organization's goals within a specific target market, taking into consideration all the major functional areas of the business that must be coordinated, such as production, marketing, finance, and human resource management.

tactics Techniques, practices, or methods salespeople use during face-to-face interactions with customers.

strategies The things that salespeople do as the result of pre-call planning to ensure that they call on the right people, at the right time, and with the right tactics to achieve positive results.

Today's customer wants a quality product and a quality relationship. Salespeople who build partnering-style relationships will be rewarded with repeat business and referrals.

analysis helps you determine what products the restaurant needs to prepare the items it serves to customers.[15] With this information you can select the most appropriate selling tactic (method), which might be to present samples of food and beverage items the restaurant is currently not buying from you.

Strategic planning sets the stage for a value-added form of consultative selling that is more structured, more focused, and more efficient. The result of this value added is better time allocation, more precise problem solving, and a greater chance that there will be a good match between your product and the customer's needs. Andrew Parsons, director of consumer marketing for McKinsey and Company, notes that in the current selling environment salespeople must choose from a sophisticated range of alternatives. He points out in general terms that personal selling has moved from "a game of checkers to a game of chess." For many salespeople, strategic planning is not an option, but the key to survival.

THE STRATEGIC/CONSULTATIVE SELLING MODEL

When you study a value-added approach to personal selling that combines strategic planning, consultative selling practices, and partnering principles, you experience a mental exercise that is similar to solving a jigsaw puzzle. You are given many pieces of information that must ultimately form a complete picture. Putting the parts together isn't nearly as difficult if you can see the total picture at the beginning. Therefore a single model has been developed to serve as a source of reference throughout the entire text. Figure 1.5 shows this model.

The Strategic/Consultative Selling Model features five steps, and each step is based on three prescriptions. The first step involves the development of a personal selling philosophy. Each of the other steps relates to a broad strategic area of personal selling. Each makes an important and unique contribution to the selling–buying process. A brief introduction to each strategic area is presented here.

DEVELOPING A RELATIONSHIP STRATEGY

Success in selling depends heavily on the salesperson's ability to develop, manage, and enhance interpersonal relations with the customer. People seldom buy products or services from someone they dislike or distrust. Harvey B. Mackay, chief executive officer of Mackay Envelope Corporation, says, "People don't care how much you know until they know how much you care." Most customers are more apt to openly discuss their needs and wants with a salesperson with whom they feel comfortable.

A **relationship strategy** is a well-thought-out plan for establishing, building, and maintaining quality relationships. This type of plan is essential for success in today's marketplace, which is characterized by vigorous competition, look-alike products, and customer loyalty dependent on quality relationships as well as quality products. The relationship strategy must encompass every aspect of selling, from the first contact with a prospect to servicing the sale once this prospect becomes an established customer. The primary goal of the relationship strategy is to create rapport, trust, and mutual respect, which will ensure a long-term partnership. To establish this type of relationship, salespeople must adopt a double-win philosophy (that is, if the customer wins, I win); project a professional image; and practise communication-style flexing (see Fig. 1.5). These topics will be discussed in detail in Chapters 3 and 16.

relationship strategy A well-thought-out plan for establishing, building, and maintaining quality relationships.

Some people think that the concept of *relationships* is too soft and too emotional for a business application; these people think that it's too difficult to think about relationships in strategic terms. In fact this is not the case at all. Every salesperson can and should formulate a strategic plan that will build and enhance relationships.

DEVELOPING A PRODUCT STRATEGY

product strategy A well-conceived plan that emphasizes acquiring extensive product knowledge, learning to select and communicate appropriate product benefits that will appeal to the customer, and positioning the product.

Products and services represent problem-solving tools. The **product strategy** is a plan that helps salespeople make correct decisions concerning the selection and positioning of products to meet identified customer needs. The development of a product strategy begins with a thorough study of one's product (see Fig. 1.5) using a feature-benefit analysis approach. Product features such as technical superiority, reliability, fashionableness, design integrity, or guaranteed availability should be converted to benefits that will appeal to the customer. Today's high-performance salespeople strive to become product experts. Chapter 5 focuses on company, product, and competition knowledge needed by salespeople.

A well-conceived product strategy for the age of information also requires that decisions be made concerning product positioning. The positioning of a product refers to the decisions, activities, and communications that establish and maintain a firm's intended product concept in the customer's mind. The goal of salespeople at a Lexus dealership, for example, is to create the perception that their automobiles are the best in the high-performance luxury category and that the company will stand behind its products with an excellent customer service program. The brokers at Nesbitt Burns strive to create the perception that

commodity A product that is nearly identical to or appears to be the same as competing products in the customer's mind.

Building Quality Partnerships

ADDING VALUE IN COMMODITY SALES

We use the term **commodity** to describe products that are nearly identical or that appear to be the same in the customer's mind. A good example of a commodity is the standard business envelope. There are more than 200 envelope companies in North America selling basically the same product. Mutual funds have become another modern-day commodity. Canadian investors can choose from more than 2500 different funds. Commodities are often sold by marketers who have adopted a transactional selling strategy. A common way to increase market share in a competitive commodity industry and thus escape a transactional sale is to use a form of personal selling that adds value to look-alike products. This can be accomplished by creating a truly distinctive offering, either by product innovation or by developing distinctive services that appeal to customers. Dennis Courtney, chief information officer at Dunlop Tire Corporation, offers this advice on how to add value to commodity sales:

The products that a supplier offers are only a small part of the equation. Generally, we could get what we need from several places, so it's not unique. What we're looking for goes beyond the product. We're looking for business understanding, we're looking for whether they can adapt to our special needs or whether they can advise and help us. We want their salespeople to add something worthwhile on their own account.

As Courtney notes, salespeople are in a position to add value to commodities. For example, a salesperson who is viewed as a trusted adviser, capable of giving prompt and dependable service, can give a product a measure of uniqueness in the eyes of the customer. When customers face increasing choices and feel overwhelmed by information overload, they value the assistance of a well-informed salesperson. Knowledge can add value.[a]

Strategic/Consultative Selling Model*

Strategic step	Prescription
DEVELOP A PERSONAL SELLING PHILOSOPHY	● ADOPT MARKETING CONCEPT ● VALUE PERSONAL SELLING ● BECOME A PROBLEM SOLVER/PARTNER
DEVELOP A RELATIONSHIP STRATEGY	● ADOPT DOUBLE-WIN PHILOSOPHY ● PROJECT PROFESSIONAL IMAGE ● PRACTISE COMMUNICATION-STYLE FLEXING
DEVELOP A PRODUCT STRATEGY	● BECOME A PRODUCT EXPERT ● SELL BENEFITS ● CONFIGURE VALUE-ADDED SOLUTIONS
DEVELOP A CUSTOMER STRATEGY	● UNDERSTAND BUYER BEHAVIOUR ● DISCOVER CUSTOMER NEEDS ● DEVELOP PROSPECT BASE
DEVELOP A PRESENTATION STRATEGY	● PREPARE OBJECTIVES ● DEVELOP PRESENTATION PLAN ● PROVIDE OUTSTANDING SERVICE

*Strategic/consulative selling evolved in response to increased competition, more complex products, increased emphasis on customer needs, and growing importance of long-term relationships.

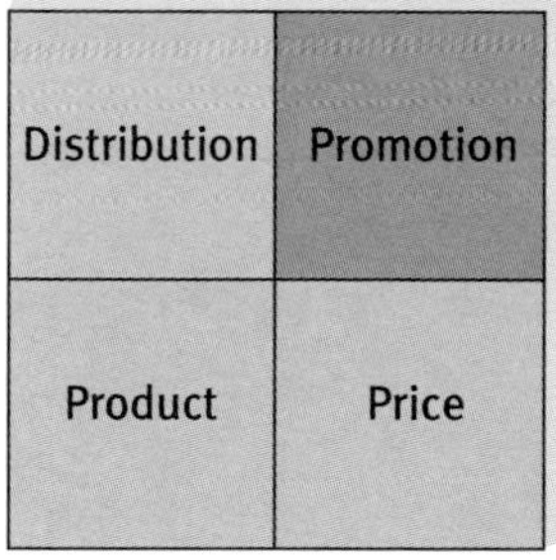

Distribution	Promotion
Product	Price

Figure 1.5   The Strategic/Consultative Selling Model is an extension of the marketing concept.

they are well-informed consultants and that the company is able to service its accounts to maximize customer satisfaction. The positioning of products and other product-related sales strategies is the major focus of Chapter 6.

The development of a product strategy often requires thoughtful decision making. Today's more knowledgeable customers seek a cluster of satisfactions that arise from the product itself, from the manufacturer or distributor of the product, and from the salesperson. The "new" product that customers are buying today is the sum total of the satisfactions that emerge from all three sources. The "cluster of satisfactions" concept will be discussed in more detail in Chapter 6. The three prescriptions for the product strategy are: become a product expert; sell benefits; and position product.

DEVELOPING A CUSTOMER STRATEGY

Customers have become increasingly sophisticated in their buying strategies. More and more, they have come to expect value-added products and services and long-term commitments.[16] Selling to today's customer starts with getting on the customer's agenda and carefully identifying his or her needs, wants, and buying conditions.

customer strategy A carefully conceived plan that will result in maximum responsiveness to the customer's needs.

A **customer strategy** is a carefully conceived plan that will result in maximum responsiveness to the customer's needs. This strategy is based on the fact that success in personal selling depends, in no small measure, on the salesperson's ability to learn as much as possible about the prospect.[17] It involves the collection and analysis of specific information for each customer. When developing a customer strategy, the salesperson should develop a broad understanding of buying behaviours, discover individual customer needs, and build a strong prospect base (see Fig. 1.5). The first two parts of the customer strategy will be introduced in Chapter 7. Suggestions regarding ways to build a solid prospect base will be discussed in Chapter 8.

Many of the most progressive companies in Canada have well-established customer strategies. Windsor Factory Supply, with seven locations in Ontario, provides a good example of a marketer that has adopted a commodity management strategy for many of its customers. Windsor Factory Supply salespeople encourage large customers, particularly ones with multiple locations, to source all of their MRO (maintenance, repair, and operating) supplies from them. When successful, commodity management contracts result in stable, long-term relationships between suppliers and customers, to the benefit of both parties. These contracts require salespeople to collect and analyze information on the specific needs of each customer, and to make frequent inventory adjustments, "custom fitting" their inventory to guarantee delivery requirements and meet the needs of these important customers (see Fig. 1.6).[18]

Figure 1.6 Windsor Factory Supply's customer strategy loop illustrates how salespeople obtain information on ways to better serve their customer.

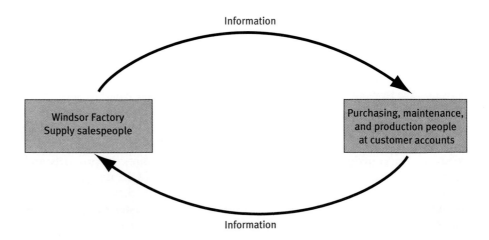

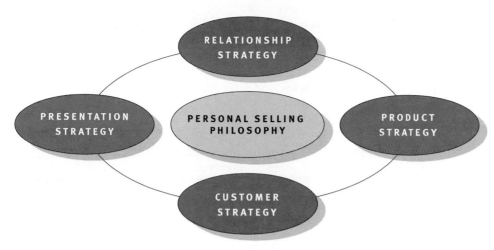

BUILDING QUALITY PARTNERSHIPS

Figure 1.7 **The major strategies that form the Strategic/Consultative Selling Model are by no means independent of one another. The focus of each strategy is to satisfy customer needs and build quality partnerships.**

DEVELOPING A PRESENTATION STRATEGY

Typical salespeople spend about 30 percent of their time in actual face-to-face selling situations. However, the sales presentation is a critical part of the selling process. The **presentation strategy** is a well-developed plan that includes preparing the sales presentation objectives, preparing a presentation plan that is needed to meet these objectives, and renewing one's commitment to provide outstanding customer service (see Fig. 1.5).

The presentation strategy usually involves developing one or more objectives for each sales call. For example, a salesperson might update personal information about the customer, provide information on a new product, and close a sale during one sales call. Multiple-objective sales presentations, which are becoming more common, will be discussed in Chapter 9.

Presale presentation plans give salespeople the opportunity to consider those activities that will take place during the sales presentation. For example, a salesperson might preplan a demonstration of product features to use when meeting with the customer. Presale planning ensures that salespeople will be well organized during the sales presentation and prepared to offer outstanding service.

presentation strategy A well-conceived plan that includes three prescriptions: establishing objectives for the sales presentation; preparing the presale plan needed to meet these objectives; and renewing one's commitment to providing outstanding customer service.

INTERRELATIONSHIP OF BASIC STRATEGIES

The major strategies that form the Strategic/Consultative Selling Model are by no means independent. The relationship, product, and customer strategies all influence development of the presentation strategy (Fig. 1.7). For example, one relationship-building practice might be developed for use during the initial face-to-face meeting with the customer, and another for possible use during the negotiation of buyer resistance. Another relationship-building method might be developed for use after the sale is closed. The discovery of customer needs (part of the customer strategy) will greatly influence planning for the sales presentation.

ELECTRONIC COMMERCE AND THE COMPLEX SALE

Electronic commerce is a modern methodology that addresses the use of information technology as an essential enabler of business.[19] Most organizations involved in sales and marketing use electronic commerce to support external

electronic commerce The use of information technology to facilitate the exchange of goods and services between buyers and sellers. For the sales organization, it can support both external activites such as personal selling, and internal activities such as customer service.

business activities such as personal selling, and internal activities such as customer service. A complex sale will almost always require the use of several forms of information technology to gather and distribute information to customers. These tools, described in selected chapters, include electronic product catalogues, product configurators, and sales proposal writers (Chapter 5); contact management systems (see ACT! references throughout the book); PowerPoint and Excel spreadsheet software (Chapter 11); Internet and extranet applications (Chapter 14); and electronic mapping software (Chapter 15).

Electronic commerce, in its many forms, promises to enhance strategic selling in the years ahead. A recent survey conducted by *Sales & Marketing Management* magazine reports that 85 percent of the respondents regard electronic commerce strategies as vital to their marketing and sales success.[20]

The Evolution of Partnering

In the early 1990s we witnessed the demise of the product solution in many major industries. A growing number of customers began buying relationships, not products. This trend is the result of a situation where the products of one company in an industry are becoming nearly identical to those of the competition. When a given industry (service, retail, wholesale, or manufacturing) is dominated by look-alike products, the product strategy becomes less important than the relationship strategy.

relationship selling   Salespeople who have adopted relationship selling work hard to build and nourish long-term partnerships. They rely on a personal, customized approach to each customer.

The term **relationship selling,** popularized over the past several years, recognizes the growing importance of relationships in selling. Salespeople who

OEB
INTERNATIONAL
Public Relations / Public Affairs

10 Lower Spadina Avenue, Suite 500
Toronto, Ontario, M5V 2Z2

Contact: Eric Cunningham, President
Telephone: (416) 260-6000
Facsimile: (416) 260-2708
E-mail: eric@oeb.com

Few marriages last as long...

Client relationships are a lot like marriages. They require loyalty, understanding, skill — and hard work. At OEB International, we're proud that our very first client has been with us for 60 years...

- *Founding member of The WORLDCOM Group Inc. with offices throughout Canada and the world.*

- *Member companies: OEB Strategies, HealthWatch, Mahoney International*

- *Niagara Region office*

OEB International is a service company that understands the evolution of selling from "peddling to partnering." The company shows it is capable of managing long-term relationships.

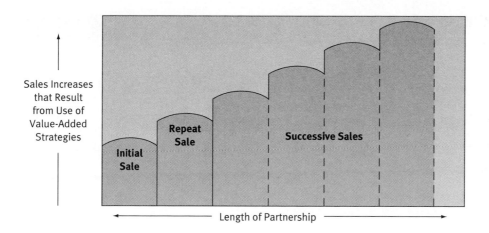

Figure 1.8 The Partnering Model. Partnering is a strategically developed, long-term relationship that solves the customer's problem. A successful partnering effort results in repeat sales, and referrals that expand the prospect base. The strength of the partnership increases each time the salesperson uses value-added selling strategies.

have adopted relationship selling work hard to build and nourish long-term partnerships. They rely on a personal, customized approach to each customer.[21] This approach stands in stark contrast to the more traditional *transaction-oriented* selling.

Today's customer wants a quality product *and* a quality relationship. Salespeople willing to abandon short-term thinking and invest the time and energy needed to develop a high-quality, long-term relationship with customers will be strongly rewarded. A strong partnership serves as a barrier to competing salespeople who want to sell to your accounts. Salespeople who are able to build partnerships enjoy more repeat business and referrals. Keeping existing customers happy makes a great deal of sense from an economic point of view. Many experts in the field of sales and marketing agree with Stanley Brown, Partner in Charge, International Centre of Excellence in Customer Satisfaction, Coopers & Lybrand, Toronto (now PricewaterhouseCoopers), who said: "Remember that if you lose that customer, it costs you 5 to 12 times more to get a new customer than to keep an existing one."[22] Even small increases in customer retention can result in major increases in profits.

Partnering is a strategically developed, long-term relationship that solves the customer's buying problem. A successful long-term partnership is achieved when the salesperson is able to skilfully apply the four major strategies and thus add value in various ways (see Fig. 1.8). Sales professionals stay close to the customer and constantly search for new ways to add value. The salespeople at Mackay Envelope Corporation achieve this goal by making sure they know more about their customers than the competitors do. Salespeople who work for Xerox Corporation are responding to a sales orientation that emphasizes postsale service. Bonuses are based on a formula that includes not just sales, but customer satisfaction as well.

partnering Selling that is strategically focused on building closer, longer-term relationships that solve customers' buying problems.

PARTNERING IS ENHANCED WITH HIGH ETHICAL STANDARDS

In the field of selling there are certain pressures that can influence the ethical conduct of salespeople, and poor ethical decisions can weaken or destroy partnerships. To illustrate, let us assume a competitor makes exaggerated claims about a product. Do you counter by promising more than your product can deliver? What action do you take when there is a time management problem and you must choose between servicing past sales and making new sales? What if a

Building Relationships through Technology

INTRODUCING CUSTOMER RELATIONSHIP MANAGEMENT

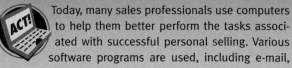

Today, many sales professionals use computers to help them better perform the tasks associated with successful personal selling. Various software programs are used, including e-mail, electronic spreadsheets, word processors, configuration systems, presentation packages, fax managers, and customer relationship management (CRM) systems. A basic CRM system consists of a database containing information about the people with whom a salesperson maintains relationships, such as customers, prospects, co-workers, and suppliers. For your use with the CRM studies in this text, a basic Windows-based CRM system is available for you to download at www.selling-today.com/casestudy (see the exercise Downloading CRM Software on page 24 for more information). You can learn the fundamentals of CRM with this software, including searching for customer and product-related information, managing time and priorities, communicating, forecasting sales, and estimating your commissions.

Caterpillar continues to promote its superior value—"serious machines"—but also its desire to create long-term customer satisfaction—"serious commitment."

superior urges you to use a strategy that you consider unethical? These and other pressures must be dealt with every day.

Although pressures exist in every selling position, most salespeople are able to draw the line between ethical and unethical behaviour. This is especially true of those who have taken a long-range view of sales work that emphasizes building partnerships. These people know that the best way to ensure repeat business is to deal honestly and fairly with every customer.

Although Chapter 16 is devoted to ethical considerations in personal selling, it should be noted that ethics is a major theme of the entire text. The topic of ethics has been interwoven throughout several chapters. The authors believe that ethical decisions must be made every day in the life of a salesperson, so this important topic cannot be covered in a single chapter.

PARTNERING IS ENHANCED WITH SALES AUTOMATION

Many companies are using some form of sales automation to enhance partnerships with customers. **Sales automation** is the term used to describe

sales automation   A term used to describe those technologies used to improve communications in a sales organization and to improve customer responsiveness. These activities are used to improve the productivity of the sales force and the sales support personnel.

Clearnet PCS attributes part of its success to strategic partnering with Lucent Technologies.

those technologies used to improve communications in a sales organization and improve customer responsiveness. Recent improvements in sales automation reflect the changes taking place in the age of information. New technologies are needed to process the massive amounts of information available to salespeople. New technologies also help salespeople stay connected to customers, sales support personnel, and other key people.

Strategic Alliances—The Highest Form of Partnering

strategic alliance The highest form of partnering relationship where two or more firms whose products or services fit well together team up to gain a competitive advantage in the marketplace.

Throughout the past decade we have seen the growth of a new form of partnership that is often described as a **strategic alliance.** The goal of a strategic alliance is to achieve a marketplace advantage by teaming up with another company whose products or services fit well with your own. Alliances are often formed by companies that have similar business interests and thus gain a mutual competitive advantage. It is not uncommon for several companies to form an alliance, or for a company to form several alliances. Digital Equipment Corporation has partnered with several small companies that have been able to deliver technological breakthroughs. Other examples include Xerox and Microsoft (integrated office products); American Express and AT&T (unified credit card and calling card); Motorola, Hitachi, and Sony (multimedia workstations and home entertainment systems).[23] Rosabeth Moss Kanter, a Harvard Business School professor, says "do-it-together" is the next great growth strategy.[24]

Strategic alliances have created a new selling environment. The first step in building an alliance is to learn as much as possible about the proposed partner. This study takes place long before face-to-face contact. The second step is to meet with the proposed partner and explore mutual benefits of the alliance. At this point the salesperson (or account manager) is selling advice, assistance, and counsel, not specific products.[25] Strong interpersonal and communication skills are needed to build an alliance that has long-term benefits to both partners. Building win-win partnerships requires the highest form of consultative selling. Very often, the salesperson is working with a company team made up of persons from such areas as research and development, finance, and distribution. Presentations and proposals usually focus on profit impact and other strategic account benefits.

Summary

As the global economy has shifted from one of excess demand to one of excess supply, competition has increased, both within North America and from foreign competitors. Vigorous sales promotion, including personal selling, will be a key factor in stimulating global demand for products.

Personal selling is the process of developing customer relationships, discovering customer needs, matching the appropriate products (physical goods, services, or ideas) with those needs, and communicating benefits through informing, reminding, or persuading. The *marketing concept* is the belief that a firm should dedicate all of its policies, planning, and operation to the satisfaction of the customer. The marketing concept has grown in popularity throughout the age of information.

The marketing era that began in Canada and the United States in the 1950s looked first at customer needs and wants, and then created goods and services to meet those needs and wants. (Previously, during the industrial age, the emphasis had been on creating products and then building customer interest in those products.) Consultative selling emerged in the late 1960s and early 1970s as an approach that emphasizes identification of customer needs through effective communication between the salesperson and the customer. Strategic selling evolved in the 1980s and involved the preparation of a carefully conceived plan to accomplish sales objectives. In the 1990s, the development of partnership selling involved providing customers with a quality product *and* a quality, long-term relationship.

Strategic selling is based on a company's strategic market plan, which takes into consideration the coordination of all of the major functional areas of the business—production, marketing, finance, and human resources. The four broad strategic areas in the Strategic/Consultative Selling Model (after development of a personal selling philosophy) are developing a relationship strategy, developing a product strategy, developing a customer strategy, and developing a presentation strategy.

Partnering is the creation of long-term relationships with customers, which requires salespeople to continuously search for ways to add quality to their selling relationships. The quality improvement process reinforces partnering through the firm's search for ways to provide a higher quality, lower cost product, and the salesperson's attempt to continuously improve the quality of customer service.

Ethical considerations are particularly important in the field of personal selling because the salesperson represents his or her company to the buyer. The salesperson may encounter pressures to "bend" principles of honesty or straightforwardness, so it is necessary to consider and develop ethical principles that will be the guidelines for one's entire career.

Key Terms

Personal Selling 5
Product 5
Personal Selling Philosophy 6
Marketing Concept 6
Marketing Mix 9
Consultative Selling 9
Transactional Selling 10
Strategic Market Plan 12
Tactics 12
Strategies 12

Relationship Strategy 13
Product Strategy 14
Commodity 14
Customer Strategy 16
Presentation Strategy 17
Electronic Commerce 17
Relationship Selling 18
Partnering 19
Sales Automation 21
Strategic Alliance 22

Review Questions

1. Explain how personal selling can help solve the problem of information overload.

2. According to the Strategic/Consultative Selling Model (Fig. 1.2), what are the three prescriptions for developing a successful personal selling philosophy?

3. Why is peddling or "pushing products" inconsistent with the marketing concept?

4. What is consultative selling? Give examples.

5. Diagram and label the four-step Consultative Sales Presentation Guide.

6. List and briefly explain the four broad strategic areas that make up the selling process.

7. Briefly describe the evolution of partnering. Discuss the forces that contributed to this approach to selling.

8. Read the Building Quality Partnerships box on p. 14 and then discuss ways to add value when selling a commodity.

9. Explain why the ethical conduct of salespeople has become so important.

10. Briefly describe why some organizations are developing strategic alliances.

Application Exercises

1. Assume that you are an experienced professional salesperson. A professor who teaches at a nearby university has asked you to speak to a consumer economics class about the social and economic benefits of personal selling. Make an outline of what you will say.

2. A friend of yours has invented a unique and useful new product. This friend, an engineer by profession, understands little about marketing and selling this new product. She does understand, however, that "nothing happens until somebody sells something." She has asked you to describe the general factors that need to be considered when you market a product. Prepare an answer to her question.

3. When Brenda Fisher received her B.Ed., she thought she would like to teach. However, a pharmaceutical firm offered her a sales position. This position would require her to call on doctors and pharmacists to explain her product line. Describe the similarities and the differences between the two positions.

 4. To learn more about the sales training programs currently offered by the Canadian Professional Sales Association, Learning International, Wilson Learning Corporation, Dale Carnegie Training, and Zig Ziglar Corporation, search the Internet and review the offerings.

CRM Application Exercise

Downloading CRM Software

The CRM system that is available for you to download is a demonstration version of the best-selling software called ACT!, a product of SalesLogix. This version of ACT! includes a database of information about prospective customers for a company that sells network systems. In the case study and exercises ahead, you will assume the role of a salesperson who is selling these network systems. To download the software, log on to the *Selling Today* Web page and follow the instructions.

www.pearsoned.ca/
manning

ACT! is a database program, which means that it uses records and fields. *Records* are the screens that contain information about each person. *Fields* are the boxes on the records for entering and displaying data, such as the name of the person, Bradley Able. ACT! is also known as a contact management program because it maintains a record for each contact (person). Some CRM systems offer a separate record for each organization.

You can experiment with ACT! without concern about damaging the program. If you inadvertently delete information in the database, you can simply download the software again. To get acquainted with the ACT! version of CRM, click on the various menu items and icons and observe the functions that are available to you. Experimenting with this software will give you a feel for the potential power of using technology to enhance your sales career. Test ACT!'s reporting capabilities by printing a phone list: select Report and Phone; in the Prepare Report box choose Active Group and Printer; then print the list.

As you experiment with ACT!, you can obtain help at any time by pressing the F1 function key. (See the exercise Learning CRM Software on page 42 for more information.)

Case Problem

Windsor Factory Supply Limited (WFS) is a large, general-line industrial distributor that started as a two-man operation in Windsor, Ontario, in 1955. It now has 174 employees, including 32 outside salespeople across its seven branches. Sales in 1999 are expected to be $82-million. Many customers remain loyal to WFS because they want good service, a broad range of general industrial products, and a supplier that will help them solve their purchasing problems. The success of WFS can be traced to a number of factors:

➤ A company philosophy that is based on the belief that being able to service existing accounts is more important than gaining new accounts. According to Wes Delnea, president of WFS, "Growth is important, but sometimes you have to keep your desire to grow in check if you do not have the ability to maintain superior service to your existing accounts."

➤ A desire to build as many relationships and the strongest relationships possible with all customers. WFS frequently moves people to new positions within the company. A warehouse person may become an outside salesperson and later be transferred to inside sales. An outside salesperson may be transferred to purchasing, or back to inside sales. This creates maximum flexibility within the company, but more important, it means that inside salespeople know the difficulties that outside salespeople face, and they often have personal contacts within customer firms. It also means that outside salespeople have had the benefit of training and learning while in the warehouse and on the inside sales desk. As a result, customers frequently have strong relationships with and trust in several WFS employees who they know can help them.

➤ A strong belief that work should be rewarding for all employees. "Happy employees help make happy customers," says Wes Delnea. Employees share many experiences, from going to major sporting events, to having company parties and picnics, to going together to Las Vegas. Twice, all of the employees shared an expense-paid trip to Las Vegas, with about 25 percent of them going per weekend on consecutive weekends. Employees have an excellent benefits package, which also includes education and recreation allowances. This employee investment has been rewarded many times over. At one point, the company had gone four years without a single absentee day. Employees even provide important input on management. In fact, a nine-member management committee, including the president, is elected each year. Confidence in the committee is high; six members have been on the committee since it was formed several years ago.

➤ An investment in customer service and a strong service culture. The company has invested in computer equipment and programming, and is able to tell customers immediately how much inventory it has and where that inventory is located. Purchasing, payables, invoicing, receivables, account profiles, sales and other financial reports, and vehicle maintenance schedules are all computerized. Employees are empowered to make decisions whenever customer service is an issue. On one occasion, two employees took a company van and left Windsor to get some material in Pittsburgh, Pennsylvania, for a customer who urgently needed it, and they returned immediately with the material. If the delivery truck has left for the day but a customer calls to order something that is urgently needed, they are never told that they have to wait for the next delivery. According to Wes Delnea, "We will get it to them. If the salesperson can't deliver it, someone will."

➤ An investment and improvement in service processes. Many large accounts have online order entry capabilities as they are connected to Windsor Factory Supply through an electronic data interface, or EDI. For example, Ford Motor Company of Canada can order from WFS directly via computer. WFS has also established a program of commodity management whereby it manages all of the general supply items for companies with multiple locations. WFS is always willing to add additional items to its inventory for customers who will buy them; an increasing number of customers are taking advantage of this service.[26]

Questions

1. Does it appear that the management and members of the sales force at Windsor Factory Supply Limited have adopted the three prescriptions of a personal selling philosophy (see Fig. 1.2)? Explain your answer.

2. What are the characteristics of the product strategy adopted by Windsor Factory Supply Limited? How will this strategy contribute to the company's long-term success?

3. How would you describe the customer strategy developed by Windsor Factory Supply Limited? How does this strategy contribute to long-term success?

4. Windsor Factory Supply Limited salespeople are paid by straight salary and do not get a commission. Why has the company decided on this compensation plan? What would be the advantages and disadvantages of each type of compensation plan for Windsor Factory Supply Limited?

5. Does it appear that Windsor Factory Supply Limited has adopted the four broad strategic areas that are part of the Strategic/Consultative Selling Model? Explain.

Partnership Selling: A Role Play/Simulation   (see Appendix C, p. 419)

[If your instructor has chosen to use the Partnering Role Play/Simulation exercise that accompanies this text, these boxes will alert you to your Role Play/Simulation assignments. Your instructor will also provide you with needed information.]

Preview the role play simulation materials in Appendix C. These materials are produced by the Park Inn International Hotel and Convention Centre, and you will be using them in your role as a new sales trainee (and, at times, as the customer) for the hotel and its convention services.

The role-play exercises will begin in Chapter 5, as you begin to create your product strategy. However, in anticipation of the role play, you can begin to imagine yourself in the role of an actual salesperson. Start to think about how you will develop your personal selling philosophy. What are some ethical guidelines that you may wish to adopt for yourself? (Ethics is also the subject of Chapter 16, Ethics — The Foundation for Relationships in Selling.) What skills will you need to develop to become a partner with your prospective customers?

The Park Inn has implemented a Quality Improvement process. How will this affect your role as a sales representative?

2

Personal Selling Opportunities in the Age of Information

LEARNING OBJECTIVES

When you finish reading this chapter, you should be able to

1. Describe how personal selling skills contribute to work performed by knowledge workers

2. Discuss the rewarding aspects of personal selling careers

3. Describe the opportunities for women and minorities in the field of personal selling

4. Discuss the characteristics of selling positions in four major employment settings: service, retail, wholesale, and manufacturing

5. Identify the four major sources of sales training

Personal selling attracts people from many different professions. Debbie Hanlon and Susan Green are both real estate brokers for Coldwell Banker and own international award-winning offices. Debbie Hanlon spent two years in hotel food and beverage management and, for a short period, owned and operated a fitness centre that left her financially bankrupt. She turned to real estate sales in 1993, and soon became one of the most successful real estate agents in Canada. In her second year, she sold more units than any of the more than 200 other salespeople who compete in her city. A few years later, she started Coldwell Banker Hanlon Inc. and now has approximately 20 agents working for her.[1]

Susan Green received her B.A. and B.Ed. from Acadia University and spent 10 years as a teacher before joining her mother in the real estate business. When her mother became ill, Susan was faced with a decision to take over the business or let it close down. Her office now has 10 agents, and she doesn't regret her decision. She says, "I have more freedom to be creative and I'm financially much better off. I love this business. Many people think that real estate is about selling houses, but it's really about providing a service to clients, both buyers and sellers. That may explain why so many successful real estate agents come from teaching and nursing careers."[2]

Personal selling skills are no less important in the life of Bobbie Gaunt, president and CEO of Ford of Canada. While a university student, she got a temporary position in a Chevrolet dealership where, she says, "I became fascinated with the process of selling cars." She later began employment at Ford as a stenographer, and eventually commenced its management training program. Her experiences in marketing and sales positioned her to lead the Canadian operations. While most production decisions are made in the U.S., Canadian operations focus on marketing and sales.[3]

Personal Selling Opportunities in the Age of Information

Stanley Marcus, chairman emeritus of the prestigious Neiman Marcus retail company, said "Sooner or later in business, everybody has to sell something to somebody." He noted that even if you are not in sales, you must know how to sell a physical product, a service, an idea, or yourself.[4] His views have garnered a great deal of support among observers of the age of information. Today's workforce is made up of millions of knowledge workers who succeed only when they add value to information. The new economy is about the growing value of knowledge, making it the most important ingredient of what people buy and sell.[5] One way to add value to information is to collect it, organize it, clarify it, and present it in a convincing manner. This skill, used every day by professional salespeople, is invaluable in a world that is overloaded with information.

As noted in Chapter 1, relationships began to become more important at the beginning of the age of information. In many cases, information does not have value unless people interact effectively. As president and CEO of her company, Bobbie Gaunt has access to information concerning product development, customer preferences and buying behaviours, competitor marketing activities, and much more. All of this information, however, has little value unless it can be analyzed properly and communicated effectively to those who value and need it. Even then, the information may have little value unless there is a good relationship among all of the parties involved, as communications may break down. John Naisbitt was right on target when he noted that in the age of information "the game is people interacting with other people."[6]

Today personal selling skills contribute in a major way to four groups of knowledge workers who usually do not consider themselves salespeople:

- Customer service representatives

- Professionals (accountants, consultants, lawyers, etc.)

- Entrepreneurs

- Managerial personnel

CUSTOMER SERVICE REPRESENTATIVES

customer service representative
Processes reservations, accepts orders by phone or other means, delivers products, handles customer complaints, provides technical assistance, and assists full-time sales representatives.

Assigning selling duties to employees with customer service responsibilities has become quite common. The term **customer service representative** (CSR) is used to describe people who process reservations, accept orders by phone or other means, deliver products, handle customer complaints, provide technical assistance, and assist full-time sales representatives. Some companies are teaming CSRs and salespeople. After the sale is closed, the CSR helps process paperwork, checks on delivery of the product, and engages in other customer follow-up duties. Here are some examples of companies that are moving customer service representatives into the proactive role of selling.

➤ **Item:** Bell Atlantic has trained its CSRs to suggest new services and features to customers when they call. One example cited by the company was a customer who phoned to get phone service installed. After hearing young voices in the background, the CSR queried the customer and found there were teenagers in the home. The CSR then suggested call waiting and successfully sold the additional service. Since Bell Atlantic began this more proactive approach, sales of ancillary products have increased by 30 percent.[7]

➤ **Item:** Alex Martin, a manager with Royal Trust's Wealth Management Operations, says that everyone who is a client impact person—a person who comes in contact with clients or potential clients—gets a business card. "In our organization, the culture is going through some rapid changes. The only reason we are in business is to sell our services, and nearly everyone who works for us has some client impact responsibility."[8]

Assigning sales duties to customer service representatives makes sense when you consider the number of contacts customers have with CSRs. When a customer seeks assistance with a problem or makes a reservation, the CSR learns more about the customer and often provides the customer with needed information. Customer needs often surface as both parties exchange information. It is important to keep in mind advice offered by the author of *Selling the Invisible*: "Every act is a marketing act. Make every employee a marketing person."[9]

PROFESSIONALS

Today's professional workers include lawyers, designers, programmers, engineers, consultants, dietitians, counsellors, doctors, accountants, and many other specialized knowledge workers. Our labour force includes nearly two million professional service providers, persons who need many of the skills used by professional salespeople. Clients who purchase professional services are usually more interested in the person who delivers the service than the firm that employs the professional. They seek expert diagnosticians who are truly interested in their needs. The professional must display good communication skills and be able to establish a relationship built on trust.

Technical skills are not enough in the age of information. Many employers expect the professional to bring in new business in addition to keeping current customers satisfied.[10] Employers often screen professional applicants to determine their customer focus and ability to interact well with people.

Many firms are providing their professional staff with sales training. The accounting firm Ernst & Young sets aside several days each year to train its professional staff in personal selling. Faced with increased competition and more cost-conscious customers, a growing number of law, accounting, engineering, and architectural firms are discovering the merits of personal selling as an auxiliary activity.[11] Providers of financial planning services, property management, landscape design, and health care services are also discovering that personal selling can be used to obtain and keep customers.

While many professional service firms are trying to train their employees to sell, others have been hiring professional salespeople to assist or team up with their service professionals. A common approach is to use a team-selling strategy that involves a salesperson and a service professional who has received training in team selling.[12]

ENTREPRENEURS

There were 10 800 Canadian businesses that filed for bankruptcy in 1998.[13] Fortunately, the number of new businesses exceeded the number of bankruptcies. As noted previously, people who start a new business frequently need to sell their plan to investors and others who can help get their firm established. Many new businesses rely on personal selling by the owners to grow and remain viable.

When Edmonton-based Three Blondes and a Brownie came up with recipes for low-fat brownies and muffins, the owners began by selling small quantities of baked goods to local cafés. In the company's first year, 1994, revenues were $100 000. Eventually, a sales call to McDonald's Restaurants of Canada resulted in the sale of frozen batter that could be shipped throughout the entire chain. Today, Three Blondes and a Brownie also sells through food distributors to restaurants, grocery stores, and hospitals across Canada, and 2001 projected revenues could reach $3.5-million.[14]

MANAGERIAL PERSONNEL

People working in managerial occupations represent another large group of knowledge workers. They are given such titles as *executive*, *manager*, or *administrator*. Leaders are constantly involved in capturing, processing, and communicating information. Some of the most valuable information is acquired from customers. This helps explain the rapid growth in what is being described as "executive selling." Chief executive officers and other executives often accompany salespeople on sales calls to learn more about customer needs and in some cases assist with presentations. Manny Fernandez of the Gartner Group, a technology consulting firm, spends more than half his time travelling on sales calls.[15] Leaders must also articulate their ideas in a persuasive manner and win support for their vision.

Increasingly, work in the information economy is understood as an expression of thought. At a time when people change their careers eight times during their lives, selling skills represent important transferable employment skills.[16]

Your Future in Personal Selling

According to Statistics Canada there are 1.3 million sales jobs in Canada. More than 9 percent of the Canadian workforce is employed in sales positions.[17] In addition, the number of sales positions is increasing in most industrialized countries. A close examination of these positions reveals that there is no single "selling" occupation. Our labour force includes hundreds of different selling careers, and chances are there are positions that match your interests, talents, and ambitions. The diversity within selling will become apparent as you study the career options discussed in this chapter.

Although many college students will ultimately become salespeople, it's often not their first career choice. Students tend to view sales as dynamic and active, but feel a selling career will require them to engage in deceitful or dishonest practices. The good news is that old stereotypes about sales are gradually going by the wayside.[18] Students who study the careers of highly successful salespeople discover that ethical sales practices represent the key to long-term success.

A professional selling position encompasses a wide range of tasks (Fig. 2.1), and therefore salespeople must possess a variety of skills. A salesperson representing Federal Express (FedEx) will make numerous sales calls each day in an attempt to establish new accounts and provide service to established accounts. There are a wide range of potential customers who can use FedEx delivery services. A salesperson working for a Caterpillar construction equipment dealer may make only two or three sales calls per day. The products offered by the dealer are expensive and are not purchased frequently.

Just as selling occupations differ, so do the titles by which salespeople are known. Their titles reflect, in part, the variety of duties they perform. A survey of current job announcements indicates that fewer and fewer companies are using the word *salesperson* to refer to the people they employ to sell their products. Instead they are using such titles as these:

Account Executive	Sales Consultant
Account Representative	Relationship Manager
Sales Account Manager	Sales Associate
Client Development Manager	Marketing Representative
District Representative	Territory Manager

Salespeople who call on supermarkets make eight to ten calls during a single day.

Figure 2.1 How salespeople spend their time during an average 46.9-hour workweek (Source: *Selling*, February 1997, p. 4)

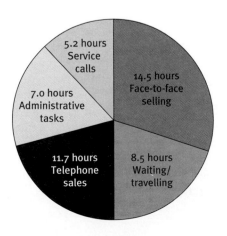

- 5.2 hours Service calls
- 14.5 hours Face-to-face selling
- 7.0 hours Administrative tasks
- 11.7 hours Telephone sales
- 8.5 hours Waiting/travelling

Salespeople, regardless of title, play an important role in sustaining the growth and profitability of organizations of all sizes. They also support the employment of many non-selling employees. A recent study indicates that in service and manufacturing firms, one salesperson creates enough sales revenue to pay for nine other jobs within the company.[19]

REWARDING ASPECTS OF SELLING CAREERS

Gene Fay, account manager for Avid Sports, sells digital video and software systems to professional and college baseball, basketball, football, and hockey teams in Canada and the United States. The job offers him many rewards. Not only does he sell a very innovative product that improves team play, he gets to meet well-known sports executives he has admired for years. His $1.8-million sales in 1997 included a sale to the Vancouver Canucks. However, his biggest sale to date was to the Orlando Magic, a US$370 000 deal.[20]

From a personal and an economic standpoint, selling can be a rewarding career. Careers in selling offer financial rewards, recognition, security, and opportunities for advancement to a degree that is unique compared with other occupations.

ABOVE-AVERAGE INCOME

Studies dealing with incomes in the business community indicate that salespeople earn significantly higher incomes than most other workers. Some salespeople actually earn more than their sales managers and other executives within the organization. The high level of compensation (whether from base salary, bonus, or incentives) is justified for good performance. Three major definitions for sales position categories and the compensation (salary plus incentives) earned by each type of salesperson follow.

> ➤ **Junior Salesperson.** Junior salespeople often sell a limited variety of non-technical products or services within a limited area, and may have one or two years of experience. They solicit additional sales from existing clients, or may solicit new clients by mail or telephone. Compensation range is $20 800 to $54 100.[21]

> ➤ **Intermediate Salesperson.** Intermediate salespeople often sell to medium or larger customers in an assigned territory, and typically have three to four years of experience. They are fully qualified salespeople who work under general supervision and are accountable for achieving specific sales objectives. They solicit additional sales from existing clients, or may solicit new clients by mail, by telephone, or in person. Compensation range is $37 000 to $57 700.[22]

> ➤ **Senior Salesperson.** Senior salespeople often sell to larger and more complex accounts, possibly even key accounts. They typically have many years of sales experience, and they may even supervise more junior sales representatives. They are often accountable for achieving specific sales objectives in major territories. Compensation range is $39 500 to $85 200.[23]

The amount earned by salespeople is clearly tied to their selling skill and the amount of effort put forth. Unlike many other workers, salespeople are rewarded financially when they give extra effort. This effort is often triggered by commissions, bonuses, incentives, and other rewards.

psychic income Consists of factors that provide psychological rewards; helps to satisfy these needs and motivates us to achieve higher levels of performance.

ABOVE-AVERAGE PSYCHIC INCOME

Two major psychological needs common to all people are recognition and security. **Psychic income,** which consists of factors that provide psychological rewards, helps satisfy these important needs and motivates us to achieve higher levels of performance. The need for recognition has been established in numerous studies that have examined human motivation. Workers from all employment areas indicate that recognition for work well done is an important morale-building factor.

In selling, recognition will come more frequently and with greater intensity than in most other occupations. Because selling contributes so visibly to the success of most business firms, the accomplishments of sales personnel will seldom go unrecognized.

Most people want to achieve some measure of security in their work. Selling is one of those occupations that usually provides job security during both good and bad times. A recent survey of more than 1100 human resources managers revealed that sales professionals and marketers are among the most sought-after employees.[24] An increasing number of companies are reducing the size of their labour force, and this trend will continue. Workers who contribute directly to the value of the enterprise through research, product development, manufacturing, and sales are most likely to avoid these layoffs.

OPPORTUNITY FOR ADVANCEMENT

Each year, thousands of openings appear in the ranks of supervision and management. Because salespeople work in positions of high visibility, they are in an excellent position to be chosen for advancement to positions of greater responsibility. The presidents of many of today's companies began their marketing careers in the ranks of the sales force.

Of course, not all salespeople can become presidents of large corporations, but in the middle-management ranks there are numerous interesting and high-paying positions in which experience in selling is a prime requisite for advancement. Information on careers in sales management will be presented in Chapter 17.

OPPORTUNITIES FOR WOMEN

Prodded by a growing awareness that gender is not a barrier to success in selling, business firms are recruiting qualified women in growing numbers. The

Brenda Fisher, a sales representative with Janssen-Ortho Inc. (see pages 198 and 220), loves her work and loves her family. She must make regular sales trips away from home. However, she has considerable flexibility to schedule when she will be home and when she will be away, and she enjoys the freedom she has while home to manage family obligations, and to bond with her two-year-old son, Matthew.

Building Relationships in a Diverse World

OPPORTUNITIES FOR WOMEN IN SALES

In a world that is beginning to value diversity we are seeing growing opportunities for women in sales. However, some misinformation regarding women in sales still exists. Here are four myths.

Myth: Women will not relocate or stick around long enough to repay the firm's hiring and training expenses. Today, working women make up nearly half of the workforce and they have made significant gains in a wide range of traditionally male-dominated areas. About 50 percent of working women contribute more than half of their family's income. Most of the women in this group need to work, want to work, and seek rewarding career opportunities.

Myth: Women will earn significantly less in sales than their male counterparts. Although a pay gap between men and women exists in the field of sales, it is relatively small compared to the earnings gap for women who work full time in the workforce as a whole.

Myth: Buyers are less accepting of female salespeople. In the field of personal selling, perceived expertise, likeability, and trustworthiness can have a major influence on purchase decisions. Women who project these qualities seldom face rejection based on gender.

Myth: Women face special problems when assigned to selling positions in foreign countries. The truth is, recent research suggests that women often enjoy a significant edge over their male counterparts when given overseas assignments.[a]

percentage of women in the sales force has increased considerably in recent years. Although women are relative newcomers to industrial sales, they have enjoyed expanded career opportunities in such areas as real estate, insurance, advertising services, investments, and travel services. In fact, the most marked increase was in services selling, where there are 89 100 women employed in sales positions.[25] A growing number of women are turning to sales employment because it offers excellent economic rewards and in many cases a flexible work schedule. Flexible schedules are very appealing to women who want to balance career and family.

OPPORTUNITIES FOR MINORITIES

From a historical perspective the field of selling has not provided equal opportunity to minorities. In the past it was not easy for a member of a minority group to obtain a sales position. Today the picture has changed, and more firms are actively recruiting employees from minority groups. Although equal opportunity legislation can be credited, in part, for bringing about changes in hiring practices, many firms now view the recruitment and training of minority employees simply as good business. Minority salespeople have become top producers in many organizations.

In recent years, several trade journal reports have highlighted the under-representation of minority employees in sales. Many companies recognize that shifting population demographics required a re-examination of hiring practices. The biggest population gains have been made by women, minorities, and immigrants. Many companies realize the need for a diverse sales force that can gain access to the diverse clientele that make up certain market segments.[26] This philosophical shift should open doors for Canada's growing population of minorities.

Opportunities for minorities exist in a variety of selling careers.

Employment Settings in Selling Today

Careers in the field of selling may be classified in several ways. One of the broadest differentiations is based on whether the product is a tangible or an intangible. Tangibles are physical goods such as furniture, homes, and data processing equipment. Intangibles are non-physical products or services such as stocks and bonds, insurance, and consulting services. This chapter will classify selling careers according to employment setting. We will explore the following four major employment settings and identify some of the unique characteristics of each:

Selling a service

Selling for a retailer

Selling for a wholesaler

Selling for a manufacturer

SELLING A SERVICE

Melinda Hancock has been selling transportation services for Eimskip since 1994. In business since 1914, Eimskip specializes in temperature-controlled cargo, but it provides total transport service, including ground operation, warehousing, coastal service, trucking, and intermodal service, between 14 ports in North America and Europe. Like many people in sales positions, Melinda Hancock did not plan a sales career; it just happened. When she finished school, she took a two-year secretarial course at a local community college. After working for several organizations as a secretary/receptionist, Melinda realized that she was not learning as much as she wanted, and she felt she was capable of doing more. She decided to take a position at Eimskip in 1991, shortly after the company began operations in Canada. Melinda Hancock credits the fact that she started out in a very small office with giving her the knowledge and background to eventually move into sales. "I was the receptionist, the secretary, the accountant, and the documentation clerk. I got to know the routes, the rates, and all of our customers, and now that the branch has grown, I have a full-time sales position, and the only sales position at this branch." Melinda Hancock knows what it takes to be successful at selling and has the determination to succeed. "You have to be a people-person. You have to be able to communicate with people, and you have to have a strong desire to help people solve problems. To do that, you need to know your company and the service you can provide. I network as much as possible at luncheons and trade shows, where I often get excellent sales leads. It helps to work for a company that is dedicated to providing unconditionally good service."[27]

In recent years the number of consumer and business dollars spent on services in our society has steadily increased. Customers feel the need for assistance from a knowledgeable salesperson when making purchases of many types of services. Statistics Canada reports that there are 219 750 people employed selling services.[28] We will look briefly at some of the opportunities in the service field.

➤ **Financial services.** This is one of the hottest areas of sales growth. Sales jobs in the securities and financial services field are expected to increase at least 35 percent by 2005.[29] Banks, brokerage firms, and other businesses are branching out, selling a broader range of financial planning and investment services.

➤ **Radio and television advertising.** Revenue from advertising supports the radio and television broadcasting industry. Every station must employ a force of salespeople whose job is to call on current and prospective advertisers. Each client's needs are unique, and meeting them makes the work of a media sales representative interesting. Additionally there is a creative side to media sales, for members of the sales staff often help develop commercials.

➤ **Newspaper advertising.** There are more than 1000 daily and weekly newspapers in Canada. Each newspaper is supported by both local and national advertisers and must sell advertising space to stay in business. Many business firms rely heavily on media sales personnel for help in developing effective advertising campaigns.

➤ **Hotel, motel, and convention centre services.** Each year, thousands of seminars, conferences, and business meetings are held throughout Canada. Most of these events are hosted by hotels, motels, or convention centres. By diversifying their markets and upscaling their services these marketers are catering to business clients in many new and exciting ways. The salespeople employed by these firms play an important role in attracting meetings. They sell room space, food, beverages, and other services needed for a successful meeting. (See the job description of a convention centre salesperson on p. 426 of Appendix C.)

➤ **Real estate.** Buying a home is a monumental undertaking. It is usually the single largest expenditure in the average consumer's lifetime. The purchase of commercial property by individual investors or business firms is also a major economic decision. Therefore the people who sell real estate assume an important responsibility. Busy real estate salespeople often hire assistants who help hold open houses or perform other duties.

➤ **Insurance.** Selling insurance has always been one of the most rewarding careers in sales. Common forms of insurance sold include fire, liability, life, health, automobile, casualty, and homeowner's. There are two broad

Hotel, motel, and convention centre salespeople play a key role in attracting meetings. They are often rewarded with repeat business and referrals.

Selling in Action

PITNEY BOWES' CERTIFICATION SETS HIGH STANDARDS

David Munro is the first graduate of the Pitney Bowes Certified Postal Consultant (CPC) program in Canada. The goal of this intensive certification program is to improve the level of assistance given to customers who want to upgrade their mail processes. The CPC program has been endorsed by both Canada Post and the U.S. Postal Service. Members of the 4000-person Pitney Bowes sales force sell both products (postage meters) and services. Before salespeople can complete the CPC program, they must tour a postal distribution centre, subscribe to an industry publication, demonstrate effective use of *The Canada Post Guides I & II*, write two case studies that illustrate how their postal consulting skills resulted in business, and study other materials that cover every aspect of the mail process. They then must pass a 90-minute written exam. Those who score 95 percent or higher can advance to the final oral exam. This exam comprises only three questions, which continually change due to changes in postal regulations. Candidates must score 100 percent to earn the designation Certified Postal Consultant. Earning the CPC certification has given David Munro greater confidence, improved earnings, and has helped him win national recognition. He says, "What I have learned in this program has really been a benefit to me."[b]

groups of insurance salespeople. One group is employed by major companies such as Manulife, Clarica, Sun Life, or London Life. The second group is made up of independent insurance agents who serve as representatives for a number of companies. The typical independent agency will offer a broad line of personal and business insurance services.

➤ **Banking.** The banking industry is very competitive today. Most banks have a sales promotion program, and personal selling is one of their key strategies. An increasing number of bank officers and customer service representatives are involved in personal selling activities. They develop new accounts and service established accounts. Bank personnel are completing sales training courses in record numbers these days.

➤ **Business services.** The heavy volume of business mergers and corporate downsizing has increased demand for business services provided by outside contractors. Some of the business services purchased today are computer programming, training, printing, credit reporting, payroll, and recruiting. Sales positions in the business services field are expected to increase by at least 50 percent by 2005.[30]

The list of careers involving the sale of services is much longer. We have not explored the expanding fields of home and business security, travel and recreation, pest control, and transportation. As the demand for services increases, so will the employment opportunities for salespeople.

SELLING FOR A RETAILER

In 1998, at the age of 26, Ruth Bell Steinhauer received the BDC Young Entrepreneur Award, recognizing her as one of Canada's outstanding young business people. When she completed her university degree in psychology, Ruth Bell Steinhauer decided that she wanted a career in retailing. She convinced a

St. John's, Newfoundland, retailer to hire her on commission to visit customers in their homes, look at their wardrobes, and help them update and accessorize their clothing. After three months, she was promoted to assistant buyer, where she learned about fashion lines and dealt directly with manufacturers. Her big opportunity came in 1997, when the owner went out of business. Bell Steinhauer bought the mailing lists and clothing racks, and re-opened the business under a new name—Bellissima.

In the first 11 months, Bellissima sold more than $1 000 000 in women's fashions, ranging from glamorous evening wear to casual sportswear. Bell Steinhauer credits her success to customer service. Bellissima is a retailer that visits stroke patients and other shut-ins in their homes, allows people to take items home "on approval," will open its doors after hours for people who cannot get in during the regular working hours, and guarantees 24-hour-or-less in-store alterations. The customer database keeps track of all customers, what they purchased, and important information about their preferences. "When customers come in the store," she says, "we greet them quickly and in a friendly manner. We try to have several of our salespeople develop relationships with each customer. That way, whenever a customer visits the store, they can find someone who is familiar with them and how best to serve them."[31]

The **retail salesperson** usually engages in full-time professional selling and is paid well for his or her contributions to the business. Products sold at the retail level range from exotic foreign automobiles to fine furniture. Here is a partial list of retail products that usually require a high degree of personal selling:

retail salesperson A salesperson who is employed at the retail level to help prospects solve buying problems. This person is usually involved in selling higher priced, technical, and specialty retail products.

Automobiles	Recreational Vehicles
Musical Instruments	Television and Radio Receivers
Photographic Equipment	Furniture/Decorating Supplies
Fashion Apparel	Tires and Related Accessories
Major Appliances	Microcomputers

Today, traditional retailers are facing new competition from online retailers. Canadian consumers are spending millions of dollars on Internet purchases, a clear sign that electronic commerce is here to stay. Traditional retailers must offer customers more than products. Robert Plant, a retail expert and chairman of Toronto-based Karabus Consulting Management Inc., says that today's biggest spenders are tired of humdrum shopping. Retailers must win them over by delivering more in-store thrills.[32] Customers today are looking for more. They want a combination of product, value, and experience. Well-trained salespeople can add value to the traditional shopping experience.

SELLING FOR A WHOLESALER

Sean Donovan is a field representative for Medis Health and Pharmaceutical Services Inc. (Medis), a national pharmaceutical distributor with distribution centres serving every part of Canada. Medis sells more than 30 000 products from more than 2000 suppliers to approximately 6000 customers.

There are 54 389 wholesaler locations in Canada, and they generate more than $307 billion in annual sales.[33] Wholesalers play an important role in making channels of distribution efficient. Full-service wholesalers, such as Medis, offer a wide variety of services to their customers, including inventory management solutions, gathering and interpreting market information, extending credit, distributing goods, and providing promotional activities. As a salesperson for Medis, Sean Donovan sells to both retail pharmacies and directly to hospitals. He must be familiar with his company's product line, and with the value-added programs Medis has developed to assist its customers with purchasing and inventory management.[34] Many wholesalers employ two kinds of salespeople: "inside" and "outside."

INSIDE SALESPERSON

inside salesperson A salesperson who solicits orders over the telephone. In addition to extensive product knowledge, the inside salesperson must be skilled in customer relations, merchandising, and suggestion selling.

The **inside salesperson** relies almost totally on telephone orders and follows a strict timetable of customer contact. Because of the escalating cost of personal selling, selling by telephone is growing in popularity. This selling method has become so popular that some companies are taking their salespeople off the road and bringing them back to headquarters, where they are retrained to sell by telephone. Jim Domanski, Canada's most quoted telemanagement consultant, estimates that contacting a customer by telephone costs one tenth of what it costs to make the same contact in person, and that a telemarketer can make as many sales calls in a day as a field salesperson can make in a week.[35]

OUTSIDE SALESPERSON

outside salesperson A salesperson who must have knowledge of many products and be able to serve as a consultant to the customer on product or service applications. This position usually requires an in-depth understanding of the customer's operation.

The duties of an **outside salesperson** vary from one wholesale firm to another. Some specialize in a single area, such as electronics or small appliances, while others sell a wide range of product lines. The typical outside salesperson must have knowledge of many products and be able to serve as a consultant to the customer. For example, a sales representative for a pharmaceutical wholesaler calling on retail stores will need to be familiar with advertising and display techniques, store layout, and other merchandising strategies. Most importantly, this person must be completely familiar with the customer's operation.

SELLING FOR A MANUFACTURER

David Vokey is a senior client manager in the higher-education industry group of IBM Canada. Vokey led the sales team that helped Acadia University become Canada's first "ThinkPad University." While selling in Nova Scotia and Prince Edward Island, he grew IBM's sales from $1.5-million in 1994 to $11-million in 1998; in 1999 he was placed in charge of academic clients in all four Atlantic provinces.[36] In his role as senior client manager, Vokey manages IBM's relationships with many of its most important customers.

Manufacturers employ sales and sales support personnel in many different capacities. Field salespeople, sales engineers, and detail salespeople are outside salespeople who interact face to face with prospects and customers. Inside salespeople rely primarily on the telephone to identify prospects and engage in other selling activities.

FIELD SALESPERSON

field salesperson A salesperson employed by a manufacturer who handles well-established products that require a minimum of creative selling. The position usually does not require a high degree of technical knowledge.

A **field salesperson** sells to new customers and increases sales to current ones. These salespeople must be able to recognize buyer needs and prescribe the best product or service to meet these needs. Field salespeople who provide excellent service find their customers to be a good source of leads for new prospects.

SALES ENGINEER

A **sales engineer** must have detailed and precise technical knowledge and the ability to discuss the technical aspects of his or her products. Expertise in identifying, analyzing, and solving customer problems is of critical importance. A sales engineer may be responsible for introducing a new product that represents a breakthrough in technology and must be prepared to answer a wide range of highly technical questions with conviction.

DETAIL SALESPERSON

The primary goal of a **detail salesperson** is to develop goodwill and stimulate demand for the manufacturer's products. This person is usually not compensated on the basis of the orders obtained, but receives recognition for increasing the sale of goods indirectly. The detail salesperson calls on wholesale, retail, and other customers to help improve their marketing. In a typical day this salesperson may help train a sales staff or offer advice to a firm that is planning an advertising campaign. Detail salespeople also collect valuable information regarding customer acceptance of products. They must be able to offer sound advice in such diverse areas as credit policies, pricing, display, store layout, and storage. The detail salesperson is sometimes referred to as a *missionary salesperson*.

INSIDE SALESPERSON

As face-to-face sales costs increase, many manufacturers have developed an inside sales force. At IBM, about 15 percent of members of the sales force never leave the office. They make calls to smaller customers, take orders, and in some cases provide support to field salespeople.[37] Some marketers are finding that only the initial sale of the product requires face-to-face contact. Inside salespeople can handle repeat contacts.

sales engineer A person who must have detailed and precise technical knowledge and the ability to discuss the technical aspects of his or her products. The sales engineer sometimes introduces new products that represent a breakthrough in technology.

detail salesperson A salesperson representing a manufacturer, whose primary goal is to develop goodwill and stimulate demand for a product or product line. This person usually assists the customer by improving the customer's ability to sell the product.

Sales engineers must have detailed and precise technical knowledge.

Learning to Sell

"Are salespeople made or are they born?" This classic question seems to imply that some people are born with certain qualities that give them a special advantage in the selling field. This is not true. The principles of selling can be learned and applied by people whose personal characteristics are quite different.

In the past few decades, sales training has expanded on four fronts. These four sources of training are corporate-sponsored training, training provided by commercial vendors, certification studies, and courses provided by colleges and universities.

Hundreds of business organizations, such as Xerox Corporation, IBM, Maytag, and Zenith, have established or expanded training programs. These large corporations spend millions of dollars each year to develop their salespeople. *Training* magazine, which conducts an annual analysis of employer-provided training, indicates that salespeople are among the most intensively trained employee groups. The typical salesperson completes 38 hours of training a year, which is 10 hours more than senior executives receive.[38]

The programs designed by firms specializing in the development of sales personnel are a second source of sales training. Some of the most popular courses are offered by Wilson Learning Corporation, The Forum Corporation, Dale Carnegie Training, Learning International, and Zig Ziglar Corporation. These training programs have proved to be a good investment for many individuals and business firms.

The trend toward increased professionalism in personal selling has been the stimulus for a third type of training and education initiative. Many salespeople are returning to the classroom to earn certification in a sales or sales-related area. In real estate, financial planning, and life insurance sales, there are professional designations for salespeople. The Canadian Professional Sales Association (CPSA) Sales Institute Certification Program offers certification for salespeople who undertake training offered at several colleges and universities throughout Canada. The CPSA also offers a number of professional development seminars in selling and sales management.

www.cpsa.com

Building Relationships through Technology

LEARNING CRM SOFTWARE

Many salespeople are at first apprehensive about using computers, yet research shows a high degree of acceptance. Salespeople are often heard remarking, "I don't know how I got along without it."

Following the instructions in this text's CRM application exercises and case studies will give you a good understanding of basic CRM. This knowledge can be valuable as you enter today's selling environment. Many sales organizations are using CRM, and your understanding of the basics will help you learn the particular system that is used by your potential employer. Some people, after following these instructions, list their use of CRM on their résumé.

Many users of CRM enter information about friends and family into their database and use it to enhance all of their relationships. CRM helps people remember the status of relationships, steps to take, and pending events, such as anniversaries and birthdays. (See the application exercise on learning CRM software on page 46 for more information.)

The Canadian Professional Sales Association offers many benefits including professional development programs designed to help salespeople improve selling and relationship-management skills.

The fourth source of sales training is offered by universities and colleges throughout Canada. A large number of universities offer courses in sales management in their undergraduate business programs, while many community colleges and technical schools offer courses in personal or professional selling. These courses are attracting more interest among business majors in these institutions. Some university instructors are beginning to add a larger personal selling component to their sales management courses as the business community increasingly asks for more selling skills from graduates of business programs. According to Trevor Adey, vice-president of commercial sales at Stratos Mobile Networks, "It is unfortunate that more university business students do not get any sales training in their undergraduate business programs. They study a lot of marketing. When I think about opportunities now, I see many small- and medium-sized organizations that need good salespeople who understand marketing, more than they need good marketing people who might be able to sell."[39]

www.stratos.ca

Summary

Today's workforce is made up of millions of knowledge workers who succeed only when they add value to information. The new economy rewards salespeople and other knowledge workers who collect, organize, clarify, and present information in a convincing manner. Selling skills contribute in a major way to four groups of knowledge workers who usually do not consider themselves salespeople: customer service representatives, professionals (accountants, consultants, lawyers, etc.), entrepreneurs, and managerial personnel.

Selling careers offer many rewards not found in other occupations. Income, both monetary and psychic, is above average, and there are many opportunities for advancement. Salespeople enjoy job security, mobility, and independence. Opportunities in selling for members of minority groups and for women are growing. In addition, selling is very interesting work, because a salesperson is constantly in contact with people. The redundant adage "No two people are alike" reminds us that sales work will never be dull or routine.

The text described each of the four major employment settings in the field of personal selling. We have provided a brief introduction to the variety of employment opportunities in service, retail, wholesale, and manufacturer's sales. Keep in mind that each category features a wide range of selling positions, which vary in terms of educational requirements, earning potential, and type of customer served. The discussion and examples should help you see which kind of sales career best suits your talents and interests.

Key Terms

Customer Service Representative 30	*Inside Salesperson* 40
Junior Salesperson 33	*Outside Salesperson* 40
Intermediate Salesperson 33	*Field Salesperson* 40
Senior Salesperson 33	*Sales Engineer* 41
Psychic Income 34	*Detail Salesperson* 41
Retail Salesperson 39	

Review Questions

1. List and describe the four employment settings for people who are considering a selling career.

2. Explain the meaning of *psychic income*.

3. Explain why personal selling is an important auxiliary skill needed by lawyers, engineers, accountants, and other professionals.

4. What future is there in selling for women and minorities?

5. Develop a list of retail products that require well developed personal selling skills.

6. Some salespeople have an opportunity to earn certification in a sales or sales-related area. How can a salesperson benefit from certification?

7. Describe the two types of wholesale salespeople.

8. List four titles commonly used to describe manufacturing salespeople. Describe the duties of each.

9. Develop a list of eight selling career opportunities in the service field.

10. List and briefly describe the four major sources of sales training.

Application Exercises

1. Examine a magazine or newspaper ad for a product or service that you have never seen before. Evaluate its chances for receiving wide customer acceptance. Will this product require a large amount of personal selling effort? What types of salespeople (service, manufacturing, wholesale, or retail) will be involved in selling this product?

2. Ten things that have been proposed as important indicators of sales aptitude include:

highly persuasive	honest
reliable	sociable
enthusiastic	obviously ambitious
high verbal skills	well organized
general sales experience	specific sales experience

Rank the three qualities that you think are most important (1 = most important). Rank the three that you think are least important (1 = least important). Be prepared to defend your answer.

3. Interview a salesperson from one of the four major employment settings (service, retail, wholesale, manufacturing), and ask the following questions:

a. Why did you decide on a sales career?
b. What do you like most about your job?
c. What do you like least about your job?
d. What is a typical sales day like?
e. What are the most important things for sales success?

4. Shelly Jones, a vice-president and partner in the consulting firm Korn/Ferry International, has looked into the future and he sees some new challenges for salespeople. He recently shared the following predictions with *Selling* magazine:

a. Salespeople will spend more time extending the range of applications or finding new markets for the products they sell.
b. The selling function will be less pitching your product and more integrating your product into the business equation of your client. Understanding the business environment in which your client operates will be critical.
c. In the future you will have to be a financial engineer for your client. You need to understand how your client makes money and be able to explain how your product or service contributes to profitable operation of the client's firm.

Interview a salesperson who is involved in business-to-business selling (a manufacturer's representative, for example) and determine if this person agrees with the views of Shelly Jones.

5. There are many information sources on selling careers and career opportunities on the Internet. Search the Internet for information on selling careers. Use your search engine to find career information on a pharmaceutical representative, a field sales engineer, and a retail salesperson.

CRM Application Exercise

Learning CRM Software

Launch the CRM software that you have downloaded from www.pearsoned.ca/manning to become acquainted with the layout and features of the ACT! program. Start by pressing the F1 function key, which displays the contents of the help file. Clicking on the first entry, ACT! Screens, shows information about the program's three main screens: contact screens (records with information about people), word processing screens, and the query screen. Print the ACT! screens page by selecting File, Print Topic. At the bottom of this page is a row of icons, essentially a small version of the toolbar icons found on the main contact screen. Click on each of these icons for an explanation of its function.

Next, select the underlined link The Contact Screens to learn about the two screens where you can view information about a contact (person). At the top of this screen, click on the link labelled Status Area to read a description of the information found along the side of the contact screens. Here you will learn to determine the number of records in the database, how to use the card index icon to navigate, and how to discover whether there are notes, history information, or activities scheduled for this contact.

Browse through the help screens to learn more about the structure and functions of this CRM software.

Case Problem

At 31 years of age, Valerie Howe was considering a career change. She had spent nearly eight years of her life—her whole career—working for the public sector. Valerie Howe started work as a small-business consultant and after one year she moved to a position as an industrial development officer with the provincial government, Department of Industry, Trade and Technology (DITT). She spent the next seven years working with the oil and gas sector to build local industrial capabilities and to promote the province's burgeoning sector to international markets. The job involved travel to interesting locations within Canada, and also to the United States, Scotland, Norway, and Russia. After seven years without a salary increase, few opportunities for advancement, and uncertainty due to provincial government downsizing, DITT provided an exciting opportunity for Valerie Howe—a secondment to the cabinet secretariat, working with the lead economic analysts who advised the premier and cabinet on matters of provincial economic policy. This career move offered additional challenges and more opportunities for career advancement. It seemed as though Valerie Howe's career prospects were about to improve.

Just four months after her career move, Valerie Howe was presented with another exciting opportunity—a position with a growing information technology (IT) company. The company, **xwave solutions**, was launched in 1999 as the result of a merger of several dynamic and profitable IT companies. It was looking for an account manager, and Valerie Howe was considering the opportunity. She was a bit apprehensive about working in the private sector, and particularly in sales, where she had no experience. Valerie, however, agreed to an interview to learn more about the company and the opportunities it offered. The information was quite exciting and the opportunity was certainly worth consid-

www.xwavesolutions. com

ering: **xwave solutions** was the largest IT company in Atlantic Canada, and one of the top five Canadian-owned IT companies. It had 1200 employees in St. John's, Halifax, Ottawa, Calgary, Edmonton, and Dallas, Texas. There appeared to be tremendous growth potential for the company. The job would involve business development and account management for private-sector clients. One sector of particular relevance was the oil and gas sector—a logical fit for Valerie Howe given her background and experience. The challenges and opportunities for professional development seemed endless.

Valerie Howe had many factors to consider. After a number of years, the public sector had finally opened up opportunities for career advancement and, while there were no guarantees, she believed things would continue to progress over time. On the other hand, if she did not take advantage of the opportunity with **xwave solutions**, it might be many years before another opportunity such as this would come along. Valerie Howe was eager to make use of the knowledge she had gained from her recent business program. She was sure it would bene-fit her in either position, but the private sector recognized her value and appeared willing to compensate her accordingly. There were also possibilities for incentive compensation, such as bonuses. The sales environment, however, was not an area where Valerie Howe had experience. Her position with the provincial public service involved marketing and promotion, but she did not have direct sales responsibility. An **xwave solutions** account manager would be front and centre with clients and would face considerable competition for sales from sales managers of other IT companies.[40]

Questions

1. What factors should Valerie Howe consider when making a decision on her career choice?

2. If you were Valerie Howe, what questions would you ask during your ini-tial interview?

Part II

Developing a Relationship Strategy

High-performance salespeople are generally better able to build and maintain relationships than moderate performers. Part II focuses on the person-to-person relationship-building strategies that are the foundation for personal development and for relationships with customers that result in repeat business and referrals.

RELATIONSHIP STRATEGY

PRESENTATION STRATEGY

PERSONAL SELLING PHILOSOPHY

PRODUCT STRATEGY

CUSTOMER STRATEGY

BUILDING QUALITY PARTNERSHIPS

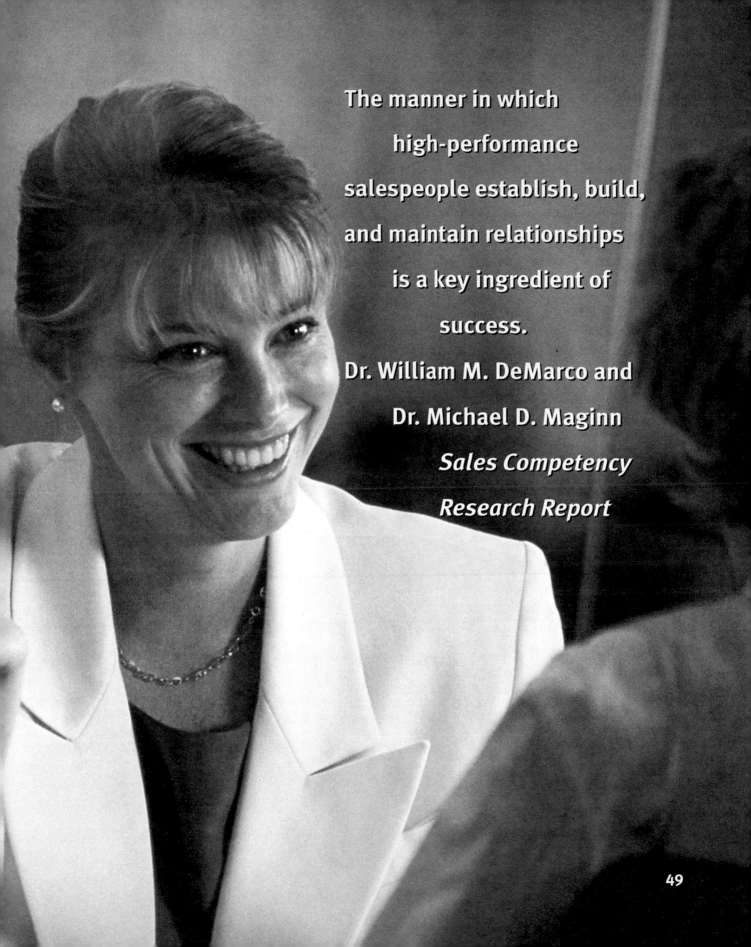

> The manner in which high-performance salespeople establish, build, and maintain relationships is a key ingredient of success.
>
> Dr. William M. DeMarco and Dr. Michael D. Maginn
> *Sales Competency Research Report*

49

Creating Value with a Relationship Strategy

LEARNING OBJECTIVES

When you finish reading this chapter, you should be able to

1. Explain the importance of developing a relationship strategy

2. Define partnering and describe the partnering relationship

3. Identify the four key groups with which the salesperson needs to develop relationship strategies

4. Discuss how self-image forms the foundation for building long-term selling relationships

5. Describe the importance of a double-win relationship

6. Identify and describe the major nonverbal factors that shape our sales image

7. Describe conversational strategies that help us establish relationships

8. Explain how to establish a self-improvement plan based on personal development strategies

The salespeople who work for Premdor Inc. understand the importance of developing relationship strategies to build long-term partnerships with their customers. The Mississauga-based manufacturer produces more than 100 000 doors per day in its plants in five countries, and sells them in more than 40 countries through a well-established wholesale and retail distribution system.

To demonstrate their commitment to service, Premdor salespeople develop "relationship plans" in consultation with their customers. Philip Orsino, president and CEO of Premdor, says that the process of developing and committing these plans to paper ensures that they understand each customer's needs and that they have clearly defined objectives for serving each customer. The customized plans also outline how the salespeople will meet their objectives for each customer, and how their performance will be measured. According to Orsino, the number-one comment from customers who have been presented with a written relationship plan has been "No one has ever done this with us before."

Premdor is creating value with its relationship strategy.[1]

Developing a Relationship Strategy

To develop and apply the wide range of interpersonal skills needed in today's complex sales environment can be challenging. Daniel Goleman, author of the best-selling books *Emotional Intelligence* and *Working with Emotional Intelligence*, notes that there are many forms of intelligence that influence our actions throughout life. One of these, **emotional intelligence**, refers to the capacity for recognizing our own feelings and those of others, for motivating ourselves, and for managing emotions well in ourselves and in our relationships. People with a high level of emotional intelligence display many of the qualities needed in sales work: self-confidence, trustworthiness, adaptability, initiative, optimism, empathy, and well-developed social skills.[2] The good news is that emotional intelligence can be enhanced with a variety of self-development activities. We discuss many of these activities in this chapter.

Selling in the age of information involves three major relationship challenges. The first major challenge is building new relationships.[3] Salespeople who can quickly build rapport with new prospects have a much greater chance of achieving success in personal selling. Needless to say, building new relationships starts with the communication of positive impressions during the initial contact. The second major challenge is transforming relationships from the personal level to the business level. Once rapport is established, the salesperson is in a stronger position to begin the need identification process. The third major challenge is management of relationships. Dr. Charles Parker—a noted consultant and sales trainer—says, "In order to achieve a high level of success salespeople have to manage a multitude of different relationships."[4] Salespeople must develop relationship management strategies that focus on four key groups. These groups are discussed later in this chapter.

Ongoing development of a **relationship strategy** should be the goal of every salesperson; customers tend to buy from people they like and trust, so we must learn how to establish and build relationships. In this chapter we introduce the double-win philosophy and discuss the importance of projecting a profes-

emotional intelligence The capacity for recognizing our own feelings and those of others, for motivating ourselves, and for managing emotions well in ourselves and our relationships.

relationship strategy A well-thought-out plan for establishing, building, and maintaining quality relationships.

Partnering is a strategically developed, high quality, long-term relationship that focuses on solving the customer's buying problem. Partnering involves establishing, re-establishing, and maintaining relationships with customers.

Figure 3.1 Every salesperson should have an ongoing goal of developing a relationship strategy that adds value to the sale.

Strategic/Consultative Selling Model	
Strategic step	**Prescription**
DEVELOP A PERSONAL SELLING PHILOSOPHY	✓ ADOPT MARKETING CONCEPT ✓ VALUE PERSONAL SELLING ✓ BECOME A PROBLEM SOLVER/PARTNER
DEVELOP A RELATIONSHIP STRATEGY	● ADOPT DOUBLE-WIN PHILOSOPHY ● PROJECT PROFESSIONAL IMAGE ● PRACTISE COMMUNICATION-STYLE FLEXING

sional image. Chapter 4 explains how an understanding of communication styles can help us better manage the relationship process. Chapter 16 focuses on the importance of maintaining high ethical standards in order to build long-term relationships with the customer (Fig. 3.1).

RELATIONSHIPS ADD VALUE

Denis Waitley, in his book *Empires of the Mind*, describes recent developments in the business community. He says, "Yesterday value was extra. Today value is everything."[5] Customers have become more sophisticated and more demanding in their buying strategies. They have come to expect partnering, and selling strategies that add value to the purchase. Consequently, salespeople need to become more sophisticated in their selling strategies. The Canadian Professional Sales Association, Learning International, Wilson Learning Corporation, Dale Carnegie Training, Zig Ziglar Corporation, and The Forum Corporation offer sales training that stresses a style of selling favouring a close, trusting, long-term relationship over the quick sell. A representative of Forum noted, "The philosophy is to serve the customer as a consultant, not as a peddler."

The manner in which salespeople establish, build, and maintain relationships is no longer an incidental aspect of personal selling; in the age of information it is a key to success. A satisfied customer will recommend you to many other prospects, and a disgruntled customer can be counted on to complain about you to numerous prospects.[6]

The salesperson who is honest, accountable, and sincerely concerned about the customer's welfare brings added value to the sale. These characteristics give the salesperson a competitive advantage—an advantage that is becoming increasingly important in a world of look-alike products and similar prices.

PARTNERING—THE HIGHEST QUALITY SELLING RELATIONSHIP

Salespeople today are encouraged to think of everything they say or do in the context of their relationship with the customer. They should constantly strive to build a long-term partnership. In a marketplace characterized by increased levels of competition and greater product complexity, we see the need to adopt a relationship strategy that emphasizes the "lifetime" customer. High quality relationships result in repeat business and important referrals. A growing number of salespeople recognize that the quality of the partnerships they create is as important as the quality of the products they sell. Today's customer wants a quality product *and* a quality relationship. One example of this trend is the J. D. Power and Associates Automotive Studies research. The Initial Quality Study conducted by this marketing information firm measures the number and type of problems experienced by new car owners. The Sales Satisfaction Study, also conducted by J. D. Power, examines factors that impact on sales satisfaction such as treatment by auto sales representatives and customer experience when the auto was delivered.[7]

Partnering can be defined as a strategically developed, high quality, long-term relationship that focuses on solving the customer's buying problem.[8] Traditional industrial-age sales training programs emphasized the importance of creating a good first impression and then "pushing" your product. Partnering emphasizes building a strong relationship during every aspect of the sale and working hard to maintain a quality relationship with the customer after the sale. Personal selling today must be viewed as a process, not an event.[9]

Larry Wilson, a noted author and sales consultant, identifies partnering as one of the most important strategic thought processes needed by salespeople. He points out that the salesperson who is selling a "one-shot" solution cannot compete against the one who has developed and nurtured a long-term, mutually beneficial partnership. Wilson believes there are three keys to a partnering relationship:

➤ The relationship is built on shared values. If your client feels that you both share the same ideas and values, it goes a long way toward creating a powerful relationship.

➤ Everyone needs to clearly understand the purpose of the partnership and be committed to the vision. Both the salesperson and the client must agree on what they are trying to do together.

➤ The role of the salesperson must move from selling to supporting. The salesperson in a partnership is actively concerned with the growth, health, and satisfaction of the company to which he or she is selling.[10]

Salespeople who are willing to abandon short-term thinking and invest the time and energy needed to develop a high quality, long-term relationship with customers will be rewarded with greater earnings and the satisfaction of working with repeat customers. Sales resulting from referrals will also increase.

partnering A strategically developed, high quality relationship that focuses on solving the customer's buying problem.

Building Relationships through Technology

COMMUNICATING USING CRM

Customer relationship management (CRM) software can be used to enhance the quality of your relationships. A good example is the software's ability to enhance communications between you and your contacts. With the ACT! software, for example, you can quickly prepare and send a letter, fax, or e-mail to one or more people who have records in the database. Recipients of your appointment confirmations, information verifications, company or product news, or brief personal notes, will recognize and appreciate your effort to keep them informed. The written word conveys consideration and helps avoid misunderstandings and miscommunications. CRM empowers you to easily use the written word to advance your relationship building. (See the exercise Preparing Letters with CRM on page 70 for more information.)

RELATIONSHIP STRATEGIES FOCUS ON FOUR KEY GROUPS

Establishing and maintaining a partnering-type relationship internally as well as with customers is a vital aspect of selling. High-performance sales personnel build strong relationships with four groups (Fig. 3.2):

1. *Customers.* As noted previously, a major key to success in selling is the ability to establish working relationships with customers in which mutual support, trust, and goals are nurtured over time. Salespeople who maintain regular contact with their customers and develop sound business relationships based on mutual trust are able to drive up sales productivity.[11]

   John Franco, former president of Learning International, says that in some cases the salesperson must move beyond the role of trusted consultant to gain full acceptance by the customer. He says that in today's highly competitive business climate the salesperson needs to be perceived as someone who is working on the customer's team as a member of the customer's organization.[12]

2. *Secondary decision makers.* High-performance salespeople understand the importance of building relationships with the people who work with customers. In many selling situations the first person the salesperson meets is a receptionist, secretary, or assistant to the primary decision maker. These persons can often facilitate a meeting with the prospect. Also, the prospect may involve other people in making the buying decision. For example, the decision to buy a new copy machine may be made by a team of persons including the buyer and persons who will actually use the machine.

3. *Company support staff.* The maintenance of relationships internally is a vital aspect of selling. Support staff may include persons working in the areas of market research, product service, credit, training, or shipping. Influencing these people to change their priorities, interrupt their schedules, accept new responsibilities, or fulfill any other request for special attention is a major part of the salesperson's job. Most sales personnel will readily admit that their productivity depends on the contributions of these people.

4. *Management personnel.* Sales personnel usually work under the direct supervision of a sales manager, department head, or some other member of the firm's management team. Maintaining a good relationship with this person is important.

Figure 3.2 An effective relationship strategy helps high-performing salespeople to build and maintain win-win relationships with four key groups.

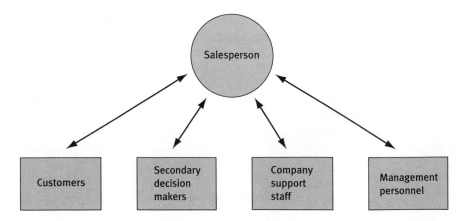

A Selling Partner

P   **Prepares strategically** for a long-term, high quality relationship that solves the customer's problems

A   **Asks questions** to get on the customer's agenda

R   **Restates customer needs** with confirmation questions

T   **Teams** with support people to custom-fit solutions

N   **Negotiates double-win solutions** with joint decision making

E   **Exceeds customer expectations** whenever possible

R   **Re-examines** the ongoing quality of the relationship frequently

Developing Thought Processes that Enhance Your Relationship Strategy

Industrial-age folklore created the myth of the "born" salesperson—a dynamic, outgoing, highly assertive individual. Experience acquired during the age of information has taught us that many other factors determine sales success. Key among these factors are a positive self-image and the ability to relate to others in effective and productive ways. With the aid of knowledge drawn from the behavioural sciences we can develop the relationship strategies needed in a wide range of selling situations.

SELF-IMAGE—AN IMPORTANT DIMENSION OF THE RELATIONSHIP STRATEGY

Self-image is shaped by the ideas, attitudes, feelings, and other thoughts you have about yourself that influence the way you relate to others. Psychologists have found that, once we form a thought process about ourselves, it serves to edit all incoming information and influence our actions. Let us consider a salesperson who has come to believe that he cannot build strong relationships with high-level decision makers. Once this mental picture, or self-image, has been formed, it is unlikely that this salesperson will be able to influence high-level executives in a sales situation. Essentially, this person is programmed to fail in attempts to build relationships at this level. There is no anticipation of improvement, so the negative self-image becomes a self-fulfilling prophecy. You simply cannot succeed at something unless you think you are going to succeed at it.

self-image A set of ideas, attitudes, and feelings you have about yourself that influences the way you relate to others.

SELF-IMAGE AND SUCCESS

Self-image is a powerful thought process influencing the direction of our lives. It can set the limits of our accomplishments, defining what we can and cannot do. Realizing the power of self-image is an important breakthrough in our understanding of the factors that influence us.

A pioneer in the area of self-image psychology was the late Dr. Maxwell Maltz, author of *Psycho-Cybernetics* and other books devoted to this topic. We are indebted to him for two important discoveries that help us understand better the "why" of human behaviour:

1. *Feelings and behaviour are consistent with the self-image.* The individual who feels like a "failure" will likely find some way to fail. There is a definite relationship between self-image and accomplishments at work. Generally speaking, the more positive your self-image, the greater your prospects for achieving success, because a positive self-image helps generate the energy needed to get things done.

2. *The self-image can be changed.* Numerous case histories show that you are never too young or too old to change your self-image and thereby achieve new accomplishments.[13]

A positive self-image (high self-esteem) is an important prerequisite to success in selling. According to a study conducted by Sentry Insurance, high self-esteem mixed with candour is the vital ingredient in the makeup of top salespeople.[14] Low self-esteem, according to Nathaniel Branden, author of *Self-Esteem at Work*, correlates with resistance to change and with clinging to the known and familiar. He notes that low self-esteem is economically disadvantageous in an information economy where knowledge and new ideas count for almost everything.[15]

How can you develop a more positive self-image? How can you get rid of self-destructive ways of thinking? Bringing your present self-image out into the open is the first step in understanding who you are, what you can do, and where you are going. Improving your self-image will not happen overnight, but it can happen. A few practical approaches are summarized here.

1. *Focus on the future and stop being overly concerned with past mistakes or failures.* We should learn from past errors, but we should not be immobilized by them.

Building Relationships in a Diverse World

BUSINESS ETIQUETTE FOSTERS QUALITY RELATIONSHIPS

A diverse workforce often creates new challenges for those who want to practise good manners. To illustrate, what do you do if a client comes into your office in a wheelchair? Do you rise? A man and a woman of equal corporate status walk down an office corridor and arrive at a door. If the woman reaches the door first, should the man move ahead to open it for her?

Changing technology also creates questions in the mind of the person who wants to avoid a violation of the rules of good etiquette. Should you switch on speaker phones without letting the caller know that others are present in the room and listening? Should you leave personal messages on voice mail if several others have access to the messages?

The growth of multinational companies has created the need to understand international business etiquette. Many companies realize that their employees need to prepare for assignments that take them to foreign countries.

If your travels take you to Japan, it's helpful to know that prolonged eye contact is considered offensive. In cultures where handshakes tend to linger longer than typical American handshakes, pulling your hand away too soon is interpreted as a rejection. Dorthea Johnson, director of The Protocol School of Washington, says, "If you have good manners, people notice. And if you have bad manners, people notice that too, especially in the international arena." Quality is a central concept in most organizations, and displaying good manners is a central part of delivering on the quality mission.

If you are not able to complete a business-etiquette training course, consider books such as *Letitia Baldrige's New Complete Guide to Executive Manners* by Letitia Baldrige, *Miss Manners' Guide for the Turn-of-the-Millennium* by Judith Martin, *Business Etiquette in Brief*, by Ann Marie Sabath, and *Complete Business Etiquette Handbook* by Barbara Pachter and Marjorie Brody.[a]

2. *Develop expertise in selected areas.* By developing "expert power" you not only improve your self-image but also increase the value of your contributions to your employer and your customers.

3. *Learn to develop a positive mental attitude.* To develop a more positive outlook, read books and listen to audiotapes that describe ways to develop a positive mental attitude. Consider materials developed by Denis Waitley, Stephen Covey, Brian Tracy, Dale Carnegie, and Zig Ziglar.

Later in this chapter you will learn how to develop and initiate a plan for self-improvement. If you want to improve your self-image, consider adopting this plan.

THE DOUBLE-WIN

Denis Waitley—consultant, national speaker, and author of several books—provides us with a brief and simple definition of the term **double-win:** "If I help you win, I win, too."[16] Both the customer and the salesperson come out of the sale feeling a sense of satisfaction. The salesperson not only obtains the order, but sets the stage for a long-term relationship, repeat business, and future referrals. Here is how one author described this "win-win" approach:

> *Both you and the Buyer "Win." That is, you both come out of the sale feeling satisfied, knowing that neither of you has taken advantage of the other and that both of you have profited, personally and professionally, from the transaction.*[17]

The double-win strategy is based on such irrefutable logic that it is difficult to understand why any other approach would be used. However, some salespeople still have not accepted the merits of the win-win approach. They have adopted a win-lose approach, which means that the salesperson wins at the buyer's expense. When a salesperson sells a product that is not the best solution to the buyer's problem, the win-lose strategy has been used.

We can adopt the win-win attitude that is one of the principles of partnering-style selling. The starting point to development of a double-win philosophy is to

double-win The view that "if I help you win, I win too."

This salesperson's clothing and facial expression project a professional image. A pleasant smile and eye contact convey friendliness to the customer.

compare the behaviours of persons who have adopted the win-lose approach with the behaviours of persons who have adopted the win-win approach (Fig. 3.3).

CHARACTER AND INTEGRITY

Your character and integrity strongly influence your relationships with others. **Character** is composed of your personal standards of behaviour, including your honesty, integrity, and moral fibre.[18] Your character is based on your internal values and the resulting judgments you make about what is right and what is wrong. When your behaviour is in tune with your professed standards and values—when you practise what you believe in—you have **integrity**. In a world of uncertainty and rapid change, integrity has become a valuable character trait. Salespeople with integrity can be trusted to do what they say they will do. One way to achieve trustworthiness in personal selling is to avoid deceiving or misleading the customer. More will be said about this topic in Chapter 16, which examines the ethical conduct of salespeople.

Nonverbal Strategies that Improve Relationships

The first contact between a salesperson and a prospect is very important. During the first few minutes—or seconds in some cases—the prospect and the salesperson form impressions of each other that will either facilitate or detract from the sales call.[19] It is very difficult to rebound from a poor first impression.

Every salesperson projects an image to prospective customers, and this image influences how a customer feels about the sales representative. The image you project is the sum total of many verbal and nonverbal factors. The quality of your voice, the clothing you wear, your posture, your manners, and your communication style represent some of the factors that contribute to the formation of your image. We discuss body language, voice quality, and manners in this chapter. Communication style is examined in Chapter 4.

THE EFFECT OF BODY LANGUAGE ON RELATIONSHIPS

Body language is a form of nonverbal communication that has been defined as *messages without words* and *silent messages.* For example, a purchasing agent who continually glances at his watch is communicating a concern for time without using the spoken word. A salesperson who leans forward in her chair while talk-

character Your personal standards of behaviour, including your honesty and integrity. Your character is based on your internal values and the resulting judgments you make about what is right and what is wrong.

integrity Part of your character; what you have when your behaviour is in accordance with your professed standards and personal code of moral values.

body language A form of nonverbal communication that has been defined as "messages without words" and "silent messages."

Figure 3.3   The starting point to developing a double-win philosophy is to compare behaviours of win-lose salespeople with those of salespeople who have adopted the win-win approach. (Adapted from a list of losers, winners, and double winners in *The Double Win* by Denis Waitley.)

Win-lose people	Win-win people
• See a problem in every solution	• Help others solve their problem
• Fix the blame	• Fix what caused the problem
• Let life happen to them	• Make life a joyous happening for others and themselves
• Live in the past	• Learn from the past, live in the present, and set goals for the future
• Make promises they never keep	• Make commitments to themselves and to others and keep them both

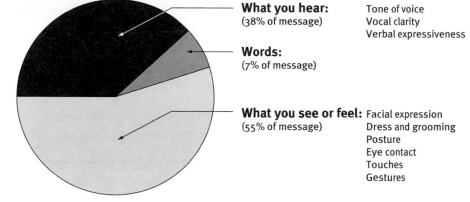

What you hear: (38% of message)

Tone of voice
Vocal clarity
Verbal expressiveness

Words: (7% of message)

What you see or feel: (55% of message)

Facial expression
Dress and grooming
Posture
Eye contact
Touches
Gestures

Figure 3.4   When someone else is speaking, your understanding of what is said depends heavily on what you see or feel. (Source: Moravian Study of Nonverbal Communication.)

ing to a customer (as opposed to slouching) is more likely to communicate a feeling of concern to this person.

Research indicates that, when two people communicate, nonverbal messages convey much more impact than verbal messages. Words play a surprisingly small part in the communication process. Studies indicate that, in a typical two-person conversation, only about 7 percent of our understanding comes from words spoken by the other person.

About 38 percent of our understanding comes from what we hear. Does the other person sound sincere, credible, and knowledgable? Every spoken message has a vocal element, coming not from *what* we say, but from *how* we say it. The voice communicates in many ways: through its tone, volume, and speed of delivery. A salesperson wishing to communicate enthusiasm needs to use a voice that is charged with energy.

About 55 percent of the meaning we attach to communication efforts by others is based on what we see or feel (Fig. 3.4). A positive message can be communicated to a customer with a smile, a firm handshake, good eye contact, and a professional appearance.[20]

Nonverbal messages can reinforce or contradict the spoken word. When your verbal message and body language are consistent, they give others the impression that you can be trusted and that what you say reflects what you truly believe. When there is a discrepancy between your verbal and nonverbal messages, you are less apt to be trusted.[21]

Ruth Bell Steinhauer (see pp. 38–39): A pleasant smile sends a positive nonverbal message.

ENTRANCE AND CARRIAGE

As noted earlier, the first impression we make is very important. The moment a salesperson walks into a client's office, the client begins making judgments. Susan Bixler, author of *The Professional Image* and *Professional Presence*, makes this comment:

> *All of us make entrances throughout our business day as we enter offices, conference rooms, or meeting halls. And every time we do, someone is watching us, appraising us, sizing us up, and gauging our appearance, even our intelligence, often within the space of a few seconds.*[22]

Bixler says that the key to making a successful entrance is simply believing—and projecting—that you have a reason to be there and have something important to offer the client. You can communicate confidence with a strong stride, good posture, and a friendly smile. A confident manner communicates to the client the message, "This meeting will be beneficial to you."

SHAKING HANDS

An inadequate handshake is like dandruff: no one will mention it, but everyone will notice it. The handshake is an important symbol of respect, and in most business settings it is the proper greeting.[23]

In the field of selling the handshake is usually the *first* and frequently the *only* physical contact one makes during a sales call. The handshake can communicate warmth, genuine concern for the prospect, and an image of strength. It can also communicate aloofness, indifference, and weakness to the customer. The message we communicate with a handshake will be determined by a combination of five factors:

1. *Eye contact during handshake.* Eyes transmit more information than any other part of the body, so maintaining eye contact throughout the handshaking process is important when two people greet each other.

2. *Degree of firmness.* Generally speaking, a firm handshake will communicate a caring attitude, while a weak grip (the dead-fish handshake) communicates indifference.

3. *Depth of interlock.* A full, deep grip will communicate friendship to the other person.

4. *Duration of grip.* There are no specific guidelines to tell us what the ideal duration of a grip should be. However, by extending the duration of the handshake we can often communicate a greater degree of interest and concern for the other person. Do not pump up and down more than once or twice.

The best time to present your name is when you extend your hand.

5. *Degree of dryness of hands.* A moist palm not only is uncomfortable to handle but also can communicate the impression that you are quite nervous. Some people have a physiological problem that causes clammy hands, and they should keep a handkerchief within reach to remove excess moisture. A clammy hand is likely to repel most customers.[24]

The best time to present your name is when you extend your hand. When you introduce yourself, state your name clearly and then listen carefully to be certain you hear the customer's name. To ensure that you will remember the customer's name, repeat it. In some cases you will need to check to be sure you are pronouncing it properly.[25]

FACIAL EXPRESSIONS

If you want to identify the inner feelings of another person, watch facial expressions closely. The face is a remarkable communicator, capable of accurately signalling emotion in a split second and capable of concealing emotion equally well. We can tell in a blink of an eye if our customer's face is registering surprise, pleasure, or skepticism (Fig. 3.5). Facial expressions are largely universal, so people around the world tend to "read" faces in a similar way. It is worth noting that the smile is the most recognized facial signal in the world and it can have a great deal of influence on others. George Rotter, professor of psychology at Montclair University, says, "Smiles are an enormous controller of how people perceive you." People tend to trust a smiling face.[26] Get in the habit of offering a sincere smile each time you meet with a prospect.

THE EFFECT OF APPEARANCE ON RELATIONSHIPS

We form opinions about people based on a pattern of immediate impressions conveyed by appearance. The clothing we wear, the length and style of our hair, the fragrances we use, and the jewellery we display all combine to make a statement about us to others—a statement of primary importance to anyone involved in selling.

According to many of the top image consultants, clothing is particularly important. John T. Molloy, author of *Dress for Success*, *New Dress for Success*, and other books, was one of the first to acknowledge publicly the link between dress and the image we project to others. He is credited with introducing the term *wardrobe engineering*, a concept that was later refined by William Thourlby,

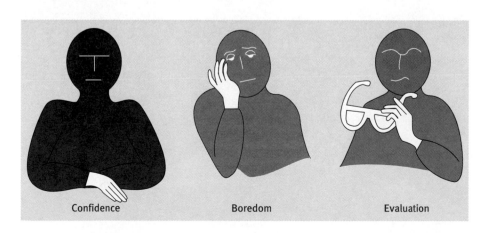

Confidence   Boredom   Evaluation

Figure 3.5   Our subtle facial gestures are continuously sending messages to others.

wardrobe engineering Combining the elements of psychology, fashion, sociology, and art into clothing selection.

unconscious expectations Certain views concerning appropriate dress.

Jacqueline Thompson, Emily Cho, Susan Bixler, and other noted image consultants. **Wardrobe engineering** combines the elements of psychology, fashion, sociology, and art into clothing selection. The position taken by Molloy and others is that clothing can evoke a predictable response.[27]

We all have certain views, or **unconscious expectations,** concerning appropriate dress. In sales work we should try to anticipate the expectations of our clientele. The clothing worn by salespeople does make a difference in terms of customer acceptance because it communicates powerful messages. The clothing we wear can influence our credibility and likeability. Martin Siewert, a member of the business development team for Axiom Management Consulting, has adopted a flexible approach to dress. His company's policy favours an informal dress code, so he usually wears casual clothing at work unless he is meeting with a client. When he calls on customers, most of whom are Fortune 500 companies, he wears a suit and tie. "I want to show that I respect their culture," he says.[28]

Most image consultants agree that there is no single "dress for success" look. The appropriate wardrobe will vary from one city or region to another and from company to company. However, there are some general guidelines that we should follow in selecting clothing for sales work. Four key ideas should govern our decisions: simplicity, appropriateness, quality, and visual integrity.

SIMPLICITY

The colour of our clothing, as well as design, will communicate a message to the customer. Some colours are showy and convey an air of casualness. In a business setting we want to be taken seriously, so flashy colours should usually be avoided.

APPROPRIATENESS

Selecting appropriate clothing for sales work can be a challenge. We must carefully consider the clients we serve and decide what will be acceptable to them. Many salespeople are guided by the type of products they sell and the desired image projected by their employer.

Body language, voice quality, and manners shape much of the image we project to others.

QUALITY

The quality of our wardrobe will also influence the image we project to customers. A salesperson's wardrobe should be regarded as an investment, with each item carefully selected to look good and fit well. Susan Bixler says, "If you want respect, you have to dress as well as or better than your industry standards."[29]

VISUAL INTEGRITY

Visual presence must have a certain amount of integrity and consistency. The images you project are made up of many factors and lack of attention to important details can negate your effort to create a good impression. Too much jewellery, a shirt that does not fit well, or unshined shoes can detract from the professional look you want to project. People often are extra alert when meeting someone new, and this heightened consciousness makes every detail count.[30]

THE EFFECT OF VOICE QUALITY ON RELATIONSHIPS

As noted previously, voice quality contributes about 38 percent of the meaning attached to spoken messages. On the telephone, voice quality is even more important because the other person cannot see your facial expressions, hand gestures, and other body movements. You cannot trade in your current voice for a new one. However, you can make your voice more pleasing to others. How?

Here are two suggestions.

1. *Do not talk too fast or too slowly.* Rapid speech often causes customers to become defensive. They raise psychological barriers because a "rapid-fire monologue" is associated with high-pressure sales methods. Peter Urs Bender, a noted Canadian business speaker and author of *Secrets of Power Presentations*, says 85 percent of presenters begin too fast. He says, "Remember, it's better to go slower than faster as this will make you look more confident. Also, be sure you incorporate some appropriately long pauses between sentences, particularly at the beginning."[31] The slower presentation allows others to follow, and it allows the speaker time to think ahead—to consider the situation and make judgments. Another good tip is to vary the speed of your speech.

 www.peterursbender.com

2. *Avoid a speech pattern that is dull and colourless.* The worst kind of voice has no colour and no feeling. Enthusiasm is a critical element of an effective sales presentation. It is also contagious. Your enthusiasm for the product will be transmitted to the customer. Your tone of voice mirrors your emotional state and physical well being. When you are feeling good and enjoying a positive mental state, your voice will naturally sound upbeat, energetic, and enthusiastic. However, the normal stresses and strains of life can be reflected in your voice. Sometimes you have to manipulate your tone of voice to communicate greater warmth and enthusiasm. Before you make that important phone call or meet with a prospect, reflect on your state of mind. To drain tension from your voice, inhale and tense every muscle. Hold for a count of five, and then exhale for a count of ten. If you want to sound warm and friendly, smile while speaking.[32]

With today's affordable video camcorders you can easily find out how you look and sound. To evaluate the quality of your voice, tape it while talking to another person. Play back the tape, and rate yourself in the previously described areas.

THE EFFECT OF MANNERS ON RELATIONSHIPS

The study of manners (sometimes called *etiquette*) reveals a number of ways to enhance your relationship strategy. Salespeople who possess knowledge of the rules of etiquette can perform their daily work with greater poise and confidence. Think of manners as a universal passport to positive relationships and respect.[33]

With practice, anyone can have good manners without appearing to be "stiff" and at the same time win the respect and admiration of others. Space does not permit a complete review of this topic, but we cover some of the rules of etiquette that are especially important to salespeople.

1. *Avoid the temptation to address a new prospect by first name.* In a business setting, too much familiarity too quickly can cause irritation.

2. *Avoid offensive comments or stories.* Never assume that the customer's value system is the same as your own. Rough language and off-colour stories can do irreparable damage to your image.

3. *Do not express personal views on political or religious issues.* There is seldom a "safe" position to take in these areas, so it is better to avoid these topics altogether.

4. *When you invite a customer to lunch, do not discuss business before the meal is ordered unless the client initiates the subject.* Also, order food that is easily controlled, and avoid items such as ribs, chicken, and lobster.

5. *When you use voice mail, leave a clear, concise message.* Do not speak too fast or mumble your name and number.

It has been said that good manners make other people feel better. This is true because good manners require that we place the other person's comfort ahead of our own. One of the best ways to develop rapport with a customer is to avoid behaviour that might be offensive to that person.

Conversational Strategies that Enhance Relationships

The foundation for a long-term relationship with the customer is frequently a "get acquainted" type of conversation that takes place before any discussion of business matters. Within a few minutes it is possible to reduce the relationship tension that is so common when two people meet for the first time. This informal visit with the customer provides the salesperson with an opportunity to apply three of Dale Carnegie's guidelines for building strong relationships:

➤ Become genuinely interested in other people.

➤ Be a good listener. Encourage others to talk about themselves.

➤ Talk in terms of the other person's interests.[34]

In a relaxed and friendly atmosphere, the customer is more apt to open up and share information that will help the salesperson determine customer needs. A casual conversation is frequently the first step in developing a trusting relationship.

The length of this conversation will depend on your sense of the prospect's reaction to your greeting, how busy the prospect appears to be, and your awareness of topics of mutual interest. In developing conversation the following three areas should be considered.

COMMENTS ON HERE AND NOW OBSERVATIONS

Observant salespeople are aware of the things going on around them. These observations can be as general as unusual developments in the weather or as specific as noticing unique artifacts in the prospect's office.

COMPLIMENTS

When you offer a *sincere* compliment to your prospect, you are saying, "Something about you is special." Most people react positively to compliments because they appeal to the need for self-esteem. Your admiration should not be expressed, however, in phony superlatives that will seem transparent. The prospect may suspect ulterior motives, which are unwelcome.

SEARCH FOR MUTUAL ACQUAINTANCES OR INTERESTS

A frequent mode for establishing rapport with a new prospect is to find friends or interests you have in common. If you know someone with the same last name as your prospect, it may be appropriate to ask whether your friend is any relation. Anything you observe in the prospect's office or home might suggest an interest that you and your prospect share. Such topics of conversation appeal to your prospect's social needs.

Strategies for Self-Improvement

Orson Welles, a well-known and highly respected actor, once said, "Every actor is very busy getting better or getting worse." To a large extent, salespeople are also "very busy getting better or getting worse." To improve, salespeople must develop an ongoing program for self-improvement. It is important to keep in mind that all improvement is self-initiated. Each of us controls the switch that allows personal growth and development to take place.

At the beginning of this chapter we introduced the concept of emotional intelligence. We noted that this form of intelligence can be increased with the aid of self-development activities. Would you like to develop a more positive self-image? Improve your ability to develop double-win relationships? Develop

Selling in Action

BUILDING RELATIONSHIPS WITH FREQUENT DEPOSITS

Building relationships in sales can be compared to making deposits in the bank. Regular bank deposits have a compounding effect, so over time you see steady growth in your account. Each of the following contacts with a customer or prospect is a deposit that can build the relationship:

- Send articles or reports of interest to your contacts. Be sure they are accompanied by a personal note.

- Send cards to celebrate an event, such as a birthday or anniversary.

- Contact customers after the sale to check on their level of satisfaction with the product.

- Express appreciation for purchases with a card, letter, or phone call.

Don't forget to make contact with secondary decision makers, support staff, and appropriate management personnel.[b]

Observant salespeople are aware of the things going on around them. EMBARC offers computer-based wireless information technology.

effective nonverbal communication skills? Improve your speaking voice? These relationship-building strategies can be achieved if you are willing to follow these steps:

Step one: set goals. Goal setting, as noted previously, is an important element of any self-improvement plan. The goal-setting process requires that you be clear about what you want to accomplish. If your goal is too general or vague, progress toward achieving that goal will be difficult to observe. An important step in the goal-setting process is to put the goal in writing.

Step two: practise visualization. To make your goals a reality, engage in visualization. Forming a mental picture of yourself succeeding in goal attainment will actually affect your behaviour. Mary Lou Retton and many other Olympic stars have used visualization. She described her preparation for the gymnastics event this way:

When I visualized myself going through a beam routine, I didn't imagine myself falling. I visualized myself on the beam — perfect. Always picture it perfect.[35]

You can work the same "mental magic" in goal setting by visualizing yourself as the person you want to be. For example, spend time developing mental pictures of successful experiences with prospective or established customers.

Step three: monitor your self-talk. Shad Helmstetter, author of *What to Say When You Talk to Yourself*, defines **self-talk** as "a way to override our past negative programming by erasing or replacing it with conscious, positive new directions."[36] It is an effective way to get rid of barriers to goal achievement. Helmstetter suggests that we develop specific positive self-talk statements and repeat them often to keep ourselves on target in terms of goal attainment.

Step four: recognize your progress. When you see yourself making progress toward a goal, or achieving a goal, reward yourself. This type of reinforcement is vital when you are trying to change a behaviour. There is nothing wrong with taking pride in your accomplishments.

Self-improvement efforts can result in new abilities or powers, and they give us the motivation to utilize more fully the talents we already have. As a result, our potential for success is greater.

This salesperson has set a fitness goal. Physical fitness can be an important part of a self-improvement program.

self-talk An effort to override past negative mental programming by erasing or replacing it with conscious, positive new directions. It is one way to get rid of barriers to goal achievement.

Summary

The manner in which salespeople establish, build, and maintain relationships is a major key to success in personal selling. The key relationships in selling include management personnel, company support staff, secondary decision makers, and customers.

The concept of *partnering* was defined and discussed in detail. Partnering emphasizes building a strong relationship during every aspect of the sale and working hard to maintain a quality relationship with the customer after the sale.

An understanding of the psychology of human behaviour provides a foundation for developing relationship strategies. In this chapter we discussed the link between self-image and success in selling. Self-imposed fears can prevent salespeople from achieving success.

We have described several factors that influence the image you project to customers. The image others have of us is shaped to a great extent by nonverbal communication. We may choose the right words to persuade a customer to place an order, but aversive factors communicated by our clothing, handshake, facial expression, tone of voice, and general manner may prejudice the customer against us and our product or service.

There are few absolute standards for defining aversive factors. Beyond obvious things like slovenly dress and rude manners you must develop your own awareness of geographic and social factors, as well as your knowledge of particular customers, to know what might be considered aversive.

We also discussed the importance of self-improvement. A four-step self-improvement plan was described.

Key Terms

Emotional Intelligence 51
Relationship Strategy 51
Partnering 53
Self-Image 55
Double-Win 57
Character 58

Integrity 58
Body Language 58
Wardrobe Engineering 62
Unconscious Expectations 62
Self-Talk 67

Review Questions

1. List the three prescriptions that serve as the foundation for development of a relationship strategy.

2. How important are establishing, building, and maintaining relationships in the selling process? List the four groups of people with whom sales personnel must be able to work effectively.

3. Define the term *partnering*. Why has the building of partnerships become more important today?

4. Defend the statement, "Successful relationships depend on a positive self-image."

5. Describe the double-win or win-win approach to selling.

6. How is our self-image formed? Why is a positive self-image so important in personal selling?

7. Describe the meaning of the term *emotional intelligence*.

8. Identify three conversational methods that can be used to establish relationships.

9. Describe the meaning of the term *body language*.

10. List and describe each step in the four-step self-improvement plan.

Application Exercises

1. Select four salespeople you know and ask them if they have a relationship strategy for working with customers, management personnel, secondary decision makers, and company support staff.

2. The partnering style of selling has been emphasized in Chapters 1 and 3. To gain more insight into the popularity of this concept, use an Internet search engine to key in the words "partnering + selling." Notice the large number of documents related to this query. Examine several of these documents to learn more about this approach to selling.

3. Complete the following etiquette quiz. Your instructor will provide you with answers so you can check your responses.

   a. On what side should you wear your name tag?
   b. Is it appropriate to drink beer from a bottle at a reception?
   c. When introducing a female salesperson to a male prospect, whose name should be spoken first?
   d. At the table, when should you place your napkin in your lap?

e. Is it ever proper to comb, smooth, or touch your hair while seated at a restaurant table?

4. Move quickly through the following list of traits. Use a check mark beside those that fit your self-image. Use an *X* to mark those that do not fit. If you are unsure, indicate with a question mark.

_____ I like myself.
_____ People trust me.
_____ I usually say the right thing.
_____ I dislike myself.
_____ I waste time.
_____ I put up a good front.
_____ I use my talents.
_____ I feel hemmed in.
_____ I use time well.
_____ I enjoy people.
_____ I usually say the wrong thing.
_____ I am discouraged about life.
_____ I have not developed my talents.

_____ People like to be around me.
_____ I trust myself.
_____ I often do the wrong thing.
_____ People avoid me.
_____ I enjoy work.
_____ I control myself.
_____ I enjoy nature.
_____ I am dependent on others for ideas.
_____ I am involved in solving community problems.
_____ I do not use my talents fully.
_____ I do not like myself.
_____ I do not like to be around people.

Now look at the pattern of your self-assessment.

a. Is there a pattern?
b. Is there a winner or loser pattern?
c. What traits would you like to change? (List them.)
d. Pick the trait you would like to change the most and prepare a plan to achieve this change.

5. It has been pointed out in this chapter that clothing communicates strong messages. In this exercise you will become more aware of whether or not your clothes communicate the messages you want them to communicate.

a. Make a chart like the one that follows:

Item of clothing being analyzed	What I want my clothes to say about me to others	What others think my clothing says

b. In the first column, list the clothing you are now wearing (for example, dress slacks, dress shoes, and sweater; athletic shoes, jeans, and T-shirt; or suit, tie, and dress shoes).
c. In the middle column, describe the message you would like the clothes you have chosen to say. For example, "I want to be comfortable," "I want people to notice me," or "I want people to understand how proper and organized I am."

d. Have somebody else fill in the third column by describing what they think your clothes say about you.

e. Compare the two columns. Do your clothes communicate what you want them to?

Do the same exercise for social dress, casual dress, business attire, and hairstyle.

CRM Application Exercise

Preparing Letters with CRM

 Load the ACT! software and look up My Record. This screen identifies the person using the database—which in this case was Pat Silva, and now will be you. Replace Pat Silva's name with your own.

The ACT! software demonstrates how customer relationship management programs are designed to be used by people who are in a hurry or who don't have extensive typing skills. Menu choices can be made by using the mouse, by typing simple key combinations, or by selecting an icon. This means that a procedure, such as preparing and printing correspondence, can be started by (a) selecting with a mouse the word Write, then the word Letter, from the menus; by (b) pressing the Alt key and the W (Write) key at the same time (Alt+W), and then pressing the L (Letter) key; or by (c) selecting the Letter icon ⬚ with the mouse.

On your screen will appear a blank letter with the date, inside address, salutation, closing line, your name, and your title. All you need to do is begin typing. If you have a printer connected to your computer, you can print your letter by selecting Print from the File menu. With the File menu open, note that the right column displays key combinations, such as Ctrl+P to print.

Find the record for Brad Able by choosing Lookup, Last Name, type in "Able," and press Enter. With Brad Able's record on the screen, choose the letter icon or, from the menus, Write and Letter. Prepare, then print, a brief letter to Brad Able confirming an appointment to meet at his office next Thursday at 9:00 a.m. to discuss his training needs. Your letter should feature the double-win approach discussed in this chapter.

CBC ◉ ## Video Case

Craig Proctor sells houses. In fact, Craig Proctor sells more houses than any other Re/Max agent in Canada. He was named "# 1 Sales Achiever" by Re/Max International in 1991 and 1996; he was number two in 1994, 1995, and 1997; he was number six in 1998. Craig Proctor was recently married and now has two small children, but he continues his success while working regular 40-hour weeks.

Wherever you go around Newmarket, Ontario, you may see the name "Craig Proctor." It is on milk jugs, on park benches, and on real estate signs. His promise, "Your home sold in under 120 days, or we buy it," can be seen on his large billboard advertisement, or on his Web site. Craig uses the Internet to add value for his clients. He is now thinking of adding video clips to his Web site, showing properties that he has listed; prospective clients will be able to better view these properties, inside and out. While many real estate agents sell only 10

www.craigproctor.com

to 20 properties each year, Craig Proctor sold 332 in 1998. He does it by creating special relationships with his customers. First, he makes sure that everyone knows the Craig Proctor name. He has spent hundreds of thousands of dollars marketing his name. He has done so well at establishing name recognition that other agents now sell under the Craig Proctor name, and he shares their commissions. Even so, each of these six agents earned over $100 000 in 1998. For $1000 a day, Craig Proctor will even let you in on some of his secrets.

How does he manage it all? Creating name recognition is only the first step. Having a successful track record builds client confidence. It says to clients that he can sell, that he is trustworthy and professional. Craig Proctor reinforces this image when he meets prospective clients, whether he is trying to sell someone a new home or trying to convince someone that he can sell their home for them. Often, before he meets prospective clients, members of the Craig Proctor team have already contacted them. Telemarketers often make cold calls by telephone to identify clients who may want to list houses. When prospective clients are identified, Craig Proctor meets and greets them, and explains how he and his team can help them. But he doesn't accept all potential clients. To be successful, Craig says, "Don't waste time." There are people who don't know the value of what they are selling, and they want too much. Does this mean he will only sell houses that are priced low? Apparently not, as his ads claim he will "sell for more money and in less time," getting an average of 2.01% higher prices for his clients (that's $4020 on a $200 000 home).

His other prescription is, "Stay in touch." But it's not always Craig Proctor that stays in touch. That's where his team comes in. Someone continually keeps in touch with clients throughout the process, making sure that a positive and happy relationship is maintained. Every Monday morning the Craig Proctor team has a sales meeting at the office, where anything can be discussed—from past performance, to handling sales with clients who are from different ethnic backgrounds, to advertising and promotion strategies, to who will contact current clients, and when, and what they will attempt to do for them.

Craig Proctor has found a formula for success, and he credits that partly to not knowing much about real estate sales when he started. According to Craig Proctor, "The tendency is, if you know anything at all about a business, to copy what others are doing. But that just gets you the same results as everyone else." Craig is certainly not like everyone else in real estate sales. He has increased efficiency for sales agents by developing a system that lets them do what they do best: sell. Team members manage all of the other things that could take time away from selling: cutting keys, posting signs, prospecting, etc. More and more, agents are looking at how Craig Proctor does it, and they too are increasing their efficiency.[37]

Questions

1. Does it appear that Craig Proctor supports the three prescriptions that serve as a foundation of the relationship strategy? (See the Strategic/Consultative Selling Model.) Explain your answer.

2. Why should real estate salespeople spend time developing a relationship strategy? What might be some long-term benefits of this strategy?

3. Is it ever appropriate to touch your client other than a handshake? Explain your answer.

4. What are some benefits to the salesperson who can mirror the behaviour of a prospect?

5. What are some precautions to take when preparing a meeting with a foreign-born prospect?

Communication Styles: Managing the Relationship Process

Saturn Corporation, owned by General Motors, has been positioning itself as "a different kind of company, a different kind of car." Since production began in 1990, its unique culture has forged unparalleled relationships among management, labour, suppliers, and customers. However, while other North American automakers have been experiencing tremendous growth, Saturn's sales have declined 17 percent over the past five years.

To help turn the company around, Saturn introduced new car and wagon models in 1999, and is now designing a sport-utility vehicle (SUV). It also has a new chair and president, Cynthia Trudell, the first woman ever to head a fully integrated subsidiary of a North American car manufacturer. Trudell grew up in Saint John, New Brunswick, where her father was a sales manager at several car dealerships. She received her chemistry degree at the University of Windsor before starting employment in 1979 in the auto industry. She was impressed with one particular general manager she worked with early in her career. He stressed the importance of solid technical product knowledge, and also tried to forge good relationships between management and labour. Trudell says, "I saw that the people who made the

LEARNING OBJECTIVES

When you finish reading this chapter, you should be able to

1. Discuss communication-style bias and how it influences the relationship process

2. Explain the benefits derived from an understanding of communication styles

3. Identify the two major dimensions of the communication-style model

4. List and describe the four major communication styles in the communication-style model

5. Learn how to identify your preferred communication style and that of your customer

6. Learn to overcome communication-style bias and build strong selling relationships with style flexing

product were the people we all needed to support. They were the ones who made the money for us and everybody else was high-priced overhead."[1]

Cynthia Trudell's friendly smile and gregarious character have made her popular among workers on the plant floor. *Automotive News*, often critical of GM, described Trudell's appointment as "perfect for Saturn."[2] Trudell appears to display the characteristics of the Supportive communication style, one of the four styles of communication discussed in this chapter. To help her manage relationships between Saturn and GM, Trudell will need communication-style flexibility, the ability to adjust her communication style to meet the needs of other people. She will need to manage the interface between two very different corporate cultures.

Communication Styles—An Introduction to Managing Selling Relationships

Almost everyone has had the pleasant experience of meeting someone for the first time and developing instant mutual rapport. There seems to be something about some people that makes you like them instantaneously—a basis for understanding that is difficult to explain. On the other hand, we can all recall meeting people who "turn us off" almost immediately. Why do these things happen during the initial contact? To answer this question we must understand a unique form of bias that can surface in almost any social or business setting. The information presented in this chapter can help you reduce tension and increase trust in all types of business relationships.

COMMUNICATION-STYLE BIAS

Bias in various forms is quite common in our society. In fact, governments at all levels have passed many laws to curb blatant forms of racial, age, and sex bias. We also observe some degree of regional bias when people from various parts of the country meet.

The most frequently occurring form of bias is not commonly understood in our society. What has been labelled **communication-style bias** is a state of mind that almost every one of us experiences from time to time, but we usually find it difficult to explain the symptoms. Communication-style bias develops when we have contact with another person whose communication style is dif-

communication-style bias A state of mind we often experience when we have contact with another person whose communication style is different from our own.

ferent from our own. For example, a purchasing agent was overheard saying, "I do not know what it is, but I just do not like that sales representative." The agent was no doubt experiencing communication-style bias but could not easily describe the feeling.

Your communication style is the "you" that is on display every day—the outer pattern of behaviour that others see. If your style is very different from the other person's, it may be difficult for the two of you to develop rapport. All of us have had the experience of saying or doing something that was perfectly acceptable to a friend or co-worker and being surprised when the same behaviour irritated someone else. However, aside from admitting that this happens, most of us are unable to draw meaningful conclusions from these experiences to help us perform more effectively with people in the future.[3]

In recent years, thousands of sales professionals have learned to manage their selling relationships more effectively through the study of communication styles. Books such as *People Styles at Work* by Robert Bolton and Dorothy Grover Bolton, and *The Versatile Salesperson* by Roger Wenschlag serve as good references. Many training companies offer seminars that provide enrollees with a practical understanding of communication-style theory and practice. This practical theory of human behaviour, based on research by the Swiss psychoanalyst Carl Jung and others, helps them achieve improved sales productivity. The psychology of behaviour patterns is a practical blend of concepts taken from the fields of psychology, communication, and sociology.

COMMUNICATION-STYLE PRINCIPLES

The theory of behavioural- or communication-style bias is based on a number of underlying principles. A review of these principles will be beneficial before we examine specific styles.

1. *Individual differences exist and are important.* It is quite obvious that we all differ in terms of physical characteristics such as height, shoe size, facial features, and body build, but the most interesting differences are those patterns of behaviour that are unique to each of us. We all display individual combinations of nonverbal characteristics. Voice patterns, eye movement, facial expression, and posture are some of the components of our communication style. Additional characteristics are discussed later in this chapter.

2. *A communication style is a way of thinking and behaving.* It is not an ability, but rather, a preferred way of using abilities one has. This distinction is very important. *Ability* refers to how well someone can do something. *Style* refers to how someone likes to do something.[4]

3. *Individual style differences tend to be stable.* Our communication style is based on a combination of hereditary and environmental factors. Our style is somewhat original at the time of birth; it takes on additional individuality during the first three to five years of life. By the time we enter elementary school, the teacher should be able to identify our communication style. This style remains fairly constant throughout life.

4. *There is a finite number of styles.* Most people display one of several clusters of similar behaviours, and this allows us to identify a small number of behavioural categories. By combining a series of descriptors we can develop a single "label" that will describe a person's most preferred communication style.

Group sales presentations can be very challenging because in most cases you are attempting to relate to several different communication styles.

5. *Everyone makes judgments about people based on communication style.* As noted in Chapter 3, when people meet you for the first time they form an immediate and distinct impression of you. This impression tends to influence how others communicate with you.

The ability to identify another person's communication style, and to know how and when to adapt your own preferred style to it, can afford you a crucial advantage in dealing with people. Differences between people can be a source of friction. The ability to "speak the other person's language" is an important relationship-management skill.[5]

IMPROVING YOUR RELATIONSHIP-MANAGEMENT SKILLS

Anyone who is considering a career in selling will benefit greatly from the study of communication styles. These concepts provide a practical method of classifying people according to communication style and give the salesperson a distinct advantage in the marketplace. A salesperson who understands communication-style classification methods and learns how to apply them can avoid common mistakes that threaten interpersonal relations with customers. Awareness of these methods greatly reduces the possibility of tension arising during the sales call. Tony Alessandra and Michael O'Connor, authors of *People Smart*, state, "If we don't think first of the other person, we run the risk of unintentionally imposing a tension-filled win-lose or lose-lose relationship on them."[6]

The first major goal of this chapter is to help you better understand your own most preferred communication style. The second goal is to help you develop greater understanding and appreciation for styles that are different from your own. The third goal is to help you manage your selling relationships more effectively by learning to adapt your style to fit the communication style of the customer. This practice is called "style flexing."

Building Quality Partnerships

LIFO DEVELOPS NEW GOLDEN RULE

Communication-style principles and practices serve as the foundation for High Performance Selling, a sales training program offered by Stuart Atkins Incorporated (SAI), a California-based training company. This training program is a version of LIFO Training that has been completed by 2 million people in over 10 000 organizations. LIFO training invites self-examination and promotes self-development. At the beginning of the High Performance Selling program, enrollees complete the LIFO Survey. This self-scoring instrument helps each participant identify his or her most preferred communication style and least preferred communication style. There are four basic styles or ways of seeing problems, people, and situations. The most preferred style represents the person's primary selling strengths. These are the factors that contribute the most to one's success in selling. Our least preferred style represents a source of untapped strengths that can be used to increase sales.

The High Performance Selling program reminds us that often we are selling products and services to a person who has a different preferred style than our own. If we always rely on our major selling strengths (most preferred style), we will not achieve our full potential. This is especially true if the customer's most preferred style is our least preferred style. Salespeople often overuse their favourite selling strengths to the point of unproductive excess.

High Performance Selling provides an emphatic reminder that customers have communication-style preferences. If we can identify the customer's most preferred style, we can adjust our approach to meet his or her needs. Most of us have been taught to use the Golden Rule, which is, "Do unto others as you would have them do unto you." In recognition of the fact that not everybody wants to be sold to the same way, the creators of High Performance Selling developed a new golden rule for salespeople: Do unto others as they want to be done unto.[a]

Communication-Style Model

This section introduces you to the four basic communication styles. One of these will surface as your most preferred style. The communication-style model that defines these styles is based on two important dimensions of human behaviour: dominance and sociability. We look at the dominance continuum first.

DOMINANCE CONTINUUM

Dominance can be defined as the tendency to control or prevail over others.[7] Dominant people tend to be quite competitive. They also tend to offer opinions readily and to be decisive and determined. Each of us falls somewhere on the dominance continuum illustrated by Figure 4.1.

A person classified as being high in dominance is generally a "take charge" type of person who makes a position clear to others. A person classified as being low in dominance is usually more reserved, unassertive, and easygoing. Dominance has been recognized as a universal behavioural characteristic. David W. Johnson developed the Interpersonal Pattern Exercise to help people achieve greater interpersonal effectiveness. He believes that people fall into two dominance categories:

1. *Low dominance:* These people have a tendency to be quite cooperative and eager to assist others. They tend to be low in assertiveness.

2. *High dominance:* These people tend to give advice freely and frequently initiate demands. They are more aggressive in dealing with others.[8]

dominance Reflects the tendency to influence or exert one's will over others in a relationship. Each of us falls somewhere on this continuum.

Figure 4.1   The first step in determining your most preferred communication style is to identify where you are on the dominance continuum.

Low   High

The first step in determining your most preferred communication style is to identify where you fall on the dominance continuum. Do you tend to rank low or high on this scale? To answer this question, complete the Dominance Indicator form in Table 4.1. Rate yourself on each scale by placing a check mark on the continuum at the point that represents how you perceive yourself. If most of your check marks fall to the right of centre, you are someone who is high in dominance. If most of your check marks fall to the left of centre, you are someone who is low in dominance. Is there any best place to be on the dominance continuum? The answer is no. Successful salespeople can be found at all points along the continuum.

SOCIABILITY CONTINUUM

sociability Reflects the amount of control one exerts over emotional expressiveness. People who are high in sociability tend to express their feelings freely, while people who are low on this continuum tend to control their feelings.

Sociability reflects the amount of control we exert over our emotional expressiveness.[9] People who are high in sociability tend to express their feelings freely,

Table 4.1 Dominance Indicator

Rate yourself on each scale by placing a check mark on the continuum at the point that represents how you perceive yourself.

I PERCEIVE MYSELF AS SOMEWHAT

Cooperative				Competitive
Submissive				Authoritarian
Accommodating				Domineering
Hesitant				Decisive
Reserved				Outgoing
Compromising				Insistent
Cautious				Risk-taking
Patient				Hurried
Complacent				Influential
Quiet				Talkative
Shy				Bold
Supportive				Demanding
Relaxed				Tense
Restrained				Assertive

while people who are low in this dimension tend to control their feelings. Each of us falls somewhere on the sociability continuum illustrated in Figure 4.2.

Sociability is also a universal behavioural characteristic. It can be defined as the tendency to seek and enjoy interaction with others. Charles Margerison, author of *How to Assess Your Managerial Style*, says that high sociability is an indication of a person's preference to interact with other people. He says that low sociability is an indicator of a person's desire to work in an environment where the person has more time alone instead of having to make conversation with others.[10] The person who is classified as being low in the area of sociability is more reserved and formal in social relationships.

The second step in determining your most preferred communication style is to identify where you fall on the sociability continuum. To answer this question, complete the Sociability Indicator form shown in Table 4.2. Rate yourself on each scale by placing a check mark on the continuum at the point that represents how you perceive yourself. If most of your check marks fall to the right of centre, you are someone who is high in sociability. If most of your check marks fall to the left of centre, you are someone who is low in sociability. Keep in mind

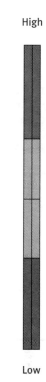

High

Low

Figure 4.2   The second step in determining your most preferred communication style is to identify where you are on the sociability continuum.

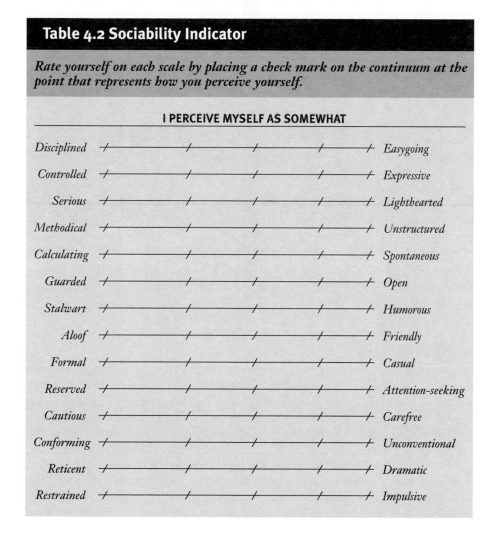

Table 4.2 Sociability Indicator

Rate yourself on each scale by placing a check mark on the continuum at the point that represents how you perceive yourself.

I PERCEIVE MYSELF AS SOMEWHAT

Disciplined	Easygoing
Controlled	Expressive
Serious	Lighthearted
Methodical	Unstructured
Calculating	Spontaneous
Guarded	Open
Stalwart	Humorous
Aloof	Friendly
Formal	Casual
Reserved	Attention-seeking
Cautious	Carefree
Conforming	Unconventional
Reticent	Dramatic
Restrained	Impulsive

that there is no best place to be. Successful salespeople can be found at all points along this continuum.

With the aid of the dominance and sociability continuums we are now prepared to discuss a relatively simple communication-style classification plan that has practical application in the field of selling. We will describe the four basic styles: Emotive, Director, Reflective, and Supportive.

FOUR STYLES OF COMMUNICATION

By combining the two dimensions of human behaviour—dominance and sociability—we can form a partial outline of the communication-style model (Fig. 4.3). Dominance is represented by the horizontal axis and sociability is represented by the vertical axis. Once the two dimensions of human behaviour are combined, the framework for communication-style classification is established.

Figure 4.3   When the dominance and sociability dimensions of human behaviour are combined, the framework for communication-style classification is established.

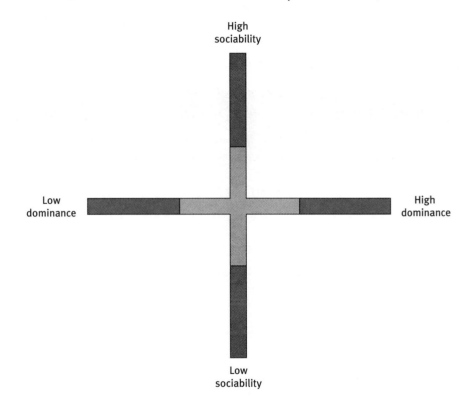

THE EMOTIVE STYLE

The upper right-hand quadrant of Figure 4.4 defines a style that combines high sociability and high dominance. We will call this the **Emotive style** (see Fig. 4.5). Emotive people like Jesse Jackson and Jay Leno usually stand out in a crowd. They are expressive and willing to spend time maintaining and enjoying a large number of relationships.[11] Oprah Winfrey, the well-known television personality, talk show host David Letterman, Canadian actor Jim Carrey, and sports personality Don Cherry provide excellent models of the Emotive communication style. Actress Sandra Bullock provides still another example. They are outspoken, enthusiastic, and stimulating. Larry King, a popular talk show host, and U.S. president Bill Clinton also project the Emotive communication

Emotive style A communication style that displays the following characteristics: appears to be quite active, takes the social initiative in most cases, likes to encourage informality, and expresses emotional opinions.

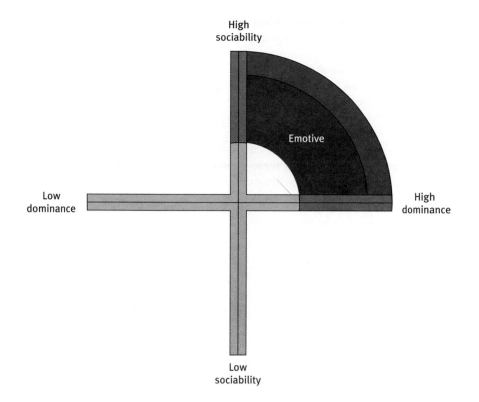

Figure 4.4   The Emotive style combines high sociability and high dominance.

style. The Emotive person wants to create a social relationship quickly and usually feels more comfortable in an informal atmosphere. Some of the verbal and nonverbal clues that identify the Emotive person follow:

1. *Appears quite active.* This person gives the appearance of being busy. A person who combines high dominance and high sociability is often restless. The Emotive person is likely to express feelings with vigorous movements of the hands and a rapid speech pattern.

2. *Takes the social initiative in most cases.* Emotives are the classic extroverts. When two people meet for the first time, the Emotive person will be more apt to initiate and maintain the conversation as well as to initiate the handshake. Emotives rate high in both directness and openness.

3. *Likes to encourage informality.* The Emotive person will move to a "first name" basis as soon as possible (too soon in some cases). Even the way this person sits in a chair will communicate a preference for a relaxed, informal social setting.

4. *Expresses emotional opinions.* Emotive people generally do not hide their feelings. They often express opinions dramatically and impulsively.

THE DIRECTOR STYLE

The lower right-hand quadrant of Figure 4.6 defines a style that combines high dominance and low sociability. We will call this the **Director style** (Fig. 4.7).

To understand the nature of people who display the Director communication style, picture in your mind's eye the director of a Hollywood film. The person you see is giving orders in a loud voice and is generally in charge of every

Emotive people like Jim Carrey are enthusiastic, outspoken, and stimulating.

Figure 4.5   Key words for the Emotive style

Sociable	Personable
Unstructured	Stimulating
Spontaneous	Persuasive
Excitable	Emotional
Zestful	Dynamic

Director style A communication style that displays the following characteristics: appears to be businesslike, displays a serious attitude, and voices strong opinions.

Jean Chrétien is known for his frank, demanding, and aggressive communication style.

facet of the operation. Everyone on the set knows this person is in charge. Although the common stereotyped image of the Hollywood film director is probably exaggerated, this example will be helpful as you attempt to become familiar with the Director style.

Lee Iacocca, Sam Donaldson (television commentator), and Prime Minister Jean Chrétien project the Director style. Television commentator Barbara Walters and interviewer Pamela Wallin typify this communication style. They may be described as frank, demanding, aggressive, and determined.

In the field of selling you will encounter a number of customers who are Directors. How can you identify these people? What verbal and nonverbal clues can we observe? A few of the behaviours displayed by Directors follow:

1. *Appears to be quite busy.* The Director generally does not like to waste time and wants to get right to the point.

2. *May give the impression of not listening.* In most cases the Director feels more comfortable talking than listening. Judy Sheindlin of the "Judge Judy" television show displays this behaviour.

3. *Displays a serious attitude.* A person who is low in sociability usually communicates a lack of warmth and is apt to be quite businesslike and impersonal. Mike Wallace, one of the stars on the popular "60 Minutes" television show, seldom smiles or displays warmth.

4. *Likes to maintain control.* The person who is high on the dominance continuum likes to maintain control. During meetings the Director will seek to control the agenda.[12]

Figure 4.7   Key words for the Director style

Aggressive	Pushy
Determined	Impatient
Intense	Serious
Frank	Bold
Requiring	
Opinionated	

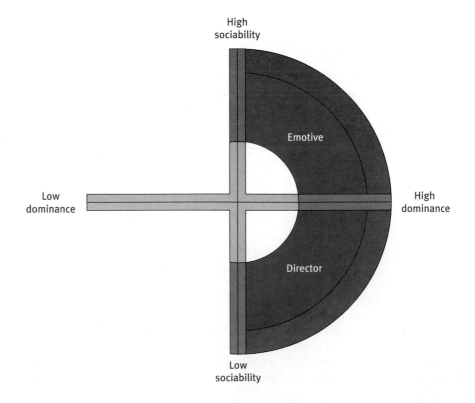

Figure 4.6   The Director style combines high dominance and low sociability.

THE REFLECTIVE STYLE

The lower left-hand quadrant of Figure 4.8 features a combination of low dominance and low sociability. We call this the **Reflective style** (see Fig. 4.9).

The Reflective person tends to examine all the facts carefully before arriving at a decision. Like a cautious scientist, this individual wants to gather all available information and weigh it carefully before taking a position. The Reflective type is usually a stickler for detail.[13] Former prime ministers Pierre Trudeau and Joe Clark fit the description. Pierre Berton and David Suzuki are two more well-known Canadians who display the characteristics of the Reflective type.

The Reflective communication style combines low dominance and low sociability; therefore people with this classification tend to be reserved and cautious. Some additional behaviours that characterize this style follow:

1. *Controls emotional expression.* Reflective people tend to curb emotional expression and are less likely to display warmth openly.

2. *Displays a preference for orderliness.* The Reflective person enjoys a highly structured environment and generally feels frustration when confronted with unexpected events.

3. *Tends to express measured opinions.* The Reflective individual usually does not express dramatic opinions. This communication style is characterized by disciplined, businesslike actions.

4. *Seems difficult to get to know.* The Reflective person tends to be somewhat formal in social relationships and therefore is viewed as aloof by many people.

Reflective style A communication style that displays the following characteristics: controls emotional expression, displays a preference for orderliness, tends to express measured opinions, and seems difficult to get to know.

Persons with the Reflective style, such as David Suzuki, tend to control their emotions and examine all the facts when making a decision.

Figure 4.9   Key words for the Reflective style

Precise	Serious
Scientific	Disciplined
Deliberate	Industrious
Preoccupied	Aloof
Questioning	Stuffy

High
sociability

Emotive

Low
dominance

High
dominance

Reflective

Director

Low
sociability

Figure 4.8   The Reflective style combines low dominance and low sociability.

In a selling situation the Reflective customer does not want to move too fast. This person wants the facts presented in an orderly and unemotional manner and does not want to waste a lot of time socializing.

THE SUPPORTIVE STYLE

The upper left-hand quadrant of Figure 4.10 defines a style that combines low dominance and high sociability. We call this the **Supportive style** (see Fig. 4.11). These people find it easy to listen and usually do not express their views in a forceful manner. The late Princess Di and entertainers Kevin Costner, Rita MacNeil, Anne Murray, and Meryl Streep display the characteristics of the Supportive style.

Low visibility generally characterizes the lifestyle of Supportive people. They complete their tasks in a quiet, unassuming manner and seldom draw attention to what they have accomplished. In terms of assertiveness, persons with the Supportive style rank quite low. Someone who ranks high on the dominance continuum is likely to view the Supportive individual as being too easygoing. In some cases Supportive people are too agreeable; they often do not state their opinions because they want to avoid conflict. This behaviour may be viewed as a sign of weakness by the Director, who seldom avoids taking a position. Other behaviours that commonly characterize the Supportive person follow:

1. *Gives the appearance of being quiet and reserved.* People with the Supportive behavioural style can easily display their feelings, but not in the assertive manner common to the Emotive individual.

Supportive style A communication style that displays the following characteristics: appears quiet and reserved, listens attentively to other people, tends to avoid the use of power, and makes decisions in a thoughtful and deliberate manner.

Figure 4.10 The Supportive style combines low dominance and high sociability.

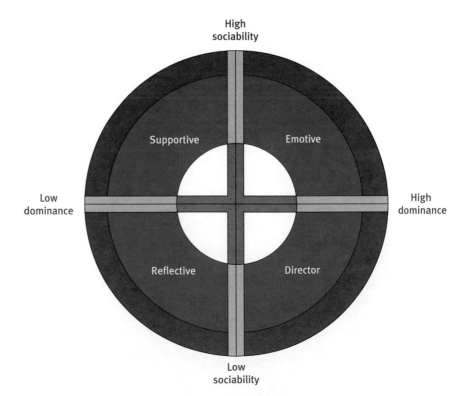

Figure 4.11 Key words for the Supportive style

Lighthearted	Relaxed
Patient	Warm
Reserved	Compliant
Sensitive	Docile
Passive	Softhearted

2. *Listens attentively to other people.* In selling, good listening skills can be a real asset. This talent comes naturally to the Supportive person.

3. *Tends to avoid the use of power.* Whereas the Director may rely on power to accomplish tasks, the Supportive person is more likely to rely on friendly persuasion.

4. *Makes decisions in a thoughtful and deliberate manner.* The Supportive person usually takes longer to make a decision.

POPULARITY OF THE FOUR-STYLE MODEL

We are endlessly fascinated by ourselves, and this helps explain the growing popularity of the four-style model presented in this chapter. To satisfy this insatiable appetite for information, many training and development companies offer training programs that present the four social or communication styles. Figure 4.12 features the approximate equivalents of the four styles presented in this chapter.

People with the Supportive communication style are usually quiet and unassuming.

DETERMINING YOUR COMMUNICATION STYLE

You now have enough information to identify your own communication style. If your location on the dominance continuum is right of centre and your position on the sociability continuum is below the centre mark, you fall into the Director quadrant. If your location on the dominance continuum is left of centre and your position on the sociability continuum is above the centre mark, then your most preferred style is Supportive. Likewise, low dominance matched with low sociability forms the Reflective communication style, and high dominance matched with high sociability forms the Emotive style.

Of course, all of us display some characteristics of the Emotive, Director, Reflective, and Supportive communication styles. However, one of the four styles is usually predominant and readily detectable.[14]

Some people who study the communication-style model for the first time may initially experience feelings of frustration. They find it hard to believe that one's behavioural style tends to remain quite uniform throughout life. People often say, "I am a different person each day!" It is certainly true that we sometimes feel different from day to day, but our most preferred style remains stable.

The Supportive person might say, "I sometimes get very upset and tell people what I am thinking. I can be a Director when I want to be!" There is no

Supportive (Manning/Reece/MacKenzie) Amiable (Wilson Learning) Supportive-Giving (Stuart Atkins Inc.) Relater (People Smarts) Steadiness (Personal Profile System)	Emotive (Manning/Reece/MacKenzie) Expressive (Wilson Learning) Adapting-Dealing (Stuart Atkins Inc.) Socializer (People Smarts) Influencing (Personal Profile System)
Reflective (Manning/Reece/MacKenzie) Analytical (Wilson Learning) Conserving-Holding (Stuart Atkins Inc.) Thinker (People Smarts) Cautiousness/Compliance (Personal Profile System)	Director (Manning/Reece/MacKenzie) Driver (Wilson Learning) Controlling-Taking (Stuart Atkins Inc.) Director (People Smarts) Dominance (Personal Profile System)

Figure 4.12   The four basic communication styles have been used in a wide range of training programs. For comparison purposes the approximate equivalents to the four communication styles discussed in this chapter are listed.

argument here. Just because you have a preferred communication style does not mean you will never display the behavioural characteristics of another style. Some people use different styles in different contexts and in different relationships.[15] Reflective people sometimes display Emotive behaviour, and Emotive people sometimes display Reflective behaviour. We are saying that each person has one most preferred and habitually used communication style.

Managing Communication-Style Bias

The most important reason for our discussion of communication styles is this: communication-style bias is a barrier to success in selling. This form of bias is a common problem in sales work simply because salespeople deal with people from all four quadrants. You cannot select potential customers on the basis of their communication style. You must be able to develop rapport with people from each of the four quadrants. When people of different styles work together but don't adjust to one another, serious problems can develop.[16]

HOW COMMUNICATION-STYLE BIAS DEVELOPS

To illustrate how communication-style bias develops in a sales situation, let us observe a sales call involving two people with different communication styles. Mary Wheeler entered the office of Dick Harrington with a feeling of optimism. She was sure that her product would save Mr. Harrington's company several hundred dollars a year. She had done her homework and was 99 percent certain that the sale would be closed. Thirty minutes after meeting Mr. Harrington, she was walking out of his office without the order. What went wrong?

Mary Wheeler is an "all business" type who is a Director in terms of communication style. Her sales calls are typically fast-paced and focused. She entered the office of Mr. Harrington, a new prospect, and immediately began to talk business. Mr. Harrington interrupted to ask if she wanted coffee. She declined the offer and continued her sales presentation. Mr. Harrington asked Mary if she enjoyed selling. After a quick glance at her watch, she responded by saying that selling was a rewarding career and then quickly returned to her sales presentation.

Mr. Harrington's communication style is Supportive. He feels uncomfortable doing business with strangers and likes slow-paced interactions with people. He felt tension when Mary failed to establish a social relationship. He also felt she was moving at a pace that was too fast. If she had spent a few minutes socializing with Mr. Harrington, his preferred approach to communication would have become apparent. The "all business" approach she used would have been more appropriate for the Director or Reflective communication style.

One of the most important steps in mastering the sales process is for the salesperson to adapt his or her selling behaviour to the customer's communication style. Communication is *always* the responsibility of the salesperson. This is not a responsibility that can be shared.[17]

DEVELOPING STYLE FLEXIBILITY

When people are introduced to communication styles for the first time, they often label certain styles as being "more favourable" or "less favourable" for selling careers. The truth is, there is no one best place to be on the communication-style model because there are no best types of personality.[18] As noted previously, a style refers to how someone likes to do something, not how well someone can do something. Successful salespeople come from all four quadrants. What these high achievers have in common is style flexibility.

MATURE AND IMMATURE BEHAVIOUR

There is a mature and an immature side to each behavioural style. Let us examine the Emotive style to illustrate this point. People with this style are open, personable individuals who seem genuinely friendly. The natural enthusiasm displayed by the mature Emotive is refreshing. On the other hand, an Emotive person may be too talkative and too emotional, and may lack the ability to listen to others; this is the immature side of the Emotive communication style.

You will recall that we used the words *industrious* and *precise* to describe the Reflective style. These are words that apply to the mature side of the Reflective person. We also used the words *aloof* and *stuffy*. These words describe the immature side of the Reflective.

The good news is that we all have the potential for developing the mature side of our communication style. Our most preferred communication style does not change, but it matures as we mature.

STRENGTH/WEAKNESS PARADOX

It is a fact of life that your greatest strength can become your greatest weakness. If your most preferred style is Reflective, people will likely respect your well-disciplined approach to life as one of your strengths. However, this strength can become a weakness if it is exaggerated. The Reflective person can be too serious, too questioning, and too inflexible.

People with the Director style are open and frank. They express their true feelings in a direct manner. When J. P. Bryan, president and CEO of Gulf Canada Resources Ltd., was asked why he stayed away from Calgary's Petroleum Club, he stated: "I stayed away because I didn't want to get friendly with people in the oil patch. I'm not bound by these traditional relationships, so we can go after people as we see fit, and I'm not worried about ruining a friendship."[19] In most cases we appreciate candour, but we do not like to be around people who are too straightforward or too blunt in expressing their views. When people come across as opinionated, they tend to antagonize others. We should avoid pushing our strengths to the point of unproductive excess.[20]

To illustrate how strengths become weaknesses in excess, let us add more detail to our communication-style model. Note that it now features three zones that radiate out from the centre (Fig. 4.13). These dimensions might be thought of as *intensity zones*.

Zone one People who fall within this zone display their unique behavioural characteristics with less intensity than those in zone two. The Emotive person, for example, is moderately high on the dominance continuum and moderately high on the sociability continuum. As you might expect, zone one communication styles are more difficult to identify because there is less intensity in both dimensions (dominance and sociability).

Zone two Persons who fall within this zone display their unique behavioural characteristics with greater intensity than persons in zone one. The zone two Reflective, for example, falls within the lowest quartile of the dominance continuum and the lowest quartile of the sociability continuum.

Figure 4.13 The completed communication-style model provides important insights needed to manage the relationship process in selling.

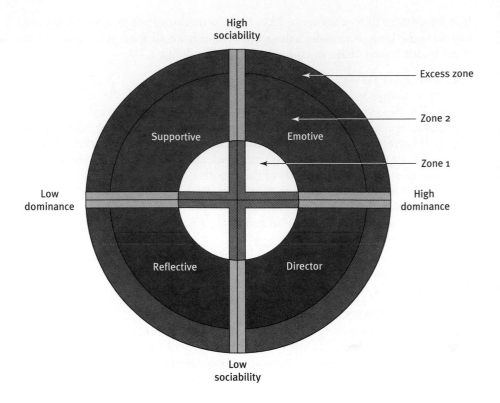

The boundary line that separates zone one and zone two should not be seen as a permanent barrier restricting change in intensity. Under certain circumstances we should abandon our most preferred style temporarily. A deliberate move from zone one to zone two, or vice versa, is called style flexing.

Excess zone The excess zone is characterized by a high degree of intensity and rigidity. When people allow themselves to drift into this zone, they become very inflexible, which is often interpreted by others as a form of bias toward their style. In addition, the strengths of the inflexible person become weaknesses. Extreme intensity in any quadrant is bound to threaten interpersonal relations.

We are apt to move into the excess zone and exaggerate our style characteristics under stressful conditions. Stress tends to bring out the worst in many people. Here are some of the behaviours that salespeople and customers may display when they are in the excess zone:

Emotive style	Expresses highly emotional opinions
	Stops listening to the other person
	Tries too hard to promote own point of view
	Becomes outspoken to the point of being offensive
	Uses exaggerated gestures and facial expressions to make a point
Director style	Gets impatient with the other person
	Becomes dictatorial and bossy
	Will not admit being wrong
	Becomes extremely competitive
	Is cold and unfeeling when dealing with people

The excess zone is characterized by a high degree of intensity and rigidity. We are more apt to move into the excess zone under very stressful conditions.

Reflective style	Becomes stiff and formal during social interactions
	Is unwilling to make a decision
	Avoids displaying any type of emotion
	Displays a strong dislike for change
	Is overly interested in detail
Supportive style	Agrees with everyone
	Is unable to take a strong stand
	Becomes overly anxious to win approval of others
	Tries to comfort everyone
	Constantly seeks reassurance

Developing Communication-Style Flexibility

Style flexing is the deliberate attempt to adjust one's communication style to accommodate the needs of the other person. You are attempting to communicate with the other person on his or her own "channel." Ron Willingham, in his book *Integrity Selling*, reminds us that "People are more apt to buy from you when they perceive you view the world as they view the world."[21] In a selling situation you should try to determine the customer's most preferred style and flex your own accordingly. If your preferred communication style is Director, and your customer is Supportive, try to be more personal and warmer in your presentation. Once you know the customer's style, flexing your style can make the difference between a presentation that falters and one that exceeds your

style flexing The deliberate attempt to adjust one's communication style to accommodate the needs of the other person.

expectations.[22] Style sensitivity and flexing are not developed overnight, of course. It takes practice.

Throughout the preapproach you should learn as much as possible about the customer and try to determine their style. Once you are in the customer's presence watch and listen for clues that reveal their predominant style.

When you are meeting with a customer do not become preoccupied analyzing the person's style. If you are trying hard to analyze the person's style, you may not listen closely enough to what he or she is trying to tell you. If you are truly tuned in to the customer, you will absorb many clues that will help you determine their style. After the sales call, analyze the communication and record your findings. Use this information to plan your next contact with the customer.[23]

Listen closely to the customer's tone of voice. A Supportive person will sound warm and friendly. The Reflective customer's voice is more likely to be cautious and deliberate. Pay particular attention to gestures. The Emotive individual will use his or her hands to communicate thoughts and ideas. The Director also uses gestures to communicate but is more controlled and less spontaneous. The Reflective person will appear more relaxed, less intense. The Emotive individual is an open, impulsive communicator, while the Reflective person is quite cautious. The Supportive type will be personal and friendly, while the Reflective person may seem difficult to get to know. To avoid relationship tension, consider the following suggestions for each of the four styles:

SELLING TO EMOTIVES

If you are attempting to sell products to an Emotive person, keep in mind the need to move at a pace that will hold the attention of the prospect. Be enthusiastic, and avoid an approach that is too stiff and formal. Take time to establish goodwill and build relationships. Do not place too much emphasis on the facts and details. To deal effectively with Emotive people, plan actions that will provide support for their opinions, ideas, and dreams.[24] Plan to ask questions concerning their opinions and ideas, but be prepared to help them get "back on track" if they move too far away from the topic. Maintain good eye contact and, above all, be a good listener.

SELLING TO DIRECTORS

The key to relating to Directors is to keep the relationship as businesslike as possible. Developing a strong personal relationship is not a high priority for Directors. In other words, friendship is not usually a condition for a good working relationship. Your goal is to be as efficient, time disciplined, and well organized as possible, and to provide appropriate facts, figures, and success probabilities. Most Directors are goal-oriented people, so try to identify their primary objectives and then determine ways to support and help with these objectives. Early in the sales presentation, ask specific questions and carefully note responses. Look for specific points you can respond to when it is time to present your proposal.

SELLING TO REFLECTIVES

The Reflective person will respond in a positive way to a thoughtful, well-organized approach. Arrive at meetings on time and be well prepared. In most cases it will not be necessary to spend a great deal of time building a social rela-

Building Relationships in a Diverse World

VERSATILITY IS KEY

One way to increase sales and enjoy selling more is to reduce the tension between you and the prospect. Personal selling is almost never a tension-free activity, but there are effective ways to control the tension that is likely to surface during the selling process. Dr. David Merrill, one of the early pioneers in development of communication-style instruments and training programs, uses the term *versatility* to describe our ability to control the tension we create in others. He believes it is important to understand your preferred communication style, but you must also be willing to control personal behaviour patterns and adapt to the people with whom you have contact. In jobs such as selling, which require a high degree of interpersonal effectiveness, versatility can be the key to success.

Roger Wenschlag, author of *The Versatile Salesperson*, defines versatility as "The degree to which a salesperson is perceived as developing and maintaining buyer comfort throughout the sales process." This does not mean you must become "another person" and display behaviours that make you uncomfortable. However, you should be able to adjust your behaviour temporarily to fit the buyer's style. Versatility displayed by the salesperson sends the message, "I care about the relationship."

Versatility has another benefit, according to Tony Alessandra, author of *People Smarts*. He notes that this quality enables you to interact more productively with difficult people.

The wonderful thing about versatility is that it can be learned. We can learn to control what we say and do to make others more comfortable.[b]

tionship. Reflective people appreciate a no-nonsense, businesslike approach to personal selling. Use specific questions that show clear direction. Once you have information concerning the prospect's needs, present your proposal in a slow, deliberate way. Provide as much documentation as possible. Do not be in too big a hurry to close the sale. Never pressure the Reflective person to make quick decisions.

SELLING TO SUPPORTIVES

Take time to build a social relationship with the Supportive person. Spend time learning about the things that are important in this individual's life—family, hobbies, and major interests. Listen carefully to personal opinions and feelings. Supportive individuals like to conduct business with sales personnel who are professional but friendly. Therefore, study their feelings and emotional needs as well as their technical and business needs. Throughout the presentation, provide personal assurances and support for their views. If you disagree with a Supportive person, curb the desire to disagree too assertively; Supportive people dislike interpersonal conflict. Give them the time to contemplate your proposal. Patience is important.

As you develop your communication-style identification skills and become more adept at style flexing, you will be better able to manage the relationship process. With these skills you should be able to open more accounts, sell more to established customers, and more effectively meet the pressures of competition. Most important, your customers will view you as a person better able to understand and meet their needs.

A WORD OF CAUTION

It is tempting to put a label on someone and then assume the label tells you everything you need to know about that person. If you want to build an effective partnering-type relationship with a prospect, you must acquire additional information about that person. Stuart Atkins, a respected authority on communication styles and author of *The Name of Your Game*, says that it requires real effort to look beyond the label and to experience the whole person as a dynamic process.[25] You must also be careful not to let the label you place on yourself become the justification for your own inflexible behaviour. Try not to let the label justify or reinforce why you are unable or unwilling to communicate effectively with others.[26]

Summary

The primary objective of this chapter is to introduce communication-style bias and examine the implications of this concept for salespeople. Many sales are lost because salespeople fail to communicate effectively with the prospect. Communication-style bias contributes to this problem. Every salesperson who is willing to develop style sensitivity and engage in appropriate style flexing can minimize one of the most common barriers to success in selling.

The communication-style model is based on two continuums that assess two major aspects of human behaviour: dominance and sociability. By combining them as horizontal and vertical continuums, we create quadrants that define four styles of communication. We have called these the Emotive, Director, Reflective, and Supportive styles. With practice in observation you should be able to increase your sensitivity to other people's styles. Practice in self-awareness and self-control will give you the ability to flex your own style and to help others feel at ease.

Key Terms

Communication-Style Bias 74
Dominance 77
Sociability 78
Emotive Style 80

Director Style 81
Reflective Style 83
Supportive Style 84
Style Flexing 89

Review Questions

1. What is the most prominent form of bias in our society? Explain.
2. Describe the five major principles that support communication-style theory.
3. What are the benefits to the salesperson who understands communication style?
4. What two dimensions of human behaviour are used to identify communication style?
5. Describe the person who tends to be high in sociability.
6. What are the four communication styles? Develop a brief description of each of the styles.
7. What is the reaction of most people who study communication styles for the first time? Why does this reaction surface?

8. What is the major reason for introducing communication styles in a text-book on selling?

9. Explain the statement, "Your greatest strength can become your greatest weakness."

10. The Building Relationships in a Diverse World box on p. 91 suggests that we should try to control what we say and do to make others more comfortable. Is it realistic to expect salespeople to follow this advice? Explain your answer.

Application Exercises

1. Oprah Winfrey is one of the best known talk show hosts.

   a. On the dominance continuum on p. 78, mark where you think her television personality belongs.

   b. On the sociability continuum on p. 79, mark where you think her television personality belongs.

   c. Using the two continuums to form the communication-style model, what is Oprah Winfrey's television communication style? Does Oprah Winfrey possess style flexibility? Explain this in terms of (i) the different styles of guests on her program and (ii) her apparent popularity with millions of people.

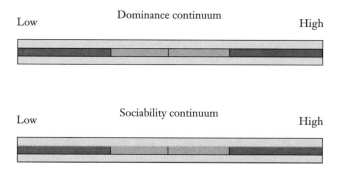

   d. Describe Oprah Winfrey's personality using statements and terms from this chapter.

   e. Have you ever observed Oprah Winfrey slipping into her excess zone? Explain.

2. Many salespeople, after being introduced to communication-style psychology, attempt to categorize each of their customers. They report that their relationships become mutually more enjoyable and productive. Select five people whom you know quite well (supervisor, subordinate, customer, teacher, friend, or member of your family). Using the two behavioural continuums in this chapter, determine these people's communication styles. Using your own descriptive terminology in conjunction with terminology in this chapter, develop a descriptive behavioural profile of each of these people. Explain how this information will improve your relationship with each of these people.

3. Self-awareness is important in personal selling. As we get to know our-selves, we can identify barriers to acceptance by others. Once you have identified your most preferred communication style, you have taken a big step in the direction of self-awareness. If you have not yet determined your most preferred communication style, take a few minutes to complete the Dominance Indicator form (Table 4.1) and the Sociability Indicator form (Table 4.2). Follow the instructions provided on pp. 77 to 80.

4. Myers-Briggs Personality Types and Jungian Personality Types are two very popular descriptions of the material in this chapter. Using your search engine, access the Internet sites that refer to these concepts. Type in "Jungian" + "personality profiles" to access the Jungian personality types. To access the Myers-Briggs types, type in "Myers-Briggs" + "personality profiles." Does the number of hits indicate anything about the validity and popularity of these theories? Examine Web sites that discuss both of these theories. Do you see a relationship between these two theories and the material in this chapter?

Case Problem

When Sonia Ajem finished high school, she had no idea she would like a career in sales. She took a course at community college, hoping to become a legal secretary. After one year she left to take a job as a file clerk at Kingsway Transport. Sonia worked with several transportation companies, gaining promotions to sales account coordinator and finally to outside sales representative. Now, at 29 years old, and after two years of sales experience with a competitor, she manages about 500 accounts for Epic Express. Her territory extends from Rexdale, Concord, and Woodbridge, north to Barrie, Orillia, and Midland, Ontario.

Sonia describes herself as a congenial, easy-to-get-along-with person. When asked why she has done so well in sales, she says, "I'm also very organized and thorough. I take promises very seriously, and I know how to listen." Sonia Ajem displays the characteristics of the Supportive communication style.

Shortly after Sonia Ajem started to sell for Epic Express, she got a telephone call from Terence Anderson, Manager of Purchasing, Stores, and Traffic for a large manufacturer in her territory. He said that he wanted to speak to her about his transportation needs, to see if Epic Express was capable of handling his outgoing freight across Quebec and Ontario. Terence, as he called himself, seemed pleasant enough on the telephone, but he also seemed to be very formal. In preparing for her visit, Sonia Ajem asked some friends what they knew about him. She was not able to get a lot of assistance because Mr. Anderson had apparently been recently transferred to this position from another location. She did find out that he was currently completing courses with the Purchasing Management Association of Canada, and that he was not much older than herself, having received a number of rapid promotions within his firm.

Since her appointment was a week away, Sonia Ajem decided to write Mr. Anderson a letter, and to include some background information on Epic Express. She also thanked him for his interest in her company and told him that she looked forward to meeting him at 3:45 p.m. as he requested.[27]

Questions

1. If Mr. Anderson displays the characteristics of the Director communication style, how should Sonia conduct herself during the meeting? Be specific as you describe those behaviours that would be admired by Mr. Anderson.

2. If Mr. Anderson wants to build rapport with Sonia Ajem, what behaviour should he display?

3. As Sonia Ajem learns more about communication styles, what three goals should she be working on to improve her relationship management skills?

Part III

Developing a Product Strategy

Part III examines the important role of complete and accurate product, company, and competitive knowledge in personal selling. Lack of knowledge in these areas will impair the salesperson's ability to achieve maximum customer service. Part III also describes several value-added selling strategies.

BUILDING QUALITY PARTNERSHIPS

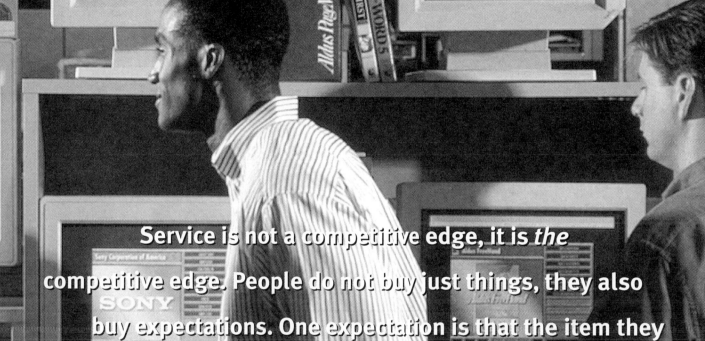

Service is not a competitive edge, it is *the* competitive edge. People do not buy just things, they also buy expectations. One expectation is that the item they buy will produce the benefits the seller promised. Another is that if it doesn't, the seller will make good on the promise.

Karl Albright and Ron Zemke

Service America: Doing Business in the New Economy

Creating Product Solutions

Michael Tulk is a general manager with Xerox Canada. He started with the company immediately after his graduation with a business degree in 1988. In 1994 he was promoted to sales manager and was transferred to New Brunswick. Xerox eliminated the position of sales manager across Canada in 1996. Michael Tulk then became a sales coach for Ottawa and for the four Atlantic provinces. Finally, in 1997, he was transferred to St. John's, Newfoundland, as the general manager—a new position within Xerox Canada, and one he still holds today. At Xerox, general managers are responsible for sales, service, and administration—basically everything within their territory. However, Michael Tulk still has some specific account responsibilities.

How did he move from an entry-level sales position to become a general manager in less than nine years? Michael Tulk credits a lot of his success to the development of a successful product selling strategy. He has taken every opportunity to enhance his knowledge of Xerox: the company, its history and philosophy, how Xerox does business, and the products and services Xerox provides as superior customer solutions.[1]

Developing a Product Solution

Creating the right product solution with the right price for the customer is the most important part of the salesperson's job. The task has become more difficult in recent years because of changing customer expectations. A growing number of customers are seeking a customized product solution. The industrial-age model of making things cheaper by making them the same is no longer acceptable in many markets. The customized product solution appeals to the customer's desire for choices. Noted author and speaker Regis McKenna says choice has become a higher value than brand.[2]

As noted in Chapter 1, a product strategy helps salespeople make correct decisions concerning the selection and positioning of products to meet identified customer needs. The **product strategy** is a well-conceived plan that emphasizes becoming a product expert, selling product benefits, and positioning the product (Fig. 5.1). Positioning the product refers to the decisions, activities, and communications that establish and maintain a firm's intended product concept in the customer's mind. Product positioning is discussed in detail in Chapter 6.

THE EXPLOSION OF PRODUCT OPTIONS

The domestic and global markets are overflowing with a vast array of goods and services. In some industries the number of new products introduced each year is mind-boggling. Consider these examples:

➤ Each year grocery stores introduce more than 10 000 new items. If you are a salesperson employed by a major food wholesaler such as Serca Foodservice, you face a real challenge when introducing a new product.

➤ Many companies develop and introduce new products to generate additional revenues. A good example is Rubbermaid, which has more than 5000 products. Rubbermaid introduces an average of one new product every day.[3]

➤ We have seen an explosion of new products in the securities and financial

product strategy A well-conceived plan that emphasizes acquiring extensive product knowledge, learning to select and communicate appropriate product benefits that will appeal to the customer, and positioning the product.

 www.rubbermaid.com

Figure 5.1   Developing a product strategy enables the salesperson to custom fit products or services to the customer's needs.

Strategic/Consultative Selling Model	
Strategic step	**Prescription**
DEVELOP A PERSONAL SELLING PHILOSOPHY	✓ ADOPT MARKETING CONCEPT ✓ VALUE PERSONAL SELLING ✓ BECOME A PROBLEM SOLVER/PARTNER
DEVELOP A RELATIONSHIP STRATEGY	✓ ADOPT DOUBLE-WIN PHILOSOPHY ✓ PROJECT PROFESSIONAL IMAGE ✓ PRACTISE COMMUNICATION-STYLE FLEXING
DEVELOP A PRODUCT STRATEGY	○ BECOME A PRODUCT EXPERT ○ SELL BENEFITS ○ CONFIGURE VALUE-ADDED SOLUTIONS

services field. In one segment, mutual funds, Canadians can choose from more than 2500 products.[4]

For the customer, this much variety creates a "good news–bad news" situation. The good news is that almost all buyers have a choice when it comes to purchasing a product or service; people like to compare various options. The bad news is that having so many choices often complicates the buying process.

As we have noted in previous chapters, the new economy is about the growing value of knowledge. However, salespeople must do more than supply the customer with large amounts of information; they must provide the buyer with the specific knowledge needed to make the best possible buying decision. One of the most important roles of the salesperson is to simplify the customer's study of the product choices. Later in this chapter we discuss how product features (information) can add value when converted into specific benefits (knowledge) that can help the buyer make an intelligent buying decision.

CREATING SOLUTIONS WITH PRODUCT CONFIGURATION

product configuration If the customer has complex buying needs, then the salesperson will perhaps have to bring together many different parts of the company's product mix to develop a custom-fitted solution. The product selection process is often referred to as *product configuration*.

The challenge facing both customers and salespeople in this era of information overload is deciding which product applications, or combination of applications, will solve the customer's buying problem. If the customer has complex buying needs, then the salesperson may have to bring together many parts of the company's product mix to develop a custom-fitted solution. The product selection process is often referred to as **product configuration.** Salespeople representing Cadalyst Resources, a computer supplier, develop customer solutions that combine computer hardware, software, installation, and training. After a careful needs assessment, the Cadalyst sales representative prepares a proposal that illustrates how the different parts of the company's product mix come together to solve the customer's buying problem.

Product configuration is no less important in retail situations where the salesperson is selling a complex product. Assembling a professional wardrobe, preparing an interior design for a home or office, or putting together an automobile lease plan involves product configuration.

Many companies are using product configuration software to develop customized product solutions quickly and accurately. Product configuration software incorporates product selection criteria and associates them directly with customer requirements. Members of the sales force can use the sales configurator to identify product options, prices, delivery schedules, and other parts of the product mix, while working interactively with the customer. Most of today's product configuration software can be integrated with contact management software programs such as ACT!, Goldmine, and Maximize. In addition to improving the quality of the sales proposal, this software reduces the time-consuming process of manually preparing written proposals.

PREPARING WRITTEN PROPOSALS

written proposals A specific plan of action based on the facts, assumptions, and supporting documentation included in the sales presentation. Written proposals vary in terms of format and content.

Written proposals are frequently part of the salesperson's product strategy. It is only natural that some buyers will want the proposed solution put in writing. *Written proposals* can be defined as a specific plan of action based on the facts, assumptions, and supporting documentation included in the sales presentation.[5] A well-written proposal adds value to the product solution and can set you apart from the competition. It offers the buyer reassurance that you will deliver what has been promised. Written proposals vary in terms of format and content. Many government agencies, and some large companies, issue a request for proposal (RFP) that specifies the format of the proposal. Most effective proposals include the following parts:

Budget and overview. Tell the prospect the cost of the solution you have prescribed. Be specific as you describe the product or service features to be provided, and specify the price.

Objective. The objective should be expressed in terms of benefits. A tangible objective might be "to reduce payroll expense by 10 percent." An intangible objective might be stated as "increased business security offered by a company with a reputation for dependability." Focus on benefits that relate directly to the customer's need.

Strategy. Briefly describe how you will meet your objective. How will you fulfill the obligations you have described in your proposal? In some cases this section of your proposal includes specific language: "Your account will be assigned to Susan Murray, our senior lease representative."

Schedule. Establish a time frame for meeting your objective. This might involve the confirmation of dates with regard to acquisition, shipping, or installation.

Rationale. With a mixture of logic and emotion, present your rationale for taking action now. Once again, the emphasis should be on benefits, not features.[6]

Selling in Action

WRITING EFFECTIVE SALES LETTERS

Sales letters are increasingly being used by salespeople to describe features and benefits, to position products, to build relationships, and to provide assurances to customers. There are several standard rules that apply to all written sales letters. These include:

1. Sales letters should follow the standard visual format of a business letter. They should contain, in the following order, either a letterhead or sender's address, date, inside address (the same as on the outside of the envelope), salutation, body of letter, complimentary closing, typed name and handwritten signature of sender, and a notation of enclosures (if there are any).

2. Placement of the letter on the paper should provide balanced white space bordering the entire letter. Three to five blank lines should separate the date and inside address; a single blank line should separate the inside address and the salutation, the salutation and the opening paragraph of the letter, and each paragraph. A single blank line should separate the last paragraph and the complimentary closing. Single spacing should generally be used within the paragraphs.

3. Proper business punctuation includes a colon after the salutation and a comma after the complimentary closing.

4. Most sales letters include at least three paragraphs. The first paragraph should indicate why you are writing the letter, the second paragraph should be a summary of the benefits proposed, and the third paragraph should state what the next action step will be for either the salesperson, customer, or both.

5. Proper grammar and spelling must be used throughout the entire letter. Business letters provide an opportunity to build a stronger relationship with the customer and close the sale. Improper placement, punctuation, spelling errors, or weak content conveys a negative impression to the reader and may result in a lost sale.

Product knowledge training is an ongoing activity in the life of a salesperson.

The proposal should be printed on quality paper and free of any errors in spelling, grammar, or punctuation. Before completing the proposal, review the content one more time to be sure you have addressed all of the customer's concerns. Also, determine if you have incorporated enough persuasion into the proposal. Did you use words and sentences that will get the prospect's attention and build interest in your product solution?[7] Tips on how to develop a persuasive presentation are presented in Chapter 10.

PRODUCT KNOWLEDGE ADDS VALUE

Company-sponsored sales training programs are giving increased emphasis to product knowledge because it can give a sales force a competitive advantage. Salespeople who can add value are in a strong position to close sales even when they do not have a price advantage. John Cady, an account manager with Revere Electric Supply Company, continually monitors orders placed by his customers to identify alternative products or technologies. While working with the purchasing agent at Abbott Laboratories he was able to recommend a new technology that was lower in price and more efficient. The estimated cost savings amounted to $122 000 for a one-year period. This is the type of assistance that builds strong partnerships.[8]

The remainder of this chapter is divided into five major sections. The first two sections examine the kinds of product information and company information required by the salesperson. The third section describes the type of information about the competition that is helpful to salespeople. Sources of information are covered in the fourth section, and the fifth section describes how product features can be translated into buyer benefits.

Becoming a Product Expert

Jubilee Ford Sales Ltd. has become Saskatchewan's largest car dealership. Sales for 1996 were over $60 million, nearly double 1993 sales. Vaughn Wynant, the president, encourages his salespeople to take courses and attend seminars. He attributes success to his "product specialists," who know everything from technical specifications to competitor offerings.[9]

Ideally, a salesperson will possess product knowledge that meets and exceeds customer expectations. This section reviews some of the most common product information categories: (1) product development and quality improvement processes; (2) performance data and specifications; (3) maintenance and service contracts; and (4) price and delivery. Each is important as a potential source of knowledge concerning the product or service.

PRODUCT DEVELOPMENT AND QUALITY IMPROVEMENT PROCESSES

Companies spend large amounts of money in the development of their products. In **product development** the original idea for a product or service is tested, modified, and retested several times before it is offered to the customer. Each of the modifications is made with the thought of improving the product. Salespeople should be familiar with a product's development history. Often this information will set the stage for stronger sales appeals.

> **product development** Testing, modifying, and retesting an idea for a product several times before offering it to the customer.

Pacific Safety Products, Inc., of Kelowna, B.C., encloses survey questionnaires with each product to encourage feedback on quality and service. Customer suggestions have resulted in new products and improvements to existing products. As one example, the company added a hard detachable bottom to its portable medical emergency kits after customers complained the kits were wearing quickly from being dragged across rough surfaces. The company has a strong commitment to R&D, to continuous product development and improvement.[10]

Quality improvement continues to be an important long-term business strategy for most successful companies. Salespeople need to identify quality improvement processes that provide a competitive advantage and be prepared to discuss this information during the sales presentation. Motorola and Xerox provide examples of companies that have won awards for implementing important quality controls. **Quality control,** which involves measuring products and services against established standards, is one dimension of the typical quality improvement process. At Pfizer Inc., salespeople in the pharmaceutical group receive extensive training as an important quality control. Sales representatives must demonstrate their ability to present product information to physicians accurately and effectively.[11]

> **quality control** The evaluation or testing of products against established standards. This has important sales appeal when used by the salesperson to convince a prospect of a product's quality.

Many companies are investing a great deal of time and money to achieve ISO certification because purchasers recognize that it assures a level of quality. The ISO designation was developed by the International Organization for Standardization and certifies the processes a company uses to develop a product or service. ISO9001 applies to companies that have a design function (usually manufacturers), while ISO9002 applies to companies from service industries. Independent auditors are used to verify that a company is in compliance with the established quality standards, and there are follow-up audits every six or 12 months.[12] Merlin Motors Inc. is an example of a company that has met ISO quality assurance standards (see p. 104).

 www.merlinford.com

PERFORMANCE DATA AND SPECIFICATIONS

Most potential buyers are interested in performance data and specifications. Here are some typical questions that might be raised by prospects:

Merlin Motors Inc. of Saskatoon became the first Ford dealership in North America to become ISO certified.

"What is the frequency response for this stereo loudspeaker?"

"What is the anticipated rate of return on this mutual fund?"

"What is the energy consumption rating for this appliance?"

"Are all your hotel and conference centre rooms accessible to persons with physical disabilities?"

A salesperson must be prepared to address these types of questions in the written sales proposal and the sales presentation. Performance data are especially critical in cases in which the customer is attempting to compare the merits of one product with another.

In many fields today there are testing programs that provide comparative data concerning various products. For example, Natural Resources Canada administers the EnerGuide Program. All major household appliances imported into Canada, or manufactured in one province and shipped to another, must have an EnerGuide verification label (see p. 106). The label shows the annual energy consumption of each appliance based on standardized test procedures. Customers can make more informed purchase decisions as they can consider the energy cost associated with the operation of each appliance. Natural Resources Canada prepares a yearly directory that gives the energy consumption of products based on the manufacturer or brand name and model number.

MAINTENANCE AND SERVICE CONTRACTS

Prospects often want information concerning maintenance and care requirements for the products they purchase. The salesperson who can quickly and accurately provide this information will have the edge. Proper maintenance will usually extend the life of the product, so this information should be provided at the time of the sale.

Today, many salespeople are developing customized service agreements that incorporate the customer's special priorities, feelings, and needs. They work hard to acquire a real understanding of the customer's specific service criteria. If call-return expectations are very important to the customer, the frequency and quantity of product-related visits per week or month can be included in the service contract. Customized service agreements add value to the sale and help protect your business from the competition.[13]

PRICE AND DELIVERY

Potential buyers expect salespeople to be well versed in price and delivery policies on their products. This information is needed to develop both a written

Table 5.1   Quantifying the Solution

Quantifying the solution often involves a carefully prepared cost-benefit analysis. This example compares the higher priced Phoenix semitruck trailer with the lower priced FB model, which is a competing product.

COST SAVINGS OF THE PHOENIX VERSUS FB MODEL FOR A 10-YEAR PERIOD (ALL PRICES ARE APPROXIMATE)

	Cost Savings
• *Stainless steel bulkhead (savings on sandblasting and painting)*	$ 425.00
• *Stainless steel rear door frame (savings on painting)*	425.00
• *Air ride suspension (better fuel mileage, longer tire life, longer brake life)*	3 750.00
• *Hardwood or aluminum scuff (savings from freight damages and replacement of scuff)*	1 000.00
• *LED lights (lasts longer; approximate savings: $50 per year × 10 years)*	500.00
• *Light protectors (save $50 per year on replacement × 10 years)*	500.00
• *Threshold plate (saves damage to entry of trailer)*	200.00
• *Internal rail reinforcement (saves damage to lower rail and back panels)*	500.00
• *Stainless steel screws for light attachment (savings on replacement cost)*	200.00
• *Domestic oak premium floor—$1\frac{3}{8}$ (should last 10 years under normal conditions)*	1 000.00
• *Doors—aluminum inner and outer skin, outside white finish, inside mill finish, fastened by five aluminum hinges (savings over life of trailer)*	750.00
• *Five-year warranty in addition to standard warranty covers bulkhead rust, LED lights, floor, scuff liner, glad hands, rear frame, mud flap assembly, and threshold plate (Phoenix provides a higher trade-in value)*	1 500.00
Total approximate savings of Phoenix over 10-year period (All the preceding is standard equipment on a Phoenix; this trailer will sell for $23 500; an FB standard trailer would sell for $19 500)	$10 750.00
Less additional initial cost of Phoenix over FB standard	4 000.00
Overall cost savings of Phoenix over FB trailer	$ 6 750.00

sales proposal and a verbal sales presentation. The professional salesperson should also have similar information for competing products. Price objections represent one of the most common barriers to closing the sale.

quantifying the solution The process of determining if a sales proposal adds value. Quantifying the solution is especially important in situations where the purchase represents a major buying decision.

In most situations the price quotation should be accompanied by information that creates value in the mind of the customer. The process of determining whether or not the proposal adds value is often called **quantifying the solution**. When the purchase represents a major buying decision, such as the purchase of a new computer system, quantifying the solution is important. One way to quantify the solution is to conduct a cost–benefit analysis to determine the actual cost of the purchase and savings the buyer can anticipate from the investment (Table 5.1).

The complexity of price information will vary from one selling situation to another. In some cases the price is the same for all suppliers, and discounting is not a common practice. In other situations the price will depend on the size of the purchase, payment plan, delivery method, and other factors. The salesperson must be able to price each part of the product configuration. Some salespeople must also be prepared to discuss leasing options. The salesperson

EnerGuide label. (Reproduced with the permission of the Minister of Public Works and Government Services Canada, 1997.)

ENER**G**UIDE

Energy consumption / Consommation énergétique

624kWh
per year / par année

▼ This model / Ce modèle

535 kWh   1052 kWh

Uses least energy /   **Uses most energy /**
Consomme le moins   **Consomme le plus**
d'énergie   **d'énergie**

Similar models   **Built-in / Encastré**   Modèles similaires
compared   comparés
                          Standard / Ordinaire

Model number   **00000000**   Numéro du modèle

Removal of this label before first retail purchase is an offence (S.C. 1992, c. 36).
Enlever cette étiquette avant le premier achat au détail constitue une infraction (L.C. 1992, ch. 36).

who cannot compute and supply price information quickly and accurately is at a serious disadvantage. In Chapter 6 we discuss how to position products according to price.

Know Your Company

A growing number of companies are recognizing that sales personnel are often the firm's closest point of contact with the customer, and therefore they need to be well informed. Often the customer's mental image of the organization is formed entirely through contact with a sales representative. In the eyes of the customer the salesperson is the company.

The decision to purchase a product or service will often depend on the prospect's feeling about the company. We should never underestimate information about the company itself as a strong appeal that can be used during the sales presentation. This is especially true in situations in which products are similar. Life insurance, for example, can be purchased from a large number of firms at nearly identical rates.

In the telecommunications industry, competitive pricing is very important.

Some companies, such as Campbell's Soup, Coca-Cola, and IBM, have what might be called "brand power." These companies, and the products offered to consumers, are quite well known. However, if you are selling loudspeakers made by Klipsch or financial services offered by Integrated Financial Concepts Inc., you may find it necessary to spend considerable time providing information about the company.

Acquiring knowledge about your company is an important step toward developing complete product knowledge. In this section we examine the types of information needed in most selling situations.

COMPANY CULTURE AND ORGANIZATION

Many salespeople take special pride in the history of the company they work for. At Procter and Gamble (P & G), a company founded in 1837, employees note with pride that the hallmark of this highly successful firm is brands that enjoy market dominance. The authors of *The 100 Best Companies to Work for in America* note, "If a P & G brand does not hold down first place in its market, it's close to the top."[14] Pride can also develop in much younger companies such as SCC Environmental in St. John's, Newfoundland. The company was ranked in the top 10 among 67 companies that applied to assist the government of Kuwait with a multi-million-dollar environmental cleanup following the Gulf War. SCC Environmental is currently pursuing business on five continents. Paul Antle, president and CEO, says: "This business is dear to my heart, and our employees are proud to be part of a progressive, growing company that helps turn environmental problems and tragedy into opportunities that offer economic and social benefits throughout the world."[15]

organizational culture A collection of beliefs, behaviours, and work patterns held in common by people employed by a specific firm.

Every organization has its own unique culture. **Organizational culture** is a collection of beliefs, behaviours, and work patterns held in common by people employed by a specific firm. Most organizations over a period of time tend to take on distinct norms and practices. At Johnson & Johnson, employees are guided by a statement of core values that communicates what is held important by the company. Research indicates that the customer orientation of a firm's salespeople will be influenced by the organization's culture. A supportive culture that encourages salespeople to offer tailor-made solutions to buyer problems will set the stage for long-term partnerships.[16]

Many prospects will use the past performance of a company to evaluate the quality of the current product offering. If the company has enjoyed success in the past, there is good reason to believe that the future will be bright. At least this is the way most prospects view an organization.

COMPANY SUPPORT FOR PRODUCT

"Service after the Sale" is the theme of many marketing programs. Companies with this philosophy keep in touch with customers to determine if they are satisfied. For example, Nissan Canada surveys customers four times over three years, and the data are used by the company and its dealers to track customer satisfaction. This focus on satisfaction has helped increase Nissan's share of the Canadian market.[17] Husky Injection Molding Systems Ltd. of Bolton, Ontario, is a world-class manufacturer of injection molding machinery. The company frequently sends teams of sales and technical specialists to call on major accounts. Mike Urquhart, vice-president of sales, says: "Our spare parts manager is one of the key people we often include in our sales presentations. It's his

Our Credo

We believe our first responsibility is to the doctors, nurses and patients,
to mothers and fathers and all others who use our products and services.
In meeting their needs everything we do must be of high quality.
We must constantly strive to reduce our costs
in order to maintain reasonable prices.
Customers' orders must be serviced promptly and accurately.
Our suppliers and distributors must have an opportunity
to make a fair profit.

We are responsible to our employees,
the men and women who work with us throughout the world.
Everyone must be considered as an individual.
We must respect their dignity and recognize their merit.
They must have a sense of security in their jobs.
Compensation must be fair and adequate,
and working conditions clean, orderly and safe.
We must be mindful of ways to help our employees fulfill
their family responsibilities.
Employees must feel free to make suggestions and complaints.
There must be equal opportunity for employment, development
and advancement for those qualified.
We must provide competent management,
and their actions must be just and ethical.

We are responsible to the communities in which we live and work
and to the world community as well.
We must be good citizens — support good works and charities
and bear our fair share of taxes.
We must encourage civic improvements and better health and education.
We must maintain in good order
the property we are privileged to use,
protecting the environment and natural resources.

Our final responsibility is to our stockholders.
Business must make a sound profit.
We must experiment with new ideas.
Research must be carried on, innovative programs developed
and mistakes paid for.
New equipment must be purchased, new facilities provided
and new products launched.
Reserves must be created to provide for adverse times.
When we operate according to these principles,
the stockholders should realize a fair return.

Johnson & Johnson

Companies like Johnson & Johnson have published statements like this one that make its core values clear to customers, vendors, employees, and shareholders.

Valerie Howe (p. 46) uses her cellular phone to communicate with customaers when she is away from her office.

role to say, 'Here's how we back you up. Here's how we can help you when you have problems.' This is one way we convince customers that we are committed to helping them before, during, and after the sale."[18]

Know Your Competition

Acquiring knowledge of your competition is another important step toward developing complete product knowledge. Salespeople who have knowledge of their competitors' strengths and weaknesses are better able to understand their own position, and adjust their selling strategy accordingly.[19] Prospects often raise specific questions concerning competing firms. If we cannot provide answers or if our answers are vague, the sale may be lost.

YOUR ATTITUDE TOWARD YOUR COMPETITION

Regardless of how impressive your product is, the customer will naturally seek information about similar products sold by other companies. Therefore, you must acquire facts about competing products before the sales presentation. Once armed with this information, you are more confident in your ability to handle questions about the competition.

Xerox Corporation believes that education contributes to the success of its customers. Many of the Xerox courses are offered at the International Center for Training and Management Development, pictured here.

The attitude you display toward your competition is of the utmost importance. Every salesperson should develop a set of basic beliefs about the best way of dealing with competing products. Here are a few helpful guidelines:

1. In most cases, do not refer to the competition during the sales presentation. Doing so will shift the focus of attention to competing products, which is usually not desirable. Always respond to direct questions, but do not initiate the topic.

2. Never discuss the competition unless you have all your facts straight. Your credibility will suffer if you make inaccurate statements. If you do not know the answer to a specific question, simply say, "I do not know." It is also best to avoid generalizations about the competition.

3. Avoid criticizing the competition. You may be called on to make direct comparisons between your product and competing products. In these situations, stick to the facts and avoid emotional comments about apparent or real weaknesses. Prospects tend to become suspicious of salespeople who initiate strong criticism of the competition.

Customers appreciate an accurate, fair, and honest presentation of the facts. They generally resent highly critical remarks about the competition. Avoid mudslinging at all costs. Fairness is a virtue that people greatly admire.

BECOME AN INDUSTRY EXPERT

Lee Boyan, sales consultant, suggests that salespeople become experts in an appropriate niche of an industry or a group of industries.[20] If the sales force includes several persons, each might assume responsibility for a specific area.

Salespeople should closely examine the sources of information about their products and the industries where these products are used.

One member of an office equipment sales team might, for example, concentrate on the banking industry. This person would read the appropriate trade journals and become active in professional associations that serve bankers' needs.

Sources of Product Information

There are several sources of product information available to salespeople. Some of the most common include: (1) product literature developed by the company, (2) sales training meetings, (3) plant tours, (4) internal sales and sales support team members, (5) customers, (6) the product, (7) the Internet, and (8) publications.

PRODUCT LITERATURE

Most companies prepare materials that provide a detailed description of their product. This information is usually quite informative, and salespeople should review it carefully. If the company markets a number of products, a sales catalogue is usually developed. To save salespeople time, many companies give them computer software that provides a constantly updated, online product catalogue. Advertisements, promotional brochures, and audio cassettes can also be a valuable source of product information. Some salespeople develop their own product literature with the aid of electronic marketing encyclopedias. These libraries put a wide range of sales and marketing information at your fingertips. EnCyc Inc., for example, has developed an encyclopedia that allows salespeople to create PowerPoint presentations automatically by pulling the right slides from an organized database.[21]

Distributor salespeople for Rich's Bakery are provided with a free audio cassette that features tips on how to sell their product.

SELLING
FRESH BAKED PRODUCTS FROM
FROZEN DOUGHS
IS ALMOST AS EASY AS

LISTENING
TO THIS TAPE.

BAKERY BASICS

HOT TIPS – COOL PROFITS

If you think frozen doughs are a difficult sell, we'd like to put your mind at ease. In just eight minutes, our *free cassette* will teach you all you need to know about the simplicity of handling Rich's® Frozen Doughs. You'll learn about the major sales opportunities that await by taking business from local bakeries and the benefits your customers will gain from selling baked-on-premise products.

It's easy listening. It's easy baking. It's easy selling. So call us toll free at 1-800-659-5251.

RICH'S Bakery

Rich Products Corporation, Food Service Division, 1150 Niagara Street, Buffalo, New York 14213 U.S.A.

CIRCLE 137 FOR MORE INFORMATION

SALES TRAINING MEETINGS

As noted previously, company-sponsored sales training programs frequently focus on product knowledge. Sales and marketing executives tend to view product knowledge training as a basic element of any sales training program.

New technology is providing long-distance learning opportunities for many salespeople. David Wilkins, owner of Avalon Ford Sales 1996 Ltd. of St. John's, Newfoundland, encourages his salespeople to participate in training courses that are provided through an interactive distance learning network called Fordstar. Salespeople can sit in their own office and learn via satellite from Oakville, Ontario, and various other Ford Motor Company locations.[22]

PLANT TOURS

Many companies believe that salespeople should visit the manufacturing plant and see the production process first-hand. Such tours not only provide valuable

Surveys indicate that product knowledge training should be a basic element of any sales training program.

product information but also increase the salesperson's enthusiasm for the product. A new salesperson may spend several days at the plant getting acquainted with the production process. Experienced personnel within the organization can also benefit from plant tours.

INTERNAL SALES AND SALES SUPPORT TEAM MEMBERS

Amir Moussavian, senior vice-president of sales at Giga Trend, Incorporated, believes professional salespeople learn from each other. He credits the success of his company to building a team knowledgeable about computer technology. Giga Trend's salespeople are not reluctant to communicate their interests and share talents, because commissions are pooled. The pooled commissions provide an incentive to help each other and learn from each other.[23] Team selling has become more popular, in part, because many complex sales require the expertise of several sales and sales support personnel.

Building Relationships through Technology

STARTING FAST WITH CRM

New salespeople can be overwhelmed by the amount of information they need to master. This includes information about the company and its processes, products, and customers. Companies can now make learning easier with information technology. Information about the company and its processes can be stored on the company's network, on its virtual private network (VPN), or on CD-ROM. Computer-based training (CBT) permits new employees to learn at their own pace about a product's specifications, features, benefits, uses, and selling points.

Companies can now provide salespeople with software that they can use to accurately and effectively create product solutions. Electronic configuration software allows salespeople to select the components necessary to assemble a custom-tailored solution to meet their prospects' needs. This software guides users through the product selection process while ensuring that the components will be compatible with one another.

Companies can deliver to new salespeople a rich body of customer information through a strong commitment to the use of customer relationship management software. The salesperson who carefully records her business and relationship contacts with customers and prospects will, over time, accumulate a valuable store of information. A new salesperson taking over these accounts can quickly come up to speed with these people and their needs. (See the exercise Finding Product Information in CRM on page 120 for more information.)

CUSTOMERS

Persons who actually use the product can be an important source of information. They have observed its performance under actual working conditions and can provide an objective assessment of the product's strengths and weaknesses. Some companies collect testimonials from satisfied customers and make this persuasive information available to the sales staff.

THE PRODUCT

The product itself should not be overlooked as a source of valuable information. Salespeople should closely examine and, if possible, use each item they sell to become familiar with its features. Investigation, use, and careful evaluation of the product will provide a salesperson with additional confidence.

THE INTERNET

Many companies are using the Internet to showcase the features and benefits of their products. The Internet is also an excellent source of technical reports on various products. Some salespeople turn to the Internet to access information concerning competing products.

PUBLICATIONS

Trade and technical publications such as *Supermarket Business* and *Advertising Age* provide valuable product information. Popular magazines and the business section of the newspaper also offer salespeople considerable information about their products and their competition. A number of publications such as *Consumer Reports* test products extensively and report the findings in nontechnical language for the benefit of consumers. These reports are a valuable source of information.

A WORD OF CAUTION

Is it possible to be overly prepared? Can salespeople know too much about the products and services they sell? The answer to both questions is generally no. Communication problems can arise, however, if the salesperson does not accurately gauge the prospect's level of understanding. There is always the danger that a knowledgeable salesperson will overwhelm the potential buyer with facts and figures. This problem can be avoided when salespeople adopt the feature-benefit strategy.

Adding Value with a Feature-Benefit Strategy

Charles Revson, founder of the Revlon Company, once said, "In the factory we make cosmetics. In the store we sell hope." Throughout this chapter we stress the importance of acquiring information on the features of your product, company, and competition. Now it is important to point out that all successful sales presentations translate product features into buyer benefits. The "hope" that Charles Revson mentioned is a good example of a buyer benefit. It is only when a product feature is converted to a buyer benefit that it makes an impact on the customer. People do not buy features; they buy benefits.

DOONESBURY   by Garry Trudeau

Copyright 1982, G. B. Trudeau. Reprinted with permission of Universal Press Syndicate. All rights reserved.

DISTINGUISH BETWEEN FEATURES AND BENEFITS

To be sure we understand the difference between a product feature and a benefit, let us define these two terms.

A **product feature** is anything that can be felt, seen, or measured. A feature answers the question, "What is it?" Features include such things as craftsmanship, durability, design, and economy of operation. In most cases these are technical facts about the product. They reveal how the product was developed and manufactured. Product features are often described in the technical section of the written sales proposal and in the literature provided by the manufacturer.

A **product benefit** is whatever provides the consumer with personal advantage or gain. It answers the question, "How will I benefit from owning or using the product?" If you mention to a prospect that a certain tire has a four-ply rating, you are talking about a product feature. If you go on to point out that this tire will provide greater safety, last longer, and improve gas mileage, you are pointing out benefits.

Nortel Networks is a Canadian company that has become a world leader in communication technology. One of its products, the Companion C3050 portable telephone, is part of a system to provide communication in the workplace. One feature is its low power consumption; the benefit is that users obtain more talk and standby time between recharges. Another feature is that it can be paired with a regular telephone and can share the same extension number with it; the benefit to users is that both phones will ring but either can be answered. This means that users can answer their regular telephone when in their office but can answer their Companion telephone when away from their office. This provides additional advantages to users as customer service and sales improve, and expenses are reduced as more long-distance phone calls are answered and do not have to be returned. As you see, features become more appealing to customers once they are converted to benefits they can appreciate.

Jerry Vass, consultant and sales trainer, says the buyer has three questions about the product you sell: So what? What's in it for me? and Can you prove it? He cautions salespeople to avoid burying the prospect with features that, by themselves, would not answer any of these questions. Vass also believes that very few salespeople have the ability to sell benefits rather than features.[24]

product feature Anything that a customer can feel, see, hear, taste, smell, or measure to answer the question, "What is it?" Features include things such as craftsmanship, durability, design, and economy of operation.

product benefit Whatever provides the customer with personal advantage or gain. This usually answers the question, "How will the customer benefit from owning or using the product?"

Many forms of product knowledge and sales support tools are available to distributor salespeople.

USE BRIDGE STATEMENTS

We know that people buy benefits, not features. One of the best ways to present benefits is to use a bridge statement. A **bridge statement** is a transitional phrase that connects a statement of features with a statement of benefits. This method permits customers to connect the features of your product to the benefits they will receive. A sales representative for Allied Food Group might use a bridge statement to introduce a new snack food:

> "This product is nationally advertised, *which means* you will benefit from more presold customers."

Some companies prefer to state the benefit first and the feature second. When this occurs, the bridge statement may be a word such as "because." For example:

> "You will experience faster turnover and increased profits *because* the first order includes an attractive display rack."

bridge statement A translational phrase that connects a statement of features with a statement of benefits. This method permits customers to connect the features of your product to the benefits they will receive.

Selling in Action

NEW PRODUCT SALES SUCCESS REQUIRES A CUSTOMER-CENTRED FOCUS

Robert Cooper of McMaster University is one of the world's leading researchers on new products. According to Cooper, products less than five years old account for about 32 percent of sales and 30 percent of profits, up from 22 percent of profits between 1976 and 1981. New products have a lot of advantages: competitive lead time, management commitment, and sales force enthusiasm. Unfortunately, some fail—and failures are costly.

When Xerox introduced the 9200 mega-copier, sales were far below expectations. Buyers initially interested in the copiers became more resistant as sales presentations proceeded, a surprising finding. A questionnaire administered to the sales force found a negative correlation between enthusiasm and sales. That is, salespeople who were less enthusiastic sold more copiers than those who had higher enthusiasm, another surprising finding.

When researchers made sales calls with Xerox salespeople, they discovered two differences between how salespeople tried to sell the new copiers and how they sold more established products. First, they asked 40 percent fewer questions. Second, they provided three times as many product details. Instead of being customer-centred and asking questions to discover customer needs,

the salespeople were product-centred, performing "feature dumps."

One theory was that salespeople would introduce new products to customers as the products were introduced to them. That is, if management described all the "bells and whistles" to the salespeople, they would do the same to customers. To test this theory, researchers intervened in a new product launch for a Kodak blood analyzer. Researchers described to 12 randomly chosen salespeople how the product solved customer problems, without describing any of the product's bells and whistles. The salespeople were further coached to avoid describing product features, and to ask questions that uncovered needs. After one year, the salespeople in the experimental group achieved sales 54 percent higher than a matched group who had experienced the company's standard product launch—one with all the bells and whistles.

These examples support David Milliken's views. The national director of business development at Deloitte & Touche says, "Any minute you spend talking about a product or feature that doesn't connect to an explicit need is a minute wasted."[a]

IDENTIFY FEATURES AND BENEFITS

A careful analysis of the product will help identify both product features and buyer benefits. Once all the important features are identified, arrange them in logical order. Then write beside each feature the most important benefit the customer will derive from that feature. Finally, prepare a series of bridge statements to connect the appropriate features and benefits. Using this three-step approach, a hotel selling conference and convention services, and a manufacturer selling electric motors used to power mining equipment, developed feature-benefit worksheets (Tables 5.2 and 5.3). Notice how each feature is translated into a benefit that would be important to someone purchasing these products and services. Table 5.2 reminds us that company features can be converted to benefits. Product analysis helps you decide what information might be included in the sales presentation. Research indicates that high-performance salespeople present recommendations more in terms of customer benefits than in terms of product features.[25]

FEATURE-BENEFIT APPROACH COMPLEMENTS CONSULTATIVE SELLING

Identifying product features and then converting these features to buyer benefits is an integral part of consultative selling. The salesperson should approach the customer with complete knowledge of the product or service. With the aid of questions the customer's buying needs are identified. Once the needs are known, the salesperson should discuss the features and benefits that specifically apply to that person. In this way the sales presentation is individualized for each customer. Everyone likes to be treated as an individual. A sales presentation tailored to individual customers communicates the message, "You are important and I want you to be a satisfied customer."

Table 5.2 Convert Features to Benefits

Salespeople employed by a hotel can enhance the sales presentation by converting features to benefits.

FEATURE	BENEFIT
Facilities	
The hotel conference rooms were recently redecorated.	*Which means all your meetings will be held in rooms that are attractive as well as comfortable.*
All of our guest rooms were completely re-decorated during the past six months and many were designated as non-smoking rooms.	*Which means your people will find the rooms clean and attractive. In addition, they can select a smoking or non-smoking room.*
Food Services	
We offer four different banquet entrées pre-pared by our executive chef, who was recently selected Chef of the Year by the Canadian Federation of Chefs and Cooks.	*Which means your conference will be enhanced by delicious meals served by a well-trained staff.*
Our hotel offers 24-hour room service.	*Which means your people can order food or beverages at their convenience.*

Table 5.3 Convert Features to Benefits

Here we see company features translated into customer benefits.

FEATURE	BENEFIT
Our company has . . .	**Which means to you . . .**
1. The best selection of motors in the area	• *Choice of the best models to interface with your current equipment*
	• *Equipment will operate more efficiently*
2. Certified service technicians	• *Well-qualified service personnel keep your equipment in top running condition*
	• *Less downtime and higher profits*

Summary

A salesperson whose product knowledge is complete and accurate is better able to satisfy customers. This is without doubt the most important justification for becoming totally familiar with the products you sell. It is simply not possible to provide maximum assistance to potential customers without this information. Additional advantages to be gained from knowing your product include greater self-confidence, increased enthusiasm, improved ability to overcome objections, development of stronger selling appeals, and the preparation of more effective sales proposals.

A complete understanding of your company will also yield many personal and professional benefits. The most important benefit, of course, is your ability to serve your customer most effectively. In many selling situations, customers inquire about the company's business practices. They want to know things about support personnel, product development, credit procedures, warranty plans, and product service after the sale. When salespeople are able to provide the necessary company information, they gain respect. They also close more sales.

This chapter also stresses knowing your competition. It pays to study other companies that sell similar products to determine whether they have competitive advantages or disadvantages.

Salespeople gather information from many sources. Company literature and sales training meetings are among the most important. Other sources include factory tours, customers, competition, sales support personnel, the Internet, publications, and actual experience with the product itself.

In the sales presentation and when preparing the written sales proposal, your knowledge of the product's features and your company's strengths must be presented in terms of the resulting benefits to the buyer. The information and benefits you emphasize will depend on your assessment of the prospect's needs and motivation.

Key Terms

Product Strategy 99
Product Configuration 100
Written Proposals 100
Product Development 102
Quality Control 103

Quantifying the Solution 105
Organizational Culture 108
Product Feature 115
Product Benefit 116
Bridge Statement 116

Review Questions

1. Provide a brief description of the term *product strategy*.

2. Some sales managers state, "Training given to sales personnel should stress product knowledge over any other area." List three reasons that support this view.

3. What is *product configuration*? Provide an example of how this practice is used in the sale of commercial stereo equipment.

4. Review the Johnson & Johnson statement of corporate values on p. 109 and explain how its core values can contribute to a salesperson's career success.

5. Define the term *organizational culture*. How might this company information enhance a sales presentation?

6. Basic beliefs underlie the salesperson's method of handling competition. What are three guidelines a salesperson should follow in developing basic beliefs in this area?

7. Explain what the customer's expectations are concerning the salesperson's attitude toward competition.

8. List and briefly describe the five parts included in most written sales proposals.

9. What are the most common sources of product information?

10. Distinguish between *product features* and *buyer benefits*.

Application Exercises

1. Obtain, if possible, a copy of a customer-oriented product sales brochure or news release that has been prepared by a marketer. Many salespeople receive such selling tools. Study this information carefully, then develop a feature-benefit analysis sheet.

2. Today many companies are automating their product configuration and proposal writing activities. Go to the Internet and find these providers of software: www.qwikquote.com (for simple sales configuration); www.results-online.com (for moderately complex sales configuration); and www.exactium.com (for complex sales configuration). Click on each company's demonstration software and study the design of each product.

www.qwikquote.com
www.results-online.com
www.exactium.com

3. Select a product you are familiar with and know a great deal about. (This may be something you recently shopped for and purchased, such as a compact disc player or an automobile.) Under each of the categories listed, fill in the required information about the product.
   a. Where did you buy the product? Why?
   b. Did product design influence your decision?
   c. How and where was the product manufactured?
   d. What different applications or uses are there for the product?
   e. How does the product perform? Are there any data on the product's performance? What are they?
   f. What kinds of maintenance and care does the product require? How often?
   g. Could you sell the product you have written about in items *a* through *f*? Why or why not?

CRM Application Exercise

Finding Product Information in CRM

Providing immediate access to product information can increase a salesperson's efficiency and responsiveness to customer requests. Computers excel at the task of quickly providing information. An example can be found in the ACT! CRM case study software. Basic information about networks is available in the Reference Library, a feature of this version of ACT!: select <u>V</u>iew, <u>R</u>eference Library, to view the networking information. Print this information by selecting <u>F</u>ile, <u>P</u>rint. While in the Reference Library, other library documents can be opened by selecting <u>F</u>ile, <u>O</u>pen, and double-clicking on one of the files that ends with "wpd." When finished, these ACT! word processing files can be closed by selecting <u>F</u>ile, <u>C</u>lose (Alt+F C).

Case Problem

When Michael Tulk (introduced at the start of this chapter) was near graduation, he was looking forward to not having to study any more. After four years in university, he thought he had seen enough books. He was excited when he got his employment offer from Xerox Canada, and he was looking forward to starting his sales career. But, according to Michael Tulk, "Before I even received my degree, I received a huge box of books, and I knew immediately that my studying days were far from over."

Shortly after new salespeople are hired at Xerox Canada, they go to Toronto or to Leesburg, Virginia, for three weeks of basic sales school. Here they learn about company history and culture, the importance of ethics, and the basic selling process—even the importance of appearance and the expected dress code. It is an excellent beginning for new recruits, and they leave highly motivated to get on with their careers.

After they have been in sales for a year, salespeople may get to take a course on strategic selling. This course reinforces what they have already learned and builds upon it by focusing on, among other things, large or key accounts, selling to buying teams, how to identify people influential in the buying decision, how to identify and nurture a "coach" or "champion" within the buying firm, and how to get to the decision maker early in the selling process.

Some salespeople get to go to a high-volume training session, where they learn about high-volume duplicators and how to sell in the offset print world. Another specialized session trains salespeople to sell document production systems or print systems. Some of these units can range from $250 000 to $750 000 or more.

Another session that salespeople get to attend after they have been in sales for a year or more is referred to as focus school. Michael Tulk thinks this is one of the best experiences he has had since beginning his training with Xerox Canada. At this session each participant must discuss five specific sales experiences, three where they were successful and two where they were unsuccessful, with reasons why.

While the basic training may be done in Canada or the United States, the more advanced training is frequently done only at Leesburg. It is here that Xerox Corporation has the most modern facilities, with virtually every piece of their competitors' equipment. Xerox sales specialists take the machines apart to see exactly how they are built, how they operate, and what weaknesses they have. This becomes important product knowledge for salespeople, who can then see exactly what they are selling against and how best to position Xerox solutions in each instance. Michael Tulk says this is very important, even for the simplest solutions. "When your customer wants a simple photocopier that will produce 50 copies per minute, you have to know who your competitors are and how your recommendations will better serve the customer's needs."

The training at Xerox is becoming more complicated as technology becomes more complex. Xerox is no longer just a photocopier supplier; it supplies document solutions for all types of businesses, large and small. Sales now frequently combine hardware, software, installation, and support services. This means that training beyond the basic sales level has become very specialized. Many salespeople must rely on support specialists to help them make a sale, emphasizing the need for effective team-selling strategies.

Michael Tulk also points to that as one of his keys to success. He says, "I was fortunate, I think, to have been in sales in Atlantic Canada. It means you have to work harder and learn more because you have to be just a bit more self-reliant. You don't always have the resources at your fingertips that you would have in a larger centre, so you have to take more responsibility for what you do. At one point I was a Centralized Solutions Consultant, a Colour Sales Executive, and a High Volume Sales Executive, all in one. I now know a lot about a few things and a little about a lot of things. But in this business you have to work hard to stay on top because the technologies and competitors are constantly evolving."

Questions

1. Does Michael Tulk appear to utilize the three prescriptions for a product selling strategy? Explain.

2. In addition to the actual product strategy developed by Michael Tulk, how important will company information (history, culture, ethical position, performance, product support, etc.) be in closing the sale?

3. Why are sales support specialists becoming so important in this industry? What are the implications for salespeople?

4. Should Michael Tulk invest a lot of his time in learning about the competition? Explain. What should be his attitude toward the competition?

5. Is Michael Tulk's sales career one where becoming an industry expert would be important? Explain.

Partnership Selling: A Role Play/Simulation (see Appendix C, p.419)

DEVELOPING A PRODUCT STRATEGY

Read *Employment Memorandum 1* on p. 423, which introduces you to your new training position with the Hotel Convention Centre. You should also study the product strategy materials that follow the memo to become familiar with the company, product, and competitive knowledge you will need in your new position.

Read *Customer Service/Sales Memorandum 1* on p. 444 and complete the three-part customer/service assignment provided by your sales manager. In item 1 you are to complete a feature-benefit worksheet; in item 2 you are to configure a price/product sales proposal; and in item 3 you are to write a sales cover letter for the sales proposal. Note that the information presented in the price/product sales proposal will consist of product facts/features, and the information presented in your sales cover letter should present specific benefit statements. These three forms should all be custom fitted to meet your customer's—B. H. Rivera's—specific needs. All the product information you will need is in the product strategy materials provided as enclosures and attachments to *Employment Memorandum 1*.

Developing Product-Selling Strategies

Strategic Technologies Inc. of Surrey, B.C. has a problem. It manufactures the "Mercedes-Benz" of electronic-curfew tagging equipment, and competes in an industry dominated by Chevys and Fords. When your product is priced 40 percent higher than your competition, you have to develop a product-selling strategy that adds value. Doug Blakeway, president and CEO of Strategic Technologies, encourages potential clients to test drive his equipment and to compare it to the competition. One value-added feature is a visual display monitor that informs convicts under house arrest when they have a scheduled meeting with their parole officer, or when their curfew time has arrived. The display also allows corrections officials to leave time- and date-stamped messages without having to phone the convict. Strategic Technologies also provides value by supplying its equipment only on a rental basis. This means the equipment is regularly upgraded, and salespeople have an opportunity to keep in contact with clients. The company's 100-percent lifetime warranty adds additional value. Customers receive new equipment while their equipment is being serviced.

Strategic Technologies has positioned itself as a provider of superior equipment and service. When customers make

LEARNING OBJECTIVES

When you finish reading this chapter, you should be able to

1. Describe positioning as a product-selling strategy

2. Discuss product differentiation in personal selling

3. Explain how today's customer is redefining the product

4. Describe how to position products at various stages of the product life cycle

5. Explain how to position your product with a price strategy

6. Explain how to position your product with a value-added strategy

7. Describe the four dimensions of the total product

head-on comparisons, and when price is not the overriding factor, Strategic Technologies almost always wins. Doug Blakeway says, "If an [corrections] agency is looking strictly at the attributes, we always come out on top."[1]

Product Positioning—A Personal Selling Strategy

product positioning Decisions, activities, and communication strategies that are directed toward trying to create and maintain a firm's intended product concept in the customer's mind.

Long-term success in today's dynamic global economy requires the continual positioning and repositioning of products. **Product positioning** involves those decisions and activities intended to create and maintain a certain concept of the firm's product in the customer's mind. A product's "position" is the customer's concept of the product's attributes relative to their concept of competing products.[2] In a market that has been flooded with various types of sport-utility vehicles, Land Rover has been positioned as a dependable vehicle that can climb a steep, rock-covered hillside with ease. Every effort has been made to create the perception of safety, durability, and security. To give sales representatives increased confidence in the Land Rover, the company has arranged plant tours and the opportunity to observe actual testing of Land Rover vehicles under extremely demanding conditions.

Good positioning means that the product's name, reputation, and niche are well recognized. However, a good positioning strategy does not last forever. The positioning process must be continually modified to match the customer's changing wants and needs.[3]

THE ESSENTIALS OF PRODUCT POSITIONING

Salespeople make important contributions to the process of product positioning. Most companies use a combination of marketing and sales strategies to give their products a unique position in the marketplace. Every salesperson needs a good understanding of the fundamental practices that contribute to product positioning. This chapter begins with a brief introduction to the concept of product differentiation. This introduction is followed by an explanation of how products have been redefined in the age of information. The remainder of the chapter is devoted to three product-selling strategies that can be used to position a product. Emphasis is placed on positioning your product with a value-added strategy. In the age of information, salespeople who cannot add value to the products they sell will diminish in number and influence.

Achieving Product Differentiation in Personal Selling

One of the basic tenets of sales and marketing is the principle of product differentiation. The competitors in virtually all industries are moving toward differentiating themselves on the basis of quality, price, convenience, economy, or some other factor. Salespeople, who are on the front line of many marketing efforts, assume an important role in the product differentiation process.

Many of the fastest-growing companies are creating strong positions in specific market segments. Some examples are described here:

Item: Edmonton-based ZCL Composites Ltd. is a manufacturer of fibreglass-reinforced underground fuel storage tanks. To compete against approximately 150 other tank manufacturers, the company had to find a way to differentiate itself. President and CEO Ven Côté says, "We began to offer entire systems that included not just the tank but all the accessories that go with it. Through vertical integration we positioned ourselves not as a tank manufacturer, but as a whole solution provider." This positioning strategy has allowed the company to grow regionally, nationally, and internationally.[4]

 www.zcl.com

Item: Prince Edward Island-based Padinox Inc. has been manufacturing high quality stainless steel Paderno brand and Chaudier brand cookware since 1979. This cookware is used by many world-class chefs and can be found at Sussex Drive and aboard Air Force One. Padinox Inc. sells through 250 stores across North America and, in addition, has eight factory outlets. As a free service the company will affix an assist handle on any piece of cookware for arthritic or elderly customers.[5]

 www.padinox.ca

Item: Toronto-based Castek Software Factory Inc. has cultivated an image as a provider of a quality product that's delivered on time and on budget. Ray Lavitt, vice-president of business development, says: "The IT industry, for a variety of reasons, does not have a real good record for the delivery of software.... Providing on-time, on-budget complex applications development is the way we differentiate ourselves from everyone else." Their standout reputation for service and reliability has helped Castek grow from sales of $1.1 million in 1992 to expected sales of $40 million in 2000.[6]

 www.castek.com

Notice that all these businesses are selling their products and services in highly competitive markets. Also, each is attempting to achieve product and service differentiation. Personal selling has helped each company achieve success.

Positioning ZCL Composites as a whole-solution provider has allowed Ven Côté, president and CEO, to grow the company both within Canada and internationally.

Redefining "Product" in the Age of Information

Ted Levitt, former editor of the *Harvard Business Review*, says that products are problem-solving tools. People buy products if they fulfill a problem-solving need. Today's better-educated and more demanding customers are seeking a *cluster of satisfactions*. **Satisfactions** arise from the product itself, from the company that makes or distributes the product, and from the salesperson who sells and services the product.[7] Figure 6.1 provides a description of a three-dimensional Product Selling Model.

To illustrate how the cluster of satisfactions concept works in a business setting, let us examine a complex buying decision. Stora Port Hawkesbury Ltd., a major pulp and paper mill in Nova Scotia, recently purchased nine cranes from Konecranes Canada Inc. The contract, worth approximately $7 million, was part of a $750-million expansion, to allow Stora to produce magazine-quality paper at this mill.[8]

The buying decision at Stora Port Hawkesbury Ltd. was complex because the products, in various configurations, were available from several crane manufacturers, and even from some distributors or agents. This purchase decision was a very important one that would have long-term implications for the mill. Several potential suppliers presented proposals. Here are some of the questions that the Stora people had to answer before making the buying decision:

Questions Related to the Product

What product is best for our type of operation?

Does the product have a good reputation for quality?

Given the cost of this product, will Stora Port Hawkesbury receive a good return on investment?

Questions Related to the Company

Does this company provide the most advanced technology?

What is the company's reputation for manufacturing quality products?

What is the company's reputation for standing behind the products it sells?

Questions Related to the Salesperson

Does this salesperson possess the knowledge and experience needed to recommend the right product?

Can this salesperson be trusted?

Will this salesperson provide support services after the sale?

The purchase of a service may be no less complicated. Let us assume that you are planning a retirement banquet for the president of your company. The location of the banquet would likely depend on the type of food and beverage service available at hotels and restaurants in your community. This would be the *product* decision. The qualifications of the food and beverage salesperson or sales manager would also influence your buying decision, because this is the person who describes the food, beverage, and meeting room options and works with you after the buying decision. You must be convinced that this person has the experience and skills necessary to do the job. In the final analysis you would

satisfactions The positive benefits that customers seek when making a purchase. Satisfactions arise from the product itself, from the company that makes or distributes the product, and from the salesperson who sells and services the product.

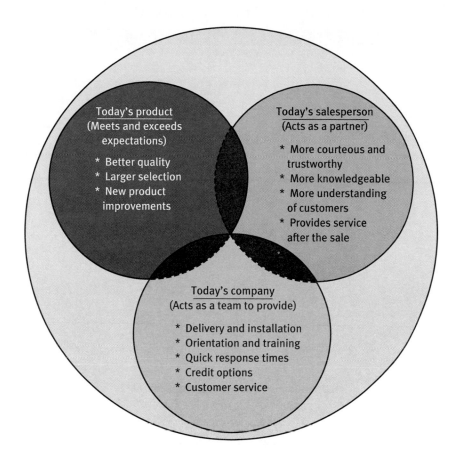

Figure 6.1   Product Selling Model. The product strategy should include a cluster of satisfactions that meet the needs of today's better educated and more demanding customers. Drawing from this cluster, the salesperson can custom fit presentations to meet a wide range of needs.

make a buying decision based on your perception of the "whole product," which provides a cluster of satisfactions.

Product Positioning Options

Product positioning is a concept that applies to both new and existing products. Given the dynamics of most markets, it may be necessary to reposition products several times in their life, because even a solid, popular product can lose market position quickly. Salespeople have assumed an important and expanding role in positioning products. To succeed in our overcommunicated society, marketers must use a more direct and personalized form of communication with customers. Advertising directed toward a mass market will often fail to position a complex product.

Throughout the remainder of this chapter we discuss specific ways to use various product-positioning strategies. We explain how salespeople can (1) position new and emerging products versus well-established products, (2) position products with price strategies, and (3) position products with value-added strategies.

POSITIONING NEW AND EMERGING PRODUCTS VERSUS MATURE AND WELL-ESTABLISHED PRODUCTS

In many ways, products are like human beings: they are born, grow up, mature, and grow old. In marketing this process is known as the **product life cycle.** The

product life cycle   Stages of a product from the time it is first introduced to the market until it is taken off the market, including the stages of introduction, growth, maturity, and decline.

Sales representatives from Paine Webber are encouraged to look beyond the customer's immediate basic needs to build a long-term relationship.

product life cycle includes the stages a product goes through from the time it is first introduced to the market until it is discontinued. As the product moves through its cycle, the strategies relating to competition, promotion, pricing, and other factors must be evaluated and possibly changed. The nature and extent of each stage in the product life cycle are determined by several factors, including:

1. The product's perceived advantage over available substitutes;
2. The product's benefits and the importance of the needs it fulfills;
3. Competitive activity, including pricing, substitute product development and improvement, and effectiveness of competing advertising and promotion; and
4. Changes in technology, fashion, or demographics.[9]

As we attempt to develop a product-selling strategy, we must consider where the product is positioned in terms of the life cycle. The sales strategy used to sell a new and emerging product will be much different from the strategy used to sell a mature, well-established product (Fig. 6.2).

SELLING NEW AND EMERGING PRODUCTS

Sometimes a promising new product enters the marketplace to high hopes, but initial sales are disappointing. This was the case when the Ricoh MV715 was first introduced. The MV715 was a multifunctional office product that gave users the capability to fax, copy, and print from one station. Potential customers were skeptical that a single product could take the place of several others. Ricoh Corporation decided to interview customers who had purchased the MV715 to determine how they used the product and if it had made their offices more efficient. After careful analysis of interviews with 200 buyers, the company discovered that salespeople had not adjusted their selling style to fit the new product. They had failed to position the product so that it appealed to buyers.[10]

Price is just one factor to consider when you are selling a new product such as the Ricoh MV715. A product that is both new and innovative will often require the efforts of a highly motivated salesperson who has received intensive sales and technical training.[11] Selling strategies used during the new and emerging stage (see Fig. 6.2) are designed to develop a new level of expectation, change habits, and in some cases establish a new standard of quality. The goal is to build desire for the product.

SELLING MATURE AND WELL-ESTABLISHED PRODUCTS

Mature and well-established products are usually characterized by intense competition as new brands enter the market. At this point, customers accept the products and are aware of competing products. With new and emerging products, salespeople may initially have little or no competition and may dominate the market. However, this condition may not last long.

Sun Life Assurance Company of Canada regularly provides its 1500 independent sales agents with new products. Yet the company finds that its new products are quickly copied by competing insurance companies. When

---

Building Relationships through Technology

MANAGING NEW PRODUCT INFORMATION WITH CRM

Today, salespeople are challenged to manage a steady stream of information about customers (needs) and products (solutions). From this stream of information, the sales professional must select product information that will be relevant to a specific customer and deliver the information in a manner that the customer can understand. CRM assists the busy salesperson by providing tools that can collect information and link it to those who need it. Most CRM systems can receive and organize information from e-mail, from Web sites, and from the files of reference material that are kept within a company's information system. Sales professionals can add value to this information by summarizing, combining, and tailoring the information to meet a customer's needs.

When new product information is received, databases of customer data can be quickly searched to find those customers who might have an interest. The new product information can be merged into an e-mail, fax, or letter to that customer, along with other information (benefits) that help the customer assess its value. Later, the CRM system can display a follow-up alert, while reminding the sales professional of the information that was shared with the customer. (See the exercise Informing Customers with CRM on page 143 for more information.)

Figure 6.2 Product-selling strategies for positioning new and emerging products versus mature and well-established products

Product selling strategy	Product selling strategy
• Develop new levels of expectations • Change habits • Establish new standards • Build desire for product • Focus on creating new markets	• Emphasize brand superiority • Emphasize company superiority • Point out unique features • Provide outstanding customer service • Focus on sustaining existing market share

SELL QUALITY
...without saying a word.
Heinz
America's Favorite Ketchup

Salespeople who sell mature and well-established products emphasize brand superiority. In this promotion piece, Heinz is positioning its brand name.

competing products enter the market, Sun Life sales agents must adopt new strategies. One positioning strategy is to emphasize the company's 125 years of superior service to policyholders and its undeniable financial strength. Agents often describe Sun Life as a supportive company that gives high priority to service after the sale, and a stable company that will be around to service future needs.[12] The objective is to create an awareness in the customer's mind that Sun Life is a solid company with a long history of good service to policyholders.

The relationship strategy is often critical in selling mature and well-established products. To maintain market share and ward off competitors, many salespeople work hard to maintain a strong relationship with the customer. At Sun Life, salespeople have found that good service after the sale is one of the best selling strategies because it builds customer loyalty.

POSITIONING PRODUCTS WITH A PRICE STRATEGY

Price, promotion, product, and distribution are the four elements that make up the marketing mix. Pricing decisions must be made at each stage of the product life cycle. Therefore, setting the price can be a complex process. The first step in establishing price is to determine the firm's pricing objectives. Some firms set their prices to maximize their profits; they aim for a price as high as possible without causing a disproportionate reduction in unit sales. Other firms set a market share objective; management may decide that the strategic advantage of an increased market share outweighs a temporary reduction in profits. Many of the new companies doing business on the Internet have adopted this approach.

Pricing strategies often reflect the product's position in the product life cycle. When compact disc players were in the new and emerging stage, customers who wanted this innovative equipment were willing to accept the $1000 per unit price tag.

TRANSACTIONAL SELLING TACTICS THAT EMPHASIZE LOW PRICE

Some marketers have established a positioning plan that emphasizes low price and the use of transactional selling tactics. These companies maintain a basic strategy that focuses on meeting competition. If the firm has meeting competition as its pricing goal, it makes every effort to charge prices that are identical or close to those of the competition. Once this positioning strategy has been adopted, the sales force is given several price tactics to use. Salespeople can alter (lower) the base price through the use of discounts and allowances. Discounts and allowances can take a variety of forms. A few of the more common ones follow:

Quantity discount. The **quantity discount** allows the buyer a lower price for purchasing in multiple units or above a specified dollar amount.

Time-period pricing. With **time-period pricing** the salesperson adjusts the price up or down during specific times to spur or acknowledge changes in demand.[13] Off-season travel and lodging prices provide an example.

Promotional allowances. A **promotional allowance** is a price reduction given to a customer who participates in an advertising or a sales support program. Many salespeople give supermarkets promotional allowances for advertising or displaying a manufacturer's products.

Another option available to salespeople facing a buyer with a low price buying strategy is to "unbundle" product features. Let's assume that a price-conscious customer wants to schedule a conference that will be accompanied by a banquet-style meal, thereby eliminating the need for servers. This product configuration involves less cost to the seller, and the cost savings can be passed on to the buyer. A salesperson representing a line of computer products might reduce the selling price by altering or eliminating certain assurances and/or warranties.

These examples represent only a small sample of the many discounts and allowances salespeople use to compete on the basis of price. Price discounting is a competitive tool available to large numbers of salespeople. Excessive focus on low prices and generous discounts, however, can have a negative impact on profits and sales commissions.

CONSEQUENCES OF USING LOW-PRICE TACTICS

Pricing is a critical factor in the sale of many products and services. In markets where competition is extremely strong, setting a product's price may be a firm's most complicated and important decision.

The authors of *The Discipline of Market Leaders* encourage business firms to pick one of three disciplines—best price, best product, or best service—and then do whatever is necessary to outdistance the competition. However, the authors caution us not to ignore the other two disciplines: "You design your business to excel in one direction, but you also have to strive to hit the minimum in the others."[14] Prior to using low-price tactics, everyone involved in sales and marketing should answer these questions:

- *Are you selling to high- or low-involvement buyers?* Some people are emotionally involved with respected brands, such as BMW, Sony, and American Express. A part of their identity depends on buying the product they consider the best. Low-involvement buyers care mostly about price.[15]

- *How important is quality in the mind of the buyer?* If buyers do not fully understand the price-quality relationship, they may judge the product by its price. For a growing number of customers, long-term value is more important than short-term savings that result from low prices. A broad-based desire for high quality and "value" as opposed to the lowest possible price suggests that price alone is an inadequate competitive tool.[16]

quantity discount A price reduction made to encourage a larger volume purchase than would otherwise be expected.

time-period pricing Adjusting prices up or down during specific times to spur or acknowledge changes in demand.

promotional allowance A price reduction given to a customer who participates in an advertising or sales support program.

Building Quality Partnerships

HOW DO CUSTOMERS JUDGE SERVICE QUALITY?

In the growing service industry there is intense price competition. From a distance one gets the impression that every buyer decision hinges on price alone. However, a closer examination of service purchases indicates that service quality is an important factor when it comes to developing a long-term relationship with customers.

How do customers judge service quality? Researchers at Texas A&M University have discovered valuable insights about customer perceptions of service quality. They surveyed hundreds of customers in a variety of service industries and discovered that five service-quality dimensions emerged:

1. *Tangibles* are things the customers can see, such as the appearance of personnel and equipment.

2. *Reliability* is the ability to perform the desired service dependably, accurately, and consistently.

3. *Responsiveness* is the willingness of sales and customer service personnel to provide prompt service and help customers.

4. *Assurance* includes the employees' knowledge, courtesy, and ability to convey trust and confidence.

5. *Empathy* means the provision of caring, individualized attention to customers.

Customers apparently judge the quality of each service transaction in terms of these five quality dimensions. Companies need to review these service-quality dimensions and make sure that each area measures up to the customer's expectations. Salespeople should recognize that these dimensions have the potential to add value to the services they sell.[a]

- *How important is service after the sale?* For many buyers, service after the sale is a critical factor. In some cases, low-price tactics mean less service. If low price results in fewer services after the sale or a reduction in the quality of service, some customers will be less likely to buy the product.

THE INFLUENCE OF ELECTRONIC BUSINESS ON PRICING

Companies large and small are racing to discover new sales and marketing opportunities on the Internet. Products ranging from personal computers, to airline tickets, to equity stocks and mutual funds can now be purchased online. Salespeople who are involved primarily in transactional selling, and add little or no value to the sales transaction, will often not be able to compete with online vendors. To illustrate, consider the purchase of stocks online from one of Canada's many discount brokers. At the present time it's possible to make an online purchase for a fraction of the cost of using a full-service broker. A well-informed buyer, willing to visit several Web sites, can make decisions based on online information and investing tools that were beyond the understanding of the average investor only a few years ago. Persons who need little or no assistance buying stocks can visit Canada's largest discount broker, TD Waterhouse, or one of the many others, including E*Trade Canada, Royal Bank Action Direct, Bank of Montreal InvestorLine, CIBC Investor's Edge, or Scotia Discount Brokerage, to name only a few of the many choices available to informed consumers. The person who wants help selecting a stock can turn to a full-service broker such as Merrill Lynch, CIBC Wood Gundy, Nesbitt Burns, or Scotia McLeod. Full-service broker revenues are still about five times that of discount brokers, but their share is decreasing.[17] They will survive and prosper only as long as they continue to add value to the sales transaction.

Customers who buy airline tickets online, however, may pay higher prices than they would through a travel agent. While the airlines do not charge a premium for online purchases, they also do not advise customers of less expensive routings or travel days. Customers who want online convenience must ensure they are making informed decisions if they wish the best prices. Online ticket purchases are increasing, particularly among frequent flyers, but they still account for only a very small percentage of sales.

The new economy is reshaping the world of commerce, and every buyer continues to have more choices.

POSITIONING YOUR PRODUCT WITH A VALUE-ADDED STRATEGY

Many progressive marketers have adopted a market plan that emphasizes **value-added strategies**. Companies add value to their product with one or more intangibles such as better-trained salespeople, increased levels of courtesy, more dependable product deliveries, better service after the sale, and innovations that truly improve the product's value in the eyes of the customer. In today's highly competitive marketplace these value-added benefits give the company a unique niche and a competitive edge.

value-added strategies Relationship, product, or service strategies that a company uses that add value for the customer.

When Raytheon Company began selling IBM computer clones, salespeople emphasized the lower price and similarities in the products. However, price discounting alone proved insufficient when competing with a well-established brand name. Once the salespeople began to emphasize the differences in the products, especially features that improved the efficiency of users, sales improved. In the buyer's mind, productivity, more than price, added value to the Raytheon computers.[18]

Customers who visit Alive & Well Canada Inc. in Markham, Ontario are introduced to a value-added shopping experience. The store specializes in discount women's wear, but it also has a large selection of men's and children's

www.shopcanada.com/
alive&well.html

© Edgar Argo.

"WE HAVE QUALITY AND WE HAVE LOW PRICES...
WHICH DO YOU WANT?"

Hewlett-Packard uses a value-added selling strategy and reminds customers that price is only the tip of the iceberg.

wear, and gifts and housewares. Each department offers a wide selection of top-quality products, and shoppers are waited on by well-trained salespeople who are courteous and knowledgeable. Shoppers are offered free beverages, electric reclining massage chairs, and infant change tables in the washrooms, all designed to help make the shopping experience an enjoyable one. There is also a nine-metre pirate ship with a lookout tower, children's videos, and free strollers for shoppers who visit with small children.[19]

VALUE ADDED—A NEW CHALLENGE FOR SALESPEOPLE

Salespeople are usually in the best position to explain the features and benefits that add value to a product or service. Adding value starts with building a knowledge base. Dan Kosch, president of a sales consulting and training company, says, "Show customers that you understand their business, their concerns, and what they hope to accomplish."[20] This knowledge will help you direct the customer's attention from price to value.

In a business-to-business selling situation the most powerful value-added strategy is often one that enhances the customer's profitability. The salesperson describes features, programs, and services that affect the customer's profits by enhancing revenues, reducing costs, or helping deflect future costs.[21] Sales representatives employed by Airgas, North America's leading supplier of industrial, medical and specialty gases and related equipment, emphasize to customers the value of doing business with a vendor that can meet all of their primary needs: quality products that are delivered on time; orders that are complete; and bills that are accurate. They explain that doing business with a single vendor can reduce procurement costs. Once the customer's needs are determined, salespeople identify the cost savings, put a dollar figure on those savings, and then support the numbers with documentation. Airgas does not attempt to be a low-price vendor. The strategy is to show the customer the difference between buying a product that's a one-time, low-price solution and developing a long-term relationship with a dependable and efficient full service provider.[22]

In some cases the salesperson can add value by doing something extra for the customer. For example, the salesperson might offer to help a customer identify ways to make his or her business more efficient. Suggestions that result in improved cash flow, more effective use of equipment, or expansion of the customer base will certainly be appreciated. This assistance will add value to the relationship between the salesperson and the customer.

Selling the Value-Added Product

To understand fully the importance of the value-added concept in selling, and how to apply it in a variety of selling situations, it helps to visualize every product as being four-dimensional. The *total product* is made up of four "possible" products: the generic product, the expected product, the value-added product, and the potential product[23] (Fig. 6.3).

GENERIC PRODUCT

generic product Describes only the basic substantive product being sold.

The **generic product** is the basic, substantive product you are selling. *Generic product* describes only the product category, for example, life insurance, rental cars, clothing, hotels, or personal computers. Every Ritz-Carlton hotel offers guest rooms, food and beverage service (restaurants, bars, and banquet space), meeting rooms, guest parking, and other basic services. Alive & Well, mentioned earlier in this chapter, provides categories of goods traditional to a discount specialty retailer.[24] The generic products at a bank are money that can be loaned to customers and basic chequing account services.

The capability of delivering a generic product simply gives the marketer the right to play in the game, to compete in the marketplace.[25] Generic products, even the lowest priced ones, often cannot compete with products that are "expected" by the customer.

EXPECTED PRODUCT

Every customer has minimal purchase expectations that exceed the generic product itself.[26] Ritz-Carlton must offer not only a comfortable guest room, but also a clean one. Some customers expect a "super" clean room. The **expected product** is everything that represents the customer's minimal expectations. The customer at Alive & Well will *expect* current fashions, a good selection, discount prices, and well-informed salespeople.

expected product Everything that represents the customer's minimal expectations.

The minimal purchase conditions vary among customers, so the salesperson must acquire information concerning the expected product that exists in the customer's mind. Every customer will perceive the product in individualized terms, which a salesperson cannot anticipate. To say that every customer is unique might seem trite, but when salespeople fully accept this fundamental of personal selling, they are better prepared to apply the value-added concept.

When the customer expects more than the generic product, the generic product can be sold *only* if those expectations are met.[27] To determine each customer's expectations requires the salesperson to make observations, conduct background checks, ask questions, and listen to what the customer is saying. We are attempting to discover both feelings and facts.

Research reported in the *Harvard Business Review* indicates that it is very difficult to build customer loyalty if you are selling only the expected product. Customer satisfaction and loyalty do not always move in tandem. The customer who purchases the services of a consulting firm may feel satisfied after the project is completed, but may choose a different consulting firm the next time. Customer loyalty is more likely to increase when the purchase involves a "value-added" product.[28]

VALUE-ADDED PRODUCT

The **value-added product** exists when salespeople offer customers more than they expect. When you make a reservation at one of the Ritz-Carlton hotels and request a special amenity such as a tennis lesson, a record of this request is maintained in the computer system. If you make a reservation at another Ritz-Carlton at some future date, the agent will inform you of the availability of a tennis court. The guest who buys chocolate-chip cookies in the lobby gift shop in New Orleans may find a basket of them waiting in his room in Boston two weeks later. The hotel company uses modern technology to surprise and delight guests, and provide a value-added product.[29] Alive & Well provides many things to enhance customers' shopping experiences. Most retailers will not allow food or beverages in their stores. Being offered free beverages is certainly more than most customers expect. They too are getting a value-added product.

value-added product Product that exists when salespeople offer the customer more than they expect.

Saturn has adopted a value-added product strategy that emphasizes the ability of salespeople to solve customers' problems.

Figure 6.3 The Total Product Concept. An understanding of the four "possible" products is helpful when the salesperson develops a presentation for specific types of customers.

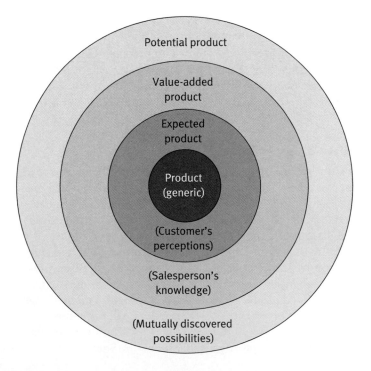

As competition intensifies, and as products and prices become more similar, companies must work harder to distinguish themselves and their products from the competition. They must increase their efforts to find out what customers need and then satisfy those needs with added value. In most cases, the salesperson delivers the value-added product.[30]

How can a salesperson create a value-added product or service? Larry Wilson, noted author and sales consultant, says that adding value means *always* working outside your job description to exceed customer expectations.[31] Salespeople who have adopted the value-added philosophy routinely meet clients' expectations and then do things that exceed those expectations.

The value-added product strategy will vary from one situation to another. Eileen Tertocha, a sales representative with Skipper Morrison Realtors, has developed a unique value-added strategy for new homeowners:

> *I give my customers first-class treatment on moving day, including plenty to eat for both the family and the movers. Then, on a regular day-to-day basis, I check to see if everything is going okay or if they need any help from me or anyone else.*[32]

Eileen Tertocha's goal is to make moving as easy as possible. She goes beyond the customer's expectations to take care of a variety of details.

One of the most powerful value-added strategies is personalized service. This **interpersonal value** is win-win relationship-building with the customer (as described in Chapter 3) that results from keeping that person's best interests always at the forefront. Marilyn Carlson Nelson, CEO of Carlson Companies Inc., one of the largest privately held companies in the world, says personal selling is really about proving that you are a good match for your customer and then backing your claim with facts. She also views selling as a service:

> *Selling is not about peddling a product. It's about wrapping that product in a service—and about selling both the product and the service as an experience. That approach to selling helps create a vital element of the process: a relationship.*[33]

interpersonal value Win-win relationship building with the customer that results from keeping that person's best interest always at the forefront.

POTENTIAL PRODUCT

After the value-added product has been developed, the salesperson should begin to conceptualize the **potential product.** The potential product refers to what may remain to be done; that is, what is possible.[34] As the level of competition increases, especially in the case of mature products, salespeople must look into the future and explore new possibilities.

In the highly competitive food services industry, restaurant owners like to do business with a distribution sales representative (DSR) who wants to help make the business profitable. The DSR who assumes this role becomes a true partner and looks beyond the customer's immediate and basic needs. The potential product might consist of a careful study of the restaurant's current menu and appropriate recommendations to the owner. To deliver the potential product a salesperson must discover and satisfy new customer needs, which requires imagination and creativity.

Steelcase Incorporated, a leading manufacturer of office furniture, recently developed the Personal Harbor Workspaces. The product is designed to be clustered around common work areas that invite teamwork and collaboration. These circular workstations offer buyers a twenty-first-century version of the traditional office cubicle. The podlike workstation is such a departure from con-

potential product Refers to what may remain to be done; that is, what is possible.

Selling in Action

SETTING YOUR PROFESSIONAL FEES

The age of information has created many career opportunities for people who want to sell professional services. Strong demand for professional services has surfaced in such diverse fields as telecommunications, banking, computer technology, training, and health care. Dana Martin spent 18 years working in the human resources division of Allstate Insurance. His specialty was the design and delivery of training programs. Recently he decided to leave the corporate environment and start his own training firm. Martin, like thousands of other professional service providers, had to decide how much to charge for his service. Should he price his service on an hourly basis or on a project basis? Here are some things to consider when determining fees:

- *Experience:* In the case of Dana Martin, new clients benefit from what he has learned during his many years at Allstate.

- *Exclusivity:* If you are one of only a small number of people with a particular capability, you may be able to charge more. Specialists often charge higher fees than generalists.

- *Target Market:* Some markets are very price sensitive. If you are selling your services to large corporations that are used to paying high fees, you may be able to set your fees higher. If you are providing your services to small business clients, expect resistance to high fees.

- *Value:* How important is your service to the client? In the late 1990s many companies needed help preparing their computers for transition to the year 2000. This was known as the Y2K problem. Some firms were willing to pay high fees for this assistance. Some service providers charge higher fees because they add value in one form or another.[b]

ventional office design that customers were initially unable to comprehend its potential. Salespeople quickly learned that a traditional product-oriented presentation would not work. Meetings between Steelcase salespeople and customers involved discussions of concepts such as team building, organizational communication, and employee interaction. Steelcase developed "advanced solution teams" that adopted a true consultative role. These teams meet with people in the organization who are more interested in the potential of the Personal Harbor Workspaces than in their price.[35]

The potential product is more likely to be developed by salespeople who are close to their customers. Many high-performing salespeople explore product possibilities with their customers on a regular basis. Potential products are often mutually discovered during these exchanges.

Adding Value—A Future Perspective

There is every indication that product selling strategies that add value will become more important in the future. New-product life cycles have shrunk by half or more during the past decade. A life cycle of six months is not uncommon.[36] Value-added selling strategies can be very effective during the new and emerging stage. Some companies that have experienced low profits with low-priced products will be reinventing their products. They will develop products that provide benefits people think are worth paying for. Maytag Corporation developed the environment-friendly Neptune washer, which has been popular among affluent customers. Priced at nearly $1600, the Neptune costs about twice as much as a conventional washer.[37]

General Mills is emphasizing a value-added strategy by supplying independent distributor salespeople with training materials and programs.

Products have always been characterized by their fixed and uniform design, whereas services are much easier to customize.[38] The new economy is primarily a service economy that very often gives buyers a customized solution to their problem. Many buyers are searching for a solution that includes the right combination of value-added attributes.

Summary

Success in today's dynamic global economy requires the continual positioning and repositioning of products. Product positioning involves those decisions and activities intended to create and maintain a certain concept of the firm's product in the customer's mind. Salespeople can make an important contribution to the process of product positioning. In many cases they assume an important role in product differentiation.

We noted that today's better-educated customers are often seeking a cluster of satisfactions. They seek satisfactions that arise from the product itself, from the company that makes or distributes the product, and from the salesperson who sells and services the product.

We introduced the major product-positioning strategies available to salespeople: positioning new and emerging products versus mature and well-established products; positioning with a price strategy, and positioning with a value-added strategy.

Part of this chapter was devoted to the total product concept. The total product is made up of four possible products. This range of possibilities includes the generic product, the expected product, the value-added product, and the potential product.

Key Terms

Product Positioning 124	*Value-Added Strategy 133*
Satisfactions 126	*Generic Product 136*
Product Life Cycle 127	*Expected Product 137*
Quantity Discount 131	*Value-Added Product 137*
Time-Period Pricing 131	*Interpersonal Value 139*
Promotional Allowance 131	*Potential Product 139*

Review Questions

1. Why has product differentiation become so important in sales and marketing?
2. According to Ted Levitt, what is the definition of a product? What satisfactions do customers want?
3. Explain what is meant by *positioning* as a product-selling strategy.
4. Why have salespeople assumed an important role in positioning products? What major economic developments have influenced product positioning?
5. Briefly describe the influence of electronic business on pricing. What types of products are sold on the Internet?
6. What are the possible consequences a salesperson might experience when using low-price tactics?

7. Read the Building Quality Partnerships insight titled How Do Customers Judge Service Quality on page 132. How might this information help a salesperson who wants to adopt the value-added selling strategy?

8. What are some of the common ways salespeople add value to the products they sell?

9. What are the four possible products that make up the *total product* concept?

10. Describe the differences between a generic product and a value-added product.

Application Exercises

1. Obtain catalogues from two competing industrial supply firms or two competing direct mail catalogue companies. Assume one of the represented businesses is your employer. After studying the catalogues, make a comparative analysis of your company's competitive advantages.

2. The Delta Hotels & Resorts chain illustrates the total product concept discussed in this chapter. Research value-added information on the Delta Whistler Resort by visiting Delta's Web site. Click on Delta Whistler Resort and examine the information presented on conference facilities, restaurants and lounges, golf packages, skiing, etc.

 www.deltahotels.com

3. Interview the manager of a local supermarket that sells a large assortment of national brands such as Nabisco, Kellogg's, and McCain. Ask this person what kinds of appeals are used by sales representatives of national brand products when they request more shelf space. Determine how frequently they offer trade or advertising allowances.

4. Call a local financial services representative who specializes in stock, bond, or equity fund transactions. Ask what percentage of clients rely on the information given to make complex decisions on their investments. Also ask this person if customers feel that advice in custom fitting investment programs adds value to their decision making. Find out whether financial products are getting more or less complex and what effect this will have on providing value-added service in the future.

CRM Application Exercise

Informing Customers with CRM

The notes in the ACT! database software contain two references to extranets, another system offered by SimNet Systems. One account is a prospective buyer of an extranet who needs more information. The other account has an extranet and is willing to show it to others. The Reference Library also contains information about private virtual networks, including extranets. Find the two accounts by selecting Lookup, Keyword, type "Extranet", check Notes, uncheck Contact, and press Enter.

After searching, ACT! will display two records. An examination of the notes will show the account with an extranet and the one with an interest. Make a note of the name of the organization now using an extranet. Close the notes screen (File, Close) and use the Page Up or Page Down key to display the account that needs information. Select <u>V</u>iew, <u>R</u>eference Library to display the information about networks. Page Down to the last paragraph of that document, entitled VPN. Highlight the paragraph with your mouse and select <u>E</u>dit, <u>C</u>opy. Select <u>F</u>ile, <u>C</u>lose to close the library.

Select <u>W</u>rite, <u>L</u>etter, and enter the following: "You might find this of interest." Press Enter twice to begin a new paragraph. Select <u>E</u>dit, <u>P</u>aste to add the information from the Reference Library. Press Enter twice again for a new paragraph and type "If you wish, I can arrange for you to look at the extranet in use at" then enter the name of the person and organization using the extranet. Select <u>F</u>ile, <u>P</u>rint (Ctrl+P) to print the letter and <u>F</u>ile, <u>C</u>lose to close the letter window.

Video Case

In 1988, Greg Brophy had $32 000 and he was looking for a business. He borrowed an additional $160 000 and bought a large truck and a paper shredder. Today, in his mid-30s, he is president and owner of Shred-it Canada Corporation, which has more than 300 trucks operating from more than 70 offices in major cities throughout Canada, the United States, England, Belgium, Singapore, Hong Kong, and Argentina. Systemwide sales for 1999 were $112 million, and sales for 2000 are expected to be $145 million.

Greg Brophy understands the consultative selling process, and he makes sure that his salespeople do, too. There is no question that timing was important to the success of Shred-it, but Greg Brophy's sales ability and his selling philosophy also played a key role. He says, "Administrative work can always be done at night. The day is for selling." That's why Greg Brophy still regularly spends time visiting major accounts or making sales calls with salespeople. He has developed a series of videos to help train Shred-it salespeople, and he requires all senior executives to visit customers as well.

When a salesperson first visits a potential customer, they spend about two minutes talking about Shred-it and its history. Then they ask about the customer's situation, how satisfied they are with it, and what they would change if they could. The salesperson carefully records the responses. "It is super important that they take notes, and that the customer sees them taking notes," says Greg Brophy. Throughout this process the salesperson identifies the customer's buying motives, then describes the Shred-it service in greater detail, molding the presentation to the needs of each customer. According to Greg Brophy, "If the customer is interested in environmental issues and recycling, we talk about how we manage recycling. If the customer has no interest, we don't waste a lot of time talking about it."

At this stage the salesperson always asks to tour the customer's office. This provides a lot of knowledge concerning the size of the operation, who the key people are, where the main paper collection points are, and which areas have confidential information. Throughout the tour the salesperson clarifies how the customer handles paper waste and what their concerns are with respect to waste management, all the while continuing to take notes and promoting the benefits of the Shred-it service in terms of the customer's needs.

Finally, when the salesperson feels comfortable enough to make an offer, they recommend the number and size of containers that the customer will need. They continue to identify the customer's needs with respect to how often the customer would like Shred-it to come, and what days of the week and times of the day would be most appropriate. This allows the salesperson to make a final price offer for the service. The salesperson then tries to close the sale. The customer is offered the service at a specified price, is reminded about the benefits of using Shred-it, and is given the opportunity to try the service for one month. Greg Brophy says, "We are so sure that customers will be satisfied with our service that we guarantee satisfaction. We tell them that if we cannot cut their costs by 25 percent and if they are not completely satisfied with our service after one month, we will remove the containers from their office and we will shred the invoice so there is no charge to them." Since promising that guarantee, salespeople have improved their ability to close sales from 30 percent to 70 percent of prospects.[39]

Questions

1. To fulfill a problem-solving need, salespeople must often be prepared to communicate effectively with customers who are seeking a cluster of satisfactions (see Fig. 6.1). Is it likely that a customer who is considering buying on-site shredding services will seek information regarding all three dimensions of the Product Selling Model? Explain, using Shred-it Canada as an example.

2. Should Shred-it Canada position itself with a price or a value-added strategy? Explain.

3. Using Shred-it Canada as an example, explain the total product concept. What would be the generic, expected, and value-added products?

Part IV

Developing a Customer Strategy

With increased knowledge of the customer, the salesperson is in a better position to achieve sales goals. This part presents information on understanding buyer behaviour, discovering individual customer needs, and developing a prospect base.

BUILDING QUALITY PARTNERSHIPS

One of the two
sustainable strategic
advantages
in the new
global marketplace
is an obsession
with customers.
Customers, not
markets.

Tom Peters
Thriving on Chaos

7

Understanding Buyer Behaviour

LEARNING OBJECTIVES

When you finish reading this chapter, you should be able to

1. Discuss the meaning of a customer strategy

2. Understand the complex nature of customer behaviour

3. Discuss the social and psychological influences that shape customer buying decisions

4. Discuss the power of perception in shaping buying behaviour

5. Distinguish between emotional and rational buying motives

6. Distinguish between patronage and product buying motives

7. Explain three commonly accepted theories that explain how people arrive at a buying decision

8. Describe three ways to discover individual customer buying motives

The final decade of the twentieth century was characterized by a major power shift in the direction of the customer. The new economy not only gives the customer more choices, it provides more information needed to make those choices. Granted, information overload often creates confusion in the marketplace, but we must not lose sight of the power shift.

We know that new products must satisfy the customer's needs, but identifying these needs can be very challenging. Pembina Dodge Chrysler, one of five Chrysler dealerships in Winnipeg, understands this challenge. Several times it has won the President's Challenge Award that requires superior performance in three areas: parts, service, and sales.

Ron Trudel, a senior salesperson at the dealership, has been recognized many times as one of the best Chrysler Canada dealer salespeople. In an environment that has been growing increasingly competitive with both new product introductions and strong global competitors, Ron Trudel continues to be successful because he understands the customer buying decision process and how to satisfy customer needs. He has a clearly focused customer strategy.[1]

Developing a Customer Strategy

The greatest challenge to salespeople in the age of information is to improve responsiveness to customers. In fact, a growing number of sales professionals believe the customer has supplanted the product as the driving force in sales today.[2] As noted by Larry Wilson, "The products of one company in an industry are becoming more and more similar to those of the competition."[3] The salesperson can distinguish between similar products and services and help the customer to perceive important differences.

ADDING VALUE WITH A CUSTOMER STRATEGY

A **customer strategy** is a carefully conceived plan that will result in maximum customer responsiveness. One major dimension of this strategy is to achieve a better understanding of the customer's buying needs and motives. When salespeople take time to discover these needs and motives, they are in a much better position to offer customers a value-added solution to their buying problem.

customer strategy A carefully conceived plan that will result in maximum customer responsiveness.

Every salesperson who wants to develop repeat business should figure out a way to collect and systematize customer information. As part of the customer strategy, many salespeople use some type of customer profile. The authors of *Reengineering the Corporation* discuss the importance of collecting information about the unique and particular needs of each customer:

> *Customers—consumers and corporations alike—demand products and services designed for their unique and particular needs. There is no longer any such notion as* the *customer; there is only* this *customer, the one with whom a seller is dealing at the moment and who now has the capacity to indulge his or her own personal tastes.*[4]

The first prescription for developing a customer strategy focuses on buyer behaviour (Fig. 7.1). Every salesperson needs a general understanding of why and how people buy, which is the topic of this chapter. The second prescription emphasizes the discovery of individual customer needs. The third prescription for developing a customer strategy emphasizes building a strong prospect base, which is discussed in Chapter 8.

The Complex Nature of Customer Behaviour

The forces that motivate customers can be complex. Arch McGill, a former vice-president of IBM, reminds us that individual customers perceive the product in their own terms, and that these terms may be "unique, idiosyncratic, human, emotional, end-of-the-day, irrational, erratic terms."[5] Different people doing the same thing (for example, purchasing a personal computer) may have different needs that motivate them, and each person may have several motives for a single action.

The proliferation of market research studies, public opinion polls, surveys, and reports of "averages" makes it easy to fall into the trap of thinking of the customer as a number. The customer is a person, not a statistic. Companies that fully accept this basic truth are likely to adopt a one-to-one marketing strategy. The one-to-one strategy is based on a bedrock concept: Treat different customers differently. The one-to-one marketer focuses on cultivating a long-term relationship with each customer in order to sell that customer many products

Figure 7.1 The greatest challenge to salespeople today is to improve responsiveness to customers. Understanding why and how customers buy and knowing who prospects are forms the foundation blocks for the salesperson to develop a highly responsive customer strategy.

Strategic/Consultative Selling Model	
Strategic step	**Prescription**
DEVELOP A PERSONAL SELLING PHILOSOPHY	✔ ADOPT MARKETING CONCEPT ✔ VALUE PERSONAL SELLING ✔ BECOME A PROBLEM SOLVER/PARTNER
DEVELOP A RELATIONSHIP STRATEGY	✔ ADOPT DOUBLE-WIN PHILOSOPHY ✔ PROJECT PROFESSIONAL IMAGE ✔ PRACTISE COMMUNICATION-STYLE FLEXING
DEVELOP A PRODUCT STRATEGY	✔ BECOME A PRODUCT EXPERT ✔ SELL BENEFITS ✔ CONFIGURE VALUE-ADDED SOLUTIONS
DEVELOP A CUSTOMER STRATEGY	○ UNDERSTAND BUYER BEHAVIOUR ○ DISCOVER CUSTOMER NEEDS ○ DEVELOP PROSPECT BASE

over an entire lifetime of patronage. This is a concept that works not only for the retail customer, but also for business-to-business transactions, distributors, and service providers both in the public and private sectors.[6]

Forces Influencing Buying Decisions

Figure 7.2 illustrates the many forces that influence buying decisions. Notice that individual psychological and physiological needs, combined with group social influences, shape customer perceptions and buying motives. As we explain each part of the model, a better understanding of buyer behaviour will emerge.

INDIVIDUAL NEEDS THAT SHAPE CUSTOMER BEHAVIOUR

To gain insights into customer behaviour motivated by individual needs, including physiological, security, social, esteem, and self-actualization needs, it is helpful to study the popular hierarchy of needs developed by Abraham Maslow. According to Maslow, basic human needs are arranged in a hierarchy according to their strength. His theory rests on the assumption that as each lower-level need is satisfied, the need at the next level demands attention.

Basic human needs have changed little throughout our economic history. However, the ways in which needs are fulfilled has changed greatly during the age of information.7 The starting point for developing an understanding of the forces influencing buying decisions is a review of the individual needs that shape the customer's behaviour.

Selling in Action

DEVELOPING A "SEGMENT BUSTER"

The Chrysler PT Cruiser has been described as a wacky-looking cross between a 1937 Ford and a London taxicab. Some view it as part 1920s gangster car and part 1950s hot rod. DaimlerChrysler AG describes the car as a surefire "segment buster" that combines the room of a minivan with the flair of a sport-utility vehicle and the utility of a small car. It will be built in Mexico and sold in North America and about 40 foreign markets.

DaimlerChrysler knows that some people will love the car and some will hate it. The PT (which stands for personal transportation) Cruiser is the company's first vehicle designed entirely through an unconventional market-research process known as "archetype research." The research was conducted by a French-born medical anthropologist named G. Clotaire Rapaille. The process began with a series of free-wheeling, three-hour focus-group sessions in Great Britain, France, Germany, Italy, and North America. With lights dimmed and mood music playing, participants were asked to drift back to their childhoods and jot down the memories invoked by the prototype PT Cruiser parked in the room. After the sessions, Dr. Rapaille and members of the research team pored over the stories looking for emotions sparked by the vehicle. This research led to major design changes that made the car look even more outlandish. The final design is one that thrills some and puts off others, just what the research team hoped to accomplish.[a]

PHYSIOLOGICAL NEEDS

Physiological needs, sometimes called primary needs, include the needs of food, water, and sleep. Maslow placed our physiological needs at the bottom of the pyramid. He believed that these basic needs tend to be strong in the minds of most people. As these more basic needs (hunger, thirst, sex, etc.) are satisfied, a person seeks to satisfy the higher needs. Efforts to satisfy the higher needs must be postponed until the basic physical needs are met.

Maslow describes people as "wanting" animals, who strive to satisfy higher needs after lower needs have been satisfied. People tend to satisfy their needs systematically in most cases, starting with the most basic and moving up the pyramid.

physiological needs   Primary or physical needs, including the need for food, water, sleep, and sex.

SECURITY NEEDS

After physiological needs have been satisfied, the next need level that tends to dominate is safety and security. **Security needs** represent our desire to be free from danger and uncertainty. The desire to satisfy the need for safety and security will often motivate people to purchase such items as medical and life insurance or a security alarm for their home or business. The buyer who voices a strong desire to have products delivered on time and undamaged may be motivated by security needs. For a banking customer the security need might surface as a desire for accessibility, timely hours of operation, or localized access to service.[8] Needless to say, working with a competent, trusted salesperson gives the customer a feeling of security.

security needs   These represent our desire to be free from danger and uncertainty, and include the need for clothing, shelter, and insurance.

SOCIAL NEEDS

Social needs, or the need to belong, reflect our desire for identification with a group and "social" approval from others. These needs help explain our continuing search for friendship, companionship, and long-term business relationships. This "need to belong" is more than just an urge—it is a fundamental human

social needs   Needs that reflect a person's desire for affection, identification with a group, and approval from others.

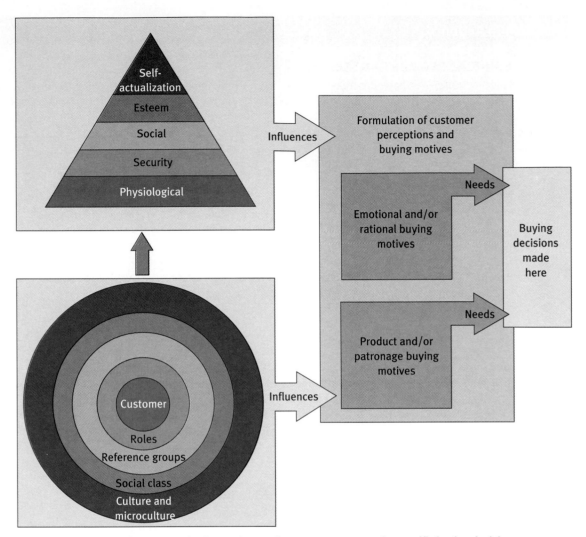

Figure 7.2 **The forces that motivate customers to make specific buying decisions are complex. This model illustrates the many factors that influence buyer behaviour. It can serve the salesperson as a guide for developing a highly responsive customer strategy.**

need.[9] This level of Maslow's hierarchy of needs helps us understand why many customers want to be treated as partners. They desire an accessible, two-way relationship.

ESTEEM NEEDS

esteem needs The desire to feel worthy in the eyes of others, to develop a sense of personal worth and adequacy or a feeling of competence and importance.

Esteem needs appear at the fourth level of Maslow's need priority model. Esteem needs reflect our desire to feel worthy in the eyes of others. We seek a sense of personal worth and adequacy, a feeling of competence. In simple terms, we want to feel that we are important. Esteem needs motivate people to seek recognition and "status" approval from others. These needs may provide the motivation to buy membership in an exclusive golf club or purchase an expensive car. When Mercedes-Benz Canada Inc. advertises its SL-Class cars with the ad copy "If Life Were Fair We Would All Have One," it is trying to appeal to prospects' esteem needs.

SELF-ACTUALIZATION NEEDS

Dr. Maslow defined the term **self-actualization** as a need for self-fulfillment, a full tapping of one's potential. It is the need to "be all that you can be," to have mastery over things you are doing. There are many forms of self-actualizing behaviour. Wanting to be better at whatever you do, whether your occupation or a hobby, is an expression of the need for self-actualization. A person who values good workmanship will purchase the highest quality tools to do the job. A person who plans to build a high quality stereo system may be very precise in the specifications of the products needed. In selling, we must be sensitive to the needs of people who are searching for a way to achieve self-actualization.

The five-level need priority model developed by Maslow is somewhat artificial in certain instances. At times, several of our needs interact within us. One example is the business lunch. Not only are you conducting business with a client, but you are also satisfying your need for food and beverages, to engage in social activities, and perhaps to seem important in your own eyes and, you hope, the eyes of your customer.[10] However, the model does provide salespeople with a practical way of understanding which need is most likely to dominate customer behaviour in certain circumstances.

self-actualization　The need for self-fulfillment; a full tapping of one's potential to meet a goal; the need to be everything one is capable of being.

Drawing by Richter; © 1977 The New Yorker Magazine, Inc.

"What do I do? I drive a Maserati."

The need to earn other people's admiration can be a strong motivating force.

GROUP INFLUENCES THAT SHAPE CUSTOMER BEHAVIOUR

As noted earlier, the people around us also influence our buying decisions. These **group influences** can be arranged into four major areas: (1) role influences, (2) reference groups, (3) social class, and (4) culture and microculture[11] (Fig. 7.3). Salespeople who understand these roles and influences can develop the type of insight customers view as being valuable.

group influences　These are the forces that other people exert on our buying behaviour.

A Certified Management Accountant designation helps people meet both esteem and self-actualization needs.

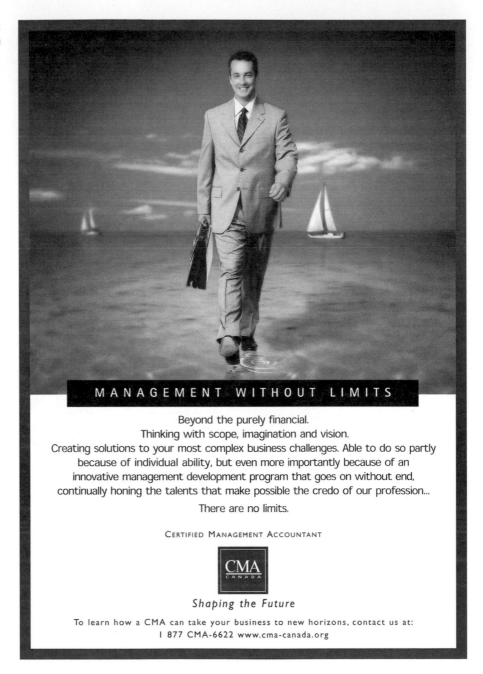

ROLE INFLUENCE

Throughout our lives we occupy positions within groups, organizations, and institutions. Closely associated with each position is a **role**: a set of characteristics and expected social behaviours based on the expectations of others. All the roles we assume (student, member of the school board, or position held at work) influence not only our general behaviour but also our buying behaviour. In today's society, for example, a woman may assume the role of mother at home and purchasing manager at work. In the manager's role she may feel the need to develop a conservative wardrobe or to attend a training course on leadership.

role A set of characteristics and expected social behaviours based on the expectations of others. All the roles we assume may influence our buying behaviour.

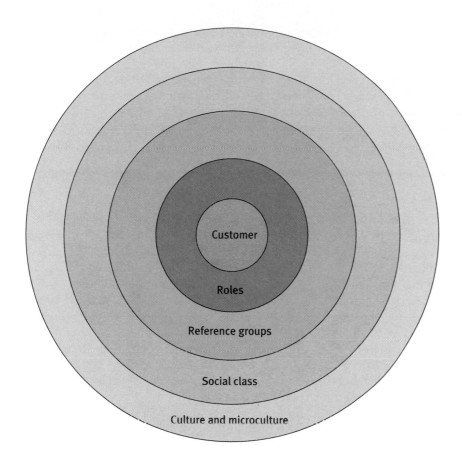

REFERENCE GROUP INFLUENCE

A **reference group** consists of the categories of people to which you see yourself as belonging and to which you habitually compare yourself. Members of a reference group tend to influence the values, attitudes, and behaviours of one another.[12] The reference group may act as a point of comparison and a source of information for the individual member. In the business community, the Canadian Professional Sales Association may provide a reference group for its members. As members of a reference group we often observe other people in the group to establish our own norms, and these norms become a guide for our purchasing activity. Of course, the degree to which a reference group influences a buying decision will depend on the strength of the individual's involvement with the group and the degree of susceptibility to reference group influence.

reference group   Two or more people who have well-established interpersonal communications and tend to influence the values, attitudes, and buying behaviours of one another. They act as a point of comparison and a source of information for a prospective buyer.

SOCIAL CLASS INFLUENCE

A **social class** consists of people who are similar in occupational prestige, values, lifestyles, interests, and behaviours.[13] The criteria used to rank people according to social class vary from one society to another. In some societies, land ownership allows entry into a higher social class; in other societies, education is a major key to achieving upper-class status. The neighbourhood we live in and the type, value, and condition of our home also represent class indicators. To some degree, individuals within social classes have similar attitudes, values, and possessions.

social class   A group of people who are similar in occupational prestige, values, lifestyles, interests, and behaviours.

How many social classes are there? There is no clear answer to that question, but sociologists usually employ between three and six categories. At one extreme is the upper class, which usually consists of "old money": people who possess inherited wealth. They buy large homes, obtain degrees from prestigious institutions, travel extensively, and tend to buy quality products. At the other extreme is the lower class, which is characterized by persons with little formal education and considerably less income. Marketers often focus attention on a specific social class. Metropolitan Life Insurance Company, a large provider of life insurance to the middle class, announced a plan to target more affluent customers for new business. Met Life assigned 300 salespeople to sell policies to individuals who earn $150 000 to $200 000 annually.[14]

CULTURAL INFLUENCE

culture The arts, beliefs, institutions, transmitted behaviour patterns, and thoughts of a community or population.

Culture can be defined as the accumulation of values, rules of behaviour, forms of expression, beliefs, transmitted behaviour patterns and the like for a group of people who share a common language and environment. Culture tends to encourage or discourage particular behaviours and mental processes.[15] We maintain and transmit our culture chiefly through language. Culture has considerable influence on buying behaviour. Today, culture is getting more attention because of the rapid increases in immigrant groups. As cultural diversity increases, companies must re-examine their sales and marketing strategies.

Within many cultures there are groups whose members share ideals and beliefs that differ from those held by the wider society of which they are a part. We call such a group a **microculture**.[16] Among the many Canadian microcultures are the teenage, elderly, and Native microcultures. Members of a microculture may have stronger preferences for certain types of foods, clothing, and housing.

microculture Within many cultures, the groups whose members share ideals and beliefs that differ from those held by the wider society of which they are a part.

A breakdown in communications, and even conflict, can arise from the differences between the culture of the sales representative and the culture of the customer. Consider the impact of culture on the daily work of pharmaceutical representatives. The culture of physicians is quite different than the culture of mainstream society. To complicate matters even further, there are microcultures within the physician group. For example, the religious convictions of one physician might keep her from prescribing a certain pharmaceutical product. A simple process of cultural awareness on the part of salespeople can prevent misunderstandings from happening.[17]

Building Relationships through Technology

MANAGING MULTIPLE CONTACTS WITH CRM

Salespeople often find that groups of their contacts have common interests and buying motives. Customers and prospects may be segmented into groups by buying influences, by the products they purchase, by the industries they are involved in, or by their size. Customer relationship management software can enable the salesperson to easily link contacts together as groups and "mass produce" information that is custom-fitted to the needs of people in a specific group. For example, each owner of a specific product may receive a telephone call, personalized letter, or report that describes the benefits of a new accessory available from the salesperson. (See the exercise Managing Multiple Contacts with CRM on page 171 for more information.)

Perception—How Customer Needs Are Formed

Perception is the process of selecting, organizing, and interpreting information inputs to produce meaning. The information inputs are sensations received through sight, taste, hearing, smell, and touch.[18] Our perception is shaped by group influences as well as by the psychological and physiological conditions within us (see Fig. 7.2). Perception determines what is seen and felt; therefore it influences our buying behaviour. The importance of perception was emphasized by Al Ries, co-author of *Positions: The Battle for Your Mind*: "It's perception that determines whether you win or lose in the marketplace."[19]

We tend to screen out or modify stimuli, a process known as *selective perception*, for two reasons. First, we cannot possibly be conscious of all inputs at one time; just the commercial messages we see and hear each day are enough to cause sensory overload. Second, we are conditioned by our social and cultural background, and by our physical and psychological needs, to use selectivity.

Buyers may screen out or modify information presented by a salesperson if it conflicts with their previously learned attitudes or beliefs. The prospect who is convinced that "I will never be able to master the personal computer" is apt to use selective perception when the salesperson begins discussing user-friendly features. Salespeople who can anticipate this problem of selective perception should acquire as much background information as possible before meeting with the prospect. During the first meeting with the customer, the salesperson should make every effort to build a strong relationship so the person opens up and freely discusses personal perceptions. Salespeople who do this have accepted one of the great truisms in sales and marketing: "Facts are negotiable. Perception is rock solid."

People involved in sales and marketing need to review their own perceptions periodically to see if they are accurate. For many years, marketers have mistakenly stereotyped older consumers as crotchety grandparents living on a

perception   A process whereby we receive stimuli (information) through our five senses and then assign meaning to them.

The image projected by Pentium, a processor from Intel, has considerable impact on buyer behaviour.

Guess who makes the Pentium processor even more fun?

modest fixed income. The truth is that many senior citizens are in the middle to high income bracket and see themselves as much younger than their chronological years.[20]

Buying Motives

buying motive An aroused need, drive, or desire that initiates the sequence of events that may lead to a purchase.

Every buying decision has a motive behind it. A **buying motive** can be thought of as an aroused need, drive, or desire. It acts as a force that stimulates behaviour intended to satisfy that aroused need. Our perceptions influence or shape this behaviour. An understanding of buying motives provides the salesperson with the reasons why customers buy.

As you might expect, some buying decisions are influenced by more than one buying motive. The buyer of catering services may want food of exceptional quality served quickly so all the guests can eat together. This customer may also be quite price conscious. In this situation the caterer should attempt to discover the **dominant buying motive** (DBM). The DBM will have the greatest influence on the buying decision.[21] If the customer is anxious to make a good impression on guests who have discriminating food tastes, then food quality may be the dominant buying motive.

dominant buying motive The motive that has the greatest influence on a customer's buying decision.

Successful salespeople have adopted a product strategy that involves discovery of the buying motives that will influence the purchase decision. In Chapter 10 we describe a need identification process that can be used to discover the customer's buying motives.

Emotional versus Rational Buying Motives

emotional buying motives Those motives that prompt the prospect to act as a result of an appeal to some sentiment or passion.

A careful study of buyer behaviour reveals that people make buying decisions based on both emotional and rational buying motives. An **emotional buying motive** is one that prompts the prospect to act because of an appeal to some sentiment or passion. When customers buy expensive Harley-Davidson motorcycles, they are paying for much more than a high-flying hog. They are purchasing entry into a community of like-minded enthusiasts who share a passion for all things Harley.[22] Emotions can be powerful and often serve as the foundation of the dominant buying motive. A **rational buying motive** usually appeals to the prospect's reason or judgment based on objective thought processes. Some common rational buying motives would include quality, price and availability of technical assistance.

rational buying motives Those motives that prompt the prospect to act because of an appeal to the prospect's reason or better judgment; include price, quality, and availability of technical assistance. Generally these result from an objective review of available information.

EMOTIONAL BUYING MOTIVES

A surprising number of purchases are guided by emotional buying motives. This is why many firms use emotional appeals. Even technology firms sometimes rely on these appeals. Compaq Computer Corporation asks, "Compaq—Has It Changed Your Life Yet?" GTE, the giant telecommunications firm, says, "We're working to help make your life easier." And ads for British Airways promote the new Club World: travellers enjoy 55 percent more legroom and unique cradle seats, which increase passenger comfort.

Doing business in Canada, or anyplace else in the world, is never purely a rational or logical process. To inspire people and move them in the right direction, you have to engage them emotionally.[23] In a world filled with look-alike products, emotional factors can have considerable influence. If two vendors have

Rational buying motives usually influence the purchase decisions of the professional buyer.

nearly identical products, then the influence of the vendors' salespeople becomes more important. The salesperson who is able to connect at a personal level will have the advantage.

It is emotions that help explain the "why" behind buying decisions. Salespeople should make every effort to discover the emotions that influence buying decisions. The salesperson who is able to identify and satisfy the customer's emotional buying motives is performing an important service.[24]

RATIONAL BUYING MOTIVES

A purchase based on rational buying motives is generally the result of an objective review of available information. The buyer closely examines product or service information with an attitude that is relatively free of emotion. Professional buyers or purchasing agents are most likely to be motivated by rational buying motives such as on-time delivery, financial gain, competent installation, saving of time, increased profits, or durability.

The buyers at Wal-Mart Canada purchase for the largest and most profitable retailer in the world. They are tough, aggressive, and focused on choosing products that will complement the selection of merchandise available at Wal-Mart stores. Eugene Dubejsky, National Sales Manager for Procter & Gamble, says: "Wal-Mart buyers also demand that salespeople are professional and knowledgeable about their products. The buyers want to do business with Canadian firms and have dramatically increased the amount of domestic merchandise in Wal-Mart stores since the company's arrival in Canada."[25]

In the face of increased competition, professional buyers such as those employed by Wal-Mart will want to partner with salespeople who can respond to their rational buying motives. This is especially true in the fields of manufacturing and processing, where salespeople are expected to offer powerful insights into helping firms make things better, faster, and cheaper.[26]

PATRONAGE VERSUS PRODUCT BUYING MOTIVES

Another way to help explain buyer behaviour is to distinguish between patronage and product buying motives. Patronage buying motives and product buying motives are learned reasons for buying. These buying motives are important because they can stimulate repeat business and referrals.

PATRONAGE BUYING MOTIVES

A **patronage buying motive** is one that causes the prospect to buy products from one particular business. The prospect has usually had prior direct or indirect contact with the business and has judged this contact to be beneficial. In those situations where there is little or no appreciable difference between two products, patronage motives can be highly important. At a time when look-alike products are very common, these motives take on a new degree of importance. Some typical patronage buying motives are:

Superior service. As noted earlier in this text, superior service adds value to the product. In many cases the value-added product builds customer loyalty.

patronage buying motive   A motive that causes the prospect to buy a product from one particular company rather than another. Typical patronage buying motives include superior service, attractive decor, product selection, and competence of the salesperson.

This advertisement helps Hewlett-Packard generate a prospect database for the sales force. It also helps the company discover the prospect's buying motives.

Now, what can Hewlett-Packard do for you?

Please check for the information you want:

☐ I want increased computing power for less cost.
☐ I want true multi-vendor connectivity.
☐ I want easier access to information.
☐ I want better service and support.

Name

Title

Company name

Street

City

State   Zip Code

MAIL TO: HEWLETT-PACKARD, Inquiries Manager, 19310 Pruneridge Ave., Dept. 740G, Cupertino, CA 95014

Or Call 1 800 752-0900, Dept. 740G

**hp HEWLETT®
PACKARD**

Selection. Some firms make every effort to carry a complete selection of products. The prospect is usually quite certain that the item needed will be available.

Competence of sales representatives. There is no doubt that the salesperson is in a unique position to develop a loyal customer following. A salesperson who knows the product and is willing to give "something extra" to the customer is an asset to any firm.

PRODUCT BUYING MOTIVES

A **product buying motive** is one that leads a prospect to purchase one product in preference to another. Interestingly enough, this decision is sometimes made without direct comparison between competing products; the buyer simply feels that one product is superior to another.

product buying motives Reasons that cause the prospect to buy one particular product brand or label over another. Typical product buying motives include brand preference, quality preference, price preference, and design or engineering preference.

3M has become a world leader by helping customers who value innovation.

1 Want a better finish?

2 Start with the colour purple.

There's just something about purple that rubs us the right way. Which is why we chose it for our state-of-the-art sandpaper. Designed specifically for wood, 3M™Regal™Abrasives take the manufacturing process to the next level by giving you what you've always wanted. Less. As in less dust. Our patented 3M™XODUST™ dust control treatment ensures a cleaner machine. Our patented 3M™Cubitron™ mineral contributes to a longer abrasive life. It's just one more colourful way we make the leap *from need to...*

Innovation

© 1999 9909-WA-10530E   *For more information, call 1-800-3M-HELPS, or internet: http//www.3m.com/Canada*

There are numerous buying motives that trigger prospects to select one product over another:

Brand preference. Many marketers seek to develop brand loyalty. Maytag, Mercedes-Benz, and United Van Lines serve as examples of companies that have developed a strong brand preference.

Quality preference. J. D. Power, founder of J. D. Power and Associates, says, "We define quality as what the customer wants."[27] Today's customer is likely to have high quality standards.

Price preference. Most prospects are price conscious to some degree. If a product has a price advantage over the competition and quality has not been sacrificed, it will probably enjoy success in the marketplace.

Design or engineering preference. Many companies are betting that superior product design will be the key to winning customers in the twenty-first century. One of these companies is Deere & Company, a maker of farm implements. The powerful 8000 model John Deere tractor, priced from $160 000 to $204 000, offers farmers design features such as an air conditioned cabin with excellent forward and rearward visibility and a four-wheel drive system that offers a tight turning radius.[28]

How Customers Make Buying Decisions

Several commonly accepted theories explain how people arrive at a buying decision. Three of the most popular theories are described here. One traditional point of view holds that the salesperson closes the sale by guiding the prospect through five mental processes. We refer to this approach as the **buyer action**

"I can't decide. I'm having a brand identity crisis."

theory. A second traditional theory is based on the assumption that a final buying decision is possible only after the prospect has answered five logical questions. This is called the **buyer resolution theory.** Both of these theories thrived during the past 40 years, when the main focus was on the product. The third explanation of how people buy is "prospect" oriented and is called the **need-satisfaction theory.** This approach to the selling–buying process gives maximum attention to a highly responsive customer strategy that ensures satisfaction of prospect needs. It has been adopted by successful marketers who realize the benefits associated with long-term partnerships.

THE BUYER ACTION THEORY

From a traditional point of view there are five mental steps that lead to a buying decision: (1) attention, (2) interest, (3) desire, (4) conviction, and (5) action. The salesperson's role is to guide the prospect through each step. These five steps have application in advertising, public relations, publicity, and sales promotion as well as in personal selling.

ATTENTION

There is no hope of selling a product unless you first get the prospect's attention. In some cases this is not an easy task. A potential buyer may be preoccupied with a variety of concerns and may view your presence as an intrusion. The salesperson can do a number of things to attract and hold a potential buyer's attention. These things are discussed in a later chapter.

INTEREST

The second step in the buying process is development of interest in the product. A salesperson must determine the best way to convert attention to interest. The manner in which this is done will vary, of course. In some selling situations the prospect's interest might be sparked by a product demonstration. In another situation the salesperson may use a series of stimulating questions to create interest.

DESIRE

Desire moves us to possess something or to experience something that we perceive as enjoyable or satisfying. It can be a compelling factor in life. We can all recall instances when the desire within us became almost overwhelming. This desire may have been kindled by the sounds of a high-quality stereo system or by the knowledge that a new computer will improve our productivity.

CONVICTION

At the conviction stage the prospect has decided that the product is a genuine value, with features that justify its price. Competing products have been ruled out. The salesperson has removed doubt from the buyer's mind. At this stage the prospect can rationalize the purchase to himself or herself and others.

ACTION

Once the buyer makes the first four decisions, the stage is set to close the sale. Sometimes the fifth decision is made quickly and effortlessly. In other cases the prospect shows signs of procrastination. In some cases a small amount of pressure applied at the right time will motivate buyer action. Several persuasive techniques available to the salesperson will be discussed later in this textbook.

buyer action theory   The five mental steps — attention, interest, desire, conviction, and action — that lead to a buying decision. This is a widely accepted theory in selling, advertising, and display that explains how customers buy.

buyer resolution theory   A selling theory that recognizes a purchase will be made only after the prospect has made five buying decisions involving specific affirmative responses to the following items: need, product, source, price, and time.

need-satisfaction theory   A selling theory that positions the salesperson as a consultant whose objective is to solve buying problems for customers. This theory is consistent with the marketing concept of discovering customer needs and then providing satisfaction, while at the same time making a profit.

PROS AND CONS OF THE BUYER ACTION THEORY

This approach to selling is most common in situations where product features and benefits are easily understood by the prospect, the product is not expensive, and the purchase does not require multiple decision makers. It is frequently used to sell clothing, jewellery, household appliances, and other consumer goods. This approach is usually not effective in those selling situations that involve complex products and multiple decision makers.

THE BUYER RESOLUTION THEORY

The buyer resolution theory (sometimes referred to as the 5-Ws theory) also recognizes that selling is a mental process. This view of the selling–buying process recognizes that a purchase will be made only after the prospect has made five buying decisions involving specific, affirmative responses to the following questions:

Progistix tries to understand its customers, and even its customers' customers, to tune its service to meet each customer's needs and expectations.

1. Why should I buy? (need)
2. What should I buy? (product)
3. Where should I buy? (source)
4. What is a fair price? (price)
5. When should I buy? (time)

WHY SHOULD I BUY?

Realistically, it is sometimes difficult to provide prospects with an answer to this question. In many cases salespeople fail in their attempt to help customers become aware of a need. Thus large numbers of potential customers are not sufficiently persuaded to purchase products that will provide them with genuine buyer benefits. Many businesses are operating with inefficient and outdated equipment. A majority of Canadians classified as "head of household" have too little insurance.

WHAT SHOULD I BUY?

If a prospect agrees that a need does exist, then you are ready to address the second buying decision. You must convince the prospect that the product being offered will satisfy the need. In most cases the buyer can choose from several competing products.

WHERE SHOULD I BUY?

As products become more complex, consumers are giving more attention to "source" decisions. In a major metropolitan area the person who wants to buy a LaserJet 3100 or a competing product will be able to choose from several sources. As we noted in Chapter 5, company features such as certified service technicians or a complete parts inventory may permit a company to enjoy a competitive advantage.

WHAT IS A FAIR PRICE?

Today's better-educated and better-informed consumers are searching for the right balance between price and value (benefits). They are better able to detect prices that are not competitive or do not correspond in their minds with the product's value. Salespeople who represent higher priced products and services, such as Mont Blanc pens (prices range from $200 to more than $19 000) or meeting and banquet space at the Banff Springs Hotel, an upscale heritage hotel owned by Canadian Pacific Hotels, must be prepared to explain the product features that justify the higher price.

WHEN SHOULD I BUY?

A sale cannot be closed until a customer has decided when to buy. In some selling situations the customer will want to postpone the purchase because of reluctance to part with the money. The desire to postpone the purchase might also exist because the customer cannot see any immediate advantage to purchasing the product now.

PROS AND CONS OF THE BUYER RESOLUTION THEORY

The buyer resolution theory recognizes that a purchase will be made only after the prospect has made all five buying decisions. The omission of any of these decisions results in no sale. One strength of this sales approach is that it focuses the salesperson's attention on five important factors that the customer is likely to consider before making a purchase. This approach helps structure the information-gathering process. Answers to these five questions provide

The buyer resolution theory recognizes that a purchase will be made only after the five "w" questions have been answered in the mind of the prospect.

valuable insights about the customer's buying strategy. One important limitation of this theory is that it is often not possible to anticipate which of the five buying decisions will be most difficult for the prospect to make. Customers often have an established buying process or cycle, and when the selling process does not mesh with the buying process, a sale is not likely.[29] Therefore, a "canned" or highly inflexible sales presentation would not be appropriate. Also, there is no established sequence in which prospects make these decisions. A decision concerning price may be made before the source decision is made. These limitations remind us that a sales presentation must be flexible enough to accommodate a variety of selling situations.

THE NEED-SATISFACTION THEORY

The need-satisfaction theory is the foundation of consultative selling, which was described in Chapter 1. This buying process theory is based on the assumption that buying decisions are made to satisfy needs. The role of the professional salesperson is to identify these needs and then recommend a product or service that will satisfy them.

The consultative selling approach, coupled with strategic planning, sets the stage for long-term partnerships that result in repeat business and referrals. Put another way, strategic planning gives us the opportunity to maximize the benefits of consultative selling. As noted earlier, salespeople who develop correct strategies are more likely to make sales presentations to the right person, at the right time, and in a manner most likely to achieve positive results.

The need-satisfaction theory encompasses the concept that salespeople should conduct a systematic assessment of the prospect's situation. This usually involves collecting as much information as possible prior to the sales call and using a series of carefully worded questions to obtain the customer's point of view during the sales call. These questions lead the customer to talk more freely and help the salesperson pinpoint the customer's needs. Each customer should be thought of as a separate target market, with the salesperson trying to adapt to each one's needs.

The need-satisfaction approach to selling is based on a series of basic beliefs about the professional salesperson's role. These beliefs help us develop our own personal philosophy of selling, which serves as our "conscience" in

Building Relationships in a Diverse World

KEEPING PACE WITH A CHANGING CUSTOMER BASE

Canada is quickly becoming a truly multicultural nation, and this diversity presents marketers with major opportunities and major challenges. Marlene L. Rossman, author of *Multicultural Marketing*, says, "While many companies have fought over slices of the tiny yuppie market, the mature market, the senior market, the woman's market, and the other slow-growth markets, they have ignored the ethnic market, the fastest growing and most profitable market of them all." The largest ethnic community in Vancouver is Chinese. The Chinese community in Vancouver is six times larger than it is in Montreal, and it is larger still in Toronto.

However, the largest ethnic community in Toronto is Italian.

Several demographic trends indicate that Canada will be characterized by even more diversity in the years ahead. According to Shirley Roberts, president of Market-Driven Solutions Inc., visible minorities are expected to account for 24 percent of the Canadian population by 2016, up from only 9 percent in 1997. As a result, she says, "We will have to understand differences rather than averages." As we begin the twenty-first century, it is important to learn how to sell to the new demographics.[b]

selling situations. The key basic beliefs that serve as foundation stones for the need-satisfaction theory follow.

1. Effective communication exists between the buyer and the seller. *Two-way communication will provide for a mutual exchange of ideas, feelings, and perceptions.*

2. Systematic inquiry is necessary to establish the individual needs of individual customers. A lengthy discussion of the product or service is postponed until the salesperson becomes well acquainted with the prospect. In almost every selling situation, information supplied by the customer is essential. We must keep in mind the importance of treating different customers differently. The mass market is disappearing, because a growing number of customers need custom solutions.

3. Salespersons take a *two-way advocacy* position, representing the interests of their company and of their clients with equal dignity and skill. High-performance salespeople bring to the sales task a genuine sensitivity for the customer's needs.

4. In some selling situations the salesperson will reach the conclusion that the product does not provide the best solution (or the entire solution) to the customer's problem. For instance, people who sell elaborate computer systems sometimes help shape a client's entire strategic business plan. These salespeople will naturally use some of their own "solutions" (their company's products). However, they may incorporate other people's solutions as well, including their competitors' products.

5. Every effort should be made to develop a *long-term relationship with the customer.* Today, customers want a partner, someone who shares the same goals. Salespeople who can suggest ways to improve productivity, increase profits, and improve service, for example, are more likely to become valued partners.

Most customers feel less stress in the presence of a salesperson who has adopted the need-satisfaction philosophy of selling. The buying process is more relaxed and less threatening. They become genuine participants in the selling–buying process and begin to view the salesperson as a partner.

A growing number of firms use some variation of consultative selling. This approach works effectively in all types of selling situations. It does not matter whether you are selling financial securities, computer systems, or training programs; it does not matter whether you are focusing on the needs of an individual or working on a strategic plan with the divisional vice-president of a corporation—you can still apply consultative selling skills. You are engaging in progressive levels of complexity, not a fundamentally different approach.[30]

Figure 7.4 provides a comparison of the need-satisfaction theory with the buyer action and buyer resolution theories. The benefits of the need-satisfaction theory to the buyer and the seller are obvious.

Discovering Individual Customer Buying Motives

Buyer behaviour changes as people assume new roles, adopt new reference groups, and experience an increase or decrease in income. This is the reason salespeople need to develop a "customer" orientation rather than a "market" orientation. What is the difference? In the words of Tom Peters and Nancy Austin, "Markets do not buy products, customers do."[31]

A customer orientation can give a salesperson a tremendous competitive advantage in the marketplace. All it takes is the right mindset. It means recognizing that customer A may well buy or not buy your product for reasons different from those of customer B. It means that we must understand customers better than they understand themselves. It means appreciating your customer's unstated and unmet needs. It means knowing their businesses or lifestyles in ways that extend beyond their use of your current product or service.[32] When we ask appropriate questions, listen to the responses, and make observations, we can often discover the customer's unique buying motives.

QUESTIONS

Salespeople should think of themselves as nondirective counsellors. They should use questions to get prospects talking about themselves and their buying needs. As prospects open up, the salesperson is given a golden opportunity to discover their wants, needs, and perceptions. In business-to-business selling situations the questions are often specific and direct: "When will you begin shipping the new product line? When will the plans for the plant expansion be finalized?" Salespeople need to recheck and verify facts constantly.[33] The questioning process is examined in detail in Chapter 10.

LISTENING

It has been said, "We cannot learn when we are talking." This point seems of particular importance as we attempt to get acquainted with prospects. By asking questions and then pausing to let the prospect talk, we can obtain a better understanding of the forces that are shaping buyer behaviour. If you let people talk and listen carefully, they will actually tell you how to sell them.

OBSERVATION

As noted in Chapter 3, we should be as observant as possible before and during the sales presentation. Before meeting with a prospect, look at the physical surroundings and try to identify clues that will tell you more about the prospect. Read the customer's trade journals. During the presentation, observe the prospect's facial expressions and body movements. Emotions are often communicated by nonverbal behaviour.

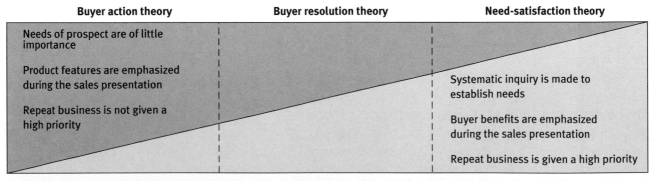

Buyer action theory	Buyer resolution theory	Need-satisfaction theory
Needs of prospect are of little importance		
Product features are emphasized during the sales presentation		Systematic inquiry is made to establish needs
Repeat business is not given a high priority		Buyer benefits are emphasized during the sales presentation
		Repeat business is given a high priority

Figure 7.4 **The need-satisfaction theory provides salespeople with the strongest foundation for developing a highly responsive customer strategy.**

In an ideal situation the information collected with questions, listening, and observations will be entered into a database that is easily accessible to people throughout the selling organization. As noted by one expert on buyer behaviour, "A business that doesn't equip itself with the capability to remember what makes each of its customers different probably won't be in business for long."[34]

As buyers become better educated and more sophisticated, it will become more critical than ever to gain an understanding of why people buy. Sales personnel must individualize each sales presentation to discover the most dominant buying motives. The most effective ways to discover individual customer buying motives and needs are discussed in Chapter 10.

Summary

The importance of developing a customer strategy was introduced in this chapter. This type of planning is necessary to ensure maximum customer responsiveness. The complex nature of customer behaviour was also discussed. We noted that buyer behaviour is influenced in part by individual (physical and psychological) needs. Maslow's popular model ranks these needs. It shows that the strongest, most basic physiological needs take precedence over the higher level needs. There are also a number of group influences that shape our psychological needs to various degrees. Buyer behaviour is influenced by the roles we assume, and our reference groups, social class, and culture.

Perception was defined as the process of selecting, organizing, and interpreting information inputs to produce meaning. We use our five senses to assign meaning to these inputs. Our perception is shaped by social influences as well as by the psychological and physiological conditions within us.

We discussed emotional and rational buying motives. Emotional buying motives prompt the prospect to act because of an appeal to some sentiment or passion. Rational buying motives tend to appeal to the prospect's reasoning power or judgment.

We also compared patronage and product buying motives. Patronage buying motives grow out of a strong relationship that has developed between the customer and the supplier. When competing products are quite similar, patronage motives can be very important. Product buying motives are usually in evidence when a prospect purchases one product in preference to another.

This chapter also presented several theories that explain the buying process. Three of the most popular theories are the buyer action theory, the buyer resolution theory, and the need-satisfaction theory. The discovery of buying motives was also discussed.

Key Terms

Customer Strategy 149	*Group Influences 153*
Physiological Needs 151	*Role 154*
Security Needs 151	*Reference Group 155*
Social Needs 151	*Social Class 155*
Esteem Needs 152	*Culture 156*
Self-Actualization 153	*Microculture 156*

Review Questions

1. According to the Strategic/Consultative Selling Model, what are the three prescriptions for the development of a successful customer strategy?

2. Explain how Maslow's hierarchy of needs affects buyer behaviour.

3. Describe the four group influences that affect buyer behaviour.

4. What is meant by the term *perception*?

5. Distinguish between emotional and rational buying motives.

6. List three commonly accepted theories that explain how people arrive at a buying decision.

7. What are the steps in the buyer action theory? To what other sales promotion methods does this theory apply?

8. List the five basic beliefs that serve as a foundation for the need-satisfaction theory.

9. List and describe three methods salespeople use to discover buying motives.

10. J. D. Power, founder of J. D. Power and Associates, says, "We define quality as what the customer wants." Do you agree or disagree with his observations? Explain your answer.

Application Exercises

1. Select several advertisements from a trade magazine. Analyze each one, and determine what rational buying motives the advertiser is appealing to. Do any of these advertisements appeal to emotional buying motives?

2. Select a magazine that is aimed at a particular consumer group, for example, *Architectural Digest*, *Chatelaine*, or *Camping Canada*. Study the advertisements and determine what buying motives they appeal to.

3. The J. D. Power and Associates company is referenced in the Product Buying Motives section of this chapter. This company provides information on customer buying satisfaction and buying habits on the Internet. Click on the "research and consulting" link on their Web site and examine their customer satisfaction reports.

www.jdpower.com

CRM Application Exercise

Managing Multiple Contacts with CRM

The ACT! database software identifies four firms involved with architecture. You can look up these firms and arrange to make contact with them. Start by selecting Lookup, Other, and, on the blank record, enter "architectural" in the Account Code field and click OK. ACT! will display four records with *architectural* in that field.

Scheduling Multiple Telephone Calls. Starting with the first record, Bryan Enterprises, select the schedule call icon ☎ or select the following menu choices: <u>S</u>chedule, <u>C</u>alls. Use your mouse to select the following Monday, pick OK, select 9:00 a.m., pick OK, and on the menu, choose Follow up, and pick OK. On the next window, called Schedule an Activity, select the box labelled "<u>C</u>ontact…," which displays another window called Select a Contact. On the Select a Contact window, pick the box labelled Lookup. This will return you to the Schedule an Activity window, where you can pick OK. To confirm that a phone call was scheduled with each person in these architectural firms, select <u>V</u>iew, <u>T</u>ask List. When the task list window appears, choose the Time Period, <u>F</u>uture. Pick OK when finished.

Creating Form Letters. You can create a form letter to send to each of the people in the four architectural firms by selecting <u>W</u>rite, <u>E</u>dit Template, typing the word "letter," and pressing Enter. A template with codes will be displayed. Type the words, "I'll call Monday," then select <u>F</u>ile, Save <u>A</u>s, and type "Form" then press Enter. Select <u>F</u>ile, <u>C</u>lose. To prepare the four letters, select <u>W</u>rite, <u>F</u>orm Letter, type "Form," and press Enter. On the next window, labelled Prepare Form Letter, choose Active <u>L</u>ookup and <u>D</u>ocument, then pick OK. The first form letter will be displayed on your screen. By pressing the Page Down key, you can review all four letters. Select <u>P</u>rint (Ctrl+P) to print the four letters and <u>F</u>ile, <u>C</u>lose to close the letter window.

Case Problem

Ron Trudel has been selling cars for Pembina Dodge Chrysler in Winnipeg since 1985. Before that, he sold farm machinery, worked in retail, owned an import company, and operated as a manufacturer's agent. Ron Trudel has been recognized by Chrysler Canada with a Senate Membership four times. This award recognizes the top 50 salespeople in Canada each year.

When asked why he has done so well, Ron Trudel says, "Selling is easy. The first thing you have to remember is the golden rule: Treat every customer like you would want to be treated. The next most important thing is enthusiasm. Customers know immediately if you don't have enthusiasm, and I think I have as much today as when I started selling. I greet customers as soon as they come into our dealership, and I try to develop some rapport within the first 35 seconds. That's important too. I ask questions and I listen. It's very important to understand customer needs before you start making recommendations. When families are involved, I always encourage the husband and wife to visit our showroom together. I also like to see the children come along. Each family member has different buying motives, and if you listen to them interact while they visit your showroom, you can easily see what buying motives each person has, and you can try to appeal to all of them. It's also nice when the whole family is involved because this is a major decision, one which everyone should enjoy, and one which everyone will remember for years to come. The first responsibility of the salesperson is to ensure that everyone has good memories of the occasion. That's why I also take such good care of my customers after the sale."

What does Ron Trudel do for his customers? He regularly calls them to see if they are happy with their purchase and the service they are getting. In fact, he even gets his customers to call him when they want service and he arranges it with the service department for them. As Ron Trudel says, "Even if they just want an oil change, I ask them to call me. If they're tied up at the office and can't get away, I'll even pick up their vehicle for them, have it serviced, and deliver it back to them when it's done."

Ron Trudel has been selling cars long enough now that he gets a lot of business from repeat customers and from referrals. Customers will come to the dealership to see him, and if he's not there, they will go away and come back again. Some have even called him at home to see if he was going to be in the next day. His effort and customer dedication have been paying off to the point where he is currently selling about twice as many vehicles as the average salesperson. And he does put in a lot of effort. Ron Trudel looks after a lot of little things. He makes sure customers leave with all the relevant information, as many customers want to think about their vehicle purchase for some time and to compare dealerships. For many customers this is a very major decision, probably the biggest after buying a home. Ron Trudel calls all prospects a few days after they visit the showroom to see if he can help them further. This has resulted in many sales for him that might otherwise have gone elsewhere.

When it comes to effort, Ron Trudel is always selling. He estimates that about 30 percent of his time is spent prospecting. One of his favourite methods is to look through old company sales slips to see which customers have bought cars from salespeople who are no longer at the dealership. Then he calls them to see if they are thinking about another purchase, or if there is anything he can do to help them. Ron Trudel is also an active member in his church group, golfs regularly, and belongs to several fraternal and service organizations, where he also networks. In fact, Ron Trudel says, "I'm always prospecting. Nothing gets mailed from our house without my business card in it. I even send one with my telephone and electricity payments each month. I've left them in restaurants, posted them on bulletin boards, and generally leave them anywhere they might get noticed."

Recently, a prospect walked into the showroom holding one of Ron's business cards. When Ron Trudel began to ask him some questions (the need-discovery process), it was quickly apparent that the customer knew exactly what he wanted. Ron quoted him a price, to which the customer responded that he had a slightly better offer from one of the other Chrysler dealerships in Winnipeg. Further questioning revealed that the customer had bought his last car from that other dealership, but the salesperson he had bought the car from no longer worked there. The new salesperson that he had been talking to didn't seem to be particularly interested in his business. While Ron Trudel was trying to decide whether to meet the price, he asked the prospective customer, "Where did you get my card?"

Questions

1. Does it appear that Ron Trudel has built his customer strategy on the three prescriptions featured in the Strategic/Consultative Selling Model? Explain.

2. If this prospective customer had already been offered a low price on a new car, why did he come to see Ron Trudel?

3. Should Ron Trudel focus on patronage or product buying motives while making his presentation to this customer? Explain.

4. What does it appear that Ron Trudel has learned about customer behaviour from his years as a car salesperson?

Developing a Prospect Base

The Stevens Company Limited has 33 sales representatives and sells medical supplies and equipment from Ontario to British Columbia. There are also two inside telemarketers who manage smaller accounts. They call inactive accounts and also new accounts that are not sufficiently large to justify the time of a field sales representative. They use ACT! contact software developed by SalesLogix. According to Jeff Stevens, the company maintains a detailed profile of customers, prospects, and all support personnel. With a single computer keystroke, staff can bring up detailed information on any of more than 8000 contacts in the database. Customer service has been improved because the ACT! software reminds the sales representatives when it's time to make a follow-up call and shows them important account information at a glance.[1]

The makers of ACT! and other software vendors such as Epicor, EDSI, and ActiveSales are helping companies develop effective customer relationship management systems. These systems are at the heart of every successful one-to-one marketing initiative. Success in selling depends on one's ability to identify prospects, gain insight into the prospect's needs, and develop an accurate picture of a prospect's value.[2]

LEARNING OBJECTIVES

When you finish reading this chapter, you should be able to

1. Discuss the importance of developing a prospect base

2. Identify and assess important sources of prospects

3. Describe criteria for qualifying prospects

4. Explain common methods of organizing prospect information

5. Name some characteristics that are important to learn about customers as individuals and as business representatives

6. Describe the steps in developing a prospecting and sales forecasting plan

Prospecting—An Introduction

Gerhard Gschwandtner, editor of *Selling Power*, says, "The main purpose of a salesperson is not to make sales, but to create customers."[3] Identifying potential customers is an important aspect of the customer strategy. In the terminology of personal selling this process is called **prospecting**. A potential customer, or **prospect,** is someone who has three basic qualifications. First, the person must have a need for the product or service. Many companies attempt to identify a target market that includes those prospects who qualify on the basis of need. Second, the individual must be able to pay for the purchase. An important fundamental of consultative selling is that prospects should not be persuaded to buy products they cannot afford. Third, the prospect must be authorized to purchase the product. Finding prospects who can make the purchase is not as easy as it sounds. In many situations the salesperson must make the sales presentation to multiple decision makers. One of these decision makers might be the technical expert who wants an answer to the question: "Does the product meet the company's specifications?" Another decision maker may be the person who will actually use the product. The employee who will use the forklift truck you are selling may be involved in the purchase decision. Of course, there is often a "purse-string" decision maker who has the ultimate authority to release funds for the purchase.[4]

The goal of prospecting is to build a **prospect base** made up of current customers and potential customers. Many successful companies find that current customers account for a large percentage of their sales. Every effort is made to keep these clients satisfied because they provide the repeat business that is necessary to maintain profitability.

THE IMPORTANCE OF PROSPECTING

Every salesperson must cope with customer attrition; that is, the inevitable loss of customers over a period of time, which can be attributed to a variety of causes. Unless new prospects are found to replace lost customers, a salesperson will eventually face a reduction in income and possible loss of employment.

To better understand the significance of prospecting, let us examine a few common causes of customer attrition.

1. The customer may move to a new location outside the salesperson's territory. The Canadian population is very mobile. This cause of attrition is especially common in the retail and service areas.
2. A firm may go out of business or merge with another company. In some areas of business the failure rate is quite high. In recent years we have witnessed a record number of mergers, which have caused massive changes in purchasing plans.
3. A loyal buyer or purchasing agent may leave the position because of promotion, retirement, resignation, or serious illness. The replacement may prefer to buy from someone else.

Some studies reveal that the average company loses 15 to 20 percent of its customers every year. Depending on the type of selling, this figure might be higher or lower. It becomes clear that many customers are lost for reasons beyond the salesperson's control. If salespeople want to keep their earnings at a stable level, they will need to develop new customers.

prospecting A systematic process of identifying potential customers.

prospect Someone who has three basic qualifications. First, the person must have a need for the product or service. Second, the individual must be able to afford the purchase. Third, the person must be authorized to purchase the product.

prospect base A list of current and potential customers.

Joe Girard, a popular sales trainer, uses the "Ferris wheel" concept to illustrate the relationship between prospecting and the loss of customers due to the attrition factors described earlier. As people get off the Ferris wheel, the operator fills their seats one at a time, moves the wheel a little, and continues this process until all the original riders have left the wheel and new ones come aboard (Fig. 8.1). In reality, of course, established customers do not come and go this fast. With the passing of time, however, many customers will be replaced.

PROSPECTING REQUIRES PLANNING

Prospecting should be viewed as a systematic process of locating potential customers. Some prospecting efforts can be easily integrated into a regular sales call. Progressive marketers are doing three things to improve the quality of the prospecting effort:

1. Increase the number of people who board the Ferris wheel. You want to see a continuous number of potential prospects board the Ferris wheel, because they are the source of sales opportunities. If the number of potential prospects declines sharply, the number of sales closed will also decline.

2. Improve the quality of the prospects who board the Ferris wheel. Companies that have adopted the quality improvement process concept view this phase of prospecting as critical. They have established quality standards that ensure a steady supply of prospects with high profit potential.[5] In the absence of such quality standards it may be necessary to "fire" an unproductive customer at a later date. This becomes necessary when customers demand more sales and service resources than their purchase volume justifies.[6]

3. Shorten the sales cycle by quickly determining which of the new prospects are *qualified* prospects—qualified as to need, ability to pay, and authority to purchase the product. Gerhard Gschwandtner says, "Time is the ultimate scorekeeper in the game of selling." He points out that many salespeople do not meet their sales goals because they do not quickly qualify new prospects.[7] Later in this chapter we examine qualifying practices and discuss how to shorten the sales cycle with sales automation methods.

In most selling situations, prospecting begins with a study of the market for your product or service. When Pitney Bowes first developed the desktop postage meter, the company conducted a careful study of the market. At first glance, equipment of this nature seemed well suited only to a large business firm. With additional market analysis the company identified many additional customers who could benefit from purchasing the product. Many small business firms use this product today.

THE PROSPECTING ATTITUDE

Attitudes serve as a foundation for our behaviour. Salespeople who view prospecting as an important key to success spend time every day on this activity. Prospecting is not thought of as a chore, but an opportunity to identify persons who can benefit from owning your product. Prospecting is viewed as a process that can take place in virtually any environment—social situations, on an airplane, while attending a professional meeting, or wherever people are present.[8]

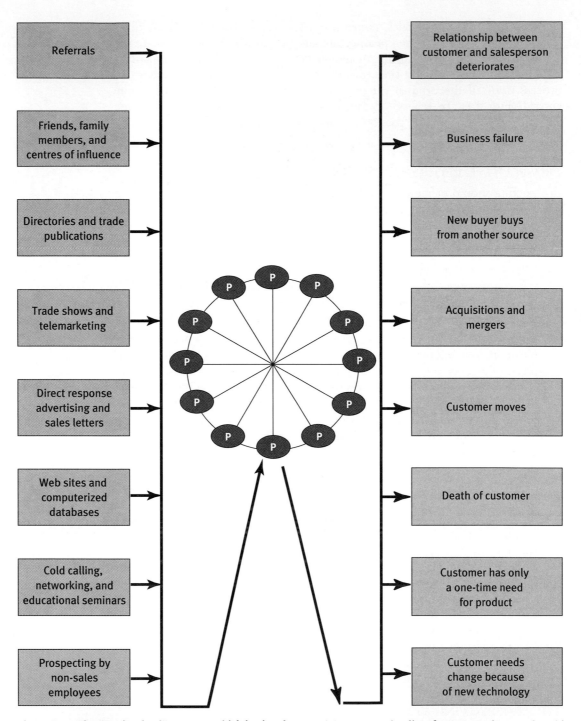

Figure 8.1 The "Ferris wheel" concept, which is aimed at supplying an ongoing list of prospects, is part of world sales record holder Joe Girard's customer strategy.

Building Relationships through Technology

USING THE SAME CRM SOFTWARE AS AT&T

AT&T implemented a customer relationship management program that resulted in major increases in productivity and improved customer service. The first stage of the automation project involved 11,000 desktop computers and the popular ACT! software. This combination of hardware and software resulted in a reported 15 to 20 percent improvement in productivity. AT&T salespeople gained easier and quicker access to account information such as the prospect's name, title, company, assistant's name, and notes concerning the account. Placing the database on a server gives all network users access to this important information.

Information in a CRM database can be reviewed prior to calling or visiting a prospect, thus ensuring a more personalized contact. By using CRM, salespeople gain a competitive edge in relating to their prospects' needs and interests.

You have the opportunity to use a demonstration version of the same software (ACT!) AT&T uses. Just as an AT&T salesperson would be, you are assigned a number of prospect accounts (20) and given individual and company information about each account's contact person in the database. Your participation in the CRM case studies and exercises will give you hands-on experience with the strategic development of a prospect base using modern sales technology. Not only will you be using the same software that is being used by thousands of salespeople, you also will be working with data that are derived from authentic selling challenges. (See the CRM case study Reviewing The Prospect Database on page 193 for more information.)

Prospecting requires self-discipline. Paul S. Goldner, author and sales trainer, suggests that you make an appointment with yourself for one hour of prospecting each day. He says the time to prospect will never be exactly right, so use the appointment to ensure that this important sales activity does not get postponed.[9]

Sources of Prospects

Every salesperson must develop a prospecting system suited to a particular selling situation. There are several sources of prospects, and each should be carefully examined.

Referrals

Friends, family members, and centres of influence

Directories

Trade publications

Trade shows

Telemarketing

Direct response advertising and sales letters

Web sites

Computerized databases

Cold calling

Networking

Educational seminars

Prospecting by non-sales employees

Trade shows are very effective for prospecting. Barry Siskind has been helping companies get the most out of trade shows for 12 years.

Featuring Barry Siskind:
North America's foremost show expert!

Making Trade Shows Work.™

Step by step.
In less than one day!

REFERRALS

The use of referrals as a prospecting approach has been successful in a wide range of selling situations. In most cases referral leads result in higher close rates, larger sales, and a shorter sales cycle. A **referral** is a prospect who has been recommended by a current customer or by someone who is familiar with the product. Satisfied customers, business acquaintances, and even prospects who do not buy can often recommend the names of persons who might benefit from owning the product. Research in the field of personal selling indicates that it takes much less time to sell a qualified, referred lead than it does to sell a non-

referral A prospect who has been recommended by a current customer or by someone who is familiar with the product.

Building Quality Partnerships

DATABASE PROSPECTING

Rick Hall, vice president of Zyga Corporation, says, "Before building a database, most companies don't know much about their customers." However, he also cautions that it is not enough to know who your best customer is, you must know why. To answer this question, Hall suggests you need a good marketing analyst. Companies are increasingly using customer databases for prospecting. The valuable customer information on their databases may allow companies to identify and target specific groups of customers, but mining databases of customer information may provide little more than fool's gold.

British Columbia Telecom decided to invite 100 of its best customers to a Vancouver Grizzlies basketball game. It was while the invitations were being printed that someone discovered the customers were all heavy 900-number users, and that a number of them were sex-line enthusiasts. It was fortunate that the company caught this mistake in time to avert a potentially embarrassing situation.[a]

qualified, nonreferred lead.[10] Endless chain referrals and referral letters and cards represent two variations of this prospecting tactic.

ENDLESS CHAIN REFERRALS

The endless chain approach to obtaining referrals is easy to use because it fits naturally into most sales presentations. A salesperson selling long-term health care insurance might say, "Miss Chen, who do you know who might be interested in our insurance plan?" This open-ended question gives the person the freedom to recommend several prospects and is less likely to be answered with a no response. Be sure to use your reference's name when you contact the new prospect—"Mary Chen suggested that I call you. . . ."

REFERRAL LETTERS AND CARDS

The referral letter method is a variation of the endless chain technique. In addition to requesting the names of prospects, the salesperson asks the customer to prepare a note or letter of introduction that can be delivered to the potential customer. The correspondence is an actual testimonial prepared by a satisfied customer. Some companies use a referral card to introduce the salesperson. The preprinted card features a place for your customer to sign the new prospect's name and his or her own name.

Using an existing customer as an intermediary has several advantages. The amount of time spent on prospecting can be reduced and the referral will make it easier to get an appointment. In addition, the views of a satisfied customer will often have a great deal of impact on the prospect. Needless to say, salespeople who are viewed as product experts, who are recognized as problem solvers and partners, are more likely to be the beneficiaries of referrals.

FRIENDS, FAMILY MEMBERS, AND CENTRES OF INFLUENCE

A person who is new in the field of selling often uses friends and family members as sources of information about potential customers. It is only natural to contact people we know. In many cases these people have contacts with a wide range of potential buyers.

The centre-of-influence method involves establishing a relationship with a well-connected, influential person who is willing to provide prospect information. This person may not make buying decisions, but has influence on other people who do. To illustrate, consider the challenge facing Gary Schneider, creator of a powerful software product that would help small farmers optimize their crop selection. After spending several years developing the product, Schneider and his wife began selling the product one copy at a time. During one cold call on a major crop insurer, he met a senior researcher who immediately saw the benefits of his product. This respected researcher is in a position to influence buying decisions at his company and provide prospect information for other crop insurers.[11]

DIRECTORIES

Directories can help salespeople search out new prospects and determine their buying potential. A list of some of the more popular national directories is provided here.

The Blue Book of Canadian Business lists 2500 medium- to large-size Canadian firms with sales over $10 million or having over 500 employees. Published by Canadian Newspaper Services International Limited.

The Canadian Key Business Directory lists and profiles the top 20 000 businesses in Canada. Available from Dun & Bradstreet.

Canadian Directory of Industrial Distributors lists industrial distributors by product specialty and geographic location. Also contains information on age of company, types of accounts serviced, main contacts within firms, etc.

Canadian Trade Index is in three volumes and lists more than 26 000 manufacturers, distributors, and industrial service companies. Published by the Alliance of Manufacturers and Exporters Canada.

Fraser's Canadian Trade Directory is published in four volumes and contains 350 000 listings designed to help you find suppliers of specific products or services, including many non-Canadian companies that have distributors or agents in Canada.

Scott's Directories are published in separate regional volumes—Atlantic, Quebec, Ontario, and Western—and are also available on CD-ROM. They are designed to help locate businesses by company name, province/city, or type of business. There is also a Greater Toronto Directory. Available from Southam Inc.

Polk City Directory provides detailed information on the citizens of a specific community. Polk, in business for over 125 years, publishes about 1100 directories covering 6500 communities in Canada and the United States. The directory can usually be obtained from the city government or chamber of commerce.

These are just a few of the better known directories. There are hundreds of additional directories covering business and industrial firms on the national, regional, and local levels. Some directories are free, while others must be purchased at a nominal fee. One of the most useful sources of free information is the telephone directory. Most telephone directories have a classified (Yellow Pages) section that groups businesses and professions by category.

If you are involved in the sale of products in the international market, the Department of Foreign Affairs and International Trade can be a valuable resource. It provides the Canadian Trade Commissioner Service, among other services. Canada has trade commissioners in more than 125 cities throughout the world. They can provide a number of essential services, including market intelligence and identification of potential customers, suppliers, or distributors and agents in foreign locations. Another valuable resource is the Export Development Corporation (EDC), a Crown corporation that helps Canadian exporters compete throughout the world. EDC provides a wide range of financial and risk management services, and country and market information on most countries where Canadians sell. You can also view Canadian export performance data by country, and view country economic and credit summaries.

www.dfait-maeci.gc.ca

www.edcinfo.com

TRADE PUBLICATIONS

Trade publications provide a status report on every major industry. If you are a sales representative employed by one of the huge food wholesalers that supply

The Scott's Directories are good sources of prospects for sales-people.

PRECISION TARGET MARKETING

Use Scott's Directories and Selectories

• for personal contact to arrange a face-to-face sales call

• to save valuable time by pinpointing hot prospects that need your product or service

• to produce mailing labels and personalized letters for sales literature and promotions

• to prepare telemarketing call sheets

• to close more sales in record time... using Scott's knowledge of company and product information for a professional and well prepared presentation!

• to build a personalized prospect database

SCOTT'S
DIRECTORIES

1450 Don Mills Road
Don Mills, Ontario M3B 2X7
(416) 442-2122, 1-800-668-2374
Fax (416) 510-6875

3300 Côte Vertu, Suite 410
Ville St-Laurent, QC H4R 2B7
(514) 339-1397, 1-800-363-1327
Fax (514) 339-1396

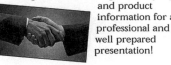

supermarkets, then you will benefit from a monthly review of *Canadian Grocer* magazine. Each month this trade publication reports on trends in the retail food industry, new products, problems, innovations, and related information. Trade journals such as *Women's Wear Daily*, *Home Furnishings*, *Canadian Dairy*, *Hardware Retailer*, *Modern Tire Dealer*, and *Oilweek* are examples of publications that might help salespeople identify prospects.

TRADE SHOWS

A trade show is a large exhibit of products that are, in most cases, common to one industry, such as electronics or office equipment. The prospects walk into the booth or exhibit and talk with those who represent the exhibitor. In some cases sales personnel invite existing customers and prospects to attend trade shows so they will have an opportunity to demonstrate their newest products.

Research studies indicate that it is much easier to identify good prospects and actually close sales at a trade show. In most cases fewer sales calls are needed to close a sale if the prospect was qualified at a trade show.[12] Some marketers use special qualifying methods at trade shows. Brian Jeffrey, president of SalesForce Training & Consulting Inc. in Carp, Ontario, prepares a list of seven questions that will quickly qualify or disqualify prospects at a trade show.[13]

TELEMARKETING

telemarketing The practice of marketing goods and services through telephone contact.

Telemarketing is the practice of marketing goods and services through telephone contact. It has become an integral part of many modern sales and marketing campaigns. One use of telemarketing is to identify prospects. A financial services company used telemarketing to identify prospects for its customized equipment leasing packages. Leads were given to salespeople for consideration. Telemarketing can also be used to quickly and inexpensively qualify prospects for follow-up. Some marketers use the telephone to verify sales leads generated by direct mail, advertisements, or some other method.

DIRECT RESPONSE ADVERTISING AND SALES LETTERS

Many advertisements invite the reader to send for a free booklet or brochure that provides detailed information about the product or service. In the category of business-to-business marketing, advertising has the greatest inquiry-generating power.[14] Some firms distribute postage-free response cards (also known as bingo cards) to potential buyers. Recipients are encouraged to complete and mail the cards if they desire additional information. In some cases the name of the person making the inquiry is given to a local sales representative for further action.

Sales letters can easily be incorporated into a prospecting plan. The prospecting sales letter is sent to persons who are in a position to make a buying decision. Shortly after the letter has been mailed (three or four days), the prospect is called and asked for an appointment. The call begins with a reference to the sales letter. To make the letter stand out, some salespeople include a promotional item. As noted in Chapter 5, all sales letters must be written with care. To get results, sales letters must quickly get the reader's attention.

WEB SITES

Web site A collection of Web pages maintained by a single person or organization. It is accessible to anyone with a computer, a modem, and Web-browser software.

Thousands of companies and business people have established Web sites on the World Wide Web. A **Web site** is a collection of Web pages maintained by a sin-

An up-to-date customer database can enhance prospecting.

gle person or organization. It is accessible to anyone with a computer, a modem, and Web-browser software. IBM Canada demonstrates the versatility of a Web site. You can find information on everything from hardware, software, services, and support to networking and small business solutions. It is easy to find product specifications, and technical support information and downloads. IBM even puts interesting news and articles related to its products on the Web so that visitors to the site can see what awards it has won and which companies have been assisted through IBM solutions. By contrast, many individual salespeople maintain less sophisticated Web sites that feature their picture, biographical information, and details of the products or services they sell.

www.can.ibm.com

COMPUTERIZED DATABASES

With the aid of electronic data processing it is often possible to match product features with the needs of potential customers quickly and accurately. In many situations a firm will develop its own computerized database. In other cases it is more economical to purchase the database from a company that specializes in collection of such information. For example, lists are available for boat enthusiasts, computer industry professionals, and subscribers to many magazines.

With the aid of a personal computer (PC), salespeople can develop their own detailed customer files. The newer PCs provide expanded storage capacity at a lower price than in the past. This means that salespeople can accumulate a great deal of information about individual customers and use this information to personalize the selling process.[15] For example, a PC can help an independent insurance agent maintain a comprehensive record for each policyholder. As the status of each client changes (marriage, the birth of children, etc.), the record can easily be updated. With the aid of an up-to-date database the agent can quickly identify prospects for various existing and new policy options.

COLD CALLING

With some products, cold call prospecting is an effective approach to prospect identification. In **cold calling** the salesperson selects a group of people who may or may not be actual prospects and then calls on each one (by phone or personal

cold calling A method of prospecting in which the salesperson selects a group of people who may or may not be actual prospects, and then calls on each one.

visit). For example, the sales representative for a wholesale medical supply firm might call on every hospital in a given community, assuming that each one is a potential customer. Many new salespeople must rely on the cold call method because they are less likely to get appointments through referrals.[16] It takes time to develop a group of established customers who are willing to give referrals.

Successful cold calls do not happen spontaneously. Some strategic thinking and planning must precede personal visits and telephone calls. Who do you contact? What will you say during the first few seconds? What message should you leave on voice mail? These and other questions will be answered in Chapter 9.

NETWORKING

networking The practice of making and using contacts. It involves people meeting people and profiting from the connections.

In simple terms, *networking* is the art of making and using contacts. **Networking** is people meeting people and profiting from the connections.[17]

Barry Siskind, an Ontario-based consultant and author of *Making Contact*, sees networking as a three-act process. In act one, you must be able to approach someone and engage them in conversation. Act two is when you "net-chat," a term Siskind uses to describe a technique to collect and give information, finding out as much as you can about the other person in the shortest time possible. Act three is where you disengage; many networkers spend too much time networking with too few people. Successful networkers must develop a number of skills. They must be able to engage people in conversation, make a good impression, gather information, disengage from conversation, and follow up on their contacts.[18] The following are some tips for networking.

1. *Be focused.* You should consider who you need to network with, and where you are likely to meet these people.

2. *Be a listener.* Listening is important to any successful interpersonal activity. Besides, you learn more when you listen.

3. *Be sincere.* If you are superficial or only wish to use people, you will quickly be shunned.

4. *Be mobile.* Move around the room and mingle. Don't get trapped in one place.

5. *Be a joiner.* Many valuable contacts are made in charity organizations, on boards of trade, and in athletic clubs.

6. *Be sensitive to cultural and physical differences.* There is a trend of increasing diversity in the workplace. Focus on the person and not on the difference. You need to have empathy, show respect, and demonstrate sensitivity to differences.

There are three types of networks salespeople should grow and nurture. Every salesperson will be well served by networking within their own organization. You never know when someone in finance or shipping will be needed to help solve a problem or provide you with important information. A second form of networking involves establishing contacts inside your industry. Make contact with experts in your field, top performers, leaders, successful company representatives, and even competitors. The third form of networking involves business contacts with people outside of your industry, such as bankers, government officials, developers, and other people in your community. The local golf course is frequently a good place to make these contacts.[19]

Many databases are now available on CD-ROM and provide an excellent way to prospect for customers.

Networking skills are of special importance to new salespeople who cannot turn to a large group of satisfied customers for referrals and leads. Professionals (accountants, lawyers, consultants, etc.), entrepreneurs, managerial personnel, and customer service representatives must also develop networking skills.

EDUCATIONAL SEMINARS

Many salespeople are using educational seminars as a method of identifying prospects. Seminars provide an opportunity to showcase your product without pressuring prospects to buy. Polaroid Canada Inc. has been conducting seminars across Canada to display and demonstrate imaging products. Approximately 150 prospects have been attending each of these seminars, where Polaroid imaging specialists ensure that prospects' toughest questions are answered and prospects are able to explore imaging solutions in a hands-on environment.[20] The purpose of these seminars is not to sell products, but to demonstrate them and to educate prospects on Polaroid solutions. Microsoft, IBM, and Xerox have all used seminar selling at many locations across Canada.[21] Many banks, investment firms, accounting firms, wine merchants, and consulting companies use seminars to generate new prospects. When inviting prospects, be clear about the seminar's content, and always deliver what you promise.[22]

PROSPECTING BY NON-SALES EMPLOYEES

Should service technicians, receptionists, bank tellers, and other non-sales personnel be involved in prospecting? In a growing number of organizations the answer is yes. Prospecting need not be the exclusive responsibility of the sales force. At Computer Specialists Incorporated, employees have been given an incentive to pass along names of prospective customers. If the prospect becomes an account, the employee receives a bonus of up to $1000, depending on the value of the job. Over a one-year period this program generated 75 leads, resulting in 9 new accounts.[23] The incentive program at Computer Specialists Incorporated helps keep everyone focused on potential customers.

Employees do not have to work in sales to identify potential customers. However, they may not be alert to opportunities unless they are given an orientation to this role. Non-sales personnel need special training to function effectively in this role. Also, an incentive program will keep them focused on new business opportunities for the organization.

COMBINATION APPROACHES

In recent years we have seen an increase in the number of prospecting approaches used by salespeople. In many cases, success in selling depends on your ability

---

Selling in Action

SEMINAR SELLING

The use of educational seminars has become an important prospecting method. You can educate prospective customers with brochures, news releases, catalogues, or your Web site, but educational seminars offer the advantage of face-to-face contact. Barbara Siskind, in her book *Seminars To Build Your Business*, identifies 15 objectives for hosting seminars. Here are a few of the most important.

Obtain sales leads. This is one of the most common objectives for seminars. You can obtain the names of attendees and arrange appointments for future sales calls. Seminars may also help identify actual product users, technical support people, or engineers who, although they may not be the decision makers, may influence the purchase decision.

Promote your place of business. Your place of business can become a destination for people who might otherwise not consider visiting it. You have an opportunity to create awareness of your company and develop a positive image for your entire operation and its capabilities.

Showcase and demonstrate your expertise. Seminars allow you to show a carefully targeted group of people that you really know your stuff. Salespeople can be supported by technical experts and others in the organization who can address clients' specific concerns.

Toronto-based Charon Systems, Inc., a systems integrator that deploys networks for organizations, regularly organizes seminars for 80 to 100 technology people from mid-sized firms. President David Fung estimates that 25 percent of prospects become clients.[b]

to use a combination of the methods described in this chapter. For example, the large number of prospects identified at a trade show might be used to develop an effective telemarketing program. Prospects are called and an effort is made to set up a personal call. Prospects identified at a trade show or educational seminar might also be sent a sales-oriented newsletter or a sales letter.

Qualifying the Prospect

Prospecting can turn up a large number of people or organizations that appear to need the product. This list should be examined to target the most promising prospects. A **target market** is a well-defined set of present and potential customers that an organization attempts to serve.[24] Refining the prospect list is essential for two reasons. First, a salesperson cannot afford to spend time calling on persons who are not real prospects. Time conservation should be a primary concern. Second, a salesperson will sometimes identify prospects who cannot place an order large enough to cover the cost of the sales call. Many companies have established ratios of sales volume to sales expense that must be taken into consideration when prospecting. The average sales call costs more than $250, so salespeople must try to avoid calls on customers who have limited buying potential.

> **target market**   A well-defined set of present and potential customers that an organization atttempts to serve.

It is important to keep in mind that calling on potential customers is much more time consuming than calling on established customers. In terms of sales closings, a new customer will require about three times the number of contacts compared with closing a sale with an established customer.[25]

Not all prospects are equal. A salesperson might begin with a list of 25 potential customers. After careful study, 10 of the names are eliminated because they do not appear to need the product. Then the salesperson estimates the potential sales that might be generated from the remaining prospects. By using this approach, the salesperson eliminates another 5 persons because the potential order would not be large enough to cover sales call expenses. The remaining names in this hypothetical situation might be ranked according to anticipated sales volume. This process of identifying prospects who should be contacted is called **qualifying**.

> **qualifying**   Examining the prospect list to identify the people who are most apt to buy a product.

In many selling situations it is possible to establish criteria that can be used to qualify prospects. To rate the names that appear on the prospect list, it is sometimes helpful to ask yourself several basic questions:

1. Does the name represent a customer who is already buying from you? If so, is there a chance you can obtain additional business?

2. Is the name a former customer? If so, do you know why the person stopped buying from you? Should you make another contact with this person?

3. Does the name represent a user of your type of product? Is this person currently buying from one of your competitors?

4. What is the amount of potential sales that can be generated from the prospect? As noted before, not all prospects are equal.

5. What is the prospect's credit rating? (Note: The *Dun & Bradstreet Reference Book* is one excellent source of credit information.)

This list can be revised to meet the needs of many different types of salespeople. A sales representative for an industrial equipment dealer will see the qualifying process differently from the person who sells commercial real estate. The main consideration is providing accurate answers to each question.

Organizing Your Prospect Information

When it comes to organizing prospect information, the salesperson has two choices. Some salespeople record prospect information on blank file cards (4 × 6 is the most popular) or on preprinted file cards that have space for specific kinds of information, or they record information in loose-leaf notebooks.

At some retail stores, for example, salespeople record information about each customer in a "personal book." Successful salespeople often have three or four bulging books that help them provide more personalized service to each customer. In addition to the customer's name, address, and account number they record the person's sizes, style preferences, hobbies and interests, birthday, previous items purchased, and any other appropriate information. With this information available, each customer becomes a "prospect" for future purchases. Sales personnel often call their customers when new products arrive.

Harvey Mackay instructs his salespeople to develop a 66-question customer profile. The form is divided into categories such as education, family, business background, special interests, and lifestyle. In the process of collecting and analyzing this information, the salesperson gets to know the customer better than competing salespeople do. Harvey Mackay describes the benefits of developing a customer profile:

> *If selling were just a matter of determining who's got the low bid, then the world wouldn't need salespeople. It could all be done on computers. The "Mackay 66" is designed to convert you from an adversary to a colleague of the people you're dealing with and to help you make sales.*[26]

He says that the 66-item customer profile helps the salesperson systematize information in a way that will make it more useful and accessible.

The use of file cards and notebooks is adequate for salespeople who deal with a small number of prospects and do not get involved in complex sales. The use of some type of computerized system is more appropriate for salespeople who deal with large numbers of prospects, frequently get involved in complex sales, and must continually network with management and members of the sales support team. A recent study conducted by *Sales & Marketing Management* magazine found that more than one-third of the companies surveyed use an automated lead management system.[27] With the aid of modern technology salespeople can retrieve data from various sources no matter where they are. Regardless of the system used, most salespeople need to collect and organize two kinds of prospect information: information about the prospect as an individual and information about the prospect as a business representative.

THE PROSPECT AS AN INDIVIDUAL

The foundation for a sales philosophy that emphasizes the building of partnerships is the belief that we should always treat the other person as an individual. Each prospect is a one-of-a-kind person with a number of unique characteristics. The only possible way we can treat the prospect as an individual is to learn as much as possible about the person. The starting point is to learn the correct spelling and pronunciation of the prospect's name. Then acquire information about the person's educational background, work experience, special interests, hobbies, and family status. Interview industry people or employees at the company to acquire personal information.[28]

In Chapter 4 you were introduced to the concept of communication-style bias and the benefits derived from an understanding of communication styles. You also learned how to overcome communication-style bias and build strong selling relationships with style flexing. If at all possible, acquire information concerning the prospect's communication style before the sales call. Business associates or close friends of the prospect can supply this helpful information.

A lasting business partnership is based in large part on a strong personal relationship. Dale Carnegie, a pioneer in the field of human relations training and author of *How to Win Friends and Influence People*, recognized the importance of taking a personal interest in others. He said, "You can make more friends in two months by becoming interested in other people than you can in two years by trying to get other people interested in you."

THE PROSPECT AS A BUSINESS REPRESENTATIVE

In addition to personal information about the prospect, it is important to collect certain business-related facts. This is especially important when the prospect is associated with a business. At the outset determine if the prospect is authorized to purchase your product or service. Salespeople must also be concerned about the prospect's ability to buy. A potential buyer's credit rating is easy to check in most cases.

Before calling on the prospect it pays to review various aspects of the company operation. Research starts with a document search for information about the company and industry.[29] What does the company manufacture or sell? How long has the firm been in business? Is the firm a leader in the field? Does the firm have expansion plans? Each company has its own, unique culture.

Most established firms have been doing business with one or more other suppliers. When possible, find out whom the company buys from and why. It always helps to know in advance who the competition is. Salespeople who take time to study personal and business facts will be in a stronger position to meet the prospect's needs. They will also close more sales.

Developing a Prospecting and Sales Forecasting Plan

A major barrier to prospecting is time. There never seems to be enough time for a salesperson to do everything that needs to be done. In many situations, less than half of the workweek is devoted to actual sales calls. The remainder of the time is spent identifying and screening prospects, travel, paperwork, planning, sales meetings, and servicing accounts. Time devoted to prospecting often means that less time is available for actual selling. Given a choice, salespeople would rather spend their time with established customers. Attrition, of course, will gradually reduce the number of persons in this category, and prospecting will be necessary for survival.

Prospecting activities can be approached in a more orderly fashion with the aid of a plan. It is difficult to prescribe one plan that will fit all selling situations; however, most situations require the following similar types of decisions:

1. *Prepare a list of prospects.* You will recall that the prospect base includes current customers and potential customers. The process of enlarging the

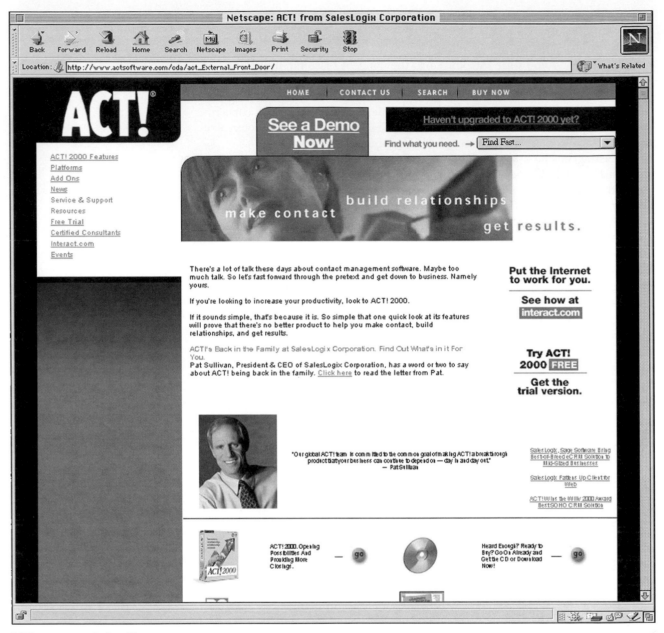

ACT! customer-relationship-management software by SalesLogix allows salespeople to organize and access prospect information.

prospect base to include potential customers will vary from one industry to another. In the food service distribution industry, salespeople often start with a territorial audit.[30] This involves the collection and analysis of information about every food service operator (restaurants, hotels, colleges, etc.) in a given territory. Important information such as the name of the operation, name of the owner or manager, type of menu, and so forth is recorded on a card or entered into a personal computer. Some salespeople in this industry pinpoint each operator on a map of the territory. When the audit is complete, the salesperson analyzes the information on each food service operator and selects those who should be contacted.

A salesperson who sells hotel and convention services could use a variation of the territorial audit. The list of prospects might include local businesses, educational institutions, civic groups, and other organizations that need banquet or conference services.

2. *Forecast the potential sales volume that might be generated by each new account for each product.* A **sales forecast** outlines expected sales for a specific product or service to a specific target group over a specific period of time. With a sales forecast the salesperson is able to set goals, establish a sales budget, and allocate resources with greater accuracy.

sales forecast Outlines expected sales for a specific product or service to a specific target group over a specific period of time.

Preparing an accurate sales forecast can be a real challenge. Jack Stack, author of *The Great Game of Business*, says sales forecasts are too often based on gut feelings and wishful thinking. Salespeople need to begin the forecasting process with a careful estimate of sales volume to current customers. This is followed by an assessment of new sales to prospects that will be identified during the sales forecast period.[31]

3. *Anticipate prospect calls when planning the sales route; a systematic routing plan saves time and reduces travel expenses.* The procedure used to determine which customers and prospects will be visited during a certain period of time is called **routing.** Consider calls on prospective customers in developing your route plan. This approach helps minimize the cost of developing new accounts.

routing The procedure used to determine which customers and prospects will be visited during a certain period of time.

A plan helps give prospect identification greater purpose and direction. It also helps reduce the cost of developing new customers. Without a plan, salespeople tend to give prospecting too little attention.

Summary

Prospect identification has been called the lifeblood of selling. A continuous supply of new customers must be found to replace those lost for various reasons. *Prospecting* is the systematic process of locating potential customers.

Analysis of both your product and your existing customers can help to identify, locate, and even profile your prospects. Important sources of new customers include referrals (both endless chain referrals and referral letters and cards); friends, family members, and centres of influence; directories; trade publications; trade shows; telemarketing; direct response advertising and sales letters; Web sites; computer databases; cold calling; educational seminars; networking; and prospecting by non-sales employees.

These prospecting techniques produce a list of names that must be evaluated using criteria developed by each salesperson. The process of prospect evaluation is called *qualifying.* Basic questions that can be used to qualify a prospect include: Is the person already buying from you? Is the person a former customer? Is the person a user of your product? and Is the person currently buying from a competitor? An estimate of the amount of sales that could be generated from this prospect, and the prospect's credit rating, should also be determined.

Information about both customers and prospects should be recorded systematically, whether on a special form, in a notebook, on cards, or in a computerized database. Information that is important to record about customers as individuals includes their correct name; their age and experience; and their education, family status, special interests and hobbies, and communication style. Information that is important to record about customers as representatives of their business includes their authority to buy, the business's ability to pay, the company operations, and the company buying practices.

Development of a prospecting and sales forecasting plan requires preparing a list of prospects, creating a forecast of potential sales volume from each new account, and anticipating prospect calls when planning a sales route.

Key Terms

Prospecting 174
Prospect 174
Prospect Base 174
Referral 178
Telemarketing 182
Web Site 182

Cold Calling 183
Networking 184
Target Market 187
Qualifying 187
Sales Forecast 191
Routing 191

Review Questions

1. What three qualifications must an individual have to become a prospect?

2. Why is an understanding of customer attrition important to salespeople? What percentage of a firm's customers are lost each year?

3. Describe three things progressive marketers are doing to improve the quality of the prospecting effort.

4. List the major sources of prospects.

5. Explain how the endless chain referral prospecting method works.

6. Discuss how direct response advertising and sales letters can be used to identify prospects.

7. What are the two most common methods of organizing prospect information?

8. What is *networking*? How might a real estate salesperson use networking to identify prospects?

9. What does the term *qualifying* mean? Why is this step in prospecting important?

10. What is *routing*? How does this relate to the prospecting plan?

Application Exercises

1. You are a sales representative for Xerox Canada. Assuming Xerox has just designed a new, less expensive, and better quality copying machine, make a list of 15 prospects you would plan to call. From the material in this chapter, identify the sources you would use in developing your prospect list.

2. You are in the process of interviewing for a sales position with Sun Life Assurance of Canada. In addition to filling out an application form and taking an aptitude test, one of the items the agency manager requests of you is to develop a list of prospects with whom you are acquainted. He informs you

that this list will represent the prospects you will be working with during the first few weeks of employment. The agency manager recommends that you list at least 50 names. Prepare a list of 10 acquaintances you have that would qualify as prospects.

3. Sales automation software is most commonly used in the prospecting phase of selling. New product releases that provide additional features and benefits to salespeople are continually being developed. The software used in this book is marketed by SalesLogix, a leader in the field. Access the SalesLogix Web site and research the latest version of ACT! Click on and examine information on this number-one-selling sales automation software.

 www.saleslogix.com

4. Locating companies to work for is a form of prospecting. Assuming you are interested in changing careers, develop a list of 10 companies for which you would like to work. Assign each company a priority according to your interest, from the most desirable (1) to the least (10). Organize your list in six columns showing the company name, telephone number, address, person in charge of hiring, prospect information, and priority. What sources did you use to get this information?

CRM Case Study

Reviewing the Prospect Database

Becky Kemley is the sales manager in the Dallas, Texas office of SimNet Systems, which sells network products and services. The productivity and the critical mission of Becky's customers can be considerably enhanced by selecting and using the correct LAN (local area network), WAN (wide area network), or VPN (virtual private network) system. Becky's company is called a value-added reseller (VAR) because its people help customers maximize the value of the products bought through SimNet.

Becky's sales and technical support people may spend several months in the sales process (sales cycle). Salespeople telephone and call on prospects to determine if they qualify for SimNet's attention. Time is taken to study the customer's needs (needs discovery). The expert opinion of SimNet's technical people is incorporated into a sales proposal that is presented to the prospective customer. The presentation may be made to a number of decision makers in the prospect's firm. The final decision to purchase may follow weeks of consideration within the firm and negotiations with SimNet.

Once a decision is made by a customer to buy from SimNet, Becky's people begin the process of acquiring, assembling, and installing the network system; they then follow through with appropriate training, integration, and support services.

Becky's company must carefully prospect for customers. SimNet may invest a significant amount of time helping a potential customer configure the right combination of products and services. This means that only the most serious prospects should be cultivated. Further, Becky's people must ascertain that if the investment of time is made in a prospective customer, the prospect will follow through with purchases from SimNet.

Becky is responsible for ensuring that prospect information is collected and used effectively. The network salespeople use the ACT! CRM software to manage their prospect information. The system, which is same as the software available for download for use with this textbook, allows salespeople to document and manage their sales efforts with each prospect.

Becky has just hired you to sell for SimNet beginning December 1. Becky has given you the files of Pat Silva, a salesperson who has just been promoted to SimNet's corporate headquarters. Becky has asked you to review the status of Pat's 20 prospect accounts. Pat's customers have been notified that Pat is leaving and that a new salesperson, you, will be contacting them. Becky wants you to review each prospect's record. You are to meet with Becky next Monday and be prepared to answer the following questions.

Questions

1. Which contact can you ignore immediately *as a prospect* for making a potential purchase?
2. Referring only to the *date close* category, which four prospects would you call immediately?
3. Referring only to the *dollar amount of sales forecasted* category, which four accounts would you call first? Does the likelihood of closing percentage category have any influence on decisions concerning which prospects to call first? Why?
4. According to information on the records and notes (View, Notes) windows, which prospecting method did Pat Silva appear to use the most? Give examples.

Case Problem

Many sales people are finding that once you have a customer, maintaining the relationship is a lot cheaper than finding a new customer. A growing number of salespeople are using contact software to improve service to existing customers. Marisa Trichilo, Ontario Accounts Coordinator for Western Inventory Service Ltd., a national company that counts inventories and fixed assets for all types of businesses across Canada, is giving her customers added value with ACT! contact software. Like most salespeople, she is trying to cope with expanded duties, faster work pace, and customers with high expectations. ACT! software helps her in the following ways:

➤ **Customer profile.** Complete information on each customer is available on-screen at the touch of a key. In addition to name, phone number, and address, she has a complete record of all past contacts. The profile also includes important personal and business information about the customer.

➤ **Organization and planning.** It is no longer necessary for Marisa to prepare a written "to do" list or a planning calendar. All of this information can easily be entered into her portable computer. In the morning she simply clicks her Day At A Glance command and she is reminded of scheduled appointments, follow-up phone calls that need to be made, and other activities. If she needs to make a call at 2:00 p.m., she can press the Set Alarm button, which serves the same purpose as an alarm clock.

➤ **Correspondence.** ACT! software features a built-in word processor that makes it easy to prepare memos, letters, and reports. To send a standard follow-up letter to a customer, she simply brings up the letter from storage, enters the customer's name, and presses the appropriate key. The word processor automatically prints the inside address and mailing label. With ACT! software you can even send and receive e-mail. Most salespeople are responsible for numerous reports. The ACT! software can be used to generate a wide range of reports with a minimum of effort. It features 30 predefined reports for use in a wide range of sales and sales support areas.

David Florence, a sales representative with Motorola-EMBARC, makes more than 100 phone calls each day. He appreciates the ACT! feature that permits automatic dialling. He simply identifies the customer's name and presses a key.

Questions

1. If your goal is to maintain long-term partnerships with each of your customers, what features of the ACT! contact software will be most helpful?

2. Let us assume you are selling copy machines in a city with a population of 100 000 people. Your territory includes the entire city. What features of the ACT! software would you use most frequently?

3. Some salespeople who could benefit from use of ACT! software continue to use a Rolodex or note cards to keep a record of their customers. What are some barriers to adoption of this type of technology?

4. Examine the first ACT! contact screen presented in Appendix B.
   a. What is Bradley Able's position within the company?
   b. What is the "date expected" for the sale to close?
   c. What is the forecasted dollar amount of this potential sale?

Part V

Developing a Presentation Strategy

The chapters included in Part V review the basic principles used in the strategic/consultative sales presentation. You will use this information as you prepare presentation objectives, develop a presentation plan, and identify ways to provide outstanding service after the sale.

RELATIONSHIP STRATEGY

PRESENTATION STRATEGY

PERSONAL SELLING PHILOSOPHY

PRODUCT STRATEGY

CUSTOMER STRATEGY

BUILDING QUALITY PARTNERSHIPS

To play any game well, you first have to learn the
rules, or principles of the game.
And second, you have to forget about them.
That is, you have to learn to play without thinking about
the rules. This is true whether the
game is chess or golf or selling. Shortcuts won't work.
Al Ries and Jack Trout
Marketing Warfare

197

Approaching the Customer

You might think that a sales force is unimportant for a pharmaceutical company that has a number of drugs needed by patients with serious health problems. Not true. Once Health Canada approves a drug, the sales force has to inform everyone who can be influential in the purchase decision for it, and they must ensure that it is available where and when needed.

Brenda Fisher is one of about 150 Canadian salespeople for Janssen-Ortho Inc., but this is not what she expected to be doing when she completed her B.Ed. "I applied for teaching positions everywhere, but I didn't even get a thank you because there were so many applicants. When I applied for this sales job, the manager was skeptical as to why I wanted to sell. I tried to convince him that selling a product is the same as teaching a concept. You have to understand what the customer needs to know, and you have to communicate knowledge about your product and company and how you can meet their needs."

On any particular day, Brenda Fisher may have to approach general practitioners, specialists, nurses, residents, interns, wholesalers, pharmacists, or any combination of these. She may have to educate them about her company, her products, or herself. She may have to persuade them to buy her products, or she may simply need to remind them about Janssen-Ortho and the products that it manufactures.[1]

As noted in Chapter 2, there is a wide range of career options in the field of personal selling. How do you know if you have selected the most suitable sales position? If the position provides you with the new energy needed each day to be a true consultant to your customers, then you have probably made the right choice. Michael Leimbach, a research director for Wilson Learning Corp., expressed his view on the salesperson's future role in *Canadian Manager*: "Salespeople have to become consultants and strategists ... A consultant brings value to the customer by better understanding the customer's business, the market they compete in and the customers they serve."[2] This chapter provides you with the information needed to assume the role of consultant when approaching the customer.

Developing the Presentation Strategy

The presentation strategy combines elements of the relationship, product, and customer strategies. Each of the other three strategies must be developed before a salesperson can develop an effective presentation strategy.

The **presentation strategy** is a well-conceived plan that includes three prescriptions: (1) establishing objectives for the sales presentation; (2) developing the presale presentation plan needed to meet these objectives; and (3) renewing one's commitment to providing outstanding customer service (Fig. 9.1, Strategic/Consultative Selling Model).

The first prescription reminds us that we need to establish one or more objectives for each sales call. High-performance salespeople like Brenda Fisher understand that it is often possible to accomplish several things during a single call. A common objective of sales calls is to collect information about the prospect's needs. Another common objective is to build relationships with those who will make the buying decision.

A carefully prepared presentation plan ensures that salespeople will be well organized during the sales presentation and prepared to achieve their objectives. A six-step presentation plan is introduced later in this chapter.

Establishment of objectives for the sales presentation and preparation of the presale presentation plan must be guided by a strong desire to offer outstanding customer service. Achieving excellence is the result of careful needs analysis, correct product selection, clear presentations, informative demonstrations, win-win negotiations, and flawless service after the sale. Salespeople who are committed to doing their best in each of these areas will be richly rewarded.

presentation strategy A well-conceived plan that includes three prescriptions: establishing objectives for the sales presentation; preparing the presale presentation plan needed to meet these objectives; and renewing one's commitment to providing outstanding customer service.

A PRESENTATION STRATEGY ADDS VALUE

The importance of planning and preparation was recognized in a national survey of 1500 sales managers and sales representatives. When they were asked to rank 14 personal selling skills in order of importance to their *long-term success*, pre-call planning was ranked as most important.[3]

How does pre-call planning add value? Value is added when you position yourself as a resource—not just a vendor. You must prove that you have important ideas and advice to offer.[4] A well-planned presentation adds value when it is based on carefully developed sales call objectives and a presentation plan needed to meet these objectives. Good planning ensures that the presentation will be customized to meet the needs of the prospect.

Figure 9.1 The Strategic/Consultative Selling Model provides the foundation for a successful consultative-style presentation strategy.

Strategic/Consultative Selling Model*	
Strategic step	**Prescription**
DEVELOP A PERSONAL SELLING PHILOSOPHY	✓ ADOPT MARKETING CONCEPT ✓ VALUE PERSONAL SELLING ✓ BECOME A PROBLEM SOLVER/PARTNER
DEVELOP A RELATIONSHIP STRATEGY	✓ ADOPT DOUBLE–WIN PHILOSOPHY ✓ PROJECT PROFESSIONAL IMAGE ✓ PRACTISE COMMUNICATION-STYLE FLEXING
DEVELOP A PRODUCT STRATEGY	✓ BECOME A PRODUCT EXPERT ✓ SELL BENEFITS ✓ CONFIGURE VALUE-ADDED SOLUTIONS
DEVELOP A CUSTOMER STRATEGY	✓ UNDERSTAND BUYER BEHAVIOUR ✓ DISCOVER CUSTOMER NEEDS ✓ DEVELOP PROSPECT BASE
DEVELOP A PRESENTATION STRATEGY	● PREPARE OBJECTIVES ● DEVELOP PRESENTATION PLAN ● PROVIDE OUTSTANDING SERVICE

* Strategic/consultative selling evolved in response to increased competition, more complex products, increased emphasis on customer needs, and growing importance of long-term relationships.

Planning the Preapproach

preapproach Activities that precede the actual sales call and set the stage for a personalized sales approach, tailored to the specific needs of the prospect. This involves the planning necessary for the actual meeting with a prospect.

Preparation for the actual sales presentation is a two-part process. Part one is referred to as the **preapproach**. The preapproach involves preparing presale objectives and developing a presale presentation plan. Part two is called the **approach** and involves making a favourable first impression, securing the prospect's attention, and developing the prospect's interest in the product (Fig. 9.2). The preapproach and approach, when handled correctly, establish a foundation for an effective sales presentation.

The preapproach should be viewed as a key step in preparing for each sales presentation. Professional salespeople complete the preapproach for every presentation, whether it involves a new account or an established customer.[5] The preapproach includes the first two prescriptions for developing a presentation strategy: establishing objectives and creating a presale presentation plan.

approach The first contact with the prospect, either face-to-face or by telephone. The approach has three objectives: to build rapport with the prospect, to capture the person's full attention, and to generate interest in the product you are selling.

ESTABLISHING PRESENTATION OBJECTIVES

Sales representatives employed by Nalco Chemical Company prepare for each sales call by filling out a 13-point pre-call planner. One section of this form requires the salesperson to identify the objectives of the call. Nalco is a compa-

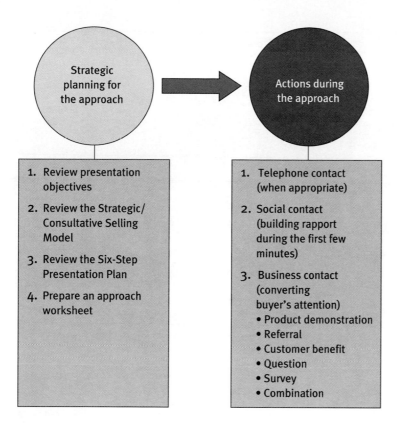

Figure 9.2   Preparing for the presentation involves planning for the activities that will occur before meeting the prospect and for the first few minutes of actual contact with the prospect.

ny that emphasizes professionalism, long-term partnerships, and staying focused on customer needs.[6] We know that most sales are not closed during the first contact with the customer, so why not establish other objectives? Here are some additional objectives that might be established during the preapproach:

1. Obtain personal and business information to update the customer's file.
2. Conduct a needs assessment to determine if your product is suitable. (A second call may not be necessary.)
3. Involve the prospect in a product demonstration.
4. Make an appointment with the prospect's boss or the individual who is the decision maker.
5. Secure a list of referrals.
6. Provide postsale service.

Setting multiple objectives helps reduce the fear of failure that salespeople often feel during the preapproach stage. It can be a confidence-raising experience. Achieving one or more objectives will engender a feeling of accomplishment. Once you have an appointment with the prospect and the presentation objectives have been established, consider sending a fax that outlines the agenda for the meeting. The fax will confirm the appointment and clarify the topics to be discussed.[7]

FACTORS INFLUENCING PRESENTATION OBJECTIVES

There are a number of factors affecting the objectives that you select for a sales presentation. Will the presentation be made to one person or a group? How

Extensive strategic planning is required for salespeople who use computer graphics tied into a desktop projection system such as this one from Proxima.

familiar is the prospect with the product? How much time will you need to spend with the prospect? Answers to these and other questions help the salesperson establish appropriate objectives.

Multicall sales presentations. The use of **multicall sales presentations** will also affect the objectives that are established. Many companies that have adopted the need-satisfaction approach to personal selling use multiple sales calls. The purpose of the first call is to collect and analyze certain basic information that is used to develop a specific proposal. Once the proposal is prepared, the salesperson makes a second appointment to present it. In many cases additional calls will be needed to close the sale. The complexity of products has led to longer sales cycles in many industries.

multicall sales presentations
A standard practice in some industries where products are complex and buying decisions are made by more than one person. The purpose of the first call is to collect and analyze certain basic information that is used to develop a specific proposal.

Multicall sales presentations have become more common in the retail field. The sale of expensive recreational vehicles, leased automobiles, boats, and quality sound systems for the home or business often requires more than one sales call. Sales personnel employed by Tom James Company, a firm that sells individually tailored suits, use a three-call plan. During the first home or office visit, the client reviews designs, picks out the fabric from a sample board of one-inch swatches, and gets measured. The suit is fitted during a second call and delivered during the third call.[8] Each of these calls may require different objectives.

TEAM VERSUS ONE-PERSON PRESENTATION OBJECTIVES

In today's ever-changing business environment, teamwork has surfaced as a major development. A recent survey of 19 000 salespeople and sales managers found that about one quarter of the people contacted use sales teams.[9] Presale planning and the actual sales presentation often require two or more people.[10] Team selling is ideally suited to organizations that sell complex or customized products and services that require direct communication between customers and technical experts. In some situations the involvement of technical experts can shorten the selling cycle. The team approach often results in more precise need identification, improved selection of the product, and more informative sales presentations. To achieve greater customization, Burlington Menswear, a fabric manufacturer, uses teams on most sales calls. Salespeople are teamed with a representative from a support area such as research and development, operations planning, or styling. These specialists often improve the need identification process and the identification of solutions to the customer's buying problem.[11] Complex problems often require pooled expertise.

As noted in Chapter 1, we are seeing the growth of strategic alliances. These long-term partnerships are especially common in business-to-business sales. Teams are often involved in forming the alliance and making purchase decisions after the alliance is established. When a customer's decision-making process is guided by a team, the seller will likely use a team-selling approach.[12]

A variation of the team approach to selling is used by some marketers. Salespeople are trained to seek the assistance of another salesperson or actually to turn the customer over to another salesperson when problems surface. The

Some presentation strategies involve a team approach. The sales team might include a technical specialist or a senior company executive.

Selling in Action

NO TECH TO HIGH TECH

Account planning by the 70 sales representatives at Sebastiani Winery used to be a time-consuming process. Without the aid of modern technology, salespeople were forced to manually analyze two monthly reports that were inches thick. Preparing for a sales call was burdensome. Some salespeople said they spent almost half their time analyzing reports. A major sales force automation (SFA) initiative was started in the late 1990s. The project had four objectives:

- Improve communication through the use of e-mail, file sharing, and intranet technology

- Provide support needed to develop multimedia presentations
- Provide data analysis capabilities
- Ease the administrative burden

Each member of the Sebastiani sales force received a laptop loaded with Windows 95, PowerPoint, e-mail, and Business Objects, the software needed for analyzing data. The new technology was introduced during a three-day training program. Today, salespeople have the ability to do account planning that is much more effective than in the past.[a]

other salesperson may bring to the selling situation greater ability to identify the customer's needs or to select the appropriate product. Salespeople who have well-prepared presale objectives know when to seek assistance from another professional.

SELLING TO A BUYING TEAM

In some cases salespeople must address and satisfy both the individual and collective concerns of each participant in a multi-buyer situation. The decision makers may be members of a well-trained buying team, a buying committee assembled for a one-time purchase, or a board of directors.

As in any type of selling situation, the salesperson should attempt to determine the various buying influences. When possible, the role of each decision maker, the amount of influence he or she exerts, and each decision maker's needs should be determined before or during the presentation. Careful observation during the presentation can reveal who will use the product, who controls the finances, and who will provide the expertise necessary to make the correct buying decision.

When you make a group selling presentation, make sure all parties feel involved. Any member of the group who feels ignored could prevent you from closing the sale. Be sure to direct questions and comments to all potential decision makers in the group.

Find out if there are any silent team or committee members. A silent member is one who will influence the buying decision but does not attend the presentation. Silent members are usually senior managers who have a major influence on the buying decision. If a silent member does exist, you must find a way to communicate, directly or indirectly, with this person.[13]

INFORMATIVE, PERSUASIVE, AND REMINDER PRESENTATION OBJECTIVES

When preparing presale presentation objectives, it is important to make a decision concerning the overall purpose of the presentation. The major purpose may be to inform, persuade, or remind. The sale of highly technical products and

Well-prepared presale objectives
will help salespeople address the
needs of each person in a group
selling situation.

services often begins with an informative sales presentation; the customer needs
to be familiar with the product before making a buying decision. In another situation, where the customer's needs have been carefully identified and your product is obviously suited to these needs, a persuasive presentation would be appropriate. In the case of repeat customers, it is often necessary to remind them of
the products and services you offer.

INFORMATIVE PRESENTATION

The objective of a presentation that involves a new or unique product is generally to inform customers of its features and explain how these features will benefit the customer. Typically, people will not purchase a product or service until
they become familiar with its application. Informative presentations are usually
more prevalent when the product is being first introduced to the market. A
detail salesperson (introduced in Chapter 2) usually spends a great deal of time
informing customers of new products and changes in existing products.

PERSUASIVE PRESENTATION

Some degree of persuasion is common to nearly all sales presentations.
Persuasion—the act of presenting product appeals so as to influence the
prospect's beliefs, attitudes, or behaviour—is a strategy designed to encourage
the buyer to make a buying decision. Persuasion can be integrated into every
phase of the sales presentation. A friendly greeting and a firm handshake at the
time of initial customer contact represent a relationship-oriented form of persuasion. An enthusiastic sales demonstration is another type of persuasion common in sales. Additional forms of persuasion include converting features to
buyer benefits, repeating feature-benefit statements, and asking for the sale.
Persuasive strategies are designed to elicit a positive response from the prospect.
It is never a good idea, however, to apply too much persuasion in an attempt to
sell a product or service. These actions can perpetuate the stereotype of the
pushy, unprofessional salesperson.

persuasion   The act of presenting
product appeals so as to influence
the prospect's beliefs, attitudes, or
behaviour.

REMINDER PRESENTATION

In some selling situations, the primary objective of the sales call will be to remind the prospect of products and services offered by the company. Without this occasional reminder the prospect may forget information that is beneficial. Computer salespeople might periodically remind customers about special services (training classes, service contracts, and customized programming, for example) available from the company they represent. An occasional reminder can prevent the competition from capturing the business.

The sale of expensive recreational vehicles, leased automobiles, boats, and quality sound systems for the home or business often require more than one sales call. Consideration of whether the overall presentation objective should be to inform, persuade, or remind will have a significant influence on your presale presentation plan and your efforts to provide outstanding service.

Developing the Six-Step Presentation Plan

Once you have established objectives for the sales presentation, the next step (prescription) involves developing the presentation plan. This plan helps you achieve your objectives.

Today, with increased time constraints, fierce competition, and rising travel costs, the opportunity for a face-to-face meeting with customers may occur less frequently. The few minutes you have with your customers may be your only opportunity to win their business, so careful planning is more critical than ever. Ken Daniels, team leader at AT&T Global Information Solutions, says, "Plan each sales call before you make it so you don't get sidetracked."[14]

In preparation for development of the presentation strategy, it is helpful to review the three broad strategic areas that have been described in previous chapters: relationship strategy, product strategy, and customer strategy. Why is this review so critical? It is because today's dynamic sales presentations require consideration of the simultaneous influences of the relationship, product, and customer strategies. A careful review of these three areas sets the stage for flexible presentations that meet the needs of the customer.

PLANNING THE PRESENTATION

six-step presentation plan
Preparation involving consideration of those activities that will take place during the sales presentation.

Once you have sufficient background information, you are ready to develop a "customized" presale presentation plan. The plan is developed after a careful review of the **six-step presentation plan** (Fig. 9.3). This planning aid is a tentative list of activities that will take place during the sales presentation. This presale activity will further strengthen your self-confidence and help avoid confusion in the presence of the prospect.

CUSTOMIZING THE PRESENTATION

Preparing a customized sales presentation can take a great deal of time and energy. Nevertheless, this attention to detail will give you added confidence and help you avoid delivering unconvincing hit-or-miss sales talks.

A well-planned sales presentation is a logical and orderly outline that features the salesperson's own thoughts from one step to the next. The presentation is usually divided into six main parts (see Fig. 9.3):

1. *Approach.* Preparation for the approach involves making decisions concerning effective ways to make a favourable first impression during the initial contact, to secure the prospect's attention, and to develop the prospect's interest in the product. The approach should set the stage for an effective sales presentation.

2. *Presentation.* The presentation is one of the most critical parts of the selling process. If the salesperson is unable to discover the prospect's buying needs, select a product solution, and present the product in a convincing manner, the sale may be lost. Chapter 10 covers all aspects of the sales presentation.

3. *Demonstration.* An effective sales demonstration helps verify parts of the sales presentation. Demonstrations are important because they provide the customer with a better understanding of product benefits. The demonstration, like all other phases of the presentation, must be carefully planned. Chapter 11 is devoted exclusively to this topic.

4. *Negotiation.* Buyer resistance is a natural part of the selling–buying process. An objection, however, does present a barrier to closing the sale. For this reason, all salespeople should become skillful at negotiating buyer concerns. Chapter 12 covers this topic.

The Six-Step Presentation Plan	
Step One: APPROACH	● Review Strategic/Consultative Selling Model ● Initiate customer contact
Step Two: PRESENTATION	● Determine prospect needs ● Select product or service ● Initiate sales presentation
Step Three: DEMONSTRATION	● Decide what to demonstrate ● Select selling tools ● Initiate demonstration
Step Four: NEGOTIATION	● Anticipate buyer concerns ● Plan negotiating methods ● Initiate double-win negotiations
Step Five: CLOSE	● Plan appropriate closing methods ● Recognize closing clues ● Initiate closing methods
Step Six: SERVICING THE SALE	● Suggestion selling ● Follow-through ● Follow-up calls
Service, retail, wholesale, and manufacturer selling.	

Figure 9.3 The Six-Step Presentation Plan. A presale plan is a logical and an orderly outline that features a salesperson's thoughts from one step to the next in the presentation. Each step in this plan will be explained in Chapters 9 to 14.

The sales presentation should be a model of good two-way communication.

5. *Close*. As the sales presentation progresses, there may be several opportunities to close the sale. Salespeople must learn to spot closing clues. Chapter 13 provides suggestions on how to close sales.

6. *Servicing the sale*. The importance of developing a long-term relationship with the prospect was noted earlier in this chapter. This rapport is often the outgrowth of postsale service. Learning to service the sale is an important aspect of selling. Chapter 14 deals with this topic.

In some cases you can assess the value of something by determining how long it has existed. A truly valuable idea or concept is timeless. The six parts of the presale presentation plan checklist have been discussed in the sales training literature for several decades; therefore, they might be described as fundamentals of personal selling. These steps are basic elements of almost every sale and frequently occur in the same sequence. Of course some sales are made without an objection, and some customers buy before the salesperson attempts to close.

Although these six selling basics are part of nearly every seminar, workshop, and course devoted to sales training, the emphasis given to each will vary depending on the nature of the selling situation.

The Approach

After a great deal of preparation it is time to communicate with the prospect, either by face-to-face contact or by telephone. We refer to the initial contact with the customer as the *approach*. All the effort you have put into developing relationship, product, and customer strategies can now be applied to the presentation strategy. If the approach is effective, you will be given the opportunity to make the sales presentation. If, however, the approach is not effective, the chance to present your sales story may be lost. You can be the best-prepared salesperson in the business, but without a good approach there may be little chance for a sale.

The approach has three important objectives. First, you want to build rapport with the prospect. Second, you want to capture the person's full attention; never begin your sales story if the prospect seems preoccupied and is not paying attention. Third, you want to generate interest in the product you are selling.

In some selling situations the first contact with the customer is a telephone call. The call is made to schedule a meeting or in some cases to conduct the sales presentation. The face-to-face sales call starts with the social contact and is followed by the business contact. The telephone contact, social contact, and business contact are discussed in this section.

ATTENTION—TODAY'S SCARCE RESOURCE

We live in a world that is threatened by an information glut. Technological advancements in the age of information have so dramatically advanced the communication process that people are often overwhelmed by too much information. Key decision makers complain that they must cope daily with message overload created by electronic mail, voice mail, faxes, memos, phone calls, and letters. Many say the communications barrage interrupts them three or more times every hour.[15]

Attention has become one of today's scarcest resources. Many of the people we need to communicate with are distracted and unable to concentrate.[16] Salespeople must learn how to connect with prospects and then figure out how to get their attention. Keeping in touch with established customers is no less important.

THE TELEPHONE CONTACT

A telephone call provides a quick and inexpensive method of scheduling an appointment. Appointments are important because many busy prospects will not meet with a salesperson who drops in unannounced. An appointment provides benefits to both the prospect and the salesperson. The prospect knows

The telephone contact can set the stage for the social and business contact. The first few seconds of the call are crucial to the image you project.

Building Relationships in a Diverse World

SELLING ACROSS CULTURES

The growth of international trade is creating some communication problems for salespeople. More firms are opening branch offices abroad or entering into joint ventures with foreign corporations than ever before. Yet all too often business travellers going overseas have little knowledge of the language and culture of the host country. There are many subtle communication traps awaiting the unwary. For example, if you are visiting with a prospect in Mexico, you should always inquire about the person's spouse and family. In Saudi Arabia, you should not inquire about a client's family. In Latin America, people are often late for scheduled meetings. In Sweden, you should try to be prompt to the second.

A buyer for Marks & Spencer's, one of England's major department store chains, reminds us that communication style may be an issue in some cultures. He says, "If you want to sell to the British, write a nice, clear, nonexaggerating letter explaining the simple facts of your business, and ask for an appointment to come over and see me. I will be busy, but British buyers, unlike American buyers, will see you. I will give you half an hour to persuade me, and if you are flamboyant, I will reject most of what you say."

Many Canadian and American organizations are beginning to realize they must prepare their foreign-based employees for the diverse aspects of the new culture in which they will be living and working. For example, female employees should be prepared to cope with far more male chauvinism than they would encounter back home. Men and women alike learn that aggressiveness may be counterproductive in some countries. In Japan, for example, people who wait and listen in a conversation earn respect.

How about business cards? Business cards are very important in most foreign countries, and it is common courtesy to have your card printed in English as well as in the local language.[b]

---

about the sales call in advance and can therefore make the necessary advance preparation. The buyer will be in a better position to give attention to the sales presentation.

Some salespeople use the telephone exclusively to establish and maintain contact with the customer. As noted in Chapter 2, inside salespeople rely almost totally on the telephone for sales. **Telesales**, not to be confused with telemarketing, includes many of the same elements as traditional sales: gathering customer information, determining needs, prescribing solutions, negotiating buyer concerns, and closing sales. Telesales is usually not scripted, a practice widely used in telemarketing. In some situations, telesales is as free-wheeling and unpredictable as a face-to-face sales call. IBM is one of several companies that is expanding the telesales concept to sell to customers in North America and throughout the world.[17]

telesales Using the telephone to acquire information about the customer, determine needs, suggest solutions, negotiate buyer concerns, close the sale, and service the sale.

In Chapter 3 we examined some of the factors that influence the meaning we attach to an oral message from another person. With the aid of this information we can see that communication via telephone is challenging. The person who receives the call cannot see our facial expression, gestures, or posture, and therefore must rely totally on the sound of our voice and the words used. The telephone caller has a definite handicap.

The telephone has some additional limitations. A salesperson accustomed to meeting prospects in person may find telephone contact impersonal. Some salespeople try to avoid using the telephone because they believe it is too easy for the prospect to say no. It should be noted that these drawbacks are more imagined than real. With proper training a salesperson can use the telephone effectively to schedule appointments. When you make an appointment by telephone, use the following practices:

From The Wall Street Journal *by permission of Cartoon Features Syndicate*

"I don't think of myself as the Jenkins Doolittle & Bloom gatekeeper. I rather prefer lead blocker."

In some cases a secretary, assistant, or receptionist will screen incoming telephone calls. Be prepared to convince this person that your call is important. Always treat the gatekeeper with respect and courtesy.

1. *Plan in advance what you will say.* It helps to prepare written notes to use as a guide during the first few seconds of the conversation. What you say will be determined by the objectives of the sales call.

2. *Politely identify yourself and the company you represent.* Set yourself apart from other callers by using a friendly tone and impeccable phone manners. This approach will help you avoid being shut out by a wary gatekeeper (secretary or receptionist).

3. *State the purpose of your call and explain how the prospect can benefit from a meeting.* In some cases, it is helpful to use a powerful benefits statement that will get the prospect's attention and whet the person's appetite for more information. Present only enough information to stimulate interest.

4. *Show respect for the prospect's time by telling the person how much time the appointment will take.* Emphasize that you know her time is valuable.

5. *Confirm the appointment with a brief note or letter with the date, time, and place of your appointment.* Enclose your business card and any printed information that may be of interest to the prospect.[18]

You should anticipate resistance from some prospects. After all, most decision makers are very busy. Be persistent and persuasive if you genuinely believe a meeting with the prospect will be mutually beneficial.

EFFECTIVE USE OF VOICE MAIL

The growing popularity of voice mail presents a challenge to salespeople. What type of message will set the stage for a second call or stimulate a return call? It's important to anticipate voice mail and know exactly what you will say if you reach a recording. The prospect's perception of you is based on what you say and your voice quality. Here is a message that almost guarantees that you will be ignored:

Ms. Simpson, I am Paul Watson and I am with Acme Property Management Services. I would like to visit with you about our services. Please call me at 862-1500.[19]

Building Relationships through Technology

PLANNING PERSONAL VISITS

Personally visiting prospects and customers helps build strong relationships, yet travelling is expensive and time consuming. A salesperson is challenged to plan visits that will optimize the investment represented by each trip. Access to CRM prospect records helps salespeople quickly identify all the accounts in a given geographic area.

CRM empowers salespeople to rapidly review and compare an area's prospects on the basis of position in sales cycle, potential size of account or purchase, likelihood of sale, and the contribution that the visit could make to information gathering and relationship building. A well-managed CRM database will provide salespeople with appropriate business and social topics to discuss when calling selected prospects for an appointment. (See the exercise Planning Personal Visits on page 220 for more information.)

Note that this message provides no compelling reason for the prospect to call back. It offers no valid item that would stimulate interest. The voice mail message should be similar to the opening statement you would make if you had a face-to-face contact with the prospect:

> *Miss Simpson, my name is Paul Watson and I represent Acme Property Management Services. We specialize in working with property managers. We can help you reduce the paperwork associated with maintenance jobs and provide an easy way to track the progress of each job. I would like the opportunity to visit with you and will call back in the morning.*[20]

Note that this message is brief and describes results that customers can receive. If Paul Watson wants a call back, then he needs to give the best time to reach him. He should give his phone number slowly and completely. It's usually best to repeat the number.

THE SOCIAL CONTACT

According to many image consultants, "First impressions are lasting impressions." This statement is essentially true, and some profitable business relationships never crystallize because some trait or characteristic of the salesperson repels the prospective customer. Sales personnel have only a few minutes to create a positive first impression. Dr. Leonard Zunin, coauthor of *Contact: The First Four Minutes*, describes what he calls the "four-minute barrier." In this short period of time a relationship can be established or denied. Susan Bixler, author of *The New Professional Image*, describes the importance of the first impression this way:

> *Books are judged by their covers, houses are appraised by their curb appeal, and people are initially evaluated on how they choose to dress and behave. In a perfect world this is not fair, moral, or just. What's inside should count a great deal more. And eventually it usually does, but not right away. In the meantime, a lot of opportunities can be lost.*[21]

To be certain your first impression is appropriate, review the material in Chapter 3. The information in this chapter is timeless and will serve you well today and in the future.

The l
prepai
buyer

QUES
The c
alway:
direct
that tl
M
manaş
to the
questi

"l

"|

These
menta
to arc
examp

"
in

"|
ot

Once
proce
then y
his or

SURV
Larry
the l
Assoc
tionn:
of his
docur
financ
the pi
chine:
cannc

T
ing w
matio
the si
treatr
Price

The
appro

DEVELOPING CONVERSATION

The brief, general conversation during the social contact should hold the prospect's attention and establish a relaxed and friendly atmosphere for the business contact that is to follow. As mentioned in Chapter 3, there are three areas of conversation that should be considered in developing a social contact:

1. *Comments on here and now observations.* These comments may include general observations about the victory of a local athletic team, an article in the *Globe and Mail*, or specific comments about awards on display in the prospect's office.

2. *Compliments.* Most customers will react positively to sincere compliments. Personal items in the prospect's office, achievements, or efficient operation of the prospect's business provide examples of things that can be praised.

3. *Search for mutual acquaintances or interests.* The discovering of mutual friends or interests can serve as the foundation for a strong social contact.

Communication on a personal basis is often the first step in discovering a common language that will improve communication between the salesperson and the prospect. How much time should be devoted to the social contact? There is no easy answer to this question. The length of the conversation will depend on the type of product or service sold, how busy the prospect appears to be, and your awareness of topics of mutual interest.

THE BUSINESS CONTACT

Converting the prospect's attention from the social contact to the business proposal is an important part of the approach. When you convert and hold your prospect's attention, you have fulfilled an important step in the selling process. Furthermore, without success in the beginning, the door has been closed on completing the remaining steps of the sale.

Some salespeople use a carefully planned opening statement or a question to convert the customer's attention to the sales presentation. A statement or question that focuses on the prospect's dominant buying motive is, of course, more likely to achieve the desired results. Buyers must like what they see and hear, and must be made to feel that it will be worthwhile to hear more.

Throughout the years, salespeople have identified and used a number of effective ways to capture the prospect's attention and arouse interest in the presentation. Five of the most common methods will be explained in the following material:

Product demonstration approach

Referral approach

Customer benefit approach

Question approach

Survey approach

We also discuss combining two or more of these approaches.

PRODUCT DEMONSTRATION APPROACH

This straightforward method of getting the prospect's attention is used by sales representatives who sell copy machines, photographic equipment, automobiles, construction equipment, office furniture, and many other products. If the

presentation strategy. With experience, salespeople learn to select the most effective approach for each selling situation. Table 9.1 provides examples of how these approaches can be applied in real-world situations.

COMBINATION APPROACHES

A hallmark of consultative selling is flexibility. Therefore a combination of approaches sometimes provides the best avenue to need identification. Sales personnel who have adopted the consultative style will, of course, use the question and survey approaches most frequently. Some selling situations, however, require that one of the other approaches be used, either alone or in combination with the question and survey approaches (Fig. 9.4). Here is an example of how a salesperson might use a referral and question approach combination:

Salesperson: Carl Hamilton at Simmons Modern Furniture suggested that I visit with you about our new line of compact furniture designed for today's smaller homes. He believes this line might complement the furniture you currently feature.

Table 9.1 Business Contact Worksheet

This illustrates how to prepare effective real-world approaches that capture the customer's attention.

METHOD OF APPROACH	WHAT WILL YOU SAY?
1. Product demonstration	1a. (Retail clothing) "We have just received a shipment of new fall sweaters from Braemar International."
	1b. (Business forms manufacturer) "Our plant has just purchased a $300 000 Harris Graphics composer, Mr. Reichart; I would like to show you a copy of your sales invoice with your logo printed on it."
2. Referral	2. (Food wholesaler) "Paula Doeman, procurement manager for St. Joseph's Hospital, suggested that I provide you with information about our computerized 'Order It' system."
3. Customer benefit	3. (Real estate) "Mr. and Mrs. Stuart, my company lists and sells more homes than any other company in the area where your home is located. Our past performance would lead me to believe we can sell your home within two weeks."
4. Question	4. (Hotel convention services) "Mrs. McClaughin, will your 2002 Annual Franchisee Meeting be held in April?"
5. Survey	5a. (Custom-designed computer software) "Mr. Pham, I would like the opportunity to learn about your accounts receivable and accounts payable procedures. We may be able to develop a customized program that will significantly improve your cash flow."
	5b. (Retail menswear) "May I ask you a few questions about your wardrobe? The information will help me better understand your clothing needs."

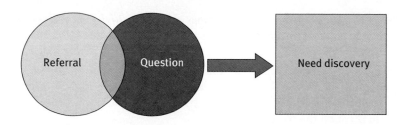

Referral   Question

Need discovery

Figure 9.4   Combination approaches provide a smooth transition to the need discovery part of the consultative-style presentation.

Customer: Yes, Carl called me yesterday and mentioned your name and company.

Salesperson: Before showing you our product lines, I would like to ask you some questions about your current product mix. First, what do you currently carry in the area of bedroom furniture?

DEALING WITH THE "BAD-TIMING" RESPONSE

If the approach is effective you will usually be given an opportunity to make the sales presentation. However, the prospect may attempt to delay the presentation with a statement such as "The time just isn't right, call me back later." Before you agree to a follow-up call, try to determine if the prospect is really interested in your product and willing to take action in the future. Your response might sound like this: "I certainly do not mind scheduling another call. But first, do you agree that my product is one you see yourself using?" You do not want to waste time on a follow-up call if the person is not a prospect. If the timing of your call is truly a problem, find out why. A real prospect has a reason and will likely explain it. This information will help you schedule your sales call at the right time.[27]

COPING WITH SALES CALL RELUCTANCE

The transition from the preapproach to the approach is sometimes blocked by sales call reluctance. Fear of making the initial contact with the prospect is a problem for rookies and veterans, and people in every selling field. Research conducted by Behavioral Sciences Research Press, Incorporated, reveals that about 40 percent of all salespeople will, at some point, experience call reluctance. For new salespeople the problem can be career-threatening.[28] Sales call reluctance may stem from concern about interrupting or intruding on the prospect, or it may stem from fear of saying the wrong thing or concern about not being able to respond effectively to the person who quickly begins asking questions. Sales call reluctance may surface because the salesperson fears rejection. Regardless of the reasons for sales call reluctance, you can learn to deal with it. Here are some suggestions:

➤ *Be optimistic about the outcome of the initial contact.* It is better to anticipate success than to anticipate failure. Martin Seligman, professor of psychology at the University of Pennsylvania and author of the best-selling book *Learned Optimism,* says that success in selling requires a healthy dose of optimism.[29] The anticipation of failure is a major barrier to making the initial contact.

➤ *Practise your approach before making the initial contact.* A well-rehearsed effort to make the initial contact will increase your self-confidence and reduce the possibility that you may handle the situation badly.

➤ *Recognize that it is normal to feel anxious about the initial contact.* Even the most experienced salespeople experience some degree of sales call reluctance.

➤ *Develop a deeper commitment to your goals.* Abraham Zaleznik, professor emeritus at Harvard Business School, says, "If your commitment is only in your mind, then you'll lose it when you encounter a big obstacle. If your commitment is in your heart and your mind, you'll create the power to break through the toughest obstacles."[30]

Summary

As one sales consultant noted, "Organization multiplies the value of anything to which it is applied." This is especially true of pre-call planning. The well-prepared salesperson approaches the sales call with an attitude of confidence and expectancy.

Developing a presentation strategy involves preparing presale objectives, developing a presale presentation plan, and providing outstanding customer service. The presentation strategy combines elements of the relationship, product, and customer strategies.

Preparation for the sales presentation is a two-part process. Part one is referred to as the *preapproach* and involves preparing presale objectives and developing a presale presentation plan. Part two is called the *approach* and involves making a good first impression, securing the prospect's attention, and developing the prospect's interest in the product.

Over the years, salespeople have identified several ways to convert the prospect's attention and arouse interest in the presentation. Some of the most common ways include the product demonstration approach, referral approach, customer benefit approach, question approach, and survey approach. This chapter also includes information on how to cope with sales call reluctance.

Key Terms

Presentation Strategy 199	*Persuasion 205*
Preapproach 200	*Six-Step Presentation Plan 206*
Approach 200	*Telesales 210*
Multicall Sales Presentation 202	

Review Questions

1. What is the purpose of the preapproach? What are the two prescriptions included in the preapproach?

2. Explain the role of objectives in developing the presale presentation plan.

3. Why should salespeople establish multiple-objective sales presentations? List four possible objectives that could be achieved during a sales presentation.

4. What is the difference between a canned and a planned sales presentation?

5. Describe the major purpose of the informative, persuasive, and reminder sales presentations.

6. What are the major objectives of the approach?

7. Review the Building Quality Partnerships box on p. 214. Why do you think Dale Carnegie's book *How to Win Friends and Influence People* appeared on the list of books that contributed most to our culture?

8. What are some rules to follow when leaving a message on voice mail?

9. What methods can the salesperson use to convert the prospect's attention to the sales presentation?

10. Discuss why combination approaches are considered an important consultative-selling practice. Provide one example of a combination approach.

Application Exercises

1. Assume that you are a salesperson who calls on retailers. For some time you have been attempting to get an appointment with one of the best retailers in the city to carry your line. You have an appointment to see the head buyer in 90 minutes. You are sitting in your office. It will take you about 30 minutes to drive to your appointment. Outline what you should be doing between now and the time you leave to meet your prospect.

2. Tom Nelson has just graduated from Algonquin College with a major in marketing. He has three years of experience in the retail grocery business and has decided he would like to go to work as a salesperson for the district office of Procter & Gamble. Tom has decided to telephone and set up an appointment for an interview. Write out exactly what Tom should *plan* to say during his telephone call.

3. Concepts from Dale Carnegie's *How to Win Friends and Influence People* are referenced in this chapter. Access the Dale Carnegie Web site and examine the courses offered. Click on the "Sales Advantage Course" and read the description. Note the books that are used with this course. Is enthusiasm and remembering names an important part of the approach?

4. Participant 1: You are a salesperson for ZCL Composites Inc. (see Chapter 6) and you are calling on a new customer who has not done business with your company before. In fact, you have found out that Brian Burns, the purchasing manager, has not even heard of your company. You believe that Mr. Burns is an Emotive (substitute Director, Reflective, Supportive; see Chapter 4). One apparoach you like to use in a situation like this is to suggest some questions to customers that they might wish to have answered. This approach allows you to plan and practise what you want to tell the customer. You begin this approach with, "Mr. Burns, in preparing for my meeting with you today, I have thought of three important questions you might like to have answered about ZCL Composites. For example, you might like to know. ..."

Participant 2: You are Brian Burns.

CRM Application Exercise

Planning Personal Visits

CRM software allows trip planners to examine the status of prospects in the geographic area to be visited. Assume that a salesperson using the ACT! software wishes to visit the city of Bedford, Texas. The software permits a fast field search capability to select and sort the records of prospects in that city: Lookup, City, type "Bedford," and press Enter. After arranging by phone to visit these people, you can print the information contained in these records and take it along: Report, Contact Report, Active Lookup, Printer, and Enter. You should now have printed information about all customers in Bedford. Salespeople today use the Internet to schedule trip transportation and lodging, and to check the weather forecast.

Case Problem

When Brenda Fisher wakes up on Monday morning, she usually has her whole week planned. She works from her office at home, and she tries to leave home with everything necessary for her weekly schedule. As a Janssen-Ortho pharmaceutical sales representative, Brenda spends most of her day visiting hospitals, medical clinics, and doctors' offices. She spends a large part of each day serving as a consultant to doctors, head nurses, pharmacists, and others who need information and advice regarding the complex medical products available from her company. As might be expected, she also spends a considerable amount of time conducting informative presentations designed to achieve a variety of objectives. In some situations she is introducing a new product and in some cases she is providing up-to-date information on an existing product. Some of her presentations are given to individual health care professionals and others are given to a group. Occasionally she even makes presentations to as many as 30 interns or residents at one time. Each of these presentations must be carefully planned.

Janssen-Ortho is owned by Johnson & Johnson, and sells in excess of $250-million worth of prescription drugs in Canada annually. Hismanol was the first drug sold in Canada by Janssen Canada when it entered the Canadian market in 1982, before the Janssen-Ortho merger. In 1993, Janssen-Ortho received a "notice of compliance" for Risperdal, an anti-psychotic drug. A notice of compliance from Health Canada is necessary before a drug can be marketed legally in this country. In the case of Risperdal, the notice of compliance was granted in 11 months, much shorter than the average $3\frac{1}{2}$ years that it takes to get approval for new drugs in Canada. The speed of approval is an indicator of both the quality of and the need for the drug. However, even with drugs that are clearly needed, management knows that a sales force is necessary to win acceptance in the marketplace. Doctors are very cautious when it comes to prescribing a new drug to their patients. They demand accurate information regarding principal uses of the drug, dosage forms and strengths, dose instructions, and possible side effects.

Brenda uses informative and reminder presentations almost daily in her work. Informative presentations are given to doctors who are in a position to prescribe her products. The verbal presentation is often supplemented with audiovisual aids and printed materials. Reprints of articles from leading medical journals are often used to explain the success of her products in treating patients. These articles give added credibility to her presentations. Some of her informative presentations are designed to give customers updates on the prescription drugs she sells. Reminder presentations are frequently given to pharmacists who must maintain an inventory of her products. She has found that it is necessary periodically to remind pharmacists of product delivery procedures and policies, and special services available from Janssen-Ortho. She knows that without an occasional reminder a customer can forget information that is beneficial.

In some cases a careful needs analysis is required to determine if her products can solve a specific medical problem. Every patient is different, so generalizations about the use of her products can be dangerous. When doctors talk about their patients, Brenda must listen carefully and take good notes. Sometimes she must get additional information from company support staff. Janssen-Ortho has a physician on staff who can be reached by calling a toll-free 800 number. Customers can get immediate expert advice and additional technical information through this important part of the Janssen-Ortho customer service program.

Brenda's career in pharmaceutical sales has required continuous learning. In the beginning she had to learn the meaning of dozens of medical terms and become familiar with a large number of medical problems. If a doctor asks, "What is the 'mode of action' of Risperdal?" she must know the meaning of the medical term and be knowledgeable regarding this Janssen-Ortho product.

Brenda also spends time learning about the people she works with. She recently said, "It is important to me to have a good relationship with our internal support staff. It makes my work more enjoyable, and my job much easier." When meeting someone for the first time, she takes time to assess their communication style and then adjusts her own style to meet their needs. She points out that in some cases the competition offers a similar product at a similar price. It is in these situations that a good relationship with the customer can influence the purchase decision.

Questions

1. If you become a pharmaceutical sales representative, how important is it to adopt the three prescriptions for a presentation strategy? Explain.

2. Brenda Fisher spends a great deal of time giving individual and group presentations. Why is it essential that she be well prepared for each presentation? Why would a "canned" presentation be inappropriate in her type of selling?

3. Salespeople are encouraged to establish multiple-objective sales presentations. What are some objectives that Brenda Fisher might achieve during a sales presentation to doctors who are not currently using her products?

4. What are some special challenges Brenda Fisher faces when she makes a group presentation? How might she enhance her group presentations?

5. Put yourself in the position of a pharmaceutical sales representative. Can you envision a situation where you might combine the elements of an informative, persuasive, and reminder presentation? Explain.

CRM Case Study

Establishing Your Approach

Becky Kemley, your sales manager at SimNet Systems, has notified Pat Silva's former prospects by letter that you will be calling on them soon. She wants to meet with you tomorrow to discuss your preapproach to your new prospects. Review the records in the ACT! database.

Questions

1. Becky wants you to call on Robert Kelly. Describe what your call objectives will be with Mr. Kelly.

2. Describe a possible topic of your social contact with Mr. Kelly and how you would convert that to a buying contact.

3. Becky has given you a reprint of a new article about using networks for warehouse applications. Which of your prospects might have a strong interest in this kind of article? How would you use this article to make an approach to that prospect?

Partnership Selling: A Role Play/Simulation (see Appendix C, p. 447)

DEVELOPING A RELATIONSHIP STRATEGY

Read *Employment Memorandum 2*, which announces your promotion to account executive. (In your new position you will be assigned by your instructor to one of the two major account categories in the convention centre market. You will be assigned to either the *association accounts market* or the *corporate accounts market*. Association accounts includes customers who are responsible for planning meetings for the association or group they are a member of or are employed by. Corporate accounts include customers who are responsible for planning meetings for the company they represent. You will remain in the account category for the rest of the role plays.)

Note the challenges you will have in your new position. Each of these challenges will be represented in the future *sales memoranda* you will be receiving from your sales manager.

Read *Sales Memorandum 1* for the account category you are assigned. (Note that the "A" means association and your customer is Erin Adkins, and "B" means corporate and your customer is Leigh Combs.) Follow the instructions in the sales memorandum and strategically prepare to approach your new customer. Your call objectives will be to establish a relationship (social contact), share an appealing benefit, and find out if your customer is planning any future conventions (business contact).

You will be asked to assume the role of a customer in the account category that you are not assigned as a salesperson. Your instructor will provide you with detailed instructions for correctly assuming this role.

Creating the Consultative Sales Presentation

When Dave Tripp, sales representative for HarperCollins publishers, won the "Sales Rep of the Year" award, his loyal customers were not surprised. To maximize service to his 30 retail and wholesale accounts, he uses the consultative-selling approach exclusively. He takes pride in his ability to look at situations through the bookseller's eyes and answer the question, "What can I do to bring more customers into this store?" Carol Erdahl, co-owner of The Red Balloon Bookshop, says, "It's his job to present what's new, but he's always looking out for us, suggesting things to promote the books.[1]

Tripp sees himself as a partner in the management of each bookstore. Drawing on his knowledge of what types of books sell well at each store, he works with buyers to predict demand for new releases. He also understands the value of building a relationship with store employees. He is on a first-name basis with salespeople at each store. He gets acquainted with their reading preferences and makes sure they get advance copies of books in their favourite genres (science fiction, how-to, poetry, etc.).

Tripp's service to his customers is really the manifestation of such qualities as product knowledge (he needs to keep on top of a list of more than 16 000 books), dependability, and service after the sale.[2]

LEARNING OBJECTIVES

When you finish reading this chapter, you should be able to

1. Describe the characteristics of the consultative sales presentation

2. Explain how to determine the prospect's needs

3. Discuss the use of questions to determine needs

4. Select products that match customer needs

5. List and describe three types of need-satisfaction presentation strategies

6. Present general guidelines for developing effective presentations

A growing number of salespeople, like Dave Tripp, have adopted the consultative sales presentation (Fig. 10.1). They support the selling philosophy expressed by Suzanne Vilardi, area sales manager for Swift Transportation:

> *Be a consultant, a partner, an extension of your client's business. Be a friend, a problem solver. Balance your client's best interests with those of your own and your company.*[3]

Figure 10.2 features key concepts related to creating the consultative sales presentation. This approach can be used effectively in all types of selling: service, retail, wholesale, and manufacturing. It results in increased customer satisfaction, more sales, fewer cancellations and returns, more repeat business, and more referrals.

The Consultative Sales Presentation

As we noted in Chapter 9, an effective approach sets the stage for the sales presentation. Once you have established rapport with the prospect, captured the prospect's full attention, and generated interest in your product, you can begin the sales presentation with confidence. To be most effective, the salesperson

Figure 10.1   Creating the sales presentation.

The Six-Step Presentation Plan	
Step One: APPROACH	✓ Review Strategic/Consultative Selling Model ✓ Initiate customer contact
Step Two: PRESENTATION	● Determine prospect needs ● Select product or service ● Initiate sales presentation
Step Three: DEMONSTRATION	● Decide what to demonstrate ● Select selling tools ● Initiate demonstration
Step Four: NEGOTIATION	● Anticipate buyer concerns ● Plan negotiating methods ● Initiate double-win negotiations
Step Five: CLOSE	● Plan appropriate closing methods ● Recognize closing clues ● Initiate closing methods
Step Six: SERVICING THE SALE	● Suggestion selling ● Follow-through ● Follow-up calls
Service, retail, wholesale, and manufacturer selling.	

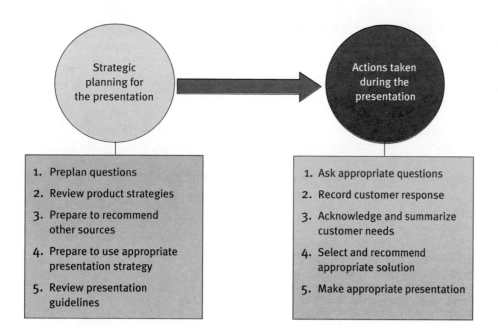

Figure 10.2   Salespeople who truly represent value to their customers plan ahead strategically for the actions taken during the presentation.

should think of the presentation as a four-part process. The Consultative Sales Presentation Guide (Fig. 10.3) features the four parts.

PART ONE—NEED DISCOVERY

A review of the behaviours displayed by high-performance salespeople helps us understand the importance of precise need discovery. They have learned how to skilfully diagnose and solve the customer's problems better than their competitors. This problem-solving capability translates into more repeat business and referrals, and fewer order cancellations and returns.

Unless the selling situation requires mere order taking (customers know exactly what they want), need discovery is a standard part of the sales presentation. It may begin during the approach, if the salesperson uses questions or a survey during the initial contact with the customer. If neither of these two methods is used during the approach, need discovery begins immediately after the approach.

The pace, scope, depth of inquiry, and time allocated, depend on a variety of factors. Some of these include the sophistication of the product, the selling price, the customer's knowledge of the product, the product applications, and, of course, the time available for dialogue between the salesperson and the prospect. Each selling situation is different, so a standard set of guidelines for need discovery is not practical. Additional information on need discovery is presented later in the chapter.

Figure 10.3   The Consultative Sales Presentation Guide. To be most successful, the salesperson should think of the sales presentation as a four-part process.

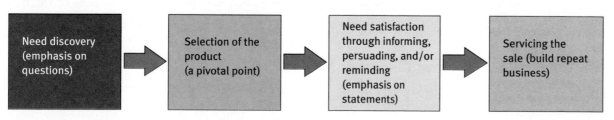

PART TWO—SELECTION OF THE PRODUCT

The emphasis in sales and marketing in the age of information is on determining customer needs and then selecting or configuring custom-fitted solutions to satisfy these needs. Therefore an important function of the salesperson is product selection and recommendation. The salesperson must choose the product or service that will provide maximum satisfaction. When making this decision, the salesperson must be aware of all product options, including those offered by the competition. A John Deere farm equipment salesperson can, for example, offer a farmer a seed planter that possesses an almost endless combination of features. Some farmers want 4-row planters; others want a 24-row planter. Some use the planter to apply liquid fertilizer; others want a planter to apply dry fertilizer. A farmer can order a planter from Deere according to more than a million permutations.[4]

Salespeople who have the ability to diagnose a need accurately and select the correct product to fill this need deliver more value to the customer and achieve the status of trusted adviser.[5] They face fewer buyer concerns and close more sales.

PART THREE—NEED SATISFACTION THROUGH INFORMING, PERSUADING, OR REMINDING

The third part of the consultative sales presentation consists of communicating to the customer, both verbally and nonverbally, the satisfaction that the product or service will provide. The salesperson places less emphasis on the use of questions and begins making statements. These statements are organized into a presentation that informs, persuades, or reminds the customer of the most suitable product or service. Later in this chapter, and in several of the remaining chapters, we discuss specific strategies used in conjunction with the demonstration, negotiating buyer concerns, and closing the sale.

PART FOUR—SERVICING THE SALE

Servicing the sale is a major dimension of the selling process. These activities, which occur after closing the sale, ensure maximum customer satisfaction and set the stage for a long-term relationship with the customer. Service activities include suggestion selling, making credit arrangements, following through on assurances and promises, and dealing effectively with complaints. This topic is covered in detail in Chapter 14.

In those cases where a sale is normally closed during a single sales call, the salesperson should be prepared to go through all four parts of the Consultative Sales Presentation Guide. However, when a salesperson uses a multicall approach, preparation for all the parts is usually not practical. The person selling computer systems or investments, for example, will almost always use a multicall sales presentation. Need discovery (part one) is the focus of the first call.

Need Discovery

A lawyer does not give the client advice until the legal problem has been carefully studied and confirmed. A doctor does not prescribe medication until the

The sales presentation can inform, persuade, or remind.

patient's symptoms have been identified. In like manner, the salesperson should not recommend purchase of a product without a thorough need identification.

Your best bet is to adopt the style used so successfully by most counsellors. You start with the assumption that the client's problem is not known. The only way to determine and confirm the problem is to get the other person talking. You must obtain information to clarify the need properly. The counsellor style requires that you be more concerned about the customer's welfare than closing the sale. This is consistent with the trend we discussed previously: the emphasis in selling has shifted from the product to the customer.

The counsellor style often creates need awareness. Many customers do not realize that they actually have a need for your product or service. Even when they are aware of their need, they may not realize that an actual solution to their problem exists.

Need discovery begins with pre-call preparation, when the salesperson is acquiring background information on the prospect. It continues once the salesperson and the customer are engaged in a real dialogue. Through the process of need discovery the salesperson establishes two-way communication by asking appropriate questions and listening carefully to the customer's responses. These responses will usually provide clues concerning the customer's dominant buying motive (Fig. 10.4).

need discovery   The salesperson establishing two-way communication by asking appropriate questions and listening carefully to the customer's responses.

ASKING QUESTIONS

Questions provide one of the most effective ways to involve the prospect. Appropriate questions reduce tension and build trust in a selling situation because they communicate interest in the other person's welfare. A sales presentation devoid of questions closes the door on meaningful two-way communication.

The art and science of using questions was discussed by Socrates more than 2300 years ago. He noted, among other things, that questions tend to make people think. Kevin Daley, CEO of Communispond, describes the benefits of the Socratic approach: "The customer opens up and gives lots of useful

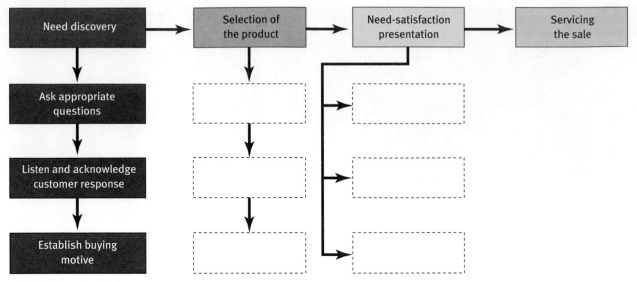

Figure 10.4   Three dimensions of need discovery.

information. A high level of trust is established, and the customer owns the decisions made."[6] In any selling situation we want the prospect to be actively thinking, sharing thoughts, and asking questions. Until the person begins to talk freely, the salesperson will have difficulty discovering dominant buying motives and perceptions. A well-planned sales presentation will include a variety of preplanned questions (Table 10.1). We will describe the four most common types of question used in the field of personal selling.

INFORMATION-GATHERING QUESTIONS

Linda Richardson, an adjunct personal selling professor at the Wharton Graduate School, has developed a corporate sales training program called Dialogue Selling. She says that the first step in the partnership-building process is to ask general questions that help you acquire important information about the prospect.[7] At the beginning of most sales presentations there is a need to collect certain basic information. **Information-gathering questions** are designed to elicit such information (see Table 10.1).

In most cases the information-gathering question is easy to answer. These questions help us acquire facts about the prospect that may reveal the person's need for the product or service. Questions of this type also help build rapport with the customer. Here are some general information-gathering questions that can be used in selected selling fields:

> "This call is not about selling, but about learning. I'd like to learn more about your situation and your needs. Could you help me with that?"

> "Can you give me a close estimate of how many people will attend your meeting? I need this information to develop a facilities plan that will meet your needs"[8]

Many salespeople use preplanned information-gathering questions. These questions are sometimes listed on a form or checklist. If the company does not provide a preprinted form or checklist, a worksheet (Table 10.2) can easily be developed. It is common practice to get the customer's permission before asking

Table 10.1 Types of Question Used in Conjunction with Consultative Selling

TYPE OF QUESTION	DEFINITION	WHEN USED	EXAMPLES
Information-gathering questions	*General questions designed to get the prospect to disclose certain types of basic information*	*Usually at the beginning of a sales presentation*	*"Can you describe the type of leasing plan you envision?"*
Probing questions	*More specific questions designed to uncover and clarify the prospect's perceptions and opinions*	*When you feel the need to obtain more specific information that is required to fully understand the problem and prescribe a solution*	*"What type of image do you want your advertising to project to current and potential customers?" (newspaper advertising)*
Confirmation questions	*Designed to find whether or not your message is understood by the prospect*	*After each important item of information is presented*	*"Do you see the merits of purchasing a copy machine with the document enlargement feature?" (office copy machine)*
Summary confirmation questions	*Designed to clarify your understanding of the prospect's needs and buying conditions*	*Usually used after several items of information have been presented*	*"I would like to summarize what you have told me thus far. You want a four-bedroom home with a basement and a two-car garage?" (real estate)*

the first question. You might simply ask, "Do you mind if I get your answers to a few questions?"

In some cases the use of certain types of information-gathering questions can have negative consequences. Prospects often expect salespeople to do their homework and acquire certain basic information from other sources prior to the sales presentation. In the eyes of a busy prospect, the salesperson who seems to be poorly prepared for the sales presentation may appear unprofessional.

PROBING QUESTIONS

Throughout the sales presentation the salesperson should make every effort to clarify the prospect's perceptions and opinions. Some prospects will have a

A good salesperson and a good doctor have one thing in common: they encourage questions.

limited vocabulary for describing their problems; they know a problem exists but have difficulty expressing their views. High-performance salespeople realize that there is a common tendency for people to speak in generalities.[9]

probing questions Help the salesperson to uncover the prospect's perceptions or opinions.

Probing questions help you to uncover and clarify the prospect's perceptions and opinions (see Table 10.1). These questions encourage customers to give you more details about their problems. The more time customers invest in talking to you about their problems, the greater your chance of seeing the total picture.

Although probing techniques will vary from one selling situation to another, there is a general format you should observe. Your probing should begin on a general basis and gradually narrow to the specifics that will ultimately give you the information needed to fully understand the problem and prescribe a solution.[10] Here are two examples of general probing questions:

"How do you feel about using a computer to keep your expense records?"

"What kinds of solutions have you already considered?"

These general probing questions are not threatening, and they give prospects a chance to talk about a problem or issue from their point of view. These questions also keep the focus of the sales presentation on the customer's agenda. General probing questions establish a rapport that is hard to achieve in any other way.

As the sales presentation progresses, you will need to use more specific probing questions that uncover the clues you need to custom fit your product or

---

Table 10.2 Need Discovery Worksheet

Preplanned questions (sometimes used with preprinted forms) are being used increasingly in service, retail, wholesale, and manufacturer selling. Salespeople who use the consultative approach frequently record answers to their questions and use this information to select and recommend correct solutions that build repeat business and referrals. (Questions taken from **Shearson Lehman Brothers Selling Skills Training Program***)*

PREPLANNED QUESTIONS TO DISCOVER BUYING MOTIVES	CUSTOMER RESPONSE
1. *"Tell me a little bit about your investment portfolio."*	
2. *"What is the history of your family income?"*	
3. *"What are your major concerns when managing your financial affairs?"*	
4. *"What are your current investment objectives?"*	
5. *"What do you expect from your financial services consultants?"*	
6.	
7.	
8.	
9.	
10.	

service to the prospect's needs. The following probing questions are more specific and more focused:

"What will be the consequences if you choose to do nothing about your current record-keeping problems?"

"Would a 20 percent reduction in turnaround time improve your profit picture?"

The best sales presentations are characterized by active dialogue. As the presentation progresses, the customer becomes more open and shares perceptions, ideas, and feelings freely. A series of good probing questions will stimulate the prospect to discover things that he or she had not considered before. Too many rapid-fire probing questions may be threatening to your customer and should be avoided.

CONFIRMATION QUESTIONS

As a ship moves from one port to another, the captain and crew must continually check instruments to be certain the ship stays on course. In a selling situation you must, from time to time, use confirmation questions to avoid the same problem. Is your language too technical? Is the prospect listening to you? Are you on target in terms of the person's needs and interests? Does the prospect agree with what you are saying? **Confirmation questions** are used throughout the presentation to determine if the message is correctly understood by the prospect (see Table 10.1). Many confirmation questions are simple and to the point:

"Do you need additional information regarding any aspect of our sales proposal?"

"If I understand you correctly, you want the Dolby 'C' noise reduction feature, is that correct?"

"Will this location appeal to your business partner?"

"Would you like me to explain how the security system is activated?"

confirmation questions Types of questions used throughout the sales presentation to find out if the message is getting through to the prospect. They check both the prospect's level of understanding and the prospect's agreement with the presentation's claims.

This real estate salesperson, with the help of a computerized database of homes, is using probing and confirmation questions to clarify the needs of the customer.

Building Quality Partnerships

SOLVING CUSTOMER PROBLEMS USING A MULTIPLE QUESTION APPROACH

Neil Rackham conducted studies of 35 000 sales calls and from this research developed the material for his book entitled *Spin Selling*. The book describes strategies for making large-ticket sales and is based on a close examination of successful salespeople. SPIN is an acronym for situation, problem, implication, and need-payoff. Rackham recommends the multiple question approach, which involves using four types of question in a specific sequence.

Situation questions. These questions are used to collect facts and background information about the customer's existing situation. Some examples of situation questions include: How long have you held this position? How many people do you currently employ? Do you usually purchase or lease your equipment? These questions help you acquire information that may be needed later in the sales presentation.

Problem questions. These questions help the salesperson uncover specific problems, difficulties, or dissatisfactions. The salesperson is searching for areas where his or her product or service can solve existing problems. Examples of problem questions are: Does your Canon copy machine make copies fast enough for you? Are you happy with your current lease plan? If the salesperson discovers a problem area, he or she uses implication questions.

Implication questions. These questions encourage the customer to think about the consequences of the problem. The objective of implication questions is to get the customer to understand the true dimensions of the problem area. If the customer who owns the Canon copy machine complains about delays caused by slow operation of the machine, the salesperson might ask this implication question: Does the slow operation of the machine have a negative impact on office productivity? How do you think a faster copy machine would improve office productivity?

Need-payoff questions. These questions build up the value or usefulness of a proposed solution in the customer's mind. Need-payoff questions focus on the solution rather than the problem. Here is an example: Would restricted phone lines provide the cost savings you desire?

UPS is one of several companies that prepares its salespeople to apply the principles of SPIN selling. Sales representatives complete a training program that prepares them to use the four types of questions at appropriate points during the sales presentation.

Confirmation questions not only maintain the prospect's attention, but also they clear up misunderstandings. In an ideal situation, the salesperson is getting feedback from the prospect throughout the presentation.

SUMMARY CONFIRMATION QUESTIONS

buying conditions Those circumstances that must be available or fulfilled before the sale can be closed.

The length of a sales presentation can vary from a few minutes to an hour or more, depending on the nature of the product, the customer's knowledge of the product, and other factors. As the sales call progresses, the amount of information available to the salesperson and the customer increases. In most cases the customer's buying conditions surface. **Buying conditions** are those qualifications that must be available or fulfilled before the sale can be closed. The customer may buy only if the product is available in a certain colour or can be delivered by a certain date. In some selling situations, product installation or service after the sale are considered important buying conditions by the customer. In a complex sale, several buying conditions may surface. The salesperson has the responsibility of clarifying and confirming each condition.

summary confirmation questions Questions used to clarify and confirm buying conditions.

One of the best ways to clarify and confirm buying conditions is with **summary confirmation questions** (see Table 10.1). To illustrate, let us consider a situation where Tammy Harris, sales manager at a major hotel, has interviewed a prospect who wants to schedule a large awards banquet. After a series of information-gathering, probing, and confirmation questions, Tammy feels confident she has collected enough information to prepare a proposal. However, to be sure that she has all the facts and has clarified all important buying conditions, she asks the following summary confirmation question:

> "Let me summarize the major items you have mentioned. You need a room that will comfortably seat 60 persons and 10 of these persons will be seated at the head table?"

If the customer responds in the affirmative, Tammy continues with another summary confirmation question:

> "You want chicken served as the main course, and the price per person for the entire meal cannot exceed $15?"

Once all the buying conditions are confirmed, Tammy can prepare a proposal that reflects the specific needs of the customer, which results in a win-win situation. The salesperson wins because the proposal will be custom fitted to meet the customer's requirements. The chances of closing the sale improve. Also, the customer wins because he or she had the opportunity to clarify buying conditions and will now be able to review a specific proposal.

ELIMINATING UNNECESSARY QUESTIONS

It is important to avoid the use of unnecessary questions during a sales call. As noted previously, salespeople need to acquire as much information as possible about the prospect before the first meeting. This preliminary information gathering is especially important when the prospect is a corporate buyer. These buyers expect the salesperson to be well informed about their operation and not waste time asking a large number of basic information-gathering questions. A growing number of corporate buyers want to establish a long-term partnership with suppliers. They assume that potential partners will conduct a careful study of their company before the first sales call.

LISTENING AND ACKNOWLEDGING THE CUSTOMER'S RESPONSE

Stephen Covey, the noted author and consultant, says that most salespeople sell products, not solutions. To correct this situation he encourages us to, "Seek first

Building Relationships through Technology

REVIEWING ACCOUNT STATUS

 Salespeople regularly review the status of their prospects' records in their CRM databases. In some cases, this is done on the computer screen. In other situations, a printed copy of the records can enhance the process.

Salespeople review their files to ascertain at what phase in the Consultative Sales Presentation Guide each prospect is in the sales cycle. Then they will decide which action to take to help move the prospect to the next phase. Sales managers can be helpful with this process,

especially for new salespeople. Managers can help salespeople evaluate the available information and suggest strategies designed to move to the next phase.

Even experienced salespeople count on their sales managers to help plan presentations. Managers can help salespeople evaluate their prospects' needs, select the best solution, and plan a presentation most likely to succeed. (See the exercise Printing the Customer Database on page 248 for more information.)

to understand, then to be understood."[11] To understand the customer we must listen closely and acknowledge every response.

The listening efficiency rate for most people is about 25 percent. This means they miss about 75 percent of the messages spoken by other people. Why has the skill of listening fallen on hard times? Good listening takes time, and time has become a scarce commodity in our fast-paced world. Also, watching television encourages passive rather than active listening. Many people spend from four to six hours a day watching television and in the process acquire passive rather than active listening skills.[12]

DEVELOPING ACTIVE LISTENING SKILLS

What does listening really mean? Listening is an active process that requires your participation. Too frequently, hearing is confused with listening.

The late Carl Rogers stated that through active listening we can understand what people mean when they speak and what they are feeling. **Active listening** is the process of sending back to the person what you as a listener think the individual meant, both in terms of content and in terms of feelings. It involves taking into consideration both verbal and nonverbal signals.[13] This approach to listening enables the salesperson to check on the accuracy of what the customer said and what the customer meant. Active listening involves three practices that can be easily learned.

active listening The process of sending back to the person what you as a listener think the individual meant, in terms of both content and feelings. It involves taking into consideration both verbal and nonverbal signals.

Focus your full attention. This is not easy, because the delivery of the messages we hear is often much slower than our capacity to listen. So we have plenty of time to let our minds roam, to think ahead, and to plan what we are going to say next. Our senses are constantly feeding us new information while someone is trying to tell us something. Staying focused is often difficult and involves maintaining eye contact with the speaker and not letting distractions interfere.[14]

Paraphrase the customer's meaning. This involves stating in your own words what you think the person meant. This technique not only helps ensure understanding but also is an effective customer relations strategy. The customer will feel good knowing that not only are you listening to what has been said but also you are making an effort to ensure accuracy. Paraphrasing also helps you remember what was said.[15]

In addition to paraphrasing the content, echo the feelings you felt were expressed or implied. It is important that we check on our perception of the customer's feelings. This step is especially helpful if the person is experiencing negative emotions such as doubt or frustration.

Take notes. Although note taking is not necessary in every sales presentation, it is important in complex sales where the information obtained from the customer is critical to the development of a good proposal. It is important that you capture your customer's major points. Make sure your notes are brief and to the point.[16] Michael Tulk, introduced in Chapter 5, never makes a sales call without a pen and notebook. He says, "Not only does note taking make sure I get accurate information, it indicates to customers that I value what they are saying and I really want to understand their situation before I recommend any solution."[17] A.T. Cross pen company has developed an electronic pen-and-notepad combination that enables the user to quickly convert handwritten notes to text.

Active listening is not easy. Gerry Mitchell, chairman of the Dana Corporation, described listening as "tough and grinding work." Like learning to give a speech, learning to listen takes practice. Many salespeople are enrolling in seminars and workshops designed to develop listening skills.

ESTABLISHING BUYING MOTIVES

The primary goal of questioning, listening, and acknowledging is to uncover prospect needs and establish buying motives. Our efforts to discover prospect needs will be more effective if we focus our questioning on determining the prospect's primary reasons for buying. When a customer has a definite need, it is usually supported by specific buying motives.

In many selling situations note taking will demonstrate a high level of professionalism.

Selection of the Product

The second part of the consultative sales presentation consists of selecting or creating a solution that satisfies the prospect's buying motives. After identifying the buying motives, the salesperson carefully reviews the available product options. At this point the salesperson is searching for a specific solution to satisfy the prospect's buying motives. Once the solution has been selected, the salesperson makes a recommendation to the prospect (Fig. 10.5).

If the sale involves several needs and the satisfaction of multiple buying motives, selection of the solution may take several days or even weeks and involve the preparation of a detailed sales proposal. A company considering the purchase of automated office equipment would likely present this type of challenge to the salesperson. The problem needs careful analysis before a solution can be identified.

MATCH SPECIFIC BENEFITS WITH BUYING MOTIVES

As we noted in Chapter 6, products and services represent problem-solving tools. People buy products when they perceive that they fulfill a need. We also noted that today's more demanding customers seek a cluster of satisfactions that arise from the product itself, from the company that makes or distributes the product, and from the salesperson who sells and services the product (see Fig. 6.1). Each of these clusters may add value to the sale. Once the customer's needs and buying motives are firmly established, the salesperson can determine which specific benefits to emphasize. The emphasis here is on *specific* rather than *general* benefits. Research indicates that the success of a sales call is related to the number of different needs discovered and the specific benefits highlighted in response to those needs.

CONFIGURE A SOLUTION

Most salespeople bring to the sale a variety of products or services. Salespeople who represent food distributors can offer customers a mix of several hundred items. Most pharmaceutical sales representatives can offer the medical community a wide range of products. The Future Shop, a large retailer of electronics, offers customers a wide range of audio and visual entertainment options. The customer who wants to purchase a sound system, for example, can choose from many combinations of receivers, speakers, and so on.

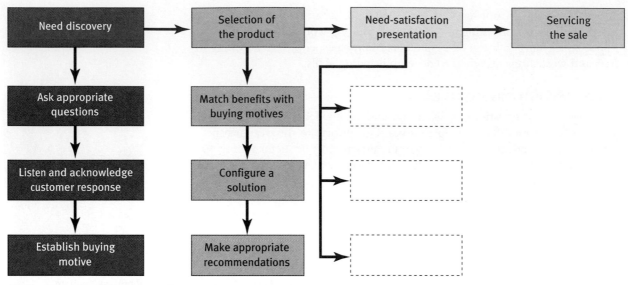

Figure 10.5 Three dimensions of product selection.

MAKE APPROPRIATE RECOMMENDATIONS

The recommendation strategies available to salespeople are similar to those used by a doctor who must recommend a solution to a patient's medical problem. In the medical field, three possibilities for providing patient satisfaction exist. In situations in which the patient easily understands the medical problem and the appropriate treatment, the doctor can make a recommendation and the patient can proceed immediately toward a cure. If the patient does not easily understand the medical problem or solution, the doctor may need to discuss thoroughly with the patient the benefits of the recommended treatment. If the medical problem is not within her medical specialty area, the doctor may recommend a specialist to provide the treatment. In consultative selling the salesperson has these same three counselling alternatives.

RECOMMEND PRODUCT—CUSTOMER BUYS IMMEDIATELY

The selection and recommendation of products to meet customer needs may occur at the beginning of the sales interview, such as in the product approach; during the interview, just after the need discovery; or near the end, when minor concerns have been dealt with. At any of these three times, presentation of products that are well matched to the prospect's needs may result in an immediate purchase.

RECOMMEND PRODUCT—SALESPERSON MAKES
NEED-SATISFACTION PRESENTATION

This alternative requires a full presentation of product benefits, including demonstrations and handling of any objections, before the sale is closed. In this situation the customer may not be totally aware of a buying problem, and the solution may not be easily understood or apparent. Because of this, the salesperson will need to make an in-depth presentation to define the problem and communicate a solution to the customer.

RECOMMEND ANOTHER SOURCE

Earlier in this book we indicated that professional salespeople may recommend that a prospect buy a product or service from another source, maybe even a

cathy® by Cathy Guisewite

competitor. If, after a careful needs assessment, the salesperson concludes that the products represented will not satisfy the customer's needs, the consultative salesperson should recommend another source.

Need Satisfaction—Selecting a Presentation Strategy

Decisions concerning which presentation strategy to emphasize have become more complex. This is due to several factors discussed in previous chapters: longer sales cycles, multiple buying influences, emphasis on repeat sales and referrals, greater emphasis on custom fitting products, and building of long-term partnerships. Conducting business in the new economy, which is based on the assets of knowledge and information, requires that we think about ways to improve the sales presentation. Here is how one author described this challenge:

> As we move from the rutted byways of the Industrial Age to the electronic thoroughfares of the Information Age, business presentations become a measure of our ability to adapt to new surroundings. The most successful and forward-thinking companies already have assigned presentations a new, fundamental and strategic importance.[18]

Today we need a broader range of presentation strategies. Today, the need-satisfaction strategy involves assessing the customer's needs; selecting the product; and deciding whether to use an informative, persuasive, or reminder presentation (Fig. 10.6).

INFORMATIVE PRESENTATION STRATEGY

To be informative, a message must be clearly understood by the customer. Of course, clarity is important in any presentation, but it needs special attention in a presentation whose primary purpose is to inform. The **informative presentation** emphasizes factual information often taken from technical reports, company-prepared sales literature, or written testimonials from persons who have used the product. This type of presentation is commonly used to introduce new products and services. This strategy emphasizes clarity, simplicity, and directness.

informative presentation Emphasizes factual information, which is often taken from technical reports, company-prepared sales literature, or written testimonials from people who have used the product.

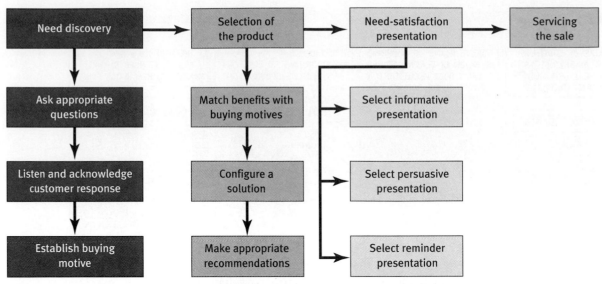

Figure 10.6 The three strategies to use in developing an effective need-satisfaction presentation.

A variety of factors motivate sales personnel to adopt the informative presentation. Some have discovered that this strategy works best when you sell highly complex products that have to be custom fitted to unique needs. In addition, if the product's price is quite high, a factual presentation, devoid of emotion, may be the best approach. Some salespeople simply think that it is not appropriate to use persuasion during the sales presentation. They believe that a product should stand on its own merits and that persuasion should not be necessary to sell it.

Within most major industries, new products are appearing at a rapid rate. Many of these products are introduced through informative sales presentations.

PERSUASIVE PRESENTATION STRATEGY

persuasive presentation A sales strategy that influences the prospect's beliefs, attitudes, or behaviour, and encourages buyer action.

Many salespeople believe that, when a real need for their product exists, the stage is set for a persuasive presentation. The major goal of the **persuasive presentation** strategy is to influence the prospect's beliefs, attitudes, or behaviour and to encourage buyer action. Persuasive sales presentations include a subtle transition stage where the dialogue shifts from an intellectual emphasis to an emotional appeal.

Persuasion is commonly used in all professions. Medical doctors routinely use persuasion to influence patient behaviour. In fact, doctors involved in the growing field of preventive medicine rely heavily on persuasion to encourage patients to adopt certain health practices. Teachers use persuasion to encourage students to complete assignments. Lawyers use persuasion to influence clients' feelings and opinions.

In the field of personal selling, persuasion is an acceptable strategy once a need has been identified and a suitable product has been selected. When it is clear that the buyer will benefit from ownership of the product or service, an enthusiastic and persuasive sales presentation is usually appropriate.

The persuasive presentation strategy requires a high level of training and experience to be effective, because a poorly planned and delivered persuasive presentation may raise the prospect's anxiety level. The persuasive presentation, when handled properly, does not trigger fear or distrust.

REMINDER PRESENTATION STRATEGY

Studies show that awareness of a company's products and services declines as promotion is stopped. This problem represents one of the reasons many companies employ missionary salespeople to maintain an ongoing awareness of and familiarity with their product lines. Other types of salespeople also use this presentation strategy. Route salespeople rely heavily on **reminder presentations** (sometimes called *reinforcement presentations*) to maintain their market share. They know that, if they do not make frequent calls and remind customers of their products, the competition will likely capture some customers. The 12 800 Frito-Lay salespeople are in a strong position to use the reminder presentation strategy because they use handheld computers to manage orders. It takes only a minute or two to review a programmed product list in the presence of a customer.[19]

The reminder presentation also has many applications at the retail level. Sales personnel working with repeat customers are in a good position to remind them of products or services offered in their own department or another department located in some other area of the store.

Reminder presentations assume that in most cases the prospect understands at least the basic product features and buyer benefits. Salespeople using this strategy understand the value of repetition. They know that many of their recommendations will not be accepted until the second, third, or fourth time.

In some cases the reminder presentation will focus on factors other than a specific product or service. The presentation may include information that will indirectly influence the sale. For example, a salesperson might describe a new automated package and delivery system that will improve service to customers.

reminder presentation Sometimes called the reinforcement presentation. Assumes that the prospect has already been involved in an informative or persuasive presentation and understands at least the basic product features and buyer benefits.

Guidelines for Developing a Persuasive Presentation Strategy

There are many ways to incorporate persuasion into a sales presentation. In this section we review a series of guidelines that should be followed during preparation of a persuasive presentation.

PLACE SPECIAL EMPHASIS ON THE RELATIONSHIP

Throughout this book we have emphasized the importance of the relationship strategy in selling. Good rapport between the salesperson and the prospect is a necessary foundation for the use of a persuasive sales presentation. Jennifer Low, writing in *Profit*, says: "Today's sales mantra is: 'Selling is about relationships.' Unfortunately, too many people think that means a lot of backslapping. It's really about servicing customers and building a record of trust and credibility."[20] People seldom purchase products from salespeople they dislike or distrust.

You can cultivate relationships even when you are speaking to a group. When you are speaking to a group, you want each member to feel as if you're talking directly to them. Throughout the presentation make eye contact with various group members and involve them when appropriate. Eye contact tends to bond you to your audience.[21] Also, you should stand during most presentations. Standing tends to add energy to your presentation because you have more options in terms of body language.

SELL BENEFITS AND OBTAIN CUSTOMER REACTIONS

People do not buy things, they buy what the things will do for them. They do not buy an auto battery, they buy a sure start on a cold morning. Office managers do not buy laser printers, they buy better-looking letters and reports. Every product or service offers the customer certain benefits. The benefit might be greater comfort, security, a feeling of confidence, or economy.

Some salespeople make the mistake of emphasizing only product features; they fail to translate these features into buyer benefits. If you are selling Allstate insurance, for example, you should become familiar with the service features. One feature is well-trained employees, and another is the convenient location of Allstate offices across Canada. The benefit to customers is greater peace of mind in knowing that they will receive good service at a nearby location.

After you state the feature and convert it into a buyer benefit, obtain a reaction from the customer. You should always check to see if you are on the right track and if your prospect is following the logic of your presentation. The reactions can be triggered by a simple confirming question. Here are some examples:

Feature	Benefit	Confirming question
Commercial-size package	Money saved	"You are interested in saving money, are you not?"
Automatic climate control system for automobile	Temperature in car not varying after initial setting	"Would you like the luxury of setting the temperature and then not worrying about it?"

The feature-benefit-reaction (FBR) approach is used by many high-performance salespeople. Involving the customer with a confirmation question helps you maintain two-way communication with the customer.

MINIMIZE THE NEGATIVE IMPACT OF CHANGE

As we noted earlier, salespeople are constantly threatening the status quo. They sell people the new, the different, and the untried. In nearly all selling situations the customer is being asked to consider change of some sort, and in some cases it is only natural for the person to resist change.

Whenever possible we should try to help the customer view change in a positive and realistic way. Change is more acceptable to people who understand the benefits of it and do not see it as a threat to their security. The prospect must be given realistic expectations about the products they are buying.[22] If the salesperson creates unrealistic expectations by exaggerating buyer benefits, long-term problems will likely surface. The credibility of the salesperson and of the company he or she represents may suffer.

PLACE THE STRONGEST APPEAL AT THE BEGINNING OR END

Research indicates that appeals made at the beginning or end of a presentation are more effective than those given in the middle. A strong appeal at the beginning of a presentation, of course, will get the prospect's attention and possibly develop interest. Made near the end of the presentation, the appeal sets the stage for closing the sale.

TARGET EMOTIONAL LINKS

An important key to successful persuasion is a good understanding of your prospect so you know which emotion links to target. **Emotional links** are the connectors between your messages and the prospect's emotions.[23] Some common emotional links in the business community are quality improvement, on-time delivery, increased market share, innovation, customer service, and reduction of operating expenses. Targeting just a few emotional links can increase your chances of closing the sale. When you target emotional links use persuasive words such as *proven, efficient, save, convenient, world-class, new* and *improved*. Also, use the language that your prospect is most tuned in to.

emotional links   The connectors that link a salesperson's message to the customer's internal emotions and increase the chances of closing a sale — for example, quality improvement, on-time delivery, service, innovation.

USE METAPHORS, STORIES, AND TESTIMONIALS

Metaphors, sometimes referred to as *figurative language*, are highly persuasive sales tools. Metaphors are words or phrases that suggest pictorial relationships between objects or ideas. With the aid of metaphors you can paint vivid, visual pictures for prospects that will command their attention and keep their interest. The success of the metaphor rests on finding common ground (shared or well-known experiences) so that your message gets a free boost from a fact already known or believed to be true. A salesperson presenting a new computer system that has a very fast data analysis capability might say, "The speed of our system, compared to what you are used to, would be like comparing an Olympic sprinter to a toddler just learning to walk."[24]

Donald J. Moine, noted speaker and sales trainer, says that stories will not only help you sell more products, but they will also help you enrich relationships with your customers. A good story not only focuses the customer's attention, it can effectively communicate the value of a product or service. Xerox and IBM represent just two examples of companies that use stories to inspire the selling effort.[25]

Many salespeople find it beneficial to quote a specific third party. Third-party testimonials from satisfied clients can help a prospect feel confident about using your product.

Guidelines for Creating Effective Presentations

There are many ways to make all three need-satisfaction presentation strategies more interesting and valuable. A more effective presentation can be developed using the following general guidelines. Each of these guidelines will be discussed in more detail in Chapters 11 to 14.

STRENGTHEN THE PRESENTATION STRATEGY WITH AN EFFECTIVE DEMONSTRATION

The need-satisfaction presentation can be strengthened if the salesperson pre-plans effective demonstrations that clarify the product features and benefits.

Many salespeople encounter doubt or skepticism during the sales presentation. The prospect often wants some kind of assurance or proof. We must be prepared to substantiate our claims with factual information. This information can be provided in several ways. The following list of proof strategies is explained in detail in Chapter 11.

The product itself

Models

Photos and illustrations

Portfolios

Testimonials and case histories

Reprints

Graphs, charts, and test results

Laptop computers and demonstration software

Audiovisual technology

Bound paper presentations

PREPLAN METHODS FOR NEGOTIATING AND CLOSING THE SALE

It is a good idea to assume that customers want to make the most efficient use of the time they spend purchasing goods and services. To make your presentation as concise and to the point as possible, you should preplan methods for negotiating misunderstandings or resistance that often surface during the presentation. You need to bring some degree of urgency to the selling environment by presenting focused solutions.[26] In most cases the focus of the negotiation will be on one of the following areas:

➤ *Need* awareness is vague or nonexistent.

➤ *Price* does not equal perceived value.

➤ The buyer is satisfied with present *source*.

➤ The *product* does not meet the buyer's perceived requirement.

Methods used to negotiate buyer resistance in each of these areas are introduced in Chapter 12.

Sales Force Automation. Salespeople can enhance their presentation strategy with proof devices produced using computer software packages such as the popular Microsoft PowerPoint.

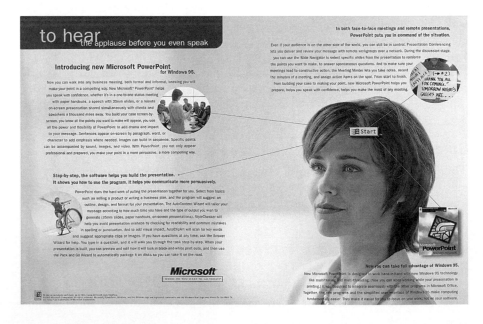

It is also important to preplan closing and confirming the sale. This planning should include a review of closing clues that may surface during the sales presentation and of methods for closing the sale. This and other topics are discussed in Chapter 13.

PLAN FOR THE DYNAMIC NATURE OF SELLING

The sales presentation is a dynamic activity. From the moment the salesperson and the customer meet, the sales presentation is being altered and fine-tuned to

Consultative selling skills	**Parts of the Sales Presentation**			
	Need discovery	**Selection of the product**	**Need-satisfaction presentation**	**Servicing the sale**
Questioning skills	• As a question approach • To find needs and buying motives • To probe for buying motives • To confirm needs and buying motives	• To confirm selection	• To confirm benefits • To confirm mutual understanding	• To make suggestions • To confirm delivery and installation • To handle complaints • To build goodwill • To secure credit arrangements
Presenting benefits	• As a benefit approach • To discover potential benefits	• To match up with buying • motives	• To present and summarize features effectively	• To make suggestions • To use credit as a close
Demonstrating skills	• As a product approach • To clarify need	• To clarify selection	• To strengthen product claims	• When making effective suggestions
Negotiating skills	• To overcome initial resistance to sales interview • To overcome buyer's need concerns	• To overcome buyer's product concerns	• To overcome buyer's source, price, and time concerns	• In handling complaints • To overcome buyer's financing concerns
Closing skills	• When customer has made buying decision	• When buyer immediately recognizes solutions	• Whenever buyer presents closing signals	• After suggestion • To secure repeats and referrals

Figure 10.7   The Selling Dynamics Matrix. Salespeople can select from a variety of skills throughout the sales presentation.

reflect the new information available. During a typical presentation the salesperson will ask numerous questions, discuss several product features, and describe the appropriate product benefits. The customer is also asking questions and, in many cases, voicing concerns. The successful sales presentation is a good model of two-way communication. Because of the dynamic nature of the sales presentation, the salesperson must be prepared to apply several different selling skills to meet the variety of buyer responses. Figure 10.7 illustrates how the various selling skills can be applied during all parts of the sales presentation. In creating effective presentations the salesperson should be prepared to meet a wide range of buyer responses with effective questions, benefit statements, demonstrations, negotiating methods, and closing methods.

KEEP YOUR PRESENTATION SIMPLE AND CONCISE

Numerous surveys have found that customers like sales presentations that are concise and free of unnecessary complexity. When the salesperson gives clients too much information or discusses topics that do not deal with their individual needs, clients simply stop paying attention.[27]

The best way to achieve conciseness is to preplan your sales call. Think ahead of time about what you are going to say and do. Anticipate questions and objections the prospect may voice, and be prepared with accurate information and concise answers.

In many selling situations there is a certain amount of time pressure. Rarely does a salesperson have an unlimited amount of time to spend with the customer. Figure 10.8 illustrates an ideal breakdown of time allocation between the salesperson and the prospect during all three parts of the sales presentation. In terms of involvement the prospect assumes a greater role during the need-discovery stage. As the salesperson begins the product selection process, the prospect's involvement decreases. During the need-satisfaction stage the sales-

The dynamic nature of selling requires that the salesperson be prepared to respond to a wide variety of questions from the customer.

person is doing most of the talking, but note that the prospect is never excluded totally.

In addition to preplanning the sales presentation, consider a "dress rehearsal" in front of your colleagues. A less threatening approach might be to practise in front of your spouse or a close friend. Videotaping the rehearsal can help you see how you really look. Do you appear too stiff and motionless? Do you talk too fast or too slow? It's a good idea to practise presentations with specific customers in mind.[28]

THE CONSULTATIVE SALES PRESENTATION AND THE TRANSACTIONAL BUYER

Throughout this chapter you have been given a comprehensive introduction to the consultative sales presentation. It is important to keep in mind that the fundamentals of consultative selling must be customized to meet the individual needs of the customer. For example, some of the guidelines for developing an effective presentation must be abandoned or greatly altered when you are working with a transactional buyer. In Chapter 1 we described transactional selling as a process that most effectively matches the needs of the buyer who is primarily interested in price and convenience. In most cases the transactional buyer understands what product they need and when they need it. In many situations they are interested only in the product itself and not what the company or salesperson can do to create additional value. The customer may even resent time spent with the salesperson, especially time spent on need discovery. The Internet has armed many transactional buyers with a great deal of information, so the salesperson that spends time asking information-gathering questions or making a detailed informative presentation may be wasting the customer's time. Most of these buyers want the salesperson to configure a product solution that focuses on pricing and delivery issues.[29]

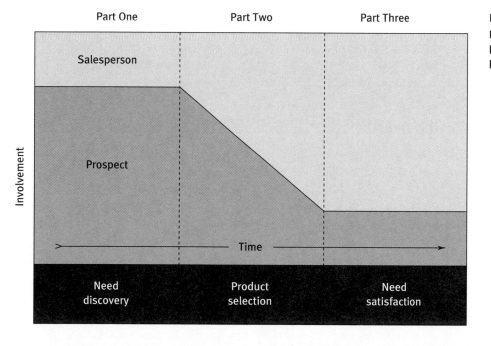

Figure 10.8   Time used by salesperson and customer during each part of the consultative sales presentation.

Summary

A well-planned and well-executed presentation strategy is an important key to success in personal selling. To be most effective, the presentation should be viewed as a three-part process: need discovery, selection of the product, and need satisfaction through informing, persuading, or reminding.

The most effective sales presentation is characterized by two-way communication. It should be a dialogue between the salesperson and the prospect, whose involvement should be encouraged with information-gathering, probing, confirmation, and summary confirmation questions. Beware of assuming things about the prospect, and be sure the language of your presentation is clearly understood. Listen attentively as the prospect responds to your questions or volunteers information.

After making a good first impression during the approach and getting the customer's full attention, the salesperson begins the presentation. The salesperson's ability to emphasize will be tested during this part of the sale, because this is where the prospect's buying motives are established. The salesperson's ability to verbalize product benefits will also be tested during this part of the sale.

Once you have selected a product or service that matches the customer's needs, you must decide which presentation strategy to emphasize. Need satisfaction can be achieved through informing, persuading, or reminding. The salesperson will, of course, use a combination of these presentation strategies in some cases. An effective presentation is an important part of the sales call and will often determine the ease or difficulty of proceeding through the rest of the steps to a successful sale.

Key Terms

Need Discovery 227
Information-Gathering Questions 228
Probing Questions 230
Confirmation Questions 231
Buying Conditions 232
Summary Confirmation Questions 232

Active Listening 234
Informative Presentation 237
Persuasive Presentation 238
Reminder Presentation 239
Emotional Links 241

Review Questions

1. List and describe the four parts of the Consultative Sales Presentation Guide.

2. List and describe the four types of question commonly used in the selling field.

3. Define the term *buying conditions*. What are some common buying conditions?

4. What is the listening efficiency rate of most people? Describe the process of active listening and explain how it will improve the listening efficiency rate.

5. Discuss the major factors that should be considered during the product selection phase of the consultative-style sales presentation.

6. Distinguish between the three types of need-satisfaction presentations: informative, persuasive, and reminder.

7. What are the guidelines to follow when developing a persuasive sales presentation?

8. What are some advantages of using the feature-benefit-reaction (FBR) approach?

9. Discuss those factors that contribute to the dynamic nature of selling. What skills are used by salespeople to cope with the dynamic nature of personal selling?

10. Read the opening vignette that begins on p. 223 and then evaluate Dave Tripp's practice of building a close relationship with salespeople who work in the bookstores he visits. Does this practice represent appropriate use of Tripp's limited time? Explain.

Application Exercises

1. Assume that you are a salesperson working in each of the following kinds of selling careers, and assume further that the prospect has given you no indication of what he or she is looking for. Identify the kinds of question you will use to find your prospect's specific needs.
   a. Personal computer
   b. Carpet
   c. Financial planning

2. You are a department manager and have called a meeting with the five staff members in your department. The purpose of your meeting is to inform your staff of a new procedure your company has adopted. It is important that you develop understanding and support. What steps can you take to enhance communication with the group?

3. Pick a job that you would really like to have and for which you are qualified. Assume you are going to be interviewed for this job tomorrow afternoon. You really want this position and therefore want to be persuasive in presenting your qualifications. List facts about your qualifications, including where you have worked previously, how much education you have, and what hobbies and activities you have been involved in. Use a feature-benefits worksheet like the one in Chapter 5 (Table 5.2) as a guide to convert these employee facts to employer benefits in the form of selling statements.

4. The explosion of product options and the complex needs of today's customer make the salesperson's task of product selection more challenging. On the Internet, access Cincom Systems Inc., a leading international supplier of information technology. From their home page click on the general listing of "Products." From this list examine functions available with the "Sales Automation—CONTROL:Acquire" product. Carefully study the Acquire Sales Configurator and the Acquire Bid Management descriptions.

5. Participant 1: You are a salesperson for Shred-it Canada (see Chapter 6) and you are calling on the largest hospital in your territory. You have a meeting to see Ms. Joan Tanner, the manager of administrative services. A friend of

yours who does business with Ms. Tanner has described her as a Reflective (substitute Emotive, Director, Supportive; see Chapter 4). Prepare several questions (information-gathering, probing, and confirmation questions) to use during your consultative sales presentation to Ms. Tanner. Your goal is to discover the prospect's needs and to establish her buying motives.

Participant 2: You are Joan Tanner.

CRM Application Exercise

Printing the Customer Database

Sales managers regularly help salespeople review the status of their accounts. These strategic account review meetings often involve examining all of the information available on the salespeople's most promising prospects. The sales manager and salesperson will each have a copy of all information currently available for the accounts either on their computer screens or on paper. To produce a paper record of the information contained in the ACT! database, select Lookup, Everyone, Report, Contact Report, Active Group, Printer, and Enter. Approximately 40 pages of information will be printed.

Case Problem

Annette Peterson is a real estate salesperson for Canwest Homes, Inc. A young couple, John and Beth Reems, was referred to Annette by the sales manager. John and Beth are being transferred to the city due to John's job as a manager of a local men's clothing store. Beth had been a computer systems analyst in a department store and will be looking for a similar position after the move.

Annette had no opportunity to visit with John and Beth until they arrived in the city today. The sales manager set up an appointment for them to meet at the office at 1:00 p.m. Following their arrival the following sales presentation occurred:

Annette: Good afternoon, Mr. and Mrs. Reems. My name is Annette Peterson.

John: Good afternoon. I'm John Reems and this is my wife, Beth.

Beth: Good afternoon, Mrs. Peterson, we've been looking forward to meeting you.

Annette: Please call me Annette. And how was your flight?

John: Oh, we had a lovely flight and got a wonderful view of the city as we circled for landing.

John: I enjoyed the flight also, and am looking forward to seeing the city and driving around to see the homes for sale. Our flight back leaves at 8:30 p.m. so we are not going to have a lot of time. Our looking is going to have to move rather quickly.

Annette: My sales manager told me you would have limited time, so I've prepared an agenda for us to follow this afternoon. I have four homes that I have selected from our computerized database. I picked up the keys for all four of them so we can drive out and take a look. Before we get going, though, I would like to show you a picture of each home and tell you a little about it. I am sure you will find all four of them very appealing.

John and Beth: Oh!

Annette: Here is the first one. It is priced at $146 000, has 2000 square feet, and is a two-storey. This house has two bathrooms and is located on a 65 by 135 foot lot. It was built in 1975 and has Acan windows.

John and Beth: Uh-huh! [Beth looks for a pencil in her purse.]

Annette: Now here is a picture of the second house. I do not like this one as well as the first, but I thought you might like to see it. This home was built in 1987 and is priced at $140 000. The taxes are $3000 a year. It has 1600 square feet and has vinyl siding on it. It also has an attached 22 by 24 foot garage. The lot is 80 by 140 feet. It is a ranch-style home.

John and Beth: We do like ranch-style homes.

Annette: This picture is the third home that I chose. I really like this one. It is a split-level, priced at $138 900. The taxes are—oh, I'm sorry, the taxes do not seem to be listed for this one. I am sure we can find out what they are, however, if you are interested.

John: Well, we really are not interested in split-level homes. There are too many stairs to climb. By the way, how far are these homes from the store?

Annette: Well, most customers I have worked with do not concern themselves with how far, but rather how long it will take them to get to work. You will find that the city has an excellent system of streets with rapid uncongested travelling. The homes I am going to show you are all located in a suburb called Majestic Oaks. It will take you about 20 minutes to get from there to your store.

John: I see. [John looks at his watch.]

Annette: Here is the fourth home I picked out [showing a picture of the fourth home]. This one is also a two-storey and has a 24 by 24 foot garage. The price is $139 000 and it has an assumable mortgage of $80 500 with two years remaining at 6.5 percent interest. The home is located on a cul-de-sac, with a 90 by 160 foot lot. I went through this house last week and remember that it has oak wainscoting in the family room and also vinyl siding. It has a high-efficiency furnace, air conditioner, and Maytag appliances.

Questions

1. Describe what you think John and Beth's impressions are of Annette.
2. Evaluate the strength of Annette Peterson's presentation strategy.
3. Evaluate the weaknesses of this presentation strategy.
4. Assume you are Annette Peterson. Prepare an outline that you would follow in giving your sales presentation.
5. Assuming that Annette Peterson follows the same pattern in the demonstration and close that she has already established in the presentation thus far, is she likely to close the sale? Why or why not?
6. Select five features brought out by Annette and convert them to buyer benefits. Use the forms presented in Chapter 5 (Tables 5.2 and 5.3).

CRM Case Study

Planning Presentations

Becky Kemley, your sales manager at SimNet Systems, wants to meet with you this afternoon to discuss the status of your accounts. It is common for prospects to have several contacts with SimNet before ordering a network system. These multiple call contacts, or sales cycle phases, usually include getting acquainted and prequalifying, needs discovery, proposal presentation, closing, and account maintenance. Becky wants to know what phase each account is in and, particularly, which accounts may be ready for a presentation.

Questions

1. Which five accounts have already had a need discovery? Which two accounts are scheduled for a need discovery? Which six accounts are likely to buy but have not yet had a need discovery?

2. Which two accounts have had a need discovery and now need a product solution configured?

3. Which three accounts do not now have a network and appear to be ready for your sales presentation?

4. For those accounts listed next that are ready for your sales presentation, which strategy would you use for each: informative, persuasive, or reminder?

   Able Profit Machines   International Studios

   Big Tex Auto Sales   Lakeside Clinic

5. Which accounts appear to be planning to buy without a need discovery or product configuration/proposal? What risks does this pose?

Partnership Selling: A Role Play/Simulation (see Appendix C, p. 454)

UNDERSTANDING YOUR CUSTOMER'S BUYING STRATEGY

Read *Sales Memorandum 2 ("A" or "B" depending on the account category you were assigned in Chapter 9).* Your customer has called you back because you made such a good approach in call 1, and he or she wants to visit with you about a convention recently assigned. In this call you are to use the information gathered in sales call 1 to re-establish a good relationship, discover your customer's convention needs, and set an appointment to return and make a presentation.

Follow the instructions carefully and prepare information-gathering questions prior to your appointment. Keep your information-gathering questions general and attempt to get your customer to share information openly. Use probing questions later during the appointment to gain more insight. Be careful about doing too much of the talking. In the need discovery your customer should do most of the talking, with you taking notes and using them to ask confirmation and summary confirmation questions in order to check the accuracy of your perceptions concerning what the customer wants. After this meeting you will be asked to prepare a sales proposal from the information you have gathered.

Your instructor may again ask you to assume the role of a customer in the account category that you are not assigned as a salesperson. If so, you will receive detailed customer instructions, which you should follow closely. This will provide you with an opportunity to experience the strategic/consultative/partnering style of selling from a customer's perspective.

Custom Fitting the Sales Demonstration

Judith Tatar and Darren Alexander, owners of Tatar/Alexander Photogallery in Toronto, have created a unique method to present art to their clients. They created digital images of 1500 pieces of art, and carry their "inventory" to their clients' locations for viewing. Clients can search the database by artist, by price, or by subject, whichever they prefer. Darren Alexander says: "Our key client base—corporate clients, art consultants, and interior designers—love the increased accessibility and portability of our system; we have also enabled them to work more efficiently using this high-tech selection tool which was specifically designed with their requirements in mind."

Previously, dealers would have to rely on clients visiting their gallery, or they would have to carry artwork to potential clients' offices, often returning four or five times to make a sale. Now, sales can often be made on the first visit. "Never before attempted in Canada's traditional gallery network, this system was part of our initial business plan and helped us get the financing we needed to start," adds Darren Alexander. "Since then, it has helped us continually meet or exceed our sales targets."[1]

LEARNING OBJECTIVES

When you finish reading this chapter, you should be able to

1. Discuss the important advantages of the sales demonstration

2. Explain the guidelines to be followed when planning a sales demonstration

3. Complete a demonstration worksheet

4. Develop selling tools that can strengthen your sales presentation

5. Discuss how to use audiovisual presentations effectively

The Importance of the Sales Demonstration

demonstration A sales and marketing technique that adds sensory appeal to the product. It attracts the customer's attention, stimulates interest, and creates desire.

Trying to get a message through to an information-overloaded customer is one of the major challenges facing salespeople today. If the customer isn't paying attention, there is little chance of closing the sale.[2] The increase in look-alike products and greater competition present additional challenges. The sales demonstration has become a more important communication tool. A well-planned **demonstration** adds sensory appeal to the product (Fig. 11.1). It attracts the customer's attention, stimulates interest, and creates desire. It is usually not possible to make this type of impression with words alone.

A product demonstration contributes in a positive way to the selling–buying process. Both the customer and the salesperson benefit. The prospect can evaluate the product or service more effectively. The salesperson finds it easier to show what the product will do and how it will fit the customer's needs. Strategic planning, of course, sets the stage for an effective demonstration that will add value to the sale (Fig. 11.2). Some of the most important benefits of the sales demonstration are discussed here.

Figure 11.1 Conducting the sales demonstration.

The Six-Step Presentation Plan	
Step One: APPROACH	✔ Review Strategic/Consultative Selling Model ✔ Initiate customer contact
Step Two: PRESENTATION	✔ Determine prospect needs ✔ Select product or service ✔ Initiate sales presentation
Step Three: DEMONSTRATION	● Decide what to demonstrate ● Select selling tools ● Initiate demonstration
Step Four: NEGOTIATION	● Anticipate buyer concerns ● Plan negotiating methods ● Initiate double-win negotiations
Step Five: CLOSE	● Plan appropriate closing methods ● Recognize closing clues ● Initiate closing methods
Step Six: SERVICING THE SALE	● Suggestion selling ● Follow-through ● Follow-up calls
Service, retail, wholesale, and manufacturer selling.	

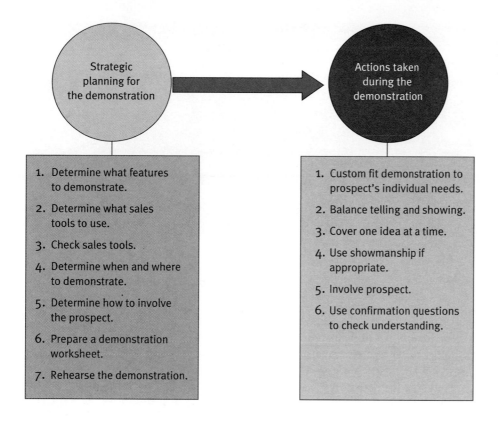

Figure 11.2   Poorly conducted demonstrations usually result from a lack of strategic planning and preparation.

Strategic planning for the demonstration

Actions taken during the demonstration

1. Determine what features to demonstrate.
2. Determine what sales tools to use.
3. Check sales tools.
4. Determine when and where to demonstrate.
5. Determine how to involve the prospect.
6. Prepare a demonstration worksheet.
7. Rehearse the demonstration.

1. Custom fit demonstration to prospect's individual needs.
2. Balance telling and showing.
3. Cover one idea at a time.
4. Use showmanship if appropriate.
5. Involve prospect.
6. Use confirmation questions to check understanding.

IMPROVED COMMUNICATION AND RETENTION

In the previous chapter we noted the limitation of the verbal presentation; words provide only part of the meaning attached to messages that flow between the salesperson and the prospect. When we try to explain something with words alone, people frequently do not understand our messages.

Why is communication via the spoken word alone so difficult? One major reason is that we are visually oriented from birth. We grow up surrounded by the influence of movies, television, commercial advertising, road signs, and all kinds of visual stimulation. People are accustomed to learning new things through the sense of sight or through a combination of seeing and hearing.

Many sales representatives recognize the limitations of the spoken word. When talking to prospects about the economic benefits of delivering training programs with a satellite system, a salesperson used a table (Table 11.1) to illustrate savings. With the aid of this table, prospects can visualize the economic benefits of the satellite delivery system compared with a competing system using high-bandwidth terrestrial lines.

In many selling situations the buyer does not make an immediate buying decision. The decision to buy may be made several days or weeks after the presentation. Therefore, retention of information is important.

When we rely on verbal messages alone to communicate, retention of information will be minimal. A number of studies provide evidence to support this important point. Research conducted at Harvard and Columbia universities found that retention increases from 14 to 38 percent when the spoken word is

Strategic selling today involves customizing a product demonstration to each customer's unique set of buying conditions.

accompanied with effective visuals. In addition, the time needed to present a concept can be reduced by up to 40 percent with the use of appropriate visuals.[3]

PROOF OF BUYER BENEFITS

A well-planned and well-executed sales demonstration is one of the most convincing forms of proof. This is especially true if your product has dramatic points of superiority.

Salespeople representing Epson, Canon, Hewlett-Packard, and other manufacturers can offer the customer a wide range of printers. What is the real difference between a $300 basic printer and a $1000 laser printer? The laser equipment will print a neater and more attractive letter or report. The most effective way to provide proof of this buyer benefit is to show the customer material that has been printed on both printers. By letting the prospect compare the examples, the salesperson is converting product features to a buyer benefit. Be prepared to prove with tests, findings, and performance records every claim you make.

FEELING OF OWNERSHIP

Many effective sales demonstrations give the prospect a temporary feeling of ownership. This pleasant feeling builds desire to own the product. Let us con-

Table 11.1 Sample table to illustrate potential savings to a prospect.

How Much Can a Satellite System Save You?			
TYPE OF SYSTEM **PER PERSON COST 20 SITES**	**PER PERSON COST 30 SITES**	**PER PERSON COST 40 SITES**	**PER PERSON COST 50 SITES**
Satellite delivery system $10.70	$9.90	$9.00	$8.20
High-bandwidth terrestrial lines $9.70	$10.10	$10.50	$11.00

These cost estimates are based on current satellite broadcast rates and rates for use of terrestrial lines. The per person cost is based on an audience size of 25 trainees at each site.

Building Relationships in a Diverse World

DO YOU NEED A VOICE COACH?

African, Asian, and aboriginal North Americans, and recent immigrants to North America, often face special challenges in verbal communication. New arrivals may have a strong accent because the phonetic habits of the speaker's native language are carried over to his or her new language. Many people born and raised in North America have a strong regional accent. Should this uniqueness be viewed as a problem? Kim Radford had to answer this question when he took a position as a stockbroker soon after graduating from college. Radford, who is black, conducted most of his business on the telephone and seldom met clients face to face. Early on, someone said, "Kim, you need to get that black accent out of your voice if you're going to be successful in this business."

Radford faced a real dilemma: he wanted to be successful, but he did not want to compromise his personal integrity. He talked to several people, black and white, and the advice he received boiled down to this guideline:

> Stay honest to yourself, but communicate and be understood. There's no need to clean up the fact that you sound different as long as you're articulate and your diction's good and people can understand you.

It is a fact of life that people in every community feel certain that the way they talk is the "natural" way. So if you feel that your accent and dialect need to be changed, or you want to improve pronunciation, consider seeking help from a voice coach.[a]

sider the person who enters a men's clothing store and tries on a Hart Shaffner and Marx suit. During the few moments the customer is wearing the suit, a feeling of pride is apt to develop. If the suit fits well and looks good, desire to own it will probably build.

Successful automobile salespeople encourage prospects to go for a demonstration ride. The new car almost always seems superior to the buyer's older model. Without a demonstration ride, of course, the opportunity to build desire would be lost.

Many firms offer prospects an opportunity to enjoy products on a trial basis. This is done to give people a chance to assess the merits of the product in their own home or business. Some firms that sell office equipment and office furniture use this sales strategy.

OTHER BENEFITS

Most salespeople gain added self-confidence when they incorporate an effective demonstration into the sales presentation. This is especially true of new salespeople who have not polished their verbal sales story. It is reassuring to know that it will not be necessary to rely completely on verbal skills.

Planning Effective Demonstrations

An effective sales demonstration is the result of both planning and practice. Planning gives the salesperson a chance to review all the important details that should be considered in advance of the actual demonstration. Practice (or rehearsal) provides an opportunity for a trial run to uncover areas that need additional polish. During the planning stage it helps to review a series of guidelines that have helped salespeople over the years to develop effective demonstrations.

USE CUSTOM-FITTED DEMONSTRATIONS

In nonmanipulative selling, each presentation is custom tailored because individual client problems and priorities are unique.[4] In other words, every aspect of the sales presentation, including the demonstration, should relate to the needs or problems mutually identified by the prospect and the salesperson.

It is possible to develop a sales demonstration so structured and so mechanical that the prospect feels like a number. We must try to avoid what some veteran marketing people refer to as the *depersonalization* of the selling–buying process. If the demonstration is overly structured, it cannot be personalized to meet specific customer wants and needs.

Shape Industries Inc., located in Winnipeg, is a contract manufacturer for commercial seating products. The president, Ryan Smith, often uses custom-fitted demonstrations to promote the company's newest products and designs. Using digital technology, he is able to produce customized electronic catalogues for customers or send a presentation to customers, either on diskette or through e-mail. This way, customers get to see only what they want to see. Ryan Smith says, "We used to do a catalogue, but I was always philosophically opposed to the concept. A catalogue shows where you have been. We're always progressing and moving ahead." Another important advantage to customizing these presentations is that it buys time: when catalogues appear, copycat products soon follow.[5]

CHOOSE THE RIGHT SETTING

The location of the sales demonstration can make a difference. Some companies routinely rent space at a hotel, motel, or conference centre so that the demonstration can be conducted in a controlled environment free of noise and other interruptions.

A firm selling modern log homes frequently conducts an open house at the site of a newly completed house. Potential customers are invited by letter or personal contact to tour the home at appointed times. After touring the home, prospects view a 20-minute video that explains how the homes are constructed. Pictures of other homes built by the company are also shown.

Many salespeople visit the prospect's office and talk to the person across the desk. David Peoples, author of *Selling to the Top*, believes there is a better setting for the presentation. He suggests a one-on-one stand-up presentation in a conference room that ensures privacy. This approach puts the customer on a pedestal and gives the person a feeling of being very special.[6]

CHECK SALES TOOLS

Be sure to check every item to be used in conjunction with the sales demonstration. If you are using audiovisual equipment, be certain that it is in good working condition. When using a projector, always carry an extension cord and a spare bulb. If you are selling real estate, the most critical aspect of preparing for the demonstration is becoming familiar with the property. Never show a home you have not seen.[7]

COVER ONE IDEA AT A TIME

Pace the demonstration so that the customer does not become confused. Offer one idea at a time, and be sure the customer understands each point before mov-

Selling in Action

TRACKING DOWN A SALE

Care Trak is a product designed to locate patients suffering from the effects of brain injuries or Alzheimer's disease who have wandered away from a care centre and gotten lost. During a sales call at one nursing home, a sales representative was explaining the benefits of Care Trak when a doubting staff member picked up the transmitter and asked the salesperson to wait 20 minutes, then try to find him. After a 20-minute wait, the salesperson began the search under the watchful eyes of the nursing home administrator and members of the nursing staff.

After tracking the staff member to a specific location, the locator signal became very strong in spite of the fact that they were standing in the middle of an empty hallway. At that point the staff members began having doubts about the value of the equipment. Then the salesperson pointed the directional antenna straight up to the ceiling. He pushed aside a ceiling tile to reveal the nursing home employee in his hiding place. The nursing home placed an order for the product that day.[b]

ing on. This practice is especially important if the primary purpose of your sales presentation is to inform. When you neglect this practice, there is the danger that the customer's concentration will remain fixed on a previous point. Some demonstrations are ruined by a salesperson who moves too rapidly from one point to another. A good rule of thumb is to use a confirmation question to get agreement on each key point before moving on to the next. This approach will make closing easier because you have secured agreement on key points throughout the demonstration. Make the customer a part of every step.

APPEAL TO ALL SENSES

In conducting a sales demonstration, it is a good idea to appeal to all appropriate senses. Each of the five senses—sight, hearing, smell, touch, and taste—represents an avenue by which the salesperson can attract the prospect's attention and build desire.

Although sight is considered the most powerful attention-attracting sense, it may not be the most important motivating force in every selling situation. When presenting a food product, the taste and aroma may be critical.

Christa-Lee McWatters understands the importance of reaching the prospect through as many senses as possible. She sells 28 different wines bottled by Sumac Ridge Estate Winery Ltd. in Summerland, British Columbia to beer and wine stores, restaurants, and even to individuals and companies.[8] The sales presentation for a quality wine usually highlights four areas:

 www.sumacridge.com

Consumer demand. The wine's sales potential is described in realistic terms.

Marketing strategies. Suggested ways to merchandise the wine are discussed.

Bouquet. The distinctive fragrance of the wine is introduced.

Taste. A sample of the wine is given to the prospect in a quality wineglass.

Note that a sales presentation featuring these appeals will reach the prospect through four of the five senses. Collectively, these appeals develop a strong motivating force. When you involve more than one sense, the sales presentation is more informative and persuasive.

Comprehension and retention can be enhanced with visual images.

BALANCE TELLING, SHOWING, AND INVOLVEMENT

Some of the most effective sales demonstrations combine telling, showing, and involvement of the prospect. To plan an effective demonstration, consider developing a demonstration worksheet. Simply divide a sheet of paper into three columns. Head the first column, "Feature to be demonstrated." Head the second column, "What I will say." Head the third column, "What I or the customer will do." List the major features you plan to demonstrate in proper sequence in the first column. In the second column, describe what you will say about the feature, converting the feature to a customer benefit. In the third column, describe what you (or the customer) will do at the time this benefit is discussed. A sample demonstration worksheet appears in Figure 11.3.

Prospects can be involved in many demonstrations. Two retail examples follow:

Furniture: To prove comfort or quality, have the buyer sit in a chair, lie on a mattress, or feel the highly polished finish of a coffee table.

Clothing: Have the customer try on garments to highlight style, fit, and comfort features. This involvement is especially important in the sale of quality garments.

If it is not possible for the prospect to participate in the demonstration or handle the product, place sales literature, pictures, or brochures in the person's hands. After the sales call these items will remind the prospect of not only who called, but why.

Some information-age demonstrations will involve the customer in some type of virtual reality. DaimlerChrysler AG is developing what it calls Virtual Vehicle, which uses virtual reality to let customers assess different combinations of colours, fabrics, and wheel designs on Mercedes-Benz cars. Holding a flat, colour touch screen, a customer can walk around a computer-generated image of a car and click on various options. Click on the seat and you can change the fabric at lightning speed. Click on the radio and you can alter the speaker con-

Demonstration Worksheet		
Feature to Be Demonstrated	**What I Will Say (Include Benefit)**	**What I or the Customer Will Do**
Special computer circuit board to accelerate drawing graphics on a colour monitor screen.	"This monitor is large enough to display multiple windows. You can easily compare several graphics."	Have the customer bring up several windows using the computer keyboard.
Meeting room setup at a hotel and conference centre.	"This setup will provide a metre of elbow space for each participant. For long meetings, the added space provides more comfort."	Give the customer a tour of the room and invite her to sit in a chair at one of the conference tables.

Figure 11.3 The demonstration worksheet enables the salesperson to plan strategically and then rehearse demonstrations that strengthen the presentation.

figuration; you hear the sound immediately. Once all the decisions are made, the customer can get a binding delivery date straight from the factory.[9]

DEVELOP CREATIVE DEMONSTRATIONS

Presenting product features and buyer benefits in an interesting and appealing way requires some creativity. One recent study found that 90 percent of the salespeople who were surveyed agreed that creativity is critical in selling.[10] Creativity is needed to develop a sales demonstration that will gain attention and increase desire. The ability to come up with problem-solving answers or different ways of looking at things is greatly valued in today's fast-changing business environment. Some of the creative skills we need to cultivate include capacity for divergent thinking, ability to break problem-solving habits (mental sets), persistence in problem solving, and willingness to take risks.[11] One way to develop a more creative approach to sales demonstrations is to ask "What if….?" questions, and then record your answers. This exercise is best done when you feel relaxed and rested. Relaxation enhances the creative process.[12]

REHEARSE THE DEMONSTRATION

While you are actually putting on the demonstration, you will need to be concentrating on a variety of things. The movements you make and the multitude of things you do should be so familiar to you that each response is nearly automatic. To achieve this level of skill, you will need to rehearse the demonstration.

Rehearse both what you are going to say and what you are going to do. Merrie Spaeth, consultant and author of *Marketplace Communication*, says, "…if you don't rehearse, the best-conceived idea can go wrong."[13] Say the words aloud exactly as if the prospect were present. It is surprising how often a concept that seems quite clear as you think it over becomes hopelessly mixed up when you try to discuss it with a customer. Rehearsal is the best way to avoid this embarrassing situation. Whenever possible, have your presentation/demonstration videotaped before you give it; this is perhaps the best way to perfect what you will say and do.

The 5th Wave   By Rich Tennant

Courtesy of Rich Tennant

"GET READY, I THINK THEY'RE STARTING TO DRIFT."

Sales Tools for Effective Demonstrations

Nearly every sales organization provides its staff with sales tools or proof devices of one kind or another. Many of these, when used correctly, augment the sales effort. If the company does not provide these items, the creative salesperson secures or develops sales tools independently. In addition to technology-based presentations, sales personnel can utilize a wide range of other selling aids. Creative salespeople are continually developing new types of sales tools. The following section summarizes some of the most common tools used today.

THE PRODUCT ITSELF

Without a doubt the best selling aid is often the product itself. In the growing market for ergonomic office chairs, ranging in price from $700 to $2900, furniture makers know the best way to close the sale is to provide an opportunity for the customer to sit in the chair. With growing awareness of the hazards of poor sitting posture and bad ergonomics, more people are searching for a comfortable work chair.[14]

When demonstrating the actual product, be sure it is typical in terms of appearance and operation. Try to avoid a situation in which it becomes necessary to apologize for appearance, construction, or performance. Of course, you should be able to demonstrate the product skilfully.

MODELS

Sometimes it is not practical to demonstrate the product itself because it is too big or immobile. In such cases it is easier to demonstrate a small-scale model or cross section of the original equipment. A working model, like the actual product, can give the prospect a clear picture of how a piece of equipment operates.

With the aid of modern technology it is possible to create a model in picture form. ClosetMaid, a manufacturer of ventilated wire for commercial closets and other storage products, uses desktop visualization software to create a 3-D presentation that allows customers to see exactly what the finished facility will look like. Sales representatives can print out a hard copy so the customer has a picture of the custom-designed model for future reference. With the aid of this visualization technology, ClosetMaid salespeople can modify closet layouts on screen and produce a detailed bill of materials for each project.[15]

PHOTOS AND ILLUSTRATIONS

The old proverb "One picture is worth a thousand words" can be put into practical application by a creative salesperson. A great deal of information can be given to the prospect with the aid of photos and illustrations. Consider these creative uses of photos:

➢ Amir Hooda of Anar Jewellers Inc. in Toronto takes Polaroid pictures and gives them to clients who have tried on jewellery but who are not ready to make a purchase. Amir Hooda says, "I don't pressure them. I just take a photo and attach my card. People don't throw away photos and it almost always results in business."[16]

➢ Reardon Construction & Development Ltd. of St. John's, Newfoundland, has been involved in numerous building and renovation projects over the years. Customers who visit its Web site can see dozens of pictures representing numerous new home construction projects, including large homes, bungalows, and split-level homes; renovation/conversion projects, including office fitups, building expansions, home extensions, and condominiums; and commercial projects, including strip malls, shopping plazas, fast food outlets, daycare centres, subdivisions, and retirement villages.[17]

 www.reardons.com

Some salespeople organize photographs in a presentation album or portfolio. Either option provides the flexibility needed by salespeople.

PORTFOLIO

A **portfolio** is a portable case or loose-leaf binder containing a wide variety of sales-supporting materials. The portfolio is used to add visual life to the sales message and to prove claims. A person who sells advertising might develop a portfolio including the following items:

Successful advertisements used in conjunction with previous campaigns

Selected illustrations that can be incorporated into advertisements

A selection of testimonial letters

One or more case histories of specific clients who have used the media with success

portfolio A portable case or loose-leaf binder containing a wide variety of sales-supporting materials. It is used to add visual life to the sales message and to prove claims.

The portfolio has been used as a sales aid by people who sell interior design services, insurance, real estate, securities, and convention services. It is a flexible sales aid that can be revised at any time to meet the needs of each customer.

REPRINTS

Leading magazines and journals sometimes feature articles that directly or indirectly support the salesperson's product. A reprint of the article can be a forceful selling aid. It is also an inexpensive selling tool. Pharmaceutical and medical sales representatives often use reprints from journals that report on research in the field of medicine. A few years ago, Closure Medical Corporation received approval to sell Dermabond, a surgical glue used to close cuts. This innovative product received national attention when the prestigious *Journal of the American Medical Association* concluded that gluing a wound could be just as effective as sewing it shut. Salespeople representing Dermabond used the article to help educate doctors on the product's merits and applications.[18]

The most effective demonstrations include telling, showing, and customer involvement. The use of sales tools can help with the process.

In many cases the prospect will be far more impressed with the good points of your product if they are presented by a third party rather than you. A reprint from a respected journal can be very persuasive.

GRAPHS, CHARTS, AND TEST RESULTS

Graphs and charts can be used to illustrate change of some variable such as payroll expense, fuel consumption, or return on investment. For example, a bar graph might be used to illustrate the increase in fuel costs over a 10-year period.

Although graphs are usually quite descriptive, the layperson may misunderstand them. It is best to interpret the graph for the prospect. Do not move too fast, because the full impact of the message may be lost. A variety of charts have been developed to be used in conjunction with the sales demonstration. One popular type of chart is the flip chart, which consists of illustrations or messages on individual sheets of paper. The salesperson can face the prospect while turning pages. A variety of illustrations and printed messages can be put on the various pages.

Test results from a reliable agency can often be convincing. This is especially true when the test results are published by a respected independent agency, such as J. D. Power and Associates.

LAPTOP COMPUTERS AND DEMONSTRATION SOFTWARE

As noted previously, a growing number of companies have started equipping salespeople with small, portable computers weighing only a few kilograms. With the aid of these small computers a salesperson can compute financial options on the spot and close sales that might otherwise be lost. Another benefit of portable computers is that salespeople who use computers to send electronic messages or to get information from the corporate mainframe can spend less time in the office and more time on the road.

Thanks to modern computer technology, it's possible to conduct impressive multiple, simultaneous product demonstrations without leaving your office. Let's assume you are presenting a new employee disability insurance plan to members of the 3M Canada human resources staff. One key decision-maker is based in London, Ontario, and the other is in the United States. With the aid of Pixion PictureTalk software or a similar product you can use the Internet to conduct the demonstration for both persons in real time. A sales manager might use this same approach to train members of her sales team in remote offices.

Personal computers have played an important role in increasing sales force productivity. Salespeople have instant access to customer data, so it is often easier to customize the sales presentation. Many salespeople report that PC-based presentations, using graphics software, are very effective. Today's personal computer can produce striking visuals and attractive printed material that can be given to the customer for future reference.

ENHANCING DEMONSTRATIONS WITH POWERPOINT

The PowerPoint software program from Microsoft is a popular presentation package that is included in the Microsoft Office suite of software programs. PowerPoint is so common that many prospects will find the standard presentation graphics very familiar. Salespeople who want their demonstration to look unique can create their own corporate template, animate their logo, or put video clips of their own company information into a PowerPoint presentation.[19] A video can be embedded in the corner of the screen along with a picture of the salesperson, so the electronic demonstration is more personalized. The help files that are available with PowerPoint and competing software, such as LMSoft, offer salespeople many ways to enhance their demonstrations. Members of the 500-person Goodyear Tire and Rubber Company sales force can customize their PowerPoint presentations by using some of the 450 photo assets that can be obtained from the company intranet.[20]

CREATING ELECTRONIC SPREADSHEETS

For many years, salespeople have been using electronic spreadsheets to prepare sales proposals. The electronic spreadsheet is an excellent tool to organize the numbers involved in preparing quotes, such as quantities, costs, and prices. The electronic spreadsheet allows the user to answer "what if" questions about the effects of lowering costs or raising prices. Once the preparation work is finished, the electronic spreadsheet itself can be printed and used as the proposal or to accompany the proposal.[21]

Many computers sold today include an electronic spreadsheet program. The leading electronic spreadsheet, Excel, is part of Microsoft's Office suite of products. If you have access to Excel, or any other electronic spreadsheet software, you can explore the power of this tool for preparing proposals.

AUDIOVISUAL TECHNOLOGY

A large number of companies provide their salespeople with audiovisual aids such as videotapes, 35-mm slides, and computer-based presentations. There are several reasons why audiovisual presentations have become more commonplace. First, there have been major advances in the development of hardware and software. The equipment is more reliable, more compact, and easier to operate. Software is continuously improving. Many of today's videos, software packages, and transparencies feature professional actors, top-notch photography, and attractive graphics.

Many companies find that audiovisual presentations, although expensive to produce, can be a good investment. These presentations often reveal product

A growing number of salespeople are using portable computers in conjunction with sales presentations.

uses, values, features, and benefits in an interesting manner that encourages the prospect to listen and ask questions. When GTE began selling its new digital Airfone system to various airlines, the sales staff used a multimedia program that included video, sound, animation, and other high-tech wizardry. The sales team needed a powerful visual presentation that would deliver a wealth of technical information in an entertaining manner.[22]

When an audiovisual presentation fails to live up to expectations, some companies find that salespeople are not using the materials correctly. Most salespeople are not audiovisual experts and need training. Below are some suggestions on how to use audiovisual presentations to achieve maximum impact.

1. Be sure the prospect knows the purpose of the presentation. Preview the material and describe a few highlights. Always try to build interest in advance of the audiovisual presentation.

2. Be prepared to stop the presentation to clarify a point or to allow the prospect to ask questions. Do not permit the audiovisual presentation to become a barrier to good two-way communication.

Selling in Action

DEVELOPING PROFESSIONAL-LOOKING PRINTED MATERIALS

The assistance needed to develop an attractive portfolio or bound paper presentation may be closer than you think. Major office products retailers, such as Staples or Office Depot, and quick printers, such as Kinko's, offer a variety of services needed by salespeople. They maintain a large inventory of supplies needed to make presentation materials attractive and professional looking. You can purchase high-quality paper and plastic sheet protectors that will improve the effectiveness of your portfolio presentation. These service centres are equipped with the newest printers and copy machines, so quality materials can be prepared quickly.

Computer-based presentations can be enhanced with the use of an LCD projection panelbook.

3. At the conclusion of the audiovisual presentation, review key points and allow the prospect an opportunity to ask questions.

Finally, realize that the audiovisual presentation cannot do the selling for you. Audiovisual technology provides support for the major points in your presentation. No matter how exotic the sales tool, you are still the central figure in the selling situation.

BOUND PAPER PRESENTATIONS

Although many salespeople are using some type of presentation technology in conjunction with the sales demonstration, paper is still widely used. For many sales and marketing organizations, bound paper presentations continue to be the most popular medium.[23] With the aid of computer-generated graphics it is easy to print attractive graphs, charts, and other proof information. Product guarantees and warranties are sometimes included in a bound paper presentation. Some marketers use guarantees and warranties to differentiate their products from competing products. Customer testimonials represent another common element of bound paper presentations. A testimonial letter from a prominent satisfied customer provides persuasive evidence that the product has support in the industry. Here, proof letters describing tangible benefits of the product can also enhance credibility. Prospects like bound paper presentations because the document is readily available for future reference.

Summary

In selling, the prospect is moving from a known quantity (the money in hand or an obligation for future payment) to something of an unknown quantity (amount of satisfaction to be gained from the potential purchase). With most people this process produces anxiety and insecurity. The professional salesperson reduces prospect anxiety and insecurity by supplying proof of product performance. The objective of the demonstration part of the sale is to supply this proof.

People perceive impressions through the five senses. In the presentation the salesperson communicates verbally to the prospect primarily through the sense of sound. In the demonstration the salesperson broadens the communication strategy to include as many of the other senses as possible. Generally, the more senses we appeal to, the more believable our sales appeal becomes.

In the demonstration the senses of hearing and sight are combined when we tell the prospect about a product benefit and show the product—or a visual presentation of the product—at the same time. When we ask the prospect to personally operate the product or to examine a sales tool, we simultaneously introduce a third sense—the sense of touch. If appropriate, the salesperson should also appeal to the senses of taste and smell.

Nearly every marketing-driven organization provides its salespeople with a variety of sales tools to use in the demonstration. A partial list of these tools includes the product itself, models, photos, reprints, portfolios, graphs, charts, test results, testimonials, case histories, audiovisual presentations, laptop computers, demonstration software, and bound paper presentations.

Key Terms

Demonstration 252
Portfolio 261

Review Questions

1. List the benefits of using a sales demonstration during the presentation of a product or service.

2. What effect does showing (appealing to the sense of sight) have on retention when combined with an oral presentation?

3. Discuss the advantages of using the demonstration worksheet.

4. Explain why a salesperson should organize the sales presentation so that it appeals to as many of the five senses as possible.

5. List the guidelines to follow in planning an effective demonstration.

6. Develop a list of the sales tools that the salesperson should consider when planning a sales demonstration.

7. Describe the merits of a bound paper presentation. What can be done to strengthen the persuasive power of a bound paper presentation?

8. Explain how magazines and trade journals can be used to assist the salesperson in a persuasive sales presentation.

9. Explain why audiovisual presentations are becoming more popular as a means of support for sales demonstrations.

10. What are some of the common sales functions performed by laptop computers and demonstration software?

Application Exercises

1. In many selling situations it is difficult, if not impossible, to demonstrate the product itself. List means other than the product itself that can be used to demonstrate the product features and benefits.

2. Develop a list of sales tools you could use in a job interview situation. What tools could you use to demonstrate your skills and capabilities?

3. As noted in this chapter, demonstration software is becoming increasingly popular. Real estate products are often showcased on the Web. Access the Toronto Real Estate Board home page. Assume you have just taken a job in Waterloo. Click on "Find a Home" and select "Waterloo" (Southwestern Ontario) region for information that describes the home you would like and examine the properties that match your request. Select the home you personally like best from among the ones that were found by the search. Click on it and examine the information available.

 www.realestate.ca/ toronto

4. Participant 1: You have been hired as a part-time recruiter for your school. Bob Thompson, a local lawyer, is visiting you along with his daughter, Kimberley. You have discovered from a previous telephone conversation with Mr. Thompson that his daughter is particularly interested in a marketing career, and he is willing to send her to the school that will best prepare her for her chosen profession. You are to demonstrate to Mr. Thompson and Kimberley that your school is the best choice for them. You have freedom to create testimonials, charts, brochures, data, or anything else that will help you with your demonstration. Be sure to consider how you will involve them in your demonstration.

Participants 2 and 3: You are Bob and Kimberley Thompson.

Case Problem

Jack Alber is a manufacturer's sales representative for the Mayflower Appliance Company. Jack recently graduated from college with a major in marketing and went to work for Mayflower shortly thereafter. Mayflower manufactures and markets a line of small home appliances. As a sales representative, Jack calls on wholesalers and retailers that distribute small electrical appliances. Recently Mayflower introduced in limited test markets a new line of small food processors. The company selected the name Orkan Food Processor for its new product line. After careful analysis of consumer, retailer, and wholesaler reactions in the test markets, Mayflower made several product improvements. Mayflower planned a full-scale introduction of the improved Orkan Food Processor for autumn. The promotion was planned to coincide with the important gift-buying season from October to December.

To accomplish the sales goal of 1 million units during the first year, Mayflower began its distribution promotion in June. In a national sales meeting, all sales representatives, including Jack Alber, were introduced to the new product line. The sales representatives were informed that the sales promotion for the Orkan Food Processor would be the biggest in the company's history. Included in the sales promotion program were the following:

1. A million-dollar advertising campaign including the "Oprah" television show
2. Sales banners and window stickers for retailers, to develop point-of-purchase promotions
3. A package that featured four-colour printed pictures of the Orkan Food Processor and shelf signs
4. A sales kit for each of the sales representatives that included the following: (a) the Orkan Food Processor itself; (b) the package; (c) sales banners, newspaper advertising slicks, and catalogue specification sheets; and (d) a notebook computer and CD-ROM presentation software. The multimedia presentation contained a sales message from Mayflower's vice-president of sales that outlined test market results, projected profit potential of the Orkan Food Processor, comments from consumers and retailers, and film clips of Oprah Winfrey making commercials for Orkan. The multimedia presentation was designed to be shown to retailers and wholesalers who were prospective dealers and distributors for the Orkan Food Processor.

This was the first time Jack had come into contact with audiovisual equipment in a sales presentation. Jack was a persuasive communicator and felt his best presentation was based on one-to-one communication with the prospect. Jack felt reluctant about trying to integrate multimedia into his presentation, even though he felt it was well prepared. Jack thought that it would be awkward to carry in, set up, and plug in the equipment and that he would lose the personal touch he had been so successful with in the past. As Jack flew home from the sales meeting, he decided he would try to introduce the new product line in his territory without using the multimedia presentation.

Questions

1. Based on Jack's strong personal selling skills, do you agree or disagree with his decision not to use the multimedia presentation? Why?

2. Describe how you would organize the presentation *without* the use of the multimedia components. Indicate where you would use each of the sales tools.

3. Describe how you would organize the presentation *with* the use of the multimedia components.

4. Describe the benefits you would emphasize in selling the Orkan Food Processor to (a) the wholesaler, (b) the retailer, and (c) the ultimate consumer.

5. Describe the senses you could appeal to in demonstrating the Orkan Food Processor. Explain how you would make each of these appeals.

6. How could you involve the prospect in demonstrating the Orkan Food Processor?

CRM Case Study

Custom Fitting the Demonstration

Your SimNet Systems sales manager, Becky Kemley, has asked you to meet with her to discuss demonstrations. She wants you to tell her if any of your accounts needs a demonstration, and, if so, what type of demonstration.

Questions

1. Which two accounts need a demonstration of the speed and power capabilities of the recommended network?

2. Which account needs to be shown that the recommended network product configuration will meet the account's specifications?

3. Which account with many sites will need a demonstration of SimNet's ability to put together a complex solution?

4. Which account seeking a low price needs a testimonial of SimNet's value-added ability to help customers maximize the power of their network?

5. Which account needs a demonstration of SimNet's financial stability?

Partnership Selling: A Role Play/Simulation (see Appendix C, p. 458)

DEVELOPING A SALES PRESENTATION STRATEGY—THE DEMONSTRATION

Read *Sales Memorandum 3* ("A" or "B" depending on the category you were assigned in sales call 1).

In this role play your call objectives are to make a persuasive presentation, negotiate any customer concerns, and close and service the sale.

At this time you should complete item 1 of the presentation plan and prepare and price a product solution. This will include completing the sales proposal form. Also, you should obtain a three-ring binder with pockets in the front and back for the development of a portfolio presen-tation. In this binder you should prepare your presentation and demonstration, following the instructions in items 2a, 2b, 2c, and 2d under the presentation plan. The presentation and demonstration materials (use the product strategy materials, i.e., photos, price lists, menus, awards, etc., provided to you with *Employment Memorandum 1*) should be placed in the three-ring binder as a part of your portfolio presentation. You may want to select a person as your customer and rehearse the use of these materials.

Negotiating Buyer Concerns

LEARNING OBJECTIVES

When you finish reading this chapter, you should be able to

1. Describe common types of buyer concerns

2. Outline general strategies for negotiating buyer concerns

3. Discuss specific methods of negotiating buyer concerns

4. Describe ways to deal effectively with buyers who are trained in negotiating

The Banff Centre for Management (BCM) is a not-for-profit organization dedicated to training and developing executives, managers, and professionals. It is acclaimed as the best organization of its type in Canada, and one of the five best in North America. Operating for more than 46 years, it has delivered programs to more than 250 000 participants from Canada and around the world.

Doug Macnamara, the general manager, has a ready response when prospective clients raise concerns about external training programs such as the ones offered by the BCM. He describes their ability to provide innovative, experiential, and unforgettable learning in exceptional facilities situated in one of the most attractive locations in the world. The BCM has developed a network of faculty who are experienced at the mid- to senior-executive level and who are superior learning facilitators. Of course, some forms of sales resistance are not communicated to Doug by prospective clients. He must often work hard to identify the resistance, clarify it, then overcome it.[1]

Negotiating Buyer Concerns and Problems

Today, people like Doug Macnamara are more likely to anticipate buyer concerns and plan negotiating methods (Fig. 12.1). The person who makes the buying decision is not only better educated in most cases but also better prepared to make a decision.

NEGOTIATION—PART OF THE WIN-WIN RELATIONSHIP STRATEGY

Frank Acuff, negotiations trainer and author of *How to Negotiate Anything with Anyone, Anywhere Around the Globe*, says, "Life is a negotiation."[2] Negotiating skills have application almost daily in our personal and professional lives.

Some of the traditional personal selling books discussed how we should "handle" buyer objections. The message communicated to the reader was that personal selling is a "we versus they" process: somebody wins and somebody loses. The *win-win* solution, where both sides win, was not offered as an option.

Too often we were led to believe that buying problems or objections needed to be handled with some type of manipulation. Ron Willingham, author of

The Six-Step Presentation Plan	
Step One: APPROACH	✔ Review Strategic/Consultative Selling Model ✔ Initiate customer contact
Step Two: PRESENTATION	✔ Determine prospect needs ✔ Select product or service ✔ Initiate sales presentation
Step Three: DEMONSTRATION	✔ Decide what to demonstrate ✔ Select selling tools ✔ Initiate demonstration
Step Four: NEGOTIATION	○ Anticipate buyer concerns ○ Plan negotiating methods ○ Initiate double-win negotiations
Step Five: CLOSE	○ Plan appropriate closing methods ○ Recognize closing clues ○ Initiate closing methods
Step Six: SERVICING THE SALE	○ Suggestion selling ○ Follow-through ○ Follow-up calls
Service, retail, wholesale, and manufacturer selling.	

Figure 12.1   Negotiating customer concerns and problems

Double-win salespeople have learned to anticipate certain objections and prepare a well-planned and well-executed presentation.

Integrity Selling, notes the important difference between negotiation and manipulation:

> *We don't view negotiation as manipulation. We don't see it as outtalking, outsmarting, or outmaneuvering people. We don't view it as combat or as an adversary relationship. Instead we view negotiating as a win-win activity—where seller and buyer sit down together and attempt to work out the best solution for both sides.*[3]

In negotiations there are only two possible outcomes: win-win and lose-lose. The win-lose scenario is a deception. When the salesperson wins and the customer loses, it is a double loss. If the customer wins and the salesperson loses, it is also a double loss.[4] When the salesperson makes too many concessions and feels like a loser, service after the sale is likely to suffer. In fact, the salesperson may avoid dealing with the customer in the future. Win-win negotiations result in mutual respect, stronger relationships, and greater loyalty on the part of the salesperson and the customer.

negotiation Working to reach an agreement that is mutually satisfactory to buyer and seller.

What is **negotiation**? One definition is "working to reach an agreement that is mutually satisfactory to both buyer and seller." It involves building relationships rather than making one-time deals.[5] As we noted in Chapter 1, the salesperson increasingly serves as a consultant or resource and provides solutions to buyers' problems. The consultant seeks to establish and maintain long-term relationships with customers. The ability to negotiate problems or objections is a necessary skill for all salespeople who adopt the consultative approach to personal selling. Figure 12.2 outlines the steps a salesperson can take to anticipate and negotiate problems.

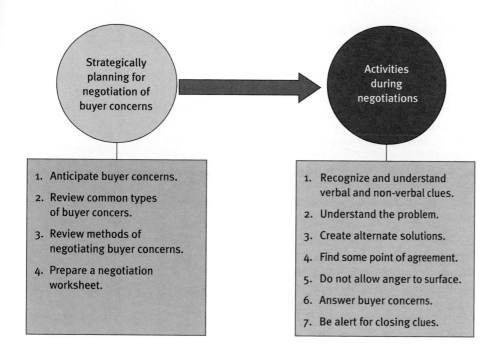

Figure 12.2   Today salespeople must be prepared to anticipate and negotiate buyer concerns and problems.

NEGOTIATION IS A PROCESS

It is important to keep in mind that negotiations often take place throughout the sales process—not just at the closing stage. Early negotiations may involve the meeting location, who will attend the sales presentation, or the amount of time available for the first meeting. Salespeople sometimes make early concessions to improve the relationship. This approach may set a costly precedent for later in the sale.[6] Some concessions can have a negative influence on the sales presentation. If, for example, you need 40 minutes for an effective product demonstration, do not agree to a 20-minute meeting.

Establishing a strategic alliance, described in Chapter 1 as the highest form of partnering, requires lengthy negotiations. These negotiations may extend over several months. Once the alliance is finalized, negotiations will continue when concerns voiced by one party or the other surface.

Common Types of Buyer Concerns

Salespeople learn that patterns of buyer resistance exist, and they can therefore anticipate that certain concerns will arise during the sales call. With this information it is possible to be better prepared for each meeting with a customer. The great majority of buyer concerns fall into five categories: need, product, source, price, and time.

CONCERNS RELATED TO NEED FOR THE PRODUCT

If you have done your homework satisfactorily, then the prospect you call on probably has a need for your product or service. You can still expect, however, that the initial response may be, "I do not need your product." This might be a conditioned response that arises nearly every time the prospect meets with a sales representative. It may also be a cover-up for the real reason for not buying, which might be lack of funds, lack of time to examine your proposal carefully, or some other reason.

In some selling situations you can anticipate with great accuracy that concerns will surface. Take, for example, the person selling a new type of office telephone equipment. This equipment is very advanced in terms of design and makes most existing equipment obsolete. Although the equipment offers the buyer many special features, resistance may still arise. Potential customers who already own reliable equipment are apt to say, "We are happy with our current system." Potential customers who own basic equipment may say, "We can get along well without this equipment." In both cases the salesperson has encountered indifference related to need.

Sincere need resistance is one of the great challenges that face a salesperson. Think about it for a moment. Why would any customer want to purchase a product that does not seem to provide any real benefits? Unless we can create need awareness in the prospect's mind, there is no possible way to close the sale.

If you are calling on business prospects, the best way to overcome need resistance is to prove that your product is a good investment. Every privately owned business hopes to make a profit. Therefore you must demonstrate how your product or service will contribute to that goal. Will your product increase sales volume? Will it reduce operating expenses? If the owner of a hardware store says, "I already carry a line of high quality tools," point out how a second line of less expensive tools will appeal to another large segment of the buying public. With the addition of the new line the store will be in a better position to compete with other stores (discount merchandise stores and supermarkets) that sell inexpensive tools.

In some selling situations you must help the prospect solve a problem before you have any chance of closing the sale. Suppose the prospect says, "I am already overstocked." If you call on wholesalers or retailers, expect to hear this objection

The desire to buy low is quite common. However, faced with information overload, buying decisions become more difficult. When concerns surface, salespeople need to explain the benefits that add value and use skilful negotiations to gain acceptance of the selling price. If the selling price is too low, profit margins will suffer.

BOUGHT LOW,
SOLD HIGH,
LEFT A BEAUTIFUL
PORTFOLIO

Reprinted by permission of Roz Chast

quite frequently. Often the prospect is unwilling to buy additional merchandise until older stock is sold. If there is no demand for the older merchandise, then a real problem exists. In this situation your best bet is to offer the buyer one or more solutions to the problem. Here are some tactics:

1. Suggest that the prospect hold a special sale to dispose of the unsold merchandise. It may even be necessary to sell the stock at a loss to recover at least part of the original investment. Closeouts can be painful, but may be the best option.

2. Ask the prospect to accept a trial offer on a guaranteed sale or consignment basis. This option will allow the customer to acquire new merchandise without an initial cash investment and will open the door for your product.

3. If company policy permits, consider negotiating the purchase of the prospect's inventory. Give the customer a credit against a minimum opening order.

The key to negotiating need resistance in many cases is creative problem solving. Work closely with the prospect to overcome the barrier that prevents closing the sale.

CONCERNS ABOUT THE PRODUCT

In some cases the product itself becomes the focal point of buyer resistance. When this happens, try to discover specific reasons why the prospect has doubts about your product. Often you will find that one of the following factors has influenced the buyer's attitude:

1. The product is not well established. This is a common form of buyer resistance if you are selling a new or relatively new product. People do not like to take risks. They need plenty of assurance that the product is dependable. Use laboratory test results, third-party testimonials from satisfied users, or an effective demonstration to illustrate the product's strong points.

2. The product will not be popular. If the product is for resale, discuss sales results at other firms. Discuss the success other firms have had with your product. Also, discuss any efforts your company has taken to increase demand. For example, show the prospect sample advertisements that have appeared in the newspaper, or commercials that have appeared on television.

3. Friends or acquaintances did not like the product. It is not easy to handle this form of buyer resistance. After all, you cannot say, "Your friend is all wet—our product is the best on the market!" Move cautiously to acquire more information. Use questions to pinpoint the problem, and clarify any misinformation that the person may have concerning your product.

4. The present product is satisfactory. Change does not come easily to many people. Purchasing a new product may mean adopting new procedures or retraining employees. In the prospect's mind the advantages do not outweigh the disadvantages, so buyer resistance surfaces. To overcome this resistance we must build a greater amount of desire in the prospect's mind. Concentrate on superior benefits that give your product a major advantage over the existing product or reconfigure the product to better meet the customer's needs.

CONCERNS RELATED TO SOURCE

One of the hardest problems for a salesperson to overcome is the source objection. This is especially true if prospects feel genuine loyalty to their present supplier. We should not be surprised to hear a prospect say, "I have been buying from the Ralston Company for years, and their people have always treated me right." After all, the Ralston Company sales staff has no doubt taken great care to develop close ties with this prospect.

When dealing with the loyalty problem, it is usually best to avoid direct criticism of the competing firm. Negative comments are apt to backfire because they damage your professional image. It is best to keep the sales presentation focused on the customer's problems and your solutions.

There are positive ways to cope with the loyalty objection. Here are some suggestions:

1. Work harder to identify problems your company can solve with its products or services. With the help of good questions you may be able to understand the prospect's problems better than your competitors can.[7]

2. Point out that the business may profit from the addition of a second line. You do not expect the person to drop the present supplier, but you do want the person to try your product.

3. Point out the superior benefits of your product. Here you hope the logic of your presentation will overcome the emotional ties that may exist between the prospect and the present supplier.

4. Encourage the prospect to place a trial order and then evaluate the merits of your product. Again, you are not asking the person to quit the present supplier.

5. Point out that the prospect's first obligation is to the business. As owner or manager, the person should continually be searching for ways to maintain or increase profits.

Try to stay visible and connected. Every contact with the prospect is one more step in building a relationship. David Haslam, president of Toronto-based Presidential Plumbing Ltd., devotes time to a number of community projects. He says, "I believe in community involvement, but I'm also gaining invaluable experience, getting contacts."[8] One subtle way to regularly keep in touch with a large number of contacts is with a newsletter.

Source concerns can also be directed toward your company. For reasons that may be difficult to uncover, the prospect simply may not want to do business with your firm. Try to get the person to be specific about problems with your company. You must deal decisively with perceptions that are not accurate.

CONCERNS RELATED TO PRICE

There are two important points to keep in mind concerning price resistance. It is one of the most common forms of buyer resistance in the field of selling. Therefore you must learn to negotiate skilfully in this problem area. The price objection is also one of the most common excuses. When people say, "Your price is too high," they probably mean, "You have not sold me yet." In the eyes of most customers value is more important than price.

Building Quality Partnerships

APPLYING NEGOTIATION SKILLS IN THE JOB MARKET

Chester L. Karrass, creator of the Effective Negotiating seminar, says, "In business, you don't get what you deserve, you get what you negotiate." This is good advice for the job seeker. Most employers will not propose the highest wage possible at the beginning of the offer. If you want a higher starting wage, you must ask for it. Employers often have a predetermined range for each position and the highest salary is reserved for the applicant who brings something extra to the job. To prepare for a productive negotiation, you must know your own needs and you must know something about the worth of the position. Many employers will tell you the salary range prior to the interview. The Internet can be a good source of salary information for certain types of job. In terms of your needs, try to determine what you care about the most. Interesting work? Future promotion? Flexible work schedule? If you are willing to negotiate, you can increase your pay by hundreds or even thousands of dollars. Be prepared to sell yourself, negotiate the salary you feel is appropriate, and achieve a win-win solution in the process.[a]

Although price may not be the real barrier to closing the sale, do not overlook its importance. It is a major concern for many people. The professional buyer has no other choice than to search for the best possible buy. The typical prospect is also value conscious. It is important to keep in mind that, in almost every selling situation, getting the order depends on the right combination of price and quality.[9]

COPING WITH BUYERS WHO ARE TRAINED IN NEGOTIATION

In recent years we have seen an increase in the number of training programs developed for professional buyers. For example, the Purchasing Management Association of Canada (PMAC) offers a two-day seminar designed to enhance the negotiating skills of purchasing people. Enrollees learn how to negotiate with salespeople. Some salespeople are also returning to the classroom to learn negotiation skills. SalesForce Training & Consulting Inc., of Carp, Ontario, offers a one-day seminar called "Win-Win Negotiating for Salespeople," which covers many of the negotiating techniques that salespeople need to know. The Canadian Professional Sales Association offers a popular seminar, "The Persuasive Communicator: Motivating People to Buy," which is designed to help salespeople negotiate buyer concerns.

Professional buyers often learn to use specific tactics in dealing with salespeople. Homer Smith, author of *Selling through Negotiation*, provides these examples:

Budget limitation tactic.[10] The buyer may say, "We like your proposal, but our budget for the convention is only $8500." Is the buyer telling the truth, or is he or she testing your price? The best approach here is to take the budget limitation seriously and use appropriate negotiation strategies. One strategy is to reduce the price by eliminating some items. In the case of a fleet truck sale the salesperson might say, "We can deliver the trucks without radios and thus meet your budget figure. Would you be willing to purchase trucks without radios?"

Take-it-or-leave-it tactic.[11] How do you respond to a buyer who says, "My final offer is $3300, take it or leave it"? A price concession is, of course, one option. However, this will likely reduce profits for the company and lower your commission. An alternative strategy is to confidently review the superior benefits of your product and make another closing attempt. Appealing to the other person's sense of fairness may also move the discussion forward. If the final offer is totally without merit, consider calling a halt to the negotiation to allow the other party to back down from his or her position without losing face.[12]

Let's split the difference tactic.[13] In some cases the salesperson may find this price concession acceptable. If the buyer's suggestion is not acceptable, then the salesperson might make a counter-offer.

These tactics represent only a sample of those used by professional buyers. To prepare for these and other tactics, salespeople need to plan their negotiating strategies in advance and have clear goals. To avoid falling prey to negotiating tricks, study all relevant information related to the sale and decide in advance on the terms you will (and will not) accept.[14]

NEGOTIATING PRICE WITH A LOW-PRICE STRATEGY

As noted in Chapter 6, some marketers have positioned their products with a price strategy. The goal is to earn a small profit margin on a large sales volume. Many of these companies have empowered their salespeople to use various low-price strategies such as quantity discounts, trade discounts, seasonal discounts, and promotional discounts. Some salespeople are given permission to match the price of any competitor. As noted in Chapter 6, one of the consequences of using low-price tactics may be lower commissions and lower profits.

HOW TO DEAL WITH PRICE CONCERNS

As we have noted, price concerns are common, so we must prepare for them. There are some important "do's and don'ts" to keep in mind when the price concern surfaces.

Do add value with a cluster of satisfactions. As noted in Chapter 6, a growing number of customers are seeking a cluster of satisfactions that includes a good product, a salesperson who is truly a partner, and a company that will stand behind its products (see Fig. 6.1). Many business firms are at a competitive disadvantage when the price alone is considered. When you look beyond price, however, it may become obvious that your company offers more value for the dollar.

Stephen Smith, senior account manager for Bell Atlantic, says that price is like the tip of the iceberg—it is often the only thing the customer sees. Salespeople need to direct the customer's attention to the value-added features that make up the bulk of the iceberg that is below the surface (Fig. 12.3).[15] Do not forget to sell yourself as a high-value element of the sales proposal. Emphasize your commitment to customer service after the sale.

Do not make price the focal point of your sales presentation.
You may need to discuss price, but do not bring it up too early. The best time to deal with price is after you have reviewed product features and discussed buyer benefits. Unfortunately, many salespeople volunteer a price reduction without

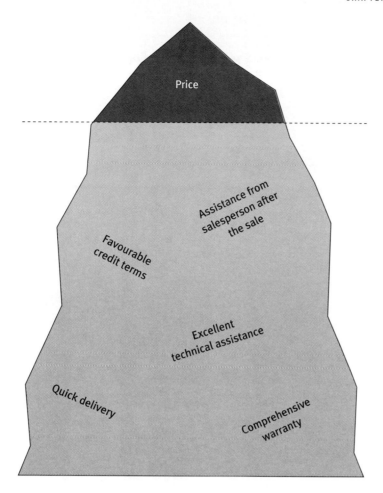

Figure 12.3   A sales proposal is sometimes like an iceberg. The customer sees the tip of the iceberg (price) but does not see the value-added features below the surface.

being asked. In most cases, this happens because the salesperson does not fully understand the benefits that add value to their product.[16]

You increase the chances for a win-win outcome by increasing the number of issues you can resolve. If you negotiate price along with delivery date, support services, or volume purchases, you increase the opportunities for a trade-off so you and the customer both win something of value.[17]

Do not apologize for the price. When you do mention price, do so in a confident and straightforward manner. Do not have even a hint of apology in your voice. Convey to the prospect that you believe your price is fair and make every effort to relate price to value. Many people fear paying too much for a product or service. If your company has adopted a value-added strategy, point this fact out to the prospect. Then discuss how you and your company add value.

Do point out the relationship between price and quality. In our highly competitive, free enterprise economy, there are forces at work that tend to promote fair pricing. The highest quality can never be obtained at the lowest price. Quality comes from the Latin word *qualitas*, meaning "what is the worth." When you sell quality, price will more likely be secondary in the prospect's

LiteCo is a distributor of ABB drives. It tries to overcome resistance related to source (LiteCo is ISO-registered), and to price (customers who compare its ABB drives to others are comparing apples to oranges).

ABB AC and DC Drives from Liteco

ABB Drive technology   Their drive technology

Liteco is a fully authorized business partner of ABB Drives We carry the full line of ABB AC and DC variable speed drives from 3/4 up to 1500 HP, including the new ACS 600 Direct Torque Control Drives.

Liteco is your complete value added source with integration & engineering services, on-site startup & commissioning & technical support and training. Liteco is also a ABB Designated Service Station (DSS) with full repair and warranty service.

ABB Automation and Drives

ABB Industrial Control Products

Litetec is a fully authorized business partner with ABB Control and carries a complete line of control products including Contactors, Pilot Devices, Molded Case Circuit Breakers, Miniature Circuit Breakers and Disconnect Switches.

Litetec is also an authorized ABB Capacitor Bank Assembler.

Contactors & Accessories

Molded Case Circuit Breakers

Pilot Devices

Capacitor and Harmonic Filter Banks

Miniature Circuit Breakers

Disconnect Switches

ABB **LITECO**

LiteCo and LiteTec are now ISO 9001 Registered

Saint John   Moncton   Fredericton   Sussex   Charlottetown
(506)458-9333

mind. Always point out the value-added features that create the difference in price. Keep in mind that cheap products are built down to a price rather than up to a standard.[18] Some salespeople like to point out to customers that while they can pay too much for a product, they can also pay too little. Customers who pay a higher price risk only the price difference they have paid over the cheaper alternative. Customers who pay too little risk the entire price if the product they buy does not meet their needs. If you believe in your product and understand its unique features, price resistance will not bother you.

Do explain the difference between price and cost. *Price* represents the initial amount the buyer pays for the product; *cost* represents the amount the buyer pays for a product as it is used over a period of time. The price–cost comparison is particularly relevant with a product or service that lasts a long time or is particularly reliable. If one product requires servicing once a year and a lower-priced competing product requires servicing three times a year, the extra service calls must be part of the price–cost equation. In this case the product with the lower initial *price* may *cost* more because of the two extra service calls.[19]

Do not make concessions too quickly. Give away concessions methodically and reluctantly, and always try to get something in return. A concession given too freely can diminish the value of your product. Also, giving a concession too easily may send the signal that you are negotiating from a position of weakness.[20]

When the pressure to make price concessions builds, consider unbundling product features in order to achieve a more competitive price. As we have noted in previous chapters, many transactional buyers are primarily interested in price and convenience, so consider eliminating features that contribute to a higher selling price. If the buyer is only interested in the lowest possible price, and you represent a marketer committed to a value-added sales strategy, consider withdrawing from negotiations.

CONCERNS RELATED TO TIME

If a prospect says, "I want time to think it over," you may be encountering resistance related to time. Resistance related to time is often referred to as the **stall.** D. Forbes Ley, author of *The Best Seller*, states that a stall signals conflict. He says, "The conflict is the agony of indecision between the desire to have your product versus feelings of uncertainty and anxiety."[21] A stall usually means the customer does not yet perceive the benefits of buying now. In most cases the stall indicates that the prospect has both positive and negative feelings about your product. Consider using questions to determine the negative feelings: "Is it my company that concerns you?" "Do you have any concerns about our warranty program?" "Does anyone else need to approve this purchase?"

Take a few moments to review the benefits of your product. Prospects may only need additional assurance that the product meets their needs. Review the superior benefits that build a case for owning your product.

It is all right to be persuasive if the prospect can truly benefit from buying now. If the price will soon rise, or if the item will not be available in the future, then you should provide this information. You must, however, present this information sincerely and accurately. It is never proper to distort the truth in the hope of getting the order.

stall   Resistance related to time. A stall usually means the customer does not yet perceive the benefits of buying now.

General Strategies for Negotiating Buyer Concerns

The successful negotiation of buyer concerns is based in large part on understanding human behaviour (Table 12.1). This knowledge, coupled with a good measure of common sense, will help us overcome most forms of buyer concerns. It is also helpful to be aware of general methods for negotiating buyer hesitation.

Table 12.1 Negotiating Buyer Concerns

BUYER'S CONCERN	SOURCE OF HESITATION	REQUEST FOR
"Price too high."	Perceived cost vs. benefit	Value articulation
"Think about it."	Afraid to make a bad decision	Create comfort, provide proof
"Talk to boss."	Unable to justify decision	Risk reduction, benefit review
"Need more quotes."	Unsure you're the best option	Targeted solutions, value
"Set with current supplier."	Doesn't see benefit of change	Differentiation
"Bad history."	Past experience is affecting current review	Offer proof of change

When buyers express concerns, they are often simply requesting more information to justify the buying decision. The concerns can tell us a lot about the real source of hesitation and what type of information the customer is seeking. (Adapted from "Hide-and-Seek," a table in "Objections are a 'Yes' About to Happen," by Nancy J. Stephens, *Selling*, November 1998, p. 3.)

ANTICIPATE BUYER CONCERNS

Many people who sell, such as Doug Macnamara for the Banff Centre for Management, have learned to anticipate certain problems and forestall them with a well-planned and well-executed presentation. Although buyer resistance is by no means insurmountable, it is a good idea to take preventive measures whenever possible. By anticipating problems we can approach the prospect with greater confidence and often save valuable time.

Salespeople frequently anticipate buyer resistance and plan ways to deal with it.

KNOW THE VALUE OF WHAT YOU ARE OFFERING

It is important that we know what is of real value to the customer and not consider value only in terms of purchase price. The real value of what you are offering may be a value-added intangible such as superior product knowledge, good credit terms, or prompt delivery. An important aspect of the negotiation process is discovering what is of utmost importance to the buyer. The focus of personal selling today should be the mutual search for value. This process is called **added-value negotiating** because it seeks to add more value to any sale so both the salesperson and the customer feel comfortable.[22] Some salespeople make the mistake of offering a lower price the moment buyer resistance surfaces. In the customer's mind price may be of secondary importance compared with the quality of service after the sale. As noted previously, do not be in a hurry to make price concessions.

added-value negotiating A negotiating process where both the seller and the customer search for mutual value so they both feel more comfortable after a sale.

PREPARE FOR NEGOTIATIONS

It helps to classify possible resistance with the aid of a negotiations worksheet. To illustrate how this form works, let us review an example from the food industry. Mary Turner is a salesperson for Durkee Famous Foods. She represents more than 350 products. Mary calls on supermarkets daily and offers assistance in the areas of ordering and merchandising. Recently her company decided to offer retail food stores an allowance of $1 per case of olives if the store purchased 15 or more cases. Prior to talking with her customers about this offer, Mary sat down and developed a negotiations worksheet, shown in Figure 12.4.

Figure 12.4   Before the presentation it is important to prepare a negotiations worksheet.

Negotiations Worksheet		
Buyer's concern	**Type of concern**	**Possible response**
"Fifteen cases of olives will take up valuable space in my receiving room. It is already crowded."	Product	Direct denial: "You will not have to face that problem. With the aid of our merchandising plan you can display 10 cases immediately on the sales floor. Only 5 cases will become reserve stock. You should move all 15 cases in about two weeks."
"This is a poor time of the year to buy a large order of olives. People are not buying olives at this time."	Time	Indirect denial: "I agree that it has been a problem in the past, but consumer attitudes seem to be changing. We have found that olives sell well all year long if displayed properly. More people are using olives in the preparation of omelettes, pizza, and other dishes. Of course, most relish trays feature olives. We will supply you with point-of-purchase material that suggests new ways to use this high-profit item."
"I would rather not tie up my money in a large order."	Price	Superior benefit: "As you know, olives represent a high-profit item. The average margin is 26 percent. With the addition of our $1 per case allowance the margin will rise to about 30 percent. This order will give you a good return on your investment."

We cannot anticipate every possible problem, but it is possible to identify the most common problems that are likely to arise. The negotiations worksheet can be a useful tool.

UNDERSTAND THE PROBLEM

We have already noted that the prospect occasionally misunderstands the salesperson. It is just as easy for the salesperson to misunderstand the prospect. Therefore an important step in dealing with a problem is to make sure you understand it. Be certain that both you and the prospect are clear on the true nature of what needs to be negotiated. When the prospect begins talking, listen carefully without interrupting, even when you think you know what the prospect is going to say. It is only common courtesy to give people the opportunity to express their point of view. With probing questions, you can fine-tune your understanding of the problem.

CREATE ALTERNATIVE SOLUTIONS

When the prospect finishes talking, it is a good practice to validate the problem, using a confirmation question. This helps to isolate the true problem and reduce the chance of misunderstanding. The confirmation question might sound like this: "I think I understand your concern. You feel the warranty does not provide you with sufficient protection. Is this correct?" By taking time to ask this question, you accomplish two important things. First, you are giving personal attention to the problem, which will please the customer. Second, you gain time to think about the best possible response.

The best possible response is very often an alternative solution. Many of today's customers do not want to hear that there is only one way or a single solution. In the age of information, people have less time to manage their work and their lives, so they expect new levels of flexibility. In the area of computers, Gateway, Dell, Compaq and several other companies were quick to respond to this trend. Some of today's most successful companies recognize that customers expect options.[23]

FIND SOME POINT OF AGREEMENT

Negotiating buying problems is a little like the art of diplomacy. It helps to know what points of agreement exist. This saves time and helps establish a closer bond between you and the prospect. At some point during the presentation you might summarize by using a confirmation question: "Let us see if I fully understand your position. You think our product is well constructed and will provide the reliability you are looking for. Also, you believe our price is fair. Am I correct on these two points?"

Once all the areas of agreement have been identified, there may be surprisingly few points of disagreement. The prospect suddenly sees that the advantages of ownership far outweigh the disadvantages. Now that the air is cleared, both the salesperson and the customer can give their full attention to any remaining points of disagreement.

DO NOT DESTROY YOUR RELATIONSHIP STRATEGY WITH ANGER

In most situations the relationship between the salesperson and the prospect contains the seeds of conflict and disagreement. Negotiations can get emotional.

Building Relationships in a Diverse World

NEGOTIATING ACROSS CULTURES

Negotiations in the international arena will vary from one country to another because of cultural differences. German buyers are more apt to look you in the eye and tell you what they do not like about your product. Japanese buyers, on the other hand, do not want to embarrass you and therefore will bury their concerns beneath several layers of courtesy. In China, negotiations are more straightforward. People who have been doing business in China for many years suggest a very direct approach to negotiations. However, do not become antagonistic. Do get involved in native business rituals that are intended to create a friendly atmosphere.

When we enter into negotiations in foreign countries,

it is important to understand and accommodate the customer's culture. You may not get every detail exactly right, but you will win respect by trying.

In most cases you don't have the luxury of making mistakes and learning from experience. Seek advice from someone who has first-hand experience with the culture.

Selling in certain cultures often requires more time in bonding and building rapport. Several meetings may be needed to lay the groundwork for the actual sale.

In some cultures no may not mean no, and yes may not mean yes. Take time to validate your understanding so you know exactly what has been accepted or rejected.[b]

Conflict can arise when the salesperson and prospect fail to agree on need, price, credit terms, or other factors. When the customer becomes impatient or angry, the salesperson must be careful not to fuel this emotion. Most people's natural response when under attack is to defend themselves or to counterattack. Both of these tactics will usually fuel an upward spiral of heated disagreement.[24] If you want to earn the customer's trust and respect, avoid becoming defensive and argumentative. Ask questions and keep the customer talking so you learn more about the true nature of the problem. Also, listen to what the customer is saying. Listening without defending helps to defuse any anger.[25]

Specific Methods of Negotiating Buyer Concerns

There are seven specific methods of negotiating buyer concerns. In analyzing each problem, we should try to determine which method will be most effective. In most cases we will use a combination of the following methods to negotiate buyer resistance.

DIRECT DENIAL

Direct denial involves refuting the opinion or belief of a prospect. The direct denial of a problem is considered a high-risk method of negotiating buyer concerns. Therefore you should use it with care. People do not like to be told they are wrong. Even when the facts prove the prospect is wrong, resentment can build if we fail to handle the situation properly.

When a prospect offers buyer resistance that is not valid, we sometimes have no option other than to disagree openly. If the person is misinformed, we must provide accurate information. For example, if the customer questions the product's quality, meet the concern head-on with whatever proof seems appropriate. It is almost never proper to ignore misinformation. High-performance salespeople counter inaccurate responses from the prospect promptly and directly.

direct denial   Involves refuting the prospect's opinion or belief. The direct denial of a problem is considered a high-risk method of negotiating buyer concerns.

The manner in which you state the denial is of major importance. Use a win-win approach. Be firm and sincere in stating your beliefs, but do not be offensive. Above all, do not patronize the prospect. A "know-it-all" attitude can be irritating.

INDIRECT DENIAL

indirect denial Often used when the prospect's concern is completely valid, or at least accurate to a large degree. The salesperson bends a little and acknowledges that the prospect is at least partially correct.

Sometimes the prospect's concern is completely valid, or at least accurate to a large degree. This method is referred to as the **indirect denial.** The best approach is to bend a little and acknowledge that the prospect is at least partially correct. After all, if you offered a product that is objection-proof, you would likely have no competitors. Every product has a shortcoming or limitation.[26] The success of this method is based in part on the need most people have to feel that their views are worthwhile. For this reason the indirect denial method is the most widely used.

Here is an exchange that features the use of this approach. The salesperson is a key account sales representative for Tele-Direct Atlantic.[27]

Salesperson: The total cost of placing your one-quarter-column ad in the Yellow Pages of the five different directories you have chosen is approximately $10 000.

Prospect: As a builder I want to reach people who are planning to build a home. I am afraid my ad will be lost among the hundreds of ads featured in your directories.

Salesperson: Yes, I agree the Yellow Pages in our directories do feature hundreds of ads, but the section for general contractors features fewer than 30 ads. Our design staff can prepare an ad that will be highly visible and will set your company apart from ads placed by other contractors.

Note that the salesperson used the words "Yes, I agree . . ." to reduce the impact of denial. The prospect is less likely to feel his or her point of view has been totally disproved.

FEEL—FELT—FOUND

Successful salespeople are sensitive to clues that indicate the client feels something is wrong. One way to empathize with the client's concerns is to use the "feel—felt—found" strategy. George Hutchison, chairman and CEO of North Bay, Ontario-based Equisure Financial Network Inc., is an ace negotiator who regularly uses this method. When someone raises a major concern, he will often say to the person, "I know how you *feel*. Others have *felt* the same way. However, we've *found* that. ..." Hutchison says that, besides offering empathy, this method reassures the person that others have successfully overcome the same concerns.[28]

www.equisure.ca

QUESTIONS

Another effective way to negotiate buyer resistance is to convert the problem into a question. Let us say that a prospect wants to trade used office equipment for new equipment but objects to the low trade-in allowance. The salesperson responds in this way: "Do you agree that our trade-in allowance, which is slightly lower than what you expected, will be more than offset by the extra service and dependability of our company?"

Suppose a prospect interested in purchasing four new tires objects to the price, which is about $20 higher per set than the price of a competing firm. The salesperson uses a question to minimize the price difference: "Do you agree that the convenience of our nationwide dealer network more than offsets the small price difference?" In this example the question is designed to encourage the tire buyer to weigh the disadvantage of a slightly higher price against the advantage of a national system of dealers who can provide convenient service. Questions often motivate the prospect to think in more depth about the salesperson's offer. Prior to a sales presentation, make a list of the concerns you expect to hear from the prospect and next to each one list the questions you can use to minimize it.

THE SUPERIOR BENEFIT

Sometimes the customer raises a problem that cannot be answered with a denial. For example: "Your copy machine does not feature an automatic document feed mechanism. This means that our employees will have to spend more time at the machine." You should acknowledge the valid objection and then discuss one or more superior benefits: "We have not included the automatic feature because it is less reliable than the manual approach. As you know, downtime is not only costly but also inconvenient." A **superior benefit** is a benefit that will, in most cases, outweigh the customer's specific concern.

superior benefit   A benefit that will, in most cases, outweigh the customer's specific concern.

DEMONSTRATION

If you are familiar with your product as well as that of your competition, this method of negotiating buyer concerns is easy to use. You know the competitive advantages of your product and can discuss these features with confidence.

The product demonstration is one of the most convincing ways to overcome buyer skepticism. With the aid of an effective demonstration you can overcome specific concerns.

Sometimes a second demonstration is needed to overcome buyer skepticism. This demonstration will provide additional proof. High-achieving sales personnel know when and how to use proof to overcome buyer concerns.

TRIAL OFFER

A **trial offer** involves giving the prospect an opportunity to try the product without making a purchase commitment. The trial offer (especially with new products) is popular with customers because they can get fully acquainted with your product without making a major commitment. Assume that a buyer for a large restaurant chain says, "I am sure you have a good cooking oil, but we are happy with our present brand. We have had no complaints from our managers."

trial offer   Involves giving the prospect an opportunity to try the product without making a purchase commitment.

Building Relationships through Technology

AUTOMATED SORTING AND PRODUCTIVITY

The notes of a busy salesperson can quickly become extensive. Paper notes make it difficult, if not impossible, to cross reference important information within those notes. The notes in a CRM system give salespeople immediate access to records containing needed words or phrases. This feature offers users many advantages, including a method of quickly finding information about buyers with similar interests or concerns. (See the exercise Finding Keywords in a CRM Database on page 292 for more information.)

In response to this comment you might say, "I can understand your reluctance to try our product. However, I do believe our oil is the finest on the market. With your permission I would like to ship you 125 litres of our oil at no cost. You can use our product at selected restaurants and evaluate the results. If our oil does not provide you with superior results, you are under no obligation to place an order."

In the case of office equipment the customer may be given the opportunity to use the product on a trial basis. An office manager might respond to the salesperson who sells dictation equipment in this manner: "I would not feel comfortable talking to a machine." In response to this issue a salesperson might say, "I can understand how you feel. How about using one of our demonstration models for a few days?"

THIRD-PARTY TESTIMONY

Studies indicate that the favourable testimony of a neutral third party can be an effective method of responding to buyer resistance. Let us assume that the

Aramark lists several of its larger customers in this ad, a form of third-party testimony.

WHO'S GOT THE SOLUTIONS FOR MORE EFFICIENT OFFICE SYSTEMS?

We're ARAMARK Office Services and while our name is new, we bring our clients years of experience in providing total office management solutions. Our point of difference lies in our approach to your business, which is solutions based supported by technology and equipment, not the other way around.

Our range of services includes on-site print on demand, copy centre, mail centre management, Electronic Document Management Systems, distribution, fulfilment and stationery and forms control. ARAMARK provides you with the most advanced equipment available with dedicated specialists in each area.

In addition, ARAMARK's unique "Unlimited Partnership" culture offers a wide range of managed services from food service to cleaning to office coffee. All designed for cost effectiveness and to save you time, time that can be focused on your core business.

Now isn't that the best solution of all.

ARAMARK
Managed Services, Managed Better.
FORMERLY VERSA SERVICES

*ARAMARK® Managed Services for Business, Education, Healthcare, Sports & Entertainment, Offshore and Remote, and Government:
Food, Refreshment, Office Management, and Facility Services. Visit us at www.aramark.ca*

owner of a small business states that he or she can get along without a personal computer. The salesperson might respond in this manner: "Many small business owners think the way you do. However, once they use a personal computer, they find it to be an invaluable aid. Mark Williams, owner of Williams Hardware, says that his PC saves him several hours a week. Plus, he has improved the accuracy of his record keeping."

Third-party testimony provides a positive way to solve certain types of buying problems. The positive experiences of a neutral third party will almost never trigger an argument with the prospect.

COMBINATION METHODS

As noted previously, consultative selling is characterized by flexibility. A combination of methods sometimes proves to be the best way to deal with buyer resistance. For example, an indirect denial might be followed by a question: "The cost of our business security system is a little higher than the competition. The price I have quoted reflects the high-quality materials used to develop our system. Wouldn't you feel better entrusting your security needs to a firm with more than 25 years of experience in the business security field?" In this situation the salesperson might also consider combining the indirect denial with an offer to arrange a demonstration of the security system.

Summary

Sales resistance is natural and should be welcomed as an opportunity to learn more about how to satisfy the prospect's needs. Buyers' concerns often provide salespeople with precisely the information they need to close a sale.

Concerns may arise from a variety of reasons, some related to the content or manner of the presentation strategy and others related to the prospect's own concerns. Whatever the reasons, the salesperson should *negotiate* sales resistance with the proper attitude, never making too much or too little of the prospect's concerns.

General strategies for negotiating buyer concerns include anticipating them, knowing the value of what you are offering, preparing for negotiations, understanding the problem, creating alternative solutions, finding some point of agreement, and avoiding anger.

The best strategy for negotiating sales resistance is to anticipate it and pre-plan methods to answer the prospect's concerns. If a salesperson uses a negotiations worksheet, then it will be much easier to deal with buyer resistance.

We discussed the various types of problems likely to surface during the sales presentation. Most objections can be placed in one of five categories: need, product, source, price, and time.

Specific methods and combinations of methods for negotiating resistance will vary depending on the particular combination of salesperson, product, and prospect. We have described several common methods, but you should remember that practice in applying them is essential and that there is room for a great deal of creative imagination in developing variations or additional methods. With careful preparation and practice, negotiating the most common types of buyer concerns should become a stimulating challenge to each salesperson's professional growth.

Key Terms

Negotiation 272
Stall 281
Added-Value Negotiating 283
Direct Denial 285

Indirect Denial 286
Superior Benefit 287
Trial Offer 287

Review Questions

1. Explain why a salesperson should welcome buyer concerns.

2. List the common types of buyer concerns that might surface in a presentation.

3. How does the negotiations worksheet form help the salesperson prepare to negotiate buyer concerns?

4. Explain the value of using a confirmation question as a general strategy for negotiating buyer concerns.

5. List seven general strategies for negotiating buyer concerns.

6. John Ruskin says that it is unwise to pay too much when making a purchase, but it is worse to pay too little. Do you agree or disagree with this statement? Explain.

7. What is usually the most common reason prospects give for not buying? How can salespeople deal effectively with this type of concern?

8. Professional buyers often learn to use specific negotiation tactics in dealing with salespeople. List and describe two tactics that are commonly used today.

9. When a customer says, "I want time to think it over," what type of resistance is the salesperson encountering? Suggest ways to overcome this type of buyer concern.

10. What are some positive ways to cope with the loyalty objection?

Application Exercises

1. During an interview with a prospective employer the interviewer raises the objection that you are not qualified for the job for which you are applying. On the basis of your observation you do not believe the interviewer fully understands the amount of experience you have or that you really have the ability to perform the job requirements. Write how you would overcome the objection the interviewer has raised.

2. Your negotiation of sales resistance can be compared in part with how you manage interpersonal conflicts. In learning how to deal with conflicts constructively, the first step is to become aware of your present and past style of managing conflict. Think back over the interpersonal conflicts you may have been involved in during the past few years. These conflicts may have been with customers, friends, parents, spouse, teachers, boss, or subordinates. In the space provided, list five major conflicts you can remember and how you resolved them.

Conflict   Resolution of Conflict

1.

2.

3.

4.

5.

Analyze your basic style of conflict management from these five examples. Do you tend to back away from conflicts (the "flight method" of conflict resolution), or do you look for conflict and stand your ground no matter what happens (the "fight method" of conflict resolution)? Would salespeople who have a flight style of handling objections close many sales? How about the salesperson who has a fight style? Which style would the salesperson who always used the direct denial method of negotiating tend to possess—flight or fight? Is the indirect denial a fight, a flight, or a somewhere-in-between style? Explain.

3. Assume you have decided to sell your own home. During an open house a prospect, whom you are showing through the house, begins to criticize every major selling point about your home.

    a. You have taken excellent care of your home, believe it to be a good home, and have done a lot of special projects to make it more enjoyable. What will be your emotional reaction to this prospect's criticisms? Should you express this emotional reaction?

    b. You think this prospect is really interested in buying your home, despite this surface criticism. How would you negotiate the buyer's concerns he or she is showing?

4. Acclivus Corporation is a leading supplier of sales training programs. One of its most popular programs is the "Acclivus Sales Negotiation System." Access the Acclivus Web site and click on the "What We Offer" link. Study the information on the Negotiation training program. Also, click on the Advertising link and study Acclivus' "R3evolution" concept. What is this concept? Click on the "Success Stories" link and examine what organizations say about the negotiations training they have received.

 www.acclivus.com

5. Participant 1: You are a salesperson for Windsor Factory Supply Limited (see Chapter 1), and you are about to make a sales call on Elizabeth Pujera, a senior buyer for one of your major automotive accounts. Ms. Pujera has just transferred to your territory from one of your customer's U.S. locations. You have heard that she is a tough negotiator, always looking for ways to save money for her company. You have submitted a quotation for her annual supply of safety clothing, and she has advised you during a follow-up phone conversation that she expects a reduction of at least 20 percent from the prices you have quoted. You know that her request will be impossible to meet as, on average, you are making just over 12 percent on the products you are offering. You are about to meet in her office to discuss your quotation. You should be creative in dealing with her price objection.

Participant 2: You are Elizabeth Pujera.

CRM Application Exercise

Finding Keywords in a CRM Database

During sales training this week, your sales manager, Becky Kemley, led a discussion about negotiating buyer resistance and managing objections. The discussion included methods of identifying and responding to price concerns. You wish to find those contacts who might have a price objection so that you can better prepare for working with them. Using the ACT! software, access all records containing the word "price" by selecting Lookup, Keyword, type "price," check Notes, and press Enter. After searching, ACT! will display three records in which price is an issue. Print contact reports for these three records by selecting Report, Contact Report, Active Lookup, Printer, and OK.

Video Case

www.banffmanagement. com

Each year, private and public organizations across Canada, including not-for-profit agencies, send thousands of employees to management training seminars. Training has become a multi-million-dollar business, and the number of programs has been growing rapidly. Some of the largest providers of management training and related services are catering to clients in new and exciting ways. The Banff Centre for Management (BCM; introduced at the beginning of this chapter) provides a good example of this type of service provider. The goal of the BCM is to advance the state of leadership excellence in both individuals and organizations across Canada.

In total, the BCM offers about 150 programs yearly, in areas such as executive development, general leadership and management, not-for-profit and community leadership, aboriginal leadership, and environmental leadership. The program-design staff members each work with approximately 10 to 15 partnered client organizations annually to develop customized programs. They promise an unforgettable experience, with guaranteed results. Part of the process includes individual competency measurement, and if improvement cannot be demonstrated six to twelve months after the program, the BCM will refund that person's portion of the learning costs, or will re-engage with that individual free of charge.

The BCM has a wide range of accommodations for participants, including 433 guestrooms in five facilities. There is a resource room with a printer and computers with Internet connections, and a full range of current management books and periodicals. Classrooms are equipped with the latest in multimedia technology. The BCM has a 500-seat dining room, six private function rooms that can be configured for various-sized groups for banquets or receptions, and numerous lounges that are licensed for private functions. There are outstanding indoor recreational facilities for swimming, squash, racquetball, weight training, track, and aerobic training. Outdoor sports are also available, including fishing, hiking, climbing, kayaking, river rafting, skiing, trail riding, golfing, mountain biking, and more. Participants can also attend a number of cultural events provided by the Banff Centre for the Arts.

In an ideal situation, Doug Macnamara, general manager of the BCM, likes to guide prospects through the facilities. This tour in some ways fulfills the function of a sales demonstration. He describes special amenities and services that the BCM can offer, and uses this time to become better acquainted with the prospect's needs. Then he escorts the prospect back to his office and completes a needs assessment, before preparing a detailed sales proposal. In most cases the proposal will be presented to the prospect at a second meeting. The proposal needs to contain accurate and complete information because, when signed, it becomes a legally enforceable sales contract.

Rarely will the sales proposal for a program be accepted without negotiating some modifications. Some clients Doug Macnamara deals with are experienced negotiators, and they often press for concessions that might include a lower daily participant rate, lower rates for accommodations or meals, complimentary barbecues or receptions, or passes for cultural or sporting events.

Of course some buyer concerns are not easily identified. Doug Macnamara says he follows three steps in dealing with buyer concerns:

1. He locates the concerns. Some prospects are reluctant to accept a sales proposal, but the reason may be unclear. Doug has discovered some clients are concerned whether instructors can relate "theoretical" material to the real world of business, and whether they can relate to adult learners who often need a more active style of learning rather than simply lecture-based learning. Once these perceptions are uncovered, Doug knows how to deal with them.

2. He clarifies the concerns. If a prospect says, "I like your facilities and your program, but your price is too high," Doug must clarify what the prospect means. Is the prospect seeking a major price concession or a very small price concession?

3. He overcomes the buyer concerns. Doug says, "You must know the value of what you are offering. The BCM must be able to cover its costs, so concessions can only be made after careful consideration. Sometimes there are things included in the proposal that the prospect does not value or need, and removing them allows both parties to win: the client gets a program configured to meet their specific needs, and the BCM controls its costs."

Doug Macnamara's ability to configure value-added solutions for clients and to negotiate buyer concerns have helped the BCM achieve its goals.[29]

Questions

1. If you were selling management training programs to businesses, what types of buyer concerns would you expect from a new prospect?

2. Let's assume that you are representing the Banff Centre for Management and you are meeting with a new prospect in her office. She is located some distance from Banff and cannot visit your facilities. What are some tools that you might use during the sales presentation? What proof devices might you use to support your claims?

3. If you meet with a professional buyer who is trained in negotiations, what tactics can you expect the person to use? How would you respond to each of these tactics?

CRM Case Study

Negotiating Resistance

Becky Kemley has asked you to review Pat Silva's former prospect accounts. She wants you to look for accounts with which you might anticipate objections during a presentation.

Questions

1. Which account might voice a time objection and say, "We want to put off our decision for now," and how would you propose dealing with this objection?

2. Which account is most likely to try to get you to agree to a lower price and how would you respond?

3. Which account might you anticipate would use the phrase "we want to shop around for a good solid supplier." What would be your response?

Partnership Selling: A Role Play/Simulation (see Appendix C, p. 458)

DEVELOPING A SALES PRESENTATION STRATEGY—NEGOTIATING

Refer to *Sales Memorandum 3* and strategically plan to anticipate and negotiate any objections and/or concerns your customer may have to your presentation. You should prepare a negotiations worksheet to organize this part of your presentation.

The instructions for item 2e direct you to prepare negotiations for the time, price, source, and product objections. You will note that your price is approximately $200 more than your customer budgeted for this meeting. You will have to be very effective in negotiating a value-added strategy because your convention centre is not a low-price supplier (see Chapter 6 on value-added product strategies).

During the presentation you should use proof devices from the product strategy materials provided in *Employment Memorandum 1* to negotiate concerns you anticipate. You may also want to use a calculator to negotiate any financial arrangements such as savings on parking, airport transportation, etc. Place these materials in the front pocket of your three-ring binder (portfolio) so you can easily access them during your presentation. You may want to ask another person to be your customer, instructing them to voice the objections you have anticipated and then responding with your negotiation strategies. This experience will provide you with the opportunity to rehearse your negotiation strategies.

Closing the Sale and Confirming the Partnership

Dana Bengtson, sales representative for Ryder Commercial Leasing & Services, understands the importance of patience in selling. It took him two years to convince a major food distributor to replace its in-house truck fleet with leased trucks from Ryder. Soon after his first contact he arranged for efficiency studies of the prospect's existing transportation system. With this information he was able to demonstrate the cost advantages of leasing. Although he seemed to be moving toward a close, the prospect's officials let it be known that they did not want to continue talks about leasing, at least for the time being. Bengtson realized it was time to slow down negotiations and be patient. In his words, it was time to "do nothing." Later Bengtson resumed his closing efforts. He sent the officials articles on long-term vehicle leasing and information on the food distribution business. He restructured his proposal to make it more appealing. After six more months of hard work he was rewarded with a seven-year lease agreement worth more than $4 million annually to Ryder. Dana Bengtson closed this sale because he knew when to speed up and when to slow down negotiations.[1]

LEARNING OBJECTIVES

When you finish reading this chapter, you should be able to

1. Describe the proper attitude to display toward closing the sale

2. List and discuss selected guidelines for closing the sale

3. Explain how to recognize closing clues

4. Discuss selected methods of closing the sale

5. Explain what to do when the buyer says yes and what to do when the buyer says no

Developing an Attitude toward Closing the Sale

The excitement and personal satisfaction Dana Bengtson feels after closing a sale are common among both new and experienced salespeople. When the prospect says yes, the salesperson receives both a personal and an economic reward. The amount of personal satisfaction received on closing the sale depends on the salesperson's attitude toward the product. Salespeople who believe strongly in their product enjoy converting prospects to customers. They also look forward to a continuing partnership with the new customer.

Closing the sale is less difficult if everything is handled properly throughout the sales presentation. A strategically prepared salesperson approaches the close with confidence (Fig. 13.1). Closing is usually more difficult when some aspect of the sales presentation has not been handled properly. Maybe a negative first impression still lingers in the prospect's mind. Perhaps the sales demonstration did not go smoothly. Maybe buyer concerns were not negotiated effectively. These and other factors can serve as barriers to closing the sale.

Some sales are lost because the salesperson attempts to close too early or too late. Sometimes salespeople try to close before the prospect is ready to buy. An early closing attempt may be interpreted as "pressure" selling. We must take

Figure 13.1 Effective closing methods require careful planning.

The Six-Step Presentation Plan	
Step One: APPROACH	✔ Review Strategic/Consultative Selling Model ✔ Initiate customer contact
Step Two: PRESENTATION	✔ Determine prospect needs ✔ Select product or service ✔ Initiate sales presentation
Step Three: DEMONSTRATION	✔ Decide what to demonstrate ✔ Select selling tools ✔ Initiate demonstration
Step Four: NEGOTIATION	✔ Anticipate buyer concerns ✔ Plan negotiating methods ✔ Initiate double-win negotiations
Step Five: CLOSE	○ Plan appropriate closing methods ○ Recognize closing clues ○ Initiate closing methods
Step Six: SERVICING THE SALE	○ Suggestion selling ○ Follow-through ○ Follow-up calls
Service, retail, wholesale, and manufacturer selling.	

care to avoid giving the prospect a feeling of anxiety about being sold something.

It is also possible to close too late by ignoring obvious closing clues. Sometimes salespeople keep on talking long after buyers have decided to make the purchase. When this happens, customer attitudes sometimes change, and sales are lost.

Another barrier to closing the sale is the early "retreat." When the buyer says no, the salesperson may give up too soon. These and other barriers are discussed in this chapter.

LOOKING AT CLOSING FROM THE PROSPECT'S POINT OF VIEW

Closing the sale will no doubt be easier if you look at this aspect of selling from the prospect's point of view. Recognize the concerns that may surface in the person's mind.

Do I really need this product?

Does this product measure up to the competition?

Should I postpone buying?

Will this supplier stand behind the product?

What will my friends think if I buy this item?

These may be genuine concerns that could prevent the buyer from saying yes to your proposal. It is best to anticipate these concerns and develop a strategic sales presentation that will eliminate them.

CLOSING THE SALE—THE BEGINNING OF THE PARTNERSHIP

Closing should be viewed as part of the selling process—the logical outcome of a well-planned presentation strategy. There is a building process that begins with an interesting approach and need discovery. It continues with effective

A strategically prepared salesperson approaches the close with confidence.

Selling in Action

DETERMINATION IS THE KEY

Joe Batten, author of the popular sales training film *Ask for the Order and Get It,* believes that determination is a major key to success in personal selling. He describes determination as a firm, unyielding stand never to let a sale you have worked to make go unasked for. Determination prevents you from taking a quick no for an answer. Determination keeps you from mistaking a customer's doubt for refusal, recognizing that the word *no* may mean "no for now" or "no based on what I currently know."[a]

---

product selection and presentation of benefits, which build desire for the product. After a well-planned demonstration and after dealing with sales resistance, it is time to ask for the sale. Closing should be thought of as the beginning of a long-term partnership.

The image of a salesperson who makes a quick pitch, writes up an order, and disappears has faded into history. In the new information-age economy the customer realizes the need for a partner, someone to be there when needed, to consistently advise and to help solve problems on a continuing basis.[2]

Guidelines for Closing the Sale

A number of factors increase the odds that you will close the sale (Fig. 13.2). These guidelines for closing the sale have universal application in the field of selling.

FOCUS ON DOMINANT BUYING MOTIVES

Most salespeople incorporate the outstanding benefits of their product into the sales presentation. This is only natural. However, be alert to the *one* benefit that generates the most excitement. The buying motive that is of greatest interest deserves the greatest emphasis. Vince Peters, director of sales training and development for Wyeth-Ayerst International, tells his 8000 pharmaceutical salespeople that the key to closing "is to find out exactly what a prospect is looking for."[3]

Zig Ziglar, author of *Secrets of Closing the Sale*, reminds us that when closing it is important to give prospects a reason to buy, or some information so that they can act in their own best interests. He says, "This helps you move closing from being *selfish* on your part to being *helpful* to the prospect."[4] To apply this premise, focus your close on the point of greatest interest and give the prospect a reason for buying.

NEGOTIATE THE TOUGH POINTS BEFORE ATTEMPTING THE CLOSE

Many products have what might be thought of as an Achilles heel. In other words, the product is vulnerable or appears to be vulnerable in one or more areas. Negotiate a win-win solution to the tough points before you attempt to close the sale. Such factors can lose the sale if you ignore them. The close should

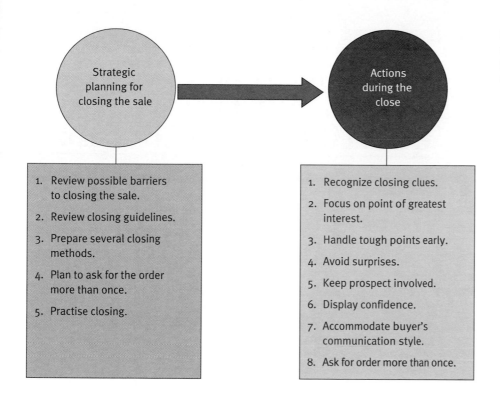

Figure 13.2 The presentation strategy should include reviewing these guidelines for closing and confirming the sale.

Strategic planning for closing the sale

1. Review possible barriers to closing the sale.
2. Review closing guidelines.
3. Prepare several closing methods.
4. Plan to ask for the order more than once.
5. Practise closing.

Actions during the close

1. Recognize closing clues.
2. Focus on point of greatest interest.
3. Handle tough points early.
4. Avoid surprises.
5. Keep prospect involved.
6. Display confidence.
7. Accommodate buyer's communication style.
8. Ask for order more than once.

be a positive phase of the sales presentation. This is not the time to deal with a controversial issue or problem.

In the case of Maytag washing machines, Rolex watches, Lexus automobiles, or Banff Springs Hotel conference facilities, the Achilles heel may be price. Each of these products may seem expensive in comparison with competing ones. People who sell them find ways to establish the value of their product before attempting the close.

LONGER SELLING CYCLES REQUIRE MORE PATIENCE

Longer selling cycles have become a fact of life in recent years. One reason for this change is that more people are involved in purchasing some products. The purchase of highly technical products such as computers, security equipment, and robotics may involve persons from many areas of the organization. In some cases the buyer has more options than in the past. These customers are likely to take more time to make a buying decision, and the amount of time will likely increase as the purchase price increases.

The partnership between IBM and Acadia University provides a case study in patient selling. Before David Vokey (introduced in Chapter 2) successfully closed the deal that made Acadia Canada's first "ThinkPad University," there were many sales calls, many people were involved from both organizations, and a considerable amount of time and effort was required to make the buying decision. Acadia carefully evaluated 12 companies that wanted to be its primary technological partner. According to Acadia president Dr. Kelvin Ogilvie, the university needed "to have absolute confidence that the technology being provided would meet the objectives and standards required for our program, and that the company would be in business in the long term to provide us with

ServiceMaster of Canada recognizes that different customers can have different dominant buying motives. Focusing on dominant buying motives helps close sales.

critical long-term support. Then once you get beyond that absolute requirement, you get into your confidence in your ability to work with the corporation in a partnership arrangement."[5]

AVOID SURPRISES AT THE CLOSE

Some salespeople make the mistake of waiting until the close to reveal information that may come as a surprise to the prospect. For example, the salesperson quotes a price but is not specific concerning what the price includes. Let us assume that the price of a central air-conditioning unit is $1800. The prospect believes that the price is competitive in relation to similar units on the market and is ready to sign the order form. Then the salesperson mentions casually that the installation charge is an extra $225. The prospect had assumed that the $1800 fee included installation. Suddenly the extra fee looms as a major obstacle to closing the sale.

The surprise might come in the form of an accessory that costs extra, terms of the warranty, customer service limitations, or some other issue. Do not let a last-minute surprise damage the relationship and threaten the completion of a sale.

DO NOT ISOLATE THE PROSPECT DURING THE SALE

Adults are self-directing people. They are most comfortable when they have a voice in matters that influence their lives. Do not forget this important point at the time you attempt to close. Involve the customer in the close if at all possible. Sometimes it is possible to involve the prospect in some type of "doing" activity. The prospect might be asked to hold the sales proposal as the salesperson explains the details. A salesperson selling carpet might hand the prospect a sample case and ask the person to pick out her favourite colour.

You can achieve involvement with questions. You might summarize points of agreement with carefully phrased confirmation-type questions. Here are some examples:

"Ms. Hansen, you seem to agree that this model combines good looks with durability. Is that right?"

"Mr. Walker, you do agree that your current electric bills are too high. Is that right?"

You might also let the prospect summarize the positive aspects of your product. This might be done by using the following types of question:

"What features of our product do you like best?"

"What aspects of our customer service program do you find most appealing?"

DISPLAY A HIGH DEGREE OF SELF-CONFIDENCE AT THE CLOSE

Do you believe in your product? Do you believe in your company? Have you identified a genuine need? If you can answer yes to each of these questions, then there is no need to display timidity. Look the prospect in the eye and ask for the order. Do not be apologetic at this important point in the sales presentation. The salesperson who confidently asks for the sale is displaying the boldness that is often needed in personal selling.

ASK FOR THE ORDER MORE THAN ONCE

Too often, salespeople make the mistake of not asking for the order or asking just once. If the prospect says no, they give up. Michael LeBoeuf, author of *How to Win Customers and Keep Them for Life*, reports that almost two thirds of all sales calls conclude without the salesperson asking for the order. He also says that a majority of customers say no four times before saying yes.[6] Some of the most productive salespeople ask for the order three, four, or even five times. A

Building Quality Partnerships

AN INSPIRING EXAMPLE

Ben Feldman was an unlikely candidate to earn the title "Greatest Life-Insurance Salesperson in History." He talked softly, hesitantly, and had a deceptively sleepy appearance. He was so shy that he once insisted on standing behind a screen when he spoke to an audience of fellow insurance salespeople. This quiet demeanour seemed to appeal to most customers, because he closed thousands of sales. He joined New York Life Insurance Company in the early 1940s and soon started making his mark. In the 1950s he became the first agent to write a million dollars in new business a month. In the 1960s he was the first salesperson to write a million a week. When he was in his prime, Feldman's income approached $5 million (U.S.) a year.

He sold life insurance by talking about life, not death. He focused his attention on owners of small industrial corporations. Feldman appealed to their need to protect their assets with large amounts of life insurance. He would show prospects his "tax book," a loose-leaf binder that contained the financial histories of people whose businesses or property had to be sold because they died without enough life insurance to pay estate taxes. Taped inside were a $1000 bill and a few pennies. He would point to the pennies and say, "For these you can get this"—the bill. This sales tool helped him close many sales.

In 1993, New York Life marked Ben Feldman's 50th year with the company by proclaiming "Feldman's February." The company initiated a national competition in which agents were encouraged to sell their best to honour Feldman. The winner of the Feldman February competition was Ben Feldman. Working the phones as he recovered from a health problem, he recorded sales of more than $15 million (U.S.).[b]

surprising number of yes responses come on the fourth or fifth attempt. Of course, not all of these closing attempts necessarily come during one call.

Many customers will think more highly of you if you have the courage to ask for the order. Do not be timid. If you beat around the bush, they may begin to question your commitment to the product. If you are fearful of asking for the order, or ask once and give up, you will never achieve success in personal selling.

RECOGNIZE CLOSING CLUES

closing clue An indication, either verbal or nonverbal, that the prospect is preparing to make a buying decision.

As the sales presentation progresses, you need to be alert to closing clues (sometimes called *buying signals*). A **closing clue** is an indication, either verbal or nonverbal, that the prospect is preparing to make a buying decision. It is a form of feedback, which is so important in selling. When you detect a closing clue, it may be time to attempt a close.

Many closing clues are quite subtle and may be missed if you are not alert. This is especially true in the case of nonverbal buying signals. If you pay careful attention—with your eyes and your ears—many prospects will tell you how to close the sale. As we have noted earlier in this text, one of the most important personality traits salespeople need is empathy, the ability to sense what the other person is feeling. In this section we will review some of the most common verbal and nonverbal clues.

VERBAL CLUES

Closing clues come in many forms. Spoken words (verbal clues) are usually the easiest to perceive. These clues can be divided into three categories: (1) questions, (2) recognitions, and (3) requirements.

Questions. One of the least subtle buying signals is the question. You might attempt a trial close after responding to one of the following questions:

"Do you have a credit plan to cover this purchase?"

"What type of warranty do you provide?"

"How soon can our company get delivery?"

Recognitions. A recognition is any positive statement concerning your product or some factor related to the sale, such as credit terms or delivery date. Some examples follow:

"We like the quality control system you have recommended."

"I have always wanted to own a boat like this."

"Your delivery schedule fits our plans."

Requirements. Sometimes customers outline a condition that must be met before they will buy. If you are able to meet this requirement, it may be a good time to try a trial close. Here are some requirements that the prospect might voice:

"We will need shipment within two weeks."

"Our staff will need to be trained in how to use this equipment."

"All our equipment must be certified by the plant safety officer."

In some cases, verbal buying clues will not jump out at you. Important buying signals may be interwoven into normal conversation. Listen closely whenever the prospect is talking.

NONVERBAL CLUES

Nonverbal buying clues will be even more difficult to detect. Once detected, this type of signal is not easy to interpret. Nevertheless, you should be alert to body movement, facial expression, and tone of voice. Here are some actions that suggest that the prospect may be prepared to purchase the product:[7]

The prospect's facial expression changes. Suddenly the person's eyes widen and genuine interest is clear in the facial expression.

The prospect begins showing agreement by nodding.

The prospect leans forward and appears to be intent on hearing your message.

The prospect begins intently to examine the product or study the sales literature.

When you observe or sense one of these nonverbal buying clues, do not hesitate to ask for the order. Keep in mind that the modern approach to selling holds that there may be several opportunities to close throughout the sales presentation. Important buying signals may surface at any time. Do not miss them.

Specific Methods for Closing the Sale

There is no *best* closing method. Your best bet is to preplan several closing methods and use the ones that seem appropriate (Fig. 13.3). Given the complex nature of many sales, it is often a good idea to be prepared to use a combination of closing methods. Do keep in mind that your goal is not only to close the sale but also to develop a long-term partnership. A win-win closing strategy results in repeat business and the opportunity to obtain referrals.

TRIAL CLOSE

Charles B. Roth, noted sales consultant, once said, "Start your presentation on a closing action, continue it on a closing action, and end it on a closing action." This may be overdoing it a little, but Mr. Roth does make an important point: you should not postpone attempts to close until your sales presentation is completed.

A **trial close,** also known as a *minor point close*, is a closing attempt made at an opportune time during the sales presentation to encourage the customer to reveal readiness or unwillingness to buy. When you are reasonably sure that the prospect is about to make a decision but is being held back by natural caution, the trial close may be appropriate. It is a good way to test the buyer's attitude toward the actual purchase. A trial close is often presented in the form of a probing or confirmation question. Here are some examples:

> "We can arrange an August-first shipment. Would this date be satisfactory?"

> "Which do you prefer, the dark green or the blue finish?"

> "Would you rather begin this plan on July first or July fifteenth?"

trial close A closing attempt made at an opportune time during the sales presentation to encourage the customer to reveal readiness or unwillingness to buy.

Figure 13.3 Preparing for the close requires the preplanning of several closing methods. Research indicates that in many selling situations several closing attempts will be necessary.

Closing Worksheet		
Closing clue (prospect)	**Closing method**	**Closing statement (salesperson)**
"That sounds fine."	**Direct appeal close**	"Good, may I get your signature on this order form?"
"What kind of financing do you offer?"	**Multiple options close**	"We have two financing methods available: 90-day open credit or two-year long-term financing. Which of these do you prefer?"
"Well, we don't have large amounts of cash available at this time."	**Assumption close**	"Based on your cash position, I would recommend you consider our lease-purchase plan. This plan allows you to pay a very small initial amount at this time and keep the cash you now have for your everyday business expenses. I will be happy to write up your order on the lease-purchase plan."

"Do you want one of our staff members to supervise the installation?"

"Will a $250 down payment be possible at this time?"

Some salespeople use the trial close more than once during the sales presentation. After the salesperson presents a feature, converts that feature to a buyer benefit, and confirms the prospect's agreement that the benefit is important, it would be appropriate to use a trial close.[8]

In broader terms, it would be appropriate to attempt a trial close after steps two, three, or four of the six-step presentation plan (Fig. 13.4).

SUMMARY-OF-BENEFITS CLOSE

Let us assume that you have discussed and demonstrated the major benefits of your product and you detect considerable buyer interest. However, you have covered a great deal of material. There is a chance that the prospect will not be able to put the entire picture together without your help. At this point you should provide a concise summary of the most important buyer benefits. Your goal in the **summary-of-benefits close** is to re-emphasize the benefits that will help bring about a favourable decision. For maximum sales success, focus on those benefits that satisfy the personal concerns of the buyer.[9]

Let us see how this closing method works in the management education industry. Bill Morrissey, manager of the Centre for Management Development, Memorial University of Newfoundland, recently called on Mr. Ray Busch, director of marketing for a large corporation. Near the end of the sales presentation, Bill summarized the major benefits in this manner: "Mr. Busch, we can provide you with a state-of-the-art seminar room that will seat 30 people comfortably and four smaller rooms for the workshops you have planned. Our staff will serve a noon lunch, and the cost will be $195 per person, including the instructor's fees. Finally, we will see that each of your employees receives a pad of paper, a pen, and a copy of the conference program. Should I go ahead and reserve these facilities for November 24?" In the process of reviewing all the important points, you provide the buyer with a positive picture of the proposal.

summary-of-benefits close Involves summarizing the most important buyer benefits, re-emphasizing the benefits that will help bring about a favourable decision.

ASSUMPTION CLOSE

The **assumption close** assumes the customer is going to buy.[10] This closing approach comes near the end of the planned presentation. If you have identified a genuine need, presented your solutions in terms of buyer benefits, presented an effective sales demonstration, and negotiated buyer concerns satisfactorily, it may be natural to assume the person is ready to buy. In the assumption close you actually assume that the prospect has already bought the product and then ask one or more questions about a minor point. Here are some examples:

"Do you want this purchase added to your charge account?"

"Will next Friday be OK for delivery, or will you need it sooner?"

In place of asking a question, the salesperson may start doing something such as writing up the order. The order might be completed and handed to the prospect along with a pen. The salesperson says, "Can I get your signature here?" or some similar statement. This must be done with a positive mental

assumption close   After the salesperson identifies a genuine need, presents solutions in terms of buyer benefits, conducts an effective sales demonstration, and negotiates buyer concerns satisfactorily, the assumption that the prospect has already bought the product. The closing activity is based on the assumption that a buying decision has already been made.

Figure 13.4 The trial close should be attempted at an opportune time during the sales presentation. It is appropriate to initiate a trial close after steps two, three, or four of the six-step presentation plan.

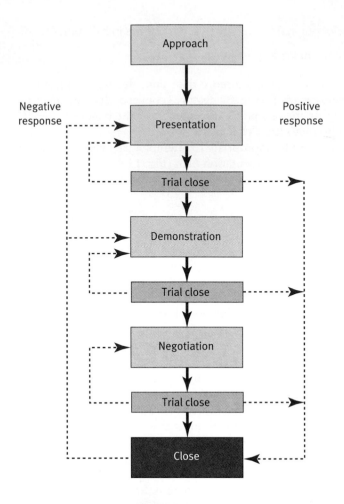

When you are making a group sales presentation, closing the sale may offer a greater challenge.

attitude. You are confident that the prospect is ready to buy and you are only bringing the selling–buying process to a close.

SPECIAL CONCESSION CLOSE

The **special concession close** offers the buyer something extra for acting immediately. A special inducement is offered if the prospect will agree to sign the order. The concession may be part of a low-price strategy such as a sale price, a quantity discount, a more liberal credit plan, or an added feature that the prospect did not anticipate.

> **special concession close**
> Offers the buyer something extra for acting immediately.

You should use this closing approach with care, because some customers are skeptical of concessions. This is especially true when the concession comes after the salesperson has made what appears to be the final offer. Let us assume that a customer is interested in buying a certain piano. The salesperson says in a firm voice, "The price is $5800." The customer says, "The price seems awfully high." After a few minutes of discussion the customer seems to be losing interest in the purchase. The salesperson says, "I think that price is firm, but let me check with the boss." A few minutes later the salesperson returns and says, "You are in luck. We can cut the price by $400."

What will be the impact of the $400 price concession? It may be the factor that motivates the buyer to say yes. On the other hand, it may have a negative influence on the person's attitude. Here are some thoughts that might surface in the prospect's mind:

> I wonder why the salesperson had to discuss the price with the boss.
>
> Why was the lower price not quoted in the first place?
>
> Maybe if I start to leave, the salesperson will lower the price again.
>
> If she is willing to lower the price, maybe there is something wrong with the product.

If the $5400 figure provides the store with an adequate profit margin, it may be best to quote this price in the first place. It is difficult to establish specific guidelines for every selling situation, but a good rule of thumb is to avoid gimmicks. Today's better educated buyer is not fooled easily.

MULTIPLE OPTIONS CLOSE

In many selling situations it is a good idea to provide the prospect with options. As noted in the previous chapter, today's customer expects new levels of flexibility. In the **multiple options close,** allow the person to examine several different options and try to assess the degree of interest in each one. As you near the point where a close seems appropriate, remove some of the options. This will reduce confusion and indecision.

> **multiple options close**   When the salesperson gives the prospect several options to consider and tries to assess the prospect's degree of interest in each.

You often see the limited choice technique used in office equipment sales. If a small business owner wants to purchase a copy machine, most vendors will offer several models for consideration. Let us assume that the prospect has examined four models and seems to be uncertain about which one would be the best choice. The salesperson might determine which copier is least appealing and eliminate it as an option. Now the prospect can choose among three copiers. If the prospect seems to favour one copier, it would be appropriate to ask for the order.

Instantaneous information can be very helpful in closing the sale. Toshiba's notebook computers offer salespeople easy access to information.

When using the limited choice close, follow these simple steps:

1. Cease showing new products when it appears that the prospect has been given ample selection. Too many choices can result in confusion and indecision.

2. Remove products that the prospect does not seem genuinely interested in and concentrate on the options the prospect does seem to be interested in.

DIRECT APPEAL CLOSE

direct appeal close Involves simply asking for the order in a straightforward manner. It is the most direct closing approach.

The **direct appeal close** has the advantages of clarity and simplicity. This close involves simply asking for the order in a straightforward manner. It is the most direct closing approach, and many buyers find it attractive. Realistically, most customers expect salespeople to ask for the sale.

The direct appeal should not, of course, come too early. It should not be used until the prospect has displayed a definite interest in the product or service.

The salesperson must also gain the prospect's respect before initiating this appeal. Once you make the direct appeal, stop talking. Raymond Slesinski, Digital Equipment sales trainer, tells his trainees, "After asking a closing question, do not speak, even if the prospect doesn't answer quickly." His advice is to give the prospect time to think about your offer.[11]

A variation of the direct appeal close involves using a question to determine how close the customer is to making a buying decision. The question might be "How close are we to closing the sale?" This direct question calls for a direct answer. The customer is encouraged to reflect on the progress of the sale.[12]

COMBINATION CLOSES

In some cases the most effective close is a **combination close** that combines two or more of the closing methods we have discussed. To illustrate, let us observe Colleen White as she attempts to close a sale in the office of a buyer for a large department store. Colleen represents a firm that manufactures a wide range of leather clothing and accessories. Near the end of her planned presentation she senses that the prospect is quite interested in her products but seems reluctant to make a decision. This is how she handles the close: "Ms. Taylor, I have described two benefits that seem especially important to you. First, you agree that this line will be popular with the fashion-conscious shoppers your store caters to. Second, you indicated that the prices I quoted will allow you excellent profit margins. If we process your order now, you will have the merchandise in time for the pre-Christmas buying period. We can guarantee the delivery at this point." Notice that this close starts with a summary of benefits and ends with a special concession.

combination close   When the salesperson tries to use two or more closing methods at the same time.

Practise Closing

Your success in selling will depend in large part on learning how to make these six closing methods work for you. You will not master these approaches in a few days or a few weeks, but you can speed up the learning process with preparation and practice. Role playing is the best-known way to experience the feelings that accompany closing, and practise the skills needed to close sales. To prepare the role play, anticipate various closing scenarios and then prepare a written script.[13] Find someone (your sales manager, friend, or spouse) to play the role of the customer and give them a script to act out. Practise the role plays in front of a video recorder, and then sit back and observe your performance. The video monitor provides excellent feedback. Use the closing worksheet (see Fig. 13.3) to prepare for practice sessions. You need to learn these methods so well that you can use them without consciously thinking about them.

One of the most important outcomes of practice is increased self-confidence. Think about Larry Wilson's views on the importance of confidence: "Fear of failure and fear of rejection are the most significant barriers to success and fulfillment in selling."[14]

Confirming the Partnership when the Buyer Says Yes

Congratulations! You have closed the sale and have established the beginning of what you hope will be a long and satisfying partnership with the customer.

When the customer says yes, take a few moments to express appreciation and to congratulate the person for making a wise decision.

confirmation step Reassuring the customer after the sale has been closed, pointing out that he or she has made the correct decision. This may involve describing the satisfaction of owning the product.

buyer's remorse Feelings of regret, fear, or anxiety that a buyer may feel after placing an order.

Before preparing to leave, be sure that all details related to the purchase agreement are completed. Check everything with the buyer, and then ask for a signature if necessary.

Once the sale has been closed, it is important to take time to reassure the customer. This is the **confirmation step** in closing the sale. Before you leave, reassure the customer by pointing out that he or she has made the correct decision, and describe the satisfaction that will come with ownership of the product. The reason for doing this is to resell the buyer and to prevent buyer's remorse. **Buyer's remorse** is an emotional response that can take various forms such as feelings of regret, fear, or anxiety.[15] It's common to wonder whether or not we have made the right decision. Compliment the customer for making a wise decision. Once the sale is closed, the customer may be required to justify the purchase to others. Your words of reassurance will be helpful.

Before leaving, thank the customer for the order. This is very important. Everyone likes to think that a purchase is appreciated. No one should believe that a purchase is taken for granted. Even a small order deserves words of appreciation. In many cases a follow-up thank-you letter is appropriate.

In several previous chapters we said that a satisfied customer is one of the best sources of new prospects. Never hesitate to ask, "Do you know anyone else who might benefit from owning this product?" or a similar question. Some customers may even agree to write an introductory letter on your behalf.

After you complete the sale, you should do everything possible to make sure the customer receives maximum satisfaction from the purchase. This may require a detailed explanation of how to operate and maintain the product. Some sales representatives make it a practice to be present when the product is delivered. They want to make sure the customer does not have any problems with the new product. How to "service" a sale properly is described fully in Chapter 14.

What to Do when the Buyer Says No

High-performance salespeople learn to manage disappointment. Abraham Zalezik, professor emeritus at the Harvard Business School, says the way we handle disappointment is often more important in reaching success than our focus on success itself. Learning to cope with disappointment forces people to learn more about themselves and better manage future disappointments.[16]

Never treat a lost sale as a defeat. When you adopt the win-win relationship strategy, there is never a winner and a loser. When the sales interview is over, both the customer and the salesperson should feel like winners. A strong display of disappointment or resentment is likely to close the door to future sales.

Faced with the possibility of a failed presentation strategy, some salespeople abandon their relationship and customer strategies and turn to selling methods that are unethical, illegal, or both. Sometimes sales representatives will imply that, if the prospect postpones signing the order, the item may not be available. If in fact the company has a large surplus of these products, the salesperson has been dishonest. Another unethical practice is suggesting that the price will soon increase sharply when in all likelihood the price will not change. If the customer finds out later that your information was not correct, you are likely to lose the opportunity for repeat business.

In some selling situations it is proper to reopen the presentation. If you are preparing to leave and think of an effective approach to closing the sale, do not hesitate to use it. You might recall an important point that was overlooked earlier. For example, you might want to review a testimonial from a satisfied customer. A third-party opinion might reopen the door and set the stage for the close.

PREPARE THE PROSPECT FOR CONTACT WITH THE COMPETITION

Some prospects refuse to buy because they want to take a close look at the competing products. This response is not unusual in the field of selling. You should do everything possible to help the customer make an intelligent comparison.

It is always a good practice to review your product's strong points one more time. Give special emphasis to areas in which your product has a superior advantage over the competition. To illustrate, let us assume you are selling a high quality welding machine designed for heavy production. The prospect seems to like your product but insists on looking at a competing product before making a buying decision. At this point you should review the exclusive features of your product and encourage the customer to remember these points when making a comparison. Make it easy for the person to buy your product at some future date.

Building Relationships through Technology

ADDING AND DELETING PROSPECTS

 Prospect and customer databases are continually changing. Promotions, transfers, mergers, and many other events require additions and deletions to a salesperson's automated data. Most CRM software makes this an easy process and warns users against the inadvertent removal of an account. (See the exercise Adding and Deleting Prospects on page 314 for more information.)

Selling in Action

I CLOSEM

Many sales managers will tell you that the difference between a good salesperson and a great salesperson is their ability to close sales. Tom Budd, a Calgary-based investment banker with Griffiths McBurney & Partners, is one of Canada's most successful deal closers. In 1997, Budd was lead adviser in 18 mergers and takeovers, and participated in 26 corporate financings. In *Titans*, Peter C. Newman estimates Tom Budd's annual income at about $5 million; Budd claims the estimate is "conservative."

How does Budd do it? Gene McBurney, a founding partner of Griffiths McBurney, says, "He's a great team player. He has very high standards, and he expects his partners to live up to similar high standards." His clients respect and trust him because he treats them honestly and always has their best interest at heart. Budd claims the key to success in his business "is to know the different personalities in the oil patch and anticipate their needs." When you combine his credibility and customer knowledge with his charisma, tireless work habits, and competitive desire to run faster, jump higher, and leap further, it's easy to see why Tom Budd comes out on top. Calgary oilman Harold Pederson says, "He's got a real nose for deals and he can close them effectively."

Tom Budd developed his closing skills from the time he was a student. To pay his tuition at the University of New Brunswick, he started a painting company. Budd would spend the day painting one house, then get dressed up at night and visit a neighbour to explain to the owner why his house didn't look as good as the one he had just painted. His technique helped Tom Budd close many painting contracts and shows he understood a lot about customer behaviour even then. He has continued to close deals throughout his career and he has earned the vanity plate on his car: ICLOSEM.[c]

ANALYZE LOST SALES

When you experience a no-sale call, try to benefit from the experience. A lost sale can be a good learning experience. Take a good, objective look at your presentation and try to identify any weaknesses. Were you able to arouse genuine interest early? Did you ask well-thought-out questions? Was the sales demonstration handled properly? Were you able to deal effectively with buyer resistance? If you do pinpoint a weakness, consider how to avoid this problem in the future. When you experience a no-sale call, salvage as much as possible from the experience. If you anticipate a return call, do record any new information you have learned about the prospect. This might include personal information, company information, or purchase priorities. Callbacks frequently yield good results, so avoid the temptation to give up after a single call on a prospect.

Do not spend *too much* time analyzing lost sales. Jack Falvey, author and sales consultant, says that we get no's for many unknown or subjective reasons, so a time-consuming study of every no-sale call may not be cost effective. He cautions salespeople to avoid dwelling on rejection and to keep moving forward.[17] Learning how to deal with no's is an important key to success in selling.

Summary

Closing the sale is usually not difficult if everything is handled properly throughout the sales presentation. When the sales presentation is well organized and well delivered, the close is part of the process that results in a sale.

The salesperson must be alert to closing clues from the prospect. These clues fall into two categories: verbal and nonverbal. Verbal clues are the easiest to recognize, but they may be subtle as well. Here again it is important to be an attentive listener. The recognition of nonverbal clues is more difficult, but practice in careful observation will help in detecting them.

Several closing methods may be necessary to get the prospect to make a buying decision; therefore it is wise for the salesperson to preplan several closes. These closing methods should be chosen from the list provided in this chapter, and then customized to fit the product and type of buyer with whom the salesperson is dealing. In some selling situations the use of combination closes is very effective.

The professional salesperson is not discouraged or offended if the sale is not closed. Every effort should be made to be of further assistance to the prospect; the sale might be closed on another call. Even if the sale is lost, the experience may be valuable if analyzed to learn from it.

Key Terms

Closing Clue 302	*Multiple Options Close 307*
Trial Close 304	*Direct Appeal Close 308*
Summary-of-Benefits Close 305	*Combination Close 309*
Assumption Close 305	*Confirmation Step 310*
Special Concession Close 307	*Buyer's Remorse 310*

Review Questions

1. List some aspects of the sales presentation that can make closing and confirming the sale difficult to achieve.

2. Explain why sales cycles are longer today. How should salespeople respond to this trend?

3. What guidelines should a salesperson follow for closing the sale?

4. Why is it important to look at closing from the prospect's point of view?

5. What three verbal clues can the prospect use to indicate that it is time to close the sale? What nonverbal clues should the salesperson be alert to?

6. Explain how the multiple options close might be used in the sale of men's and women's suits.

7. Is there a best method to use in closing the sale? Explain.

8. What is meant by a trial close? When should a salesperson attempt a trial close?

9. Explain the summary-of-benefits close.

10. What confirming steps should a salesperson follow when the customer says yes? What should be done when the customer says no?

Application Exercises

1. Which of the following statements, often made by prospects, would you interpret as buying signals?

   a. "How much would the payments be?"
   b. "Tell me about your service department."

    c. "The company already has an older model that seems good enough."

    d. "We do not have enough cash flow right now."

    e. "How much would you allow me for my old model?"

    f. "I do not need one."

    g. "How does that switch work?"

    h. "When would I have to pay for it?"

2. You are an accountant who owns and operates an accounting service. You have been contacted by the president of an advertising agency about the possibility of your auditing her business on a regular basis. The president has indicated that she investigated other accounting firms and thinks they price their services too high. With the knowledge you have about the other firms, you know you are in a strong competitive position. Also, you realize her account would be profitable for your firm. You really would like to capture this account. How will you close the deal? List and describe two closing methods you might use in this situation.

www.ryder.com

3. Ryder Commercial Leasing and Services is the topic of the opening material in this chapter. Access this company's Web site and view the information provided. Examine articles in the company news section and determine if any of this information would be helpful in closing the sale. Examine the business services section. Does it appear that Ryder is able to partner with its potential customers?

4. Participant 1: You are making a presentation on behalf of the Canadian Professional Sales Association (see Chapter 2) to Mr. Albert Hong, director of sales for Western Canadian Freight Services. You believe that Mr. Hong is a Director (substitute Emotive, Reflective, Supportive; see Chapter 4). Mr. Hong has indicated that he might be interested in purchasing a membership for his seven salespeople, and you have already sent him information by mail. You are about to meet Mr. Hong in his office. Your goal is to close the sale. Be prepared to try several closes that might appeal to Mr. Hong.

Participant 2: You are Mr. Albert Hong.

CRM Application Exercise

Adding and Deleting Prospects

Adding and deleting contacts is easy with the ACT! software, as it is with most CRM software. Create a contact record for B. H. Rivera by selecting Edit, New Contact or by pressing the Insert key (Ins on some keyboards). This will display a blank record that can be completed by selecting fields with the mouse or by using the Tab key to move from field to field. In the Company field, type "Graphic Forms" and type 3195556194 (no hyphens) into the Phone field. "2134 Martin Luther King" is the address, and the city, state, and zip code are Atlanta, GA, and 61740.

Most CRM software permits you to save time and avoid errors by selecting field data from menus. For example, point at the ID/Status field label and double-click with your mouse on the label, not the field. A menu of choices should appear. Another way to obtain this menu is to place the cursor in the field and press the F2 function key. From this menu, select Prospect as the ID/Status for the B. H. Rivera record.

You have just added a new record to the ACT! database. The demonstration version of the ACT! software limits the number of contacts to 25. The full version of ACT! has no such limit. Do not enter more than 25 contacts into this demonstration version. Print this new record by selecting Report, Contact Report, Active Contact, Printer, and OK.

To remove a contact, select Edit, Delete Contact. The window is displayed with a box for Contact, Lookup, and Cancel. Picking Contact will cause the individual record to be deleted, Lookup will delete all records currently being looked up, and Cancel will terminate the procedure without making changes. Choosing to delete a record will cause a warning window to be displayed. This window asks if you are sure that you wish to delete the contact. Caution is advised when deleting records or using the delete function. Press the F1 function key to display the appropriate help screen.

Case Problem

Ruan and Clark Distributing is a respected wholesale-broker of building products, including a quality line of carpeting. Three years ago, Bob Thompson graduated from college and accepted a sales position with Ruan and Clark as the representative for the carpet line.

During the past six months Bob has been calling on Woodside Building and Supply Company, one of the firms in his territory. Woodside already carries carpet lines from several of Bob's competitors. Woodside dominates its trading area in several product lines, including carpet. Bob has called on the buyer, Jim Cooney, four times. However, he has not been able to close the sale. Recently, Ruan and Clark took a new line of carpet that Bob felt offered his dealers an excellent buy.

In calling on Woodside for the fifth time, Bob decided to use the new product line to try to close the sale. The following sales presentation took place:

Bob: Hello, Jim. It's good to see you.

Jim: [In a warm, friendly tone of voice] Good to see you again, Bob, but I'll tell you right up front, I don't have a budget to buy additional goods! I would like to find out what you have, but even if you *gave* me a roll of carpet, I wouldn't be able to find a place here to store it.

Bob: I'm sorry to hear that, because we have just added another product line that we think is going to revolutionize the carpet industry. [Bob shows Jim a sample of the new line—a toast colour with alternating rows of cut and uncut yarn.] Our carpet mill took the popular traditional candy stripe, built it up to a higher quality, and changed its styling to appeal to more of your customers. In short, with this new toast-coloured, 10-year-guaranteed carpet you will no longer have to compete with your competitors on the same product. This will give your salespeople a strong competitive advantage in their sales presentation. Our sales forecasting indicates that within 12 months this new product will take over 25 percent of the traditional market.

Jim: Bob, this is an appealing line.

Bob: [Handing the sample to Jim] Because of our mill's innovation in construction you get a much better feel in the surface yarns, don't you?

Jim: Yes, it does feel good.

Bob: This construction feature, along with the improved rubber backing, will give your customers a better-quality piece of goods. In addition, Jim, the mill has been able to hold the price on these goods to a competitive level. What do you think of it?

Jim: [Inspecting the goods a second time] I like it, Bob, but as I said before . . .

Bob: [Breaking in and focusing on the space problem] Jim, I can appreciate your space problem, but I am in a position to ship you as little as one roll now, so you can get into the market immediately and find out how well this product is suited for your situation.

Jim: [Showing more interest] Well, I would like to try it, but I just cannot see how I can do it today.

Bob: That is too bad, Jim, because we are running this new line at a special introductory price. The regular price on these goods is $8.99 a metre, but we are introducing it at $6.99. [Bob feels he now has Jim wanting the goods. However, he thinks Jim may want to put the sale off until later.]

Jim: That is a good price, Bob, but I am just . . .

Bob: [Interrupting Jim] Also, we will pay the freight at $6.99, which will save you an additional 15 percent. [Bob really wants to open the Woodside account because of the high sales Woodside will experience and the future profitability his company will achieve. Under any other circumstances he would not have offered to pay the freight at this price.]

Jim: [In a quiet voice] That sure sounds like something I should take advantage of.

Questions

1. Based on the information given, do you think this sale can be closed?
2. Assume you are Bob. After Jim's last comment, which close would you use next? Why?
3. What appeared to be the major obstacle to closing this sale?
4. Did Jim give any closing clues? Identify them.
5. Did Bob use any trial closes? Identify them.
6. What did you like and what did you dislike about the way Bob attempted to close this sale?

CRM Case Study

Forecasting the Close

You are interested in discovering what your commissions may be for the next few months from Pat Silva's former accounts. To do this, you will review the information on each contact record. There are four fields on the first page of the contact screen from which you can forecast your expected sales:

Network Need, Likelihood, Dollar Amount, and Date Close. When working with these accounts, Pat entered the information found in each of these fields: in the Network Need field, Pat entered the type of network that the prospect might order; in the Likelihood field, Pat estimated the percentage of possibility that the account might place an order (0.80 means 80 percent); the Dollar Amount field refers to how much Pat thought the account would spend; the month Pat felt they would order is in the Date Close field (01/31 means January).

You can estimate each month's likely sales by multiplying the Dollar Amount field number times the Likelihood field percentage number. An 80 percent chance of a $100,000 sale is a forecast of $80,000 in sales. If the Date Close field for several accounts is 12/31, you can calculate the sales for that month (December) by totalling the forecasts for each account. For an estimate of your commission income, multiply each month's forecast by 10 percent.

Pat did not show that any forecasted sales were 100 percent. Pat recognized that the sales might not close, the amount anticipated (Dollar Amount) might not be achieved, and the close might not take place during the month projected. Pat knew that these transactions would not close themselves; certain steps would have to be taken to increase the possibility that the prospect would place an order. To collect your commissions, you have to discover the steps most likely to close these sales.

Questions

1. What would your commission income be for all Pat's accounts if you closed them as Pat forecasted?

2. What kind of special concession might be necessary to close the sale with Quality Builders?

3. What kind of close may be necessary to get an order from Computerized Labs?

4. What kind of close would be appropriate for the Lakeside Clinic?

Partnership Selling: A Role Play/Simulation (see Appendix C, p. 458)

DEVELOPING A SALES PRESENTATION STRATEGY—CLOSING THE SALE

Refer to *Sales Memorandum 3* and strategically plan to close the sale with your customer. To consider the sale closed you will need to secure the signature of your customer on the sales proposal form. This will guarantee your customer the accommodations listed on the form. These accommodations may change depending on the final number of people attending your customer's convention. This is an important point to keep in mind when closing the sale; however, you still must get the signature to guarantee the accommodations.

Follow the instructions carefully, and prepare a closing worksheet listing at least four closes using the methods outlined in this chapter. Two of these methods should be the summary of benefits and the direct appeal. Remember that it is not the policy of your convention centre to cut prices, so your methods should include value-added strategies.

Use proof devices to make your closes more convincing, and place them in the front pocket of your three-ring binder/portfolio for easy access during your presentation. You may want to ask another person to be your customer and practise the closing strategies you have developed.

Servicing the Sale and Building the Partnership

Never underestimate the power of indifference. This time-proven fundamental has universal support in the business community, yet many sales and marketing professionals still do things that give the customer an emotional slap in the face. Aurora Pucciarello, CEO of Max Distribution, describes how a valued customer was lost due to indifference. Near the end of a lucrative three-year contract, the client indicated a desire to renew it. All Aurora and her sales staff had to do was complete a basic proposal. "We were told to just fill out the same numbers as before. We thought great, we've got them in our pocket." The proposal was filed away and forgotten. Later, a phone call from the client let Pucciarello know she had missed the proposal deadline and lost the business. This client accounted for 10 percent of her total sales. She cried that day.[1]

Building Long-Term Partnerships with Customer Service

Customer service is the key to building customer loyalty. In the past some organizations were able to survive without fully embracing this fundamental, but times have changed. In a world of increased global competition and narrowing profit margins, customer retention through value-based initiatives can mean the difference between increasing or eroding market share. Progressive marketers are searching for ways to differentiate their service from competitors and build emotional loyalty through value.[2]

Customer service can be defined as those activities that enhance or facilitate the purchase and use of the product (Fig. 14.1). In good times and bad, quality customer service builds profits by attracting new accounts and keeping old ones active. The point of view that "service pays" is accepted by successful firms that have adopted the marketing concept and seek to establish long-term partnerships with customers.

A sales organization that can develop a reputation for servicing each sale will be sought out by customers who want a long-term partner to help them with their buying needs. Satisfied customers represent an "auxiliary" sales force—a group of people who will recommend customer-driven organizations to others.

customer service All those activities enhancing or facilitating the sale and use of a product or service, including suggestion selling, delivery and installation, assistance with the warranty or service contract, securing credit arrangements, and making postsale courtesy calls.

The Six-Step Presentation Plan	
Step One: APPROACH	✔ Review Strategic/Consultative Selling Model ✔ Initiate customer contact
Step Two: PRESENTATION	✔ Determine prospect needs ✔ Select product or service ✔ Initiate sales presentation
Step Three: DEMONSTRATION	✔ Decide what to demonstrate ✔ Select selling tools ✔ Initiate demonstration
Step Four: NEGOTIATION	✔ Anticipate buyer concerns ✔ Plan negotiating methods ✔ Initiate double-win negotiations
Step Five: CLOSE	✔ Plan appropriate closing methods ✔ Recognize closing clues ✔ Initiate closing methods
Step Six: SERVICING THE SALE	⬤ Suggestion selling ⬤ Follow-through ⬤ Follow-up calls
Service, retail, wholesale, and manufacturer selling.	

Figure 14.1 Servicing the sale involves three steps: suggestion selling, follow-through, and follow-up calls.

Craig Proctor (see Chapter 3) owes part of his success to his ability to manage many relationships.

Some companies, such as Quebecor Printing, recognize that customer service is an excellent way to achieve a competitive advantage in a highly competitive market, and that people are important in maintaining service quality.

If customers are pleased with the service they receive after the sale, be assured that they will tell other people. Recent research shows that when someone has a good customer service experience, he tells an average of six people; when he has an outstanding experience, he tells twice as many.[3]

RESPONDING TO INCREASED POSTSALE CUSTOMER EXPECTATIONS

People buy expectations, not things, according to Ted Levitt, author of *The Marketing Imagination*. They buy the expectations of benefits you promised.

Once the customer buys your product, expectations increase. Levitt points out that after the sale is closed, the buyer's attitude changes.

> *The fact of buying changes the buyer. He expects the seller to remember the purchase as having been a favor bestowed on him by the buyer, not as something earned by the seller. Hence it is wrong to assume that to have gained an account gives you an advantage by virtue of having gotten "a foot in the door." The opposite is increasingly the case. If the buyer views the sale as a favor conferred by him on the seller, then he in effect debits the seller's account. The seller owes him one. The seller is in the position of having to rebuild his relationship from a deficit position.*[4]

Increased customer expectations after the sale is closed require a strategic plan for servicing the sale. Certain aspects of the relationship, product, and customer strategies can have a positive influence on the customer's heightened expectations.

How do we respond to a customer who has increased expectations? First, we should be certain our customer strategy is on target. We must fully understand the needs and wants of the customer. We have to know what the customer is trying to accomplish and how we can help him or her do it better. Successful salespeople are driven by a close-to-the-customer orientation and they frequently test their assumptions regarding levels of customer satisfaction. In some cases this means asking the customer questions that might make the salesperson uncomfortable. The answers to these questions serve as an early warning system for things that are going wrong.[5] Unresolved postsale problems open the door to competitors.

Second, we should re-examine our product strategy. In some cases we can enhance customer satisfaction by suggesting related products or services. If the product is expensive, we can follow through and offer assistance in making credit arrangements. If the product is complex, we can make suggestions concerning use and maintenance. Each of these forms of assistance may add value to the sale.

THE HIGH COST OF CUSTOMER ATTRITION

Financial institutions, public utilities, airlines, retail stores, restaurants, manufacturers, and wholesalers face the problem of gaining and retaining the patronage of clients and customers. These companies realize that keeping a customer happy is a good strategy. To regain a lost customer can be four to five times more expensive than keeping a current customer satisfied.[6]

There is no longer any doubt that poor service is the primary cause of customer attrition. A surprisingly small number of customers (12 to 15 percent) are lost due to product dissatisfaction. No more than 10 to 15 percent of lost customers leave due to price considerations. Most research indicates that from 50 to 70 percent of customer attrition is due to poor service.[7] A carefully developed strategic plan to reduce customer defection will pay big dividends.

Larry Rosen, president of Harry Rosen Gentlemen's Apparel, fully embraces the customer-for-life philosophy of doing business. Rosen's obsession with customer service has enabled the store to expand to several Canadian cities, and Harry Rosen now has a licensing agreement with Hugo Boss to open 20 boutiques in the United States over the next few years. Rosen says, "We don't look at a person that walks into our store as an immediate sale. We look at him with a potential lifetime value."[8]

Current Developments in Customer Service

In his book *Business @ The Speed of Thought*, Bill Gates predicts that in the new millennium customer service will become the primary value-added function.[9] He recognizes that customer service is the primary method of building and extending the partnership. Customer service, in its many forms, nourishes the partnership and keeps it alive. The age of information has ushered in a series of customer service initiatives that affect the daily work of salespeople. We will discuss three of these current developments.

- *Salespeople are spending more time monitoring customer satisfaction.* There is a growing trend in which companies rely on their salespeople to continually monitor their customers' needs, concerns, and future plans. In the past many salespeople would live or die by the number of sales closed, and too little attention was given to service after the sale. Eastman Chemical Company provides a good example of a company that involves its salespeople in the customer service process. Eastman developed the "customer advocacy" program, which is designed to objectively measure customer satisfaction levels and give salespeople the responsibility for improving and maintaining that performance. Members of the sales force conduct ongoing surveys to assess levels of customer satisfaction. The survey form is delivered by a salesperson who emphasizes the importance of helping Eastman improve sales and service performance.[10]

  Salespeople who have direct contact with the customer are in an excellent position to assess the health of the partnership. Mack Hanan, author of *Consultative Selling*, encourages salespeople to seek answers to several questions:[11] Is the customer still growing because of your products and your expertise? How much more growth can take place in the future? How much is the partner growing you? In other words, is your company benefiting enough from the partnership? When the partnership involves a strategic alliance, answers to these questions are especially important.

- *Customer knowledge is viewed by sales and sales support personnel as an important key to improving customer service.* Bob Johnson, vice-president of Information Technology Services Marketing Association, says the ability to manage your customer knowledge is the number one lesson for anyone who wants to build customer loyalty:

  > *If you can't capture, manage and leverage customer history (as well as information regarding current and future needs), you can forget about loyalty. Limited knowledge management capability fosters the sense that the company has no real interest in the customer—or his repeat patronage.*[12]

  Once you acquire knowledge about your customer, you can tailor your customer service initiatives for them. Canadian Pacific Hotels found that business travellers valued recognition of their individual quirks and preferences, and it began a frequent-guest club to customize service. For example, customers could state their preference for bed size, or even a specific drink in their mini-bar, and CP hotels would ensure they got it. Following implementation of this program, CP Hotels saw its share of business travel grow by 16 percent in a year that the market as a whole grew by only 3 percent. Much of the growth was due to increased customer loyalty,

Building Quality Partnerships

THE MOMENT OF MAGIC

Tony Alessandra, a well-known sales trainer and consultant, says that there are three possible outcomes when a customer does business with an organization.

The moment of truth. In these selling situations the customer's expectations were met. Nothing happened to disappoint the customer, nor did the salesperson do anything to surpass the customer's expectations. The customer is apt to have somewhat neutral feelings about his relationship with the salesperson. The moment of truth will usually not build customer loyalty.

The moment of misery. This is the outcome of a selling situation where the customer's expectations were not met. The customer may feel a sense of disappointment or even anger. Many customers who experience the moment of misery will share their feelings with others and often make a decision to "fire" the salesperson.

The moment of magic. This is the outcome of a sale where the customer received more than she expected. The salesperson surpassed the customer's expectations by going the extra mile and providing a level of service that added value to the customer/salesperson relationship. This extra effort is likely to establish a foundation for increased customer loyalty.[a]

as many club members stopped spreading their business among competing hotels.[13]

- *Customer-friendly, computer-based systems will frequently be used to enhance customer service.* Computers give both the salesperson and the customer ready access to information and problem solving alternatives. In the future, human involvement in service will shift from routine, low-value tasks to a high-value, personal consultancy on important customer problems or desires.[14] We will see greater use of technology to gather information on unhappy customers and technology will quickly drive this information to people who can deal with the problem. Computer-based systems will also enhance information sharing. General Electric has begun to create for its 12 operating units a very large extranet. An **extranet** is a private Internet site that enables several companies to securely share information and conduct business.[15]

> **extranet** A private Internet site that enables several companies to securely share information and conduct business.

Customer Service Methods that Strengthen the Partnership

Sales & Marketing Management magazine states that customer service encompasses all activities that enhance or facilitate the sale and use of one's product or service. The skills required to service a sale are different from those required prior to the sale (Fig. 14.2). High-performance sales personnel do not abdicate responsibility for delivery, installation, and warranty interpretation, or other customer service responsibilities. They continue to strengthen the partnership with suggestion selling, follow-through on promises, and follow-up activities.

ADDING VALUE WITH SUGGESTION SELLING

Suggestion selling is an important form of customer service. This is the process of suggesting merchandise or services that are related to the main item sold to the customer. The suggestion is made when, in the salesperson's judgment, the added item will provide the customer with additional satisfaction.

> **suggestion selling** The process of suggesting merchandise or services that are related to the main item being sold to the customer. This is an important form of customer service.

A follow-up phone call to thank the customer and find out if he or she is pleased with the product will strengthen the relationship after the sale.

Figure 14.2 The completed Consultative Sales Presentation Guide illustrates the ways in which high-performance salespeople use value-added strategies to service the sale and build repeat business and referrals. Customer service provides many opportunities to strengthen the partnership.

The salesperson who is genuinely interested in helping customers solve their problems can enhance the relationship with suggestion selling. Some of the best ways to engage in suggestion selling follow.

Suggest related items In some cases there are related products or services that will add to the customer's satisfaction. An illustration is the sale of townhouses. Many real estate firms offer the customer a basic dwelling plus a

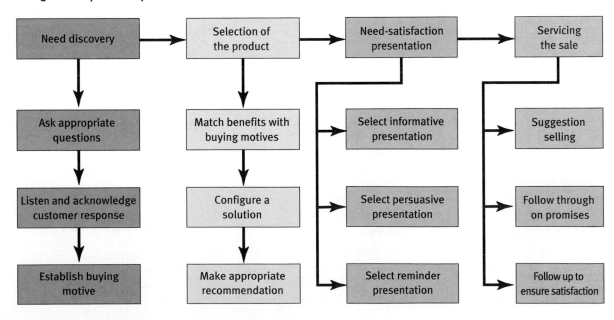

Need discovery	Selection of the product	Need-satisfaction presentation	Servicing the sale
Ask appropriate questions	Match benefits with buying motives	Select informative presentation	Suggestion selling
Listen and acknowledge customer response	Configure a solution	Select persuasive presentation	Follow through on promises
Establish buying motive	Make appropriate recommendation	Select reminder presentation	Follow up to ensure satisfaction

choice of options. The option list might include a fireplace, a screened patio, or an outdoor gas grill.

Selling related merchandise at an auto agency is quite common. Most customers can choose from a long list of options including special trim, upscale stereo systems, anti-lock braking system, and a host of other items.

Suggestion selling is no less important when selling services. For example, a travel agent has many opportunities to use suggestion selling. Let us assume that a customer purchases a two-week vacation in Germany. The agent can offer to book hotel reservations or schedule a guided tour. Another related product would be a rental car.

Sometimes a new product is simply not "right" without related merchandise. A new business suit may not look right without a new shirt and tie. An executive training program held at a fine hotel can be enhanced with a refreshment break featuring a variety of soft drinks, fresh coffee, and freshly baked pastries. That new stereo receiver may not sound right until it is matched with a set of quality speakers.

Suggest new items. New products and services are being introduced at a record pace. Some are brand-new features, while others are variations of existing items. Many buyers need help in keeping up with new product introductions. In most cases the salesperson who has already established a relationship with the customer is in the best position to introduce new products. John Morrison, branch manager of Tenaquip Ltd.'s Mississauga (Ontario) office, encourages his field salespeople to mention new products on each sales call. Tenaquip has 50 000 items in its product assortment, so new products are a logical way to increase business, and they always provide salespeople with something new to present to customers.[16]

Suggest a larger quantity. The customer can benefit in several ways from buying a larger quantity. Economy is one of the most common benefits. Many companies offer a discount on large orders. A grocer may be offered a 10-case shipment at $9.90 a case. If the person buys 15 cases, the price is $0.60 per case cheaper. In the retail food business a price reduction of this amount is significant.

Sometimes a large order is a good hedge against rising prices. The prices of oil, sugar, paper, antifreeze, and other products have increased in recent years. When a salesperson is sure that prices will rise in the near future, it is a good policy to suggest a larger quantity.

Convenience is another value-added benefit associated with large orders. The customer is saved the inconvenience of running out of the item at a critical time.

Suggest better quality products. Quality can be described as the degree of excellence inherent within a product or service. Many firms offer the customer a choice of products that vary in terms of quality and price. This is a good marketing strategy because most people like to have a choice when making a purchase. Also, higher priced products often provide the customer with added value.

The effort to sell better quality goods is known as *trading up* or *upgrading* in the field of selling. It is an important selling method that often benefits the customer. The higher priced item may be the best buy when such factors as durability, comfort, or trade-in value are considered.

HOW AND WHEN TO USE SUGGESTION SELLING

Customers will view suggestion selling as a form of value-added service when it is presented correctly. There is a right way and a wrong way to make suggestions. Here are some guidelines to follow (Fig. 14.3):

1. *Plan for suggestion selling during the preapproach step.* Before meeting with the customer, develop a suggestion selling plan that includes your objectives for this important dimension of selling. This may involve writing down a list of items that you might suggest after you close the sale. Suggestion selling is easier when you are prepared.

2. *Make suggestions after you have satisfied the customer's primary need.* If you make suggestions too early, the customer may become confused or fail to give your proposal full attention.

3. *Make your suggestion thoughtful and positive.* "We just received a new order

Figure 14.3 Customers will view suggestion selling as a form of value-added service when it is presented according to this suggested selling guide.

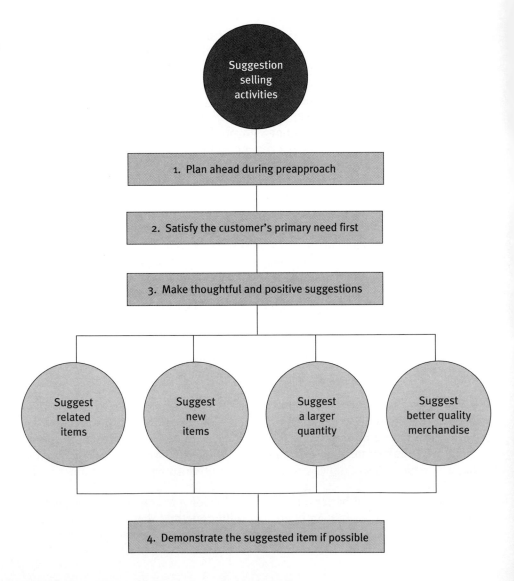

of silk ties that would go well with your new shirt. Let me show you the collection." Avoid questions like, "Can we ship anything else?" This question invites a negative response.

4. *Demonstrate the suggested item if at all possible, or use sales tools to build interest.* If you have suggested a shirt to go with a new suit, allow the customer to see it next to the suit. In industrial selling, show the customer a sample, or at least a picture if the actual product is not available.

Suggestion selling is a means of providing value-added service. When you use it correctly, customers will thank you for your thoughtfulness and extra service. It is also a proven sales-building strategy. Use it often.

CROSS SELLING USED TO GROW SALES

In recent years we have seen an increase in the use of cross selling to grow sales volume. **Cross selling** involves selling products that are not directly related to products that you have sold to an established customer. A bank customer who has a home equity loan might be contacted and asked to consider purchase of a mutual fund. The customer who has purchased a townhouse might be a candidate for a security service. One financial services company, Quick & Reilly, has trained its 600 customer service representatives to use cross selling when customers call regarding their current investments. By completing the cross selling training programs, the representatives learned how to assess the caller's financial goals and develop a tailored proposal of products and services. Quick & Reilly achieved a 35 percent sales increase after developing the cross-selling program.[17]

cross selling   Selling to an established customer products that are not directly related to products the customer has already bought.

Cross selling is most effective in those situations where the customer has a positive attitude toward the selling organization. Also, the salesperson (or customer service representative) must propose only products that are tailored to solve the specific problem the customer has confirmed. If cross selling fulfills a genuine customer need, the result will be a stronger partnership.

Cross selling has become a major phenomenon in the age of information. Customers often have too much information and they need help deciding which information has value. In many cases, the information needed requires only a telephone call. A well-informed and well-trained customer service representative can strengthen the partnership.

ADDING VALUE WITH FOLLOWING THROUGH

A major key to an effective customer service strategy is follow-through on assurances and promises that were part of the sales presentation. Did your sales presentation include claims for superior performance; promises of speedy delivery; assistance with credit arrangements; guaranteed factory assistance with installation, training, and service?

Most sales presentations are made up of claims and promises that the company can fulfill. However, fulfillment of these claims will depend to a large degree on after-sale action. Postsale follow-through is the key to holding that customer you worked so hard to develop.

COMMON POSTSALE PROBLEMS

Every salesperson should become familiar with the most common postsale problem areas. Identify the leading problem areas in your company and be aware of possible solutions. Many studies indicate that customer-related problems after the sale are most likely to be in one of the following areas:

Making credit arrangements. Credit has become a common way to finance purchases. This is true of industrial products, real estate, automobiles, home appliances, and many other products. Closing the sale will often depend on your ability to develop and present attractive credit plans to the customer. Even if you do not get directly involved in the firm's credit and collection activities, you must be familiar with how the company handles these matters. Salespeople need to establish a relationship with the credit department and learn how credit analysts make their decisions.

Several agencies can supply up-to-date credit information. A credit bureau is available in most large cities. Dun & Bradstreet Incorporated publishes credit books for each region. Sometimes, local bank personnel will provide helpful information.

Making credit decisions gets a lot tougher when you are conducting business in foreign countries. Overseas transactions can be complex, and in some cases there is little recourse if a customer does not pay. Doron Weissman, president of Overseas Brokers, a freight forwarder and export brokerage firm, says, "When I sell my services, I automatically qualify the account to make sure they're financially able to meet my demands. If not, I move on."[18]

Late deliveries. Many organizations are adding value with on-time deliveries. A late delivery can be a problem for both the supplier and the customer. To illustrate, let us assume that the supplier is a manufacturer of small appliances and the customer is a department store chain. A late delivery may mean lost sales due to out-of-stock conditions, cancellation of the order by the department store, or loss of future sales.

The causes of late delivery may be beyond your control. It is not your fault if the plant closes because of labour trouble or weather conditions. It is your responsibility, however, to keep the customer informed of any delays. You can also take steps to prevent a delay. Check to be sure your order was processed correctly. Follow up to see if the order was shipped on time. Above all, keep the customer informed.

Improper installation. Buyer satisfaction is often related to proper installation of the product. This is true of consumer products such as security systems, central air-conditioning, solar heating systems, and carpeting. It is also true of industrial products such as electronic data processing equipment and air quality control systems. Some salespeople believe it is to their advantage to supervise product installation; they are then able to spot installation problems. Others make it a practice to follow up on the installation to be sure no problems exist.

Customer training in the use or care of the product. For certain industries it is essential that users be trained in how to use the new product. This is true of office duplication equipment, electronic cash registers, farm implements, and a host of other products. Technology has become so complex that many suppliers must provide training as part of the follow-up to ensure customer satisfaction. Most organizations that sell microcomputers and other types of electronic equipment for office use now schedule training classes to

Salespeople often assist with credit arrangements and provide counsel to prospective customers.

ensure that customers can properly use and care for the products. These companies believe that users must be skilled in handling their equipment.

Price changes. Price changes need not be a serious problem if they are handled correctly. The salesperson is responsible for maintaining an up-to-date price list. As your company issues price changes, record them accurately. Customers expect you to quote the correct price the first time.

PREVENTING POSTSALE PROBLEMS

There are ways to prevent postsale problems. The key is conscientious follow-up to be sure everything has been handled properly. Get to know the people who operate your shipping department. They are responsible for getting the right merchandise shipped on time, and it is important that they understand your customers' needs.

Become acquainted with people in the credit department. Be sure that they maintain a good, businesslike relationship with your customers. This is a delicate area; even small mistakes (a "pay now" notice sent too early, for example) can cause hurt feelings. If your company uses a customer support staff to resolve postsale problems, be sure to get acquainted with the people who provide this service.

CUSTOMER FOLLOW-UP METHODS

Customer follow-up methods usually have two major objectives. One is to express appreciation for the purchase and thus to enhance the relationship established during the sales presentation. You no doubt thanked the customer at the time the sale was closed, but it would not hurt to say thank-you again a few days later. The second purpose of the follow-up is to determine if the customer is satisfied with the purchase. Both of these methods will strengthen the buyer–seller relationship and build a partnership that results in additional sales.

In survey after survey, poor service and lack of follow-up after the sale are given as primary reasons people stop buying from a particular supplier. Most customers are sensitive to indifferent treatment by the sales representative. With this fact in mind you should approach follow-up in a systematic and businesslike way. There are five follow-up methods.

Selling in Action

EFFECTIVE DESIGN AND USE OF THE BUSINESS CARD

The business card continues to be a powerful tool for salespeople. It provides a personal touch in our high-tech world. The business card is a convenient way to communicate important information to customers, sales support personnel, and others. When you develop your business card, keep these tips in mind.

- Use eye-catching items such as your picture, your company logo, raised letters, colours, and textured paper. The card should be tasteful and pleasing to the eye.

- The card should feature all current contact information such as your e-mail address, telephone numbers, and mailing address.
- Consider using both sides of the card. You might print your customer service philosophy on the back of the card or list the products you sell.

Give your cards generously to anyone who might need to contact you later. Always offer your business card when networking. The card is useful when the contact tells others about your products or services.[b]

PERSONAL VISIT

This is usually the most costly follow-up method, but it may produce the best results. It is the only strategy that allows face-to-face, two-way communication. When you take time to make a personal visit, the customer knows that you really care.

Use the personal follow-up to keep the customer informed of new developments, new products, or new applications. This information may pave the way for additional sales. When you do make a personal visit, do not stay too long. Accomplish the purpose of your visit as quickly as possible and then excuse yourself.

TELEPHONE CALL

The telephone provides a quick and efficient way to follow up a sale. A salesperson can easily make 10 or 12 phone calls in a single hour, and the cost will be minimal. If you plan to send a thank-you card or letter, follow it up with a thank-you call. The personal appeal of the phone call will increase the effectiveness of the written correspondence. The telephone call has one major advantage over written correspondence: it allows for a two-way exchange of information. Once an account is well established, you may be able to obtain repeat sales by telephone.

E-MAIL MESSAGE

In many cases it is a lot quicker to send an e-mail message than to make a phone call. Salespeople report that they waste a lot of time playing "phone tag." Some customers prefer e-mail messages and may become irritated if you do not adhere to their wishes. If you know that a customer is not in the habit of checking their e-mail all that often, use the telephone as a back-up method. When in doubt, use parallel channels of communication.

LETTER OR CARD

Written correspondence is an inexpensive and convenient form of customer follow-up. Letters and cards can be used to thank the customer for the order and to promise continued service.[19] Some companies encourage their salespeople to use a formal letter typed on company stationery. Other companies have designed special thank-you cards, which are signed and sent routinely after a sale

Building Relationships through Technology

ISLANDS OF INFORMATION

 Companies often use many different software programs to manage information about customers. The firm will have customer purchase and payment history in its accounting system. Customer service problems may be recorded in the service department's software. A help desk program may be used by people in customer support.

The company's salespeople may be using one software program to manage their contacts with customer personnel, another program to prepare quotes, and yet another for correspondence with customers. To reduce these "islands" of customer information, more companies are finding ways to merge this information or acquiring software that performs more than one of these functions. Some CRM systems are combining a number of these functions into one integrated package. (See the CRM case study Servicing the Sale with CRM on page 337 for more information.)

is closed. The salesperson may enclose a business card. These thank-you cards do have one major limitation: they are mass produced and therefore lack the personal touch so important to customer satisfaction.

CALL REPORT

The **call report** is a form that serves as a communications link with persons who can assist with customer service. The format varies, but generally it is a simple form with only four or five spaces. The sample call report form that appears in Figure 14.4 is used by a company that installs security systems at banks and other financial institutions. A form like this is one solution to the problem of communication between the company personnel and the customer. It is a method of follow-through that triggers the desired action. It is simple, yet businesslike.

Follow-up programs can be as creative or ingenious as you wish, according to Nancy Friedman, president of a national telephone training company. She suggests you customize your follow-up program to meet the needs of your customer.[20] Every sales organization competes on value, so you must continually think of new ways to add value. Creative use of your interpersonal communication skills will keep your messages fresh and personalized. Keep in mind that people buy both from the head and the heart. Let the customer know how much you care about their business.[21] You can use these five methods independently or

call report A written summary that provides information on a sales call to people in the sales organization so that follow-up action can be taken as necessary.

Figure 14.4 The Call Report

Sales Call Report

Date: October 26, 2002
To: Walt Higgins, service engineer
From: Diane Ray, sales representative

Action Promised: Visit Canspec Manufacturing within the next week to check on installation of our security system.

Assistance Needed: System B-420 was installed at Canspec Manufacturing on October 24. As per our agreement, you should make a follow-up call to check the installation of the system and provide Canspec personnel with a Form 82 certification checklist. The form should be given to Mr. Kurt Heller, president.

Copies to: Mr. Kurt Heller

Figure 14.5 Servicing the Sale Worksheet. Suggestion selling, follow through on assurances and promises, and customer follow-up methods must be carefully planned. Use of this worksheet will help you preplan ways to add value.

Servicing the Sale Worksheet

Method of Adding Value	What You Will Say or Do
Suggestion Selling Suggest the purchase of global position-ing system (GPS) technology to enhance use of seed research equipment.	"GPS technology will enable you to track all of your research and plot the findings on your computer screen."
Follow through Set up a secure Web site or extranet so the client can track the production and delivery of the custom-engineered seed research equipment.	Set up the secure Web site in a timely manner and then contact the customer when it is operational. Explain how to access the Web site and review the bene-fits of using this source of assistance.
Schedule training for persons who will be using the new technology.	Send training schedule to customer and confirm the dates with a follow-up call.
Follow-up Send a thank-you letter to each member of the team that made the purchase deci-sion.	Express sincere appreciation for the pur-chase and explain the steps you will take to ensure a long-term partnership.
Check to be certain that the training was effective.	Visit the customer's research facility and talk with the employees who completed the training. Answer questions and pro-vide additional assistance as needed.

in combination. Your main consideration should be some type of appropriate follow-up that (1) tells customers you appreciate their business and (2) deter-mines if they are satisfied with the purchase.

PREPLAN YOUR SERVICE STRATEGY

Servicing the sale is a very important dimension of personal selling, so a certain amount of preplanning is essential. It helps to preplan your service strategy for each of the three areas we have discussed: suggestion selling, follow through, and follow-up. You cannot anticipate every aspect of the service, but you can preplan important ways to add value once the sale is closed. Develop a "servicing the sale" worksheet, like the one shown in Figure 14.5, prior to each sales presentation.

Partnership-Building Strategies Should Encompass All Key People

Some salespeople do a great job of communicating with the prospect but ignore other key people involved in the sale. To illustrate how serious this prob-lem can be, let us look at the approach used by Jill Bisignano, a sales represen-tative for a major restaurant supply firm. Jill had called on Bellino's Italian Restaurant for several years. Although she was always very friendly to Nick Bellino, she treated the other employees with nearly total indifference. One day she called on Nick and was surprised to learn that he was retiring and had decid-ed to sell his restaurant to two long-time employees.

Building Quality Partnerships

BUTTERFLY BEHAVIOUR

In *The Butterfly Customer,* Susan O'Dell and Joan Pajunen, two Toronto-based management consultants, describe a customer who would rather switch than fight. This "butterfly customer" is one who flits from business to business, from relationship to relationship, always looking for the latest, the closest, the cheapest.

There is, however, a special butterfly that businesses should value. That is the monarch, the one butterfly that returns to the same place, year after year, with total loyalty. O'Dell and Pajunen describe five characteristics of monarch butterflies to help you identify them so you can encourage their loyalty.

1. *Monarch butterflies always return—sooner or later!* You need to keep regular staff who will recognize them, who will make them feel welcome and important, and who can communicate with them to find out where they have been if they have not patronized you recently, and what has brought them back.
2. *Monarch butterflies often send others in their place.* Even if they do not continue to patronize your business, monarch butterflies refer others to you. You need to train your staff to find out why new customers come to your business, where they have heard about it.
3. *Monarch butterflies have opinions.* They not only

have opinions, monarch butterflies freely express them. These customers are highly involved with your business, and motivated to help you improve it. What appears as a "nuisance" complaint may be a monarch butterfly who is committed to your business. To reward these customers, you need to ensure your staff and system can provide feedback on every complaint.
4. *Monarch butterflies share their homework.* Monarch butterflies are curious and informed, and love to provide you with details on what your competitors are doing. You must ensure your staff members have appropriate listening skills, and that they know what to do with this information when they receive it.
5. *Monarch butterflies are forgiving and giving.* Monarch butterflies will allow you to screw up occasionally, and will pitch in and help you with your service delivery when the going gets rough. They don't mind helping themselves, and may even help you service other clients.

According to O'Dell and Pajunen, trust is what leads to monarch behaviour. Trust is gained by consistently delivering what you promise, how you promised it. High-profit, low-maintenance customers are your reward for being trustworthy.[c]

As you might expect, it did not take the new owners long to find another supplier. Jill lost a large account because she failed to develop a good personal relationship with other key employees. It pays to be nice to everyone.

Here is a partial list of people in your company and in the prospect's company who can influence both initial and repeat sales:

1. *Receptionist.* Some salespeople simply do not use common sense when dealing with the receptionist. This person has daily contact with your customer and may schedule most or all calls. To repeatedly forget this individual's name or display indifference in other ways may cost you dearly. Display a friendly but businesslike attitude toward this person. Do not be patronizing or aloof.

2. *Technical Personnel.* Some products must be cleaned, lubricated, or adjusted on a regular basis. Take time to get acquainted with the people who perform these duties. Answer their questions, share technical information with them if necessary, and show appreciation for the work they are doing.

3. *Stock Clerks or Receiving Clerks.* People who work in the receiving room are often responsible for pricing incoming merchandise and making sure that

these items are stored properly. They may also be responsible for stock rotation and processing damage claims.

4. *Management Personnel.* Although you may be working closely with someone at the departmental or division level, do not forget the person who has the final authority and responsibility for this area. Spend time with management personnel occasionally and be alert to any concerns they may have.

This is not a complete list of the people you may need to depend on for support. There may well be other key people who influence sales. Always look beyond the customer to see who else might have a vested interest in the sale.

Solving the Customer's Problem

In recent years we have learned more about the impact of customer complaints. Research indicates that unhappy customers often do not initiate a verbal or written complaint. This means that postsale problems may not come to the attention of salespeople or other personnel within the organization. We also know that unhappy customers do share their negative experiences with other people. A dissatisfied customer will often tell eight to ten people about their problem.[22] A double loss occurs when the customer stops buying our products and takes steps to discourage other people from buying our products. When complaints do surface, we should view the problem as an opportunity to strengthen the business relationship. To achieve this goal, follow these suggestions:

1. *Give customers every opportunity to disclose their feelings.* Companies noted for outstanding customer service rely heavily on telephone systems—like toll-free "hotlines" to ensure easy access. At Federal Express, Cadillac Division of General Motors, and IBM, to name a few companies, specially trained advisers answer the calls and offer assistance.[23] When a customer purchases a Ford vehicle, the salesperson introduces the customer to service staff who play a key role in providing postsale service. The goal is to personalize the relationship with another member of the service team. Ford has discovered that after-sale contact builds a perception of value.[24] When customers do complain, by telephone or in person, encourage them to express all their anger and frustration. Do not interrupt. Do not become defensive. Do not make any judgments until you have heard all the facts as the customer sees them.[25] If they stop talking, try to get them to talk some more. Most of us feel better once we have had the opportunity to express our concerns fully.

2. *As the customer is talking, listen carefully and attentively.* You will need accurate information to solve the problem. One of the biggest barriers to effective listening is emotion. Do not become angry, and do not get into an argument. Once you feel the customer has fully vented, paraphrase what he or she said to prove you cared enough to listen.[26]

3. *Keep in mind that it does not really matter whether a complaint is real or perceived.* If the customer is upset, you should be polite and sympathetic. Do not yield to the temptation to say, "You do not really have a problem." Remember, problems exist when customers perceive they exist.[27]

4. *Do not alibi.* Avoid the temptation to blame the shipping department, the installation crew, or anyone else associated with your company. Never tear

down the company you work for. The problem has been placed in your hands, and you must accept responsibility for handling it. "Passing the buck" will only leave the customer with a feeling of helplessness.

5. *Politely share with the customer your point of view concerning the problem's cause.* At least explain what you think happened. The customer deserves an explanation. At this point a sincere apology is usually appropriate.

6. *Decide what action must be taken to remedy the problem.* Take action quickly and offer a value-added atonement. Don't just do what is expected; delight the customer by exceeding their expectations. Winning customer loyalty today means going beyond making it right.[28]

The value of customer complaints can emerge in two forms. First, complaints can be a source of important information that may be difficult to obtain by other means. Second, customer complaints provide unique opportunities for companies to *prove* their commitment to service. Loyalty builds in the customer's mind if you do a good job of solving his or her problem.[29]

Summary

Servicing the sale is a major dimension of the selling process, with the objectives of providing maximum customer satisfaction and establishing a long-term partnership. Good service ensures that the product will meet the customer's needs, and also satisfies the needs for security and recognition discussed in Chapter 7 (see Maslow's hierarchy of needs). A reputation for good service is essential in attracting new accounts and keeping old ones.

In this chapter, we reviewed several current developments in customer service. Salespeople are spending more time monitoring customer satisfaction. Customer knowledge is an important key to improving customer service, and computer-based systems are being used to enhance customer service. The goal is to develop lifetime customers.

The customer service strategy is made up of four activities: adding value with suggestion selling, adding value with cross selling, following through on assurances and promises, and using appropriate follow-up strategies. These activities create a positive impression of the salesperson and the company, which results in increased patronage buying.

A salesperson depends on the support of many other people in servicing a sale. Maintaining good relationships with support staff members who help service your accounts is well worth the time and energy required. This chapter also includes information on ways to effectively solve the customer's problem. Regular and objective self-evaluation is also a valuable practice. Efficient performance of the functions involved in customer service is important to ensure continuing customer satisfaction and should be a matter of professional pride.

Key Terms

Customer Service 319
Extranet 323
Suggestion Selling 323

Cross Selling 327
Call Report 331

Review Questions

1. What two powerful motivators can a salesperson appeal to with a well-planned customer service program? Explain the significance of each one.

2. Define *customer service*. List the activities associated with this phase of personal selling.

3. Explain how suggestion selling fits into the definition of customer service. How does suggestion selling differ from cross selling?

4. Explain some of the reasons customer service is considered a profit stimulator.

5. List and describe three current developments in customer service.

6. How does credit become a part of servicing the sale?

7. This chapter describes the value of the lifetime customer. Is it realistic to believe that people will become lifetime customers in our very competitive marketplace?

8. List and describe five customer follow-up methods.

9. What types of customer service problem might be prevented with the use of a call report?

10. List five self-evaluation questions a salesperson should regularly review to improve customer service.

Application Exercises

1. You are a salesperson working in the paint department at a Canadian Tire store. A customer has just purchased 75 litres of house paint. Assume that your store carries everything in the painting line, and list as many items as you can think of that could be used for suggestion selling. Explain how your suggestions of these items could be a service to the customer.

2. You work as a wholesale salesperson for a plumbing supply company. One of your customers, a contractor, has an open line of credit with your company for $10 000 worth of products. He is currently at his limit; however, he is not overdue. He just received word that he has been awarded a $40 000 plumbing contract at the local airport. The contract requires that he supply $9000 worth of plumbing products. Your customer does not have the cash to pay for the additional products. He informs you that, unless you can provide him with some type of financing, he may lose the contract. He says that he can pay you when he finishes his next job in 60 days. Explain what you will do.

3. You have just interviewed for a job that you really would like to have. You have heard it is a good idea to follow up an interview with a thank-you note or letter and an indication of your enthusiasm for the position. Select the strategy you will use for your follow-up and explain why you chose it.

4. Using your search engine, examine the Internet for information on customer satisfaction. Type in "customer satisfaction" + selling. Are you surprised by the number of hits on this subject? Examine some of the hits related to what customers have said about specific company customer service programs.

5. Participant 1: You are the store supervisor (choose Emotive, Director, Reflective, Supportive; see Chapter 4) at Great Canadian Pulp, and you are responsible for ordering standard inventory items that your plant keeps in stock to support maintenance and operations. You have recently had a situation where your plant foreperson needed a valve urgently to replace a damaged one. When you checked your inventory, you found that there were none in stock, but there was a shipment due several days previously from your supplier. This was not the first time this particular supplier had let you down on its delivery promise. You have just scheduled a meeting with Shirley Jones, their salesperson, and Jim Baker, their sales manager, to discuss what can be done.

Participants 2 and 3: You are Shirley Jones and Jim Baker.

CRM Case Study

Servicing the Sale with CRM

You have taken over a number of accounts of another salesperson, Pat Silva. Most of these accounts are prospects, which means that they have not yet purchased from SimNet. Two accounts did purchase networks from Pat: Ms. Karen Murray, of Murray D'Zines, and Ms. Judith Albright, owner of Piccadilly Studio. You now want to be sure that these sales are well serviced.

Questions

1. Whom should you speak with, within SimNet, before following through and contacting each of the customers? What do you need to discover?

2. What will be your follow-up strategy for each customer?

3. Does the fact that these customers initiated their orders (they were not sold the products, they bought them) influence your follow-up strategy?

4. Might other customers or prospects be affected by your service activities? How will this influence your activities? Could customer service be your competitive edge?

5. Do you see any suggestion selling opportunities with these two accounts? Which suggestion selling methods should you consider?

Video Case

Good renovators are often distinguished by their ability and willingness to service the customer after a sale has been made. Garnet Kindervater has been a renovator for more than 25 years and has earned an excellent reputation among his clients and peers. In 1998, he won a Canadian Home Builders' Association National Sam Award in the Home Renovation Award category–over $100 000. In 1999, he won the "Renovator of the Year Award" in St. John's, Newfoundland, in the under $25 000 category. He currently serves as president of the Canadian Home Builders' Association in Ottawa.

Garnet describes the renovation business as a highly personal one. His sees his role as renovator to manage the client from the time a project is started until after its completion. When he receives the first phone call from a potential

www.chba.ca

client, Garnet likes to get as much information as he can during the conversation. "Just by knowing their address, often I can picture their house and even its layout. I have been in this business so long that I know what has been built throughout the city and when various neighbourhoods were constructed. I can usually tell simply from the address how much work might be involved, and what additional problems might be uncovered once work is started. It's also important to find out how much planning the client has done; that is, where are they in the purchase decision stage, and whether they are actually serious about having the work completed. If there is exterior work involved, I sometimes take a drive past the property for a quick assessment before I actually meet with the client.

"In the earliest stage, the client often has a general idea that they want something done, but it is often only at the concept stage and has not been clearly defined in their own mind. Renovators must be careful here to fill only a consultative role, making sure that the client knows what can be done and what will be involved. If the client talks to several renovators at this stage, the concept might change as the client continues to discuss it with more and more people. Sometimes, the final renovation that the client decides on may have little resemblance to what was initially discussed. When renovators quote on exactly the same job, price differences are usually not very great.

"I generally refuse to play a price game with clients. I think there is a real trap you can fall into as you then think about how you can manage a project to come in under cost. Quality gets sacrificed, the client becomes unhappy, and your reputation suffers. I always try to ensure the client gets superior value and that there are no surprises once work has been started. If there might be additional work necessary, it is a good idea to let the client know before work starts. For example, you might be replacing a wall in a bathroom and notice once you have started that a window has been leaking and is in very bad shape. That could add several hundreds of dollars to the project. Sometimes, clients will ask for changes to the project once a contract is signed. I accepted a job last week, and even before I started, the customer decided to make additional changes to the main entranceway, including new floor covering. In situations like this, you need to be sure the client understands and accepts any additional costs that will be involved.

"When there are major renovations, there are often a number of tradesmen involved in the project, such as plumbers, roofers, plasterers, or electricians. Any of them may have contact with the client. As the renovator, I must make sure the client is happy not only with the work the tradesmen do, but how they manage the process while they do it. Tradesmen need to be sensitive to the fact that they are working in someone's home and they need to be aware of things such as appearance, language, cleanliness, and courtesy. Clients can't always judge the quality of work that is done, but they can certainly tell whether they are happy with who did it and how it was done.

"When the project is completed, I always ask the client to develop a deficiency list, anything that may still need to be done or that they are dissatisfied with. Then, we do a walk-through together to ensure we agree on whatever actions should be taken. If the project is handled properly throughout the renovation process, there is seldom anything that the client is unhappy with at this stage. I did, for a period in the 1980s, begin to see more client problems. I had tried to grow my business too fast. At one point I had as many as 50 people working for me, but I found that it was impossible to properly manage all my clients. As problems continued to increase, I realized it was better to serve a smaller number of clients and do it well. Reputation is what gets you renovation business, and I guard my reputation carefully. I only work with tradesmen who have my standards of workmanship, and who are good at relationship management. If all they can offer is technical competence, I let them work with someone else. Quality workmanship is important in this business, but the ability to communicate with clients and to service the sale is even more so."[30]

Questions

1. Explain why it is so important for renovators to manage the renovation process rather than to wait for the end of the project to service the sale.

2. Should a renovator use suggestion selling? What problems might arise for a renovator who uses suggestion selling improperly?

3. Would you consider the following-through of assurances and promises and customer follow-up to be examples of superior customer service? Explain.

Partnership Selling: A Role Play/Simulation (see Appendix C, p. 458)

DEVELOPING A SALES PRESENTATION STRATEGY—SERVICING THE SALE

Refer to *Sales Memorandum 3*, and strategically plan to service the sale with your customer. After closing the sale (getting the customer's signature) there are several steps to add value and build customer confidence and satisfaction. These steps are important to providing total quality customer service and should provide for repeat sales and a list of referred customers.

Following the instructions in item 2g of your presentation plan, you need to schedule a future appointment to telephone or personally call and confirm the number of people attending the convention, and final room and menu needs (see the convention centre policies). Also, during this conversation you might suggest beverages for

breaks, audiovisual needs, and any other items that will make this an outstanding convention for your customer.

You should have your calendar available to suggest and write down dates and times for this future contact. Any special materials, such as a calendar, can be placed in the back pocket of your portfolio. You may want to ask another person to be your customer and practise the customer service strategies you have prepared.

At this point you should be strategically prepared to make the presentation to your customer outlined in *Sales Memorandum 3*. Your instructor will provide you with further instructions.

Part VI

Management of Self and Others

Personal selling requires a great deal of

self-discipline and self-direction.

Chapter 15 examines the four dimen-

sions of self-management. Chapter 16

focuses on ethics, an important topic for

both individual salespeople and sales

organizations. The final chapter

examines the fundamentals of sales

force management.

BUILDING QUALITY PARTNERSHIPS

Joyful people exude a humble self-confidence gained from mastering a succession of situations. They are enthusiastic, energetic, creative, and fun to be around. They welcome changes, ignore rivalry, enjoy life, enjoy their work, and enjoy other people.

Derek A. Newton, *Feed Your Eagles: Building and Managing a Top-Flight Sales Force*

Management of Self: The Key to Greater Sales Productivity

Many people go through life hoping for an enjoyable and successful career. Elli Davis has certainly found hers, but it wasn't the first one she tried. Elli Davis started as a teacher with the Metropolitan Toronto public school system, but it didn't take too many years for her to decide that she didn't want to retire from there with a pension. She thought about other careers, possibly interior decorating or sales, and eventually focused on real estate sales. This has proven to be very fortunate for her and for Royal LePage, where she started her career. In 1998, Elli Davis was named Royal LePage's #1 Residential Sales Representative for the twelfth consecutive year. She has chosen to be an "expert" in one particular niche—luxury condominiums in the Toronto market—but she still achieves quite a few upscale home sales. Elli Davis is a person who has managed herself and her career with meticulous detail; her success is not an accident.[1]

A salesperson is much like the individual who owns and operates a business. The successful sales representative, like the successful entrepreneur, depends on good self-management. Both of them must keep their own records, use self-discipline in scheduling their time, and analyze their own performance.

High-performance salespeople and successful entrepreneurs have one more characteristic in common. They realize that all development is really self-development.[2]

Management of Self—A Four-Dimensional Process

What makes a salesperson successful? Some people believe the most important factor is hard work. This is only partly true. Some people work hard but do not accomplish much. They lack purpose and direction. This lack of organization results in wasted time and energy.

Wasting time and energy is the key to failure in the age of information. Many salespeople are drowning in information and the flood of messages each day leaves little time to think and reflect. Sales and sales support personnel, like most other knowledge workers, are working under tighter deadlines. The response time to customer inquiries has been shortened and customers are less tolerant of delays.

In this chapter we approach management of self as a four-dimensional process consisting of the following components:

1. *Time management.* There are only about 250 business days per year. Within each day there is only so much time to devote to selling. Selling hours are extremely valuable. A group of 1300 salespeople was asked to evaluate 16 challenges they face in their work. "Not enough time" was ranked first; "Achieving balance between work and family" was ranked second; "Dealing with information overload" was ranked third.[3]

2. *Territory management.* A sales territory is a group of customers and prospective customers assigned to a single salesperson. Every territory is unique. Some territories consist of one or two cities or counties, while others encompass several provinces. The number of accounts within each territory will also vary. Today, territory management is becoming less of an art and more of a science.

3. *Records management.* Every salesperson must maintain a certain number of records. These records help to "systematize" data collection and storage. A wise salesperson never relies on memory. Some of the most common records include planning calendars, prospect forms, call reports, summary reports, and expense reports.

4. *Stress management.* A certain amount of stress comes with many selling positions. Some salespeople have learned how to take stressful situations in stride. Others allow stress to trigger anger and frustration. Learning to cope with various stressors that surface in the daily life of a salesperson is an important part of the self-management process.

Time Management

A salesperson can increase sales volume in two major ways. One is to improve selling effectiveness, and the other is to spend more time in face-to-face selling

Most people who achieve success in selling have a strong work ethic. They are "self-starters" who are committed to more than the 8-hour day or the 40-hour week.

situations. The latter objective can best be achieved through improved time and territory management.

Improving the management of both time and territory is a high-priority concern in the field of selling. These two closely related functions represent major challenges for salespeople.

Let us first look closely at the area of time management. There is definitely a close relationship between sales volume and number of customer contacts made by the salesperson. You have to make calls to get results.

TIME-CONSUMING ACTIVITIES

Some salespeople who have kept careful records of how they spend their time each day are surprised to learn how little is spent in face-to-face selling situations. The major time-consuming activities in personal selling are travel, time spent waiting to see a customer, completion of sales records, casual conversation, time spent on customer follow-through and follow-up, and time spent in face-to-face selling. Salespeople need to examine carefully each of these activities and determine whether too much or too little time is spent in any area. One way to assess time use is to keep a time log. This involves recording, at the end of every hour, the activities in which you were engaged during that time.[4] At the end of the week, add up the number of minutes spent on the various activities and ask yourself, "Is this the best use of my time?"

Once you have tabulated the results of your time log, it should be easy to identify the "time wasters." Pick one or two of the most wasteful areas and then make plans to correct the problem. Set realistic goals that can be achieved. Keep in mind that wasting time is usually a habit. To manage your time more effectively, you will need to form new habits.

© 2000 Edgar Argo

TIME MANAGEMENT METHODS

Sound time management methods can pave the way to greater sales productivity. The starting point is forming a new attitude toward time conservation. You must view time as a scarce resource not to be wasted. The time-saving strategies presented here are not new, nor are they unique. They are being used by time-conscious people in all walks of life.

DEVELOP A SERIES OF PERSONAL GOALS

According to Alan Lakein, author of *How to Get Control of Your Time and Your Life*, the most important aspect of time management is knowing what your goals are. He is referring to all goals: career goals, family goals, and life goals. People who cannot or will not sit down and write out exactly what they want from life will lack direction.

The goal-setting process requires that you be clear about what you want to accomplish. If your goal is too general or vague, progress toward achieving that goal will be difficult to observe. Goals such as "I want to be a success" or "I desire good health" are much too general. Goals should also reflect the values that govern your life. For example, if one of your governing values is "I love my family," then you may commit yourself to spending quality time with family members.

Goals have a great deal of psychological value to people in selling. Sales goals, for example, can serve as a strong motivational force. To illustrate, let us assume that Mary Paulson, sales representative for a cosmetic manufacturer, decides to increase her sales by 15 percent over the previous year. She now has a specific goal to aim for and can begin identifying specific ways to achieve the new goal. Goals often help us form new habits.

PREPARE A DAILY TO-DO LIST

Sales professionals who complete the time management course offered by Franklin Covey are encouraged to engage in event control. This technique

Date_____
DAILY TO-DO LIST

Priority	Items to do
3 ←	— Call Fanshawe College to check on installation of copy machine.
2 ←	— Call Price Optical to make an appointment for product demonstration.
4 ←	— Attend Chamber of Commerce at 3:00 P.M.
1 ←	— Call Simmons Furniture and deal with customer complaint.

Notes for tomorrow:

Figure 15.1   A daily list of activities can help us set priorities and save time.

involves planning and prioritizing events every day.[5] Start each day by thinking about what you hope to accomplish. Then write down the activities (Fig. 15.1). Putting your thoughts on paper forces you to clarify your thinking. Moff D. Warren, president of Intellective Innovations, says, "If you write down exactly what needs to be done, not only does it make you psychologically ready for the day, it also helps you think broadly as you develop strategies for your business."[6] It is much easier to coordinate activities written in black and white than to try to carry them around in your head.

Now you should rank these activities from most important to least important. Make sure that daily activities are related to attaining the goals you have established. Begin each day with the highest priority task. Resist the urge to relegate the tasks you dislike to the bottom of the list.[7]

Preparing a daily to-do list should become a habit. Try not to let busywork crowd planning out of your schedule. After all, preparation of a to-do list will usually require only 5 to 10 minutes. This small investment of time will pay big dividends.

MAINTAIN A PLANNING CALENDAR

Ideally, a salesperson needs a single place to record daily appointments (personal and business), deadlines, and tasks. Unfortunately, many salespeople write daily tasks on any slip of paper they can find: backs of envelopes, three-by-five cards, napkins, or Post-it notes. Hyrum W. Smith, author of *The 10 Natural Laws of Successful Time and Life Management*, calls these pieces of paper "floaters."

> *They just float around until you either follow through on them or lose them. It's a terribly disorganized method for someone who wants to gain greater control of his or her life.*[8]

The use of floaters often leads to the loss of critical information, missed appointments, and lack of focus. Select a planning calendar design (the Franklin Covey Day Planner is one option) that will bring efficiency to your daily planning efforts. You should be able to determine at a glance what is coming up in the days and weeks ahead (Fig. 15.2).

Some salespeople use electronic pocket organizers to store hundreds of names, addresses, and phone numbers. These organizers can be used to keep track of appointments and serve as a perpetual calendar. You simply key in a birthday or anniversary and a gentle beep will jog your memory on the appropriate date. The electronic organizer can also be used to keep track of appointments.

ORGANIZE YOUR SELLING TOOLS

You can save valuable time by finding ways to organize sales literature, business cards, order blanks, samples, and other items needed during a sales call. You may waste time on a callback because some item was not available during your first call. You may even lose a sale because you forgot or misplaced a key selling tool.

If you have a great deal of paperwork, invest in one or more file cabinets. Some salespeople purchase small, lightweight cardboard file boxes to keep their materials organized. These boxes can easily be placed in your car trunk and moved from one sales call to another. The orderly arrangement of selling tools is just one more method of time conservation.

The key to regular use of the four time-saving techniques described previously is *commitment*. Unless you are convinced that efficient time management is important, you will probably find it difficult to adopt these new habits. A salesperson who fully accepts the "time is money" philosophy will use these techniques routinely.

SAVING TIME WITH TELEPHONES, FAX MACHINES, E-MAIL, AND ELECTRONIC DATA INTERCHANGE

As the cost of a sales call increases, more and more salespeople are asking the question, "Is this trip necessary?" In many situations a telephone call can replace a personal visit. The telephone call may be especially useful in dealing with accounts that are marginal in terms of profitability. Some customers actually prefer telephone contact for certain types of business transaction. Here are some situations in which the phone call is appropriate:

Call the customer in advance to make an appointment. You will save time and the customer will know when to expect you.

Use the telephone to keep the customer informed. A phone call provides instant communication with customers at a low cost.

Build customer goodwill with a follow-up phone call. Make it a practice to call customers to thank them for buying your product and to determine if the customer is satisfied with the purchase.

Some customers prefer to be contacted by e-mail, and it would be a mistake to ignore their preference. Busy people often discourage telephone calls to minimize interruptions. They review e-mail messages only at specific times of the day.

Voice mail automated telephone systems are now being used by companies of all sizes. These systems not only answer the phone and take messages but also provide information-retrieval systems that are accessible by telephone. This

The cellular telephone has become a convenient and time-saving sales tool.

June '02

NOTES

	MAY 2002					
S	M	T	W	T	F	S
			1	2	3	4
5	6	7	8	9	10	11
12	13	14	15	16	17	18
19	20	21	22	23	24	25
26	27	28	29	30	31	

	JULY 2002					
S	M	T	W	T	F	S
	1	2	3	4	5	6
7	8	9	10	11	12	13
14	15	16	17	18	19	20
21	22	23	24	25	26	27
28	29	30	31			

SUNDAY	MONDAY	TUESDAY	WEDNESDAY	THURSDAY	FRIDAY	SATURDAY
2	**3**	**4** 10:30 Wheat First Securities 12:00 Lunch with Ray Williams 3:00 Farrell's Service Centre	**5** 9:00 Demonstration at Conestoga College 11:00 Demo at Millis, Inc. 3:30 Meet with Helen Sisson	**6** 9:00 Austin & Son Storage 10:30 Demo at CMP Sporting Goods 1:00 Attend Computer Trade Show	**7** 9:00 Sales Meeting at Holiday Inn 1:30 Demo at Omega Homes	**8** 10:00 Take Dana to soccer game
9	**10** 8:00 to 12:00 Sales Training 1:30 Meet with M.I.S. staff at Mohawk College	**11** 9:30 Park Realty 11:00 White Tire Service 2:00 Demo at Ritter-Seaford	**12** 9:00 Demonstration at Ross accounting services 11:00 Prospecting 2:30 Meet with technical support staff	**13** 8:30 Meet with Helen Hunt 12:00 Lunch with Tim 1:00 Demo at Collins Wholesale 4:00 Parent-Teacher conference	**14** 9:00 Demo at Fanshawe College 1:00 to 5:00 Update sales records	**15** 9:00 10-K run (starts at YMCA building)
16	**17**	**18**	**19**	**20**	**21**	**22**

Figure 15.2 Monthly Planning Calendar sample. Shown are the first 15 days of a monthly planning calendar for a computer service sales representative.

Building Relationships through Technology

CONFIRMING IMMEDIATELY

Sharing close-up and personal information creates a core on which successful relationships may be built and sustained. Friends have long supplemented their personal visits with notes, letters, and telephone calls.

Contemporary technology offers new ways save time in addition to enhancing and extending relationship-rich communications. Enlightened salespeople use the fax and computer modem as fast, thus effective, methods to give information to their customers. The fax function can be particularly useful to quickly convey temporary messages that confirm, affirm, or verify. (See the exercise Corresponding with CRM on page 361 for more information.)

technology is especially useful for salespeople who need to exchange information with others.[9] For many salespeople the cellular telephone has become a convenient and time-saving sales tool. A pager can also be used to facilitate communication with customers and the main office.

The fax machine takes telecommunication a step further. With the aid of a fax machine, salespeople can send and receive documents in seconds, using standard public or cellular telephone lines. Detailed designs, charts, and graphs can be transmitted across the country or around the world.

Electronic data interchange (EDI) provides a fast and efficient way of exchanging common documents such as purchase orders, invoices, sales reports, and fund transfers. EDI is meeting the needs of companies that no longer want to transfer information on paper. In today's fast-paced world, if you do business only on paper some firms will not buy your products. Most Fortune 500 companies are using EDI today.[10]

With a fax machine, salespeople can send and receive documents in seconds.

territory The geographic area where prospects and customers reside.

Territory Management

Many marketing organizations have found it helpful to break down the total market into manageable units called sales territories. A **territory** is the geographic area where prospects and customers reside. Although some firms have developed territories solely on the basis of geographic considerations, a more common approach is to establish a territory on the basis of classes of customers. Territories are often classified according to sales potential. Some marketers assign sales representatives to key industries. The *Ottawa Citizen* newspaper divides its customer base into major business lines such as real estate and automotive.[11] Regardless of how the sales territory is established, it is essentially a specific number of present and potential accounts that can be called on conveniently.

WHAT DOES TERRITORY MANAGEMENT INVOLVE?

To appreciate fully the many facets of territory management, it will be helpful to examine a typical selling situation. Put yourself in the shoes of a salesperson who has just accepted a position with a firm that manufactures a line of high quality tools. You are responsible for a territory that covers Alberta and Saskatchewan. The territory includes 88 auto supply firms that carry your line of tools. It also includes 38 stores that do not carry your tools. On the basis of this limited information, how would you carry out your selling duties? To answer this question, it will be necessary to follow these steps:

STEP 1: CLASSIFY ALL CUSTOMERS

If you classify customers according to potential sales volume, then you must answer two questions: What is the dollar amount of the firm's current purchases? What amount of additional sales might be developed with greater selling effort? Store A may be purchasing $3000 worth of tools each year, but potential sales for this firm amount to $5000. Store B currently purchases $2000 worth of tools a year, and potential sales amount to $2500. In this example, store A clearly deserves more time than store B.

It is important to realize that a small number of accounts may provide a majority of the sales volume. Many companies get 75 to 80 percent of their sales volume from 20 to 25 percent of their total number of customers. The problem lies in accurately identifying which accounts and prospects fall into the top 20 to 25 percent category. Once this information is available, you can develop customer classification data that can be used to establish the frequency of calls.

The typical sales territory is constantly changing, so the realignment of territories from time to time is necessary. Software, such as MapInfo ProAlign, is now available to help sales managers realign sales territories. Accounts can be segmented based on industry, size, dollar volume, and complexity. The sales manager enters a variety of account information and then produces maps that show accounts in different configurations.[12]

STEP 2: DEVELOP A ROUTING AND SCHEDULING PLAN

Many salespeople have found that travel is one of their most time-consuming nonselling activities. A great deal of time can also be wasted just waiting to see a customer. The primary objective of a sales routing and scheduling plan is to increase actual selling by reducing time spent travelling between accounts and waiting to see customers.

Building Quality Partnerships

OUTSTANDING RELATIONSHIP MANAGEMENT

When Xerox Canada president Kevin Francis was a sales manager, he convinced Joe Murphy to join the company. He had no way of knowing that his friend from St. Francis Xavier University would eventually earn the name "Joe Xerox." Like most new hires, Joe began his career making cold calls on smaller accounts. He soon was given responsibility for larger customers, eventually including Memorial University of Newfoundland and government accounts. Joe was kept busy with these few accounts; managing them proved to be quite challenging.

Joe had to continually prospect for new opportunities, as there were many departments within each major account, and carefully plan each sales call. "You can't see people without a purpose. If you waste their time, they soon get tired of seeing you," says Joe. "I planned my call cycles so that I would regularly see everyone, and so I would keep current with everyone's needs. Managing customer satisfaction is critical when you have only a few accounts. One dissatisfied person could result in lost sales throughout the entire organization."

When Joe Murphy decided to retire in 1999, Memorial held a retirement party for him. People from across the university who had dealt with Joe over his career were invited to attend and wish him well. Memorial's president honoured Joe by signing a "retirement" certificate for him, recognizing the outstanding service he had provided the university over the 21 years he managed the account.[a]

If a salesperson called on only established accounts and spent the same amount of time with each customer, routing and scheduling would not be difficult. In most cases, however, you need to consider other variables. For example, you may be expected to develop new accounts on a regular basis. In this case, you must adjust your schedule to accommodate calls on prospects. Another variable involves customer service. Some salespeople devote considerable time to adjusting warranty claims, solving customer problems, and paying goodwill visits.

There are no precise rules to observe in establishing a sales routing and scheduling plan, but the following guiding principles apply to nearly all selling situations:

With mapping software, salespeople can perform rapid analyses of sales opportunities in Europe.

1. Obtain or create a map of your territory, and mark the location of present accounts with pins or a marking pen. Each account might be colour coded according to sales potential. This will give you a picture of the entire territory. Many companies are using mapping software to create a territory picture that can be viewed on the computer screen. With the aid of geographic information system (GIS) mapping software, salespeople can perform rapid analyses of sales opportunities in a geographic area and create a territory plan.[13]

2. If your territory is quite large, consider organizing it into smaller subdivisions. You can then plan work in terms of several trading areas that make up the entire territory.

3. Develop a routing plan for a specific period of time. This might be a one- or two-week period. Once the plan is firm, notify customers of your anticipated arrival time by telephone, letter, or e-mail.

4. Develop a schedule that accommodates your customers' needs. Some customers appreciate getting calls on a certain day of the week or at a certain hour of the day. Try to schedule your calls in accordance with their wishes.

5. Think ahead, and establish one or more tentative calls in case you have some extra time. If your sales calls take less time than expected or if there is an unexpected cancellation, you need optional calls to fill in the void.

6. Decide how frequently to call on the basis of sales potential. Give the greatest attention to the most profitable customers.

SALES CALL PLANS

You can use information from the routing and scheduling plan to develop a **sales call plan.** This proposal is a weekly action plan, usually initiated by the sales manager. Its primary purpose is to ensure efficient and effective account coverage.

The form most sales managers use is similar to the one shown in Figure 15.3. One section of the form is used to record planned calls. A parallel section is for completed calls. Additional space is provided for the names of firms called on.

The sales manager usually presents the sales call plan to individual members of the sales staff. Some salespeople may be asked to allocate calls across all categories of customers; sometimes the sales manager may ask senior or field salespeople to call on one category of account, and more junior or inside salespeople to call on another category of account. The Royal Bank of Canada, for example, segmented its customers into A, B, and C accounts on the basis of dollar activity and profitability. Account managers were asked to focus on larger accounts,

sales call plan   A plan developed with information taken from the routing and scheduling plan. The primary purpose of the plan is to ensure efficient and effective account coverage.

offering them additional products and services. As a result, the average profit per A account increased 268 percent and the number of A accounts increased 292 percent over a two-year period.[14]

The plan's success will depend on how realistic the goals appear to the sales staff, how persuasive the sales manager is, and what type of training accompanies the plan's introduction.

Records Management

Although some salespeople complain that paperwork is too time consuming and reduces the amount of time available for actual selling, others recognize that accurate, up-to-date records actually save time. Their work is better organized,

Figure 15.3 Sales call plan

Sales Call Plan

Salesperson _____   For week ending _____

Territory _____   Days worked _____

Planned Calls	**Total Completed Calls**
Number of planned calls _____	Number of calls only _____
Number of planned presentations _____	Number of presentations _____
Number of planned telephone calls _____	Number of telephone calls _____
Account Category Planning	Number of orders _____
A. Account calls _____	Total miles travelled _____
B. Account calls _____	A. Account calls _____
C. Account calls _____	B. Account calls _____
	C. Account calls _____

Companies called on	Address	Date	Customer rating	Comments about call

and quick accessibility of information often makes it possible to close more sales and improve customer service.

A good record-keeping system gives salespeople useful information with which to check their own progress. For instance, an examination of sales call plans at the end of the day provides a review of who was called on and what was accomplished. The company also benefits from complete and accurate records. Reports from the field help management make important decisions. A company with a large sales force operating throughout a wide geographic area relies heavily on information sent to the main office.

COMMON RECORDS KEPT BY SALESPEOPLE

A good policy is never to require a record that is not absolutely necessary. The only records worth keeping are those that provide positive benefits to the customer, the salesperson, or the personnel who work in sales-supporting areas of the company. Each record should be brief, easy to complete, and free of requests for useless detail. Where possible, the format should provide for the use of check marks as a substitute for written responses. Completing sales record forms should not be a major burden.

What records should you keep? The answer to this question will vary depending on the type of selling position. Some of the most common records kept by salespeople are described in this section.

CUSTOMER AND PROSPECT CARD FILES

Most salespeople find it helpful to keep records of customers and prospects. Each of these cards has space for name, address, and phone number. Other information recorded might be the buyer's personal characteristics, the names of people who might influence the purchase, or appropriate times to make calls. Of course, many salespeople have replaced their card files with computerized record systems.

CALL REPORTS

The call report (also called an activity report) is a variation of the sales call plan described earlier in this chapter. It is used to record information about the people you have called on and what took place. The call report is one of the most basic records used in the field of selling. It provides a summary of what happened during the call and an indication of what future action is required. The call reports (daily and weekly) featured in Figure 15.4 are typical of those used in the field.

We are seeing less emphasis on call reports that require only numbers (calls made each day, number of proposals written, etc.). Companies that emphasize consultative selling are requesting more personal information on the customer (information that will expand the customer profile) and more information on the customer's short- and long-range buying plans.[15]

EXPENSE RECORDS

Both your company and the government agencies that monitor business expenses will require a record of selling expenses. These usually include such items as meals, lodging, travel, and in some cases entertainment expenses. Several expense-reporting software packages are now available to streamline the expense reporting process. Automated expense reports save the salesperson a great deal of time and allows them to be reimbursed while still on the road.

Personal organizers such as Palm allow salespeople to access address, phone, fax, e-mail, appointment, and to-do lists.

Photography by Timothy Greenfield-Sanders.

SALES RECORDS

The records used to report sales vary greatly in design. Some companies require daily reports, others weekly ones. As you would expect, one primary use of the sales report is to analyze salespeople's performance.

You can take certain steps to improve a reporting system. Some records should be completed right away, while you can easily recall the information. Accuracy is always important. It can be embarrassing to have an order sent to the wrong address simply because you have transposed a figure. Take time to

Figure 15.4   Call report, expense voucher, and weekly sales report. These are three of the most common records kept by 3M salespeople.

proofread forms for accuracy. Neatness and legibility are also important when you are preparing sales records.

You should re-examine your territory management plan continually. Update it often so it reflects the current status of your various accounts. When possible, use a portable computer and appropriate software to improve your records management system. Computers can help you to achieve increased selling time and to enhance customer service.

Stress Management

Personal selling produces a certain amount of stress. This is due in part to the non-routine nature of sales work. Each day brings a variety of new experiences, some of which will cause stress. Prospecting, for example, can be threatening to some salespeople. Long hours on the job, the loss of leisure time, and too little time for family members can also be stressful.

Although "variety is the spice of life," there is a limit to how much diversity one can cope with. One of the keys to success in selling is learning how to bring order to the many facets of the job. Figure 15.5 provides an action plan to reduce stress. We must be physically and mentally prepared to handle work-related stress.

stress The response of the body or mind to demands on it, in the form of either psychological or physiological strain.

Stress can be defined as the behavioural adjustments to change that affect you physically and psychologically. It is a process by which your body and mind mobilize energy for coping with change and challenge.[16] Repeated or prolonged stress can trigger a variety of warning signs. Physical signs might take the form of headaches, loss of appetite, hypertension, or fatigue. Psychological symptoms include anxiety, depression, irritability, and reduced interest in personal relationships.[17] The latter problem can be a serious barrier to success in sales. Some stress is beneficial because it helps keep us motivated, but too much stress can be unhealthy if left unchecked.

Stress might be caused by trying to figure out ways to meet a sales quota or how to schedule travel throughout a sales territory. Missed appointments, presentations before large groups, and lack of feedback concerning your performance can also create stress. Ironically, some of the time-saving tools used by salespeople (fax machines, car phones, and electronic mail) make it difficult for them to escape the pressures of their job. Many salespeople feel they are "on call" 24 hours a day.

As noted in Chapter 1, information surplus has replaced information scarcity as an important new problem in the age of information. A growing number of knowledge workers report tension with colleagues, loss of job satisfaction, and strained personal relationships as a result of information overload. Too much information also crowds out quiet moments needed to restore balance in our lives.[18]

It is not possible to eliminate stress from your life, but you can adopt stress management strategies that will help you cope with the stress in your life. Three stress management strategies are discussed here.

MAINTAIN AN OPTIMISTIC OUTLOOK

Researchers evaluated the coping strategies of 101 salespeople from three companies. They found that those who faced job-related stress with an optimistic outlook fared better than those with a pessimistic attitude. The research team found that optimists used "problem-focused" coping strategies while pessimists used "emotion-focused" techniques. The optimistic salespeople most frequently focused on various ways to solve the problem. Pessimists were more likely to try to avoid the problem and to direct their feelings toward other people.[19]

PRACTISE HEALTHY EMOTIONAL EXPRESSION

When stress occurs, you may undergo physiological and psychological changes. The heartbeat quickens, the blood pressure rises, and tension builds. To relieve the pressure you may choose a *fight* or *flight* response. Fighting the problem may mean unleashing an avalanche of harsh words or ignoring the other person. These reactions, of course, are not recommended. This behaviour may damage relationships with team members, customers, or customer support personnel.

Flight is the act of running away from the problem. Rather than face the issue squarely, you decide to turn your back on it. The flight response is usually not satisfactory; the problem will seldom go away by itself. If you feel stress from an impractical quota, talk to your sales manager and try to get the quota reduced. Don't just give in to the feeling of being overwhelmed. If you are spending too much time away from family, take a close look at your territory management plan and try to develop a more efficient way to make sales calls.

MAINTAIN A HEALTHY LIFESTYLE

An effective exercise program—jogging, tennis, golf, racquetball, walking, or some other favourite exercise—can "burn off" the harmful chemicals that build up in your bloodstream after a prolonged period of stress. Ron Sakkal, a Midland Walwyn Capital Inc. stockbroker in Toronto, uses a personal trainer twice a week. Although he pays $100 per week for two sessions, Ron Sakkal says, "As a financial investment I think it's been very worthwhile. I'm full of energy and am sleeping well."[20]

The food you eat can also play a critical role in helping you manage stress. Health experts agree that the typical Canadian diet—high in saturated fats, refined sugars, additives, caffeine, and even too much protein—is the wrong menu for coping with stress. Husky Injection Molding Systems Ltd. employees in Bolton, Ontario, enjoy organic, vegetarian meals, prepared and subsidized by the company. All employees receive $500 annually for vitamins, and they have access to a massage therapist, chiropractor, naturopath, and doctor or nurse, who are usually on-site.[21]

An Action Plan to Reduce Stress

1. Take 15 minutes.
2. Make two columns on a piece of paper. Write "Work" at the top of one, "Personal" at the top of the other. Write down all the things that are driving you crazy.
3. Underline the most important things on the lists.
4. Separate them into "chronic" and "acute."
5. For each one, ask yourself: what do I need to do to reduce the stress arising from this factor right now? Some answers could be as simple as "Get a good night's sleep."
6. Take action.[b]

Figure 15.5   An action plan to reduce stress.

Exercise is an excellent way to moderate stress.

Leisure time can also provide you with the opportunity to relax and get rid of work-related stress. Jovan Vuksanovich uses billiards to help increase relaxation skills among corporate clients, frequently combining lectures and demonstrations for an entertaining, relaxing, and informative evening. Midland Walwyn Capital, Nortel, and CHUM have all been clients.[22]

One additional way to handle stress is to come to work rested and relaxed. Dr. Louis E. Kopolow, an expert in the field of stress management, says, "The best strategy for avoiding stress is to learn how to relax."[23] Fatigue will reduce

Building Quality Partnerships

FOUR MODERATORS OF STRESS

The stress-related tension that surfaces in our lives can be a barrier to effective interpersonal relations. The psychological problems that can result from too much stress are anxiety, depression, instability, and reduced interest in personal relationships. The authors of *The One-Minute Manager Gets Fit* have identified four moderators of stress. When these four are in good working order, they can help prevent stress from turning into strain.

1. *Autonomy* is a sense we get on weekends of being able to do what we want. Autonomy can also be working independently or having the necessary skills and qualifications to be able to move from one job to another.

2. *Connectedness* relates to the ties we have with those around us. People with a high sense of connectedness feel they have strong, positive relationships in all areas—at home, at work, and in the community.

3. *Perspective* has to do with the meaning of life—the direction, the purpose, the passion that you feel for what you are doing. It keeps you from letting little things get you down. Because you are looking at the big picture, normal strains of daily life do not get blown out of proportion.

4. *Tone* is your energy level, your physical well-being and appearance, and how you feel about your body. By having better tone, a person can definitely improve self-esteem and, in doing so, help moderate stress.[c]

your tolerance for dealing with stressful situations. How much sleep do you need each night? The number of hours of sleep required for good health varies from person to person, but seven or eight hours seems to be about right for most people. The critical test is if you feel rested in the morning and prepared to deal with the day's activities.

In many respects, salespeople must possess the same self-discipline as a professional athlete. Sales work can be physically demanding. Lack of proper rest, poor eating habits, excessive drinking, and failure to exercise properly can reduce one's ability to deal with stress and strain.

Summary

In this chapter we described management of self as a four-dimensional process. It involves time management, territory management, records management, and stress management.

All salespeople can learn more about their products and improve their selling skills. However, there is no way to expand time. Our only option is to find ways to improve time and territory management. The four time-saving techniques discussed in this chapter should be used by every salesperson. When used on a regular basis, they will set the stage for more face-to-face selling time.

The first step in territory management is classification of all customers according to sales volume or some other appropriate criterion. You normally should spend the most time with accounts that have the greatest sales potential. The second step requires developing a routing and scheduling plan. This plan should reduce time spent travelling between accounts. In some cases you can substitute telephone calls or e-mail messages for personal calls.

A good record-keeping system provides many advantages. Accurate, up-to-date records can actually save time because work is better organized. The company also benefits because sales reports provide an important communication link with members of the sales force. Today computers are used to develop more efficient record-keeping systems.

There is a certain amount of stress associated with sales work. This is due in part to the non-routine nature of personal selling. Salespeople must learn to cope with the factors that upset their equilibrium. Three stress management strategies were discussed.

Key Terms

Territory 349
Sales Call Plan 351

Stress 356

Review Questions

1. Describe how a salesperson is much like the individual who owns and operates a business.

2. Management of self has been described as a four-dimensional process. Describe each dimension.

3. What are the two major ways a salesperson can increase sales volume?

4. How can a salesperson use a time log to improve time management?

5. List four techniques the salesperson should use to make better use of valuable selling time.

6. Effective territory management involves two major steps. What are they?

7. What is a sales call plan? Explain how it is used.

8. Describe the most common records kept by salespeople.

9. What is the definition of stress? What are some indicators of stress?

10. The Building Quality Partnerships box on p. 358 describes four moderators of stress. Which of these four moderators do you think is most important for persons employed in the sales field? Explain.

Application Exercises

1. Deciding on a goal can be the most crucial decision of your life. It is more damaging not to have a goal than it is not to reach a goal. It is generally agreed that the major cause of failure is the lack of a well-defined purpose. A successful life results not from chance, but from a succession of successful days. Prepare a list for the following categories:

   Career goals
   1.
   2.
   3.

   Family goals
   1.
   2.
   3.

   Educational goals
   1.
   2.
   3.

   Interpersonal relationship goals
   1.
   2.
   3.

2. You have just been hired as a salesperson for a major Canadian industrial distributor. Your sales manager has told you she expects you to make sales calls 210 days per year (you get four weeks of vacation, two weeks of sales training, 10 paid holidays, and are not required to call on customers during the two weeks around Christmas). She wants all salespeople to average 3.5 calls per day. She has advised you that your best customers should see you twice each month, and you should call on every account at least once each year. She has provided you with the following information on your accounts, based on last year's sales. She wants your suggested sales call plan (how you will allocate your sales calls across customers) for next year, based on this information. How would you allocate your calls to these customers? What other recommendations would you make to your sales manager?

Accounts	Sales
Top 10 accounts	$300 200
Next 10 accounts	$180 500
Next 10 accounts	$164 200
Next 20 accounts	$135 600
Next 20 accounts	$128 800
Next 20 accounts	$ 99 300
Next 30 accounts	$135 210
Last 30 accounts	$ 53 460

3. Interview someone you know who uses a planning calendar. What kind is it—pocket, desk, or some other type? How long has the person been using it? How important is the calendar to daily, weekly, monthly, and yearly planning? Has the person ever considered discontinuing its use? What are the person's suggestions for someone who does not use one? Write your answer.

4. Time management is an important part of a successful salesperson's job. Using your search engine, examine the Internet for information on time management. Type in "time management" + selling. Examine the training products and services available on this topic.

CRM Application Exercise

Corresponding with CRM

Waiting for a client who forgot an appointment can be very time consuming. The client who promptly receives a faxed reminder note is more likely to remember and honour a commitment to meet. Quickly confirming an agreement reached by telephone is easy for CRM systems such as ACT!. Look up the contact Ian Program, select <u>W</u>rite, and <u>F</u>ax Cover to display the fax cover sheet which, by itself, may be used to convey a short confirmation message. Position the cursor at Subject and type "Lunch," then press Enter twice and type "I look forward to lunch with you Friday noon at Jimmy's." Select <u>F</u>ile, <u>P</u>rint (Ctrl+P) to print the fax cover note. If your computer is running fax software, you could send the fax cover note directly to your client's fax machine.

Case Problem

Elli Davis, introduced at the beginning of this chapter, has had one of the most distinguished careers in Canadian real estate sales. In 1983, Elli joined Royal LePage as a sales rookie, and if they had a "Rookie of the Year" award, she would have won it. She sold her first property within three weeks. She was ranked fourth in Ontario and eighth nationally at the end of her second year, and was the #1 Residential Sales Representative in Canada in 1987, her third year in the business. She hasn't lost that title since. There are a lot of things that must come together to create success at this level, but Elli Davis openly discusses some of the personal principles that have guided her career. Five factors comprise her formula for success.

Number one. Decide what you want to accomplish and stay focused on it. Elli Davis says, "I'm focused on being successful. I work hard, and I plan every day. I'm in my office every morning at 9:00 a.m. and I know what I am going to do before I get there. I'm very well organized. You should never underestimate the value of organization and planning to sales success."

Number two. Know your business. Elli Davis studied hard for her real estate sales examination and scored the highest grade her instructor had seen in his nine years of teaching. That same demand to know what is going on in her industry still drives Elli Davis. She spends every morning carefully studying the latest MLS listings of new properties on the market and decides what might appeal to her clients. She keeps track of all sales in her area, to the point where she is an "expert" resource to both sellers and buyers. Elli Davis thoroughly knows 30 to 40 buildings where she regularly has listings, and she can remember floor plans, square footage, renovations and changes, and recent market prices for all of them. She takes pride in her ability to put the right people into the right home.

Number three. Be honest and sincere, and learn to listen carefully to your clients. Elli Davis knows that professionalism requires dedication and integrity, and she remains committed to her clients throughout the whole sales process. She refuses to be dishonest to either buyers or sellers because she knows how important her reputation is to her long-term success. Elli knows that it is very important to listen to clients to fully understand their needs. You have to be able to satisfy their needs to make them happy. She is now at a point where many of her sales come from happy customers who have worked with her in the past, or from referrals they have made. Elli Davis says, "A client is a client, and they are all potential repeat clients or referrals." Her sales job often requires a lot of empathy. Not every client is making a happy purchase or sale. Sometimes clients are forced to move, and sometimes they must sell at prices well below what they paid.

Number four. Establish a good support group. Sales is a demanding job, and to be successful you must devote a lot of time and commitment to what you are doing. It is essential that you have a supportive home life and friends who understand that your first responsibility must sometimes be your clients. According to Elli Davis, "I've had to leave parties early to show properties, or to make offers to clients. Sometimes I simply can't go to social engagements when important sales could be affected, and my friends just have to accept this."

Number five. Love your career. Elli Davis says, "Anyone with a full-time career has to absorb its responsibilities. If they can't do it happily, they shouldn't be in the field." Now she takes some weekends off and arranges a few short vacations. These are necessary to prevent burnout, common to salespeople who work long hours. But she still has fun. She enjoys her day, and the enthusiasm for her job is still there after 16 years.

Questions

1. Which of Elli Davis's "five factors for success" will make the most important contribution to a career in personal selling? Explain.

2. Reflect on your own approach to accomplishing things, then select two of Elli's elements that you would find easy to adopt. Then select two elements you would find difficult to adopt. Explain your choices.

3. How might goal setting be used in conjunction with time management?

4. How might a commitment to excellence improve the territory management process? records management?

5. Do you agree or disagree that the people you associate with can influence your enthusiasm?

CRM Case Study

Managing Yourself with CRM

A key objective in managing your time is to confirm that, at any time, you are working on your highest priorities. Contacting prospective customers is the highest priority for most salespeople. The next challenge is to decide in which order prospects should be contacted. Many salespeople prioritize their accounts on the basis of their value; that is, the amount that they are likely to spend with the sales organization.

Questions

1. On the basis of the dollar amount that Pat Silva estimated that each account might spend, in what order would you contact the prospects in the ACT! database?

2. If you were to rank these prospects on the basis of your sales commission, would this priority list be different than the list developed in question 1? If so, why?

3. There are several ways that this list of prospects could be prioritized. For example: By date; dollar amount; or commission. Which of these rankings is best?

Ethics: The Foundation for Relationships in Selling

LEARNING OBJECTIVES

When you finish reading this chapter, you should be able to

1. Discuss the influence of ethical decisions on relationships in selling

2. Describe the factors that influence the ethical conduct of sales personnel

3. Compare legal versus ethical standards

4. Explain how role models influence the ethical conduct of sales personnel

5. Discuss the influence of company policies and practices on the ethical conduct of salespeople

6. Explain how values influence behaviour

7. Discuss guidelines for developing a personal code of ethics

Many companies have codes of ethics that define acceptable behaviours in relationships with their suppliers. General Motors' code states: "Both as a matter of sound procurement practice and basic business integrity, we at General Motors must make our purchase decisions solely on the basis of which suppliers offer GM the best value for the goods and services we need."[1]

However, in depositions filed during a sexual-harassment lawsuit against Markham, Ontario-based Magna International Inc., company officials claimed they often took purchasing agents from the "Big Three" automakers to strip clubs, and paid for lap dances and private dances in upstairs rooms. One Magna account manager claimed he entertained customers at topless bars on a weekly basis, took customers to play golf in Las Vegas, bought one customer a tuxedo, and gave other customers Mont Blanc pens. Another stated that many clients did not want their real names on salespersons' expense reports because their actions violated their company's code of ethics. Some Magna executives claim to have used false names on their expense reports to protect their clients' identities.[2]

Later in this chapter, we will look at a number of factors that affect the ethical conduct of salespeople.

Making Ethical Decisions

Making ethical decisions is a daily reality in the field of personal selling. In every selling situation salespeople must judge the rightness or wrongness of their actions. As in any other professional field there is the constant temptation to compromise personal standards of conduct to achieve economic goals.

Ethics are the rules that direct your conduct and moral judgments.[3] They help translate your values into appropriate and effective behaviours in your day-to-day life. Ethics reflect the moral principles and standards of the community. Kickbacks and payoffs may be acceptable practices in one part of the world, yet may be viewed as unethical practices elsewhere. Exaggerated or inaccurate sales claims may be acceptable at one company, but forbidden at another company.

There is no one uniform code of ethics for all salespeople. However, a large number of business organizations, professional associations, and certification agencies have established written codes. The Canadian Professional Sales Association (CPSA), introduced in Chapter 2, requires all persons seeking to become a Certified Sales Professional to agree to abide to the CPSA Sales Institute Code of Ethics (Fig. 16.1).

Today, we recognize that character and integrity strongly influence relationships in personal selling. As noted in Chapter 3, character is composed of your personal standards of behaviour, including your honesty and integrity. Your character is based on your internal values and the resulting judgments you make about what is right and what is wrong. The ethical decisions you make reflect your character strength.

We are indebted to Stephen Covey, author of *The 7 Habits of Highly Effective People*, for helping us better understand the relationship between character strength and success in personal selling. In his best-selling book Covey says there are basic principles that must be integrated into our character.[4] One example is to always do what you say you are going to do. Fulfilling your commitments builds trust, and trust is the most important precondition of partnering.

ethics Rules of conduct used to determine what is good or bad. They are moral principles or values concerned with what ought to be done—a person's adherence to honesty and fairness.

CHARACTER STRENGTH

Despite growing interest in business ethics throughout the past decade, unethical behaviour has become all too common. One recent survey indicates that nearly half of the workers surveyed engaged in unethical and/or illegal acts during the year preceding the study. Many of the workers who had transgressed reported that they were under pressure to act unethically or illegally on the job.[5] Richard Sennett, author of *The Corrosion of Character*, says the decline of character strength can be traced to conditions that have grown out of our fast-paced, high-stress, information-driven economy. He states that character strength builds as we display loyalty, mutual commitment, and the pursuit of long-term goals.[6] These are the very qualities needed to build strong buyer–seller relationships. Later in this chapter we will discuss how salespeople can develop a personal code of ethics.

ETHICS—A HISTORICAL PERSPECTIVE

For centuries the principal guideline for dealing with merchants was **caveat emptor,** which means, "Let the buyer beware." This meant that a buyer was expected to look the product over carefully. Once the transaction was concluded, the business relationship ended for all practical purposes. The buyer could not make any claims against the seller at some later date.

caveat emptor A philosophy that states, "Let the buyer beware." The buyer is expected to examine the product and presentation carefully. Once the transaction is concluded, the business relationship ends for all practical purposes.

Figure 16.1 The CPSA Sales Institute Code of Ethics.

The CPSA Sales Institute Code of Ethics is the set of principles and standards that a certified sales professional will strive to adhere to with customers, organizations, competitors, communities and colleagues.

The Certified Sales Professional pledges and commits to uphold these standards in all activities.

I will:

1. Maintain honesty and integrity in all relationships with customers, prospective customers, and colleagues and continually work to earn their trust and respect.
2. Accurately represent my products or services to the best of my ability in a manner that places my customer or prospective customer and my company in a position that benefits both.
3. Respect and protect the proprietary and confidential information entrusted to me by my company and my customers and not engage in activities that may conflict with the best interests of my customers or my company.
4. Continually upgrade my knowledge of my products/services, skills and my industry.
5. Use the time and resources available to me only for legitimate business purposes. I will only participate in activities that are ethical and legal, and when in doubt, I will seek counsel.
6. Respect my competitors and their products and services by representing them in a manner which is honest, truthful and based on accurate information that has been substantiated.
7. Endeavor to engage in business and selling practices which contribute to a positive relationship with the community.
8. Assist and counsel my fellow sales professionals where possible in the performance of their duties.
9. Abide by and encourage others to adhere to this Code of Ethics.

As a certified sales professional, I understand that the reputation and professionalism of all salespeople depends on me as well as others engaged in the sales profession, and I will adhere to these standards to strengthen the reputation and integrity for which we all strive. I understand that failure to consistently act according to this Code of Ethics may result in the loss of the privilege of using my professional sales designation.

www.cpsa.com/
institute.html

Source: www.cpsa.com/institute.html. Reprinted with permission.

With the evolution of the marketing era the caveat emptor philosophy of doing business fell into disfavour. This change resulted from two major forces. First, business leaders discovered that honest business dealings established a foundation for a long-term relationship with customers. The second force is consumer activism. Buyers have become more knowledgeable and more politically active. They demand high quality products and honest business dealings. Consumer activists often lobby for new laws that restrict certain types of business practices.

A close examination of the history of ethics and ethical behaviour reveals two interesting facts. The first is that it is difficult to define fundamental ethical principles to cover every business practice. What is considered wrong by one person or firm may be considered right by another. In the final analysis, each business firm must establish its own ethical standards. The second finding is that people

Selling in Action

HONESTY FROM A QUARTERBACK'S PERSPECTIVE

Jeff Kemp, a former National Football League quarterback, believes that sports can teach important moral lessons. Some of these lessons can be applied in personal selling. Here is what he says about honesty:

> The importance of honesty colours all the rest of life. Why is truth so important? It is because respect, rela-

tionships, and unity all depend on truth. If you cannot be honest with people, you cannot have healthy relationships.

Kemp found that honesty was the foundation for harmony among team members. He says, "Without truth, I couldn't trust my teammates and they couldn't trust me."[a]

are continually in the process of negotiating ethical norms. Situations keep changing, and we find it necessary to establish new standards. If a good customer is sexually harassing a salesperson and this behaviour is reported to the sales manager, what action should the manager take? The issue of third-party harassment is often not covered in written policies on sexual harassment.[7] You supervise salespeople who travel a great deal, and you discover that it is possible to obtain major airfare price reductions by requiring salespeople to stay over on Saturday. Should you require them to spend weekends away from family members? Many business firms are struggling to align their values, ethics, and principles with the expectations of their salespeople and their customers.

Factors Influencing the Ethics of Salespeople

In the field of personal selling the temptation to maximize short-term gains by some type of unethical conduct is always present. Salespeople are especially vulnerable to moral corruption because they are subject to many temptations. Here are a few examples:

> The competition is using exaggerated claims to increase the sale of its product. Should you counteract this action by using exaggerated claims of your own to build a stronger case for your product?

> You have visited the buyer twice, and each time the person displayed a great deal of interest in your product. During the last visit the buyer hinted that the order might be signed if you could provide a small gift. Your company has a long-standing policy that gifts are not to be given under any circumstances. What do you do?

> Your sales manager is under great pressure to increase sales. At a recent meeting of the entire sales staff this person said, "We have to beat the competition no matter what it takes!" Will this emotional appeal change your way of dealing with customers?

> During a recent business trip you met an old friend and decided to have dinner together. At the end of the meal you paid for the entire bill and left a generous tip. Do you now put these non-business-related expenses on your expense account?

> You are selling financial services for a bank and have developed a long list of satisfied customers. You are offered a similar position with a competing

Figure 16.2 Factors determining ethical behaviour of salespeople.

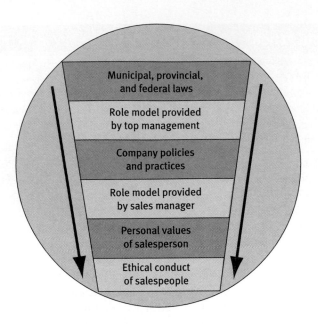

Municipal, provincial, and federal laws

Role model provided by top management

Company policies and practices

Role model provided by sales manager

Personal values of salesperson

Ethical conduct of salespeople

bank. If you accept the position, should you attempt to take your good customers with you?

These types of ethical dilemmas arise frequently in the field of selling. How do salespeople respond? Some ignore company policy, cast aside personal standards of conduct, and yield to the pressure. However, a surprising number of salespeople are able to resist. They are aided by a series of factors that help them distinguish right from wrong. Figure 16.1 outlines the positive forces that help them deal honestly and openly with prospects at all times. We will discuss each of these factors.

PROVINCIAL AND FEDERAL LAWS

In the field of selling there are both legal standards and ethical standards. A legal standard is enforced by statute; an ethical standard is an outgrowth of society's customs and attitudes. While the law regulates the minimal behavioural standards, wise salespeople recognize that operating only within legal bounds is not sufficient. In Canada, it is necessary for salespeople not only to know federal statutes but also to recognize that there are many provincial statutes, and that important differences exist between provinces.

THE COMPETITION ACT

Competition legislation is more than 100 years old in Canada. The rationale for such legislation was originally to foster competition, or to eliminate restrictive trade practices. Changes to the legislation eventually led to the *Competition Act*, passed in 1986, which defines many illegal practices throughout Canada. This Act, amended in 1992, tries to protect consumers from unfair business practices and to foster a competitive environment, while protecting companies from each other.

Here are some of the major issues relevant to salespeople:

1. *Price fixing.* Collusion occurs when sellers agree to set prices higher than they would be in a free market. In 1999, five foreign vitamin producers were fined a record $88.4-million as a result of an investigation of price fixing by Canada's Competition Bureau. In some instances, company executives can also be held liable for price-fixing conspiracy. Russell Cosburn, former vice-president of sales for Toronto-based Chinook Group Ltd., was given a nine-month sentence for his part in a conspiracy to fix prices and allocate market share for vitamin B-4.[8]

2. *Bid rigging.* A related offence, called bid rigging, is also collusion and occurs when sellers communicate with the purpose of setting prices with respect to one or more requests for proposals. In December 1997, four Toronto-based electrical contractors were fined a total of $2.55 million. Investigators for the Competition Bureau estimated that winning contracts for services were 10 to 15 percent higher than they should have been. Prosecutor James Sutton indicated that the bid-riggers, in addition to the fines, could be sued for damages by the 18 customers who paid too much for their services.[9]

3. *Price discrimination.* Price discrimination occurs when a supplier charges different prices for a like quantity and quality of goods to companies that are in competition with each other. There have been only three convictions in Canada, all since 1984. Fines have ranged from $15 000 to $50 000.[10] In the United States, functional discounts are legal; that is, it is acceptable to offer larger discounts to wholesalers versus retailers, based on the functions they perform. In Canada, wholesalers and retailers are considered competitors, and must be treated as equals with respect to pricing and related promotional allowances.

4. *Predatory pricing.* When companies set prices so low that they drive competitors from the market or deter competitors from entering the market, they may be charged with predatory pricing.

5. *Misleading advertising.* All representations, whether in print or oral (where salespeople are more likely to be involved), may be guilty of this offence. While claims may be literally true, conviction under the Act may result if any representation creates a false or misleading impression. Convictions for misleading advertising have been common in Canada. Suzy Shier Ltd. was fined $300 000 for misrepresenting discount prices on its clothing. Color Your World was also fined $225 000 for misleading advertising.[11]

6. *Double ticketing.* When any item has been marked with more than one price, the lowest price must prevail. Anyone convicted of this offence could be fined up to $10 000, imprisoned for up to one year, or both.

7. *Resale price maintenance.* It is illegal for suppliers or manufacturers to try to influence the price at which a product is to be resold by a purchaser (usually a retailer or industrial distributor). Discretionary fines or imprisonment for up to five years, or both, may be imposed.

8. *Refusal to deal.* Sellers cannot refuse to sell to legitimate buyers.

9. *Exclusive dealing.* A seller cannot require that buyers deal only or primarily in products supplied by or designated by the seller.

10. *Tied sales.* A seller cannot require a buyer to purchase another product, or refrain from purchasing a product that is not from a specific manufacturer, as a condition to being able to buy a product from the seller.

11. *Pyramid selling.* These schemes use tiers of participants (who may be called members, agents, dealers, or distributors), where each succeeding tier receives credit for revenues or commissions from sales, regardless of whether they have contributed to the sales effort. This practice is illegal; multi-level marketing plans, although similar, are not. These latter schemes do not provide compensation for the recruitment of other participants, do not require product purchase as a condition of participation (other than a specified amount of product at the seller's cost to help facilitate sales), and guarantee the right to return product in saleable condition on reasonable commercial terms.

12. *Referral selling.* It is illegal to offer price reductions or other inducements to a customer for names of other potential customers who may subsequently buy from the seller.

13. *Bait and switch selling.* It is illegal to offer a low price to attract customers and then tell them that the offered article is no longer in stock but that they can buy another, more expensive product. It is not, however, illegal to advertise limited quantities of sale items.

PROVINCIAL CONSUMER PROTECTION ACTS

Each province of Canada has its own legislation regarding the rights of buyers and sellers with respect to direct sales contracts. These sales include door-to-door sales, telephone sales, or sales through direct mail, or where the buyer has been induced to a convention or hotel, for example, for the purpose of contracting a sale for goods or services. In most provinces this legislation is referred to as either *The Direct Sellers Act* or *The Consumer Protection Act*.

One of the most important aspects of these laws is the consumer's right to contract recession, often referred to as a "cooling-off" period. The primary purpose of this provision is to allow customers an opportunity to reconsider a

Building Relationships in a Diverse World

BRIBERY SOMETIMES INFLUENCES FOREIGN DEALS

The Salt Lake City Organizing Committee has been busy polishing the image of the scandal-tainted 2002 Olympic Winter Games. It has been accused of giving International Olympic Committee (IOC) members thousands of dollars in gifts and cash to win their support for holding the games in Salt Lake City. This scandal has exposed the fact that bribery and corruption are not just problems of the Third World; the most serious allegations surround individuals and companies in advanced countries. In a 1998 study by Berlin-based Transparency International, a non-profit organization dedicated to fighting corruption, Denmark was ranked as the least corrupt among selected countries, as perceived and rated as bribe-takers. Canada ranked 6th, ahead of the United States (tied with Austria for 17th), Japan (25th), and Indonesia (80th).

As a first step to combating international bribery and corruption, many member countries of the Paris-based Organization for Economic Co-operation and Development (OECD), including Canada, signed a 1999 treaty making bribery of foreign government officials illegal. The Convention, however, does not apply to private firms where bribery remains legal. Donald Johnston, a former Canadian minister of justice and current secretary-general of the OECD, sees the need to extend the principles to the private sector. "It seems absurd that bribes offered to officials of a state-owned airline are caught by the Convention, while those to officials of a privatized airline are not," he says.[b]

buying decision made under a salesperson's persuasive influence. The cooling-off period ranges from two days to ten days depending on the province. Some provinces determine the period to begin when the contract is signed, while other provinces consider it to begin when the customer receives a copy of the contract. In addition, a notice informing the customer of the cooling-off period must be part of the contract in most provinces.

Other than Ontario and Quebec, all provinces provide for longer cooling-off periods under some conditions: if the salesperson was not licensed when the contract was negotiated, if the terms and conditions of the licence were not met, if the contract was not in accordance with the requirements of the appropriate legislation. As well, contracts may be cancelled if the goods or services are not provided in a certain period of time.

When a contract is cancelled, the seller must return money paid by the purchaser and any trade-in the purchaser may have provided (or a sum of money representing the value of the trade-in). In Manitoba, the refund must be made immediately upon demand; in most other provinces, refunds must be made in 10 to 15 days. Customer obligations to return goods also differ by province and with respect to the condition of the goods at the time of return. Salespeople should be familiar with appropriate legislation in all geographic areas where they sell.

ETHICS BEYOND THE LETTER OF THE LAW

Too often people confuse ethical standards with legal standards. They believe that if you are not breaking the law then you are acting in an ethical manner.[12] A salesperson's ethical sense must extend beyond the legal definition of what is right and wrong. To view ethics only in terms of what is legally proper encourages the question, "What can I get by with?" A salesperson must develop a personal code of ethics that extends beyond the letter of the law.

TOP MANAGEMENT AS ROLE MODEL

Ethical standards tend to filter down from the top of an organization. According to Michael Deck, principal with Toronto based KPMG Ethics & Integrity

Every leader serves as a role model. The organization's moral tone is usually established by management personnel.

Services, "Corporate integrity begins with senior executives visibly and actively setting an example of respect for the rules. In this way, senior management sends a clear message that unethical and illegal behaviours are not acceptable business practices."[13]

Employees look to company leaders for guidance. Chester Barnard, an early contributor to management thought, has stated that a leader's role is to harness the social forces in the organization, to shape and guide values. He describes good managers as value shapers concerned with the organization's informal social properties.[14] The organization's moral tone, as established by management personnel, is the most important single determinant of employee ethics. Today, top management must provide the best possible role model in the area of ethical behaviour. People at the top must realize that actions speak louder than words. They will be judged by what they do, not by what they say.

COMPANY POLICIES AND PRACTICES

Company policies and practices can have a major impact on the ethical conduct of salespeople. Two researchers at the University of Pennsylvania surveyed more than 400 industrial salespeople who were asked to make decisions concerning 14 scenarios that posed ethical dilemmas. The findings indicate that company policies can have a significant influence on employees who are faced with ethical conflicts.[15]

Developing policy statements forces a firm to "take a stand" on various business practices. Distinguishing right from wrong can be a healthy activity for any organization. The outcome is a more clear-cut philosophy of how to conduct business transactions. Research has demonstrated that companies with a defined corporate commitment to ethical practices did better financially than firms that didn't make ethics a key management component.[16]

www.kpmg.ca/ethics

In the 1999 KPMG Business Ethics Survey, 85 percent of the 203 Canadian companies that responded reported that their organization had written documents that outlined their values and principles. The presence of a senior-level manager responsible for the implementation, monitoring, and assurance of ethics initiatives was reported by 40 percent of the respondents. Most marketing companies provide salespeople with guidelines in such areas as sharing confidential information, reciprocity, bribery, gift giving, entertainment, and business defamation.

SHARING CONFIDENTIAL INFORMATION

Personal selling, by its very nature, promotes close working relationships. Customers often turn to salespeople for advice. They disclose confidential information freely to someone they trust. It is important that salespeople preserve the confidentiality of information they receive.

It is not unusual for a customer to disclose information that may be of great value to a competitor. This might include development of new products, plans to expand into new markets, or anticipated changes in personnel. A salesperson may be tempted to share confidential information with a representative of a competing firm. This breach of confidence might be seen as a means of gaining favour. In most cases this action will backfire. The person who receives the confidential information will quickly lose respect for the salesperson. A gossipy salesperson will seldom develop a trusting relationship with another business associate.

RECIPROCITY

Reciprocity is a mutual exchange of benefits, as when a firm buys products from its own customers. Some business firms actually maintain a policy of reciprocity. For example, the manufacturer of commercial sheets and blankets may purchase hotel services from firms that use its products.

Is there anything wrong with the "you scratch my back and I'll scratch yours" approach to doing business? The answer is sometimes yes. In some cases the use of reciprocity borders on commercial blackmail. Salespeople have been known to approach firms that supply their company and encourage them to buy out of obligation. The firm may be forced to buy products of questionable quality at excessive prices.

A business relationship based on reciprocity often has drawbacks. There is the ever-present temptation to take such customers for granted. A customer who buys out of obligation may take a back seat to customers who were won in the open market.

reciprocity A mutual exchange of benefits, as when a firm buys products from its own customers.

BRIBERY

The book *Arrogance and Accords: The Inside Story of the Honda Scandal* describes one of the largest commercial corruption cases in North American history. Over a 15-year period Honda officials received more than US$50 million in cash and gifts from dealers anxious to obtain fast-selling Honda cars and profitable franchises. Eighteen former Honda executives were convicted of obtaining kickbacks; most went to prison.[17]

In some cases a bribe is wrong from a legal standpoint. In almost all cases the bribe is wrong from an ethical point of view. However, bribery does exist, and a salesperson must be prepared to cope with it. It helps to have a well-established company policy to use as a reference point.

GIFT GIVING

Gift giving is a widespread practice in Canada. However, some companies do maintain a "no gift" policy. Many companies report that their policy is either no gifts or nothing of real value. At Hewlett-Packard, advertising novelties, favours, or entertainment may be given to customers and suppliers under certain conditions: they are consistent with acceptable business practice; they are of limited value and cannot be construed as a bribe or payoff; they do not violate any law,

Many businesses have firm policies to deal with ethical problem areas, such as gift giving.

government regulation, or generally accepted ethical standards; and public disclosure of the facts will not embarrass the company.[18]

There are some grey areas that separate a gift from a bribe. Most people agree that a token of insignificant price, such as a pen imprinted with a company logo or a desk calendar, is appropriate. These types of gifts are meant to foster goodwill. A bribe, on the other hand, is an attempt to influence the person receiving the gift.[19]

Are there right and wrong ways to handle gift giving? The answer is yes. The following guidelines will be helpful to any salesperson who is considering giving gifts to customers:

1. Do not give gifts before doing business with a customer. Do not use the gift as a substitute for effective selling methods.

2. Never convey the impression you are "buying" the customer's business with gifts. When this happens, the gift becomes nothing more than a bribe.

3. When gift giving is done correctly, the customer will clearly view it as symbolic of your appreciation—a "no strings attached" goodwill gesture.

4. Be sure the gift is not a violation of the policies of your firm or of your customer's firm. Some firms will not allow employees to accept gifts at all. Other firms place a dollar limit on a gift's value.

In summary, if you have second thoughts about giving a gift, do not do it. When you are sure some token is appropriate, keep it simple and thoughtful.[20]

ENTERTAINMENT

Entertainment is a widespread practice in the field of selling and may be viewed as a bribe by some people. The line dividing gifts, bribes, and entertainment is often quite arbitrary.

Salespeople must frequently decide how to handle entertaining. A few industries see entertainment as part of the approach used to obtain new accounts. This is especially true when competing products are nearly identical. A good example is the cardboard box industry. These products vary little in price and quality. To win an account may involve knowing whom to entertain and how to entertain.

Entertainment is a highly individualized process. One prospect might enjoy a professional football game while another would be impressed most by a quiet meal at a good restaurant. The key is to get to know your prospect's preferences. How does the person spend leisure time? How much time can the person spare for entertainment? You will need to answer these and other questions before you invest time and money on entertainment.

BUSINESS DEFAMATION

Salespeople frequently compare their product's qualities and characteristics with those of a competitor during the sales presentation. If such comparisons are inaccurate, are misleading, or slander a company's business reputation, such conduct is illegal.[21] Competitors have sued hundreds of companies and manufacturer's representatives for making slanderous statements while selling.

What constitutes business defamation? Steven M. Sack, coauthor of *The Salesperson's Legal Guide*, provides the following examples:

Building Relationships through Technology

THE ETHICAL MANAGEMENT OF CUSTOMER INFORMATION

Customer relationship management systems enable you to collect information about people with whom you maintain relationships, including the taking of notes. It is a good practice to record more than basic transaction information, such as personal details about your customers. Reviewing your observations about their behaviour and your recording of their statements can help you understand them and their needs. Re-reading their comments about ethical issues can assist you to assess the value of maintaining a business relationship with them.

To be fair, it is important to record only the facts regarding your observations, not necessarily your conclusions. Information in an electronic database can last a long time and, for reasons such as litigation or company acquisitions, can be "mobile." This means that others may form an opinion about your customer based on your recorded observations, with potential detrimental consequences for your customer. Since the customer may not be aware of the existence of the information in your database, that person does not have a fair opportunity to correct any erroneous conclusions. Another reason to carefully record only facts is the possibility that the information may be read by the customer. For example, there have been instances in which a customer has later joined the sales organization and gained access to the CRM system.

Most CRM systems contain scheduling functions, which means that you can set aside time on your calendar to attend meetings, make phone calls, and perform tasks. The scheduling tools usually include alarms, which will remind you that a deadline is approaching. The disciplined use of these features can help you get things done on time. Taking advantage of the system's reminder tools can be especially important when it involves fulfilling your commitments. The system can help you build trust by reminding you always to do what you said you would do. (See the exercise Preparing Mailing Labels with CRM on page 381 for more information.)

1. *Business slander.* This arises when an unfair and untrue oral statement is made about a competitor. The statement becomes actionable when it is communicated to a third party and can be interpreted as damaging the competitor's business reputation or the personal reputation of an individual in that business.

2. *Business libel.* This may be incurred when an unfair and untrue statement is made about a competitor in writing. The statement becomes actionable when it is communicated to a third party and can be interpreted as damaging the company.

3. *Product disparagement.* This occurs when false or deceptive comparisons or distorted claims are made concerning a competitor's product, services, or property.[22]

The effectiveness of company policies as a deterrent to unethical behaviour will depend on two factors. The first is the firm's attitude toward employees who violate these policies. If violations are routinely ignored, the policy's effect will soon be eroded. Second, policies that influence personal selling need the support of the entire sales staff. Salespeople should have some voice in policy decisions; they are more apt to support policies they have helped develop.

THE SALES MANAGER AS ROLE MODEL

The salesperson's actions often mirror the sales manager's behaviour and expectations. This is not surprising when you consider the relationship between salespeople and their supervisors. They look to their supervisors for guidance and direction. The sales manager is generally the company's closest point of contact with the sales staff. This person is usually viewed as the chief spokesperson for top management.

Sales managers generally provide new salespeople with their first orientation to company operations. They are responsible for interpreting company policy. On a continuing basis the sales manager monitors the salesperson's work and provides important feedback regarding conduct. If a salesperson violates company policy, it is usually the sales manager who is responsible for administering reprimands. If the moral fibre of a sales force begins to break down, the sales manager must shoulder a great deal of responsibility.

Sales managers influence the ethical behaviour of salespeople by virtue of what they say and what they do. From time to time, managers must review their expectations of ethical behaviour. Salespeople are under continuous pressure to abandon their personal ethical standards to achieve sales goals. Values such as integrity and honesty must receive ongoing support from the sales manager.

The sales manager's behaviour must be consistent with a stated philosophy. Actions do speak louder than words; any inconsistency between words and deeds is likely to have a negative influence on the attitude of the sales staff.

THE SALESPERSON'S PERSONAL VALUES

Ann Kilpatrick, a sales representative in the transportation industry, encountered something unexpected when entertaining a potential client. The client said, "Let's go to Johnny's." She was not familiar with Johnny's, but on arrival discovered it was a raunchy bar. Kilpatrick related that she sat there for five minutes and then said, "This is not what I was expecting. This is a sleazy place. Let's go somewhere else where we can talk." She was not willing to compromise her personal values to win a new account.[23]

values Your deep personal beliefs and preferences that influence your behaviour.

Values represent the ultimate reasons people have for acting as they do. **Values** are your deep personal beliefs and preferences that influence your behaviour. To discover what really motivates you, carefully examine what it is you value.[24] Sidney Simon, noted author in the field of values clarification, has said, "There's no place to hide from your values. Everything you do reflects them." Values serve as a foundation for our attitudes, and our attitudes serve as a foundation for our behaviour (Fig. 16.2). We do not adopt or discard values quickly. In fact, the development of values is a lifelong process. It is not something that is completed by early adulthood. Throughout life we are constantly making decisions, and our value system aids us in this process.

Although we live by a value system, this system is not always clear to us. One outcome of education and training is frequently the clarification of one's values. Life experiences also help people clarify their values.

Values can serve as a deterrent to unethical behaviour in a selling situation. They help to establish our own personal standards concerning what is right and what is wrong. Ron Willingham, author of *Integrity Selling*, says, "A salesperson's ethics and values contribute more to sales success than do techniques or strategies."[25] Some salespeople discover a values conflict between themselves and the employer. If you view your employer's instructions or influence as improper, you have three choices:

Figure 16.3 The relationship of values, attitudes, and behaviour.

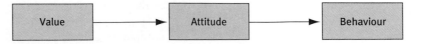

Value → Attitude → Behaviour

1. Ignore the influence of your values, and engage in unethical behaviour. The end result will likely be a loss of self-respect and a feeling of guilt. When salespeople experience conflicts between their actions and values, they also feel a loss of confidence and energy.[26] Positive energy is the result of creating value for the customer. Negative energy is experienced when salespeople fail to honour and embrace their ethical values.

2. Voice strong opposition to the practice that is in conflict with your value system. Take a stand, and state your beliefs. An anonymous author once said, "Following the path of least resistance is what makes men and rivers crooked." Your objective is to influence decisions made by your superiors.

3. Refuse to compromise your values, and be prepared to deal with the consequences. This may mean leaving the job. It may also mean that you will be fired.

Salespeople face ethical problems and decisions every day. In this respect they are no different from the doctor, the lawyer, the teacher, or any other professional. Ideally, they will make decisions on the basis of the values they hold.

Toward a Personal Code of Ethics

Many people considering a career in selling are troubled by the thought that they may be pressured into compromising their personal standards of right and wrong. These fears may be justified. The authors of *The Ethical Edge*, a book that examines organizations that have faced moral crises, contend that business firms have given too little thought to the issue of helping employees to function ethically within organizations.[27] Many salespeople wonder if their own ethical philosophy can survive in the business world. These are some of their questions:

"Will I be forced to abandon my own ethical beliefs?"

"Can good business and good ethics coexist?"

"Is honesty still a valued personal trait in the business community?"

It is becoming more difficult to provide a concise yes or no answer to these questions. Times are changing, and it is getting harder and harder to tell the "good guys" from the "bad guys." We read about the unethical use of gifts and bribes by corporate officials. Investigations of provincial medicare programs turn up overbilling and other unethical behaviours by doctors, pharmacists, and nursing home operators. Reports from colleges and universities indicate that cheating is becoming more common. Even some of our most respected political leaders have been guilty of tax fraud, accepting illegal campaign contributions, and accepting payments for questionable favours. We are tempted to ask, "Is everybody doing it?"

Our society is currently doing a great deal of soul-searching. Many people want to see a firming of ethical standards. Many leaders are keenly aware that unethical behaviour threatens the moral fabric of our free enterprise system. If the business community cannot police itself, more and more people will be looking to government for solutions to the problem. One fact we have learned from history is that we cannot legislate morality.

In the field of athletic competition the participants rely heavily on a written set of rules. The referee or umpire is ever-present to detect rule violations and assess a penalty. In the field of personal selling there is no universal code of ethics. However, some general guidelines can serve as a foundation for a personal code of business ethics.

1. *Personal selling must be viewed as an exchange of value.* Salespeople who maintain a value focus are searching for ways to create value for their prospects or customers. This value may take the form of increased productivity, greater profit, enjoyment, or security. The value focus motivates the salesperson to carefully identify the prospect's wants and needs.[28] Salespeople who accept this ethical guideline view personal selling as something you do for customers, not something you do to customers. The role of the salesperson is to diagnose buyer needs and determine if value can be created. Understanding the prospect's wants and needs should always precede any attempt to sell.[29]

2. *Relationship comes first, task second.* Sharon Drew Morgan, author of *Selling with Integrity*, says you can't sell a product unless there is a level of comfort between you and the prospect. She encourages salespeople to take the time to create a level of comfort, rapport, and collaboration that encourages open communication.[30] Placing task before relationship is based on the belief that the salesperson knows more than the customer. Morgan reminds us that "The buyer has the answers, the seller has the questions.[31] These answers will surface only when the buyer/seller relationship is characterized by rapport and trust.

3. *Be honest with yourself and with others.* To achieve excellence in terms of ethical practices, you have to believe that everything you do counts. Tom Peters, in his book *Thriving on Chaos*, says, "Integrity may be about little things as much as or more than big ones."[32] It's about accuracy in completing your expense account. There is always the temptation to inflate the expense report for personal gain. It's about avoiding the temptation to stretch the truth, to exaggerate, or to withhold information. Paul Ekman, author of *Telling Lies*, says that withholding important information is one of

Salespeople must avoid misleading sales claims. To stretch the truth is not only unethical but also illegal.

the primary ways of lying.[33] A complete and informative sales presentation may include information regarding the product's limitations. If you let your character and integrity be revealed in the little things, others will see you as one who acts ethically in all things. Any violation of honesty, however small, dilutes your ethical strength, leaving you weaker for the big challenges you will face sooner or later.[34]

Every day, salespeople make decisions that have ethical ramifications. In some cases doing the right thing may not be popular with others. Price Pritchette, author of *The Ethics of Excellence*, says:

> When you hold out for high standards, people are impressed—but they don't always like you for it. Not everybody will be on your side in your struggle to do the right thing.[35]

As you make ethical decisions, think long-term, not short-term. A serious ethical violation can be costly in terms of damage to your reputation.

Summary

At the beginning of this chapter we defined *ethics* as the rules that direct your conduct and moral judgments. Ethics help us establish standards of honesty, loyalty, and fairness. We have noted that ethics are not legally constituted guidelines. To consider only what is legally right and wrong limits our perception of morality. Laws alone will not bring a halt to unethical selling practices.

Salespeople can benefit from the stabilizing influence of good role models. Although top management personnel are usually far removed from day-to-day selling activities, they can have a major impact on salespeople's conduct. Dishonesty at the top of an organization causes an erosion of ethical standards at the lower echelons. Sales managers provide another important role model. They interpret company policies and help establish guidelines for acceptable and unacceptable selling practices.

Company policies and practices can have a strong influence on the ethical conduct of salespeople. These policies often help salespeople cope with ethical conflicts.

Finally, salespeople must establish their own standards of personal conduct. They must decide how best to serve their company and build strong partnerships with their customers. The pressure to compromise one's ethical standards surfaces almost daily. The temptation to take the easy road to achieve short-term gains is always present. The primary deterrent is a strong sense of right and wrong. Three general guidelines that can serve as a foundation for a personal code of ethics were presented.

We strongly support the premise, "Bad ethics is bad business and unethical sales practices will ultimately destroy relationships with customers." Anyone who relies on unethical sales practices cannot survive in the selling field very long. These practices undermine the company's reputation and ultimately reduce profits.

Key Terms

Ethics 365
Caveat Emptor 365
Reciprocity 373

Review Questions

1. What is the definition of *ethics*? Why is this topic receiving so much attention today?

2. What does *caveat emptor* mean? What are the two forces that have lessened the impact of this philosophy?

3. A close examination of the history of ethics and ethical behaviour reveals two interesting facts. What are they?

4. What five factors help influence salespeople's ethical conduct?

5. What is the Competition Act? Why is it needed?

6. What are the "cooling-off" laws? How do they protect customers?

7. Explain why the sales manager plays such an important role in influencing the ethical behaviour of salespeople.

8. A company policy on ethics will usually cover six major areas. What are they?

9. Is it ever appropriate to give gifts to customers? Explain.

10. List and describe three guidelines used as a foundation of a self-imposed code of business ethics.

Application Exercises

1. You find that you have significantly overcharged one of your clients. The error was discovered when you received his cheque. It is unlikely that the customer or your company will become aware of the overcharge. Because of this error, the company realized a high net profit on the sale. Your commissions are based on this profit. What, if anything, will you do about the overcharge?

2. Members of the Pharmaceutical Manufacturers Association of Canada have adopted a code of ethics to guide their relationships with their various stakeholders. Examine their code of marketing practices by accessing their Web site and searching under "About PMAC." Pay particular attention to those items that relate to the behaviours of salespeople.

www.pmac-acim.org

3. You work for a supplier of medical equipment. Your sales manager informs you that he wants you to capture a certain hospital account. He also tells you to put on your expense account anything it costs to secure the hospital as a client. When you ask him to be more specific, he tells you to use your own judgment. Up to this time you have never questioned your sales manager's personal code of ethics. Make a list of the items you feel can be legitimately charged to the company on your expense account.

4. For some time your strongest competitor has been making untrue derogatory statements about your product and about you as a salesperson. You

know for a fact that her product is not as good as yours; yet hers has a higher price. Several of your best customers have confronted you with these charges. Describe how you plan to answer them.

CRM Application Exercise

Preparing Mailing Labels with CRM

Load the ACT! software and select Report, Other. From the list of mailing label formats, choose avry5160, and press OK. In the Prepare Report window, pick Active Group and Document and press OK. The mailing information for each contact will be displayed on the screen. Select File, Print and print this list.

A friend of yours is a salesperson with a firm that installs the cables used to connect network components, a service that your company does not offer. Your friend wants to know if you will share the customer list that you just printed. What should be your response?

Case Problem

Dave MacDonald was excited when he got the unexpected phone call from Nicki Steele, a senior buyer from Halco Steel Fabricators, a local company that manufactured many items for the Canadian government. Halco had never been one of Dave's favourite accounts and, in fact, he felt that they never bought from him unless they couldn't get what they wanted elsewhere.

"I know it's been a year since we bought that prototype reel from you, but we just got a contract from the Canadian government to build ten more "bear traps" and we desperately need to hold our price on these units. Could you possibly sell us 10 new reels at the same price you charged last year?" Nicki inquired.

"I'll see what I can do and call you back today," Dave replied.

Dave immediately retrieved the file from the previous year and saw that they had supplied the reel for $6875.00, F.O.B. the customer's warehouse. There was a breakdown of the pricing in the file:

Manufacturer's list price	$6 000.00
Special engineering charge (25%)	1 500.00
Total list price	7 500.00
Distributor discount (20%)	1 500.00
Distributor net cost	6 000.00
Estimated freight per unit	300.00
Estimated distributor cost, F.O.B. destination	6 300.00
Markup (25%)	1 575.00
Selling price, F.O.B. destination	$6 875.00

There were some notes on the file that Dave reviewed. The reel was designed as part of a "bear trap" on Canadian navy ships. These bear traps would hook onto helicopters in rough weather and haul them safely onto landing pads on the ship decks. The reel was really a model SM heavy-duty steel mill reel, except some of the exposed parts were to be made of stainless steel to provide longer life in the salt-water atmosphere. There was a special engineering charge on the reel as it was a non-standard item that had to be specially engineered. The manufacturer had suggested at the time they quoted Dave that he could keep the full 20 percent discount as they thought there was only one other manufacturer capable of building a similar product that would meet the specifications, and their price would likely be much higher.

When Dave got a price from the manufacturer on the 10 new units, he was surprised that they quoted a price of only $4800.00 each, less 30/20 percent. When he asked for the price to be verified, the inside salesperson Dave was talking to clarified the pricing. First, there had been a 20 percent reduction in all SM-series reels. That made the manufacturer's list price only $4800.00. Then, because there was a large quantity, the distributor discount was increased to less 30/20 percent instead of the 20 percent that was given on the original reel. The 30 percent discount was for the large quantity, and the additional 20 percent discount was the regular distributor discount.

As Dave estimated his cost, things got better. He had estimated the freight on the original reel to be $300, but, because he would be shipping 10 reels, the freight cost would be only about $100 per reel. Dave estimated his new cost as follows:

Manufacturer's list price	$4 800.00
Distributor discount (30/20%)	2 112.00
Distributor net cost	2 688.00
Estimated freight	100.00
Estimated distributor cost, F.O.B. destination	$2 788.00

Now that he had all the figures, Dave had to decide how much he should charge Halco for the 10 reels.

Questions

1. What factors should Dave MacDonald consider when deciding on a price for the 10 new reels?
2. What price should Dave MacDonald quote to Halco Steel Fabricators?

Management of the Sales Force

Some sales managers work hard to maintain a competitive spirit among members of their sales force. Marga McNally, vice-president of sales for WRC-TV, takes a different approach. She works hard to build a sense of team effort and shared accomplishment among her 11 salespeople. McNally's management style emphasizes brainstorming and teamwork. She says, "I want salespeople who will be competitive going out the door and collaborative when they come back in the door." McNally wants her salespeople to share winning sales strategies, critique each other, and help work out what is best for the customer. She believes the best way to build a partnership with customers is to discover solutions that are right for the customer and not just right for her TV station. This is accomplished by listening without any preconceived notions. "We take a pad and pencil with us on customer calls rather than a canned presentation. Then we come back and brainstorm together on how to respond."[1]

McNally has adopted a leadership style that is very effective in the age of information. She recognizes that shared participation in problem solving and decision making is the key to individual growth and development. Collaboration also helps members of her sales team discover solutions that

LEARNING OBJECTIVES

When you finish reading this chapter, you should be able to

1. Describe the functions of a sales manager

2. List and discuss the qualities of an effective sales manager

3. Discuss recruitment and selection of salespeople

4. Describe effective orientation, training, and motivation practices

5. Develop an understanding of selected compensation plans

6. List and discuss criteria for evaluating sales performance

result in stronger partnerships with customers. She recognizes that one of the major values that has surfaced throughout the past decade is teamwork over individualism. To be an effective "team facilitator" she knows that coaching is an important part of being a leader.

Sales Management Functions

Salespeople frequently have the opportunity to advance to a management position. The first promotion for many is to the position of sales manager. Those who achieve success at this level may advance to management positions that offer even greater challenge and increased economic rewards.

The **sales manager** typically performs the functions of recruiting, training, organizing, and supervising the sales force. In companies that use team selling the sales manager must possess the knowledge and skills needed to create effective teams.[2] Managing the sales force is an external management function, focused on bringing in orders and revenue from outside the company. However,

sales manager   The person who typically performs the functions of recruiting, training, organizing, and supervising the sales force.

Besides supervising the sales force, sales managers are often involved in establishing sales quotas, developing long- and short-term forecasts, and seeing that goals are achieved.

it also requires coordination and co-operation with almost every internal department including marketing, finance, and distribution.[3]

The sales manager's duties will vary somewhat from one marketing organization to another. Today's sales manager is more likely to function in a virtual office environment. Sales force automation permits salespeople to receive data on their laptops or their home computers. The use of other technology—videoconferencing, teleconferencing, e-mail, and voice mail—reduces the need for frequent face-to-face contact with members of the sales team.[4]

Sales managers maintain a steady flow of information to salespeople and also provide a variety of selling tools and aids. Successful sales managers also help salespeople cope with the rapid change and uncertainty that permeates today's business environment.[5]

Qualities of a Good Sales Manager

Sales managers can have a dramatic influence on the salespeople they supervise. Depending on the leadership qualities adopted, sales managers can have an advantageous, neutral, or even detrimental effect on the performance of sales subordinates.[6]

Effective leadership has been discussed in hundreds of books and articles. A careful review of this material indicates that most successful supervisory-management personnel have certain behaviours in common. Writers of this material agree that there are two important dimensions of effective leadership.[7] We shall label these dimensions *structure* and *consideration*.

STRUCTURE

Sales managers who display **structure** clearly define their own duties and those of the sales staff. They assume an active role in directing their subordinates' work. Policies and procedures are clearly defined, and subordinates know what is expected of them. Salespeople also know how well they are doing because the structured supervisor evaluates their productivity and provides feedback. Members of the sales force usually appreciate the predictable nature of the highly structured sales manager. The following behaviours provide evidence of structure:

structure Sales managers clearly defining their own duties and those of the sales staff. They assume an active role in directing their subordinates.

1. *Planning takes place on a regular basis.* The effective sales manager thinks ahead and decides what to do in the future. Strategic planning is the process of determining the company's current position in the market, determining where you want to be and when, and making decisions on how to secure the position you want.[8] Strategic planning gives meaning and direction to the sales force.

2. *Expectations are clearly communicated.* Expectations of sales managers can have a positive impact on the performance of salespeople. In most cases high expectations lead to high performance.[9]

3. *Decisions are made promptly and firmly.* An effective sales manager is willing and able to make decisions in a timely way. An ineffective manager often postpones important decisions, hoping the problem will go away. Of course most decisions cannot be made until all the facts are available. A good sales manager keeps the lines of communication open and involves subordinates in making the truly important decisions.

An effective sales manager provides regular feedback. All employees want to know where they stand with the manager.

4. *Performance of salespeople is appraised regularly.* All employees want to know "where they stand" with the manager. An effective sales manager provides regular feedback. When a salesperson is not performing up to established standards, the sales manager takes immediate action.

Although structure is an important aspect of sales management, too much structure can sometimes create problems. In an effort to become better organized and more systematized, some sales organizations have developed detailed policies and procedures that rob salespeople of time and energy. Filling out endless reports and forms, for example, can cause unnecessary frustration and may reduce productivity.[10]

CONSIDERATION

consideration Sales managers who display consideration are more likely to have relationships with salespeople that are characterized by mutual trust, respect for the salesperson's ideas, and consideration for their feelings.

A sales manager who displays the dimension of **consideration** is more likely to have relationships with salespeople that are characterized by mutual trust, respect for salespeople's ideas, and consideration for their feelings. A climate of good two-way communication usually exists between the manager and the employee. The following behaviours provide evidence of consideration:

1. *Regular and effective communication receives a high priority.* The effective manager does not rely only on memos, letters, or sales reports for information sharing, but is a good listener who creates an atmosphere of cooperation and understanding through frequent face-to-face meetings. Allan Edwards, a regional manager with Lutheran Life Insurance Society of Canada in Waterloo, Ontario, frequently travels with his salespeople. He says, "We have a saying in our industry that a salesperson's altitude is determined by their attitude. If I can help them maintain a positive attitude, they will be more successful. It's my job to work in partnership with our salespeople, letting them know that I am working for them inside the organization, and I'm interested in helping them when they have concerns or problems."[11]

2. *Each salesperson is treated as an individual.* The sales manager takes a personal interest in each member of the sales force. No one is treated like a "number." The interest is genuine, not artificial. The effective sales manager does not endanger effectiveness by showing favouritism to anyone.

3. *Good performance is rewarded often.* Positive reinforcement is one of the strongest morale-building factors in the work environment. Ken Blanchard, coauthor of *The One Minute Manager*, says, "The key to developing people will always be to concentrate on catching them doing something right instead of blaming them for doing something wrong."[12] Recognition for a job well done is always appreciated.

COACHING FOR PEAK PERFORMANCE

A sales manager who develops a leadership style that combines structure and consideration behaviours possesses the skills needed to be an effective coach. **Coaching** is an interpersonal process between the sales manager and the salesperson in which the manager helps the salesperson improve performance in a specific area. The coaching process has two primary areas of focus: helping the salesperson recognize the need to improve his or her performance and developing the salesperson's commitment to improve performance.[13]

Coaching is often used to correct a specific performance problem such as ineffective prospecting, poorly developed sales presentations, or failure to provide service after the sale. We will outline a four-step coaching strategy.[14] Step one in the coaching process involves documentation of performance problems. In some cases the best approach is to observe and assess performance during actual sales calls. Step two involves getting the salesperson to recognize and agree that there is a need to improve performance in a specific area. Sales managers should never assume the salesperson sees the problem in the same way they do. Step three involves exploring solutions. At this point it's often best to let the salesperson suggest ways to improve performance. Step four involves getting a commitment from the salesperson to take action. This step may involve development of a contract (written or verbal) that clarifies the coaching goals, approaches, and outcomes. A major goal of coaching meetings is to improve performance while enabling sales managers and salespeople to maintain a relationship based on mutual respect and trust.

coaching An interpersonal process between a sales manager and a salesperson in which the manager helps the salesperson improve performance in a specific area.

Recruitment and Selection of Salespeople

Careful recruitment and selection of salespeople is very important. This is one of the most significant tasks sales managers perform. When they hire the wrong person, several problems may arise.

If the new salesperson is not a top producer, the business must absorb the cost of low productivity.

If the new employee is not able to provide good service, regular customers may be lost. Established customers represent one of the firm's most valuable assets.

If the new employee quits after a few months or must be fired, the business will suffer an economic loss. The money invested in salary, benefits, travel expenses, and training can be significant. It can cost anywhere from $10 000

Positive reinforcement is one of the strongest ways to build morale. Effective managers reward their subordinates for good performance.

to $100 000 a year in terms of training, salary and benefits, and lost productivity when the wrong person is hired.[15]

Successful salespeople are often difficult to identify. The selection of sales personnel today is, however, more of a science and less of an art. Sales managers no longer need to rely on "gut feelings." The ability accurately to identify sales aptitude can be acquired. Many progressive sales organizations recognize the need to help sales managers develop the interviewing skills necessary to make profitable hiring decisions. It is impossible to avoid occasionally hiring a poor performer, but sales managers can improve their average by using some established recruitment and selection guidelines.

DETERMINE ACTUAL JOB REQUIREMENTS

To decide what type of applicant is needed, the manager should first outline the duties the person will perform. The sales manager must have a clear picture of the job requirements before beginning the recruitment process.

Some sales managers make every effort to discover the success factors that contribute to the achievements of their high-performance salespeople. Success factors are the skills, knowledge, abilities, and behaviours considered critical for successful performance.[16] This information may be collected through interviews with salespeople or customers, by observing the salesperson during sales calls, or by some other method.

After a careful study of the duties the salesperson will perform and identification of the success factors, a job description should be prepared. A job description is an explanation of what the salesperson will do and under what conditions the work will be performed. It is a good idea to spell out in as much detail as possible the abilities and qualities that the applicant needs to be successful. This can be accomplished by answering a few basic questions about the position.

1. Will the person be developing new sales territory or assuming responsibility for an established territory?
2. Is the product or service well established, or is it new to the marketplace?
3. Will the salesperson work under the sales manager's close supervision or independently?
4. What amount of travel is required? What is the likelihood of eventual transfer? Promotion?

Once the job description is prepared, the foundation has been established to determine the type of person to be hired. There is no substitute for knowing what the job requires.

SEARCH OUT APPLICANTS FROM SEVERAL SOURCES

To identify the best possible person, it is usually best to seek applicants from more than one source. As a rule of thumb, try to interview three or more applicants for each opening. Some suggested sources of new employees follow.

1. *Candidates within the company.* One of the first places to look is within your own company. Is there someone in accounting, engineering, customer service, or some other area who aspires to a sales position? These people have

the advantage of being thoroughly familiar with the company's product offering, policies, and operations, and with what it takes to please the customer.[17]

2. *College and university students.* Many business firms are turning to college and university campuses to recruit salespeople. Placement offices are usually co-operative and often publicize openings.

3. *Trade and newspaper advertisements.* A carefully prepared newspaper advertisement will often attract well-qualified job applicants. A well-written ad should describe the job requirements *and* spell out the opportunities. All information should be accurate. The ad should "sell" the position, but it should not exaggerate its benefits.

4. *Employment agencies and listings.* There are 375 public employment offices located throughout Canada. These offices will recruit applicants and screen them according to your specifications. There is no charge for this service. There are also many private employment agencies. These firms specialize in matching applicants to the job and usually do some initial screening for employers. A fee is assessed for the services these agencies provide.

5. *Internet.* Many companies are using the Internet to recruit for sales positions. Human Resources Development Canada provides an electronic labour exchange service. Job seekers can provide personal profiles and employers can provide job profiles, and it is then possible to "match jobs to people and people to jobs." Industry Canada has also established the National Graduate Register, where recent post-secondary graduates can register in an online database and interested employers can search for candidates with specific job skills.

www.hrdc-drhc.gc.ca

ngr.schoolnet.ca

SELECT THE BEST-QUALIFIED APPLICANT

Once you have identified qualified applicants, the next step is to select the best person. This is becoming more difficult as products become more complex, customers become more sophisticated, and competitors become more aggressive. Selecting the best-qualified applicant will never be easy, but there are some qualifications and characteristics that all sales managers should look for. One of the most important qualities is a high level of interest in and enthusiasm for the job and a high degree of self-motivation. Salespeople have to be self-starters. Barry Farber, president of Farber Training Systems, says that he would hire a salesperson without experience or knowledge of the industry who is willing to give 110 percent versus someone who has experience and is highly skilled but who is not motivated.[18]

Some sales managers use a performance activity to identify the self-motivated person. For example, a potential candidate could be given a product ID and asked to make a presentation to one or more people during a subsequent meeting. The candidate's motivational level is measured by the efforts made to obtain enough information about the product and company to prepare a good presentation. Brian Jeffrey, a sales trainer and consultant, recommends that you not offer an interview to candidates who phone you for a sales position. He says, "Candidates who won't ask for an interview won't ask for an order either." He also suggests that you tell candidates you will get back to them after a few weeks, when you have interviewed other candidates. A "closer" will say, "Wait. You don't need to interview anyone else. I'm the person you need."[19]

Selling in Action

ARE YOU READY FOR THE SALES INTERVIEW?

The personal interview is an important part of the selection process when filling sales positions. When companies use a series of interviews, the first one is often used to eliminate unacceptable candidates – those who lack maturity, lack enthusiasm, or display poor appearance. Subsequent interviews are used to match people to job qualifications. At Hewlett-Packard, candidates may have as many as six interviews with various people. At Smith Kline, a team approach is used so candidates do not learn the "right" answers from one interview to the next.

While interviews will vary from one company or interviewer to another, there are some popular questions and requests that you should be prepared to handle:

- Tell me about yourself.
- Describe the sales process as you understand it.
- What books have you read recently on selling or for personal development?
- What is your greatest weakness? Strength?
- What was the most boring job you ever had, and how did you handle it?
- How do you feel about your present (or previous) employer?
- What was the biggest contribution you made to your last employer?
- Sell me this pen (laptop computer, lamp).
- Why should we hire you?

Some employers will also ask you to complete a test to demonstrate your written communication skills, or your ability to handle "the numbers." These are both important skills for a sales professional.[a]

Reliability is another quality to search for. Do not hesitate to check references to determine police records, problems at previous jobs, or patterns of instability. The applicant for a sales position must be able to earn your complete trust.

One of the greatest challenges is hiring salespeople who can develop a close, trusting, long-term relationship with customers. As we have noted previously, the manner in which salespeople establish, build, and maintain relationships is no longer an incidental aspect of personal selling. Mike Mitchell, vice-president of human resources for Tiffany & Company, says, "We look for people who feel a great sense of purpose in serving our customers. You can train people to be consultative in their approach to the point that they master the mechanics of the sales process, but you can't teach someone to care."[20]

Experts in the field of employment testing say that psychological tests can be helpful as an element of the hiring process. Psychological assessments can provide objective information about a candidate's skills and abilities. One example is the Sales Achievement Predictor developed by Western Psychological Services. This instrument assesses self-confidence, competitiveness, and other qualities deemed important in sales.[21] Test results should always be used *in conjunction with* information obtained from interviewing the candidate and from reference checks.

Orientation and Training

Once you have selected the best-qualified salesperson, two things should be done to ensure that this person becomes a productive member of your staff. First, give the new employee a thorough orientation to your business operation. Provide the orientation *before* the person begins working. This will include a review of your company's history, philosophy of doing business,

Orientation of new salespeople is one of the many duties performed by a sales manager. It's important that salespeople receive this early assistance.

mission statement, business policies, and compensation plan, as well as other important information.

Second, initiate a training program that will help the person achieve success. Sales training that is carefully planned and executed can make a major contribution to the performance of every salesperson. Study results indicate that salespeople have a more positive view about their job situation, greater commitment, and improved performance when their sales managers clarify their job role, how to execute their tasks, and how their needs will be satisfied with successful job performance.[22]

Even salespeople with great potential are handicapped when the company fails to provide adequate training. Keep in mind that, in the absence of formal training, employees will develop their own approaches to performing tasks.

Many sales managers believe that new salespeople (those with no prior sales experience) need special attention during the orientation and training period. One expert said, "They must be managed differently, compensated differently, and they must be gradually converted to the ranks of experienced sales professionals. It is often an eighteen-month process."[23]

The size of the firm should not dictate the scope of the training program. Even the smallest marketing organization should have a formal sales training program. This program should have three dimensions:

1. knowledge of the product line, company marketing strategies, territory information, and related areas;

2. attitude toward the company, the company's products and services, and the customers to be served; and

3. skill in applying personal selling principles and practices—the "doing" part of the sales training program.

An important part of the sales training program is foundation-level instruction. This aspect of sales training focuses on the *basics*. If salespeople are to plan

Building Quality Partnerships

WINNING THROUGH TEAMWORK

There is no shortage of motivational speakers who can fire up your sales force. One of the most popular speakers these days is Pat Riley, the successful coach who guided the Los Angeles Lakers to four National Basketball Association championships and later coached the New York Knicks. Hundreds of Fortune 500 companies have paid $25 000 (U.S.) to have him inspire their sales and marketing personnel. He likes to discuss with audiences the ideas presented in his book entitled *The Winner Within: A Life Plan for Team Players*. Drawing on his experience on the basketball court, Riley talks about the universal importance of co-operation and teamwork. The sales manager who wants to get the best performance from a sales force must understand one important principle of human behaviour:

> It all has to start with trust. A good manager is tough, compassionate, and deals with the truth each day. People working for that kind of leader will recognize those qualities and allow themselves to be infiltrated with a team concept.

Riley tells his audiences that success does not happen without dedication, goals, and ability to work together. He also believes that all salespeople should be rewarded for their effort. Riley encourages sales managers to develop effective competition plans.[b]

and execute a sales call successfully, they must first master certain fundamental selling skills—the skills that form the foundation for everything salespeople do in their careers. The steps that make up the Six-Step Presentation Plan (approach, presentation, demonstration, negotiation, close, and servicing the sale) represent fundamental selling skills (see Fig. 14.1).

Sales Force Motivation

It is helpful to note the difference between internal and external motivation. An **internal motivation** is an intrinsic reward that occurs when a duty or task is performed. If a salesperson enjoys calling on customers and solving their problems, this activity is in itself rewarding, and the salesperson is likely to be self-motivated.[24] Internal motivation is likely to be triggered when sales positions provide an opportunity for achievement and individual growth. **External motivation** is an action taken by another person involving rewards or other forms of reinforcement that cause the worker to behave in ways to ensure receipt of the award.[25] A cash bonus given to salespeople who achieve a sales goal provides an example of external motivation. Experts on motivation agree that organizations should attempt to provide a mix of external rewards and internal satisfaction.

internal motivation An intrinsic reward that occurs when a duty or task is performed.

external motivation Action (taken by another person) that involves rewards or other forms of reinforcement that cause the worker to behave in ways to ensure receipt of the reward.

A basic contention among too many sales managers has been that sales productivity can be improved by staging more elaborate sales contests, giving more expensive recognition awards, or picking truly exotic meeting locations. This point of view ignores the merits of internal motivation. One of the foremost critics of external rewards is Alfie Kohn, author of *No Contest: The Case against Competition* and *Punished by Rewards: The Trouble with Gold Stars, Incentive Plans, A's and Other Bribes*. Kohn states that a reward system that forces people to compete for awards or recognition may undermine co-operation and teamwork. In addition, he says that reward plans often create a situation where some salespeople are winners and some are losers. Kohn further declares, "For each person who wins, there are many others who carry with them the feeling of having lost."[26]

Experts on motivation agree that organizations should provide salespeople with a mix of external rewards and internal satisfaction. Home Depot gift cards are redeemable across Canada and allow salespeople a choice of which products they wish to receive as external rewards.

In many cases, intrinsic motivators (achievement, challenge, responsibility, advancement, growth, enjoyment of work itself, and involvement) have a longer-term effect on employee attitudes than extrinsic motivators (contests, prizes, quotas, and money). A salesperson who is intrinsically satisfied in the job will work willingly at high-performance levels.

Although criticisms of external rewards have a great deal of merit, the fact remains that large numbers of organizations continue to achieve positive results with carefully developed incentive programs. It is possible to design programs that will have long-range benefits for both the organization and the individual employee. Kirby Bonds, a regional sales manager for Avis Rent-A-Car's corporate sales division, has used sales contests to identify new accounts, build business within existing accounts, and generate endorsement letters from satisfied customers. Bonds keeps contest time frames short so that more of his salespeople have an opportunity to win.[27]

Because people bring different interests, drives, and values to the workplace, they react differently to attempts at motivation. When possible, motivation strategies should reflect the needs of the sales force. If a salesperson is not making very much money, then a cash incentive may be an effective reward. An experienced salesperson who is earning a lot of money in salary and commission might be motivated by an exciting travel or merchandise incentive. "The point of an incentive is to reward the salesperson for their work but also to make them connect the award with the company, to create some kind of bond," says Keith Robinson, vice-president of sales at Symantec Corporation. He is an avid travel incentive user because he believes winners remember trips and the enjoyment they experienced long after they return.[28]

Some sales managers are discovering that simply asking salespeople for their opinions and then following up on their suggestions, where appropriate, are excellent ways to motivate them. Effective communication is one of the most important qualities that salespeople desire from their sales manager.[29]

Many sales managers have discovered the value of communicating positive expectations to their salespeople. They recognize that most people can be greatly influenced by the expectations of others. Goethe gave some good advice that sales managers can use when he said, "If you treat a man as he is, he will remain as he is; if you treat him as if he were what he could be, he will become what he could be." With the aid of effective supervision practices and job enrichment, it is possible to release the motivation within each salesperson.

Compensation Plans

compensation plans   Pay plans for salespeople that combine direct monetary pay and indirect monetary payments such as paid vacations, pensions, and insurance plans.

Compensation plans for salespeople combine direct monetary payments (salary and commissions) and indirect monetary payments (such as paid vacations, pensions, and insurance plans). Compensation practices vary greatly throughout the field of selling. Furthermore, sales managers are constantly searching for the "perfect" sales force compensation plan. Of course, the perfect plan does not exist. Each plan must be chosen to suit the specific type of selling job, the objectives of the firm's marketing program, and the type of customer served.

Building Relationships through Technology

STAYING INFORMED

A key role of the sales manager is to provide a steady flow of information and advice to salespeople. Salespeople look to their managers for information about market trends, products, company policies, and assistance with their accounts. CRM software improves and enhances the flow of information between managers and the sales force. The same features that are used to enrich communications with customers also support the sales organization's internal communications. With direct access to a shared CRM database, for example, a sales manager can review relationships with accounts in "real time" by examining a salesperson's notes at any time. This makes it possible for the manager to enter advice about an account directly into that account's record. (See the exercise Receiving Advice through CRM on page 401 for more information.)

Recognition for success in sales can be an effective form of external motivation.

We are beginning to see some trends in the area of sales force compensation. A growing number of companies are linking sales pay to customer satisfaction. The consulting firm Hewitt Associates says that 27 percent of companies use some measure of customer service in their sales-incentive programs.[30] Many companies are following the lead of DuPont, Digital Equipment, Data General, and Tandem Computers in developing teams made up of sales representatives, engineers, and technicians. In response to this trend we are seeing the use of team compensation plans.[31] Needless to say, selecting a fair method of compensation for team members is a dilemma for many companies. Team development and outcomes may suffer if equitable compensation plans are not developed.[32]

In the field of selling there are five basic compensation plans. Here is a description of each:

Straight commission plan. The only direct monetary compensation comes from sales. No sales, no income. Salespeople under this plan are very conscious of their sales. Lack of job security can be a strong inducement to produce results. However, these people may also concentrate more on immediate sales than on long-term customer development.

Commission plan with a draw provision or guaranteed salary. This plan has about the same impact on salespeople as the straight commission plan. However, it gives them more financial security.

Commission with a draw or guaranteed salary plus a bonus. This plan offers more direct financial security than the first two plans. Therefore salespeople may adhere more to the company's objectives. The bonus may be based on sales or profits.

Fixed salary plus bonus. Salespeople functioning under this compensation plan tend to be more company centred and to have a fairly high degree of financial security if their salary is competitive. The bonus incentive helps motivate people under this plan.

Straight salary. Salespeople who work under this compensation plan are usually more company centred and have financial security.

According to *Dartnell's 29th Sales Force Compensation Survey 1996–1997*, more than 75 percent of the companies participating in the survey used some form of compensation plan that combined base salary and incentive.[33] The salary plus bonus and salary plus commission plans are both quite popular.

As might be expected, many companies are experimenting with some variation of these basic plans. In some situations, salespeople are rewarded for achieving a specific objective such as developing new accounts or improving the quality of customer service. Awards in the form of cash or points that can be used to "purchase" prizes can be used. Award programs can be styled to suit a variety of sales objectives:

Specific product movement. Bonus points can be given for the sale of certain items during specified "push" selling periods.

Percentage sales increase. Sales levels can be established with points that are given only when those levels are reached.

Establish new accounts. A block of points can be awarded for opening a new account or introducing new products through the existing outlets.

Increase sales activity. For each salesperson, points can be awarded based on the number of calls.[34]

There is no easy way to develop an effective compensation plan. There are, however, some important guidelines for your efforts to develop a good plan. First, be sure that your sales and marketing objectives are defined in detail. The plan should complement these goals. If sales and marketing objectives are in conflict with the compensation plan, problems will surely arise.

Second, the compensation plan should be field tested before full implementation. Several questions should be answered: Will the new plan be easy to administer? How does the proposed plan differ in terms of payout compared with the existing plan?

Third, explain the compensation plan carefully to the sales force. Misunderstanding may generate distrust of the plan. Keep in mind that some salespeople may see change as a threat.

Fourth, change the compensation plan when conditions in the marketplace warrant change. One reason for the poor showing of many plans is that firms fail to revise their plan as the business grows and market conditions change.[35]

Review the compensation plan at least annually to ensure that it's aligned with conditions in the market place and the company's overall marketing strategy.

Assessing Sales Force Productivity

As the cost of maintaining a sales force increases, sales managers must give more attention to measuring productivity. The goal is to analyze the profitability of each salesperson's sales volume. This task is complicated because sales territories, customers, and business conditions vary.

The problem of measuring sales force productivity is more complicated than it might appear at first glance. In most cases sales volume alone will not tell you how much profit or loss you are making on the sales of each member of the sales

Cognos Business Intelligence helps sales managers quickly assess their salespeople's profitability performance.

force. A small manufacturer was losing money until he analyzed the profitability of sales generated by each person. He found that one salesperson created a loss on almost every order. This salesperson was concentrating on a market that had become so competitive that she had to reduce the markup to make sales.

Some sales managers view the frequency of calls as an indicator of success. This information is only helpful when compared with the profit earned on each account. The number of calls made on an account should bear some relationship to the sales and profit potential of that account. In some cases it is possible to maintain small accounts without frequent personal calls.

To compare a salesperson's current productivity with the past can also be misleading. Changes in products, prices, competition, and assignments make comparisons with the past unfair—sometimes to the salesperson, sometimes to the company. It is better to measure cumulative quarterly, semiannual, or annual results in relation to established goals.

Some sales managers use performance evaluation criteria that communicate to the sales force which elements of their jobs are most important and how they are doing in each area. Evaluating salespeople involves defining the bases on which they will be evaluated, developing performance standards to determine the acceptable level of performance desired on each base, monitoring actual performance, and giving salespeople feedback on their performance.[36] Some of the most common criteria for assessing the productivity of salespeople are as follows:

Quantitative Criteria

Sales volume in dollars

Sales volume compared with previous year's sales

Sales volume by product or product line

Number of new accounts opened

Amount of new account sales

Net profit dollars

Number of customer calls

Qualitative Criteria

Attitude

Product knowledge

Communication skills

Personal appearance

Customer goodwill generated

Selling skills

Initiative

In most cases it is best to emphasize assessment criteria that can be expressed in numbers (quantitative). The preceding quantitative items are especially significant when accompanied by target dates. For example, you might assess the number of new accounts opened during a six-month period. Of course a sales manager should not ignore the other criteria listed here. The other items can affect a salesperson's productivity, and you do have to make judgments in these areas.

Some sales managers ask their salespeople to complete a self-evaluation as part of the overall evaluation process. Many salespeople feel that self-evaluation contributes to their personal development.[37]

Summary

Many capable salespeople have advanced to the position of sales manager. This job involves such diverse duties as recruiting, selecting, training, and supervising salespeople. Some sales managers are concerned solely with the management of salespeople; others have responsibility for additional marketing functions such as advertising and market research.

The sales manager is part of the management team and therefore must be concerned with leadership. An effective sales manager is an effective leader. Although the qualities of effective leaders are subject to debate, most research tells us that such people display two dimensions: structure and consideration. Sales managers who develop a leadership style that combines structure and consideration possess the skills needed to be an effective coach.

Many sales managers are involved directly or indirectly in recruiting and selecting salespeople. This is an important responsibility, because mistakes can be costly. A portion of the company's profit picture and the firm's image will be influenced positively or negatively by each member of the sales force.

Training and motivating salespeople are almost daily concerns of the sales manager. Training should always be viewed as an investment in human resources. Training helps members of the sales force reach their fullest potential.

We discussed the difference between internal and external motivation. In many cases intrinsic motivators (achievement, challenge, responsibility, involvement, and enjoyment of work itself) have a longer-term effect on employee attitudes than extrinsic motivators (contests, prizes, and money). Sales managers need to discover the individual differences between salespeople in order to select the most effective motivation strategies.

The most common compensation plans were discussed. Compensation plans should be field tested before full implementation.

Assessing sales force productivity is a major responsibility of the sales manager. Sales managers use both quantitative and qualitative criteria.

Key Terms

Sales Manager 384	*Internal Motivation 392*
Structure 385	*External Motivation 392*
Consideration 386	*Compensation Plans 394*
Coaching 387	

Review Questions

1. What is the sales manager's primary responsibility?

2. Are all sales managers' duties the same? Explain.

3. What are the two main leadership qualities displayed by most successful sales managers? Define and explain each of these qualities.

4. List and describe the four basic steps involved in coaching.

5. What is a job description? Explain the importance of job descriptions in selecting salespeople.

6. What are four sources for recruiting new salespeople?

7. What should sales managers look for in selecting new salespeople? Describe at least three important qualities.

8. What are some common criticisms of external rewards?

9. List and describe the five basic compensation plans for salespeople.

10. What are the *best* criteria for measuring a salesperson's performance? List additional criteria that should be considered in evaluating individual performance.

Application Exercises

1. Assume that you are a manager of a wholesale electrical supply business. Sales have increased to a level where you need to hire another salesperson. What sources will you use in recruiting a good professional salesperson? What criteria will you use in selecting the person you hire?

2. Carefully analyze the following types of selling position:

   a. a territory selling position for a national manufacturer that requires the salesperson to provide customer service to a large number of accounts plus open up several new accounts each month
   b. a retail sales position in the cosmetics department of a department store
   c. an automobile salesperson who sells and leases new and used cars
   d. a real estate salesperson who sells residential real estate

   Assuming that each of the preceding positions is full time, identify the type of compensation plan you think is best for each. Supply an explanation for each of your answers.

3. Schedule an appointment with two sales managers. Interview each of them, using the following questions as a guide:

   a. What are your functions as a sales manager?
   b. How do the functions of a sales manager differ from those of a salesperson?
   c. What criteria do you use in selecting salespeople?
   d. What kinds of training program do you have for new salespeople?
   e. What method of compensation do you use for your salespeople?
   f. How do you evaluate the performance of your salespeople?
   g. What personal qualities are important for becoming a sales manager?

   Write the answers to these questions. Summarize the similarities and differences of the sales managers' responses.

4. The Internet lists many sources of training in the field of sales management. Using your search engine, type in "sales management." How many hits did you come up with? Examine one or more of the training programs and list the topics that are covered. Compare this list of topics with the material presented in this chapter.

CRM Application Exercise

Receiving Advice through CRM

Becky Kemley, your sales manager at SimNet Systems, regularly reviews your progress with accounts by examining your notes. She recently entered into one of your records a note about an account's debt problems. Find her note and the two accounts she refers to by selecting Lookup, Keyword, type "debt," check Notes, and press Enter. Print the information contained in these records by selecting Report, Contact Report, Active Lookup, Printer, and Enter.

Case Problem

Hal Maybee, the Atlantic Region Sales Manager for Power & Motion Industrial Supply, Inc., was asked to make a presentation to the selling class at a local college. He told the class that his position required a lot of planning and administrative skills, and he was often called on to solve problems concerning the sales force. At the conclusion of his presentation, the course instructor asked if Hal could describe some of the more recent problems he had to solve. After a brief consideration, Hal related the following five examples:

1. About a year ago, Hal implemented a monthly contest that he thought would be fun and that would motivate the sales force. When the 10-member sales force held its monthly sales meeting, the team members would all go to a restaurant near the office for a "Steak and Beans" night. The top three salespeople got a steak dinner, and the rest of them got a plate of beans. The first few months, everyone got a laugh and seemed to enjoy it. Unfortunately, after the first few months, sales did not increase, and Jane Thompson, one of the newest salespeople, came to complain. "There really isn't much point in my trying to win," she said. "The same people win every month. As a new salesperson, it will be a long time before I can develop my territory as well as some of the senior salespeople." What should Hal do?

2. Scotia Electric had been a valued customer for more than 20 years. Hal recently assigned Sean Miske as the account manager and thought things were going well. At least, Sean reported that they were. One evening just before Hal left the office, he received a call from Larry Jordan, the purchasing manager at Scotia Electric. "I want a new salesperson. We have been a good customer of yours for a long time, but if you cannot give me another salesperson, I'm afraid I'll have to place my business elsewhere." When Hal asked him what specifically was the problem, Larry added, "Well, first, he doesn't understand our business. He is never prepared when he comes here. He talks too much and wastes everyone's time. He keeps trying to get me to go golfing with him, and I don't want to. I just want good products at good prices. I want a better salesperson." What should Hal do?

3. Hal hired Andrea Paiva, a recent college graduate, and assigned her to a territory that included Coastal Structural, one of Power & Motion's three largest accounts in the Atlantic provinces. Shortly after her first visit to the account, Andrea came to Hal to complain about one of the senior buyers.

During the visit, the buyer asked Andrea if she would like to have a tour of the plant. As they were returning to his office, while crossing a secluded area between two buildings, he placed his hands on Andrea's buttocks. According to Andrea, "I told him in no uncertain terms that his behaviour was inappropriate, and I did not appreciate it at all. It surprised him, I think, and before he had a chance to respond, I left. I stopped for a coffee before returning here, but I'm still upset." What should Hal do?

4. Robert Mendes had been the top salesperson in the Atlantic region for more than five years. He asked one day to have lunch with Hal, and during table conversation he turned quite serious. "Rumour has it that you are likely to be the next vice-president when Jim retires later this year. I just want you to know that I expect to replace you if that happens. I've been here for almost ten years now, and I know my sales are among the best in the country. I have been dedicated to this company and I know I have a lot to offer, but I can't stay around forever as simply a salesperson. I want your job and if I don't get it, I'll have to leave." Robert is correct that he is the top salesperson, and one of the best nationally. Hal was surprised by Robert's approach, and he does not believe that Robert is ready for a sales management position. As well, Hal had not been given any indication that he would be the next vice-president, although he did think it was certainly possible. What should Hal do?

5. Power & Motion had recently established a Web site, and customers were placing orders directly via the Internet. While the customers seemed pleased, the sales force was quite upset. Salespeople got commissions on sales to regular customers who ordered via the Internet, but Jim Fanning, the vice-president of marketing, decided that they would not get commissions on sales to new customers who ordered this way. Fanning's position was that sales via the Internet belonged to a "house account." When Hal approached him on behalf of his sales force, Jim advised, "If they didn't do any work for the sale, there is no reason they should get credit for the sale." What should Hal do?

Finding Employment: A Personalized Marketing Plan for the Age of Information

The principles of strategic/consultative selling can be used to prepare a personalized marketing plan to secure a high-paying, professional career position. In Chapter 1 we identify the marketing concept. This concept states that a good marketing program begins with research. After finding out the "what, where, when, why, and how much" during research, the marketing mix is developed (Fig. A.1). In designing a marketing mix, the elements of product, distribution, promotion, and price are coordinated to satisfy the job seeker's needs uncovered during the research phase. The following material describes the steps that should be followed to develop a personal marketing plan for securing a job.

Research Phase

During the research step of the personal marketing plan, the emphasis is on information gathering: (1) what type of career the individual is seeking, (2) what the market (in which that position exists) is looking for in applicants, and (3) what the market is willing to pay (Fig. A.2). This information is the starting point for the development of the rest of the personal marketing plan. Securing this basic information is fundamental to the personal marketing plan. Job seeking without this important first

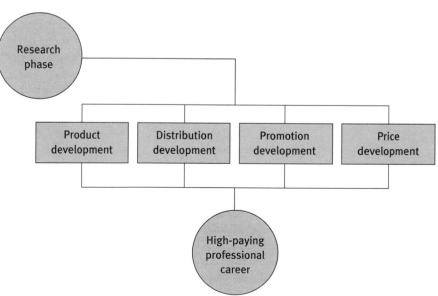

Figure A.1   The employment marketing mix

Figure A.2 Research conducted before designing a job marketing mix

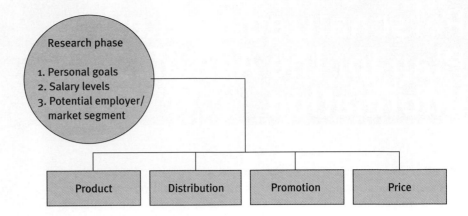

step is a waste of time. Many job seekers do not start with this first step and consequently fail to find a rewarding career position.

Deciding what you want to achieve in your career begins with a great deal of reflection on who you are and what you want to accomplish. Your future productivity and fulfillment will depend on finding employment that matches your personal beliefs and preferences. How important is it for you to earn a great deal of money early in your career? Do you want to work for a company that maintains high ethical standards? How important is it to achieve balance between time spent at work and leisure time? Do you find travel to be an energizing experience? Finding answers to these and other questions will help you set goals that are aligned with your values. The development of intermediate goals (one to two years) and long-range goals (three to five years) is an important part of your personal marketing plan.

Realistic salary goals should also be researched and established for each of these time segments (Fig. A.3). This information is extremely important because most interviewers will ask about goals during the interview.

The next step in the research process is to determine in which industries (market segments) the career opportunities exist that complement the goals you have set. This is called market segmentation. A preliminary list of 20 or more companies should be prepared. Later this list will be turned into a prospect list.

The final part of the research process is to determine what qualities the particular market segment wants in the people it selects for employees. In determining the hiring motives (see Chapter 7 on buying motives), does the market look for quantitative backgrounds, such as a minimum number of years of education or a minimum number of years of experience? Does it look for qualitative background, such as a positive attitude (see Chapter 3), a professional image

Figure A.3 Setting position and salary goals

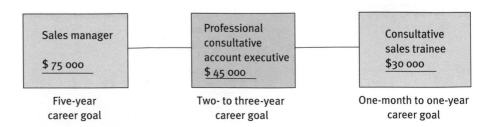

(see Chapter 3), or a certain communication skill? During this stage it is important to find out which of these qualities or combination of qualities the potential employer (market segment) is looking for, because the design of the marketing mix will be based on these findings.

Product Development

After the research phase of the personal marketing plan is complete, the next step is the development of the marketing mix. This begins with a product development program—documenting the proper amount and kind of education and job experience, fostering an appropriate appearance (packaging) and attitude, and work ethic (Fig. A.4).

It is important to take each of these areas of development and convert it into a benefit that will help the prospective employer or market segment achieve its objectives. For example, being elected an officer of a social or professional organization often means that the individual has a high energy level, tends to get along well with people, and is respected by peers (benefits). These are all important benefits that will help a prospective employer meet quotas and profit objectives (see Chapter 6).

Distribution Development

The next phase of the personal marketing mix consists of developing a sophisticated prospect base (see Chapter 8). The prospect base is made up of potential employers who offer career positions corresponding to the career goals set in the research phase. This prospect list should include the company name, address, telephone number, names and titles of individuals to be contacted concerning employment, and other background information on the company (Fig. A.5). The number of prospects will depend on the desired size of the market to be contacted. Job seekers using direct mail marketing plans may contact up to 200 prospects, while telephone and direct-contact personal marketing plans may begin with about 20 potential employers.

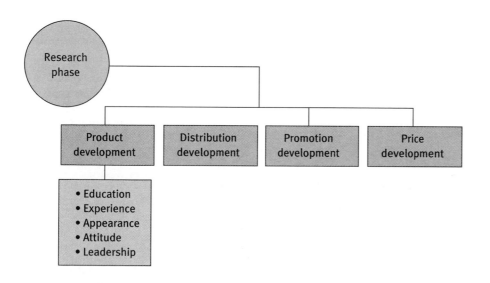

Figure A.4 Product development activities associated with finding employment

Figure A.5 Distribution development through using a prospect list

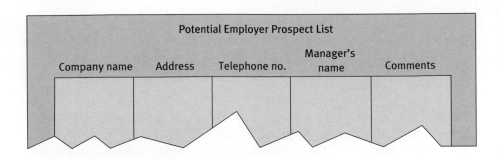

SOURCE OF POTENTIAL EMPLOYERS

The easiest source of potential employers to add to the prospect list is probably the classified section of the newspaper; however, "seldom does anything good come easy," and the newspaper is generally not the best source of prospective employers. In many cases either the best positions advertised in the newspaper are informally filled before they are advertised or the competition for them is extremely keen. It is not uncommon for a company to receive 100 to 150 résumés for jobs offering competitive salaries. In other cases, companies mass merchandise jobs that are unattractive and difficult to fill. While newspapers should not be overlooked in developing a prospect list, it is wise to use them with caution. Research findings indicate that fewer than a third of job seekers relied on classified advertising. Most job seekers contacted the prospective employer directly.

The Internet is an excellent place to start your search for job openings. More than half of companies use the Internet for job postings. Consider starting your job search with a visit to the following Web sites.

ngr.schoolnet.ca This site is the result of an alliance between CACEE (Canadian Association of Career Educators and Employers) and Industry Canada. More than 40 000 employers and 85 000 job seekers are registered in its database. Job seekers can search through more than 2000 employment opportunities each month.

www.ele-spe.org The Electronic Labour Exchange (ELE) is a free electronic service provided by Human Resources Development Canada (HRDC) that matches employers' needs to job seekers' skills, education, and experience.

jb-ge.hrdc-drhc.gc.ca Job seekers can search HRDC Job Bank for job opportunities across Canada.

www.workopolis.com This site has career postings from the *The Globe and Mail* and *The Toronto Star.* It advertises itself as "Canada's biggest job site," and boasts more than 15 000 job postings.

www.monster.ca This is another popular Canadian job search site that offers a career resource centre and links to many other interesting sites for job seekers.

In addition to these sites, many trade organizations and companies have their own online list of job openings.

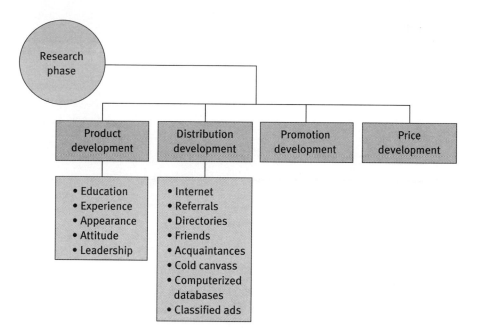

Figure A.6 Sources for developing a prospective employer list

To build a good list of prospective employers, use the Internet, directories, referrals, friends, acquaintances, classified ads, and cold calls (Fig. A.6). Most jobs will be found by visiting job fairs, talking to recruiters, networking with friends and acquaintances, and knocking on doors. (See Chapter 8 for information on these methods.)

Do not include in your list only companies with existing job vacancies. Research shows that companies frequently have openings that are not actively being recruited. Turnover also creates openings, and many firms go back into applicant files to fill these openings. In addition, many companies will create openings, especially for trainees, when a well-qualified person applies for a career-oriented position.

Promotion Development

Developing the promotional element of the personal marketing program consists of creating an effective résumé (advertisement), writing good application and thank-you letters (sales promotion), and conducting convincing job interviews (sales presentation) (Fig. A.7). The rules for developing each of these promotional concepts is much different at the professional career level than at the part-time and entry levels. They also tend to be different for acquiring a position in the private business sector than in public employment. The following promotional principles relate mainly to the professional career level in private business, although many also apply to securing entry level, part-time, or public employment positions.

Creating a good résumé should be thought of as creating an advertisement (Fig. A.8). It should be a professional, business-oriented selling aid that stands out even though it is part of a pile of 20 or more résumés. It should attract attention and interest, as a good advertisement does when a reader is looking through a magazine and stops to study one of the ads. The résumé should be long enough

FIGURE A.7 Promotional
elements used to market yourself

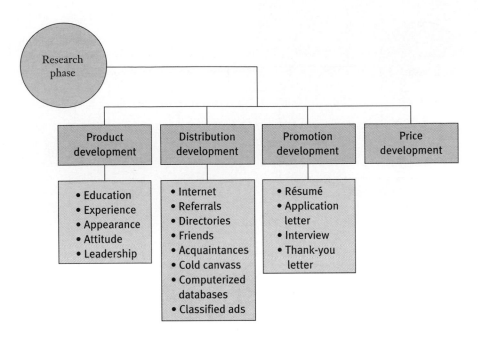

www.canadajob.com
canada.careermosaic.com

(one to two pages, depending on depth of background) and wellwritten, supplying benefits so that it gets the prospective interviewer to desire and take action to set up a personal interview. Microsoft Word software provides several résumé wizards to use when developing your résumé. You will want to consider posting your résumé online. As well as registering with the electronic services already discussed in this appendix, you can register your résumé free online. Many firms request résumés via e-mail. The letter of application and thank-you letter should also take the interviewer through the mental steps in the buying process—attention, interest, desire, conviction, and action (see Chapter 7).

THE INTERVIEW

The interview should be viewed as a strategic/consultative sales presentation (see Chapters 9 to 14). The applicant should be well prepared with preapproach information such as determination of goals, answers to challenging questions (negotiating objections), clear understanding of personal qualities and benefits, and knowledge of the interviewer and the company. When meeting the interviewer, a good first impression (good social contact) must be made. Transition from social contact to need discovery (finding out precisely what the company is looking for in an applicant) should be preplanned with well-chosen questions. Effective listening will result in productive two-way communication that maintains positive impressions. Effective listening also helps determine which parts of the interviewee's background (benefits) should be stressed. If for some reason the interviewer has not seen the résumé, the interviewee should offer it at this point to review the selling points made so far. Closing questions should be preplanned by the interviewee. These might include questions such as "When do you plan to fill this position?" or "May I call you back on Friday?" Courtesy closing statements such as "Thank you very much for an informative interview" or "I appreciate the time you spent with me, and I enjoyed our visit very much" should be preplanned. It is important to follow up the interview with a thank-you letter. This letter can be sent via e-mail or through normal mail delivery.

Figure A.8   An effective sales résumé

JANET NOREEN PURVIS

Current Address
16 Parliament Street
St. John's, NF
A1A 2Y8
(709) 739-4372

Permanent Address
13th Street
Trenton, NS
B0K 1X0
(902) 755-5992

Objectives: To secure a growth-oriented sales position in service or manufacturing industries.

Primary Skills: Have acquired background skills in selling, buying computers, and management at Drake through classroom work and on the job training

Possess progressive work experience in retail, from a small specialty store to a large department store

Have the ability to understand and apply creative design concepts through my previous classroom experience

Have the ability to work effectively and harmoniously with a wide range of people

Have the ability to rapidly learn new techniques and concepts

Summary: College graduate with a degree in marketing; enjoy working with people; willing to work hard to achieve success in chosen career

WORK EXPERIENCE

1999–Present Classy Lady, St. John's, NF

Started in a retail management trainee position; duties and responsibilities include Professional Selling, Visual Merchandising, Buying and Inventory; exposure to a broad variety of management and supervisory philosophies

1999 Lisa's Lingerie Boutique, St. John's, NF

Started as a fashion consultant for a small women's specialty store; learned basic store procedures, selling and display techniques; worked part-time during the summer while attending college

1999 Day-By-Day Services, St. John's, NF

Temporary office service, which consisted of working as a librarian for an accounting firm; also as a receptionist for a law firm; worked during the summer while attending evening classes

1997–98 Centennial Park, Trenton, NS

Park Counsellor; taught safety to young children, instructed crafts, and coached a girls' softball team; also worked as a receptionist at the main office

1996 Henry's Grandson's Place, New Glasgow, NS

Hostess at a restaurant; seated customers, cleaned tables, and ran the register; worked during the summer

EDUCATION

Memorial University of Newfoundland

Graduated with a B.Comm. with an emphasis in Marketing; major areas of study include Professional Selling and Sales Management, Advertising and Marketing Communications, Marketing Research, Business Marketing, Strategic Marketing, and Consumer Behaviour; cumulative average 81.6 ("A"). Completed one term of international study at Robert Gordon University, Aberdeen, Scotland, through student exchange program.

ORGANIZATIONS, ACTIVITIES, and INTERESTS

College: President, Marketing Society
Social Committee Member, Business Students' Association
Co-Chair, Business Day
Host, Exchange Student Program
Golf, Swimming, Tennis

Honours and Awards: Faculty of Business Administration Scholarship $3000
International Business Studies Scholarship $1000
Dean's list, last four terms

Price Development

Price development involves salary negotiations. Adequate pre-interviewing preparation is important for effective salary negotiations (Fig. A.9). The following guidelines should be followed during salary negotiations:

1. Determine the amount of money you will want to make during the first year of employment. Convert this to a range with a difference of $3000 to $5000 (*example:* $25 000 to $30 000).

2. Try to find out what salary range the position pays before the interview. As noted previously, the Internet can be your link to a large number of salary surveys.

3. Plan to state that, while starting salary is important, it is more important to know what can be made during the first year, given an excellent review.

4. As a general rule, if possible, postpone salary discussions until a job offer is made. This maintains a better bargaining position.

5. Position yourself in a strong bargaining position with a good personal marketing program.

   a. Have goals well thought out and be able to articulate them clearly.

   b. Have outstanding references.

Figure A.9   The complete marketing program used to find a high-paying professional career

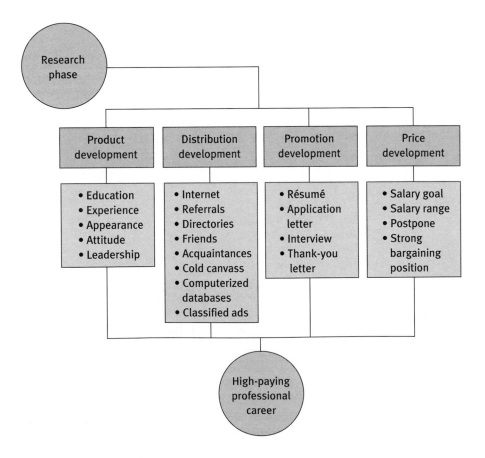

c. Have outstanding written materials that show achievement and accomplishment.

d. Possess good knowledge of the industry, company, product, personnel, and salary ranges.

e. Be currently employed with no sense of urgency to leave.

f. Sell credentials first and discuss salary second.

g. Indicate your knowledge of how to get a job.

h. Become effective in face-to-face selling situations.

Summary

From the employer's viewpoint the decision to accept the personal marketing plan of a career-oriented job seeker is a major one. An employee who stays with a company five to seven years (a statistical average) will be paid $200 000 to $280 000 in salary (five to seven years times an average annual salary of $40 000). The $200 000 to $280 000 salary plus the cost of benefits is the price the employer is paying for the marketing plan. When you make an analogy between the price of a human resource and the purchase of a piece of equipment, it becomes apparent that this is a large purchase. Therefore a company is going to examine all dimensions of the purchase carefully.

A job seeker with knowledge of the hiring and employment process realizes the dollar value of the purchase an employer is making and designs a professional personal marketing plan with this in mind. The personal marketing plan emphasizes a high quality professional approach to identifying the right product, positioning it in the right places with the right quality and quantity of promotion, and determining the right price.

Software Installation for Sales Automation Applications

A Special Note to the Student

RE: USE OF CUSTOMER RELATIONSHIP MANAGEMENT (CRM) SOFTWARE (ACT!)

Selling Today now offers you a unique opportunity to learn the reason modern software is helping to redefine sales and marketing.

You can download and use a scaled-down version of the popular ACT! software, which more than 3 million salespeople use to build relationships with their customers. The software is easy to use and includes information about more than 20 customers. You can experience first-hand how salespeople today gain the sales advantage with this new category of software.

Beginning in Chapter 1, you will find simple, easy-to-follow instructions on using this software to store and access a wide variety of business and personal information about your customers. You will discover the convenience of using this software to stay in touch with people.

The ACT! software includes important customer information that you will use in your CRM case study assignments for chapters 8-15. You will access the information in your ACT database to approach, present, demonstrate, negotiate, close and service more than $1.2 million dollars worth of sales volume.

Effectively using information technology, especially CRM, will give you a career advantage in today's highly-competitive workplace. After mastering the exercises provided, you can report your CRM experience on your résumé.

INSTRUCTIONS FOR DOWNLOADING AND USING THE CUSTOMER RELATIONSHIP MANAGEMENT (CRM) SOFTWARE.

The software that you will be using is a demonstration version of ACT!, the leading Customer Relationship Management (CRM) software. This version is limited in that no more than 25 contacts may be entered. Today, the ACT! 2000 program is much more robust, extensive, and powerful, and can manage thousands of contacts.

The software that you need is found on the Web site www.pearsoned. ca/manning. When you view the Web page with your browser, you will find a button labelled CRM. Selecting this button will display the page with the software. That page will identify the link that you will choose to begin the downloading process.

www.pearsoned.ca/manning

The software you will download is a special compressed (zipped) version. Called case_act.exe, this software file first needs to be copied to your computer then decompressed (unzipped). When decompressed, a number of files will be created that consume nearly 3 megabytes of memory, so you will need that much space available on your hard drive. The software is designed to be used with any version of Windows.

Note: This software has been successfully downloaded and used by numerous students over the years.

Sometimes, people find that any computer or software program does not perform as described or expected. If this happens to you, don't give in to frustration. Practise patience and persistence. When a problem occurs, use the software's help screens (usually the F1 key), read the user's instructions, ask for help from others, look on the Internet, or try other software commands. Learn to find solutions because computer problem solving is a very important skill.

EXPERIENCED USERS

If you are a computer user experienced with downloading and launching software, you should have no difficulty with this executable file. You can download to your hard drive and launch the software by double-clicking on it or using the Run command on the Windows Start menu. The launch pop-up window (see below) should be self-explanatory. The program will create a new folder (c:\actcase), decompress, load, and start running.

INEXPERIENCED USERS

If you are not familiar with downloading software, point at the case_act.exe file on the Web site with your cursor and click the RIGHT mouse button. If your browser is Microsoft's Internet Explorer, select the menu choice, "Save Target As." If you are using a Netscape browser, your choice will be "Save Link As." If you are using Netscape and it displays an "Unknown File Type" message, select the "Save File" button. If you are using another browser, consult its users guide for instructions.

Once you choose to download, or save the file, a window will be displayed that asks where you want to save the file. You can save this file anywhere on your hard disk drive (be sure to remember where you saved it). It is recommended that you save it to your C:\ drive (see below).

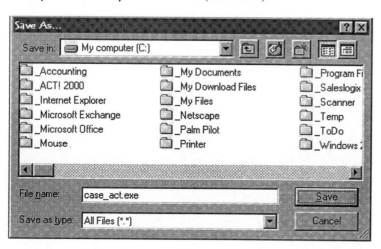

SPECIAL DOWNLOAD CHALLENGES

FILTERS

Some networks have a "filter" installed that prevents individual computer users from downloading software from the Internet. In other cases some networked systems will not allow the downloading of software files as large as ACT!. If you encounter difficulty downloading this software on a Networked computer system, consult your system administrator about these limitations. To download this software, you may need to use a computer without these limitations.

DISKETTE VERSION

A special diskette version of the software is available if you want to download to one computer and use the software on another computer. For example, if you download at a university computer center, you can then take the software home. This version has been reduced in size to fit on a $3^1/_2$ floppy diskette and is so identified on the Web site. This version of the software does not include the Help (F1 Key) functions that are described in the text.

To download the special diskette version, follow the above instructions and save the file to a $3^1/_2$ floppy diskette, known as the A: drive (see window).

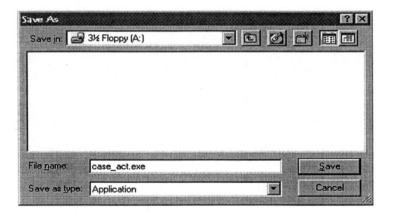

You will need a formatted $3^1/_2$ inch, 1.44 megabyte IBM-compatible diskette that has no other file on it. You can also select the diskette drive by typing "A:\" in front of case_act.exe in the above File name field.

LAUNCHING THE SOFTWARE

Once you have saved the case_act.exe file on your hard disk drive or diskette, it is easy to launch the program. The easiest way is to click the Windows Start button, then select Run, and enter "c:\case_act.exe" if you saved the file on the C:\ drive. If you saved it elsewhere on your hard disk drive, use the browse button to find it. When the file is displayed in the Run dialog box (window), click OK.

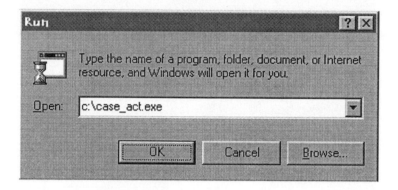

The following window will be displayed.

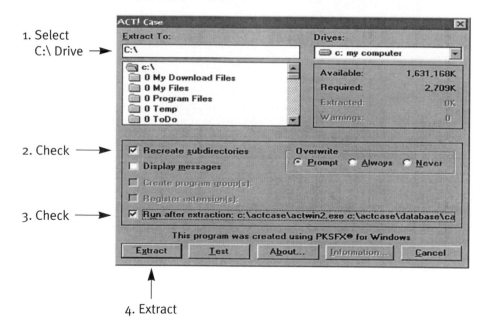

Confirm that 1, 2, and 3 above are displayed on your computer the same as in the above image. Click on 4, the button labeled Extract, and a new folder, ActCase, will be created on your computer, the files will be decompressed (unzipped), and the program will begin running. The first window that you see should look similar to the following:

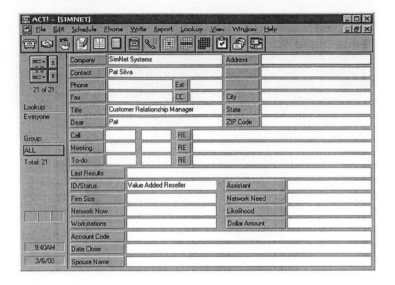

Software Status.

The program on your hard disk drive can be run as many times as you need. After completing the Sales Automation Case Study, you may choose to leave the demonstration software on your hard disk drive or you may remove it. If you saved the downloaded file on a diskette, you can reload the software from the diskette at any time. If you need another copy of the software, you may download it again from the pearsoned.ca/manning Web page.

Finding the Downloaded File

If you downloaded the file but cannot find it on your hard disk drive, you can use Windows' Find utility to search for it. Select the Windows Start button, then choose Find, and Files or Folders and enter case_act.exe.

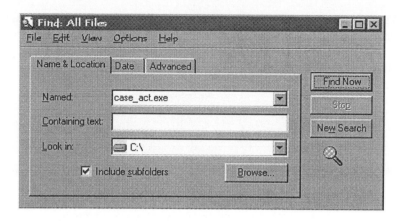

When this search utility finds and displays the file, simply select the file (case_act.exe) with your cursor and double click.

UNDERSTANDING THE SOFTWARE

ACT! is a Windows-based program and uses the standard Windows features. It is "menu driven," which means that you can operate the program by selecting from lists of choices. The main menu is displayed at the top of the screen as above displayed.

The screen that displays the information about a customer is referred to as the contact screen. ACT! has two contact screens that can be toggled by pressing the F6 function key.

You can use the arrows on the Rolodex icon (see inset) to move among the records. A single arrow moves to the next record and a double arrow displays the first (up) or last (down) record in the database. You can also use the PageUp and Page-Down keys to move between records. The records are in alphabetical order, by company name. The first record (double arrow up) in the database is for Able Profit Machines, Inc.

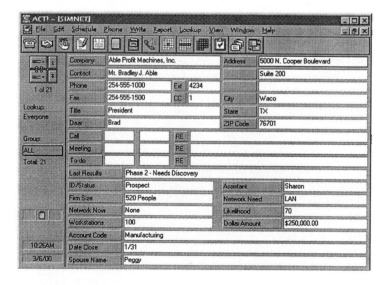

Most records contain notes taken by the previous salesperson, Pat Silva. To display these notes, press the F9 function key. When you are through examining a note, you can press the Escape key (to save changes, select File Close). The notes for the Able Profit Machines company follow.

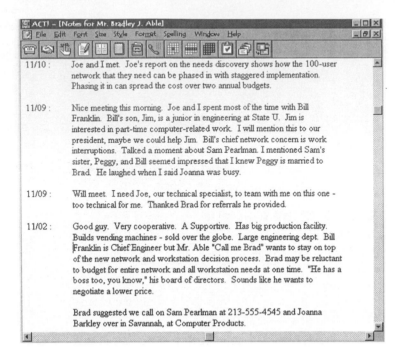

Using the ACT! Software with the CRM References throughout the Book

With the instructions provided above, you can complete any of the references to CRM located throughout the book. These references include the following:

CRM with Technology Insights. These insights, located within the chapter, describe how salespeople are using CRM software today to build relationships with customers.

CRM Application Exercises. These application exercises located at the end of the chapter provide you instructions for learning how to use the software, and gain expertise. Detailed instructions lead you through the important functions salespeople use to develop, build, and maintain relationships with customers.

CRM Case Study. The case study provides you with a database of customers supplied by a previous salesperson. You assume the role of a newly hired salesperson and with the information supplied, create relationship, product, customer, and presentation strategies to manage the sales activities in the territory you are assigned. Questions are supplied to help you plan your activities. The CRM case study starts in Chapter 8 and continues through Chapter 15.

Partnership Selling:
A Role Play/Simulation
for *Selling Today*

Contents

Introduction

Salespeople today are working hard to become more effective in such important areas as person-to-person communications, needs analysis, interpersonal relations, and decision making. This role play/simulation will help you develop these critical selling skills. You will assume the role of a new sales trainee employed by the Park Inn International Convention Centre.

PART I:

Developing a Sales-Oriented Product Strategy will challenge you to acquire the necessary product information needed to be an effective sales representative for the Park Inn (see Chapters 5 and 6). Your sales manager, T. J. McKee, will describe your new trainee position in an employment memorandum. Your instructions will include the study of materials featured on the following pages and role playing the request made in a T. J. McKee customer service/sales memorandum.

PART II:

Developing a Relationship Strategy is another major challenge in personal selling. An employment memorandum will inform you of a promotion to an account executive position. A sales memorandum will inform you of your assignment to accounts in a specific market segment. Part II also involves a role play on the development of a relationship with a new customer in your market segment (see Chapters 3 and 9). Your call objective will be to acquire background information on your new customer, who may have a need for your services.

PART III:

Understanding Your Customer's Buying Strategy involves a needs analysis role play (see Chapters 7 and 10). You will again meet with the customer, who has indicated an interest in scheduling a business conference at your convention centre. During this meeting you will acquire information to complete Part IV, which involves preparation for the sales presentation.

PART IV:

Developing a Presentation Strategy will involve preparation of a sales proposal and a portfolio presentation (see Chapters 10 to 14). This section also involves a third role play with the customer. During the role play you will reestablish your relationship with the customer, present your proposal, negotiate customer concerns, and attempt to close and service the sale.

Throughout completion of the role play/simulation, you will be guided by the employment and sales memoranda (from the sales manager) and instructions and additional forms provided by your instructor.

As you complete this simulation activity, note that the principles and practices you are learning to use have application in nearly all personal selling situations.

General Instructions for Role Playing

OVERVIEW

The primary goal of a simulation in personal selling should be to strike a balance between just enough detail to focus on the process of selling and not so much as to drown in an ocean of facts. Either too much detail or too little detail can develop anxiety in role play participants. *Partnership Selling* is designed to minimize anxiety by including only the facts needed to focus on learning the processes involved in high-performance selling.

Some anxiety will occur, however, because you are asked to perform under pressure (in terms of building relationships, securing strategic information, changing people's thinking, and getting them to take action). Learning to perform in an environment full of genuine but non-threatening pressure affords you the opportunity to practise your selling skills so that you will be prepared for real-world selling anxiety.

The following suggestions for role playing will help you develop the ability to perform under stress.

INSTRUCTIONS FOR SALESPERSON ROLE PLAYS

1. Be well prepared with product knowledge.

2. Read information for each role play ahead of time.

3. Follow specific instructions carefully.

4. Attempt to sense both the context and the facts of the situation presented.

5. Conduct a mental rehearsal. See yourself successfully conducting and completing the role play.

6. Be prepared to take notes during the role play.

7. After the role play, take note of your feelings and mentally put them into the context of what just occurred.

8. Be prepared to discuss your reaction to what occurred during the role play.

INSTRUCTIONS FOR CUSTOMER ROLE PLAYS

1. Read the instructions carefully. Be sure to note both the role play instructions and the information you are about to share.

2. Attempt to sense both the context of the buying situation and the individual facts presented in the instructions.

3. Let the salesperson initiate greetings, conversations, and concluding actions. React appropriately.

4. Supply only the customer information presented in the background description.

5. Supply customer information in a positive manner.

6. Do not attempt to throw the salesperson off track.

PART I: DEVELOPING A SALES-ORIENTED PRODUCT STRATEGY

PARK INN
INTERNATIONAL™

EMPLOYMENT MEMORANDUM 1

To: New Convention Sales Centre Trainees
From: T. J. McKee, Sales Manager
Re: Your New Sales Training Program—"Developing a Product Selling Strategy"

I am extremely happy that you accepted our offer to join the Sales and Marketing Department. Enclosed is a copy of your new position description (see p. 426). Your first assignment as a trainee will be to learn about our product and what we have recently done to provide *total quality* customer service. *To apply what you are learning, I would like you to follow up on a customer service request I recently received. (See memo p. 444.)* You will use the following product information to complete the assignment:

AN AWARD-WINNING UPDATE (See pp. 428–443)

We have recently completed a *$2.8-million investment in our convention centre.* This customer service investment included renovating all guest rooms and suites, lobby and front desk area, meeting rooms, restaurant, and lounge, and enclosure of the swimming pool. Enclosed is a copy of the "Regional Architect's Award" that our facility won. We are the only facility in the Metro area to have been presented with this award.

MEETING AND BANQUET ROOMS (See p. 437)

The Park Inn offers convention planners just over *750 square metres of award-winning meeting space* in attractive, newly renovated meeting and banquet rooms. Our Maple Park East and West rooms are conveniently located on the lobby level of the hotel. Each of these rooms can accommodate 180 people in a theatre-style setting or 80 in a classroom-style setting. They also have a divider wall that can be retracted and, with the combined rooms, can accommodate up to 370 people.

    The Top of the Park provides a spectacular view of the city through windows that surround that ballroom. This unique room, located on the top floor, can accommodate 225 classroom style, 350 banquet style, or 450 people theatre style. Also located in the Top of the Park is a revolving platform area that slowly moves, giving guests a 360-degree panoramic view of the city. The Parkview Room, which is also located on the top floor of the hotel, can accommodate 150 people theatre style and 80 people classroom style.

    In addition, for *groups booking 40 rooms or more, we provide one luxurious suite **free.*** This suite features a meeting room, bedroom, wet bar with refrigerator, and Jacuzzi.

    Be sure your clients understand that our meeting rooms *need to be reserved.* The first organization to sign a sales proposal for a specific date has the designated rooms guaranteed.

GUEST ROOM DECOR AND RATES (See pp. 434 and 438)

Our recent renovation included complete redecoration of all 250 of our large and spacious guest rooms. This includes all-new furniture, wallcoverings, drapes, bedspreads, and carpets. Our interior designer succeeded in creating a comfortable, attractive, restful atmosphere. *Seventy of our rooms are designated non-smoking.*

(continued)

ROOM RATES *(continued)*

	REGULAR RATES	*GROUP RATES*	*SAVINGS*
Single	$88	$78	$10
Double	$98	$88	$10
Triple	$106	$96	$10
Quad	$114	$104	$10

A comparison of competitive room, parking, and transportation rates is presented on p. 438.

BANQUET MEALS (See pp. 431–433)

Our executive chef, Ricardo Guido, recently won the *Canadian Federation of Chefs and Cooks' "Outstanding Chef of the Year" Award*. His winning entry consisted of the three chicken entrees featured on the enclosed menus. Ricardo has many years of experience as an executive chef. He personally oversees all our food and beverage operations. Ricardo, in my opinion, is one of the outstanding chefs in the country. His expertise and commitment to total quality customer service will help develop long-term relationships with our customers.

The enclosed dinner selections are only suggestions. We will design a special menu for your clients if they wish. A 15% gratuity or service charge is added to all group meal functions.

HOTEL/MOTEL AND SALES TAXES

All room rates are subject to *applicable sales taxes. (Sales taxes do not apply to gratuities.)*

LOCATION, TRANSPORTATION, AND PARKING (See map on p. 430)

We are located in a dynamic, growing metropolitan area of over 400 000 people. With *convenient access, just off of Highway 237 at the downtown exits*, we are within a block of the nationally recognized climate-controlled skywalk system. This 8-km system is connected to theatres, excellent shopping, the civic centre, the metropolitan convention centre, and a large selection of ethnic and fast-food restaurants. Our location offers guests the privacy they deserve during their meetings, yet is close enough to downtown to enjoy all the excitement.

Free courtesy van transportation (also known as limousine service) is provided for our overnight guests to and from the airport, as well as anywhere in the downtown area. This service saves our guests who arrive by plane from *$8.00 to $10.00 each way*.

Guests who will be driving to the hotel will find over *300 parking spaces* available to them at *no charge*. Unlike other downtown properties, our free parking saves guests up to *$6.00 per day* in parking fees. For security purposes, we have closed-circuit camera systems in the parking lot and underground parking areas.

VALUE-ADDED GUEST SERVICES AND AMENITIES

Our convention centre owners have invested heavily in the facility to provide our clients with *total quality service*, unmatched by our competition. Additional value-added services and amenities include:

- A large *indoor pool, sundeck, sauna, whirlpool, and complimentary Nautilus exercise room* in an attractive tropical atmosphere
- "Café in the Park" featuring 24-hour continental cuisine seven days a week
- "Pub in the Park" where friendly people meet, featuring *free hors d'oeuvres* Monday through Friday, 5 to 7 p.m.
- Cable television with *HBO*
- A.V. rental of most equipment in-house, at a nominal fee (see pp. 439–440)
- *Free coffee and donuts or rolls* in the lobby each morning from 6 to 8 a.m.
- A team of *well-trained, dedicated, and friendly associates* providing total quality front desk, food, and guest services
- Express check in
- Electronic key entry system
- Hair dryer, iron, and ironing board in each room
- Data port capabilities for laptop computers in each room
- Desk in each room
- Video message retrieval
- Voice mail
- On-command video (choice of 50 new-release movies)

SALES LITERATURE (See pp. 428–447)

Included in your product training materials are photos, references, letters, room schedules, sales proposals, and other information that you will use in your written proposals and verbal sales presentations. When you move into outside sales, you should use these tools to create effective sales portfolios.

TOTAL QUALITY COMMITMENT

Our convention centre is committed to *total quality customer service. Our Partnership Style of Customer Service and Selling* is an extension of our total quality process. The Total Quality Customer Glossary provides definitions of terms that describe our total quality process (see p. 427).

The hotel and convention centre industry is mature and well established. Our sales and customer service plan is to *establish strong relationships, focus on solving customer problems, provide total quality customer service, and become a long-term hotel and convention centre partner with our clients.* By utilizing this type of selling and customer service, your compensation and our sales revenue will both increase substantially.

TJM:ESS
Enclosures

POSITION DESCRIPTION — CONVENTION CENTRE ACCOUNT EXECUTIVE

COMPANY DESCRIPTION

The Park Inn Convention Centre is a total quality, full-service, equal-opportunity-employment convention centre that has recently made large investments in the physical facility, the food and beverage department, and the sales department. Company culture includes an effective and enthusiastic team approach to creating *total quality* value-added solutions for customers in a very competitive industry. The primary sales promotion tool is *Partnership Selling*, with extensive marketing support in the form of photos, reference letters, team selling, etc. The company goal is to increase revenues 20 percent in the coming year by providing outstanding customer service.

A SUCCESSFUL ACCOUNT EXECUTIVE WILL

1. Acquire necessary convention centre company, product, industry, and competitive information through company training program
2. Be committed to a total quality customer service process
3. Develop a list of potential prospects in the assigned target market
4. Develop long-term total quality selling relationships that focus on solving the meeting planner's convention centre needs
5. Achieve a sales volume of $700 000 to $800 000 annually

WORKING RELATIONSHIPS

Reports to: Sales Manager
Works with: Internal Support Team including Food Service, Housekeeping and Operations, Customer Service, and Front Desk; External Relationships including customers, professional associations, and industry personnel

SPECIFIC REQUIREMENTS

1. Must project a positive and professional sales image
2. Must be able to establish and maintain long-term relationships
3. Must be goal oriented with a plan for self-improvement
4. Must be flexible to deal effectively with a wide range of customers
5. Must be good at asking questions and listening effectively
6. Must be accurate and creative in developing customer solutions
7. Must be clear and persuasive in communicating and negotiating solutions
8. Must be good at closing the sale
9. Must follow through on promises and assurances
10. Must have math skills necessary for figuring sales proposals

SPECIFIC REWARDS

1. Attractive compensation package that includes base salary, a commission of 10 percent of sales, bonuses, and an attractive fringe benefit package
2. Pride in working for an organization that practises total quality management in employee relations and customer service
3. Extensive sales and educational support
4. Opportunity for growth and advancement

TOTAL QUALITY CUSTOMER SERVICE GLOSSARY

DIRFT—DO IT RIGHT THE FIRST TIME means being prepared, asking the right questions, selecting the right solutions, and making effective presentations. This creates repeats and referrals.

QIP—QUALITY IMPROVEMENT PROCESS means always striving to better serve our customers, resulting in high quality, long-term relationships.

TQM—TOTAL QUALITY MANAGEMENT means the commitment to support and empower people to deliver legendary customer service.

QIT—QUALITY IMPROVEMENT TEAM means a team approach to deliver outstanding customer service.

COQ—COST OF QUALITY means the ultimate lowering of cost by providing outstanding service the first time, so as to build a list of repeat and referred customers.

PONC—PRICE OF NONCONFORMANCE means the high cost of not meeting high standards. This results in correcting problems and losing customers. PONC also causes longer sales cycles and higher sales costs.

POC—PRICE OF CONFORMANCE means the lower costs of providing outstanding customer service and achieving a list of repeat or referral customers.

WIIFM—WHAT IS IN IT FOR ME means the psychic and monetary rewards in the form of personal enjoyment, higher salaries, commissions, or bonuses caused by delivering outstanding customer service.

QES—QUALITY EDUCATION SYSTEMS means internal and external educational activities designed to improve the quality of customer service.

YOU—THE MOST IMPORTANT PART OF QUALITY means the ongoing program of self-improvement that results in outstanding customer service, and personal and financial growth.

THE ALL NEW PARK INN
(with an award-winning
$2.8-million renovation)

REGIONAL ARCHITECTS ASSOCIATION

"EXCELLENCE IN RENOVATION DESIGN"

PRESENTED TO:

Park Inn International

WITH SPECIAL RECOGNITION FOR CREATING AN OUTSTANDING
CONVENTION ENVIRONMENT.

PRESENTED ON THE ELEVENTH DAY OF MARCH, 200__.

Allen Page
CHAIRPERSON, DESIGN SELECTION COMMITTEE

Patricia Burnett
PRESIDENT, REGIONAL ARCHITECTS ASSOCIATION

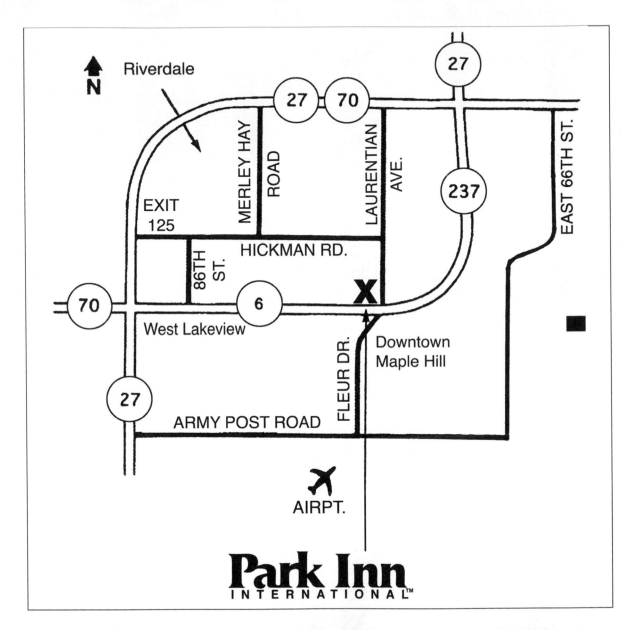

CONVENIENT, EASY TO FIND LOCATION WITH FREE PARKING

Conveniently located at Highway 6 and Laurentian Ave. Just 13 km from Maple Hill International Airport.

OUTSTANDING FOOD SERVICE

**Personally Supervised by Award-Winning
"Executive Chef of the Year"
Ricardo Guido**

CANADIAN FEDERATION OF CHEFS AND COOKS

EXECUTIVE CHEF OF THE YEAR

AWARDED TO:

Ricardo Guido

PRESENTED ON THE ELEVENTH DAY OF APRIL, 200__.

Patricia Reed

PRESIDENT, CANADIAN FEDERATION OF CHEFS AND COOKS

Ella Reed

CONFERENCE CHAIRPERSON

LITHO IN U.S.A

BANQUET STYLE MENU SELECTIONS

**All selections include tossed greens with choice of dressing,
choice of potato (baked, oven browned, au gratin, or mashed),
rice or buttered noodles, rolls with butter,
coffee, decaffeinated coffee, tea, or iced tea.**

ENTREES

CHICKEN WELLINGTON—Boneless breast of chicken topped with a
mushroom mixture, wrapped in puff pastry shell and baked to a golden brown $17.95

CHICKEN BREAST TERIYAKI—Marinated boneless breast of chicken
grilled and topped with our *special* teriyaki sauce $17.95

CHICKEN BREAST NEW ORLEANS—Baked boneless breast of chicken,
garnished with peppers, mushrooms, onions, and Monterey Jack cheese $17.95

BROILED NEW YORK STRIP STEAK—Centre cut New York strip steak
broiled to perfection, topped with our own seasoned herb butter $16.50

BROILED FILET MIGNON—A steak from the centre cut tenderloin,
broiled and served with a rich red wine sauce $24.50

SLICED PORK LOIN WITH MUSTARD SAUCE—Boneless loin of pork
oven roasted and sliced, served with a mustard sauce $17.95

GRILLED PORK CHOP—A thick cut of pork grilled to juicy perfection $18.95

BROILED ORANGE ROUGHY—A filet of orange roughy broiled
and covered with basil-lemon sauce $18.95

BROILED HALIBUT STEAK—Tender flaky halibut cut into steaks
and broiled in lemon-butter served with fresh lemon slices $19.95

Sales taxes and gratuity not included.

ATTRACTIVE, COMFORTABLE GUEST ROOMS

(All-new furnishings, HBO in every room, free *Globe and Mail* weekday and Saturday delivery, no telephone and access charges for 800 and credit card calls, and data port capabilities for laptop computers)

A TROPICAL PARADISE

For relaxation after a day's work— attractive pool, sauna, whirlpool, sundeck, and Nautilus fitness centre

BRIGHT, COMFORTABLE, AND STRATEGICALLY ARRANGED MEETING ROOMS

Everything you need for outstanding meetings

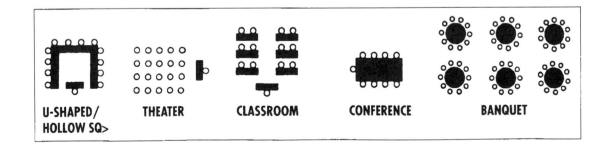

U-SHAPED/ HOLLOW SQ>   THEATER   CLASSROOM   CONFERENCE   BANQUET

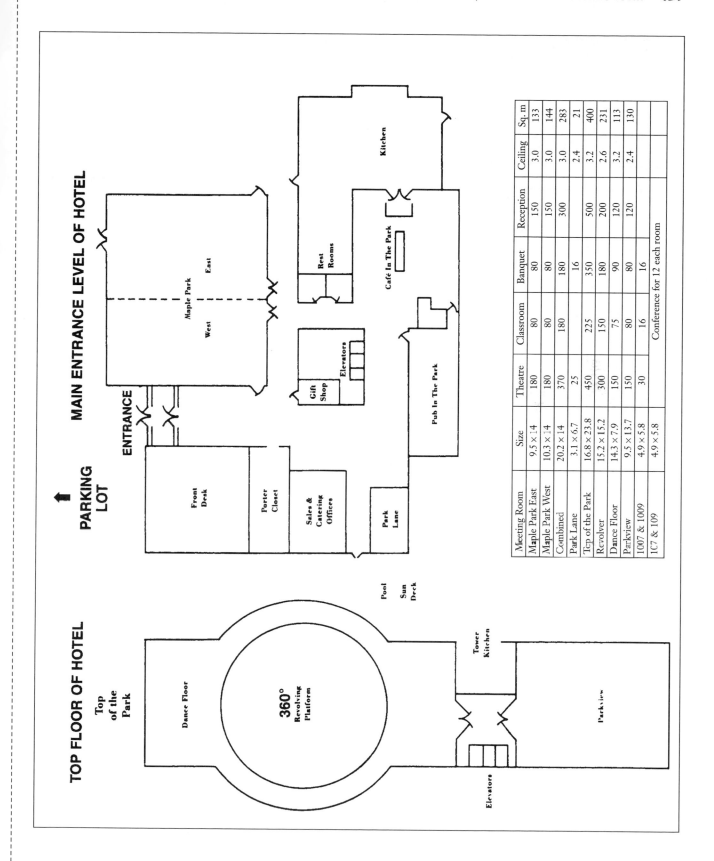

MAIN ENTRANCE LEVEL OF HOTEL

PARKING LOT

ENTRANCE

Front Desk

Porter Closet

Sales & Catering Offices

Park Lane

Gift Shop

Elevators

Pub In The Park

Rest Rooms

Maple Park — West / East

Kitchen

Café In The Park

TOP FLOOR OF HOTEL

Top of the Park

Dance Floor

360° Revolving Platform

Pool Sun Deck

Tower Kitchen

Elevators

Parkview

Meeting Room	Size	Theatre	Classroom	Banquet	Reception	Ceiling	Sq. m
Maple Park East	9.5 × 14	180	80	80	150	3.0	133
Maple Park West	10.3 × 14	180	80	80	150	3.0	144
Combined	20.2 × 14	370	180	180	300	3.0	283
Park Lane	3.1 × 6.7	25	16	16		2.4	21
Top of the Park	16.8 × 23.8	450	225	350	500	3.2	400
Revolver	15.2 × 15.2	300	150	180	200	2.6	231
Dance Floor	14.3 × 7.9	150	75	90	120	3.2	113
Parkview	9.5 × 13.7	150	80	80	120	2.4	130
1007 & 1009	4.9 × 5.8	30	16	16			
1C7 & 109	4.9 × 5.8		Conference for 12 each room				

°METRO AREA COMPETITIVE SURVEY

QUOTED GROUP RATES (IN DOLLARS) FOR HOTEL/MOTEL GUEST ROOMS

HOTEL/MOTEL	SINGLE	DOUBLE	DAILY PARKING	AIRPORT TRANS.
Park Inn	**78**	**88**	**Free**	**Free**
Marriott	80	90	6	10 each way
Sheraton	85	105	6	12 each way
Hilton	80	100	7	9 each way
Embassy	82	103	6	8 each way
Guest Quarters	84	104	Free	8 each way
Carlton	75	95	8	3 each way
Saboe	75	85	Free	12 each way
Chesterfield	70	80	Free	13 each way
Best Western	65	70	Free	15 each way
Days Inn	60	65	Free	12 each way
Sunset Inn	55	n/a	Free	12 each way

RENTAL RATES

MEETING ROOM RATES

SQUARE METRES	MEETING ROOM	4 HOURS	8 HOURS	24 HOURS
400	**Top of the Park**	**$400**	**$600**	**$900**
133	**Maple Park East**	**$150**	**$200**	**$300**
144	**Maple Park West**	**$160**	**$200**	**$300**
283	**Combined Maple Park**	**$300**	**$400**	**$500**
21	**Park Lane**	**$ 25**	**$ 40**	**$ 60**
231	**Revolver**	**$300**	**$500**	**$700**
113	**Dance Floor**	**$100**	**$175**	**$275**
130	**Parkview**	**$110**	**$185**	**$300**
28	**1007 and 1009**	**$ 40**	**$ 60**	**$ 80**
28	**107 and 109**	**$ 40**	**$ 60**	**$ 80**

- Meeting room rental charges based on set changes at 12:00 noon, 5:00 p.m., or 10:00 p.m.
- For groups of 20 or more who are reserving 20 or more guest rooms or scheduling 20 or more banquet meals, rental rates will be waived for rooms up to 150 square metres for up to 8 hours of use per day.
- For groups of 50 or more who are reserving 50 or more guest rooms or scheduling 50 or more banquet meals, rental rates will be waived for all rooms for up to 24 hours of use.

AUDIO VISUAL PRESENTATIONS GUIDE

These are the most popular audio/visual equipment items. If you require special equipment and services not listed. Please let us know. We'll do the rest!

AUDIO VISUAL EQUIPMENT PACKAGES

Saves Money • Saves Time

35mm Slides

Kodak Ektagraphic III 35mm Slide projector package features a projection stand or cart, 4" to 8" zoom lens, wireless remote control, spare 80 slide tray, all extension AC cords safely taped. Select Screens Below.
35mm Slide Projector Package $45.00

Recommended by Professional Meeting Planners:

Complet speaker freedom with
    Laser Pointer...$27.50
    Wireless Microphone................................$80.00
Groups over 75 people:
    Special Zoom Lens..................................$11.00

LCD Video Projection

LCD* Proxima Video Projector....................................$500.00
Colour Video Projector Projects Full Colour Video or Computer Images up to SVGA. Recommended for larger groups. Select Screen Below.

Video VCR/Monitor

VHS 1/2" or U-MATIC 3/4" Player/Recorder package features a roll-around 54" projection car, a 27" full-function colour video monitor/receiver. All cable connections. AC extension cords safely taped.
*VHS 1/2"...$150.00
3/4" U-MATIC $185.00

Recommended by Professional Meeting Planners:

More visibility for large groups with additional 27" video, monitor and cart, includes cables and connectors.
Each..$90.00
Full House Sound..$27.50

Overhead Projectors

Popular overhead projector package with super-wide overhead projector featuring automatic spare lamp changer. All AC extension cords safely taped. Select Screens Below.
Overhead Projector Package $40.00

Recommended by Professional Meeting Planners:

Complete speaker freedom with
    Laser Pointer...$27.50
    Wireless Microphone..............................$80.00

LCD Panel Projection

Colour Computer Data Panel $325.00
Full Colour Panel Projects Computer Images on a 6'–10' Projection Screen with Hi-Intensity Overhead Projector. Select Screen Below.

Full MotionVideo Projection

CRT Projector with VCR $550.00
Colour video projector projects full motion video on screen. Recommended for larger groups. Select screen below.

Continued

AUDIO VISUAL EQUIPMENT Á LA CARTE

Motion Picture Projection

16mm Autoload projector w/2" prime lens
with stand $40.00

Hi-Intensity Overhead Projector

4000 Lumen projector for LCD computer
        Data panel or larger groups...................$65.00

Meeting Accessories

Laser Pointer $27.50
Flip Chart Easel (No Pen) $14.00
Flip Chart Rental w/Markers $22.00
Projection carts and stands........................$16.50
Meeting accessories such as acetate rolls and sheets are
available on request.

Video Equipment

Camcorder with tripod...............................$120.00
VCR...$60.00

Audio Equipment

Cassette Player/Recorder...........................$40.00
CD Player $40.00
Portable CD/Cassette Player......................$40.00

AV Technician Services

AV Tech is on site for installation and dismantle.
Requirements for exclusive event management will be
charged these hourly rates:
Monday through Friday, 7am–5pm...........................$30.00
Evenings, Weekdays, and Holidays...........................$40.00

Microphones

Microphone, wired $22.00
Lavaliere, wired...$22.00
Wireless microphone
        (Hand held or Lavaliere) $80.00
Sound patch to house system $27.50
4 Channel mixer...$27.50

Screens

6' x 6' Tripod $22.00
8'x 8' Tripod $27.50
10' x 10' Cradle $55.00
• 7 1/2" x 10' Fast Fold $80.00
• 9' x 12' Fast fold $110.00
• Front or rear projection
Fast fold drape kits included.

THE PRINCIPAL COMPANY

2515 COLBY ROAD
KITCHENER, ONTARIO
N9L 5C7

December 15, 200_

Carroll Parez, General Manager
The Park Inn
580 King Street
Maple Hill, Ontario
K2R 4P7

Dear Carroll:

On behalf of our employees I thank you and your associates for the wonderful time we had at the Park Inn during our convention last month. Enclosed is a cheque for $22 991.23 to pay the invoice for the meeting costs.

The hospitality that we received during our time there was unparalleled. The friendliness and dedication of the staff simply made our time so enjoyable we hated to leave.

The Chicken New Orleans was superb. Our heartfelt thanks to Chef Ricardo Guido for creating the best meals we have ever had at a convention.

Without reservation I will direct anyone looking for convention space to your award-winning property. The group who gave you the award certainly knew what was important to convention planners. You may count on us to return in the future.

Sincerely,

Reggie Regan

Reggie Regan, Vice-President
Field Sales Division

Enclosures:
Schedule for our next eight convention dates
Cheque
Service Evaluation

ss

REFERENCES

COMPANY/ADDRESS	TELEPHONE NO.	DATE OF BOOKING
Association of Business and Industry 2425 Hubbell Mr. James Warner (Director)	265–8181	July 1–2
Acme Supply Company 2531 Dean Linn Compiano (Training Manager)	265–9831	July 14
Rotary International 1230 Executive Towers Mr. Roger Shannon (Executive Director)	792–4616	July 28–29
Archway Cookie Company Boone Industrial Park Mr. Bill Sorenson (Sales Manager)	432–4084	August 9
West College 4821 College Parkway Toni Bush (Athletic Director)	283–4142	September 9–11
Travellers Insurance Company 1452 29th Mr. Richard Wiese (Training Manager)	223–7500	November 14
Meredith Corporation 1716 Locust Mrs. Carol Rains (Public Relations)	284–2654	November 23–24
Pioneer Hi-Bred Incorporated 5700 Merle Highway Mrs. Sheri Sitterly (Administrative Services)	272–3660	December 12–13

CONVENTION CENTRE POLICIES AND GENERAL INFORMATION

FOOD AND BEVERAGE

- A 15% gratuity or service charge and applicable sales tax will be added to all food and beverage purchases. Any group requesting a tax exemption must submit their Certificate of Exemption prior to the event.

- There is a $25 setup fee for each meal function of 25 persons or less.

GUARANTEES

- The Convention Centre will require your menus and meeting room requirements no later than two weeks before your meeting or food function.
- Convention Centre facilities are guaranteed on a "first confirmed, first served" basis.

- A meal guarantee is required 48 hours prior to your function. This guarantee is the minimum your group will be charged for the function. If no guarantee is received by the Catering Office, we will then consider your last number of attendees as the guarantee. We will be prepared to serve 5% over your guaranteed number.

BANQUET AND MEETING ROOMS

- As other groups may be utilizing the same room prior to or following your function, please adhere to the times agreed on. Should your time schedule change, please contact the Catering Office, and every effort will be made to accommodate you.

- Function rooms are assigned by the room number of people anticipated. If attendance drops or increases, please contact the Catering Office to ensure proper assignment of rooms.

AUDIOVISUAL SERVICES

- A wide selection of audiovisual equipment and services is available on a rental basis. (See audiovisual presentation guide for details.)

CUSTOMER SERVICE/SALES MEMORANDUM 1

To: Convention Sales Trainee
From: T. J. McKee, Sales Manager
Re: Assistance with a Customer Request

A new prospect called and requested that we immediately submit a proposal for a potential meeting at our hotel. Please review the profile in our automated database (printed as follows).

CONTACT REPORT

Name: Graphic Forms   Address: 1234 Parsons Pond Road   ◄ **CONTACT SCREEN**
Contact: B. H. Rivera   :
Phone: 555–619–4879   :
  Title: President   City: Fredericton
  Sec: Province: New Brunswick
  Dear: B. H. Rivera   Postal Code: E6B 7W3

-----L-----T-----T-----T-----T-----T-----T-----T-----T-----T-----T-----T-----T-----T-----T-----R

(McKee) Visited with B. H. Rivera on the phone. Seemed very interested. Nice emotive person. Has a son, Matt, attending West College. Also knew Toni Bush of West, who is an excellent account of ours. B. H. wants a proposal ASAP to cover the following buying conditions:

1. Ten single guest rooms for two nights—Friday and Saturday
2. A meeting room for 20 people, classroom style, Friday and Saturday from 2 to 6 P.M.
3. Dinner for 20, banquet style, at 6 P.M. each night
   Friday: Grilled Pork Chops
   Saturday: Broiled Orange Roughy
4. A swimming pool

◄ **NOTES WINDOW**

Complete the following customer service/sales assignment using the material in your product sales training program (pp. 428–443) and the forms on the next two pages. (See Chapters 5 and 6 for information on developing a product strategy.)

1. *Complete the sales proposal worksheet (p. 445).*

    Our sales proposal needs to contain accurate and complete facts because, when signed, it becomes a legally enforceable sales contract. All the product and pricing guidelines have been supplied in your sales training materials. You should sign your name with your new job title "Account Executive" in the lower left-hand corner of the form.

2. *Write a sales letter (p. 446).*

    Prepare a letter that custom fits and positions the benefits that will appeal to B. H. Rivera. Be sure to list any sales literature you will be sending under the Enclosure section of your letter. (Use business letter format on p. 446.)

Make file copies of everything you prepare so our food and beverage, housekeeping, and accounting departments will have them available.

We should send or fax the proposal, cover letter, and sales literature by tomorrow afternoon.

Thank you.

Enclosures

PARK INN
INTERNATIONAL™

SALES PROPOSAL

Customer Name: _____ Title: _____

Organization Name: _____ Telephone: _____

Address: _____

Date(s) of Meetings: _____

Kind of Meetings: _____

Buying Conditions (what the customer needs—be specific): _____
_____
_____

A. Meal Functions Needed

	Time	Description	Quantity	Price	Total
Meal 1					
Meal 2					
Other		(Beverages, setup fees, etc.)			

Total _____

Sales Taxes _____

Service Charge _____

Total Meal Cost _____

B. Meeting and Banquet Rooms and Equipment Needed (describe time, date, and cost)

Total _____

Sales Taxes _____

Total Meeting/Banquet Rooms and Equipment Charges _____

C. Guest Rooms Needed

Number of Rooms Needed	Description (dates, location, special conditions)	Group Rate per Room	Total Cost

Total _____

Sales Taxes _____

Total Guest Room Charges _____

D. Total Customer Costs (from above)

A. $_____ plus **B.** $_____ plus **C.** $_____ equals **Total Charges** $ _____

Authorized Signature _____ Date _____

Customer Signature _____ Date _____

Title _____ Title _____

580 King Street, Maple Hill, Ontario K2R 4P7
555–225–0925   Fax 555–225–9386

PARTS II TO IV

PARK INN
INTERNATIONAL™

EMPLOYMENT MEMORANDUM 2

To: New Convention Centre Account Executives
From: T. J. McKee, Sales Manager
Re: Your New Sales Assignment

Congratulations on successfully completing your training program and receiving your new appointment. You will find three challenges as you partner with your accounts.

Your *first challenge will be establishing relationships* with your customers. This will require that you do strategic planning before you can call on your client for the first time. Make sure your initial meetings focus on subjects of interest to your customer.

Your *second major challenge will be to gain a complete and accurate understanding of your customer's needs.* You should prepare to ask good questions, take detailed and accurate notes, and confirm your customer's and your own understanding of their need. This process is a part of our total quality management program, which strives to provide total quality customer service.

Your *third challenge as an account executive will be to make good presentations.* Our industry, as most others these days, is competitive and is characterized by many look-alike products and some price cutting. Always *organize and deliver good presentations* that focus on (1) providing solutions to immediate and long-term customer needs, (2) negotiating double-win solutions to customer concerns, and (3) closing sales that keep our facility full. This approach will give you a competitive edge and help you maintain high quality, long-term profitable relationships.

Effectively meeting these challenges will also require that you have a program of *self-improvement.* This will enhance your career as an account executive.

Attached you will find a memorandum on an account I would like you to develop. Please follow the instructions included and provide me with appropriate feedback on your progress. I look forward to working with you on this account.

P. S. I want to compliment you on your excellent work on the B. H. Rivera account. B. H. called while you were attending a training meeting and said that your proposal and letter looked very good. Their organization was impressed with our facility, the apparent quality of our food, and your letter. Their organization will be scheduling a total of *11 more meetings* at our convention centre during the next 12 months if everything works the way you describe it. Each of these sales will be reflected in your *commission cheques.* Great work.

PART II: DEVELOPING A RELATIONSHIP STRATEGY FOR SELLING

PARK INN
I N T E R N A T I O N A L™

SALES MEMORANDUM 1A

To: **Association Account Sales**
From: **T. J. McKee, Sales Manager**
Re: **Developing the Erin Adkins, YWCA Account**
   (Call 1, Establishing a Relationship Strategy)

My sales assistant has called Erin Adkins, chairperson of the YWCA Physical Fitness Week program (see following contract report), and set up an appointment for you on Monday at 1:00 p.m. in Erin's office. During your first sales call with Erin, your *call objectives* will be to

1. Establish a strong relationship
2. Share an appealing benefit of our property to create customer interest
3. Find out if your customer is planning any conventions in the future

As we discussed during your training class, using Erin Adkins's prospect information presented later and the sales tools in your product strategy materials, your *presentation plan* should be to (see Chapters 3 and 9)

1. Use compliments, comments on observations, or a search for mutual acquaintances to determine which topics Erin wants to talk about (Erin will only want to talk about three of these topics). This should set the stage for a good relationship.
2. Take notes on the topics of interest to Erin so we can add them to our customer information data bank for future calls. (Erin will share three new items of information on each topic of interest, if you acknowledge interest.)
3. Show and describe an appealing and unique benefit of our facility so we will be considered for Erin's future convention needs. (Consider using the Architect's Award.)
4. Discuss any conventions Erin may be planning.
5. Schedule a callback appointment.

```
Name: YWCA                          Address: 16 Durham Avenue
Contact: Erin Adkins                       :
Phone: 555-515-3740                        :
   Title: Chairperson, Physical Fitness Programs   City: Maple Hill
   Sec:                               Province: Ontario
Dear: Erin                          Postal Code: K2N 4C9
-----L-----T-----T-----T-----T-----T-----T-----T-----T-----T-----T-----T-----T-----T-----R
```
◄ **CONTACT SCREEN**

(McKee) Toni Bush, the Athletic Director of West College, supplied the following information about Erin Adkins:
1. Toni and Erin have a close relationship.
2. Erin just designed and built a new home.
3. Erin appears in local TV advertising about the YWCA.
Toni reports that in Erin's office you will observe the following:
4. An autographed picture of the Chicago Bulls basketball team
5. A Schwinn Air-dyne Fitness Cycle

◄ **NOTES WINDOW**

(continued)

SALES MEMORANDUM 1A *(continued)*

Comments, Compliments, and Questions	Notes on New Items of Interest to Customer
(Toni Bush suggested you mention his name.)	1. (Example) Toni Bush is my cousin 2. 3.
	1. 2. 3.
	1. 2. 3.

PARK INN
INTERNATIONAL™

SALES MEMORANDUM 1B

To: **Corporate Account Sales**
From: **T. J. McKee, Sales Manager**
Re: **Developing the Leigh Combs, Epic Design Systems Account**
(Call 1, Establishing a Relationship Strategy)

My sales assistant has called Epic Design Systems (see following contact report) and set up an appointment for you on Monday at 1:00 p.m. in Leigh's office. During your first sales call with Leigh, your *call objectives* will be to

1. Establish a strong relationship
2. Share an appealing benefit of our property to create customer interest
3. Find out if your customer is planning any conventions in the future

As we discussed during your training class, using Leigh Combs's prospect information presented later and the sales tools in your product strategy materials, your *presentation plan* should be to (see Chapters 3 and 9)

1. Use compliments, comments on observations, or a search for mutual acquaintances to determine which topics Leigh wants to talk about (Leigh will only want to talk about three of these topics). This should set the stage for a good relationship.
2. Take notes on the topics of interest to Leigh so we can add them to our customer information data bank for future calls. (Leigh will share three new items of information on each topic of interest, if you acknowledge interest.)
3. Show and describe an appealing and unique benefit of our facility so we will be considered for Leigh's future convention needs. (Consider using the Executive Chef's Award.)
4. Discuss any conventions Leigh may be planning.
5. Schedule a callback appointment.

```
 Name:   Epic Design Systems          Address:  2142 Dominion Parkway
 Contact: Leigh Combs                        :  Suite 200
 Phone:  416-555-1000   X:    CC:             :
   Title: Customer Service Manager      City:  West Lakeview
   Sec:  Rhiannon                   Province:  Ontario
 Dear:  Leigh                    Postal Code:  K3A 9R2
-----L----T-----T-----T-----T-----T-----T-----T-----T-----T-----T-----T-----T-----T-----T-----R
```

◄ **CONTACT SCREEN**

(McKee) Linn Compiano, the Training Manager at Acme Supply Company, provided the following information about Leigh Combs:
1. Leigh has been on vacation.
2. Leigh is Linn Compiano's cousin.

Linn reports that in Leigh's office you will observe the following:
3. A large picture of Napoleon Bonaparte
4. A certificate of membership in the Canadian Marketing Society
5. An extra-large bookcase containing many business books

◄ **NOTES WINDOW**

(continued)

SALES MEMORANDUM 1B *(continued)*

Comments, Compliments, and Questions	Notes on New Items of Interest to Customer
(Linn Compiano mentioned that Leigh Combs just returned from a very enjoyable vacation.)	1. (Example) Spent one week in California 2. 3.
	1. 2. 3.
	1. 2. 3.

PRESALE PLAN WORKSHEET

SALES CALL 1 — ESTABLISHING A RELATIONSHIP

Name:_____

Your appointment for your first call is scheduled for (1) _____ at (2) _____

p.m. Your appointment was set up by (3) _____. On entering your prospect's office, you

will need to (4) _____ yourself, (5) _____ hands, and explain your

(6) _____ objectives. Your next step will be to make a (7) _____,

(8) _____, or do a search for mutual acquaintances or interests. When your customer opens

up and shares new information, you are instructed to (9) _____ _____ and

take (10) _____. If you are successful in getting your customer to talk about things in which

(s)he is interested, you should receive (11) _____ new pieces of relationship information. At

the appropriate time during your call you will convert attention from the (12) _____ to show-

ing a (13) _____ device and presenting a (14) _____, to interest your cus-

tomer in your convention centre. In completing your call (15) _____ you are asked

to (16) _____ _____ if your customer has any planned future

(17) _____. If you have not received a total of (18) _____ new pieces of

relationship information, you should go back and talk about things of interest to your customer. The

(19) _____ screen on the contact report provides factual information about your prospect

while the (20) _____ contains information that reflects your customer's interests. Erin

Adkins is active in the (21) _____. Erin also knows (22) _____

_____ of West College. Leigh Combs is a (23) _____

_____ manager and has just returned (24) _____. There are at least

two important items to (25) _____ in both Erin's and Leigh's office.

ASSESSMENT FORM 1

RELATIONSHIP STRATEGY

Salesperson's Name:_____

Date:_____

Assessment Item	Excellent		Average		Poor	Did Not Do
1. Conducted good verbal introductions (shared full name, title, and company name)	10	9	8	7	6	0
2. Made good nonverbal introduction (good entrance, carriage, handshake, and seating posture)	10	9	8	7	6	0
3. Communicated call objectives (shared why salesperson was calling)	10	9	8	7	6	0
4. Verbalized effective comments and compliments (sincerely made comments and compliments on five relationship topics)	10	9	8	7	6	0
5. Kept conversation focused on customer topics (acknowledged new information provided by customer)	10	9	8	7	6	0
6. Took effective, non-distractive notes (was organized and prepared to take notes)	10	9	8	7	6	0
7. Attractively showed material on convention centre (was well prepared with a proof device)	10	9	8	7	6	0
8. Made effective benefit statement (made a benefit statement that appealed to customer)	10	9	8	7	6	0
9. Effectively inquired about convention needs (asked good questions about future needs)	10	9	8	7	6	0
10. Effectively thanked customer (communicated appreciation, said thank you, indicated interest in prospect's future business)	10	9	8	7	6	0

Relationship Presentation:_____

Total Points

Your Name:_____

Return this form to salesperson and discuss your reaction to this presentation!

PART III: UNDERSTANDING YOUR CUSTOMER'S BUYING STRATEGY

SALES MEMORANDUM 2A

To: **Association Account Salesperson**
From: **T. J. McKee, Sales Manager**
Re: **Erin Adkins Account—phone call from customer**
         (Call 2, Discovering a Customer's Buying Strategy)

Erin Adkins from the YWCA, whom you called on recently, left a message for you to stop in about a program they are planning. Congratulations on making that first call so effectively. Apparently you established a good relationship.

As we discussed in your training program, your *call objectives* should be to

1. Re-establish your relationship
2. Discover Erin's buying conditions (the what, why, who, when, and what price needs), so we can custom fit a program for them
3. Set up an appointment to present your solution

Also, as we discussed, your *presentation plan* for this call should include (see Chapters 7 and 10)

1. In advance of your meeting, prepare general *information-gathering questions* designed to get your customer talking and to achieve your call objectives. (Use our form below.)
2. Later in your meeting, use *probing and confirmation questions* to clarify and confirm Erin's and your own perceptions of each buying condition.
3. During your sales meeting, write down each of Erin's buying conditions. (Use our form below.)
4. To end your first meeting, use your notes to construct a *summary confirmation question* to clarify and confirm all six of Erin's buying conditions.
5. Schedule a callback appointment to make your presentation and present your proposal.

Good luck!

INFORMATION-GATHERING QUESTIONS	NOTES ON BUYING CONDITIONS
(Example: Can you share with me what you had in mind?)	(Example: Needs a small meeting room)
	1.
	2.
	3.
	4.
	5.
	6.

SALES MEMORANDUM 2B

To: **Corporate Account Salesperson**
From: **T. J. McKee, Sales Manager**
Re: **Leigh Combs Account—phone call from customer**
(Call 2, Discovering a Customer's Buying Strategy)

Leigh Combs from Epic Design Systems, whom you called on recently, left a message for you to stop in about a program they are planning. Congratulations on making that first call so effectively. Apparently you established a good relationship.

As we discussed in your training program, your *call objectives* should be to

1. Reestablish your relationship
2. Discover Leigh's buying conditions (the what, why, who, when, and what price needs), so we can custom fit a program for them
3. Set up an appointment to present your solution

Also, as we discussed, your *presentation plan* for this call should include (see Chapters 7 and 10)

1. In advance of your meeting, prepare general *information-gathering questions* designed to get your customer talking and to achieve your call objectives. (Use our form below.)
2. Later in your meeting, use *probing and confirmation questions* to clarify and confirm Leigh's and your own perceptions of each buying condition.
3. During your sales meeting, write down each of Leigh's buying conditions. (Use our form below.)
4. To end your first meeting, use your notes to construct a *summary confirmation question* to clarify and confirm all six of Leigh's buying conditions.
5. Schedule a callback appointment to make your presentation and present your proposal.

Good luck!

INFORMATION-GATHERING QUESTIONS	**NOTES ON BUYING CONDITIONS**
(Example: Can you share with me what you had in mind?)	(Example: Needs a small meeting room)
	1.
	2.
	3.
	4.
	5.
	6.

PRESALE PLAN WORKSHEET

SALES CALL 2 — DISCOVERING A CUSTOMER STRATEGY

Name:_____

In call 2 your first objective is to (1) _____ _____ _____. To do this you should plan

to visit about (2) _____ information you acquired in call (3) _____.

Because your (4) _____ requested this meeting, you probably do not have to state your

(5) _____ _____ at the beginning of the call. The reason this meeting

was requested is because you apparently did a good job of (6) _____ the

_____ in call 1. In discovering your customer's needs (buying conditions) "what" refers

to services your customer needs and (7) _____ _____ refers to the

budget that your customer has. (8) _____ refers to the people coming, and

(9) _____ refers to the reason for the meeting. To secure general information you

should use (10) _____-_____ questions, and to get the details you should

use (11) _____ questions. (12) _____ questions check your

customer's and (13) _____ _____ perceptions. (14)

_____ _____ questions are used to summarize and check a list of things the

customer needs. Active listening requires that you (15) _____ _____ so you have

a record to work from in custom fitting a solution. You will also use your (16) _____

to construct your (17) _____ _____ question. When you have re-

ceived (18) _____ buying conditions from your customer, you will be prepared to set up an

(19) _____ to come back and make a (20) _____. Your second call

objective is to (21) _____, and your third call objective is to schedule an (22)

_____. Erin Adkins is in the (23) _____ accounts market, and Leigh

Combs is in the (24) _____ accounts market.

ASSESSMENT FORM 2

CUSTOMER STRATEGY

Salesperson's Name:_____

Date:_____

Assessment Item	Excellent		Average		Poor	Did Not Do
1. Effectively re-established relationship (made enthusiastic comments about information from first meeting)	10	9	8	7	6	0
2. Communicated positive body language (entrance, carriage, handshake, and seating)	10	9	8	7	6	0
3. Communicated positive verbal language (used positive words, showed enthusiasm with well-modulated voice)	10	9	8	7	6	0
4. Used customer's name effectively (used name at least three times)	10	9	8	7	6	0
5. Asked quality information-gathering questions (seemed prepared, questions were general and open ended)	10	9	8	7	6	0
6. Asked quality probing questions (followed up to secure all details)	10	9	8	7	6	0
7. Verified customer needs with good confirmation questions (wanted to be correct in interpreting customer needs)	10	9	8	7	6	0
8. Appeared to take effective notes (was organized and non-distracting, used notes in confirming needs)	10	9	8	7	6	0
9. Effectively set up next appointment (requested another meeting; suggested and wrote down date, time, and place)	10	9	8	7	6	0
10. Effectively thanked customer (communicated appreciation, said thank-you, indicated enthusiasm for next meeting)	10	9	8	7	6	0

Discovering Customer Needs Presentation:_____

Total Points

Your Name:_____

Return this form to salesperson and discuss your reaction to this presentation!

PART IV: DEVELOPING A SALES PRESENTATION STRATEGY

SALES MEMORANDUM 3A

To: **Association Account Sales**
From: **T. J. McKee, Sales Manager**
Re: **Your recent meeting on the Erin Adkins Account**
        (Call 3, Developing a Presentation Strategy)

Congratulations on doing such a thorough job of discovering Erin's buying conditions. I found that your list of buying conditions includes the kind of customer information important to increasing our sales and partnering with our clients. I would like to see a copy of Erin's proposal when you complete it.

Reviewing what we discussed during your training, your next *call objectives* are

1. Make a persuasive sales presentation that custom fits your proposal to Erin's needs
2. Negotiate any concerns Erin may have
3. Close and confirm the sale
4. Build repeat and referral business

Also, as we discussed, your *presentation plan* for this call should be to

1. Prepare and price a product solution that meets Erin's needs. *Complete the Sales Proposal Worksheet* (p. 463).
2. Before your sales call, prepare a *portfolio* presentation (see model on p. 462) that follows these guidelines.
   a. Review the relationship information and prepare for those topics you will discuss.
   b. Prepare a summary confirmation question that verifies the buying conditions secured in your second call (see Chapter 10).
   c. Select sales tools (proof devices) and create feature/benefit selling statements that appeal to Erin's buying conditions (see Chapter 11).
   d. Plan confirmation questions that verify Erin's acceptance of your solution to each buying condition. *Complete Strategic Planning Form A* (p. 466) for items b, c, and d.
   e. Prepare to negotiate the time, price, source, and product objections. *Complete Strategic Planning Form B* (p. 467) (see Chapter 12).
   f. Prepare at least four closing methods in addition to the summary of benefits. *Complete Strategic Planning Form C* (p. 468) (see Chapter 13).
   g. Plan methods to service the sale. Follow up by scheduling an appointment between now and the convention date (telephone call or personal visit) to follow through on guarantees concerning rooms and meals, suggestions about audiovisual needs, and any possible changes in the convention schedule. *Complete Strategic Planning Form D* (p. 469) (see Chapter 14).
3. During the sales call re-establish the relationship, and using your portfolio presentation
   a. Confirm all of Erin's previous buying conditions
   b. Match a proof device and feature/benefit selling statement with each buying condition
   c. Confirm Erin's acceptance of each of your proposed benefit statements
   d. Negotiate any sales resistance
   e. Close the sale
   f. Service the sale to get repeats and referrals

Good luck!

PARK INN
INTERNATIONAL™

SALES MEMORANDUM 3B

To: Corporate Account Sales
From: T. J. McKee, Sales Manager
Re: Your recent meeting on the Leigh Combs Account
           (Call 3, Developing a Presentation Strategy)

Congratulations on doing such a thorough job of discovering Leigh's buying conditions. I found that your list of buying conditions includes the kind of customer information important to increasing our sales and partnering with our clients. I would like to see a copy of Leigh's proposal when you complete it.

Reviewing what we discussed during your training, your next *call objectives* are

1. Make a persuasive sales presentation that custom fits your proposal to Leigh's needs
2. Negotiate any concerns Leigh may have
3. Close and confirm the sale
4. Build repeat and referral business

Also, as we discussed, your *presentation plan* for this call should be to

1. Prepare and price a product solution that meets Leigh's needs. *Complete the Sales Proposal Worksheet* (p. 463).
2. Before your sales call, prepare a *portfolio* presentation (see model on p. 462) that follows these guidelines:
   a. Review the relationship information and prepare for those topics you will discuss.
   b. Prepare a summary confirmation question that verifies the buying conditions secured in your second call (see Chapter 10).
   c. Select sales tools (proof devices) and create feature/benefit selling statements that appeal to Leigh's buying conditions (see Chapter 11).
   d. Plan confirmation questions that verify Leigh's acceptance of your solution to each buying condition. *Complete Strategic Planning Form A* (p. 466) for items b, c, and d.
   e. Prepare to negotiate the time, price, source, and product objections. *Complete Strategic Planning Form B* (p. 467) (see Chapter 12).
   f. Prepare at least four closing methods in addition to the summary-of-benefits close. *Complete Strategic Planning Form C* (p. 468) (see Chapter 13).
   g. Plan methods to service the sale. Follow up by scheduling an appointment between now and the convention date (telephone call or personal visit) to follow through on guarantees concerning rooms and meals, suggestions about audiovisual needs, and any possible changes in the convention schedule. *Complete Strategic Planning Form D* (p. 469) (see Chapter 14).
3. During the sales call re-establish the relationship, and using your portfolio presentation
   a. Confirm all of Leigh's previous buying conditions
   b. Match a proof device and feature/benefit selling statement with each buying condition
   c. Confirm Leigh's acceptance of each of your proposed benefit statements
   d. Negotiate any sales resistance
   e. Close the sale
   f. Service the sale to get repeats and referrals

Good luck!

PRESALE PLAN WORKSHEET

SALES CALL 3 — DEVELOPING A PRESENTATION

Name:_____

In opening your third sales call, your first activity should be to (1) _____ the relationship. To do this you will comment on topics discussed in call number (2) _____. After this step, you will make a (3) _____ type presentation. The first page in your presentation will be a (4) _____ of items discovered in call (5) _____. To present this you will use a (6) _____ _____ question. If your customer (7) _____ you will return to the (8) _____ (9) _____ condition, repeat it, and show a (10) _____ _____ from your (11) _____ strategy materials. In describing what you have shown, you will make one or more (12) _____ statements, and then you will use a (13) _____ _____ to see if your customer agrees and likes your solution. If your customer disagrees with any of your (14) _____ statements or raises a concern, you have an (15) _____ to overcome (16) _____. If your customer agrees, you will proceed through all (17) _____ buying conditions. After you have successfully gone through all the buying instructions, you are instructed to summarize the (18) _____ and (19) _____ the sale. Prior to the customer signing your sales proposal, you will need to overcome the (20) _____ concerns. After addressing each concern, you should try to (21) _____ the sale. Overcoming these concerns is best accomplished by you (22) _____ them and preparing ahead of time. After closing you will (23) _____ _____ _____ by scheduling an (24) _____ to follow up on meeting details, such as (25) _____ concerning rooms and meals.

ASSESSMENT FORM 3

PRESENTATION STRATEGY

Salesperson's Name:_____

Date:_____

Assessment Item	Excellent		Average	Poor		Did Not Do
1. Re-established a good relationship (talked sincerely and enthusiastically about topics of interest to customer) Comments:	10	9	8	7	6	0
2. Confirmed needs from previous meeting Comments:	10	9	8	7	6	0
3. Made solution sound appealing (used nontechnical, customer-oriented benefit statements) Comments:	10	9	8	7	6	0
4. Used proof devices to prove sales appeals (made product sound appealing) Comments:	10	9	8	7	6	0
5. Verified customer's understanding of solution Comments:	10	9	8	7	6	0
6. Negotiated price objection (established high value to price impression) Comments:	10	9	8	7	6	0
7. Negotiated time objection (created need to sign now using empathy) Comments:	10	9	8	7	6	0
8. Negotiated source objection (knew the competition well) Comments:	10	9	8	7	6	0
9. Asked for the order, closed sale (attempted to close after each objection) Comments:	10	9	8	7	6	0
10. Serviced the sale (established relationship that would result in referrals or repeat sales opportunities) Comments:	10	9	8	7	6	0

Presentation Points _____

Overall quality of sales portfolio and proof devices Comments:	25	20	15	10	5	0

Total Points _____

Your Name:_____

Return this form to salesperson and discuss your reaction to this presentation!

PORTFOLIO PRESENTATION MODEL

Three-ring binder with pockets recommended

PAGE 1
Summary of Customer's
Buying Conditions
1.
2.
3.
4.
5.
6.
(confirmation question)

PAGE 2
Buying Condition
1

PAGE 3
Proof Devices
(could be more than one)

(state benefits, ask
confirmation question)

PAGE 4
Buying Condition
2

PAGE 5
Proof Devices

(state benefits, ask
confirmation question)

PAGE 6
Buying Condition
3

PAGE 7
Proof Devices

(state benefits, ask
confirmation question)

PAGE 8
Buying Condition
4

PAGE 9
Proof Devices

(state benefits, ask
confirmation question)

PAGE 10
Buying Condition
5

PAGE 11
Proof Devices

(state benefits, ask
confirmation question)

PAGE 12
Buying Condition
6

PAGE 13
Proof Devices

(state benefits, ask
confirmation question)

PAGE 14
Summary of Benefits
1.
2.
3.
4.
5.
6.
(trial close)

**FRONT POCKET
MATERIALS**
Additional value-added
pages as needed to over-
come sales resistance,
close, and service the sale

**BACK POCKET
MATERIALS**
Additional value-added
pages as needed to over-
come sales resistance,
close, and service the sale

PARK INN
INTERNATIONAL™

SALES PROPOSAL

Customer Name: _____ Title: _____

Organization Name: _____ Telephone: _____

Address: _____

Date(s) of Meetings: _____

Kind of Meetings: _____

Buying Conditions (what the customer needs—be specific): _____

_____

_____

A. Meal Functions Needed

	Time	Description	Quantity	Price	Total
Meal 1 Meal 2 Other		(Beverages, setup fees, etc.)			

Total _____

Sales Taxes _____

Service Charge _____

Total Meal Cost _____

B. Meeting and Banquet Rooms and Equipment Needed (describe time, date, and cost)

Total _____

Sales Taxes _____

Total Meeting/Banquet Rooms and Equipment Charges _____

C. Guest Rooms Needed

Number of Rooms Needed	Description (dates, location, special conditions)	Group Rate per Room	Total Cost

Total _____

Sales Taxes _____

Total Guest Room Charges _____

D. Total Customer Costs (from above)

A. $_____ plus B. $_____ plus C. $_____ equals **Total Charges** $_____

_____   _____
Authorized Signature   Date   Customer Signature   Date

_____   _____
Title   Title

580 King Street, Maple Hill, Ontario K2R 4P7
555–225–0925   Fax 555–225–9386

MEETING AND BANQUET ROOM SCHEDULE OF EVENTS

1ST THURSDAY OF NEXT MONTH

Maple Park East
Open—Expect confirmation tomorrow

Maple Park West
Open—Expect confirmation tomorrow

Park Lane
10:00 a.m. C of C Membership Committee
2:00 p.m. County Central Planning Committee

Top of the Park
Open—Expect confirmation tomorrow

Revolver
Open

Dance Floor
7:00 p.m. IBM Dinner and Dance

Parkview
Open—Expect confirmation tomorrow

1007 and 1009
11:00 a.m. Advertising Profs' Luncheon
7:00 p.m. IBM Communication Seminar

107 and 109
10:00 a.m.—Expect confirmation tomorrow

ATTENTION: Phone 225–0925, ext. 8512
immediately to confirm reservations.

STRATEGIC PLANNING FORM A

MATCHING BUYING CONDITIONS WITH PROOF DEVICES AND FEATURE/BENEFITS

BUYING CONDITION	PROOF DEVICE	FEATURE	BENEFIT	CONFIRMATION QUESTION
You indicated you wanted . . .	*Here is . . .*	*which has (have) . . .*	*which means to you . . .*	*What do you think?*
1. ___ (number) guest rooms	A picture of one of our guest rooms (see p. 434)	Just been remodelled	Your people will enjoy clean, comfortable, spacious, and attractive surroundings	Is that what you had in mind?
2.				
3.				
4.				
5.				
6.				

Optional Role Play 3-A Instructions (see Chapters 10 and 11)

Step 1 Prepare your presentation plan by completing the above form.

Step 2 Organize your presentation plan by placing the above information on 8½" × 11" sheets of paper according to the portfolio presentation plan on p. 462. Select proof devices from the product strategy materials presented on pp. 428–443 and the completed proposal on p. 463.

Step 3 Using the portfolio materials you have prepared, pair off with another student who will play the role of your customer. Review your customer's buying conditions, present your solutions with benefit statements, prove your sales appeals with demonstrations, secure your customer's reactions, and summarize the benefits presented. Discuss your customer's reactions to your presentation. This exercise will help you prepare for call 3.

STRATEGIC PLANNING FORM B

ANTICIPATING AND NEGOTIATING SALES RESISTANCE WORKSHEET

PART I	ANTICIPATING SALES RESISTANCE	PART II	NEGOTIATING SALES RESISTANCE
Type	What Customer Might Say	Methods*	What You Will Say (include proof devices you will use)
Time	"I would like to take a day to think over your proposal."	Indirect denial	"I understand, but . . ." (Show p. 465, Schedule of Events.)
Price	"That price is way over my budget."		
Source	"I'm going to check with the Marriott."		
Product	"I'm concerned about the size of your meeting rooms."		

Optional Role Play 3-B Instructions

Using the preceding material you have prepared, pair off with another student who will play the role of your customer. Provide your customer with the material in Part I and instruct him or her to raise sales resistance in any order he or she chooses. Playing the role of the salesperson, you will respond with the material you prepared in Part II. Continue the dialogue until all the types of sales resistance have been successfully negotiated. Discuss with your customer his or her reaction to your methods of successfully negotiating the different types of sales resistance. This exercise will help you prepare for Sales Call 3.

*Methods of Negotiating Sales Resistance (see Chapter 12)

- Direct Denial
- Indirect Denial
- Question
- Third Party
- Superior Benefit
- Demonstration
- Trial Offer
- Feel, Felt, Found

STRATEGIC PLANNING FORM C

CLOSING AND CONFIRMING THE SALE WORKSHEET

PART I	PART II	
Verbal and Nonverbal Closing Clues	Method of Closing*	What You Will Say (include proof devices you will use)
Agreement with each benefit	Summary of the benefits and direct appeal	"Let me review what we have talked about . . . May I get your signature?" (Use p. 463, Sales Proposal.)
Agreement after an objection to price, time, or source	Assumption	
Appears enthusiastic and impatient	Trial close and assumption	
Agreement with all benefits but will not under any circum-stances go over budget	Special concession	

Optional Role Play 3-C Instructions

Using the preceding material you have prepared, pair off with another student who will play the role of your customer. Provide your customer with the appropriate closing clues from Part I and instruct him or her to provide verbal or nonverbal closing clues in any order he or she chooses. Playing the role of the salesperson, you will respond with the material you prepared in Part II. Continue the dialogue until you have responded to all the anticipated closing clues. Discuss with your customer his or her reaction to your methods of successfully closing and confirming the sale. This exercise will help you prepare for Sales Call 3.

*Methods of Closing the Sale (see Chapter 13)

- Trial Close
- Summary of the Benefits
- Assumption
- Special Concession
- Multiple Option
- Direct Appeal

STRATEGIC PLANNING FORM D

SERVICING THE SALE WORKSHEET

PART I	PART II
What You Will Do to Add Value to the Sale	What You Will Say or Write to Add Value to the Sale
1. Schedule appointments to confirm rooms and final counts on meals. Date Time 1_____ 1_____ 2_____ 2_____	"I would like to call to confirm . . ." (Show p. 443, Convention Centre Policies, and write date and time on your calendar.)
2. Make suggestions during next meeting about audiovisual equipment, beverages for breaks, etc.	
3. Provide personal assurances concerning your continuing efforts to make the meeting an outstanding success.	
4. Prepare thank-you letter concerning call 3.	

Optional Role Play 3-D Instructions

Using the preceding material you have prepared, pair off with another student who will play the role of your customer. Using the topics identified in Part I, verbally present what you have prepared in Part II on this form. Discuss with your customer his or her reaction to your methods of servicing the sale. This exercise will help you prepare for Sales Call 3.

Methods of Servicing the Sale (see Chapter 14)

- Suggestion Selling
- Follow through on Promises and Obligations
- Follow up to Ensure Customer Satisfaction

Notes

CHAPTER 1

1. Interview with Tony Woodson, Purolator Courier Ltd., May 20, 1999.
2. Correspondence from Louise McConkey, Purolator Courier Ltd., May 19, 1999.
3. John Naisbitt, *Megatrends* (New York: Warner Books, 1982), pp. 14–16.
4. Stan Davis and Christopher Meyer, *Blur: The Speed of Change in the Connected Economy* (New York: Addison-Wesley Publishers), 1998, p. 9.
5. David Shenk, *Data Smog: Surviving the Information Glut* (New York: HarperEdge, 1997), pp. 27–29.
6. "Service Earns IBM Excellence Award," *The Globe and Mail*, November 19, 1997, p. C6.
7. Chad Kaydo, "America's Best Sales Forces," *Sales & Marketing Management*, October 1997, p. 61.
8. William M. Pride, O. C. Ferrell, H. F. (Herb) MacKenzie, and Kim Snow, *Marketing: Concepts and Strategies*, Canadian Edition (Toronto: Houghton Mifflin, 1998), p. 13.
9. Montrose S. Sommers, J. G. Barnes, W. J. Stanton, M. J. Etzel, and B. J. Walker, *Fundamentals of Marketing*, 8th Canadian Edition (Toronto: McGraw-Hill Ryerson, 1998), p. 448.
10. Dennis Fox, "Ringing up Prospects," *Sales & Marketing Management*, March 1993, pp. 75–77.
11. Robert M. Peterson, George H. Lucas, and Patrick L. Schul, "Forming Consultative Trade Alliances: Walking the Walk in the New Selling Environment," *NAMA Journal*, Spring 1998, p. 11; Beth Belton, "Technology Is Changing Face of U.S. Sales Force," *USA Today*, February 9, 1999, p. 2A. Neil Rackham and John DeVincentis, *Rethinking the Sales Force* (New York: McGraw-Hill, 1999), p. 25.
12. Leslie Angello-Dean, "Converting Salespeople to Consultant/Advisors," *Sales & Marketing Training*, March–April 1990, p. 18.
13. William M. Pride, O. C. Ferrell, H. F. (Herb) MacKenzie, and Kim Snow, p. 523.
14. Robert E. Miller and Stephen E. Heiman, *Strategic Selling* (New York: Warren Books, 1985), p. 26.
15. "Menu Analysis: Key to the Sale," *Institutional Distribution*, May 15, 1990, pp. 122–124.
16. Fiona Gibb, "The New Sales Basics," *Sales & Marketing Management*, April 1995, p. 81.
17. John O'Toole, "Get Inside Your Clients' Skin," *Selling*, May 1995, p. 77.
18. Interview with Wes Delnea, president of Windsor Factory Supply Limited, March 20, 1997.
19. Stephen Hagg, Maeve Cummings, and James Dawkins, *Management Information Systems for the Information Age* (New York: Irwin McGraw-Hill, 1998), p. 15.
20. Ginger Conlon, "Business with a Capital E," *Sales & Marketing Management*, August 1999, p. 80.
21. John Heinrich, "Relationship Selling," *Personal Selling Power*, May–June 1995, p. 32.
22. Stanley A. Brown, *What Customers Value Most* (Etobicoke, ON: John Wiley & Sons Canada, 1995), p. 8.
23. Michael D. Hutt and Thomas W. Speh, *Business Marketing Management: A Strategic View of Industrial and Oranizational Markets*, 6th edition (Toronto: Harcourt Brace College Publishers, 1998), pp. 111, 120.
24. Rosabeth Moss Kanter, "The Power of Partnering," *Sales & Marketing Management*, June 1997, p. 26; Donna Fenn, "Details, Details, Details," *Inc.*, July 1997, p. 107.
25. Robert M. Peterson, George H. Lucas, and Patrick L. Schul, "Forming Consultative Trade Alliances: Walking the Walk in the New Selling Environment," *NAMA Journal*, Spring 1998, pp. 10–11, 16–19.
26. Interview with Wes Delnea, March 20, 1997; Correspondence from Wes Delnea, May 19, 1999.

SOURCES FOR BOXED INSERTS

a. James Champy, "Selling to Tomorrow's Customer," *Sales & Marketing Management*, March 1999, p. 28; "Track Funds the Easy Way with Your Mutual Friend," *The Globe and Mail*, p. C2. Neil Rackham and John DeVincentis, *Rethinking the Sales Force* (New York: McGraw-Hill, 1999), p. 28.

CHAPTER 2

1. Interview with Debbie Hanlon, April 10, 1997.
2. Interview with Susan Green, July 18, 1999.
3. John Greenwood, "Job One," *The*

Financial Post Magazine, June 1997, pp. 18–22.

4. Stanley Marcus, "Sales School," *Fast Company*, November 1998, p. 105.

5. Thomas A. Stewart, "Knowledge, the Appreciating Commodity," *Fortune*, October 12, 1998, p. 18.

6. John Naisbitt, *Megatrends* (New York: Warner Books, 1982), p. 18.

7. William Band, "The Power of Customer-Centric Thinking," *Marketing Magazine*, May 11, 1998.

8. Interview with Alex Martin, April 17, 1997.

9. Harry Beckwith, *Selling the Invisible* (New York: Warner Books, 1997), p.38.

10. Allan S. Boress, *The I Hate Selling Book* (New York: AMACOM, 1995), p.8.

11. Linda Corman, "Look Who's Selling Now," *Selling*, July–August 1996, p. 53.

12. Ibid.

13. Mark MacKinnon, "Bankruptcies Recede with Debt Levels," *The Globe and Mail*, May 3, 1999, p. B1.

14. Louie Palu, "Three Blondes and a Brownie, Edmonton," *The Financial Post Magazine*," July/August 1997, p. 11; www.interlog.com/~3blondes/The.html, accessed May 16, 1999; Donna Korchinski, "Three Blondes Cook Up Sweet Success," *The Globe and Mail*, August 4, 1999, p. B10. Correspondence from Candace Brinsmead, Three Blondes and a Brownie, March 1, 2000.

15. Beth Belton, "Technology Is Changing Face of U.S. Sales Force." *USA Today*, February 9, 1999, p. A2.

16. Mary Sykes Wylie, "Free." *Networker*, January/February 1998, p. 25.

17. Statistics Canada, 1991, Catalogue 92–339E.

18. "A Career in Sales," *Selling Power*, 1997, p. 12; "Selling Sales to Students," *Sales & Marketing Management*, January 1998, p. 15.

19. "The *Selling Power* 400," *Selling Power*, September 1998, p. 70.

20. Ken Liebeskind, "Sporting Chance," *Selling Power*, June 1998, pp. 14–16.

21. Canadian Professional Sales Association, "The CPSA Benefits Bulletin," Vol. 4, Issue 4, September 1999.

22. Ibid.

23. Ibid.

24. "Help Wanted," *Sales & Marketing Management*, July 1998, p. 14.

25. Statistics Canada, 1991, Catalogue 92–339E.

26. Eli Jones, Jesse N. Moore, Andrea J. S. Stanaland, and Rosalind A. J. Wyatt, "Salesperson Race and Gender and the Access and Legitimacy Paradigm: Does Difference Make a Difference," *The Journal of Personal Selling & Sales Management*, Fall 1998, p. 71.

27. Interview with Melinda Hancock, March 25, 1997.

28. Statistics Canada, 1991, Catalogue 92–339E.

29. Francy Blackwood, "5 Hot Fields," *Selling*, July–August 1995, p. 49.

30. Ibid., pp. 54–56.

31. "Young Entrepreneur Award Winners Have What it Takes," *The Globe and Mail*, October 26, 1998, p. C13; "Seizing the Opportunity of a Lifetime," News Release, Business Development Bank of Canada, October 21, 1998; Interview with Ruth Bell Steinhuer, May 20, 1999.

32. "Delivering the Goods," *Profit*, December–January 1999, p. 42.

33. Statistics Canada, *Wholesaling and Retailing in Canada*, Catalogue 63–236–XPB, 1995.

34. Interview with Sean Donovan, May 17, 1999. Correspondence with Annie Lalonde, Public Relations Manager, Medis Health and Pharmaceutical Services Inc., May 20, 1999.

35. Mark Stevenson, "The Lean, Mean Sales Machine," *Canadian Business*, January 1994, pp. 32–36.

36. Allan Lynch, "Secrets of a Super Salesman," *Atlantic Progress*, April 1999, pp. 5–52, 56.

37. Beth Belton, "Technology Is Changing the Face of U.S. Sales Force," p. A2.

38. "Industry Report 1998," *Training*, October 1998, p. 55.

39. Interview with Trevor Adey, April 22, 1997.

40. Interview with Valerie Howe, May 19, 1999.

SOURCES FOR BOXED INSERTS

a. Gene Koretz, "Women Swell the Workforce," *Business Week*, November 4, 1996, p. 32; Naomi Freundlich, "Maybe Working Women Can't Have It All," *Business Week*, September 15, 1997, pp. 19–22; Keith H. Hammonds, "She Works Hard for the Money," *Business Week*, May 22, 1995, p. 54; Anne Fisher, "Overseas, U.S. Businesswomen May Have the Edge," *Fortune*, September 28, 1998, p. 304.

b. Michele Marchetti, "Sales Training Even a Rep Could Love," *Sales & Marketing Management*, June 1998, p. 70. *Field Sales Training: Postal Education*. CPC Certified Postal Consultant (Pitney Bowes Canada, Sales Programs & Operations, 1998). Correspondence from David Munro, February 13, 2000.

CHAPTER 3

1. "Cold, Hard Cash," *Profit*, October–November 1997, pp. 13–14, 16, 21; www.premdor.com/about-premdor/strip-abouttext.html, May 13, 1999.

2. Daniel Goleman, *Working With Emotional Intelligence* (New York: Bantam Books, 1998), pp. 24–28, 317.

3. L. B. Gschwandtner and Gerhard Gschwandtner, "Balancing Act," *Selling Power*, June 1996, p. 24.

4. Ibid.

5. Denis Waitley, *Empires of the Mind* (New York: William Morrow, 1995), p. 3.

6. Jonathan J. Ward, "Foolish Inconsistency," *Sales & Marketing Management*, March 1993, p. 32.

7. J. D. Power and Associates, *Fact Sheet* (Los Angeles, 1993).

8. "Partnering: The Heart of Selling Today" (Des Moines: American Media Incorporated, 1990).

9. Paul S. Goldner, "How to Set the Playing Field," *Selling*, April 1998, p. 9.

10. Larry Wilson, *Selling in the 90s* (Chicago: Nightingale Conant, 1988), p. 35.

11. William Keenan, Jr. "Customer Satisfaction Builds Business," *Selling*, March 1998, p. 12.

12. Madelyn Callahan, "Teaching the Sales Relationship," *Training and Development*, December 1992, p. 35.

13. Maxwell Maltz, *Psycho-Cybernetics* (Englewood Cliffs, NJ: Prentice-Hall, 1960), p. 2.

14. "The Keys to Good Selling," *Sales & Marketing Management*, January 1990, p. 32.

15. Nathaniel Branden, *Self-Esteem at Work* (San Francisco: Jossey-Bass Publishers, 1998), pp. 20–21.

16. Denis Waitley, *The Double Win* (Old Tappan, NJ: Fleming H. Revell Company, 1985), p. 31.

17. Stephen E. Heiman, Diane Sanchez, and Tad Tuleja, *The New Strategic Selling* (New York: Warner Books, 1998), p. 73.

18. "The Strength of Character," *Royal Bank Letter*, Royal Bank of Canada, May–June 1988, p. 1.

19. Eli Jones, Jesse N. Moore, Andrea J. S. Stanaland, and Rosalind A. J. Wyatt, "Salesperson Race and Gender and the Access and Legitimacy Paradigm: Does Difference Make a Difference," *Journal of Personal Selling and Sales Management*, Fall 1998, p. 74.

20. Trumfio, "More than Words," *Sales & Marketing Management*, April 1994, p. 55.

21. "Get to the Truth of the Message," *The Pryor Report*, Vol. VI, No. 1A, p. 7.

22. Susan Bixler, *The Professional Image* (New York: Putnam Publishing Group, 1984), p. 216.

23. Barbara Pachter and Marjorie Brody, *Complete Business Etiquette Handbook* (New York: Prentice Hall, 1995), p. 14.

24. Adapted from Leonard Zunin, *Contact: The First Four Minutes* (New York: Nash Publishing, Ballantine Books, 1972), p. 109.

25. "Name That Customer," *Personal Selling Power*, January–February 1993, p. 48.

26. Deborah Blum, "Face It!" *Psychology Today*, September/October 1998, pp. 32–69.

27. John Molloy, *Dress for Success* (New York: Peter H. Wyden, 1975); *The Woman's Dress for Success Book* (Chicago: Follett Publishing, 1977); and *Live for Success* (New York: Morrow, 1981).

28. Anne M. Phaneuf, "Decoding Dress Codes," *Sales & Marketing Management*, September 1995, p. 139.

29. Susan Bixler, *Professional Presence* (New York: G. P. Putnam's Sons, 1991), p. 141.

30. Susan Bixler and Nancy Nix-Rice, *The New Professional Image*, Adams Media Corporation, 1997, p. 11–15; Barbara Pachter and Marjorie Brody, *Complete Business Etiquette Handbook*, p. 12.

31. Peter Urs Bender, *Secrets of Power Presentations*, 8th Edition (Toronto: The Achievement Group, 1999), pp. 188–189.

32. Susan Berkley, "Hone Your Sharpest Sales Weapon," *Sales & Field Force Automation*, July 1997, p. 24.

33. Barry L. Reece and Rhonda Brandt, *Effective Human Relations in Organizations*, 7th ed. (Boston: Houghton Mifflin 1999), p, 293.

34. "Sales-Related Book Picked in Top Ten for Shaping America's Culture," *Des Moines Register*, April 3, 1985, p. 3.

35. L. B. Gschwandtner, "Mary Lou Retton," *Personal Selling Power*, 15th Anniversary Issue, 1995, p. 99.

36. Shad Helmstetter, *What to Say When You Talk to Yourself* (New York: Pocket Books, 1982), p. 72.

37. Correspondence from Craig Proctor, May 20, 1999; CBC-TV "Venture" episode, Top Sellers, originally broadcast May 21, 1995.

SOURCES FOR BOXED INSERTS

a. Robert McGarvey and Scott Smith, "Etiquette 101," *Training*, September 1993, p. 51; Ann C. Humphries, "Errors Steal Power from Power Lunch," *San Jose Mercury News*, November 4, 1990, p. 2; Erika Rasmusson, "Beyond Miss Manners," *Sales & Marketing Management*, August 1997, p. 84.

b. Gerald A. Michaelson, "Build Relationships by 'Making Deposits,'" *Selling*, August 1997, p. 7.

CHAPTER 4

1. Ian Austen, "Problem Child," *Canadian Business*, March 26, 1999, p. 30.

2. Ibid., p. 24.

3. David W. Merrill and Roger H. Reid, *Personal Styles and Effective Performance* (Radnor, PA: Chilton Books, 1981), p. 1.

4. Robert J. Sternberg, *Thinking Styles* (New York: Cambridge University Press, 1997), p. 8.

5. Robert M. Hecht, *Office Systems*, February 1990, p. 26.

6. Tony Alessandra and Michael J. O'Connor, *People Smart* (LaJolla, CA: Keynote Publishing, 1990), p. 10.

7. The dominance factor was described in an early book by William M. Marston, *The Emotions of Normal People* (New York: Harcourt, 1928). Research conducted by Rolfe LaForge and Robert F. Suczek resulted in the development of the Interpersonal Checklist (ICL), which features a dominant–submissive scale. A person who receives a high score on the ICL tends to lead, persuade, and control others. The Interpersonal Identity Profile, developed by David W. Merrill and James W. Taylor, features a factor called "assertiveness." Persons classified as being high in assertiveness tend

to have strong opinions, make quick decisions, and be directive when dealing with people. Persons classified as being low in assertiveness tend to voice moderate opinions, make thoughtful decisions, and be supportive when dealing with others.

8. David W. Johnson, *Reaching Out—Interpersonal Effectiveness and Self-Actualization*, 2nd ed. (Englewood Cliffs, NJ: Prentice-Hall, 1981), p. 44.

9. The research conducted by LaForge and Suczek resulted in identification of the hostile–loving continuum, which is similar to the sociability continuum. Their Interpersonal Checklist features this scale. L. L. Thurstone and T. G. Thurstone developed the Thurstone Temperament Schedule, which provides an assessment of a "sociable" factor. Persons with high scores in this area enjoy the company of others and make friends easily. The Interpersonal Identity Profile developed by Merrill and Taylor contains an objectivity continuum. A person with low objectivity is seen as attention seeking, involved with the feelings of others, informal, and casual in social relationships. A person who is high in objectivity appears to be somewhat indifferent toward the feelings of others. This person is formal in social relationships.

10. Charles Margerison, *How to Assess Your Managerial Style* (New York: AMACOM, A Division of American Management Association, 1979), p. 49.

11. Pierce J. Howard and Jane M. Howard, "Buddy, Can You Paradigm?" *Training & Development*, September 1995, p. 31.

12. Sam Deep and Lyle Sussman, *Close the Deal* (Reading, MA: Perseus Books, 1999), p. 157.

13. Len D'Innocenzo and Jack Cullen, "Chameleon Management," *Personal Selling Power*, January–February 1995, p. 61.

14. Rod Nichols, "How to Sell to

Different Personality Types," *Personal Selling Power*, November–December 1992, p. 46.

15. Stuart Atkins, *How to Get the Most from Styles-based Training* (Beverly Hills, CA: Stuart Atkins, 1996), p. 1.

16. Robert Bolton and Dorothy Grover Bolton, *People Styles at Work* (New York: AMACOM, 1996), p. 65.

17. John Emery, "Mastering Vital Steps," *Business Outlook*, November 3, 1986, p. 14.

18. Tony Alessandra and Michael J. O'Connor, *People Smart* (LaJolla, CA: Keynote Publishing, 1990), p. 15.

19. Peter Verburg, "Jaws," *Canadian Business*, October 10, 1997, p. 52.

20. Stuart Atkins, *How to Get the Most from Styles-based Training*, p. 3.

21. Ron Willingham, *Integrity Selling* (New York: Doubleday, 1987), pp. 21–23.

22. Eric F. Douglas, *Straight Talk* (Palo Alto, CA: 1998), p. 92.

23. Ron Willingham, *Integrity Selling*, pp. 21–23.

24. David W. Merrill and Roger H. Reid, *Personal Styles and Effective Performance*, pp. 134, 135.

25. Stuart Atkins, *The Name of Your Game* (Beverly Hills, CA: Ellis & Stewart, 1981), p. 51.

26. Chris Lee, "What's Your Style," *Training*, May 1991, p. 28.

27. Interview with Sonia Ajem, March 19, 1997.

SOURCES FOR BOXED INSERTS

a. Stuart Atkins, *LIFO Personality Digest* (Beverly Hills, CA: Stuart Atkins, 1991), p. 126; *High Performance Selling* (Beverly Hills, CA: Stuart Atkins), pp. 1–10.

b. Roger Wenschlag, *The Versatile Salesperson* (New York: John Wiley & Sons, 1989), pp. 165–171. Malcolm Fleschner, "The Adaptability Factor," *Selling Power*, January/February 1997, pp. 54–56. Rod Nichols, "How to Sell to Different Personality Types," *Personal Selling Power*, November–December 1992,

pp. 46–47. David W. Merrill and Roger H. Reid, *Personal Styles and Effective Performance* (Radnor, PA: Chilton Books, 1981), p. 2. Tony Alessandra, *People Smarts* (San Diego, CA: Pfeiffer & Company, 1994), p. 55.

CHAPTER 5

1. Personal interview with Michael Tulk, May 26, 1997.

2. Erick Schonfeld, "The Customized, Digitized, Have-it-Your-Way Economy," *Fortune*, September 28, 1998, p. 116.

3. www.rubbermaid.com/corp/more/rd2main.htm

4. "Track Funds the Easy Way with Your Mutual Friend," *The Globe and Mail*, March 30, 1999, p. C2.

5. John Fellows, "A Decent Proposal," *Personal Selling Power*, November–December 1995, p. 56.

6. Adapted from John Fellows, "A Decent Proposal."

7. Joseph Conlin, "The Write Staff," *Sales & Marketing Management*, January 1998, p. 73.

8. Jim Morgan, "The Best Sales Reps Will Take on Their Bosses for You," *Purchasing*, November 7, 1996, pp. 50–52.

9. Michael G. Crawford, "Building the Perfect Sales Force," *Profit*, April–May 1997, p. 28.

10. Ian Edwards, "Safety First," *Profit*, February–March 1997, p. 22.

11. Interview with Michelle A. Reece, The Certified Medical Representative Institute, Inc., Roanoke, VA, July 19, 1996.

12. Elizabeth Church, "Service Firms Follow the Flow to ISO," *The Globe and Mail*, August 24, 1998, p. B11.

13. Ian Gelenter, "Build Satisfaction with a Service Contract," *Selling*, May 1998, p. 7.

14. Robert Levering and Milton Moskowitz, *The 100 Best Companies to Work for in America* (New York: New American Library, 1993), p. 373.

15. Interview with Paul Antle, May 13, 1997.
16. Michael R. Williams and Jill S. Attaway, "Exploring Salespersons' Customer Orientation as a Mediator of Organizational Culture's Influence on Buyer-Seller Relationships, *Journal of Personal Selling & Sales Management*, Fall 1996, pp. 33–52.
17. Gail Chaisson, "Nissan 'Stepped' into New Order," *Marketing*, November 9, 1992, p. 14.
18. Interview with Mike Urquhart, May 20, 1997.
19. Alan Test, "The Scoop on the Competition," *Personal Selling Power*, November–December 1995, p. 38.
20. "Best Advice," *Sales & Marketing Management*, January 1990, p. 34.
21. "Power Tools," *Sales & Marketing Management*, March 1999, p. 50. Matt Purdue, "Networked With ... Chip Herbert," *Sales & Field Force Automation*, January 1998, p. 18.
22. Interview with David Wilkins, May 13, 1997.
23. "Group Selling," *Success*, May 1990, p. 29.
24. Jerry Vass, "Ten Expensive Selling Errors," *Agency Sales Magazine*, July 1998, pp. 38–39.
25. Adopted from "Benchmarking the Sales Function," a report based on a study of 100 salespeople from small, medium, and large businesses, conducted by Ron Volper Group, White Plains, NY, 1996. Summary presented in the June 1997 issue of *Inc.*, p. 96.

SOURCES FOR BOXED FEATURES

a. Robert G. Cooper, *Product Leadership* (Reading, MA: Perseus Books, 1998), p. 12. Neil Rackham, "What's New," *Selling Power*, January/February 1999, pp. 90, 92–93.

CHAPTER 6

1. David Menzies, "Meeting the Challenge," *Profit*, June 1998, pp. 148–150.
2. William M. Pride, O. C. Ferrell, H. F. (Herb) MacKenzie, and Kim Snow, *Marketing: Concepts and Strategies*, Canadian ed. (Toronto: Houghton Mifflin, 1998), p. 217.
3. D. Lee Carpenter, "Return on Innovation—the Power of Being Different," *Retailing Issues Letter*, May 1998, p. 3.
4. "Secrets of the Best Sellers," *Profit*, January–February 1999, p. 21.
5. Personal correspondence from Scott Chandler, Padinox Inc., May 18, 1997.
6. David Menzies, "Meeting the Challenge," *Profit*, June 1998, p. 150. Correspondence from Karina Pollard, Castek, March 6, 2000.
7. Carl K. Clayton, "Sell Quality, Service, Your Company, Yourself," *Personal Selling Power*, January–February 1990, p. 47.
8. Personal correspondence from Patricia Dietz, Stora Port Hawkesbury Ltd., June 9, 1997.
9. J. Thomas Russell and W. Ronald Lane, *Kleppner's Advertising Procedure* (Englewood Cliffs, NJ: Prentice-Hall, 1996), pp. 46–47.
10. Andy Cohen, "Starting Over," *Sales & Marketing Management*, September 1995, pp. 40–41.
11. Lawrence Ladin, "Selling Innovation: Tips for Commercial Success," *The Wall Street Journal*, March 20, 1995, p. A14.
12. Personal correspondence from Rick Winston, Sun Life Assurance Company of Canada, June 11, 1997.
13. Michael D. Mondello, "Naming Your Price," *Inc.*, July 1992, p. 82.
14. Michael Treacy, "You Need a Value Discipline—But Which One?" *Fortune*, April 17, 1995, p. 195.
15. Robert Shulman and Richard Miniter, "Discounting Is No Bargain," *The Wall Street Journal*, December 7, 1998, p. A30.
16. Albert D. Bates, "Pricing for Profit," *Retailing Issues Letter*, Vol. II, No. 8, September 1990, p. 2.
17. Derek DeCloet, "The Good the Bad and the Ho-Hum," *Canadian Business*, September 24, 1999, p. 76; Joe Chidley, "Down and Out on Bay Street," *Canadian Business*, September 24, 1999, p. 115.
18. Thomas Petzinger, Jr., "This Former Salesman Treats Development Like a Sacred Cow," *The Wall Street Journal*, September 29, 1995, p. B1.
19. Personal correspondence from Randy Armel, Alive & Well Canada Inc., June 10, 1997.
20. Malcolm Fleschner and Charles Lee Browne, "Value Sells," *Selling Power*, March 1996, pp. 48–52.
21. "How to Win Customers and Influence Profits," *Norwest Business Advantage*, January/February 1998, p. 9.
22. Malcolm Fleschner, "We Want to Be the Biggest Small Company Around," *Selling Power*, April 1999, pp. 48–52.
23. Adopted from a model described in "Marketing Success through Differentiation—of Anything," *Harvard Business Review*, January–February 1980.
24. Tom Peters, *Thriving on Chaos* (New York: Alfred A. Knopf, 1988), p. 92.
25. Joanna Johnson, "A New Perspective on Marketing," *Construction Dimensions*, April 1990, p. 14.
26. Ted Levitt, *Marketing Imagination* (New York: Free Press, 1983), p. 80.
27. Ibid., p. 81.
28. Thomas A. Stewart, "A Satisfied Customer Isn't Enough," *Fortune*, July 21, 1997, pp. 112–113.
29. "Business Bulletin," *The Wall Street Journal*, September 24, 1998, p. A1.
30. Madalyn Callahan, "Tending the Sales Relationship," *Training and Development*, December 1992, p. 32.
31. Larry Wilson, *Changing the Game: The New Way to Sell* (New York: Simon & Schuster, 1987), p. 200.
32. Ibid., p. 31.
33. "Marilyn Carlson Nelson, Carlson Companies CEO," *Fast Company*, November 1998, p. 108.

34. Ted Levitt, *Marketing Imagination* (New York: Free Press, 1983), p. 82.

35. Francy Blackwood, "The Concept That Sells," *Selling*, March 1995, pp. 34–36.

36. Sue Shellenbarger, "The New Pace of Work Makes Taking a Break for Child Care Scarier," *The Wall Street Journal*, May 19, 1999, p. B1.

37. William C. Symonds, "Build a Better Mousetrap Is No Claptrap," *Business Week*, February 1, 1999, p. 47.

38. Stan Davis and Christopher Meyer, *Blur: The Speed of Change in the Connected Economy* (New York: Addison-Wesley Publishers, 1998), p. 47.

39. Interview with Greg Brophy, February 19, 1997. Correspondence from Judy Robson, August 26, 1999.

SOURCES FOR BOXED INSERTS

a. Adapted from discussion in Leonard L. Berry, A. Parasuraman, and Valerie A. Zeithaml, "The Service-Quality Puzzle" *Business Horizons*, September– October 1988, pp. 35–43. Robert Kreitner, *Management*, 5th ed. (Boston: Houghton Mifflin, 1992), pp. 613–614.

b. Rhonda M. Abrams, "Problem for Pros: Knowing How Much to Charge," *The Des Moines Register*, January 26, 1998, p. B2.

CHAPTER 7

1. Interview with Ron Trudel and Ike Vickar, March 5, 1997.

2. Dick Schaff and Tom Cothran, "Sales Training in the Era of the Customer," *Sales Training*, February 1998, p. 4.

3. "Six Selling Rules," *Training and Development Journal*, March 1998, p. 40.

4. Michael Hammer and James Champy, *Reengineering the Corporation: A Manifest for Business Revolution* (New York: Harper Business, 1993), p. 18.

5. Tom Peters and Nancy Austin, *A Passion for Excellence* (New York: Random House, 1985), p. 71.

6. "How Well Do You Know Your Customers?" *Sales and Field Force Automation*, January 1999, p. 141.

7. Stan Davis and Christopher Meyer, *Blur: The Speed of Change in the Connected Economy* (New York: Addison Wesley Publishers, 1998), p. 16.

8. Stanley Brown, "This Is No Psyche Job," *Sales & Marketing Management*, March 1995, p. 32.

9. "Belonging Satisfies Basic Human Need," *Menninger Letter*, August 1995, p. 6.

10. Barry L. Reece and Rhonda Brandt, *Effective Human Relations in Organizations*, 7th edition. (Boston: Houghton Mifflin Company, 1999), p. 180.

11. William M. Pride and O.C. Ferrell, *Marketing*, 4th edition. (Boston: Houghton Mifflin Company, 1985), pp. 84–92.

12. Douglas A. Bernstein, Alison Clark–Stewart, Edward J. Roy, and Christopher D. Wickens, *Psychology*, 4th edition. (Boston: Houghton Mifflin Company, 1997) p. 570.

13. William F. Schoell and Joseph P. Guillinan, *Marketing* (Boston: Allyn & Bacon, 1992), p. 164.

14. "Met Life Targets the Rich," *Des Moines Register*, June 5, 1993, p. 10.

15. Douglas A. Bernstein, Alison Clark–Stewart, Edward J. Roy, and Christopher D. Wickens, *Psychology*, 4th edition. (Boston: Houghton Mifflin Company, 1997) p. 21.

16. Metta Spencer, *Foundations of Modern Sociology* (Englewood Cliffs, NJ: Prentice–Hall, 1976), p. 64.

17. George A. Torres, "Culture — A Matter of Semantics," *NSPST Newspost*, Winter 1997, pp. 14–16.

18. William M. Pride, O.C. Ferrell, H.F. (Herb) MacKenzie, and Kim Snow, *Marketing: Concepts and Strategies*, Canadian edition. (Toronto: ON, Houghton Mifflin Company, 1998), p. 139.

19. "Focusing With Al Ries," *Sales & Field Force Automation*, July 1997, p. 120.

20. Christopher Knowlton, "Customers: A Tougher Sell," *Fortune*, September 26, 1998, p. 66.

21. Phil Kline, "Dominant Buying Motive Is the Result of Strong Emotions," *Marketing News*, May 24, 1993, p. 4.

22. Stan Davis and Christopher Meyer, *Blur: The Speed of Change in the Connected Economy*, (New York: Addison Wesley Publishers, 1998), p. 52.

23. Hal Lancaster, "It's Time to Stop Promoting Yourself and Start Listening," *The Wall Street Journal*, June 10, p. B–1.

24. Phil Kline, "Dominant Buying Motive Is the Result of Strong Emotions," *Marketing News*, May 24, 1993, p. 4.

25. Personal correspondence from Carolyn Anderson, National Public Relations (Toronto) Ltd., May 20, 1997.

26. Edith Cohen, "A View from the Other Side," *Sales & Marketing Management*, June 1990, p. 108.

27. Bill Scharfman, "The Power of Information and Quality," *Autoweek*, February 1996, p. 97.

28. Stuart F. Brown, "How Great Machines are Born," *Fortune*, March 1, 1999, pp. 164J–164R. Personal correspondence from Steven V. Bernard, Manager Pricing and Incentives, Canada, John Deere Corp., July 13, 1999.

29. "The Front Lines of Business," *Selling*, February 1997, p. 16.

30. "Consultative Selling," *Training*, May 1998, p. 80.

31. Tom Peters and Nancy Austin, *A Passion for Excellence* (New York: Random House), 1985, p. 45.

32. Michael Hammer and Stephen A. Stanton, "The Power of Reflection," *Fortune*, November 24, 1997, pp. 291–294.

33. Jack Falvey, "How the Best Get Better," *Selling*, April 1998, p. 13.

34. "How Well Do You Know Your

Customers?" *Sales and Field Force Automation*, January 1999 (Supplement to the January issue).

SOURCES FOR BOXED FEATURES

a. Adapted from Jeffery Ball, "But How Does It Make You Feel?" *The Wall Street Journal*, May 3, 1999, pp. B–1, B–4. Joseph E. DeMatio, "2001 Chrysler PT Cruiser," *Automobile Magazine*, June 3, 1999, pp. 76–82.

b. Marlene L. Rossman, *Multicultural Marketing* (New York: AMCOM, 1994). Ann Gibbon, "Vancouver's Chinese community, *The Globe and Mail*, June 7, 1999, p. B1, B4. Mark MacKinnon, "Immigrants face underemployment in Toronto, *The Globe and Mail*, May 24, 1999, p. B3. Mark MacKinnon, "High hopes fall flat for Haitians in Montreal," *The Globe and Mail*, May 31, 1999, p. B3. Harvey Schachter, "The 21st Century CEO," *Profit*, April 1999, pp. 25–34.

CHAPTER 8

1. Interview with Jeff Stevens, May 6, 1997.
2. Don Peppers, Martha Rogers, and Bob Dorf, "Is Your Company Ready for One-to-One Marketing?" *Harvard Business Review*, January–February 1999, pp. 151–154.
3. Gerhard Gschwandtner, "Thoughts to Sell By," *Personal Selling Power*, 15th Anniversary Issue, 1995, p. 122.
4. Dorothy Leeds, "Where Are the Real Decision Makers?" *Personal Selling Power*, March 1993, p. 62.
5. Gerhard Gschwandtner, "The Funnel Concept," *Personal Selling Power*, May–June 1993, p. 22.
6. Bob Donath, "Fire Your Big Customers? Maybe You Should." *Marketing News*, June 21, 1999, p. 9.
7. Ibid., p. 23.
8. Zig Ziglar, *Ziglar on Selling*, New York: Ballantine Books, 1991, pp. 70–71.
9. Paul S. Goldner, "The Ten Commandments of Prospecting," *Selling*, April 1997, p. 12.
10. Roger Pell, "It's a Fact . . . Qualified Referrals Bring More Sales to Your Company," *Personal Selling Power*, January–February 1990, p. 30.
11. Thomas Petzinger, Jr., "Selling a 'Killer App' Is a Far Tougher Job Than Dreaming it Up," *The Wall Street Journal*, April 3, 1998, p. B1.
12. Donald J. Moine, "Boothmanship," *Personal Selling Power*, May–June 1986, p. 22.
13. "How Significant Are Trade Shows to Your Marketing Efforts?" *Sales & Marketing Management*, August 1992, p. 22.
14. "Advertising Scores High in Lead Generation," *Sales & Marketing Management*, April 1994, p. 25.
15. "PCs Make Selling More Personal," *Sales and Marketing Digest*, October 1987, p. 98.
16. Alan Test, "Cold Calls Are Hot," *Agency Sales Magazine*, September 1995, p. 28.
17. Anne Baber and Lynne Waymon, "No-Nonsense Networking," *Your Company*, Summer 1993, p. 34.
18. Barry Siskind, *Making Contact* (Toronto: Macmillan Canada, 1995), pp. 1, 83.
19. Maxwell Maltz, Dan S. Kennedy, William T. Brooks, Matt Oechsli, Jeff Paul, and Pamela Yellen, *Zero-Resistance Selling*, pp. 179–180.
20. Interview with Gene Chahley, Polaroid Canada Inc., May 19, 1997.
21. Mark Stevenson, "The Lean, Mean Sales Machine," *Canadian Business*, January 1994, pp. 32–36.
22. Chad Kaydo, "Teach Your Clients Well," *Sales & Marketing Management*, April 1998, p. 83.
23. "A Company of Lead Generators," *Inc.*, September 1987, p. 111.
24. William F. Schoell and Joseph P. Guiltinan, *Marketing* (Boston: Allyn & Bacon, 1992), p. 29.
25. Tracy Emerick, "The Trouble with Leads," *Sales & Marketing Management*, December 1992, p. 58.
26. Harvey Mackay, *Swim with the Sharks* (New York: William Morrow, 1988), pp. 43, 44.
27. Tricia Campbell, "Managing Leads," *Sales & Marketing Management*, December 1998, p. 38.
28. Geoffrey Brewer, "Selling to Senior Executives," *Sales & Marketing Management*, July 1996, p. 43.
29. Gerald A. Michaelson, "Selling to the Top," *Selling*, October 1998, p. 7.
30. "Prospecting Is Where the Gold Is," *Institutional Distribution*, May 15, 1990, pp. 70–72.
31. Jack Stack, "A Passion for Forecasting," *Inc.*, 1997, pp. 37–38.

SOURCES FOR BOXED FEATURES

a. Skip Press, "Fool's Gold?" *Sales & Marketing Management*, June 1998, pp. 58–62.
b. Barbara Siskind, *Seminars to Build Your Business* (North Vancouver, BC: Self-Counsel Press, 1998), pp. 9–12; Sheldon Gordon, "Punch Up Your Profits," *Profit*, May 1999, pp. 17–22.

CHAPTER 9

1. Interview with Brenda Fisher, February 24, 1997.
2. Wilson Learning Corp., "New Study Suggests Changing Role of Salesperson Demands Sales Training Keep Pace," *Canadian Manager*, Winter 1995, p. 22.
3. Regina Eisman, "Justifying Your Incentive Program," *Sales & Marketing Management*, April 1993, p. 52.
4. Malcolm Fleschner, "Too Busy to Buy," *Selling Power*, March 1999, p. 36.
5. "6 Steps to Take Before You Sell," *Institutional Distribution*, May 15, 1990, p. 18.
6. Malcolm Fleschner, "Anatomy of a Sale," *Selling Power*, April 1998, p. 76.

7. "Set the Agenda," *Personal Selling Power*, May–June 1995, p. 79.

8. David Greising, "The Newest Wrinkle in Buying Suits," *Business Week*, April 16, 1990, p. 96.

9. Sandy Miller, "Hot Topics & Trends," *Selling Power*, April 1998, p. 73.

10. Dawn R. Detter-Schmelz and Rosemary Ramsey, "A Conceptualization of the Functions and Roles of Formalized Selling and Buying Teams," *Journal of Personal Selling & Sales Management*, Spring 1995, pp. 47, 48.

11. Charles Butler, "Why the Bad Rap?" *Sales & Marketing Management*, June 1996, p. 66.

12. Henry Canaday, "Teaming with Sales," *Selling Power*, May 1998, pp. 94–102.

13. James F. O'Hara, "Successful Selling to Buying Committees," *Selling*, February 1998, p. 8.

14. "97 Ways to Sell More in '96," *Selling*, January–February 1996, p. 50.

15. Alex Markels, "Memo 4/8/97, FYI: Messages Inundate Offices," *The Wall Street Journal*, April 7, 1997, p. B1.

16. Stan Davis and Christopher Meyer, *Blur: The Speed of Change in the Connected Economy* (New York: Addison-Wesley Publishers, 1998), pp. 167, 237.

17. Francy Blackwood, "Did You Sell $5 Million Last Year?" *Selling*, October 1995, pp. 44–53.

18. John Fellows, "Your Foot in the Door," *Selling Power*, March 1996, pp. 64–65.

19. Adapted from Art Sobczak, "Please, Call Me Back!" *Selling*, March 1999, p. 12.

20. Ibid.

21. Susan Bixler and Nancy Nix-Rice, *The New Professional Image* (Holbrook, MA: Adams Media Corporation, 1997), p. 3.

22. Melissa Campanelli, "Sound the Alarm," *Sales & Marketing Management*, December 1994, pp. 20–25.

23. James E. Lukaszewski and Paul Ridgeway, "To Put Your Best Foot Forward, Start by Taking These 21 Simple Steps," *Sales & Marketing Management*, June 1990, p. 84.

24. Abner Little, "Selling to Women Revs up Car Sales," *Personal Selling Power*, July–August 1990, p. 50.

25. "Six Great Upselling Questions," *Personal Selling Power*, April 1993, p. 44.

26. Interview with Larry Short, June 9, 1997.

27. Art Sobczak, "Dealing with the 'Bad-Timing' Brush-off," *Selling Power*, January/February 1999, p. 14.

28. "Confront Call Reluctance," *Personal Selling Power*, September 1995, p. 46.

29. Alan Farnham, "Are You Smart Enough to Keep Your Job?" *Fortune*, January 15, 1996, pp. 34–42.

30. "The Disappointment Trap," *Selling Power*, January/February 1999, p. 14.

SOURCES FOR BOXED INSERTS

a. Jay Winchester, "Ripe for Change," *Sales & Marketing Management*, August 1998, p. 81.

b. Barry L. Reece and Rhonda Brandt, *Effective Human Relations in Organizations*, 6th ed. (Boston: Houghton Mifflin, 1996), pp. 54–56; Charlene Marmer Solomon, "Global Operations Demand that HR Rethink Diversity," *Personnel Journal*, July 1994, p. 44; Lennie Copeland and Lewis Griggs, *Going International* (New York: Random House, 1985), p. 54.

c. *Des Moines Register*, April 3, 1985, p. 3.

CHAPTER 10

1. Betty Wiesendanger, "Reading His Customers Right," *Selling*, September 1996, p. 60.

2. Ibid., pp. 60–62.

3. "97 Ways to Sell More in '96," *Selling*, January–February 1996, p. 50.

4. Thomas Petzinger, Jr., "At Deere They Know a Mad Scientist May Be a Firm's Biggest Asset," *The Wall Street Journal*, July 14, 1995, p. B1.

5. James Champy, "Selling to Tomorrow's Customer," *Sales & Marketing Management*, March 1999, p. 28.

6. Kevin Daley, "Socrates on a Sales Call," *Marketing News*, May 6, 1996, p. 4.

7. Gail Gabriell, "Dialogue Selling," *Success*, May 1993, p. 34.

8. "Questions Are the Answer," *Selling Power Sales Achiever*, January/February 1999, p. 8.

9. Dorothy Leeds, "The Art of Asking Questions," *Training and Development*, January 1993, p. 58.

10. "How to Ask the Right Questions," *Agency Sales Magazine*, June 1990, p. 64.

11. "Getting into the Habit," *Sales & Marketing Management*, May 1996, p. 68.

12. Cynthia Crossen, "The Crucial Question for the Noisy Times May Just Be: Huh?" *The Wall Street Journal*, July 10, 1997, p. A1.

13. Joseph A. DeVito, *The Interpersonal Communication Book*, 4th ed. (New York: Harper & Row, 1986), p. 52.

14. Barry L. Reece and Rhonda Brandt, *Effective Human Relations in Organizations*, 7th ed. (Boston: Houghton Mifflin Company, 1999), p. 45.

15. Matthew McKay, Martha Davis, and Patrick Fanning, *Messages: The Communications Skills Book* (Oakland, CA: New Harbinger Publications, Inc., 1995), p. 15.

16. Robert A. Lupe, Jr., "Improving Your Listening Ability," *Supervisory Management*, June 1992, p. 7.

17. Interview with Michael Tulk, May 19, 1997.

18. "Presentation-Wise, We've Lost Our Tails," *Sales & Field Force Automation*, July 1999, p. 4.

19. Robert Frank, "Frito-Lay Devours Snack-Food Business," *The Wall Street Journal*, October 27, 1995, p. B1.

20. Jennifer Low, "Hot Sales in a Cold World," *Profit*, December 1994, p. 76.
21. "Eye Contact: The Overlooked Presentation Tool," *Sales & Marketing Management*, December 1998, p. 80.
22. Richard Whitely, "Do Selling and Quality Mix?" *Sales & Marketing Management*, October 1993, p. 70.
23. Stephanie G. Sherman and V. Clayton Sherman, *Make Yourself Memorable* (New York: AMACOM, 1996), pp. 58–59.
24. Art Sobczak, "How to Sell with Sizzle Stories," *Selling*, November 1998, p. 12.
25. Thomas A. Stewart, "The Cunning Plots of Leadership," *Fortune*, September 7, 1998, pp. 165–166.
26. "97 Ways to Sell More in '96," *Selling*, p. 52.
27. Michele Marchetti, "That's the Craziest Thing I Ever Heard," *Sales & Marketing Management*, November 1995, p. 77.
28. Chad Kaydo, "Lights! Camera! Sales!" *Sales & Marketing Management*, February 1998, p. 111.
29. Neil Rackham and John DeVincentis, *Rethinking the Sales Force* (New York: McGraw-Hill, 1999), p. 17

SOURCES FOR BOXED FEATURES

a. Neil Rackham, *Spin Selling* (New York: McGraw-Hill, 1998), pp. 67–89; "Tip of the Month," *Selling*, July 1998, p. 1; Dana Ray, "United They Sell," *Selling Power*, November/December 1998, pp. 19–21.

CHAPTER 11

1. Interview with Darren Alexander, June 6, 1997.
2. Larry Tuck, "Presentations That Cut Through the Information Clutter," *Sales & Field Force Automation*, June 1999, p. 86.
3. Ken Taylor, "Help Your Audience Visualize Your Message," *Selling*, April 1998, p. 10.
4. Anthony Alessandra and Phil Wexler, "The Professionalization of Selling," *Sales & Marketing Training*, February 1988, p. 42.
5. Interview with Ryan Smith, June 11, 1997.
6. David Peoples, *Selling to the Top* (New York: John Wiley & Sons, 1993), p. 197.
7. Tom Hopkins, "Demonstrating Property to Your Clients," *The Real Estate Professional*, January–February 1996, p. 70.
8. Personal correspondence from Christa-Lee McWatters, May 22, 1997.
9. Brandon Mitchener, "Mercedes Dealers Offer New Kind of Test Drive," *The Wall Street Journal*, March 26, 1998, p. B8.
10. "Country-Wide Creativity," *Selling Power*, April 1998, p. 58.
11. Douglas A. Bernstein, Alison Clarke-Stewart, Edward J. Roy, and Christopher D. Wilkens, *Psychology* (4th ed.) (Boston: Houghton Mifflin Company, 1997), p. 327.
12. Harold H. Bloomfield and Robert K. Cooper, *The Power of 5* (Emmaus, PA, Rodale Press, 1995), p. 196.
13. Merrie Spaeth, "Prop Up Your Speaking Skills," *The Wall Street Journal*, July 1, 1996, p. A14.
14. Joseph B. White, "New Ergonomic Chairs Battle to Save the Backs of Workers, for Big Bucks," *The Wall Street Journal*, June 8, 1999, p. B4.
15. Lambeth Hochwald, "Simplify," *Sales & Marketing Management*, June 1998, pp. 65–66.
16. Interview with Amir Hooda, May 29, 1997.
17. www.reardons.com, September 21, 1999.
18. David Ranii, "Dermabond's Debut Disappoints," *News & Observer*, July 31, 1999, p. D1.
19. Dana Ray, "Presentations," *Selling Power Source Book*, 1999, p. 66.
20. "Hugging the Curves of the Info Highway," *Sales & Field Force Automation*, July 1999, p. 12.
21. Gerald L. Manning and Jack W. Linge, *Selling-Today.com* (Upper Saddle River, NJ: Prentice Hall, 1998), p. 34.
22. Francy Blackwood, "Present Your Best Case," *Selling*, January–February 1995, pp. 26–28.
23. Malcolm Campbell, "All In a Day's Presentation," *Selling Power*, November/December 1998, pp. 91–93.

SOURCES FOR BOXED INSERTS

a. Marc Hequet, "Giving Good Feedback," *Training*, September 1994, p. 74; Molly McGinn, "On Your Own," *The News & Observer*, June 27, 1999; Polly Labarre, "Unit of One," *Fast Company*, June 1999, p. 103.
b. Michael Chylewski, "Memorable Sale," *Selling Power*, January/February 1999, p. 22

CHAPTER 12

1. Correspondence from Doug Macnamara, Vice-President, The Banff Centre, and General Manager, The Banff Centre for Management, September 30, 1999.
2. Hal Lancaster, "You Have to Negotiate for Everything in Life, So Get Good At It," *The Wall Street Journal*, January 27, 1998, p. B1.
3. Ron Willingham, *Integrity Selling* (Garden City, NJ: Doubleday, 1987), p. 100.
4. Tom Reiley, "Step Up Your Negotiating Success," *Personal Selling Power*, April 1990, p. 40.
5. "Powers of Persuasion," *Fortune*, October 12, 1998, p. 162
6. Gregg Crawford, "Let's Negotiate," *Sales & Marketing Management*, November 1995, pp. 28–29.
7. "The Readers Forum," *Personal Selling Power*, January–February 1993, p. 12.
8. Hilary Davidson, "5 Entrepreneurs You Need to Know," *Profit*, June 1999, p. 89.
9. John O'Toole, "Inside the Mind of

a Buyer," *Selling*, October 1994, p. 75.

10. Homer Smith, "How to Cope with Buyers Who Are Trained in Negotiation," *Personal Selling Power*, September 1988, p. 37.

11. Ibid.

12. Robert Adler, Benson Rosen, and Elliot Silverstein, "Thrust and Parry," *Training & Development*, March 1996, p. 47.

13. Homer Smith, "How to Cope with Buyers Who Are Trained in Negotiation," p. 37.

14. Robert Adler, Benson Rosen, and Elliot Silverstein, "Thrust and Parry," p. 44.

15. Joseph Conlin, "Negotiating Their Way to the Top," *Sales & Marketing Management*, April 1996, p. 58.

16. "Salespeople Can Be Their Own Worst Enemies," *Competitive Advantage*, 1996, p. 5.

17. Same Deep and Lyle Sussman, *Close the Deal: Smart Moves for Selling* (Reading, MA: Perseus Books, 1999), p. 225.

18. Roland M. Sandell, "Five Sure-Fire Methods to Overcome Objections to Price," *American Salesman*, October 1976, p. 38.

19. Alan Test, "Answering the Price Objection," *Agency Sales Magazine*, April 1996, pp. 56–57.

20. Joseph Conlin, "Negotiating Their Way to the Top," p. 62.

21. D. Forbes Ley, "The Stall—A Decision Not to Make a Decision," *Selling Advantage* (Malvern, PA: Progressive Business Publications, 1995), pp. 1, 2.

22. Steve Albrecht, "Added-Value Negotiating," *Training & Development*, July 1996, pp. 5–6.

23. John R. Graham, "Do You Know What Your Customers Expect? *Selling*, January 1998, pp. 8–9.

24. Thomas C. Keiser, "Negotiating with a Customer You Can't Afford to Lose," *Harvard Business Review*, November–December 1988, p. 31.

25. Ibid.

26. Jeff Keller, "Objections? No Problem," *Selling Power*, September 1996, pp. 44–45.

27. Adapted from Nanci McCann, "Irate Over Rates," *Selling*, July–August 1996, p. 25.

28. Rick Kang, "Management by Defiance," *Profit*, June 1999, pp. 63–64.

29. Correspondence from Doug Macnamara, Vice-President, The Banff Centre, and General Manager, The Banff Centre for Management, September 30, 1999.

SOURCES FOR BOXED INSERTS

a. Hal Lancaster, "You Have to Negotiate for Everything in Life, So Get Good At It," *The Wall Street Journal*, January 27, 1998, p. B1; Amy Lindgren, "Want a Raise? Don't Daydream; Polish Your Negotiating Skills," *Des Moines Register*, April 26, 1998, p. 1L.

b. Sarah Lubman, "Round and Round," *The Wall Street Journal*, December 10, 1993, p. R3; Urban C. Lehner, "Native Intelligence," *The Wall Street Journal*, December 10, 1993, p. R16; "Getting to Yes, Chinese Style," *Sales & Marketing Management*, July 1996, pp. 44–45; Sam Deep and Lyle Sussman, *Close the Deal* (Reading, MA: Perseus Books, 1999), pp. 279–281.

CHAPTER 13

1. Linda Corman, "The Slow and Steady Ryder Race," *Selling*, January–February 1996, pp. 56–58.

2. "How to Prosper in the New Economy," *Personal Selling Power*, January–February 1993, p. 52.

3. Andy Cohen, "Are Your Reps Afraid to Close?" *Sales & Marketing Management*, March 1996, p. 43.

4. Zig Ziglar, *Secrets of Closing the Sale* (New York: Fleming H. Revelle, 1984), p. 51.

5. Allan Lynch, "Secrets of a Super Salesman," *Atlantic Progress*, April 1999, pp. 50, 52.

6. Graham Denton, "The Single Biggest Closing Mistake," Graham Denton Skills Center (Web page)

May 4, 1999, p. 1.

7. "The Closing Moment," *Personal Selling*, October 1995, p. 48.

8. Len D'Innocenzo, "How to Close a Sale," *Personal Selling Power*, March 1990, p. 23.

9. James F. O'Hara, "The Silent Barriers to Closing the Sale," *Selling*, May 1997, p. 9.

10. Kerry L. Johnson, *Sales Magic* (New York: William Morrow, 1994), pp. 192, 193.

11. "Salestalk," *Sales & Marketing Management*, May 1990, p. 166.

12. "Selling Tips," *Selling*, May 1999, p. 13.

13. Mel Silberman, *Active Training* (New York: Maxwell Macmillan Canada, 1990), pp. 96–99.

14. Larry Wilson, *Changing the Game: The New Way to Sell* (New York: Simon & Schuster, 1987), p. 116.

15. Dian Hymer, "How Can I Cure Buyer's Remorse?" *Purchasing a New Home* (Web page) January 16, 1998, p. 1.

16. Gerhard Gschwandtner, "Dealing with Disappointment," *Selling Power*, March 1998, p. 10.

17. Jack Falvey, "Adventures in No-Man's Land," *Selling*, April 1996, pp. 83, 84.

SOURCES FOR BOXED INSERTS

a. *Training Guide: Ask for the Order and Get It* (Des Moines, IA: Creative Media Division, Batten Batten Hudson and Swab, 1977), p. 3.

b. Linda Corman, "The Best Salesman Who Ever Lived," *Selling*, June 1994, pp. 44–53.

c. Peter Verburg, "Big-Game Banker," *Canadian Business*, January 29, 1999, pp. 24–32.

CHAPTER 14

1. Susan Greco, "Five Ways to Blow a Sale," *Inc.*, September 1996, p. 101.

2. Bob Johnson, "Loyalty Lessons from the Pros," *Customer Support Management*, July/August 1999, p. 115.

3. Ibid.

4. Theodore Levitt, *The Marketing Imagination* (New York: Macmillan, 1983), pp. 117, 118.

5. Hal Lancaster, "Giving Good Service, Never an Easy Task, Is Getting a Lot Harder," *The Wall Street Journal*, June 9, 1998, p. B1.

6. Geoffrey Brewer, "The Customer Stops Here," *Sales & Marketing Management*, March 1998, pp. 31–32.

7. "Why Customers Leave," *Sales & Marketing Management*, May 1998, p. 86; Tom Peters, *The Circle of Innovation* (New York: Vintage Books, 1997), pp. 138–139.

8. Max Morden, "Service with a Smile," *In Touch* (Richard Ivey School of Business, Fall 1999), p. 37.

9. Bill Gates, *Business @ The Speed of Thought* (New York: Warner Books, 1999), p. 67.

10. Sarah Mahoney, "Look at Sales Through Your Customer's Eyes," *Selling*, March 1997, pp. 1–2.

11. Mack Hanan, *Consultative Selling*, 3rd ed. (New York: AMACOM, 1985), pp. 121–122.

12. Bob Johnson, "Loyalty Lesson from the Pros," p. 116.

13. Thomas A. Stewart, "A Satisfied Customer Isn't Enough," *Fortune*, July 21, 1997, p. 113.

14. Bill Gates, *Business @ The Speed of Thought*, p. 67.

15. Ibid., p. 218.

16. Interview with John Morrison, June 11, 1997.

17. Melinda Ligos, "The Joys of Cross-*Selling*," *Sales & Marketing Management*, August 1998, p. 75.

18. Sally J. Silberman, "An Eye for Finance," *Sales & Marketing Management*, April 1996, p. 26.

19. "How to Make Effective and Profitable Sales Calls," *Agency Sales Magazine*, June 1990, p. 43.

20. Nancy Friedman, "Follow-up or Foul-up: Service after the Sale," *Agency Sales Magazine*, October 1992, pp. 21–22.

21. Andrea Nierenberg, "Eight Ways to Stay Top of Mind," *Selling*, April 1998, p. 7.

22. "Inspirations from Michele," *Inspiring Solutions*, February 1999, p. 3.

23. "Customer Care—Phone Feedback," *Inc.*, June 1993, p. 30.

24. Bob Johnson, "Loyalty Lessons from the Pros," p. 115.

25. Bradley E. Wesner, "From Complaint to Opportunity," *Selling Power*, May 1996, p. 62

26. Sam Deep and Lyle Sussman, *Close the Deal: Smart Moves for Selling* (Reading, MA: Perseus Books, 1999), p. 252.

27. Bradley E. Wesner, "From Complaint to Opportunity," p. 62

28. Gerald A Michaelson, "When Things Go Wrong, Make It Right," *Selling*, March 1997, p. 12.

29. Michael Abrams and Matthew Paese, "Wining and Dining the Whiners," *Sales & Marketing Management*, February 1993, p. 73.

30. Interview with Garnet Kindervater, November 10, 1999.

SOURCES FOR BOXED INSERTS

a. "Relationships with Customers Must Be Job Number 1," *Food-Service Distributor*, July 1989, p. 74. Joan O. Fredericks and James M. Salter II, "Beyond Customer Satisfaction," *Management Review*, May 1995, pp. 29–32.

b. Byran Ziegler, "Your Business Card Can Be Powerful Tool," *The Des Moines Register*, August 2, 1999, p. B17.

c. Susan M. O'Dell and Joan A. Pajunen, *The Butterfly Customer* (Toronto: J. Wiley & Sons Canada, 1997).

CHAPTER 15

1. Interview with Elli Davis, April 15, 1997; Royal LePage advertisement, *The Globe and Mail*, March 12, 1999, p. A10.

2. "Sales Agency Management #17," *Agency Sales Magazine*, September 1990, p. 56.

3. "Data Trends," *Selling*, June 1999, p. 1.

4. Barry J. Farber, "Not Enough Hours in the Day," *Sales & Marketing Management*, July 1990, pp. 28, 29.

5. Ed Brown, "Stephen Covey's New One-Day Seminar," *Fortune*, January 1999, p. 138.

6. "You Said It," *Sales & Marketing Management*, July 1990, p. 24.

7. Robert H. Tardiff, "Control Your Time," *Personal Selling Power*, May–June 1995, pp. 72–73.

8. Hyrum W. Smith, *The 10 Natural Laws of Successful Time and Life Management* (New York: Warner Books, 1994), p. 108.

9. "Voice-Mail: Helping to Increase Executive Efficiency," *Black Enterprise*, March 1990, p. 35.

10. Thomas J. Wall, "The ABCs of EDI," *SMT*, June 1996, pp. 30–32.

11. Michele Marchetti, "Territories: For Optimal Performance, Segment Your Customer Base by Industry," *Sales & Marketing Management*, December 1998, p. 35.

12. Ken Liebeskind, "Where Is Everyone?" *Selling Power*, March 1998, p. 35.

13. Rich Bohn, "Territory Management: Mapping Better Sales," *Sales & Field Force Automation*, April 1998, p. 76.

14. Erika Rasmusson, "Wanted: Profitable Customers," *Sales & Marketing Management*, May 1999, pp. 28–34.

15. Nancy Arnott, "Brake Out of the Grid!" *Sales & Marketing Management*, July 1994, pp. 68–75.

16. Arnold A. Lazarus and Clifford N. Lazarus, *The 60-Second Shrink* (San Luis Obispo, California: Impact Publishers, 1997), p. 86; Howard I. Glazer, *Getting in Touch with Stress Management* (American Telephone and Telegraph, 1988), p. 2.

17. Barry L. Reece and Rhonda Brandt, *Effective Human Relations in Organizations*, 7th ed. (Boston: Houghton Mifflin, 1999), p. 370.

18. David Shenk, "Data Smog," *Perdid*, Spring 1999, pp. 5–7.

19. "Optimism Slows Job Stress," *Menninger Letter*, May 1993, pp. 1, 2.

20. Ian Cruickshank, "Walking the Talk," *Report on Business Magazine*, April 1997, p. 131.

21. Bruce Livesey, "Provide and Conquer," *Report on Business Magazine*, March 1997, pp. 34–44.

22. Robert Hough, "A Make or Break Proposition," *Canadian Business*, February 1997, p. 18.

23. Louis E. Kopolow, "Plain Talk About . . . Handling Stress," *Agency Sales Magazine*, August 1990, p. 59.

SOURCES FOR BOXED INSERTS

a. Interview with Joe Murphy, June 9, 1999.

b. Sandra Lotz Fisher, "Stress—Will You Cope or Crack?" *Selling*, May 1996, p. 29.

c. Kenneth Blanchard, D. W. Edington, and Marjorie Blanchard, *The One-Minute Manager Gets Fit* (New York: William Morrow, 1986), pp. 25–28.

CHAPTER 16

1. "GM's Gift Policy Covers the Bases—From Football to Prickly Plants," *The Globe and Mail*, September 11, 1997, p. B17.

2. Janet McFarland and Greg Keenan, "Harassment Suit Puts Heat on Big 3," *The Globe and Mail*, September 10, 1997, p. A1.

3. Vivian Arnold, B. June Schmidt, and Randall L. Wells, "Ethics Instruction in the Classrooms of Business Educators," *Delta Pi Epsilon Journal*, vol. 38, no. 4, Fall 1996, p. 185.

4. Stephen R. Covey, *The 7 Habits of Highly Effective People* (New York: Simon & Schuster, 1989), p. 18.

5. "Nearly Half of Workers Take Unethical Actions—Survey," *The Des Moines Register*, April 7, 1997, p. 18B.

6. Patrick Smith, "You Have a Job, But How about a Life?" *Business Week*, November 16, 1998, p. 30.

7. Julia Lawlor, "Stepping Over the Line," *Sales & Marketing Management*, October 1995, pp. 90–101.

8. Leonard Zehr, "Five Vitamin Giants Hit with Record Fines for Price Fixing in Canada," *The Globe and Mail*, September 23, 1999, pp. B1, B4.

9. Thomas Claridge, "Four Convicted of Rigging Bids," *The Globe and Mail*, December 20, 1997, p. B5.

10. *Competition Law* (North York, ON: CCH Canadian Limited, 1995), p. 4202.

11. Paul Brent, "Suzy Shier Fined $300 000 for Misleading Advertising," *The Financial Post*, July 18, 1995, p. 6.

12. Dawn Marie Driscoll, "Don't Confuse Legal and Ethical Standards," *Business Week*, July–August 1996, p. 44.

13. Michael Deck, "Good Intentions Aren't Enough," *The Globe and Mail*, October 23, 1997, p. B2.

14. Thomas J. Peters and Robert H. Waterman, Jr., *In Search of Excellence* (New York: Harper & Row, 1982), p. 6.

15. "Rivalries, Law Policies Take a Toll on Ethics," *The Wall Street Journal*, March 22, 1990, p. B1.

16. Corinne McLaughlin, "Workplace Spirituality Transforming Organizations from the Inside Out," *The Inner Edge*, August/September 1998, p. 26.

17. Michele Krebs, "All the Marketing Men," *Autoweek*, February 16, 1998, p. 11.

18. Dena Bunis, "Sex in Business: Scandal Generates Concerns," *Roanoke Times & World News*, August 12, 1990, p. D9.

19. Fiona Gibb, "To Give or Not to Give," *Sales & Marketing Management*, September 1994, pp. 136–139.

20. Linda Corman, "The 13 Sins of Selling," *Selling*, September 1994, p. 77.

21. Steven Sack, "Watch the Words," *Sales & Marketing Management*, July 1, 1985, p. 56.

22. Ibid.

23. Rob Zeiger, "Sex, Sales & Stereotypes," *Sales & Marketing Management*, pp. 52, 53.

24. Barry L. Reece and Rhonda Brandt, *Effective Human Relations in Organization*, 7th ed., (Boston: Houghton Mifflin Company, 1999), p. 123.

25. Ron Willingham, *Integrity Selling* (New York: Doubleday, 1987), p. xv.

26. Ron Willingham, "Four Traits All Highly Successful Salespeople Have in Common," Phoenix, AZ, 1998 (Audiotape presentation).

27. Carol Wheeler, "Getting the Edge on Ethics," *Executive Female*, May–June 1996, p. 47.

28. Ron Willingham, *Integrity Selling*, p. xv.

29. Ibid.

30. Sharon Drew Morgan, *Selling with Integrity*, San Francisco, Berrett-Koehler Publishers, Inc., 1997, pp. 25–27.

31. Ibid., pp. 27–28.

32. Tom Peters, *Thriving on Chaos* (New York: Alfred A. Knopf, 1988), p. 521.

33. Gerhard Gschwandtner, "Lies and Deception in *Selling*," *Personal Selling Power*. 15th Anniversary Issue, 1995, p. 62.

34. Price Pritchett, *The Ethics of Excellence* (Dallas, TX: Pritchett & Associates, Inc.) (no date of copyright), p. 18.

35. Ibid., p. 14.

SOURCES FOR BOXED FEATURES

a. Jeff Kemp, "Rules to Live By On and Off the Field," *Imprimis*, July 1998, p. 3.

b. Donald Johnston, "The Case for Ending Official Bribery," *The Globe and Mail*, September 25, 1998, p. 23; Alan Freeman, "Watchdog Condemns Those Who Bribe," *The Globe and Mail*, February 3, 1999, p. A19; Barrie McKenna, "Johnston Targets Unofficial Corruption," *The Globe and Mail*, March 5, 1999, p. B7.

CHAPTER 17

1. William Keenan, Jr., "These 10 Managers Show They Have What it Takes to Lead and Succeed," *Sales & Marketing Management*, August 1995, pp. 38, 39.
2. Gilbert A. Churchill, Jr. and J. Paul Peter, *Marketing*, 2nd ed. (New York: Irwin McGraw-Hill, 1998), p. 515.
3. Jack Falvey, "Fly by Night, Sell by Day," *The Wall Street Journal*, June 9, 1997, p. A18.
4. William Keenan Jr., "Death of the Sales Manager," pp. 72–79.
5. Sally J. Silberman, "Troubling Transitions," *Sales & Marketing Management*, February 1996, pp. 20–21.
6. Alan J. Dubinsky, Francis J. Yammarino, Marvin A. Jolson, and William D. Spangler, "Transformational Leadership: An Initial Investigation in Sales Management, *Journal of Personal Selling & Sales Management*, Spring 1995, pp. 17–29.
7. These dimensions are described in Edwin A. Fleischman, *Manual for Leadership Questionnaire* (Chicago, Science Research Associates, 1960), p. 3.
8. Phillip Gelman, "The Good Sales Manager," p. 56.
9. Alison Furnham, "Expect Good Work and You'll Get It," *Executive Female*, September/October 14, 1996, pp. 13–16.
10. Jack Falvey, "The Absolute Basics of Sales Force Management," *Sales & Marketing Management*, August 1990, p. 8.
11. Allan Edwards, personal interview, October 22, 1999.
12. Ken Blanchard, "3 Secrets of the One Minute Manager," *Personal Selling Power*, March 1993, p. 48.
13. Kenneth R. Phillips, "The Achilles' Heel of Coaching," *Training & Development*, March 1998, p. 41.
14. Ibid. pp. 41–44.
15. Barry J. Farber, "On the Lookout," *Sales & Marketing Management*, October 1995, pp. 34, 35.
16. Richard J. Mirabile, "The Power of Job Analysis," *Training*, April 1990, p. 70.
17. Paul Tulenko, "The Key Role of Selling," *San Jose Mercury News*, August 23, 1992, p. C1.
18. William Keenan, Jr., "Who Has the Right Stuff?" *Sales & Marketing Management*, August 1993, p. 28.
19. "Parting Company: The Right Time to Cut Bait and Run," *Personal Selling Power*, May–June 1995, p. 68.
20. Gerhard Gschwandtner, "A Jewel of the Company," *Personal Selling Power*, March 1995, p. 17.
21. Haidee Allerton, "News You Can Use," *Training & Development*, March 1996, p. 9.
22. Alan J. Dubinsky, Francis J. Yammarino, Marvin A. Jolson, and William D. Spangler, "Transformational Leadership: An Initial Investigation in Sales Management," p. 27.
23. Jack Falvey, "The Care and Feeding of New Salespeople, *Sales & Marketing Management*, February 1992, p. 22.
24. Barry L. Reece and Rhonda Brandt, *Effective Human Relations in Organizations*, 6th ed. (Boston: Houghton Mifflin, 1996), p. 153.
25. Ibid.
26. Alfie Kohn, "Why Incentive Plans Cannot Work," *Harvard Business Review*, September–October 1993, pp. 58, 59.
27. "Selling with Sales Contests," *Sales & Marketing Management*, June 1995, p. 35.
28. Nora Wood, "What Motivates Best," *Sales & Marketing Management*, September 1998, pp. 71–78.
29. Andy Cohen, "The Right Stuff," *Sales & Marketing Management*, January 1999, p. 15.
30. "Labor Letter," *The Wall Street Journal*, March 29, 1994, p. 1.
31. Ibid.
32. Dawn R. Deeter-Schmelz and Rosemary Ramsey, "A Conceptualization of the Functions and Roles of Formalized Selling and Buying Teams," *Journal of Personal Selling & Sales Management*, Spring 1995, p. 58.
33. *Dartnell's 29th Sales Force Compensation Survey 1996–97* (Chicago: Dartnell Corporation, 1996).
34. "Point Incentive Sales Programs," *SBR Update*, Volume 1, Issue 4.
35. Roger Ricklefs, "Enterprise," *The Wall Street Journal*, March 6, 1990, p. B1.
36. Donald W. Jackson, Jr., John L. Schlacter, and William G. Wolfe, "Examining the Bases Utilized for Evaluating Salespeople's Performance," *Journal of Personal Selling & Sales Management*, February 1995, p. 57.
37. "Survey of Sales Evaluation Process—What Works, What Doesn't," *Selling Power*, September 1999, p. 115.

SOURCES FOR BOXED INSERTS

a. Douglas J. Dalrymple and William L. Cron, *Sales Management: Concepts and Cases* (New York: John Wiley & Sons, 1998), pp. 344–347; William Keenan, "Time Is Everything," *Sales & Management*, August 1993, p. 61.
b. Kerry Rottenberger-Murtha, "How to Play Above the Rim," *Sales & Marketing Management*, September 1993, pp. 28, 29.

Name Index

NOTE: Boldface pages locate figures; italicized pages locate tables.

Subject Index

NOTE: Boldface pages locate figures; italicized pages locate tables.

Figure Credits

Fig. 3-3: From the book *The Double Win* by Dennis Waitley (Old Tappan, NJ: Fleming H. Revell Co., 1985). **Fig. 6-3**: Adapted and Reprinted by permission of Harvard Business Review. An exhibit from "Marketing Success through Differentiation of Anything" by Theodore Levitt (Jan/Feb 1980). Copyright (1980 by the President and Fellows of Harvard College, all rights reserved. **Fig. 15-4**: Used with the permission of 3M Corp.

Advertisement Credits

p. 18: OEB International. **p. 20**: Reprinted with permission of Caterpillar Inc. **p. 21**: Courtesy of Clearnet PCS. **p. 43**: Courtesy of Canadian Professional Sales Association. **p. 66**: Courtesy of Motorola. **p. 106**: Reproduced with the permission of the Minister of Public Works and Government Services Canada, 1997. **p. 107**: Courtesy of Microcell Solutions Inc. **p. 109**: Courtesy of Johnson & Johnson. **p. 112**: Courtesy of Rich's Products. **p. 116**: Courtesy of the Idaho Potato Commission. **p. 128**: Paine Webber Inc. **p. 130**: Courtesy of Heinz. **pp. 134–135**: Courtesy of Hewlett-Packard Company. **p. 138**: Saturn Canada. **p. 141**: Courtesy of General Mills. **p. 154**: Reprinted by permission of CMA Canada. **p. 157**: Courtesy of Intel Corporation. **p. 160**: Courtesy of Hewlett-Packard. **p. 161**: Courtesy of 3-M Innovation. **p. 164**: Ad courtesy of Progistix-Solutions Inc. www.Progistix.com. **p. 181**: Scott's Directories. **p. 185**: Reprinted with permission of Who'sWhoPublications@1999. **p. 190**: Courtesy of ACT! a division of Interact Commerce Corporation. **p. 202**: Courtesy of Proxima, San Diego, CA. **p. 242**: (Microsoft ad. **p. 265**: Courtesy of InFocus Systems. **p. 280**: LiteCo and LiteTec. **p. 288**: Aramark, formerly Versa Services. **p. 300**: SeviceMaster of Canada Limited. **p. 308**: Toshiba Company. **p. 320**: Courtesy of Quebecor Printing. **p. 354**: Photography by Timothy Greenfield-Sanders. **p. 393**: Courtesy of Home Depot. **p. 397**: Courtesy of Cognos Inc.

Photo Credits

p. 1: Al Harvey/The Slide Farm. **p. 3**: Supplied by author. **p. 8**: Blair Seitz/Photo Researchers, Inc. **p. 9**: Ken Fisher/Tony Stone Images. **p. 11**: Sepp Seitz/Woodfin Camp & Associates. **p. 12**: John Coletti/Allyn & Bacon. **p. 32**: Bill Anderson/Monkmeyer Press. **p. 34**: Supplied by author. **p. 35**: Supplied by author. **p. 37**: John Curtis/Offshoot. **p. 38**: Supplied by author. **p. 41**: Frank Steman/Omni-Photo Communications, Inc. **pp. 49-50, 57**: Romily Lockver/The Image Bank. **p. 51**: Dick Hemingway. **p. 59**: Supplied by author. **p. 60**: SuperStock/ Kwame Zikomo. **p. 62**: John Coletti/Allyn & Bacon. **p. 67**: Michael Heron /Monkmeyer. **p. 76**: SuperStock/John Smyth. **p. 81**: Archive Photos/SAGA/Deidre Davidson. **p. 82**: Courtesy of the Prime Minister's Office. **p. 83**: Canapress. **p. 85**: Timothy A. Murphy/The Image Bank. **p. 89**: John Coletti/Allyn & Bacon. **pp. 96–97**: Sam Sargent/Gamma-Liasion, Inc. **p. 102**: Jose L. Pelaez/The Stock Market. **p. 104**: Courtesy of Merlin Ford, Saskatoon, SK. **p. 109**: Supplied by author. **p. 110**: (*all three photos*) Courtesy of Xerox USA. **p. 111**: Tony Freedman/Photo Edit. **p. 113**: Michael Rosenfield/Tony Stone Images. **p. 125**: Supplied by author. **pp. 146-147**: SuperStock. **p. 159**: Supplied by author. **p. 165**: John Coletti/Stock, Boston. **p. 178**: Supplied by author. **p. 183**: John Coletti/Allyn & Bacon. **pp. 196–197**: Jeff Greenberg/Unicorn Stock Photos. **p. 203**: David Joel/Tony Stone Images. **p. 205**: John Coletti/Allyn & Bacon. **p. 208**: SuperStock. **p. 209**: Supplied by author. **p. 215**: Dick Hemingway. **p. 227**: Jose Pelaez/The Stock Market. **p. 231**: Jeffrey Shaw. **p. 235**: SuperStock. **p. 244**: Index Stock Photography, Inc. **p. 254**: Jeff Greenberg/Unicorn Stock Photos. **p. 258**: John Coletti/Allyn & Bacon. **p. 262**: Uniphoto Pictor. **p. 264**: John Riley/Tony Stone Images. **p. 272**: Vincent Serbin/DeWys, Inc. **p. 282**: John Coletti/Allyn & Bacon. **p. 297**: John Coletti/Allyn & Bacon. **p. 306**: SuperStock. **p. 310**: John Coletti/Allyn & Bacon. **p. 319**: Craig Proctor/Remax Real Estate. **p. 324**: SuperStock. **p. 329**: SuperStock. **pp. 340–341**: Index Stock Photography, Inc. **p. 343**: Jon Riley/Tony Stone Images. **p. 347**: Michael Paras/Photographic Resources. **p. 349**: Jose L. Pelaez/The Stock Market. **p. 351**: Stephen Agricola/Stock, Boston. **p. 358**: SuperStock. **p. 371**: John Coletti/Allyn & Bacon. **p. 378**: Spencer Grant/Monkmeyer Press. **p. 384**: Charles Gupton/Stock, Boston. **p. 386**: Michael Newman/Photo Edit. **p. 388**: Jonathan Nourak/Photo Edit. **p. 391**: John Coletti/Allyn & Bacon. **p. 395**: Jose L. Pelaez/The Stock Market. **pp. 428–436**, Park Inn International.